ENVIRONMENTAL POLICY

Tenth Edition

To Carol and Sandy,
For their love and support

ENVIRONMENTAL POLICY

New Directions for the Twenty-First Century

Tenth Edition

Edited by

Norman J. Vig
Carleton College

Michael E. Kraft
University of Wisconsin–Green Bay

FOR INFORMATION:

CQ Press

An Imprint of SAGE Publications, Inc.

2455 Teller Road

Thousand Oaks, California 91320

E-mail: order@sagepub.com

SAGE Publications Ltd.

1 Oliver's Yard

55 City Road

London EC1Y 1SP

United Kingdom

SAGE Publications India Pvt. Ltd.

B 1/I 1 Mohan Cooperative Industrial Area

Mathura Road, New Delhi 110 044

India

SAGE Publications Asia-Pacific Pte. Ltd.

3 Church Street

#10-04 Samsung Hub

Singapore 049483

Library of Congress Cataloging-in-Publication Data

Names: Vig, Norman J., editor. | Kraft, Michael E., editor.

Title: Environmental policy : new directions for the twenty-first century / edited by Norman J. Vig, Carleton College, Michael E. Kraft, University of Wisconsin, Green Bay.

Description: Tenth edition. | Los Angeles : CQ Press, [2019] | Includes index.

Identifiers: LCCN 2017041325 | ISBN 9781506383460 (pbk. : alk. paper)

Subjects: LCSH: Environmental policy—United States.

Classification: LCC GE180 .E546 2019 | DDC 363.7/0560973—dc23

LC record available at https://lccn.loc .gov/2017041325

This book is printed on acid-free paper.

Acquisitions Editor: Scott Greenan

Editorial Assistant: Sarah Christensen

Production Editor: Kelle Clarke

Copy Editor: Karen E. Taylor

Typesetter: C&M Digitals (P) Ltd.

Proofreader: Barbara Coster

Indexer: Maria Sosnowski

Cover Designer: Anupama Krishnan

Marketing Manager: Erica DeLuca

MIX
Paper from responsible sources

FSC® C014174

www.fsc.org

18 19 20 21 22 10 9 8 7 6 5 4 3 2 1

Contents

Preface

As we near the end of the second decade of the twenty-first century, environmental policy faces significant challenges both at home and around the world. New demands for dealing with the risks of climate change and threats to biological diversity, and for meeting the rising aspirations of the planet's seven and a half billion people, will force governments everywhere to rethink policy strategies. They need to find effective ways to reconcile environmental and economic goals and values through new approaches to sustainable development. In the United States, the early part of the decade saw a stagnant economy and persistently high unemployment, which encouraged policymakers and the business community to blame environmental policies and regulations for hindering economic growth and job creation, even where the evidence of such an impact was weak or nonexistent. The economy improved greatly by 2017, although, as economic inequality widened, the benefits of economic expansion failed to reach many who remained no better off than they were two decades earlier. Partly as a result, the dialogue over environmental policy has become even more politically contentious, and critics often blamed those policies for weakening economic growth and job creation.

Many of these criticisms continue to divide members of the two major parties deeply, as Republicans, particularly in the House of Representatives, have called for repealing, reducing, and reining in environmental policies and regulations in the face of strong Democratic defense of the same policies and actions. The result has been intense and relentless partisan debate on Capitol Hill and at the state and local levels where many of the same conflicts have been evident. Environmentalists have blamed Democrats as well for what they see as their often timid defense of environmental policy or for the ways in which they seek to balance what they see as competing economic and environmental goals even as new research demonstrates convincingly that this dichotomy represents a false choice. Political debate over the next few years may continue to be framed in these terms even as leading businesses, the scientific community, and increasing numbers of public officials recognize that the real challenge today is to find ways to meet economic and other human needs while also protecting the environment on which we depend.

The election of President Donald Trump in November 2016 brought a dramatic change in policy positions and priorities after eight years of the Barack Obama administration. Particularly in his second four-year term, Obama sought to strengthen protection of public health and the environment, foster the development of clean energy resources, and establish a viable and broadly supported path toward global action on climate change through the Paris Agreement of 2015. In contrast, early decisions in the Trump administration aimed to reverse many of Obama's major policy initiatives, especially on energy use and climate change. The differences between the two presidencies on societal values and policy priorities, key appointments to administrative agencies, budgetary support for established programs, and the use of science in decision making could hardly have been greater. What is less clear is whether the positions of the Trump presidency will win favor in Congress beyond initial actions to roll back environmental regulations, and whether the American public and the business community will support such a major reversal in public policy.

When the first environmental decade was launched in the early 1970s, protecting our air, water, and other natural resources seemed a relatively simple proposition. The polluters and exploiters of nature would be brought to heel by tough laws requiring them to clean up or get out of business within five or ten years. But preserving the life support systems of the planet now appears a far more daunting task than anyone imagined back then. Not only are problems such as global climate change more complex than recognized by early efforts to control air and water pollution, but now more than ever, the success of U.S. policies is tied to the actions of other nations. This book seeks to explain the most important developments in environmental policy and politics since the 1960s and to analyze the central issues that face us today. Like the previous editions, it focuses on the underlying trends, institutional strengths and shortcomings, and policy dilemmas that all policy actors face in attempting to resolve environmental controversies. Chapters have been thoroughly revised and updated, and one of them is new to this edition. We have also attempted to compare the positions and actions of the Trump administration to those of the George W. Bush and Barack Obama administrations and to put these differing approaches to environmental policy in the context of ongoing debates over the cost and effectiveness of past policies, as well as the search for ways to reconcile and integrate economic, environmental, and social goals through sustainable development. As such, the book has broad relevance for the environmental community and for all concerned with the difficulties and complexities of finding solutions to environmental problems at the end of this second decade of the twenty-first century.

Part I provides a retrospective view of policy development as well as a framework for analyzing policy change in the United States. Chapter 1 serves as an introduction to the book by outlining the basic issues in U.S. environmental policy since the late 1960s, the development of institutional capabilities for addressing them, and the successes and failures in implementing policies and achieving results. In Chapter 2, Barry G. Rabe considers the evolving role of the states in environmental policy at a time when the recent devolution of responsibilities may face scrutiny from new federal leaders. He focuses on innovative policy approaches used by the states and the promise of—as well as the constraints on—state action on the environment. Part I ends with a chapter by Luis E. Hestres and Matthew C. Nisbet that analyzes changes in environmental advocacy strategies in recent years and addresses a fundamental question about the capacity of environmentalists to make their case to the American public and policymakers at a time when conventional movement strategies have not been very successful and when opposition from industry and political conservatives is on the rise.

Part II analyzes the role of federal institutions in environmental policy-making. Chapter 4, by Norman J. Vig, discusses the role of recent presidents as environmental actors, evaluating their leadership on the basis of several common criteria. In Chapter 5, Michael E. Kraft examines the role of Congress in environmental policy, giving special attention to partisan conflicts over the environment and policy gridlock. The chapter focuses on recent debates and actions on national energy policy and climate change, over which Congress has struggled for much of the past decade. Chapter 6 presents Rosemary O'Leary's use of several in-depth case studies of judicial action to explore how the courts shape environmental policy. In Chapter 7, Richard N. L. Andrews examines the EPA and the way it uses the policy tools granted to it by Congress, especially its regulatory authority, to address environmental challenges. Because regulations inherently place restrictions and burdens on businesses and state and local governments, Andrews uses several case studies to illuminate how the agency implements environmental policy while addressing the concerns of these constituencies and others, such as the president, members of Congress, the news media, and the courts, about varied environmental risks and the costs and benefits of acting on them.

Some of the broader dilemmas in environmental policy formulation and implementation are examined in Part III. Chapter 8, by Edward P. Weber, David Bernell, Hilary S. Boudet, and Patricia Fernandez-Guajardo, examines disputes over national energy policy, particularly controversies surrounding hydraulic fracturing or fracking, coal mining and carbon emissions, and the interdependence of water and energy resources. In Chapter 9, Christopher Bosso and Nicole E. Tichenor examine the fascinating relationships between food and the environment, specifically the environmental impacts of the dominant food system on which the United States and other developed nations rely, the federal environmental laws that affect the production and sale of food, and the growing criticism about and ideas for change in the food system that are intended to reduce its ecological footprint while also ensuring that the nation and planet can continue to feed a growing number of people.

In Chapter 10, Sheila M. Olmstead introduces economic perspectives on environmental policy, including the use of benefit-cost analysis, and she assesses the potential of market forces as an alternative or supplement to conventional regulation. She sees great potential in the use of market-based environmental and resource policies. Chapter 11 moves the spotlight to evolving business practices. Daniel Press and Daniel A. Mazmanian examine the "greening of industry" or sustainable production, particularly the increasing use of market-based initiatives such as voluntary pollution prevention, information disclosure, and environmental management systems. They find that a creative combination of voluntary action and government regulation offers the best promise of success. Finally, in Chapter 12, Kent E. Portney examines the intriguing efforts by communities throughout the nation to integrate environmental sustainability into policy decisions in areas as diverse as energy use, housing, transportation, land use, and urban social life—considerations made even more important today in an era of higher energy costs.

Part IV shifts attention to selected global issues and controversies. In Chapter 13, Henrik Selin and Stacy D. VanDeveer survey the key scientific evidence and major disputes over climate change, as well as the evolution of the issue since the late 1980s. They also assess government responses to the problem of climate change and the outlook for public policy actions. Chapter 14 examines the plight of developing nations that are struggling with a formidable array of threats brought about by rapid population growth and resource exploitation. Richard J. Tobin surveys the pertinent evidence, recounts cases of policy success and failure, and outlines the remaining barriers (including insufficient commitment by rich countries) to achieving sustainable development in these nations. In the final chapter 15 we review the many environmental challenges that continue to face the nation and the world and discuss innovative policy instruments that might help us to better address these issues in the future.

We thank the contributing authors for their generosity, cooperative spirit, and patience in response to our editorial requests. It is a pleasure to work with such a conscientious and punctual group of scholars. Special thanks are also due to the staff of CQ Press/SAGE, including Charisse Kiino, Scott Greenan, Monica Eckman, Sarah Christensen, Jennifer Jones, Erica DeLuca, Kelle Clarke, and Olivia Weber-Stenis. We are particularly grateful for the very professional and extraordinarily thorough copyediting by Karen E. Taylor. We owe a special debt to our colleagues who graciously agreed to review previous editions of the book and offered many useful suggestions: William G. Holt, Birmingham-Southern College; Daniel Fiorino, American University; Jeff W. Justice, Tarleton State University; Jack Rasmus, St. Mary's College; Ninian Stein, Smith College; Gerald A. Emison, Mississippi State University; Rebecca Bromley-Trujillo, University of Kentucky; Sarah Anderson, University of California, Santa Barbara; Irasema Coronado, University of Texas at El Paso; Robert Duffy, Colorado State University; Erich Frankland, University of Wyoming; Raymond Lodato, University of Chicago; Melissa K. Merry, University of Louisville; and John W. Sutherlin, University of Louisiana at Monroe. We also gratefully acknowledge support from the Department of Public and Environmental Affairs at the University of Wisconsin–Green Bay. Finally, we thank our students at Carleton College and UW–Green Bay for forcing us to rethink our assumptions about what really matters. As always, any remaining errors and omissions are our own responsibility.

Norman J. Vig
Michael E. Kraft

About the Editors

Norman J. Vig is the Winifred and Atherton Bean Professor of Science, Technology, and Society emeritus at Carleton College. He has written extensively on environmental policy, science and technology policy, and comparative politics and is coeditor with Michael G. Faure of *Green Giants? Environmental Policies of the United States and the European Union* (2004) and with Regina S. Axelrod and David Leonard Downie of *The Global Environment: Institutions, Law, and Policy*, 2nd ed. (2005).

Michael E. Kraft is a professor of political science and the Herbert Fisk Johnson Professor of Environmental Studies emeritus at the University of Wisconsin–Green Bay. He is the author of *Environmental Policy and Politics*, 7th ed. (2018), and coauthor of *Coming Clean: Information Disclosure and Environmental Performance* (2011, winner of the Lynton K. Caldwell award for best book in environmental politics and policy) and of *Public Policy: Politics, Analysis, and Alternatives*, 6th ed. (2018). In addition, he is coeditor of both the *Oxford Handbook of Environmental Policy* (2013) and *Business and Environmental Policy* (2007) with Sheldon Kamieniecki and of *Toward Sustainable Communities: Transition and Transformations in Environmental Policy*, 2nd ed. (2009), with Daniel A. Mazmanian.

About the Contributors

Richard N. L. Andrews is a professor emeritus of public policy, environmental studies, environmental sciences and engineering, and city and regional planning at the University of North Carolina at Chapel Hill. A primary focus of his research and writing is the history of U.S. environmental policy. He is the author of *Managing the Environment, Managing Ourselves: A History of American Environmental Policy*, 2nd ed. (2006), "The EPA at 40: An Historical Perspective" (*Duke Environmental Law and Policy Forum*, 2011), "Reform or Reaction: EPA at a Crossroads" (*Environmental Sciences & Technology*, 1995), and many other articles on related topics.

David Bernell is an associate professor of political science in the School of Public Policy at Oregon State University and the coordinator of the energy policy concentration in the master's and PhD programs in public policy. His research and teaching focus on U.S. energy policy, energy security, and international relations. He is the coauthor with Christopher Simon of *The Energy Security Dilemma: U.S. Policy and Practice* (2016) and the author of *Constructing U.S. Foreign Policy: The Curious Case of Cuba* (2011). He formerly served with the U.S. Office of Management and Budget in the natural resources, energy, science, and water divisions, and with the U.S. Department of the Interior as an adviser on trade and the environment.

Christopher Bosso is a professor of public policy at Northeastern University. His areas of interest include food and environmental policy, science and technology policy, and the governance of emerging technologies. He is author of *Framing the Farm Bill: Interests, Ideology, and the Agricultural Act of 2014* (2017) and editor of *Feed Cities: Improving Local Food Access, Sustainability, and Resilience* (2017) and *Governing Uncertainty: Environmental Regulation in the Age of Nanotechnology* (2010). His 2005 book, *Environment, Inc.: From Grassroots to Beltway*, was cowinner of the American Political Science Association's Lynton K. Caldwell award for best book in environmental politics and policy.

Hilary S. Boudet is an assistant professor of climate change and energy in the School of Public Policy at Oregon State University. Her research interests include environmental and energy policy, social movements, and public participation in energy and environmental decision making. She coauthored, with Doug McAdam, *Putting Social Movements in Their Place: Explaining Opposition to Energy Projects in the United States, 2000–2005* (2012). Her recent work focuses on public acceptance of hydraulic fracturing and community-based interventions designed to encourage sustainable behavior.

Patricia Fernandez-Guajardo is a Fulbright Scholar and PhD student in the School of Public Policy at Oregon State University. Her master's research examined water governance and institutional capacity in Mexico. Her current research explores the water-energy nexus, specifically, the transitions from traditional irrigation systems to integrated sustainable systems in the rural American West.

Luis E. Hestres is an assistant professor of digital communication and affiliate faculty of the Center for Digital Politics Research at the University of Texas at San Antonio, where he teaches courses on digital media production; the socio-economic, cultural, and political aspects of digital media; and digital activism. His work has been published in the journals *New Media & Society*, *International Journal of Communication*, *Social Media + Society*, and *Environmental Politics*, and in *The Oxford Research Encyclopedia of Climate Change Communication*. His latest project is a book about climate change advocacy organizations and the role that digital communication technologies have played in their development. The book will be published by Lexington Books in 2019. Before earning his PhD from American University in 2014, Dr. Hestres worked as a digital strategist at the U.S. House of Representatives and for several progressive advocacy organizations in Washington, DC. Most recently, he was the Internet director for the 1Sky climate change campaign, which merged with 350.org in 2011. For more information visit www.luishestres.com.

Daniel A. Mazmanian is a professor of public policy in the Sol Price School of Public Policy at the University of Southern California. From 2000 to 2005, he served as the C. Erwin and Ione Piper Dean and Professor of the School of Policy, Planning, and Development (today, the Price School), and prior to that, he was Dean of the School of Natural Resources and Environment (today, the School for Environment and Sustainability) at the University of Michigan. Among his several books are *Can Organizations Change? Environmental Protection, Citizen Participation, and the Corps of Engineers* (1979), *Implementation and Public Policy* (1989), *Beyond Superfailure: America's Toxics Policy for the 1990s* (1992), *Toward Sustainable Communities*, 2nd ed. (2009), and *Elgar Companion to Sustainable Cities* (2014).

Matthew C. Nisbet is a professor of communication studies at Northeastern University and editor-in-chief of the journal *Environmental Communication*. The author of more than seventy-five peer-reviewed studies, book chapters, and reports, Nisbet focuses on the role of communication and the media in environmental advocacy and politics. Among awards and recognition, he has served as a Shorenstein Fellow at Harvard University's Kennedy School of Government, a health policy investigator with the Robert Wood Johnson Foundation, and a member of the National Academies consensus study committee on science communication. More information on his research and writing can be found at www.matthewnisbet.org.

Rosemary O'Leary is an environmental lawyer, Stene Chair Distinguished Professor, and director of the School of Public Affairs at the University of Kansas. She has written extensively on the courts and environmental policy. She is the winner of sixteen national research awards, including five senior scholar achievement awards (the Gaus Award, the Waldo Award, the Routledge Award, the Frederickson Award, and the Provan Award). In 2016, the article she coauthored with Susan Raines on alternative dispute resolution at the EPA was selected as one of fourteen *Public Administration Review* articles "that have made important contributions to the study of environmental policy, regulation, and governance" in the last seventy-five years. She is coeditor, with Robert Durant and Daniel Fiorino, of the MIT Press book *Environmental Governance Reconsidered: Challenges, Choices, and Opportunities*, 2nd ed. (2017).

Sheila M. Olmstead is a professor of public affairs at the Lyndon B. Johnson School of Public Affairs at the University of Texas at Austin, a visiting fellow at Resources for the Future (RFF) in Washington, DC, and a senior fellow at the Property and Environment Research Center in Bozeman, Montana. She was previously a fellow and senior fellow at RFF (2010–2013) and an associate professor (2007–2010) and assistant professor (2002–2007) of environmental economics at the Yale School of Forestry and Environmental Studies. Her research has been published in leading journals such as the *Journal of Economic Perspectives, Proceedings of the National Academy of Sciences, Journal of Environmental Economics and Management*, and *Journal of Urban Economics*. With Nathaniel Keohane, she is the author of the book *Markets and the Environment*. From June 2016 to June 2017, she served on the President's Council of Economic Advisers.

Kent E. Portney is a professor and the director of the Institute for Science, Technology, and Public Policy at the Bush School of Government and Public Service at Texas A&M University. Previously, he taught for many years at Tufts University. He is the author of *Sustainability* (2015), *Taking Sustainable Cities Seriously: Economic Development, the Environment, and Quality of Life in American Cities*, 2nd ed. (2013), *Approaching Public Policy Analysis* (1986), *Siting Hazardous Waste Treatment Facilities: The NIMBY Syndrome* (1991), and *Controversial Issues in Environmental Policy* (1992). He is also the coauthor of *Acting Civically* (2007) and *The Rebirth of Urban Democracy* (1993), which won the American Political Science Association's 1994 Gladys M. Kammerer award for best book in American politics and the American Political Science Association Organized Section on Urban Politics' 1994 award for best book in urban politics.

Daniel Press is a professor of Environmental Studies at the University of California, Santa Cruz, where he teaches environmental politics and policy. He is the author of *Democratic Dilemmas in the Age of Ecology* (1994), *Saving Open Space: The Politics of Local Preservation in California* (2002), and *American*

Environmental Policy: The Failures of Compliance, Abatement, and Mitigation (2015). California governors Gray Davis and Arnold Schwarzenegger appointed him to the Central Coast Regional Water Quality Control Board, a state agency charged with enforcing state and federal water quality laws and regulations. He served from 2001 to 2008. He currently serves as the executive director of the UC Santa Cruz Center for Agroecology and Sustainable Food Systems, the country's foremost university-based organic agriculture teaching and training farm.

Barry G. Rabe is the J. Ira and Nicki Harris Family Professor of Public Policy and the Arthur F. Thurnau Professor of Environmental Policy at the Gerald R. Ford School of Public Policy at the University of Michigan. He also serves as a nonresident senior fellow at the Brookings Institution and chaired the U.S. Environmental Protection Agency Assumable Waters Committee from 2015 to 2017. He is the author of numerous books and articles, including *Statehouse and Greenhouse: The Emerging Politics of American Climate Change Policy*, which received the 2017 Martha Derthick Book Award from the American Political Science Association for making a lasting contribution to the study of federalism. His latest book is *Can We Price Carbon?* (MIT Press, 2018), and he is also examining the politics of severance taxes and sovereign wealth funds related to oil and gas production.

Henrik Selin is an associate professor in the Frederick S. Pardee School of Global Studies at Boston University, where he conducts research and teaches classes on global and regional politics and policymaking on the environment and sustainable development. He is the author of *Global Governance of Hazardous Chemicals: Challenges of Multilevel Management* (MIT Press, 2010), coauthor of *The European Union and Environmental Governance* (Routledge, 2015), and coeditor of *Changing Climates in North American Politics: Institutions, Policymaking, and Multilevel Governance* (MIT Press, 2009) and *Transatlantic Environment and Energy Politics: Comparative and International Perspectives* (Ashgate, 2009). In addition, he has authored and coauthored more than four dozen peer-reviewed journal articles and book chapters, as well as numerous reports, reviews, and commentaries. He also serves as an associate editor for the journal *Global Environmental Politics*.

Nicole E. Tichenor is a postdoctoral research fellow at the University of New Hampshire's Sustainability Institute. Her transdisciplinary research focuses on food system sustainability and food security. She has experience in food and agricultural policy, spanning the local to national levels, through her work at the Douglas County Food Policy Council in Kansas and the National Family Farm Coalition in Washington, DC. She recently received her PhD from Tufts University's Friedman School of Nutrition Science and Policy, where she was awarded fellowships from the Friedman Foundation, the Robert and Patricia Switzer Foundation, the Horatio Alger Association of Distinguished

Americans, and the Tufts Institute of the Environment to support her research, teaching, and engagement efforts.

Richard J. Tobin has spent most of his professional career working on international development. After retiring from the World Bank, he has served as a consultant to UNICEF, the United Nations Development Programme, the United Nations Population Fund, the African Development Bank, the Asian Development Bank, the Arab Administrative Development Organization, and the Organization for Security and Co-operation in Europe. He continues to serve as consultant to the World Bank and has also worked on projects funded by the U.S. Agency for International Development, the United Kingdom's Department for International Development, and the Bill and Melinda Gates Foundation.

Stacy D. VanDeveer is a professor in the Department of Conflict Resolution, Human Security, and Global Governance at the University of Massachusetts Boston. His research and teaching interests include the global politics of resource overconsumption, international environmental policymaking and institutions, connections between environmental and security issues, and comparative and EU environmental politics. In addition to authoring and coauthoring over ninety articles, book chapters, working papers, and reports, he is the coeditor or coauthor of nine books, including *EU Enlargement and the Environment* (2005), *Changing Climates in North American Politics* (2009), *Transatlantic Environment and Energy Politics* (2009), *Comparative Environmental Politics* (2012), *Transnational Climate Change Governance* (2014), *The Global Environment*, 4th ed. (2015), *The European Union and Environmental Governance* (2015), and *Want, Waste or War?* (2015). He also coedits the journal *Global Environmental Governance*.

Edward P. Weber is the Ulysses G. Dubach Professor of Political Science in the School of Public Policy at Oregon State University. His research focuses on natural resource/environmental policymaking, policy implementation, democratic accountability, sustainability, and the design and operation of alternative decision making/governance institutions, particularly collaborative governance arrangements. He is the author of *Bringing Society Back In: Grassroots Ecosystem Management, Accountability, and Sustainable Communities* (2003), *Changing Philosophies and Policies: Endangered Species Across the Years* (2016), *New Strategies for Wicked Problems: Science and Problem Solving in the 21st Century* (2017), and over fifty articles and book chapters. He also is the former leader of the Thomas Foley Public Policy Institute at Washington State University (2001–2008).

Part I

Environmental Policy
and Politics in Transition

Chapter 1

U.S. Environmental Policy
Achievements and New Directions
Michael E. Kraft and Norman J. Vig

During the 2016 presidential election, the Republican nominee and later president, Donald Trump, frequently questioned the reality of climate change and pledged to dismantle the Obama administration's most significant environmental policy initiatives. These included the 2015 Clean Power Plan of the Environmental Protection Agency (EPA) to phase out coal-fired power plants and the adoption of new vehicle fuel economy standards embraced by the auto industry in 2012. These two rules were central components of U.S. climate policy, and they allowed the nation to meet its commitments under the global Paris Agreement on climate change that took effect in November of 2016. Trump also said during the campaign that he would end U.S. participation in the climate accord and abolish the EPA itself. He later modified the latter position to say he would work to "refocus the EPA on its core mission of ensuring clean air, and clean, safe drinking water for all Americans."[1]

In his first year in office, the new president followed through on these promises by appointing a prominent climate change denier and fierce opponent of EPA regulation, Scott Pruitt, as the agency's new administrator, proposing large budgetary and staff cuts for the EPA and signing executive orders intended to reverse both the Clean Power Plan and the fuel economy standards. He also pushed strongly for development of the nation's fossil fuel resources, among other actions to roll back Obama-era environmental policy achievements (see Chapters 4 and 8). The previous EPA administrator in the Obama administration, Gina McCarthy, described the proposed budgetary cuts as a "scorched earth budget that represents an all-out assault on clean air, water and land."[2] Further signaling his intention to reverse President Obama's climate change initiatives, on June 1, 2017, Trump announced that the United States would withdraw from the Paris climate agreement, a move widely criticized by environmentalists, governors and mayors in many states, corporate CEOs, and world leaders. Surveys indicate continued strong and bipartisan support by the American public for the accord and for regulation of greenhouse gas emissions despite the president's decision.[3]

The Democratic nominee in 2016, Hillary Clinton, offered a markedly different posture on these issues. She described climate change as an "urgent threat and a defining challenge of our time." She promised not only to maintain Obama's environmental policies but to strengthen them, and she called for "taking on the threat of climate change and making America the world's clean energy superpower." The contrast between the candidates and their party's positions could hardly have been greater.[4]

These striking differences between the two major party nominees reflect the increasing partisan and ideological polarization that had emerged on environmental and energy issues by the late 2010s.[5] These patterns differ greatly from the bipartisanship that characterized the environmental decade of the 1970s and also was evident, albeit to a lesser extent, over most of the past five decades as the nation adopted dozens of major public policies to deal with both national and global environmental problems, and provided the funds necessary to implement those policies. Today, partisanship and ideological polarization often make it exceptionally difficult to build political backing for policy adoption even when the general public is strongly supportive of it, as was the case on climate change and energy issues in 2016 and 2017.[6] Yet the political conflicts today also speak to new challenges that the nation and world now face, especially climate change, challenges requiring different kinds of governmental and private sector actions and new policy approaches that differ from those that have been relied on in previous decades.

To help address these critical questions about the appropriate role of government and public policy, this chapter provides a historical and institutional analysis that seeks to explain how policymakers have addressed environmental problems and the policy choices they have made since the modern environmental era began in the 1960s. We review the activities of government in addressing environmental problems, the structure of U.S. government that can facilitate or hinder decisions, the processes of agenda setting and policymaking, major policy decisions made over the past five decades, and what those policies have achieved since their adoption. In the concluding chapter in this volume (Chapter 15), we return to the many remaining challenges of the twenty-first century, and we explore the need for a fresh examination of environmental governance and the possible new directions in policies that better match the problems that the nation and world now face.

The Challenges of Contemporary Environmental Problems

In the late 1960s and early 1970s, environmental issues soared to a prominent place on the political agenda in the United States and other industrial nations. The new visibility was accompanied by abundant evidence, domestically and internationally, of heightened public concern over environmental threats and broad support for governmental action.[7] By the 1990s, policymakers around the world had pledged to deal with a range of important environmental problems, from protection of biological diversity to air and water pollution control. Such commitments were particularly manifest at the 1992 United Nations Conference on Environment and Development (the Earth Summit) held in Rio de Janeiro, Brazil, where an ambitious agenda for redirecting the world's economies toward sustainable development was approved, and at the December 1997 Conference of the Parties in Kyoto, Japan, where delegates agreed to a landmark treaty on global climate change. Although it received far less media coverage, the World Summit on Sustainable Development, held in September 2002 in Johannesburg, South Africa, reaffirmed the commitments made a decade earlier at the Earth Summit, with particular attention to the challenge of alleviating global poverty. The far-reaching goals of the Earth Summit and the 2002 Johannesburg meeting were revisited at the 2012 Rio+20 United Nations Conference on Sustainable Development held once again in Brazil.

Despite the notable commitments made and actions taken at these and many other comparable meetings, rising criticism of environmental programs also was evident throughout the 1990s and in the first two decades of the twenty-first century, both domestically and internationally. So too were a multiplicity of efforts to chart new policy directions. For example, intense opposition to environmental and natural resource policies arose in the 104th Congress (1995–1997), when the Republican Party took control of both the House and Senate for the first time in forty years. Ultimately, much like the earlier efforts in Ronald Reagan's administration, that antiregulatory campaign on Capitol Hill failed to gain much public support.[8] Nonetheless, pitched battles over environmental and energy policy continued in every Congress through the 115th (2017–2018). Both antiregulatory actions and fights over them were equally evident in the executive branch, particularly during the George W. Bush administration, as it sought to rewrite environmental rules and regulations to favor industry and to increase development of U.S. oil and natural gas supplies on public lands, and even more directly in the Donald Trump administration, which shared many of the same priorities (see Chapter 4). Yet growing dissatisfaction with the effectiveness, efficiency, and equity of environmental policies was by no means confined to congressional conservatives and the Bush and Trump administrations. It could be found as well among a broad array of interests, including the business community, environmental policy analysts, environmental justice groups, and state and local government officials, although without the ideological agenda that was so evident in the Bush and Trump administrations.[9]

Since 1992, governments at all levels have struggled to redesign environmental policy for the twenty-first century. Under Presidents Bill Clinton and George W. Bush, the EPA tried to "reinvent" environmental regulation through the use of collaborative decision making involving multiple stakeholders, public-private partnerships, market-based incentives, information disclosure, and enhanced flexibility in rulemaking and enforcement (see Chapters 7, 10, and 11).[10] Particularly during the Clinton administration, new emphases within the EPA and other federal agencies and departments on ecosystem management and sustainable development sought to foster comprehensive, integrated, and long-term strategies for environmental protection and natural resource management.[11] Many state and local governments have pursued similar goals with the adoption of innovative policies that promise to address some of the most important criticisms directed at contemporary environmental policy (see Chapters 2 and 12).[12] The election of President Barack Obama in 2008 brought additional attention to new policy ideas, especially in his second term of office when he pursued strong and often innovative policies on clean energy and climate change (see Chapter 4).

The precise way in which Congress, the states, and local governments—and other nations—will change environmental policies in the years to come remains unclear. The prevailing partisan polarization and policy gridlock of recent years may give way to greater consensus on the need to act; yet policy change rarely comes easily in the U.S. political system. Its success likely depends on several key conditions: the saliency of the issues and the degree of public support for action on them, the way various policy actors stake out and defend their positions on the issues, media coverage of the problems as well as the political disputes over them, the relative influence of opposing interests, and the state of the economy. Political leadership, as always, will play a critical role, especially in articulating the problems and potential solutions, mobilizing the public and policy actors, and trying to reconcile the deep partisan divisions that exist today on environmental protection and natural resource issues. Political conflict over the environment is not going to vanish anytime soon. Indeed, it may well increase as the United States and other nations struggle to define how they will respond to the latest generation of environmental problems.

The Role of Government and Politics

The high level of political conflict over environmental protection efforts in the past several decades, particularly evident at the beginning of the Trump administration, underscores the important role government plays in devising solutions to the nation's and the world's mounting environmental ills. Global climate change, population growth, the spread of toxic and hazardous chemicals, loss of biological diversity, and air and water pollution require various actions by individuals and institutions at all levels of society and in both the public and private sectors. These actions range from scientific research and technological innovation to improved environmental education and significant changes in corporate actions and individual behavior. As political scientists, we believe government has an indispensable role to play in environmental protection and improvement even as we acknowledge the importance of corporate and individual choices. Because of this conviction, we have commissioned chapters for this volume that focus on environmental policies and the government institutions and political processes that affect them. Our goal is to illuminate that role and to suggest needed changes and strategies.

Government plays a preeminent role in this policy arena primarily because environmental threats, such as urban air pollution and climate change, pose risks to the public's health and well-being that cannot be resolved satisfactorily through private actions alone. That said, there is no question that individuals and nongovernmental organizations, such as environmental groups and scientific research institutes, can do much to protect environmental quality and promote public health. There is also no doubt that business and industry can do much to promote environmental quality and foster the pursuit of national energy goals, such as improved energy efficiency and increased reliance on renewable energy sources. We see evidence of extensive and often creative individual, nonprofit, and corporate actions of this kind regularly, for example, in sustainable community efforts and sustainable business practices, as discussed in Chapters 12 and 13.

Yet such actions often fall short of national needs without the backing of public policy, without, for example, laws mandating control of toxic chemicals that are supported by the authority of government or standards for drinking water quality and urban air quality that are developed and enforced by the EPA, the states, and local governments. The justification for government intervention lies partly in the inherent limitations of the free market system and the nature of human behavior. Self-interested individuals and a relatively unfettered economic marketplace guided mainly by a concern for short-term profits tend to create spillover effects, or externalities; pollution and other kinds of environmental degradation are examples. As economists have long recognized, collective action is needed to correct such market failures (see Chapter 10). In addition, the scope and urgency of environmental problems typically exceed the capacity of private markets and individual efforts to deal with them quickly and effectively. For these reasons, among others, the United States and other nations have relied on government policies—at local, state, national, and international levels—to address environmental and resource challenges.

Adopting public policies does not imply, of course, that the voluntary and cooperative actions by citizens in their communities or the various environmental initiatives by businesses cannot be the primary vehicle of change in many instances. Nor does it suggest that governments should not consider a full range of policy approaches—including market-based incentives, new forms of collaborative decision making, and information provision strategies— to supplement conventional regulatory policies where needed. Public policy intervention should be guided by the simple idea that we ought to use those policy approaches that offer the greatest promise of working to resolve the problem at hand. Sometimes that will mean governments setting and enforcing public health or environmental standards (regulation), and sometimes it will mean relying on market incentives or information disclosure. More often than not, today, governmental agencies will employ a combination of policy tools to reach agreed-upon objectives: improving environmental quality, minimizing health and ecological risks, and helping to integrate and balance environmental and economic goals.

Political Institutions and Public Policy

Public policy is a course of government action or inaction in response to social problems. It is expressed in goals articulated by political leaders; in formal statutes, rules, and regulations; and in the practices of administrative agencies and courts charged with implementing or overseeing programs. Policy states the intent to achieve certain goals and objectives through a conscious choice of means, usually within a specified period of time. In a constitutional democracy like the United States, policymaking is distinctive in several respects: It must take place through constitutional processes, it requires the sanction of law, and it is binding on all members of society.

The constitutional requirements for policymaking were established well over two hundred years ago, and they remain much the same today. The U.S. political system is based on a division of authority among three branches of government and between the federal government and the states. Originally intended to limit government power and to protect individual liberty, this division of power translates today into a requirement that one build an often elusive political consensus among members of Congress, the president, and key interest groups for any significant national policymaking to take place. That is, fragmented authority may impede the ability of government to adopt timely and coherent environmental policy, as has been evident for some of the most challenging of modern environmental problems. Weak national climate change policy is something of a poster child for such governmental gridlock, which can be defined as an inability to act on problems because of divided authority and prevailing political conflict (see Chapter 5). Dedication to principles of federalism means that environmental policy responsibilities are distributed among the federal government, the fifty states, and tens of thousands of local governments. Here, too, strong adherence to those principles may result in no agreement on national policy action. Yet a federal structure also means that states often are free to adopt environmental and energy policies as they see fit, as has been the case for natural gas "fracking" where no major national policies have been in force. At least some of the states have a track record of favoring strong environmental policies that go well beyond what is possible politically in Washington, DC. California's adoption of a strong climate change policy and Minnesota's successful encouragement of renewable energy sources are two notable illustrations of the considerable power that states have in the U.S. political system (see Chapter 2).[13] The flip side of that coin is that some states will choose to do far less than others in the absence of national requirements.

Responsibility for the environment is divided within the branches of the federal government as well, most notably in the U.S. Congress, with power shared between the House and Senate and jurisdiction over environmental policies scattered among dozens of committees and subcommittees (see Table 1-1). For example, approximately twenty Senate and twenty-eight House committees have some jurisdiction over EPA activities.[14] The executive branch is also institutionally fragmented, with at least some responsibility for the environment and natural resources located in twelve cabinet departments and in the EPA, the Nuclear Regulatory Commission, and other agencies (see Figure 1-1). Most environmental policies are concentrated in the EPA and in the Interior and Agriculture Departments; yet the Departments of Energy, Defense, Transportation, and State are increasingly important actors as well. Finally, the more than one hundred federal trial and appellate courts play key roles in interpreting environmental legislation and adjudicating disputes over administrative and regulatory actions (see Chapter 6).

Table 1-1   Major Congressional Committees with Environmental Responsibilities[a]

Committee	Environmental Policy Jurisdiction
HOUSE	
Agriculture	Agriculture generally; forestry in general and private forest reserves; agricultural and industrial chemistry; pesticides; soil conservation; food safety and human nutrition; rural development; water conservation related to activities of the Department of Agriculture
Appropriations[b]	Appropriations for all programs
Energy and Commerce	Measures related to the exploration, production, storage, marketing, pricing, and regulation of energy sources, including all fossil fuels, solar, and renewable energy; energy conservation and information; measures related to general management of the Department of Energy and the Federal Energy Regulatory Commission; regulation of the domestic nuclear energy industry; research and development of nuclear power and nuclear waste; air pollution; safe drinking water; pesticide control; Superfund and hazardous waste disposal; toxic substances control; health and the environment
Natural Resources	Public lands and natural resources in general; irrigation and reclamation; water and power; mineral resources on public lands and mining; grazing; national parks, forests, and wilderness areas; fisheries and wildlife, including research, restoration, refuges, and conservation; marine affairs and oceanography, international fishing agreements, and coastal zone management; U.S. Geological Survey
Science, Space, and Technology	Environmental research and development; marine research; energy research and development in all federally owned nonmilitary energy laboratories; research in national laboratories; NASA, National Weather Service, and National Science Foundation
Transportation and Infrastructure	Transportation, including civil aviation, railroads, water transportation, and transportation infrastructure; Coast Guard and marine transportation; federal management of emergencies and natural disasters; flood control and improvement of waterways; water resources and the environment; pollution of navigable waters; bridges and dams
SENATE	
Agriculture, Nutrition, and Forestry	Agriculture in general; food from fresh waters; soil conservation and groundwater; forestry in general; human nutrition; rural development and watersheds; pests and pesticides; food inspection and safety

Committee	Environmental Policy Jurisdiction
Appropriations[b]	Appropriations for all programs
Commerce, Science, and Transportation	Interstate commerce and transportation generally; coastal zone management; inland waterways; marine fisheries; oceans, weather, and atmospheric activities; transportation and commerce aspects of outer continental shelf lands; science, engineering, and technology research and development; surface transportation
Energy and Natural Resources	Energy policy, regulation, conservation, research and development; coal; oil and gas production and distribution; civilian nuclear energy; solar energy systems; mines, mining, and minerals; irrigation and reclamation; water and power; national parks and recreation areas; wilderness areas; wild and scenic rivers; public lands and forests; historic sites
Environment and Public Works	Environmental policy, research, and development; air, water, and noise pollution; climate change; construction and maintenance of highways; safe drinking water; environmental aspects of outer continental shelf lands and ocean dumping; environmental effects of toxic substances other than pesticides; fisheries and wildlife; Superfund and hazardous wastes; solid waste disposal and recycling; nonmilitary environmental regulation and control of nuclear energy; water resources, flood control, and improvements of rivers and harbors; public works, bridges, and dams

Sources: Compiled from descriptions of committee jurisdictions reported in Rebecca Kimitch, "CQ Guide to the Committees: Democrats Opt to Spread the Power," *CQ Weekly Online* (April 16, 2007): 1080–83, http://library.cqpress.com/cqweekly/weeklyreport110-000002489956, and from current House and Senate committee websites.

a. In addition to the standing committees listed here, select or special committees may be created for a limited time. Each committee also operates with subcommittees (generally five or six) to permit further specialization. Committee webpages offer extensive information about jurisdiction, issues, membership, and pending actions, and include both majority and minority views on the issues. See www.house.gov/committees/ and www.senate.gov/pagelayout/committees/d_three_sections_with_teasers/committees_home.htm.

b. Both the House and Senate appropriations committees have interior and environment subcommittees that handle all Interior Department agencies as well as the Forest Service and the EPA. The Energy Department, Army Corps of Engineers, and Nuclear Regulatory Commission fall under the jurisdiction of the subcommittees on energy and water development. Tax policy affects many environmental, energy, and natural resource policies and is governed by the Senate Finance Committee and the House Ways and Means Committee.

The implications of this constitutional arrangement for policymaking were evident in the early 1980s as Congress and the courts checked and balanced the Reagan administration's efforts to reverse environmental policies of the previous decade. They were equally clear during the 1990s when the Clinton administration vigorously opposed actions in Congress to weaken environmental programs. They could be seen again in the presidency of

Figure 1-1 Executive Branch Agencies with Environmental Responsibilities

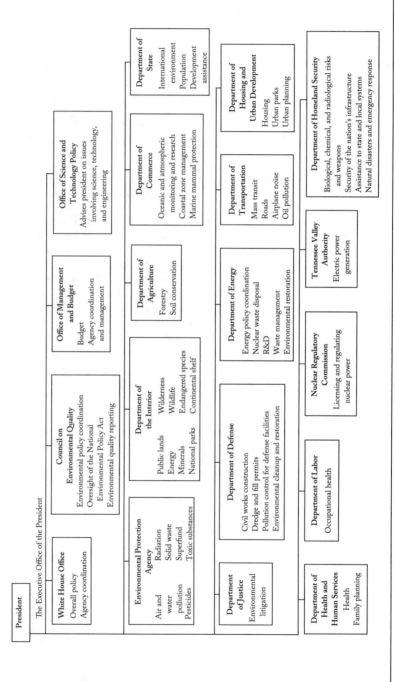

Sources: Council on Environmental Quality, *Environmental Quality: Sixteenth Annual Report of the Council on Environmental Quality* (Washington, DC: Government Publishing Office, 1987); and *The United States Government Manual 2017,* available at www.usgovernmentmanual.gov/.

George W. Bush, when Congress challenged the president's proposed national energy policy and many other environmental initiatives, particularly when the Democrats regained both houses of Congress following the 2006 election. They were just as evident in Barack Obama's presidency when the Republican House of Representatives frequently took strong exception to the president's budget recommendations and proposals for new rules and regulations in the agencies, especially the EPA's efforts to reduce toxic pollution from coal-fired power plants and to restrict release of greenhouse gases linked to climate change. Even at the beginning of the Trump administration in 2017, members of the president's own party voiced objections to the severity of his proposed budget cuts for environmental programs and scientific research.[15]

During the last two decades, the conflict between the two major parties on environmental issues had one striking effect. It shifted attention to the role of the states in environmental policy. As Barry G. Rabe discusses in Chapter 2, the states often have been at the center of the most innovative actions on environmental and energy policy, including climate change, when the federal government remained mired in partisan disputes. By 2017, for example, over half of the states had adopted some form of climate change policy, particularly to favor use of renewable energy sources, whereas Congress and the White House could reach no agreement on what to do.[16]

Generally, after broad consultation and agreement among diverse interests, both within and outside of government, divided authority typically produces slow and incremental alterations in public policy. Such political interaction and accommodation of interests enhance the overall legitimacy of the resulting public policies. Over time, however, the cumulative effect often results in disjointed policies that fall short of the ecological or holistic principles of policy design so often touted by environmental scientists, planners, and activists.

Nonetheless, when issues are highly visible or salient, the public is supportive, and political leaders act cohesively, the U.S. political system has proved flexible enough to permit substantial policy advancement.[17] As we shall see, this was the case in the early to mid-1970s, when Congress enacted major changes in U.S. environmental policy, and in the mid-1980s, when Congress overrode objections of the Reagan administration and greatly strengthened policies on hazardous waste and water quality, among others. Passage of the monumental Clean Air Act Amendments of 1990 is an example of the same alignment of forces. With bipartisan support, Congress adopted the act by a margin of 401 to 25 in the House and 89 to 10 in the Senate. Comparable bipartisanship during the mid-1990s produced major changes in the Safe Drinking Water Act and in regulation of pesticide residues in food. In 2005 and 2007, the same kind of bipartisan cooperation allowed Congress to approve new national energy policies and significantly expand protection of wilderness areas, and in 2016, it led to approval of major changes to the Toxic Substances Control Act (see Chapter 5).

Policy Processes: Agendas, Streams, and Cycles

Students of public policy have proposed several models for analyzing how issues get on the political agenda, how they are defined or framed, and how they move through the policy processes of government. These theoretical frameworks help us to understand both long-term policy trends and short-term cycles of progressive action and political reaction. One set of essential questions concerns *agenda setting*: How do new problems emerge as political issues that demand the government's attention, if they do achieve such recognition, and how are they defined in the public mind? For example, why did the federal government initiate controls on industrial pollution in the 1960s and early 1970s but do little about national energy issues until well into the 1970s, and even then only to a limited extent? Why was it so difficult for climate change to gain the attention of policymakers over the years, and why did various policy actors frame the issue in such different ways and interpret climate science in such disparate ways? Climate change's rise on the political agenda was quite slow, and then it became a significant issue by the 2008 presidential election campaign, only to fade again in prominence as the nation's attention was fixed on the economy and persistently high unemployment. In the 2016 elections, it returned as a prominent issue and was given a central role in the Trump administration as it sought to overturn the core elements in Barack Obama's climate policy (see Chapters 3 and 15).

As the case of climate change illustrates, hurdles almost always must be overcome for an issue to rise to prominence. The issue must first gain societal recognition as a problem, often in response to demographic, technological, or other social changes. It must be defined or framed as a particular kind of problem, which in turn affects the way possible solutions are developed and appraised.[18] Then it must get on the docket of government institutions, usually through the exercise of organized interest group pressure. Finally, it must receive enough attention by government policymakers to reach the stage of decisional or policy action. An issue is not likely to reach this latter stage unless conditions are ripe—for example, a triggering event that focuses public opinion sharply, as occurred with the Exxon Valdez oil spill in 1989 and again with the Deepwater Horizon oil spill in the Gulf of Mexico in 2010.[19] One model by political scientist John Kingdon analyzes agenda setting according to the convergence of three streams that can be said to flow through the political system at any time: (1) evidence of the existence of problems, (2) available policies to deal with them, and (3) the political climate or willingness to act. Although largely independent of one another, these problem, policy, and political streams can be brought together at critical times when policy entrepreneurs (key activists and policymakers) are able to take advantage of the moment and make the case for policy action.[20]

Once an issue is on the agenda, it must pass through several more stages in the policy process. These stages are often referred to as the *policy cycle*. Although terminology varies, most students of public policy delineate at least five stages of policy development beyond agenda setting. These are (1) *policy formulation* (designing and drafting policy goals and strategies for achieving them, which may involve extensive use of environmental science, economics, and policy analysis), (2) *policy legitimation* (mobilizing political support and formal enactment by law or other means), (3) *policy implementation* (putting programs into effect through provision of institutional resources and administrative decisions), (4) *policy evaluation* (measuring results in relation to goals and costs), and (5) *policy change* (modifying goals or means, including termination of programs).[21]

The policy cycle model is useful because it emphasizes all phases of policymaking. For example, how well a law is implemented is as important as the goals and motivations of those who designed and enacted the legislation. The model also suggests the continuous nature of the policy process. No policy decision or solution is final because changing conditions, new information, and shifting opinions will require policy reevaluation and revision. Other short-term forces and events, such as presidential or congressional elections or environmental accidents, can profoundly affect the course of policy over its life cycle. Thus policy at any given time is shaped by the interaction of long-term social, economic, technological, and political forces and short-term fluctuations in the political climate. All of these factors are manifest in the development of environmental policy.

The Development of Environmental Policy from the 1970s to the Twenty-First Century

As implied in the policy cycle model, the history of environmental policy in the United States is not one of steady improvement in human relations with the natural environment. Rather, it has been highly uneven, with significant discontinuities, particularly since the late 1960s. The pace and nature of policy change, as is true for most areas of public policy, reflect the dominant social values at any given time, the saliency of the issues, and the prevailing economic and political conditions.

Sometimes, as was the case in the 1970s, the combination facilitates major advances in environmental policy, and at other times, such as during the early 1980s and 2000s, we have periods of reaction and retrenchment. A third possibility, evident in the 2010s during President Obama's second term, is that no political consensus exists on what to do and consequently no major legislative actions take place. Yet, even in times like this, we see governments responding to changing environmental challenges through executive authority, rulemaking in administrative agencies, and court decisions. These responses were evident both in the Obama administration and in the first few months of the Trump administration. As noted earlier in the chapter, Trump sought to reverse many Obama initiatives through executive orders and through deep cuts in agency budgets (see Chapters 4 and 5). That is, policy change need not come only through the adoption of new legislation; it can be accomplished through administrative actions as well, and that route to policy change may be preferred when a presidential administration seeks rapid change with minimal public visibility.[22] Despite these variations in political conditions and policy responses, it is fair to say that since the late 1960s, we have seen substantial public support for environmental protection and expanding government authority to act.[23] We focus here on the major changes from that time through the middle of the second decade of the twenty-first century, and we discuss the future challenges for environmental politics and policy in the concluding chapter of the book.

Policy Actions Prior to 1970

Until about 1970, the federal government played a sharply limited role in environmental policymaking—public land management being a major exception to this pattern. For nearly a century, Congress had set aside portions of the public domain for preservation as national parks, forests, grazing lands, recreation areas, and wildlife refuges. The multiple use and sustained yield doctrines that grew out of the conservation movement at the beginning of the twentieth century, strongly supported by President Theodore Roosevelt, ensured that this national trust would contribute to economic growth under the stewardship of the Interior and Agriculture Departments.

Steady progress was also made, however, in managing the lands in the public interest and protecting them from development.[24] After several years of debate, Congress passed the Wilderness Act of 1964 to preserve some of the remaining forestlands in pristine condition, "untrammeled by man's presence." At the same time, it approved the Land and Water Conservation Fund Act of 1965 to fund federal purchases of land for conservation purposes and the Wild and Scenic Rivers Act of 1968 to protect selected rivers with "outstandingly remarkable features," including biological, scenic, and cultural value.[25]

During the mid-1960s, the United States also began a major effort to reduce world population growth in developing nations through financial aid for foreign population programs, chiefly voluntary family planning and population research. President Lyndon B. Johnson and congressional sponsors of the programs tied them explicitly to a concern for "growing scarcity in world resources."[26]

Despite this longtime concern for resource conservation and land management, and the new interest in population and development issues, federal environmental policy was only slowly extended to the control of industrial pollution and human waste. Air and water pollution were long considered to be strictly local or state matters, and they were not high on the national agenda until around 1970. In a very early federal action, the Refuse Act of 1899 required individuals who wanted to dump refuse into navigable waters to obtain a permit from the Army Corps of Engineers; however, the agency largely ignored the pollution aspects of the act.[27] After World War II, policies to control the most obvious forms of pollution were gradually developed at the local, state, and federal levels, although some of the earliest local actions to control urban air pollution date back to the 1880s and the first limited state actions to the 1890s.

By the late 1940s and 1950s, we see the forerunners of contemporary air and water pollution laws. For example, the federal government began assisting local authorities in building sewage treatment plants and initiated a limited program for air pollution research. Following the Clean Air Act of 1963 and amendments to the Water Pollution Control Act of 1948, Washington began prodding the states to set pollution abatement standards and to formulate implementation plans based on federal guidelines.[28]

Agenda Setting for the 1970s

The first Earth Day was April 22, 1970. Nationwide "teach-ins" about environmental problems demonstrated the environment's new place on the nation's social and political agendas. With an increasingly affluent and well-educated society placing new emphasis on the quality of life, concern for environmental protection grew apace and was evident across the population, if not necessarily to the same degree among all groups.[29] The effect was a broadly based public demand for more vigorous and comprehensive federal action to prevent environmental degradation. In an almost unprecedented fashion, a new environmental policy agenda rapidly emerged. Policymakers viewed the newly salient environmental issues as politically attractive, and they eagerly supported tough new measures, even when the full impacts and costs were unknown. As a result, laws were quickly enacted and implemented throughout the 1970s but with a growing concern over their costs and effects on the economy and an increasing realization that administrative agencies at all levels of government often lacked the capacity to assume their new responsibilities.

Congress set the stage for the spurt in policy innovation at the end of 1969 when it passed the National Environmental Policy Act (NEPA). The act declared that

> it is the continuing policy of the Federal Government, in cooperation with State and local governments, and other concerned public and private organizations, to use all practicable means and measures, including financial and technical assistance, in a manner calculated to foster and promote the general welfare, to create and maintain conditions under which man and nature can exist in productive harmony, and fulfill the social, economic, and other requirements of present and future generations of Americans.[30]

The law required detailed environmental impact statements for nearly all major federal actions and established the Council on Environmental Quality to advise the president and Congress on environmental issues. President Richard Nixon then seized the initiative by signing NEPA as his first official act of 1970 and proclaiming the 1970s as the "environmental decade." In February 1970, he sent a special message to Congress calling for a new law to control air pollution. The race was on as the White House and congressional leaders vied for environmentalists' support.

Policy Escalation in the 1970s

By the spring of 1970, rising public concern about the environment galvanized the 91st Congress (1969–1971) to action. Sen. Edmund Muskie, D-Maine, then the leading Democratic hopeful for the presidential nomination in 1972, emerged as the dominant policy entrepreneur for environmental protection issues. As chair of what is now called the Senate Environment and Public Works Committee, he formulated proposals that went well beyond those favored by the president. Following a process of policy escalation, both houses of Congress approved the stronger measures and set the tone of environmental policymaking for much of the 1970s. Congress had frequently played a more dominant role than the president in initiating environmental policies, and that pattern continued in the 1970s. This was particularly so when the Democratic Party controlled Congress during the Nixon and Ford presidencies. Although support for environmental protection was bipartisan during this era, Democrats provided more leadership on the issue in Congress and were more likely to vote for strong environmental policy provisions than were Republicans.[31]

The increase in new federal legislation in the next decade was truly remarkable, especially since, as we noted earlier, policymaking in U.S. politics usually takes place through incremental change. Appendix 1 lists the major environmental protection and natural resource policies enacted from 1969 to 2017. They are arranged by presidential administration primarily to show a pattern of significant policy development throughout the period, not to attribute chief responsibility for the various laws to the particular presidents. These landmark measures covered air and water pollution control (the latter enacted in 1972 over a presidential veto), pesticide regulation, endangered species protection, control of hazardous and toxic chemicals, ocean and coastline protection, improved stewardship of public lands, requirements for the restoration of strip-mined lands, the setting aside of more than one hundred million acres of Alaskan wilderness for varying degrees of protection, and the creation of a "Superfund" (in the Comprehensive Environmental Response, Compensation, and Liability Act, or CERCLA) for cleaning up toxic waste sites. Nearly all of these policies reflected a conviction that the federal government must have sufficient authority to compel polluters and resource users to adhere to demanding national pollution control standards and new decision-making procedures that ensure responsible use of natural resources.

There were other signs of commitment to environmental policy goals as Congress and a succession of presidential administrations (through Jimmy Carter's term) cooperated on conservation issues. For example, the area designated as national wilderness (excluding Alaska) more than doubled, from 10 million acres in 1970 to more than 23 million acres in 1980. Seventy-five units, totaling some 2.5 million acres, were added to the national park system in the same period. The national wildlife refuge system grew similarly. Throughout the 1970s, the Land and Water Conservation Fund, financed primarily through royalties from offshore oil and gas leasing, was used to purchase additional private land for park development, wildlife refuges, and national forests.

The government's enthusiasm for environmental and conservation policy did not extend to all issues on the environmentalists' agenda. Two noteworthy cases are population policy and energy policy. The Commission on Population Growth and the American Future recommended in 1972 that the nation should "welcome and plan for a stabilized population," but its advice was ignored. Birthrates in the United States were declining, and population issues were politically controversial. Despite occasional reports that highlighted the effect of population growth on the environment, such as the *Global 2000 Report to the President* in 1980, the issue remained largely dormant over the next four decades even as world population soared by 2017 to 7.5 billion and the U.S. population reached more than 325 million.[32]

For energy issues, we also see a pattern of inattention or neglect. Public concern over energy has tended to follow its price. When prices are low, we see little public or policymaker interest in the issues, but when they rise, people express great concern, for example, over the cost of gasoline. In addition to the historical neglect of energy issues, we have seen a pattern of policy gridlock. Here the connection to environmental policy was clearer to policymakers than it had been on population growth. Indeed, opposition to pollution control programs as well as land preservation came primarily from conflicting demands for energy production in the aftermath of the Arab oil embargo in 1973. The Nixon, Ford, and Carter administrations all attempted to formulate national policies for achieving energy independence by increasing energy supplies, with Carter's efforts by far the most sustained and comprehensive. Carter also emphasized conservation and environmental safeguards. However, for the most part, these efforts were unsuccessful. No consensus on national energy policy emerged among the public or in Congress, and presidential leadership was insufficient to overcome these political constraints until major energy policies were adopted in 1992 and again in 2005.[33]

Congress maintained its strong commitment to environmental policy throughout the 1970s, even as the salience of these issues for the public seemed to wane. For example, it revised the Clean Air Act of 1970 and the Clean Water Act of 1972 through amendments approved in 1977. Yet, by the end of the Carter administration, concerns over the impact of environmental regulation on the economy and specific objections to implementation of the new laws, particularly the Clean Air Act, began creating a backlash.

Political Reaction in the 1980s

The Reagan presidency brought to the federal government a markedly different environmental policy agenda (see Chapter 4). Virtually all environmental protection and resource policies enacted during the 1970s were reevaluated in light of the president's desire to reduce the scope of government regulation, shift responsibilities to the states, and depend more on the private sector. Whatever the merits of Reagan's new policy agenda, it was put into effect through a risky strategy that relied on ideologically committed presidential appointees to the EPA and the Agriculture, Interior, and Energy Departments and on sharp cutbacks in budgets for environmental programs.[34]

Congress initially cooperated with Reagan, particularly in approving budget cuts, but it soon reverted to its accustomed defense of existing environmental policy, frequently criticizing the president's management of the EPA and the Interior Department under Anne Gorsuch (later Burford) and James Watt, respectively; both Burford and Watt were forced to resign by the end of 1983. Among Congress's most notable achievements of the 1980s were its strengthening of the Resource Conservation and Recovery Act (Hazardous and Solid Waste Amendments, 1984); the enactment of the Superfund Amendments and Reauthorization Act (1986), which toughened the act and also established the federal Toxics Release Inventory; and amendments to the Safe Drinking Water Act (1986) and the Clean Water Act (1987; see Appendix 1 for a list of major federal environmental laws from 1969 to 2017).

As we discuss later in this chapter, budget cuts and the loss of capacity in environmental institutions took a serious toll during the 1980s. Yet even the determined efforts of a popular president could not halt the advance of environmental policy. Public support for environmental improvement, the driving force for policy development in the 1970s, increased markedly during Reagan's presidency and represented the public's stunning rejection of the president's agenda.[35] Paradoxically, Reagan actually strengthened environmental forces in the nation. Through his lax enforcement of pollution laws and prodevelopment resource policies, he created political issues around which national and grassroots environmental groups could organize. These groups appealed successfully to a public that was increasingly disturbed by the health and environmental risks of industrial society and by threats to ecological stability. As a result, membership in national environmental groups soared, and new grassroots organizations developed, creating further political incentives for environmental activism at all levels of government.[36]

By the fall of 1989, there was little mistaking congressional receptivity to continuing the advance of environmental policy into the 1990s. Especially in his first two years as president, George H. W. Bush was eager to adopt a more positive environmental policy agenda than his predecessor; this eagerness was particularly evident in his support for the demanding Clean Air Act Amendments of 1990. Bush's White House, however, was deeply divided on environmental issues for both ideological and economic reasons.

Seeking New Policy Directions:
From the 1990s to the Twenty-First Century

Environmental issues received considerable attention during the 1992 presidential election campaign. Bush, running for reelection, criticized environmentalists as extremists who were putting Americans out of work. The Democratic candidate, Bill Clinton, took a far more supportive stance on the environment, symbolized by his selection of Sen. Al Gore, D-Tennessee, as his running mate. Gore was the author of a best-selling book, *Earth in the Balance*, and had one of the strongest environmental records in Congress.

Much to the disappointment of environmentalists, Clinton exerted only sporadic leadership on the environment throughout his two terms in office. However, he and Gore quietly pushed an extensive agenda of environmental policy reform as part of their broader effort to "reinvent government," making it more efficient and responsive to public concerns. Clinton was also generally praised for his environmental appointments and for his administration's support for initiatives such as the restoration of the Florida Everglades and other actions based on new approaches to ecosystem management. Clinton reversed many of the Reagan- and Bush-era executive actions that were widely criticized by environmentalists, and he favored increased spending on environmental programs, alternative energy and conservation research, and international population policy.

Clinton also earned praise from environmental groups when he began speaking out forcefully against the antienvironmental policy decisions of Republican Congresses (see Chapters 4 and 5), for his efforts through the President's Council on Sustainable Development to encourage new ways to reconcile environmental protection and economic development, and for his "lands legacy" initiatives.[37] Still, Clinton displeased environmentalists as often as he gratified them.

The environmental policy agenda of George W. Bush's presidency is addressed in Chapter 4 and at points throughout the rest of the book, as are actions taken during Barack Obama's presidency from January 2009 through January 2017. As widely expected from statements Bush made on the campaign trail and from his record as governor of Texas, he and his cabinet departed significantly from the positions of the Clinton administration. The economic impact of environmental policy emerged as a major concern, and the president gave far more emphasis to economic development than he did to environmental protection or resource conservation.

Like his father, Bush recognized the political reality of popular support for environmental protection and resource conservation. Yet as a conservative Republican, he was also inclined to represent the views of the party's core constituencies, particularly industrial corporations and timber, mining, agriculture, and oil interests. He drew heavily from those constituencies, as well as from conservative ideological groups, to staff the EPA and the Interior, Agriculture, and Energy Departments, filling positions with what the press termed industry insiders.[38] In addition, he sought to further reduce the burden of environmental protection through the use of voluntary, flexible, and cooperative programs and to transfer to the states more responsibility for the enforcement of federal laws. Bush also withdrew the United States from the Kyoto Protocol on global climate change, significantly weakening U.S. leadership on global environmental issues. The administration's tendency to minimize environmental concerns was equally clear in its 2001 proposal for a national energy policy (which concentrated on the increased production of fossil fuels) and, throughout Bush's two terms, in many decisions on clean air rules, water quality standards, mining regulations, and the protection of national forests and parks, decisions that were widely denounced by environmentalists.[39] Many of these decisions received considerably less media coverage than might have been expected. In part, this neglect appeared to reflect the administration's strategy of keeping a low profile on potentially unpopular environmental policy actions. But the president benefited further from the sharply altered political agenda after the terrorist attacks of September 11, 2001, as well as from the decision in 2003 to invade Iraq.[40]

Barack Obama's environmental policy priorities and actions are described in some detail in Chapter 4 and in many of the chapters that follow. Hence we leave much of that appraisal until later in the volume. However, we address budgetary and administrative changes during the Obama presidency in the next section as well as comparable changes in budgets, institutions, and staffing early in the Trump administration.

Budgets and Policy Implementation

In this review of environmental policy development since 1970, we have highlighted the adoption of landmark policies and the political conflicts that shaped them. Another part of this story is the changes over time in budgetary support for the agencies responsible for implementing the policies.

Agency budgets are an important part of institutional capacity, which in turn affects the degree to which public policies might help to improve environmental quality. Although spending more money hardly guarantees policy success, substantial budget cuts can significantly undermine established programs and hinder the achievement of policy goals. For example, the massive reductions in environmental funding during the 1980s had long-term adverse effects on the government's ability to implement environmental policies. Equally sharp budget cuts proposed by Congress in the mid- to late 1990s, by the Bush administration in the 2000s, and by the Republican House between 2011 and 2017 raised the same prospect, although some of the proposed cuts failed to win approval. Changes since the 1980s in budgetary support for environmental protection merit brief comment here. More detail is provided in the appendixes.

In constant dollars (that is, adjusting for inflation), the total spending authorized by the federal government for all natural resource and environmental programs was about 30 percent higher in 2017 than it was in 1980 (see Appendix 4). However, in some program areas reflecting the core functions of the EPA, such as pollution control and abatement, spending declined substantially (about 24 percent) from 1980 to 2017, in constant dollars. In contrast, spending on conservation and land management rose appreciably between 1980 and 2017, more than tripling, again in constant dollars. For most budget categories, spending decreased during the 1980s before recovering under the administrations of George H. W. Bush and Bill Clinton, and to some extent under George W. Bush and Barack Obama.

A notable exception, other than the case of pollution control, is spending on water resources, where the phaseout of federal grant programs resulted in a steady decline in expenditures between 1980 and 2017, eventually dropping by about 40 percent.

Even when the budget picture was improving, most agencies faced important fiscal challenges. Agency responsibilities rose under environmental policies approved between the 1970s and the 2010s, and the agency staffs often found themselves with insufficient resources to implement those new policies fully and to achieve the environmental quality goals they embodied.

These constraints can be seen in the budgets and staffs of selected environmental and natural resource agencies. For example, in constant dollars, the EPA's operating budget as we calculate it (the EPA determines it somewhat differently) was only a little higher in 2017 than it was in 1980, despite the many new duties Congress gave the agency during this period (see Appendix 2). The agency's budget authority rose from 2000 to 2010, enjoying a big boost in Obama's first year in office. It then declined in 2011, rose modestly to $10.8 billion in 2012, but declined again in his last few years in office, ending at $8.3 billion in proposed spending in fiscal year 2017). In early 2017, the Trump administration proposed a 31 percent cut from this level of funding, including a 26 percent cut in the core environmental program and management budget. However, in May 2017, Congress approved a budget agreement through the end of the 2017 fiscal year that included only a 1 percent cut in EPA's budget and no reduction in its staff. The administration may well propose similar cuts for the 2018 fiscal year budget, and it remains to be seen how Congress will respond.[41]

The EPA's staff grew by a greater percentage than its budget, rising from slightly fewer than 13,000 in 1980, the last year of the Carter administration, to around 17,360 by 2011; however, the agency saw its staff decline substantially after 2011; by 2016, it stood at less than 15,400.[42] Most other agencies saw a decrease in staff from 1980 through 2010, some remained at about the same level, and a few enjoyed an increase in staff size (see Appendix 3). The Trump White House proposed a massive reduction in the EPA's staff of some 2,500 people below its modern low point in 2016, as the administration sought to diminish the agency's role in environmental protection significantly and turn over many of its responsibilities to the states, but as noted, Congress did not go along.[43] For the near term, it seems likely that both budgets and staffing levels will be sharply constrained, and these trends almost certainly will affect the capacity of agencies to implement public policies and achieve the objectives set out for them by Congress.

Improvements in Environmental Quality

It is difficult, both conceptually and empirically, to measure the success or failure of environmental policies.[44] Yet one of the most important tests of any public policy is whether it achieves its stated objectives. For environmental policies, we should ask if air and water quality are improving, hazardous waste sites are being cleaned up, and biological diversity is protected adequately. Almost always, we also want to know what these improvements cost, not just to government but for society as a whole. There is no simple way to answer those questions, and it is important to understand why that is, even if some limited responses are possible.[45]

Measuring Environmental Conditions and Trends

Environmental policies entail long-term commitments to broad social values and goals that are not easily quantified. Short-term and highly visible costs are easier to measure than long-term, diffuse, and intangible benefits, and these differences often lead to intense debates over the value of environmental programs. For example, should the EPA toughen air quality standards to reduce adverse health effects or hold off out of concern for the economic impacts of such a move? The answer often seems to depend on which president sits in the White House and how sensitive the EPA is to public concerns over the relative benefits and costs.

Variable and often unreliable monitoring of environmental conditions and inconsistent collection of data over time also make it difficult to assess environmental trends. The time period selected for a given analysis can affect the results, and many scholars discount some data collected prior to the mid-1970s as unreliable. One thing is certain, however. Evaluation of environmental policies depends on significant improvements in monitoring and data collection at both state and federal levels. With better and more appropriate data, we should be able to speak more confidently in the future about policy successes and failures. Of course, any such judgments require that policymakers examine the data objectively and evaluate programs on the evidence as opposed to acting on ideological leanings. This assumption is difficult to make today as scientific data and professional expertise are not necessarily valued as consistently by policymakers and other political actors as both were previously.

In the meantime, scientists and pundits continue to debate whether particular environmental conditions are deteriorating or improving, and for what reasons. Many state-of-the-environment reports that address such conditions and trends are issued by government agencies and environmental research institutes. For the United States, EPA and other agency reports, discussed below, are available online and offer authoritative data. Not surprisingly, interpretations of the data may differ. For instance, critics of environmental policy tend to cite statistics that show rather benign conditions and trends (and therefore little reason to favor public policies directed at them), whereas most environmentalists focus on what they believe to be indicators of serious environmental decline and thus a justification for government intervention. The differences sometimes become the object of extensive media coverage and public debate.

Despite the many limitations on measuring environmental conditions and trends accurately, it is nevertheless useful to examine selected indicators of environmental quality. They tell us at least something about what we have achieved or failed to achieve after nearly five decades of national environmental protection policy. We focus here on a brief overview of trends in air quality, greenhouse gas emissions, water quality, toxic chemicals and hazardous wastes, and natural resources.[46]

Air Quality. Perhaps the best data on changes in the environment can be found for air quality, even if disagreement exists over which measures and time periods are most appropriate. The EPA estimates that, between 1980 and 2015, aggregate emissions of the six principal, or criteria, air pollutants decreased by 65 percent even while the nation's gross domestic product (GDP) grew by 153 percent, its population grew by 41 percent, vehicle miles traveled increased by 106 percent, and energy consumption grew by 25 percent, all of which would likely have increased air pollution without federal laws and regulations.[47]

Progress generally continues. For example, between 2000 and 2015, monitored levels of the six criteria pollutants (that is, ambient air concentrations) showed improvement, with all declining during this period by between 17 and 91 percent. Ozone concentrations (using the eight-hour standard) declined by 17 percent, particulate matter by 36 percent and fine particulates (which pose a greater health risk) by 37 percent, lead by 91 percent, nitrogen dioxide (annual measure) by 45 percent, carbon monoxide by 60 percent, and sulfur dioxide by 69 percent. Consistent with these trends, the number of days with unhealthy air quality in major U.S. cities has been trending downward since 2000. The EPA celebrates these achievements, saying that the "air quality benefits will lead to improved health, longevity, and quality of life for all Americans."[48] Despite these impressive gains in air quality, as of 2015, over 120 million people (about 37 percent of the U.S. population) lived in counties with pollution levels above the standards set for at least one of these criteria pollutants, particularly ozone and fine particulates. These figures vary substantially from year to year, reflecting changing economic activity and weather patterns.[49]

One of most significant remaining problems is toxic or hazardous air pollutants, which have been associated with cancer, respiratory diseases, and other chronic and acute illnesses. The EPA was extremely slow to regulate these pollutants and had established federal standards for only seven of them by mid-1989. Public and congressional concern over toxic emissions led Congress to mandate more aggressive action in the 1986 Superfund amendments as well as in the 1990 Clean Air Act Amendments. The former required manufacturers of more than 300 different chemicals (later increased by the EPA to over 650) to report annually to the agency and to the states in which they operate the amounts of those substances released to the air, water, or land. The EPA's Toxics Release Inventory (TRI) indicates that for the core chemicals from industry that have been reported in a consistent manner over time, total releases on- and off-site decreased by over 60 percent between 1988 and 2015.

At the same time, the annual TRI reports also tell us that industries continue to release very large quantities of toxic chemicals to the environment—3.4 billion pounds a year from nearly twenty-two thousand facilities across the nation, based on the latest report. About 690 million pounds of the chemicals are released into the air, and those may pose a significant risk to public health.[50] It should be noted, however, that the TRI and related numbers on toxics do not present a full picture of public health risks. For instance, many chemicals and industries were added to TRI reporting requirements during the 1990s and 2000s, complicating the determination of change over time. Using the original or core list of chemicals obviously doesn't account for those put on the list more recently. In addition to the TRI, under the 1990 Clean Air Act Amendments, the EPA regulates 188 listed air toxics, but nationwide monitoring of emissions is not standard.

Greenhouse Gas Emissions. The United States is making significant progress in addressing climate change, largely because of improved energy efficiency, increased reliance on natural gas rather than coal for energy production, better vehicle fuel economy, and rapid growth in the use of renewable energy sources such as wind and solar power. The Obama administration advanced vehicle fuel economy standards and a Clean Power Plan designed to reduce reliance on coal-fired power plants. Although both have been challenged by the Trump administration, these new trends in energy use are likely to continue.

According to the EPA's inventory of greenhouse gases, U.S. emissions in 2015 totaled 6,586 million metric tons of CO_2 equivalent, a common way of accounting for emissions of all forms of greenhouse gases. Total U.S. emissions of greenhouse gases peaked in 2009 and declined slowly after that, with some years showing a small increase or decrease. The most notable declines in carbon dioxide releases have been in electricity generation even as there have been slight increases in emissions from transportation and industrial activity. For 2016, greenhouse gas emissions from the energy sector declined by 1.7 percent, consistent with the recent trends.[51] Projections for the next several years depend on the pace of the nation's movement away from extensive reliance on coal for generating electricity and on its shift to cleaner-burning natural gas or renewable forms of energy, such as wind and solar power.

Despite this reduction in emissions, data from the National Oceanic and Atmospheric Administration's Annual Greenhouse Gas Index (based on highly precise atmospheric measurements) show the global concentration of all greenhouse gases in the atmosphere continued to increase through 2016 and into 2017, reflecting a growth in "radiative forcing" or warming impact of 40 percent since 1990.

Measurements of carbon dioxide concentrations at Hawaii's Mauna Loa Observatory, a long-time test site, show at least five years of continuous increases, as well as a record level of 409 parts per million in May 2017. If there is any good news in these patterns, it lies in a report by the International Energy Agency that found global carbon dioxide emissions (that is, releases to the atmosphere) remained flat in 2016 for the third straight year even as the global economy continued to grow, signaling a "continuing decoupling of emissions and economic activity." The explanations for this trend include the growing reliance on renewable sources of energy, switching from coal to natural gas for electricity generation, and gains in energy efficiency.[52] In this context, it is worth adding that the United States remains by far the world's leading emitter of greenhouse gases on a per capita basis, a major factor in the Obama administration's commitment to climate change actions (see Chapter 13).

Water Quality. The nation's water quality has improved since passage of the Clean Water Act of 1972, although more slowly and more unevenly than has air quality. Monitoring data are far less adequate for water quality than for air quality. For example, the best evidence for the state of water quality can be found in the EPA's consolidation of state reports (mandated by the Clean Water Act), which are accessible at the agency website. For the most recent reporting period, the states collectively assessed only 31 percent of the entire nation's rivers and streams; 44 percent of lakes, ponds, and reservoirs; 64 percent of estuaries and bays; and a mere 8 percent of coastal shorelines and 13 percent of oceans and near coastal areas.

Based on these inventories, 47 percent of the surveyed river and stream miles were considered to be of good quality and 53 percent impaired. Some 71 percent of lakes, ponds, and reservoirs also were found to be impaired. A classification of impaired means that water bodies are not meeting or fully meeting the national minimum water quality criteria for "designated beneficial uses" such as swimming, fishing, drinking-water supply, and support of aquatic life. These numbers indicate some improvement over time, yet they also tell us that many problems remain. The same survey found that 80 percent of the nation's assessed estuaries and bays were impaired, as were 72 percent of assessed coastal shorelines and 91 percent of assessed oceans and near coastal waters.[53] The latest data on water quality show very little improvement in recent years, and in some of the categories, a decline in quality. In the face of a growing population and strong economic growth, prevention of significant further degradation of water quality could be considered an important achievement. At the same time, water quality clearly falls short of the goals of federal clean water acts.

The causes of impaired waters today are fairly well understood. The EPA reports that the leading sources of impairment of rivers and streams, for example, are agriculture, atmospheric deposition of chemicals, human modification of waterways, habitat modification, urban and stormwater runoff, and municipal discharges (in that order). That is, the causes no longer are point sources of pollution, such as industrial discharges, which have been well controlled with regulation under the Clean Water Act. Rather, they are largely nonpoint sources that are much more difficult to control and will take longer to affect.

To date, little progress has been made in halting groundwater contamination despite passage of the Safe Drinking Water Act of 1974, the Resource

Conservation and Recovery Act of 1976, and their later amendments. In its 2000 National Water Quality Inventory, still applicable today, the EPA reported that groundwater quality can be adversely affected by human actions that introduce contaminants and that "problems caused by elevated levels of petroleum hydrocarbon compounds, volatile organic compounds, nitrate, pesticides, and metals have been detected in ground water across the nation." The agency also noted that measuring groundwater quality is a complex task and data collection "is still too immature to provide comprehensive national assessments." Heading the list of contaminant sources are leaking underground storage tanks, septic systems, landfills, spills, fertilizer applications, large industrial facilities, hazardous waste sites, and animal feedlots. With about half of the nation's urban population relying on groundwater for drinking water (99 percent in rural areas), far more remains to be done.[54]

The surge in natural gas drilling around the nation through hydraulic fracturing or fracking has sparked additional concerns over groundwater quality and its possible impacts on human health. Fracking involves the injection of massive amounts of water mixed with sand and various chemicals under high pressure to release natural gas from shale formations. There were over 1.7 million active wells in the nation in recent years, and they yielded about two-thirds of natural gas production; natural gas is now the leading source of the country's electricity generation. One consequence, however, is increasing citizen concern about the risks posed by fracking's possible contamination of groundwater. Fracking is regulated primarily by the states rather than the federal government.[55]

Toxic Chemicals and Hazardous Wastes. Progress in dealing with hazardous wastes and other toxic chemicals has been the least satisfactory of all pollution control programs. Implementation of the major laws has been extraordinarily slow due to the extent and complexity of the problems, scientific uncertainty, litigation by industry, public fear of siting treatment and storage facilities nearby, budgetary limitations, and poor management and lax enforcement by the EPA. As a result, gains have been modest when judged by the most common measures.

Much the same could be said about the nation's lack of progress in addressing the challenge posed by high-level radioactive wastes from civilian nuclear power plants. Despite legislation in 1982 and again in 1987 to create a national nuclear waste repository to bury the waste, public and state opposition as well as technical uncertainties have left the country without a permanent solution to the problem. Power plant wastes continue to be stored at some seventy reactor sites across the nation with no agreement to date on a national storage site or geological repository. The Department of Energy now anticipates that it might not be able to operate such a repository until 2048. However, in 2014, the U.S. Nuclear Regulatory Commission ruled that the waste can be stored indefinitely in steel and concrete containers at reactor sites and other locations.[56]

Beyond the problem of radioactive wastes, there is the enormous task of cleaning up contaminated federal facilities, such as former nuclear weapons production plants, as well as tens of thousands of abandoned mines on federal lands in the West for which the federal government is liable for remediation. One comprehensive assessment in 2016 put the total federal environmental liability at over $400 billion, with the eventual cleanup cost likely to be much higher than that.[57]

One of the most carefully watched measures of government actions to reduce the risk of toxic and hazardous chemicals pertains to the federal Superfund program. For years, it made painfully slow progress in cleaning up the nation's worst hazardous waste sites. By the late 1990s, however, the pace of action improved. By 2016, the EPA reported that 1,439 sites on the Superfund National Priorities List had been cleaned up, but the pace in future years may well slow because of scarce federal funds for the program. In addition, some of the most costly cleanups, including chemical containments in rivers and bays, lie ahead. In prior reports, the agency noted that the "Superfund cleanup work EPA is doing today generally is more difficult, is more technically demanding, and consumes considerable resources at fewer sites than in the past." That is, the challenge is greater today, and site cleanup is also more costly and more contentious, which often translates into slower remediation of the sites.[58]

Historically, the EPA has set a sluggish pace in the related area of testing and acting on toxic chemicals, including pesticides. For example, under a 1972 law mandating control of pesticides and herbicides, only a handful of chemicals used to manufacture the fifty thousand pesticides in use in the United States had been fully tested or retested. The Food Quality Protection Act of 1996 required the EPA to undertake extensive assessment of the risks posed by new and existing pesticides. Following a lawsuit, the EPA began moving more quickly toward meeting the act's goal of protecting human health and the environment from these risks. The agency said in 2006 that it had begun a new program to reevaluate all pesticides in use on a regular basis, at least once every fifteen years.[59]

Similarly, limited progress in implementing the relatively weak Toxics Substances Control Act of 1976 finally led to the act's amendment in 2016 with congressional approval of the Frank R. Lautenberg Chemical Safety for the 21st Century Act. That act mandated that the EPA evaluate existing chemicals with a new risk-based safety standard, that it do so with clear and enforceable deadlines, with increased transparency for chemical information, and with assurances that the agency would have the budgetary resources to carry out its responsibilities for chemical safety. A list of the first ten chemicals to be studied was released in late 2016. However, it remains unclear whether the Trump administration will accord the new law the priority that Congress intended, particularly in light of the budgetary and staff cuts that are likely to hinder the act's implementation.[60]

Natural Resources. Comparable indicators of environmental progress can be cited for natural resource use. As is the case with pollution control, however, interpretation of the data is problematic. We have few good measures of ecosystem health, and controversies continue about how best to value ecosystem services. Moreover, the usual information supplied in government reports details only the area of land set aside for recreational and aesthetic purposes rather than how well ecosystem functions are being protected.[61] Nonetheless, the trends in land conservation and wilderness protection suggest important progress since the 1960s.

For example, the national park system grew from about 26 million acres in 1960 to over 84 million acres by 2017, and the number of units (that is, parks) in the system doubled. Since adoption of the 1964 Wilderness Act, Congress has set aside more than 109 million acres of wilderness through the national wilderness preservation system. Since 1968, it has designated parts of 208 rivers in 40 states as wild and scenic, with nearly 13,000 river miles protected by 2017. The Fish and Wildlife Service manages more than 150 million acres in more than 560 units of the national wildlife refuge system in all fifty states, far in excess of the total acreage in the system in 1970; about 93 million acres of this total are set aside as wildlife habitat.[62]

Protection of biological diversity through the Endangered Species Act has produced some success as well, although far less than its supporters believe essential. By 2017, forty-four years after passage of the 1973 act, more than 1,590 U.S. plant and animal species had been listed as either endangered or threatened. Over 700 critical habitats have been designated, more than 1,000 habitat conservation plans have been approved, and more than 1,050 active recovery plans were in effect. Yet only a few endangered species have recovered fully. The Fish and Wildlife Service reported in 2008 (no similar assessments have been made in more recent years) that 41 percent of those listed were considered to be stable or improving, but that 34 percent were considered to be declining in status, and that for 23 percent their status was unknown. About 2 percent were presumed to be extinct.[63]

Assessing Environmental Progress

As the data reviewed in the preceding sections suggest, the nation made impressive gains between 1970 and 2017 in controlling many conventional pollutants and in expanding parks, wilderness areas, and other protected public lands. Despite some setbacks, progress on environmental quality continues, even if it is highly uneven from one period to the next. In the future, however, further advances will be more difficult, costly, and controversial. This is largely because the easy problems have already been addressed. At this point, marginal gains—for example, in air and water quality—are likely to cost more per unit of improvement than in the past. Moreover, second-generation environmental threats such as toxic chemicals, hazardous wastes, and nuclear wastes are proving even more difficult to regulate than the "bulk" air and water pollutants that were the main targets in the 1970s. In these cases, substantial progress may not be evident for years to come, and it may well be expensive.

The same is true for the third generation of environmental problems, such as global climate change and the protection of biodiversity. Solutions require an unprecedented degree of cooperation among nations and substantial improvement in institutional capacity for research, data collection, and analysis, as well as for policy development and implementation. Hence, success is likely to come slowly and will reflect the extent to which national and international commitments to environmental protection grow and capabilities improve.

Some long-standing problems, such as population growth, will continue to be addressed primarily within nation-states, even though the staggering effects on natural resources and environmental quality are felt worldwide. By 2017, the Earth's population of 7.5 billion people was increasing at an estimated 1.2 percent (or about 89 million people) each year, with a middle-range projection for the year 2050 at about 9.9 billion. The U.S. population was growing at about 0.7 percent a year, and middle-range projections by the Population Reference Bureau put it at about 397 million by 2050 (see Chapter 14).[64]

Conclusion

Since the 1970s, public concern and support for environmental protection have risen significantly, spurring the development of an expansive array of policies that substantially increased the government's responsibilities for the environment and natural resources, both domestically and internationally. The implementation of these policies, however, has been far more difficult and controversial than their supporters ever imagined. Moreover, the policies have not been entirely successful, particularly when measured by tangible improvements in environmental quality. Further progress will likely require the United States to search for more efficient and effective ways to achieve these goals, including the use of alternatives to conventional command-and-control regulation, such as the use of flexible regulation, market incentives, and information disclosure or public education.[65] Despite these qualifications, the record since the 1970s demonstrates convincingly that the U.S. government is able to produce significant environmental gains through public policies. Unquestionably, the environment would be worse today if the policies enacted during the 1970s and 1980s, and since then, had not been in place.

Emerging environmental threats on the national and international agenda are even more formidable than the first generation of problems addressed by government in the 1970s and the second generation that dominated political debate in the 1980s. Responding to these threats will require creative new efforts to improve the performance of government and other social institutions, as well as effective leadership to design appropriate strategies to combat these threats, both within government and in society itself. Some of these strategies might include sustainable community initiatives and corporate social responsibility actions. This new policy agenda is addressed in Part IV of the book and in Chapter 15.

Government obviously is an important player in the environmental arena, and the federal government will continue to have unique responsibilities, as will the fifty states and the more than ninety thousand local governments across the nation. President Obama assembled an experienced and talented environmental policy team to address these challenges and, at the launch of his administration, vowed to make energy and environmental issues "a leading priority" of his presidency and a "defining test of our time."[66] As noted earlier, however, in 2017, the Donald Trump administration announced a dramatically different environmental policy agenda and set of priorities, the effects of which will become apparent only over the next few years. Readers can judge for themselves how well recent presidents and their appointees have lived up to the promises they made as they peruse the chapters in this volume. It is equally clear, however, that government rarely can pursue forceful initiatives without broad public support. Ultimately, society's values and priorities will shape the government's response to a rapidly changing world environment that, in all probability, will involve major economic and social dislocations over the coming decades.

Notes

1. Kyle Feldscher, "Trump Backs Off Plan to Eliminate EPA," *Washington Examiner*, September 22, 2016.
2. Coral Davenport, "E.P.A. Head Stacks Agency with Climate Change Skeptics," *New York Times*, March 7, 2017; Steven Overly, "Trump to Pull Back EPA's Fuel Efficiency Determination, Opening the Door for Reduced Standards," *Washington Post*, March 15, 2017; Alan Rappeport and Glenn Thrush, "Pentagon Grows, While E.P.A. and State Dept. Shrink in Trump's Budget," *New York Times*, March 16, 2017; and Coral Davenport, "Trump Lays Plans to Reverse Obama's Climate Change Legacy," *New York Times*, March 21, 2017. The McCarthy statement is reported in Oliver Milman, "Trump Budget Would Gut EPA Programs Tackling Climate Change and Pollution," *The Guardian, U.S. Edition*, March 16, 2017. On the impact of the cuts, see Hiroko Tabuchi, "What's at Stake in Trump's Proposed E.P.A. Cuts," *New York Times*, April 10, 2017. Ultimately, Congress rejected most of the cuts for fiscal 2017. For a somewhat more positive evaluation of Scott Pruitt's intentions for the EPA by former Republican staff at the agency, see Coral Davenport, "Scott Pruitt Is Seen Cutting the E.P.A. with a Scalpel, Not a Cleaver," *New York Times*, February 5, 2017; and Davenport, "Scott Pruitt Faces Anger From Right Over E.P.A. Finding He Won't Fight," *New York Times*, April 12, 2017.
3. Michael D. Shear and Alison Smale, "Leaders Lament U.S. Withdrawal, but Say It Won't Stop Climate Efforts," *New York Times*, June 2, 2017; Hiroko Tabuchi and Henry Fountain, "Bucking Trump, These Cities, States and Companies Commit to Paris Accord," *New York Times*, June 1, 2017; Lizette Alvarez, "Mayors, Sidestepping Trump, Vow to Fill Void on Climate Change, *New York Times*, June 26, 2017; Lyle Scruggs and Clifford Vickrey, "Most Americans Support Government Regulation to Fight Climate Change. Including in Pittsburgh," *Washington Post*, June 5, 2017; and William A. Galston, "Paris Agreement Enjoys More Support Than Donald Trump," *FIXGOV* [Brookings Institution blog], May 31, 2017, www.brookings.edu/blog/fixgov/. As expected, polls taken just after Trump's decision show most Republicans

favoring his action while the overwhelming majority of Democrats and independents were opposed to it: Scott Clement and Brady Dennis, "Post-ABC Poll: Nearly 6 in 10 Oppose Trump Scrapping Paris Agreement," *Washington Post*, June 5, 2017.

4. See Phil McKenna, "GOP and Democratic Platforms Highlight Stark Differences on Energy and Climate," *InsideClimate News*, July 26, 2016, and Clinton's positions on her website: www.hillaryclinton.com/issues/climate/. The complete party platforms for 2016 as well as earlier years can be found at www.presidency.ucsb.edu/platforms.php.

5. Riley E. Dunlap, Aaron M. McCright, and Jerrod H. Yarosh, "The Political Divide on Climate Change: Partisan Polarization Widens in the U.S." *Environment* 58, no. 5 (2016): 4–22.

6. See, for example, Galston, "Paris Agreement Enjoys More Support than Donald Trump; and Lydia Saad, "Global Warming Concern at Three-Decade High in US," available at www.gallup.com/poll/206030/global-warming-concern-three-decade-high.aspx. See also the Yale University and George Mason University joint survey conducted just after the 2016 election: Anthony Leiserowitz, Edward Maibach, Connie Roser-Renouf, Seth Rosenthal, and Matthew Cutler, *Politics and Global Warming, November 2016* (New Haven, CT: Yale Program on Climate Change Communication, 2016), available at http://climatecommunication.yale.edu/publications/politics-global-warming-november-2016/.

7. See survey data reviewed in Chapter 3; Riley E. Dunlap, "Public Opinion and Environmental Policy," in *Environmental Politics and Policy: Theories and Evidence*, 2nd ed., ed. James P. Lester (Durham, NC: Duke University Press, 1995), 63–114; Riley E. Dunlap, George H. Gallup Jr., and Alec M. Gallup, "Of Global Concern: Results of the Health of the Planet Survey," *Environment* 35, no. 9 (1993): 7–15, 33–40; and David P. Daniels, Jon A. Krosnick, Michael P. Tichy, and Trevor Tompson, "Public Opinion on Environmental Policy in the United States," in *The Oxford Handbook of U.S. Environmental Policy*, ed. Sheldon Kamieniecki and Michael E. Kraft (New York: Oxford University Press, 2013), 461–86.

8. Norman J. Vig and Michael E. Kraft, eds., *Environmental Policy in the 1980s: Reagan's New Agenda* (Washington, DC: CQ Press, 1984).

9. Robert Durant, Rosemary O'Leary, and Daniel Fiorino, eds., *Environmental Governance Reconsidered: Challenges, Choices, and Opportunities*, 2nd ed. (Cambridge, MA: MIT Press, 2017); Daniel Fiorino, *The New Environmental Regulation* (Cambridge, MA: MIT Press, 2006); Marc Allen Eisner, *Governing the Environment: The Transformation of Environmental Regulation* (Boulder, CO: Lynne Rienner, 2007); Christopher McGrory Klyza and David Sousa, *American Environmental Policy: Beyond Gridlock*, updated and expanded edition (Cambridge, MA: MIT Press, 2013); Judith A. Layzer, *Open for Business: Conservatives' Opposition to Environmental Regulation* (Cambridge, MA: MIT Press, 2012); and David M. Konisky, ed., *Failed Promises: Evaluating the Federal Government's Response to Environmental Justice* (Cambridge, MA: MIT Press, 2015).

10. Daniel A. Mazmanian and Michael E. Kraft, eds., *Toward Sustainable Communities: Transition and Transformations in Environmental Policy*, 2nd ed. (Cambridge, MA: MIT Press, 2009); Durant, O'Leary, and Fiorino, *Environmental Governance Reconsidered*; Klyza and Sousa, *American Environmental Policy*; and Michael E. Kraft, Mark Stephan, and Troy D. Abel, *Coming Clean: Information Disclosure and Environmental Performance* (Cambridge, MA: MIT Press, 2011).

11. Judith A. Layzer, *Natural Experiments: Ecosystem-Based Management and the Environment* (Cambridge, MA: MIT Press, 2008); Hanna J. Cortner and Margaret A. Moote, *The Politics of Ecosystem Management* (Washington, DC: Island Press, 1998);

Marian R. Chertow and Daniel C. Esty, eds., *Thinking Ecologically: The Next Generation of Environmental Policy* (New Haven, CT: Yale University Press, 1997); President's Council on Sustainable Development, *Sustainable America: A New Consensus for Prosperity, Opportunity, and a Healthy Environment* (Washington, DC: President's Council on Sustainable Development, 1996).

12. Kent E. Portney, *Taking Sustainable Cities Seriously: Economic Development, the Environment, and Quality of Life in American Cities*, 2nd ed. (Cambridge, MA: MIT Press, 2013).

13. The California policy is discussed in Chapter 2. On Minnesota's multifaceted and very successful energy policy, see Michel Wines, "Without Much Straining, Minnesota Reins in Its Utilities' Carbon Emissions," *New York Times*, July 17, 2014. See also Roger Karapin, *Political Opportunities for Climate Policy: California, New York, and the Federal Government* (New York: Cambridge University Press, 2016), and Barry G. Rabe, *Statehouse and Greenhouse: The Emerging Politics of American Climate Change Policy* (Washington, DC: Brookings Institution Press, 2004).

14. See Walter A. Rosenbaum, "Science, Policy, and Politics at the EPA," in *Environmental Policy*, 8th ed., ed. Norman J. Vig and Michael E. Kraft (Thousand Oaks, CA: Sage, 2013), 158–84. See also National Academy of Public Administration (NAPA), *Setting Priorities, Getting Results: A New Direction for EPA* (Washington, DC: NAPA, 1995), 124–25.

15. Glenn Thrush and Coral Davenport, "Donald Trump Budget Slashes Funds for E.P.A. and State Department," *New York Times*, March 15, 2017.

16. See Karapin, *Political Opportunities for Climate Policy* and Klyza and Sousa, *American Environmental Policy*, Chapter 7.

17. John W. Kingdon, *Agendas, Alternatives, and Public Policies*, 2nd ed. (New York: HarperCollins, 1995); Frank R. Baumgartner and Bryan D. Jones, *Agendas and Instability in American Politics* (Chicago: University of Chicago Press, 1993).

18. For a review of how this process works, see Deborah Lynn Guber and Christopher J. Bosso, "Issue Framing, Agenda Setting, and Environmental Discourse," in *The Oxford Handbook of U.S. Environmental Policy*, ed. Sheldon Kamieniecki and Michael E. Kraft (New York: Oxford University Press, 2013), 437–60.

19. Roger W. Cobb and Charles D. Elder, *Participation in American Politics: The Dynamics of Agenda-Building* (Boston: Allyn & Bacon, 1972). See also Thomas A. Birkland, *After Disaster: Agenda Setting, Public Policy, and Focusing Events* (Washington, DC: Georgetown University Press, 1997).

20. Kingdon, *Agendas*.

21. For a more thorough discussion of how the policy cycle model applies to environmental issues, see Michael E. Kraft, *Environmental Policy and Politics*, 7th ed. (New York: Routledge, 2018), Chapter 3. The general model is discussed at length in James E. Anderson, *Public Policymaking: An Introduction*, 8th ed. (Boston: Houghton Mifflin, 2014), as well as in Thomas A. Birkland, *An Introduction to the Policy Process: Theories, Concepts, and Models of Public Policy Making*, 4th ed. (New York: Routledge, 2016).

22. Klyza and Sousa, *American Environmental Policy*.

23. Dunlap, "Public Opinion and Environmental Policy"; Deborah Lynn Guber, *The Grassroots of a Green Revolution: Polling America on the Environment* (Cambridge, MA: MIT Press, 2003); and Daniels et al., "Public Opinion on Environmental Policy in the United States."

24. Paul J. Culhane, *Public Lands Politics: Interest Group Influence on the Forest Service and the Bureau of Land Management* (Baltimore: Johns Hopkins University Press, 1981), esp. Chapter 1. See also Richard N. L. Andrews, *Managing the Environment, Managing Ourselves: A History of American Environmental Policy*, 2nd ed. (New Haven, CT:

Yale University Press, 2006); and Sally K. Fairfax, Lauren Gwin, Mary Ann King, Leigh Raymond, and Laura A. Watt, *Buying Nature: The Limits of Land Acquisition as a Conservation Strategy: 1780–2004* (Cambridge, MA: MIT Press, 2005).

25. Andrews, *Managing the Environment*; Kraft, *Environmental Policy and Politics*, Chapter 4.

26. Michael E. Kraft, "Population Policy," in *Encyclopedia of Policy Studies*, 2nd ed., ed. Stuart S. Nagel (New York: Marcel Dekker, 1994), 617–42.

27. J. Clarence Davies III and Barbara S. Davies, *The Politics of Pollution*, 2nd ed. (Indianapolis, IN: Bobbs-Merrill, 1975).

28. Evan J. Ringquist, *Environmental Protection at the State Level: Politics and Progress in Controlling Pollution* (Armonk, NY: M. E. Sharpe, 1993), Chapter 2; Davies and Davies, *The Politics of Pollution*, Chapter 2. A much fuller history of the origins and development of modern environmental policy than is provided here can be found in Andrews, *Managing the Environment* and in Michael J. Lacey, ed., *Government and Environmental Politics: Essays on Historical Developments since World War Two* (Baltimore, MD: Johns Hopkins University Press, 1989).

29. Samuel P. Hays and Barbara D. Hays, *Beauty, Health, and Permanence: Environmental Politics in the United States, 1955–1985* (Cambridge, Cambridge University Press, 1987). See also Dunlap, "Public Opinion and Environmental Policy," and Robert Cameron Mitchell, "Public Opinion and Environmental Politics in the 1970s and 1980s," in *Environmental Policy in the 1980s*, ed. Norman J. Vig and Michael E. Kraft (Washington, DC: CQ Press, 1984, 51–74).

30. National Environmental Policy Act of 1969, Pub. L. No. 91–90 (42 USC 4321–4347), Sec. 101. See also Lynton Keith Caldwell, *The National Environmental Policy Act: An Agenda for the Future* (Bloomington: Indiana University Press, 1998).

31. Michael E. Kraft, "Congress and Environmental Policy," in *The Oxford Handbook of U.S. Environmental Policy*, ed. Sheldon Kamieniecki and Michael E. Kraft (New York: Oxford University Press, 2013), 280–305; Amy Below, "Parties, Campaigns, and Elections," in *The Oxford Handbook of U.S. Environmental Policy*, ed. Sheldon Kamieniecki and Michael E. Kraft (New York: Oxford University Press, 2013), 525–51; Charles R. Shipan and William R. Lowry, "Environmental Policy and Party Divergence in Congress," *Political Research Quarterly* 54 (June 2001): 245–63.

32. Kraft, "Population Policy"; Council on Environmental Quality and Department of State, *The Global 2000 Report to the President* (Washington, DC: Government Printing Office, 1980). Current population estimates can be found at the Census Bureau website: www.census.gov.

33. James Everett Katz, *Congress and National Energy Policy* (New Brunswick, NJ: Transaction, 1984); Kraft, *Environmental Policy and Politics*, Chapter 6.

34. Vig and Kraft, *Environmental Policy in the 1980s*.

35. See Riley E. Dunlap, "Public Opinion on the Environment in the Reagan Era," *Environment* 29 (July–August 1987): 6–11, 32–37; Mitchell, "Public Opinion and Environmental Politics."

36. The changing membership numbers can be found in Kraft, *Environmental Policy and Politics*, Chapter 4. See also Christopher J. Bosso, *Environment, Inc.: From Grassroots to Beltway* (Lawrence: University Press of Kansas, 2005).

37. President's Council on Sustainable Development, *Sustainable America*.

38. Katharine Q. Seelye, "Bush Picks Industry Insiders to Fill Environmental Posts," *New York Times*, May 12, 2001.

39. See Natural Resources Defense Council, *Rewriting the Rules: The Bush Administration's First-Term Environmental Record* (New York: NRDC, 2005); Bruce Barcott,

"Changing All the Rules," *New York Times Magazine*, April 4, 2004; and Margaret Kriz, "Vanishing Act," *National Journal*, April 12, 2008, 18–23.

40. Eric Pianin, "War Is Hell: The Environmental Agenda Takes a Back Seat to Fighting Terrorism," *Washington Post National Weekly Edition*, October 29–November 4, 2001, 12–13. See also Barcott, "Changing All the Rules," and Joel Brinkley, "Out of the Spotlight, Bush Overhauls U.S. Regulations," *New York Times*, August 14, 2004.

41. See Denise Lu and Armand Emamdjomeh, "Local Programs Get the Biggest Hit in Proposed EPA Budget," *Washington Post*, April 11, 2017; Marianne Lavelle, "What Slashing the EPA's Budget by One-Quarter Would Really Mean," *Inside Climate News*, March 10, 2017; and Milman, "Trump Budget Would Gut EPA Programs Tackling Climate Change and Pollution." The May decision is reported in James Hohmann, "The Daily 202: Eight Ways Trump Got Rolled in His First Budget Negotiation," *Washington Post*, May 1, 2017.

42. On the staff numbers, see EPA, *FY 2015: EPA Budget in Brief*, Publication No. EPA-190-S-14-001 (Washington, DC: EPA, Office of the Chief Financial Officer, March 2014), available at http://www2.epa.gov/sites/production/files/2014-03/documents/fy15_bib.pdf. The overall EPA budget numbers come from the Obama administration's fiscal year 2017 budget. Annual budget numbers in EPA's *FY 2017* document differ somewhat from the budget authority figures in the historical tables of the fiscal year 2017 budget. For consistency, we use the latter for comparisons over time.

43. The historical profile of the EPA's budget and staff from 1970 through 2016 can be found at the agency's website: www.epa.gov/planandbudget/budget. See also James K. Conant and Peter J. Balint, *The Life Cycles of the Council on Environmental Quality and the Environmental Protection Agency: 1970–2035* (New York: Oxford University Press, 2016).

44. Robert V. Bartlett, "Evaluating Environmental Policy," in *Environmental Policy in the 1990s*, 2nd ed., ed. Norman J. Vig and Michael E. Kraft (Washington, DC: CQ Press, 1994), 167–87; Evan J. Ringquist, "Evaluating Environmental Policy Outcomes," in *Environmental Politics and Policy*, ed. James P. Lester (Durham, NC: Duke University Press, 1995), 303–27; Gerrit J. Knaap and Tschangho John Kim, eds., *Environmental Program Evaluation: A Primer* (Champaign: University of Illinois Press, 1998).

45. One of the most thorough evaluations of environmental protection policies of this kind can be found in J. Clarence Davies and Jan Mazurek, *Pollution Control in the United States: Evaluating the System* (Washington, DC: NAPA, 1995). See also Daniel Press, *American Environmental Policy: The Failures of Compliance, Abatement and Mitigation* (Northampton, MA: Edward Elgar Publishing, 2015).

46. For a fuller account, see Kraft, *Environmental Policy and Politics*, Chapter 2.

47. U.S. Environmental Protection Agency (EPA), "Air Quality: National Summary," available at www.epa.gov/air-trends/air-quality-national-summary, accessed March 30, 2017.

48. U.S. EPA, "Air Quality."

49. U.S. EPA, "Air Quality."

50. EPA, *2015 Toxics Release Inventory: National Analysis* (Washington, DC: EPA, January 2017), available at www.epa.gov/trinationalanalysis/report-sections-2015-trinational-analysis. The volume of releases refers only to TRI facilities that reported to the EPA that year. Facilities falling below a threshold level are not required to report, nor are many smaller facilities. To view TRI data for anywhere in the United States via an interactive map, see www.epa.gov/trinationalanalysis.

51. See EPA, *Inventory of U.S. Greenhouse Gas Emissions and Sinks: 1990–2015* EPA 430-P-17-001 (Washington, DC: EPA, 2017), available at www.epa.gov/ghgemissions/

inventory-us-greenhouse-gas-emissions-and-sinks-1990-2015. The 2016 data come from a Department of Energy press release of April 10, 2017; See Energy Information Administration (EIA), "U.S. Energy-Related CO2 Emissions Fell 1.7% in 2016," *Today in Energy*, https://www.eia.gov/todayinenergy/detail.php?id=30712.

52. U.S. Department of Commerce, National Oceanic and Atmospheric Administration, *The NOAA Annual Greenhouse Gas Index* (Boulder, CO: NOAA Earth System Research Laboratory, spring 2017), available at https://esrl.noaa.gov/gmd/aggi/aggi .html. On carbon dioxide levels, see Scott Waldman, "Atmospheric Carbon Dioxide Hits Record Levels," *ClimateWire*, March 14, 2017; Justin Gillis, "Carbon in Atmosphere Is Rising, Even as Emissions Stabilize," *New York Times*, June 26, 2017; and Bob Berwyn, "Second Biggest Jump in Annual CO$_2$ Levels Reported as Trump Leaves Paris Climate Agreement," *Inside Climate News*, June 1, 2017. For some of the most useful statistics and graphic displays of trends in greenhouse gas emissions, see the webpage for the Center for Climate and Energy Solutions (www.c2es.org/ facts-figures/international-emissions) and the International Energy Agency's site for climate change (www.iea.org/topics/climatechange/).

53. U.S. EPA, "National Summary of State Information," available at https://ofmpub .epa.gov/waters10/attains_nation_cy.control#total_assessed_waters. The same page allows review of reports on each of the fifty states.

54. U.S. EPA, *National Water Quality Inventory: 2000 Report to Congress* (Washington, DC: Office of Water, EPA, 2002). After this publication, the EPA no longer included an assessment of groundwater in these reports. The U.S. Geological Survey has an extensive program of monitoring and assessing groundwater. See its website (www .usgs.gov). See also the EPA's page on groundwater: http://water.epa.gov/drink/.

55. A major study by the EPA found that "hydraulic fracturing activities can impact drinking water resources under some circumstances," but also that data gaps and uncertainties limit its ability to characterize the severity of the impacts. See U.S. EPA, *Hydraulic Fracturing for Oil and Gas: Impacts from the Hydraulic Fracturing Water Cycle on Drinking Water Resources in the United States: Final Report* EPA/600/R-16/236F (Washington, DC: Office of Research and Development, 2016), available at https:// www.epa.gov/hfstudy.

56. For a recent review of the history of policy efforts on nuclear waste, see Michael E. Kraft, "Nuclear Power and the Challenge of High-Level Waste Disposal in the United States," *Polity* 45, no. 2 (April 2013): 265–80. The Obama administration created a Blue Ribbon Commission on America's Nuclear Future to examine the challenge, but its final report led to no action. The commission's report is available at www .energy.gov/sites/prod/files/2013/04/f0/brc_finalreport_jan2012.pdf.

57. See Government Accountability Office, *Numbers of Contaminated Federal Sites, Estimated Costs, and EPA's Oversight Role*, GAO-15-830T (Washington, DC: GAO, 2015) and Government Accountability Office, *U.S. Government's Environmental Liability* (Washington, DC: GAO, 2016). The latter report was published as part of the GAO's 2017 High-Risk Series: Government Accountability Office, *Progress on Many High-Risk Areas, While Substantial Efforts Needed on Others*, GAO-17-317 (Washington, DC: GAO, February 2017), 232–47.

58. The EPA reports current achievements and challenges at its website for the Superfund program: www.epa.gov/superfund. On the cleanup of rivers, see Anthony DePalma, "Superfund Cleanup Stirs Troubled Waters," *New York Times*, August 13, 2012. For the quotation, see U.S. Environmental Protection Agency, *The Office of Solid Waste and Emergency Response: Fiscal 2010 End of the Year Report* (Washington, DC: USEPA, 2010), 12, https://archive.epa.gov/region3/ebytes/web/pdf/oswer_eoy_2010.pdf.

59. The pertinent documents can be found at the EPA's website for pesticide programs: www.epa.gov/pesticides/.

60. See Coral Davenport and Emmarie Huetteman, "Lawmakers Reach Deal to Expand Regulation of Toxic Chemicals," *New York Times*, May 19, 2016. For details about the new act, see the EPA webpage on it: www.epa.gov/assessing-and-managing-chemicals-under-tsca/frank-r-lautenberg-chemical-safety-21st-century-act.

61. Hallett J. Harris and Denise Scheberle, "Ode to the Miner's Canary: The Search for Environmental Indicators," in *Environmental Program Evaluation: A Primer*, ed. Gerrit J. Knaap and Tschangho John Kim (Champaign: University of Illinois Press, 1998), 176–200. See also Gretchen C. Daily, ed., *Nature's Services: Societal Dependence on Natural Ecosystems* (Washington, DC: Island Press, 1997); and Water Science and Technology Board, *Valuing Ecosystem Services: Toward Better Environmental Decision-Making* (Washington, DC: National Academies Press, 2004).

62. The numbers come from the various agency websites and from Kraft, *Environmental Policy and Politics*, Chapters 6 and 7.

63. The Fish and Wildlife Service website (www.fws.gov) provides extensive data on threatened and endangered species and habitat recovery plans. The figures on improving and declining species come from the U.S. Fish and Wildlife Service, *Report to Congress on the Recovery of Threatened and Endangered Species: Fiscal Years 2009–2010* (Washington, DC: Fish and Wildlife Service, January 2012), available at www.fws.gov/endangered/esa-library/pdf/Recovery_Report_2010.pdf.

64. Population Reference Bureau, "2017 World Population Data Sheet," available at www.prb.org.

65. See Mazmanian and Kraft, *Toward Sustainable Communities*; Fiorino, *The New Environmental Regulation*; Eisner, *Governing the Environment*; and Kraft, Stephan, and Abel, *Coming Clean*. A number of the chapters in Sheldon Kamieniecki and Michael E. Kraft, eds., *The Oxford Handbook of U.S. Environmental Policy* (New York: Oxford University Press, 2013), also analyze the promise of new policy approaches, as do the chapters in Durant, Fiorino, and O'Leary, *Environmental Governance Reconsidered*.

66. The quotation is from John M. Broder and Andrew C. Revkin, "Hard Task for New Team on Energy and Climate," *New York Times*, December 16, 2008. See also David A. Fahrenthold, "Ready for Challenges: Obama's Environmental Team: No Radicals," *Washington Post National Weekly Edition*, December 22, 2008–January 4, 2009, 34.

Chapter 2

Racing to the Top, the Bottom, or the Middle of the Pack?
The Evolving State Government Role in Environmental Protection

Barry G. Rabe

The problem which all federalized nations have to solve is how to secure an efficient central government and preserve national unity, while allowing free scope for the diversities, and free play to the . . . members of the federation. It is . . . to keep the centrifugal and centripetal forces in equilibrium, so that neither the planet States shall fly off into space, nor the sun of the Central government draw them into its consuming fires.

Lord James Bryce, *The American Commonwealth*, 1888

Before the 1970s, the conventional wisdom on federalism viewed "the planet States" as sufficiently lethargic to require a powerful "Central government" in many areas of environmental policy. States were widely derided as mired in corruption, hostile to innovation, and unable to take a serious role in environmental policy out of fear of alienating key economic constituencies. If anything, they were seen as "racing to the bottom" among their neighbors, attempting to impose as few regulatory burdens as possible. In more recent times, the tables have turned—so much so that current conventional wisdom often berates an overheated federal government that squelches state creativity and capability to tailor environmental policies to local realities. The decentralization mantra of recent decades has endorsed an extended transfer of environmental policy resources and regulatory authority from Washington, DC, to states and localities. Governors turned presidents, such as Ronald Reagan, Bill Clinton, and George W. Bush, extolled the wisdom of such a strategy, at least in their rhetoric. Many recent heads of the U.S. Environmental Protection Agency (EPA), including Gina McCarthy in the Obama administration and Scott Pruitt under Donald Trump, took federal office after extended state government experience and frequently endorsed the idea of shifting more authority back to statehouses. Pruitt in particular would repeatedly invoke the phrase "cooperative federalism" during his 2017 confirmation hearings in embracing a state-centered model of federalism. Of course, such a transfer would pose a potentially formidable test of the thesis that more localized units know best and has faced major political hurdles.

37

What accounts for this sea change in our understanding of the role of states in environmental policy? How have states evolved in recent decades, and what types of functions do they assume most comfortably and effectively? Despite state resurgence, are there areas in which states fall short? How will states respond to efforts by the Trump administration to reduce federal engagement and shift many environmental protection responsibilities to them? Looking ahead, should regulatory authority devolve to the states, or are there better ways to sort out federal and state responsibilities?

This chapter addresses these questions, examining evidence of state performance in environmental policy. It provides both an overview of state evolution and a set of brief case studies that explore state strengths and limitations. These state-specific accounts are interwoven with assessments of the federal government's role, for good or ill, in the development of state environmental policy.

The States as the "New Heroes" of American Federalism

Policy analysts are generally most adept at analyzing institutional foibles and policy failures. Indeed, much of the literature on environmental policy follows this pattern, with criticism particularly voluminous and potent when directed toward federal efforts in this area. By contrast, states have received much more favorable treatment. Many influential books and reports on state government and federalism portray states as highly dynamic and effective. Environmental policy is often depicted as a prime example of this general pattern of state effectiveness. Some analysts routinely characterize states as the "new heroes" of American federalism, as having long since eclipsed a doddering federal government. According to this line of argument, states are consistently at the cutting edge of policy innovation, eager to find creative solutions to environmental problems, and "racing to the top" with a goal of national preeminence in the field. When the states fall short, an overzealous federal partner is often said to be at fault.

Such assertions have considerable empirical support. The vast majority of state governments have undergone fundamental changes since the first Earth Day in 1970. Many states have drafted new constitutions and gained access to unprecedented revenues through expanded taxing powers. In turn, many state bureaucracies have grown and become more professionalized, as have staffs serving governors and legislatures. Expanded policy engagement has been further stimulated by increasingly competitive two-party systems in many regions through at least 2010, intensifying pressure on elected officials to deliver desired services. Heightened use of direct democracy provisions, such as the initiative and referendum, and increasing activism by state courts and elected state attorneys general create alternative routes for policy adoption. On the whole in recent decades, public opinion data have consistently found that citizens have a considerably higher degree of "trust and confidence" in the package of public services and regulations dispensed from their state capitals than in those generated from Washington.[1] These factors have converged to expand state capacity and commitment to environmental protection.

This transformed state role is evident in virtually every area of environmental policy. States directly regulate approximately 20 percent of the total U.S. economy, including many areas in which environmental concerns come into play.[2] The Environmental Council of the States has estimated that states operate 96 percent of all federal environmental programs that can be delegated to them.[3] Collectively, they approach that high level of engagement in the issuance of all environmental permits and the implementation of all environmental enforcement actions. Despite this expanded role, federal financial support to states in the form of grants to fund environmental protection efforts has generally declined since the early 1980s and appears likely to plunge further in the late 2010s during the Trump presidency. This continues to force states to find ways to fund most of their operations while many face significant fiscal strains.

Many areas of environmental policy are clearly dominated by states, including most aspects of waste management, groundwater protection, land use management, transportation, and electricity regulation. This state-centric role is also reflected in rapidly emerging areas, such as the protection of air, land, and water quality in view of the dramatic expansion in the exploration of shale gas and oil via hydraulic fracturing (or "fracking") techniques. In many instances, state action in these new environmental policy areas represents "compensatory federalism," whereby Washington proves "hesitant, uncertain, distracted, and in disagreement about what to do," and states respond with a "step into the breach."[4] Even in policy areas with an established federal imprint, such as air and water pollution control, states often have considerable opportunity to oversee implementation and move beyond federal standards if they so choose. In air quality alone, more than a dozen states routinely adopt policies to either exceed federal standards or fill federal regulatory gaps, often setting models for national consideration. Political scientists Christopher McGrory Klyza and David Sousa confirm that "the greater flexibility of state government can yield policy innovation, opening the way to the next generation of environmental policy."[5] That flexibility and commitment are further reflected in the institutional arrangements established by states to address environmental problems. Many states have long since moved beyond their historical placement of environmental programs in public health or natural resource departments in favor of establishing comprehensive agencies that gather most environmental responsibilities under a single organizational umbrella. These agencies have sweeping, cross-programmatic responsibilities and have grown steadily in staff and complexity in recent decades. Ironically, many of these agencies mirror the organizational framework of the much-maligned EPA, dividing regulatory activity by environmental media of air, land, and water and thereby increasing the likelihood of shifting environmental contamination back and forth across medium boundaries. Despite this fragmentation, such institutions provide states with a firm institutional foundation for addressing a variety of environmental concerns. In turn, many states have continued to experiment with new organizational arrangements to meet evolving challenges, including the use of informal networks, special task forces, and interstate compacts to facilitate cooperation among various departments and agencies.[6]

This expanded state commitment to environmental policy may be accelerated, not only by the broader factors introduced above but also by features somewhat unique to this policy area. First, a growing number of scholars contend that broad public support for environmental protection provides considerable impetus for more decentralized policy development. Such "civic environmentalism" stimulates numerous state and local stakeholders to take creative collective action independent of federal intervention. As opposed to top-down controls, game-theoretic analyses of efforts to protect so-called common-pool resources, such as river basins and forests, side decisively with local or regional approaches to resource protection. Much of the leading scholarly work of the late Elinor Ostrom, who in 2009 became the first political scientist to win the Nobel Prize in economics, actively embraced "bottom-up" environmental governance.[7] Second, the proliferation of environmental policy professionals in state agencies and legislative staff roles has created a sizable base of talent and ideas for state-level policy innovation. Contrary to conventional depictions of agency officials as shackled by elected "principals," an alternative view finds considerable policy innovation or "entrepreneurship" in state policymaking circles. This pattern is especially evident in environmental policy because numerous areas of specialization place a premium on expert ideas and allow for considerable innovation within agencies.[8] Recent scholarly work on the performance of state environmental agencies gives generally high marks to officials for professionalism, constructive problem solving, and increasing emphasis on improving environmental outcomes, albeit with considerable state-to-state variation.[9] Networks of state professionals, working in similar capacities but across jurisdictional boundaries, have become increasingly influential in recent decades. These networks facilitate information exchange, foster the diffusion of innovation, and pool resources to pursue joint initiatives. Such multistate groups as the Environmental Council of the States, the National Association of Clean Air Agencies, and the National Association of State Energy Officials also band together to influence the design of subsequent federal policies, seeking either latitude for expanded state experimentation or federal adoption of state "best practices." Other entities, such as the Northeast States for Coordinated Air Use Management, the Great Lakes Commission, and the Pacific Coast Collaborative, represent state interests in certain regions.

Third, environmental policy in many states is stimulated by direct democracy, which is not allowed at the federal level, through initiatives, referendums, and the recall of elected officials. In every state except Delaware, state constitutional amendments must be approved by voters via referendum. Thirty-one states and Washington, DC, also have some form of direct democracy for approving legislation, representing well over half the U.S. population. Use of this policy tool has grown at an exponential rate to consider a wide array of state environmental policy options, including nuclear plant closure, mandatory disclosure of commercial product toxicity, and public land acquisition. In 2016, Washington voters decisively rejected a proposal to establish the first tax in the United States on carbon dioxide emissions, a policy already in place in parts of Canada and Europe. This proposal faced significant industry opposition as well as divides between likely proponents on whether revenue from such a tax should be applied to alternative energy development or reducing other taxes. In prior years, however, Washington voters approved a ballot proposition requiring a steady increase in the amount of electricity derived from renewable sources, as was the case in Colorado and Missouri. Western states have generally made the greatest use of these provisions on environmental issues, particularly Oregon, California, and Colorado. In 2016, California voters embraced state efforts to ban plastic bags while Massachusetts voters rejected attempts to extend beverage-container deposits to a wider range of products, demonstrating that ballot propositions can be used to either expand or restrict the scope of environmental policy.

The Cutting Edge of Policy: Cases of State Innovation

The convergence of these various political forces has unleashed substantial new environmental policy at the state level. Various researchers have attempted to analyze some of this activity through ranking schemes that determine which states are most active and innovative, often tracking how policy ideas then diffuse across states. Such studies consistently conclude that certain states tend to take the lead in most areas of policy innovation, followed by an often uneven pattern of innovation diffusion across state and regional boundaries.[10] For example, the American Council for an Energy-Efficient Economy produces annual rankings of states on the basis of their adoption rates for a range of policies that offer environmental protection through more efficient energy use. In 2016, its researchers found that California and Massachusetts tied for the top ranking, followed by states located primarily on the East and West Coasts. Maine, Missouri, and Michigan were found to have made the most progress from the prior year while South and North Dakota, Kansas, and Wyoming ranked at the very bottom.[11]

Additional analyses have attempted to examine which economic and political factors are most likely to influence the rigor of state policy or the level of resources devoted to it.[12] An important but less examined question concerns the relationships between environmental policy and both environmental quality and economic growth. Emerging research has created an "eco-efficiency index" that looks across multiple areas of environmental protection over time and ranks states according to the "stress on health and ecology required to generate a given unit of income."[13] These rankings generally parallel earlier studies that track rates of policy innovation and adoption, with higher scores reflecting greater eco-efficiency (see Table 2-1). In turn, a more established body of research evidence suggests that a number of state innovations offer promising alternatives to prevailing approaches, often representing a direct response to local environmental crises and revealing shortcomings in existing policy design. Brief case studies that follow indicate the breadth and potential effectiveness of state innovation.

Table 2-1   State Air, Climate, and Energy (ACE) Index

State	Weighted Overall Score	State	Weighted Overall Score
New Jersey	47.04	Georgia	9.60
California	41.36	Minnesota	9.34
Connecticut	36.17	Utah	9.16
New York	36.03	Texas	8.84
Rhode Island	30.49	Arizona	8.54
Massachusetts	28.81	South Carolina	8.31
Delaware	26.57	Indiana	7.00
Maryland	26.18	Iowa	6.70
Washington	17.86	Idaho	6.63
Virginia	17.36	Missouri	6.56
New Hampshire	16.91	Nebraska	6.44
Hawaii	16.71	Kentucky	6.15
North Carolina	15.15	South Dakota	5.61
Pennsylvania	14.56	Alabama	5.03
Illinois	13.55	Kansas	4.93
Florida	13.10	West Virginia	4.82
Vermont	12.99	Oklahoma	4.60
Nevada	12.58	Louisiana	4.58
Oregon	11.38	Arkansas	4.53
Colorado	11.02	New Mexico	4.31
Tennessee	11.00	Mississippi	4.17
Ohio	10.28	Alaska	4.00
Michigan	10.07	Montana	3.38
Wisconsin	9.99	North Dakota	3.35
Maine	9.87	Wyoming	2.20

Source: Daniel Fiorino and Riordan Frost, "The Pilot Eco-Efficiency Index: A New State Environmental Ranking for Researchers and Government" (paper presented at the Association for Public Policy Analysis and Management's fall research conference, Washington, DC, November 4, 2016), www.researchgate.net/publication/315736703_The_Pilot_Eco-Efficiency_Index_A_New_State_Environmental_Ranking_for_Researchers_and_Government.

Anticipating Environmental Challenges

One of the greatest challenges facing U.S. environmental policy is the need to shift from a pollution control mode that reacts after damage has occurred to one that anticipates potential problems and attempts to prevent them. Growing evidence suggests that some states have launched serious planning processes and are attempting to pursue preventative strategies in an increasingly systematic and effective way. All fifty states have adopted at least one pollution prevention program. The oldest and most common of these involve technical assistance to industries and networking services that link potential collaborators. But some states have increasingly redefined pollution prevention in bolder terms, cutting across conventional programmatic boundaries with a series of mandates and incentives to pursue prevention opportunities. Thirty-four states have adopted laws that move beyond federal standards in preventing risks from chemical exposure, such as bans of specific chemicals thought to pose health risks or comprehensive chemical management systems.[14] Among the more active states, Minnesota has one of the most far-reaching programs. A series of state laws requires hundreds of Minnesota firms to submit annual toxic pollution prevention plans and give priority treatment to "chemicals of concern."[15] These plans must outline each firm's current use and release of a long list of toxic pollutants and establish formal goals for their reduction or elimination over a specified period of time. Firms have considerable latitude in determining how to attain these goals, contrary to the technology-forcing character of much federal regulation. But they must meet state-established reduction timetables and pay fees on releases. The state was also one of the first two states to ban bisphenol A, a controversial chemical used in plastics.[16] From these earlier efforts, Minnesota and other states have established multidisciplinary teams that attempt to forecast emerging environmental threats and respond before problems arise. This forward-looking approach has included pioneering efforts in recent years to review potential environmental risks from nanotechnology and its generation of staggeringly small particles that may improve product design but also harbor environmental risks.[17] Minnesota has also taken a lead role in pricing the environmental impacts of carbon dioxide emissions in long-term planning for electricity generation. This latter practice contributed to the 2007 enactment of the Next Generation Energy Act and its ambitious provisions to transition from dependence on coal toward renewables as a primary electricity source, although portions of this legislation have been reversed by federal courts after a challenge from coal interests based in North Dakota. In 2016, Minnesota embraced President Obama's proposed Clean Power Plan and launched new initiatives to ensure that it would comply with its emission reduction goals through 2030.

Colorado has taken a "race-to-the-top" approach to policy designed to anticipate and thereby minimize environmental risks from hydraulic fracturing practices. The state has a long-standing history in oil and gas extraction and has sought in recent years to balance energy development with environmental protection in the fracking era. This initiative has included pioneering steps in requiring public disclosure of chemicals used in drilling operations, water quality sampling, air quality standards, and property owner protections.[18] In turn, Colorado has undertaken a sustained process engaging diverse stakeholders to find ways to share governance responsibility across state and local levels, contrary to the more common pattern whereby states largely preempt local governments from influencing many fracking decisions.[19]

Economic Incentives

Economists have long lamented the penchant for command-and-control rules and regulations in U.S. environmental policy. Most would prefer to see a more economically sensitive set of policies, such as taxes on emissions to capture social costs or "negative externalities" and provide monetary incentives for good environmental performance. The politics of imposing such costs has proven contentious at all governmental levels, although a growing number of states have begun to pursue some form of this approach in recent years. In all, the states have enacted hundreds of measures that can be characterized as "green taxes," including environmentally related "surcharges" and "fees" that avoid the explicit use of the label "tax."[20] States use related revenues to cover approximately 60 percent of their total environmental agency expenses and, in some cases, the full costs of some popular programs such as recycling and energy efficiency.[21] A growing number of states have begun to revisit their general tax policies with an eye toward environmental purposes. For example, Iowa exempts from taxation all pollution control equipment purchased for use in the state, whereas California offers major tax incentives to purchasers of hybrid and electric vehicles. Numerous states provide a series of tax credits or low-interest loans for the purchase of recycling or renewable energy equipment or for the capital investments necessary to develop environmentally friendly technologies. Many states and localities have also developed some form of tax on solid waste, usually involving a direct fee for garbage pickup while offering free collection of recyclables.

One of the earliest and most visible economic incentive programs involves refundable taxes on beverage containers.[22] Ten states—covering 30 percent of the population—have such programs in place. Deposit collections flow through a system that includes consumers, container redemption facilities such as grocery stores, and firms that reuse or recycle the containers. Michigan's program is widely regarded as among the most successful of these state efforts and, similar to a number of others, is a product of direct democracy. Michigan's program places a dime deposit on containers—double the more conventional nickel—which may contribute to its unusually high redemption rate of 97 percent. This type of policy has diffused to other products, including scrap tires, used motor oil, pesticide containers, appliances with ozone-depleting substances, and electronic waste materials such as used computers.

States also have constitutional authority to tax all forms of energy, including transportation fuel and electricity. Many policy analysts across ideological divides have long argued that such taxation would be one of the most effective ways to deter environmental degradation, as use of conventional energy sources contributes to many environmental problems. Increasing the price of energy would likely discourage consumption and related environmental damage, just as sustained tax increases have elevated the costs of smoking and driven down rates of tobacco use in recent decades. Many states have been highly reluctant to move beyond their traditional levels of taxation for fuels such as gasoline that are commonly used to maintain highways and bridges.

But ten states have worked over the past decade to place a price on the release of carbon emissions through an auctioning process linked to an emissions cap that declines over time. Building on pioneering American work to reduce sulfur dioxide emissions, nine northeastern states have formed the Regional Greenhouse Gas Initiative (RGGI) that requires purchase, through quarterly public auctions, of allowances to emit carbon. This pricing mechanism also provides revenue whereby RGGI states can support alternative energy projects or rebate consumer electricity bills. Political scientist Leigh Raymond has argued that RGGI offers a "new model" for climate policy that is already influencing other governments in the United States and internationally.[23] California has also followed this path and has begun comparable emissions trading with the Canadian provinces of Quebec and Ontario, while other states began to explore such a "trading-ready" option in the early stages of Clean Power Plan development under President Obama.

Yet another area for state innovation based on economic incentives may be the application of severance tax revenues from oil and gas drilling operations to help alleviate related environmental impacts. Nearly all states that allow drilling have such taxes, with rates frequently highest in more conservative states. Funds generated from these taxes have soared in many states with the onset of expanded drilling through fracking techniques, and some states have explored ways to use funds to prepare for longer-term challenges once drilling declines. North Dakota, for example, has established an oil and gas Legacy Fund that sets aside 30 percent of proceeds for investment toward longer-term use while also designating funds to address drilling impacts on the environment and alternative energy development. Colorado has also been a pioneer in this area, adopting new legislation in recent years to allocate some of its severance tax revenues to water protection and other environmental protection efforts.[24] Other states, such as Connecticut, Rhode Island, Hawaii, and New York, do not produce fossil fuels and so lack severance taxes. Instead, they have created "green banks," public financial institutions that use public debt to encourage private investment in alternative energy projects.[25]

Filling the Federal Void: Reducing Greenhouse Gases

As the RGGI case demonstrates, states have proven unexpectedly active players in the fight to reduce greenhouse gas emissions to curb climate change. While most Congresses and some presidents have struggled to make any policy contribution to this problem, a number of states have attempted to fill some of the "policy gap" created by federal inaction.[26] This American "bottom-up" approach has also emerged in other federal or multilevel governmental systems, including Canada, Australia, and the European Union.[27] In Canada, for example, Prime Minister Justin Trudeau launched in 2016 plans for a "pan-Canadian" carbon price, establishing national standards but leaving considerable room for individual provinces to design their own carbon taxes or cap-and-trade programs, including ones involving possible partnerships with American states. This decentralized approach has produced an increasingly diverse set of policies that address every sector of activity generating greenhouse gases and collectively would reduce national emission levels if fully implemented.[28] Many states are responsible for substantial amounts of greenhouse gas emissions, even by global standards. If all states were to secede and become independent nations, eighteen of them would rank among the top fifty nations in the world in terms of releases. In response, many states have adopted policies that promise to reduce their greenhouse gas releases, although they tend to also pursue these policies for other environmental reasons. Twenty-nine states and Washington, DC, have enacted "renewable portfolio standards (RPS)," mandating that a certain level of state electricity must come from such renewable sources as wind, geothermal, and solar. These policies generally follow a similar structure, although they vary in terms of both the definition of eligible sources and the overall targets and timetables for expanding capacity.[29] For example, Hawaii has set a target of 100 percent renewables by 2045 whereas Vermont is committed to reaching 75 percent by 2032. Three states (California, New York, and Oregon) have set targets to reach 50 percent renewables by either 2030 or 2040. Five Midwestern states surpassed the 20 percent mark in production of electricity from wind in 2016, including Iowa at 37 percent and Kansas at 30 percent, while Texas acquired 23 percent of its power from wind during the first quarter of 2017. In turn, twenty-six states have adopted an energy-efficiency equivalent of an RPS, mandating an ongoing increase in overall energy efficiency that in some cases is integrated with renewable energy mandates. Massachusetts, Rhode Island, and Arizona have the most ambitious energy-efficiency targets, and New Hampshire is the most recent state to adopt such a policy.[30]

California has ranked among the world's most active governments in addressing climate change, developing cap-and-trade policies alongside renewable energy and energy-efficiency mandates.[31] It has adopted a number of pioneering climate statutes in recent decades, perhaps most notably the 2006 Global Warming Solutions Act (AB 32). AB 32 imposes a statutory target to reduce statewide emissions to 1990 levels by 2020 and steadily reduce them 80 percent below 1990 levels by 2050. It attempts to attain those goals through an all-out policy assault on virtually every sector that generates greenhouse gases, including industry, electricity, transportation, agriculture, and residential activity, giving extraordinary authority to the formidable California Air Resources Board in overseeing implementation. But California may have its largest impact on greenhouse gas emissions through repeated use of a unique waiver it secured through federal air legislation first adopted in 1967. On more than 100 occasions since that point, California has been able to establish more rigorous tailpipe emission standards for cars and light trucks than the rest of the nation, although its waiver frequently leads to adoption of a national standard that reflects California's preferences. This policy has resulted in substantial emission reductions per vehicle in past decades and took new form in 2009 when the Obama administration merged vehicle emission regulations with fuel economy standards, setting bold targets that would reach an average of 54.5 miles per gallon in 2025. The 2009 federal initiative followed intensive pressure from California and allied states to act after 2002 state legislation attempted to establish the world's first greenhouse gas emission standards for vehicles. This reform reflects a unique situation whereby one state can innovate within its own boundaries but leverage national-level change in the process through power granted to it through federal legislation.[32]

Taking It to the Federal Government

At the same time that states have eclipsed the federal government through new policies, they have also made increasingly aggressive use of litigation to attempt to force the federal government to take new steps or reconsider previous ones. Under the George W. Bush administration, some states pursued litigation to attempt to push the federal government into taking bolder environmental steps; under Barack Obama, some states turned to litigation to compel added federal efforts whereas others sought to thwart new steps by federal environmental agencies. In both cases, state responses have been guided by an increasingly active set of state attorneys general who have begun to develop multistate litigation strategies to influence federal policy. Unlike their federal counterpart, most state attorneys general are elected officials, and their powers have expanded significantly since the mid-1970s. They frequently represent a political party different from that of the sitting governor and often use their powers as a base from which to seek higher office, most commonly governorships.[33]

Collectively, these officials have increasingly become a force to be reckoned with, not only in their home states but also as they expand their engagement through challenges brought into the federal courts. In a 2014 Supreme Court case reviewing federal authority to establish greenhouse gas emission limits for power plants, fifteen states, including California and New York, implored the court to sustain federal regulatory authority. In turn, twelve states, including Texas and Michigan, filed a court brief that decried the federal plan as "one of the most brazen power grabs ever attempted by an administrative agency." No state has been as aggressive in combating federal environmental authority as Texas, where Attorney General Greg Abbott filed more than twenty suits attempting to block environmental actions by the Obama administration. "I go to the office in the morning," quipped Abbott in 2014, the year he was elected governor, "I sue the federal government, and I go home." One regular Abbott ally among the ranks of attorneys general hostile to federal environmental policy worked just across the Texas border in Oklahoma. Scott Pruitt built a national reputation by bringing more than a dozen well-publicized lawsuits against the EPA, although most were unsuccessful. In 2017, he was confirmed as the agency's administrator under President Trump.

State Limits

Such a diverse set of policy initiatives would seem to augur well for the states' involvement in environmental policy. Any such enthusiasm must be tempered, however, by a continuing concern over how evenly that innovative vigor extends over the entire nation. One enduring rationale for giving the federal government so much authority in environmental policy is that states appear to face inherent limitations. Rather than a consistent, across-the-board pattern of dynamism, we see a more uneven pattern of performance than conventional wisdom might anticipate. Just as some states consistently strive for national leadership, others appear to seek the middle or bottom of the pack, seemingly doing as little as possible and rarely taking innovative steps. This imbalance becomes particularly evident when environmental problems are not confined to a specific state's boundaries. Many environmental issues are, by definition, transboundary, raising important questions of interstate and interregional equity in allocating responsibility for environmental protection. These doubts about state capacity and commitment raise important concerns for any effort to shift more responsibility for environmental protection from the federal to state governments, as seems likely in the Trump era.

Uneven State Performance

Many efforts to rank states according to their environmental regulatory rigor, institutional capacity, or general innovativeness find the same subset of states at the top of the list year after year. By contrast, a significant number of states consistently tend to fall much further down the list, somewhat consistent with their placement in Table 2-1, raising questions as to their overall policy capacity and commitment. As political scientist William R. Lowry notes, "Not all states are responding appropriately to policy needs within their borders. . . . If matching between need and response were always high and weak programs existed only where pollution was low, this would not be a problem. However, this is not the case."[34] Given all the hoopla surrounding the newfound dynamism of states racing to the top in environmental policy, there has been remarkably little analysis of the performance of states that not only fail to crack top-ten rankings but may view racing to the bottom as an economic development strategy. Such a downward race may be particularly attractive during recessions, as was reflected in recent efforts in states such as West Virginia, Michigan, and Wisconsin to weaken dramatically the implementation of existing policies, efforts that had the express goal of promoting economic growth by creating a policy environment friendlier to industry.[35] What we know more generally about state policy commitment should surely give us pause over any claims that state dynamism is truly national in scope. Despite considerable economic growth in formerly poor regions, such as the Southeast, substantial variation endures among state governments in their rates of public expenditure, including their total and per capita expenditures on environmental protection.[36] Such disparities are consistent with studies of state political culture and social capital, which indicate vast differences in probable state receptivity to governmental efforts to foster environmental improvement.

Although many states have unveiled exciting new programs, nearly half have established some formal restrictions that preclude their environmental agencies from adopting regulations or standards that are more stringent than those of the federal government in such areas as air and water quality.[37] EPA Office of Inspector General reports and other external reviews generate serious questions about how effectively states handle core functions either delegated to them under federal programs or left exclusively to their oversight. Studies of water quality program implementation have found that states use highly variable water quality standards in areas such as sewage contamination, groundwater protection, nonpoint water pollution from diffuse sources, wetland preservation, fish advisories, and beach closures. Inconsistencies abound in reporting accuracy, suggesting that national assessments of water quality trends that rely on data from state reports may be highly suspect.[38] More than half of the states lack comprehensive water management and drought response plans, and several with such plans have not revised them in many years.[39] Even in many high-saliency cases, such as Everglades protection, states have sought a federal rescue rather than taking serious unilateral action. As political scientist Sheldon Kamieniecki notes, Florida's "state government, which has been continuously pressured from all sides, has waffled in its intentions to improve the wetlands ecosystem in South Florida."[40] Agricultural interests, particularly those promoting sugar production in this region, have proven formidable opponents of major restoration, which would restrict their access to massive volumes of water.[41]

Similar issues have arisen as states have struggled in recent years to formulate policies to reduce potential risks to groundwater supplies from shale gas and oil development, with some states such as Oklahoma racing in the opposite direction from Colorado's. This environmental backpedaling has included downplaying environmental concerns, such as proliferating earthquakes linked to underground wastewater injections; slashing state severance taxes; and overriding local government reservations in order to maximize immediate development. Comparable problems have emerged in state enforcement of air quality and waste management programs. Despite efforts in some states to integrate and streamline permitting, many states have extensive backlogs in the permit programs they operate and lack any real indication of facility compliance with various regulatory standards. Measurement of the impact of state programs on environmental outcomes remains imprecise in fracking as well as in many other areas. Existing indicators confirm enormous variation among states, although we likely know less about such variation than in the 1990s, given that the EPA lacks funding and staff to continue collecting state-by-state data in many areas of environmental policy. State governments—alongside their local counterparts—have understandably claimed much of the credit for increasing solid waste recycling rates from a national average of 6.6 percent in 1970 to 16 percent in 1990 to 34.6 percent in 2014. At the same time, state recycling policy design and performance appears to vary markedly, and states such as Arizona, Idaho, and Missouri prohibit cities from imposing fees or taxes on plastic bag purchases to discourage their use. Growing gaps in state and federal data gathering and dissemination capacity in recycling and many other areas raise sobering questions about the transparency of environmental policy and any ability to assess important indicators of performance.

There was also growing indication in some states during the first years of the 2010s that environmental policy faced major challenges in cases where state leaders assumed that government could be managed similarly to business and industry. Michigan shifted to total Republican control of the executive and legislative branches in 2010, and Republican Governor Rick Snyder won high marks nationally for his role in addressing fiscal concerns and assisting cities such as Detroit navigate bankruptcy en route to economic recovery. But the use of state-appointed emergency financial managers to oversee fiscally challenged municipalities backfired with tragic consequences in the case of Flint, a declining city that had once been an auto manufacturing hub.[42] The search for fiscal balance led to a 2015 decision to shift the source of Flint's water supply to save money and resulted in significant lead exposure for a city of nearly 100,000 residents. A set of state environmental and public health agencies ignored early warning signs and failed to respond to the emerging crisis, as did regional EPA authorities based in Chicago. This resulted in substantial lead contamination for Flint residents and has necessitated massive efforts to provide alternative water supplies and begin to replace damaged water infrastructure. Research on water quality trends indicates that Flint is not alone in this regard, raising questions over state and local stewardship of drinking water quality in Michigan and nationally as well as long-term challenges that may require massive new investments in modern water infrastructure that lack an obvious funding source.

Enduring Federal Dependency

More sweeping assertions of state resurgence are undermined further by the penchant of many states to cling to organizational designs and program priorities set in Washington, DC. Some states have demonstrated that far-reaching agency reorganization and other integrative policies can be pursued without significant opposition—or grant reduction—from the federal government, but the vast majority of states continue to adhere to a medium-based pollution control framework for agency organization that contributes to enduring programmatic fragmentation. Although a growing number of state officials speak favorably about shifting toward integrative approaches, many remain hard pressed to demonstrate how their states have begun to move in that direction. Many Clinton-era federal initiatives to give states more freedom to innovate were used to streamline operations rather than to foster prevention or integration. The Bush administration weakened many of these initiatives and, more generally, proved extremely reluctant to give states expanded authority or encouragement to innovate. The Obama administration was not initially seen as fostering state innovation and capacity, although it pumped considerable short-term environmental funding into states through economic stimulus support in 2009–2011. It also unveiled in its final two years a plan to reduce carbon emissions from the electricity sector that would involve states in central ways and provide them considerable incentive to tailor creative strategies that fit their particular circumstances.

Indeed, a good deal of the most innovative state-level activity has been at least partially underwritten through federal grants, which serve to stimulate additional state environmental spending.[43] In contrast, in Canada, where central government grant assistance—and regulatory presence—is extremely limited, provinces have proven somewhat less innovative than their American state counterparts. Although a number of states have developed fee systems to cover the majority of their operational costs, many continue to rely heavily on federal grants to fund some core environmental protection activities. States have continued to receive other important types of federal support, including grants and technical assistance to complete "state-of-the-state" environmental reports, undertake comparative risk assessment projects, launch inventories and action plans for greenhouse gas reductions, and implement some voluntary federal programs. On the whole, states have annually received between one-quarter and one-third of their total environmental and natural resource program funding from federal grants in recent years, although a few states (such as Colorado, Hawaii, Idaho, North Dakota, West Virginia, and Utah) relied on the federal government for between 40 and 70 percent of their total funding in the 2010s. The overall level of federal support dropped to 23 percent in 2008, increased to 30 percent three years later due to temporary injections of federal stimulus dollars, but declined to 25 percent in 2013.[44] This level appears likely to drop further due to anticipated federal budget cuts by the Trump administration. Furthermore, for all the opprobrium heaped on the federal government in environmental policy, it has provided states with at least four other forms of valuable assistance, some of which has contributed directly to the resurgence and innovation of state environmental policy. First, federal development in 1986 of the Toxics Release Inventory, modeled after programs initially attempted in Maryland and New Jersey, has emerged as an important component of many of the most promising state policy initiatives. This program has generated considerable data concerning toxic releases and provided states with a vital data source for exploring alternative regulatory approaches.[45] Many state pollution prevention programs would be unthinkable without such an annual information source. This program has also provided lessons for states to develop supplemental disclosure registries for greenhouse gases and may also do so for chemical use disclosure related to hydraulic fracturing.[46]

Second, states remain almost totally dependent on the federal government for essential insights gained through research and development. Each year, the federal government outspends the states in environmental research and development by substantial amounts, and states have shown little inclination to assume this burden by funding research programs tailored to their particular technological and informational needs.

Third, many successful efforts to coordinate environmental protection on a multistate, regional basis have received substantial federal input and support. A series of initiatives in the Chesapeake Bay, the Great Lakes Basin, and New England have received considerable acclaim for tackling difficult issues and forging regional partnerships; federal collaboration—via grants, technical assistance, coordination, and efforts to unify regional standards—with states has proven useful in these cases.[47] One model for engagement was the Great Lakes Restoration Initiative championed by the Obama administration; intended to address pressing regional environmental challenges, it was successful in accelerating ecological recovery in several areas with a legacy of heavy toxic contamination. By contrast, other major bioregions, including Puget Sound, the Gulf of Mexico, the Columbia River system, and the Mississippi River Basin, have lacked comparable federal participation and have generally not experienced creative interstate partnerships. Their experience contradicts the popular thesis that regional coordination is most likely in the absence of federal engagement, and two of the three recent regional initiatives to reduce greenhouse gases have struggled to endure in the absence of federal engagement or support.

Fourth, the EPA's ham-handedness is legendary, but its oversight of state-level program implementation looks far more constructive when we examine the role played by the agency's ten regional offices. Most state-level interaction with the EPA involves such regional offices, which employ approximately two-thirds of the total EPA workforce. Relations between state and regional officials are generally more cordial and constructive than those between state and central EPA officials, and such relations may even be, in some instances, characterized by high levels of mutual involvement and trust.[48] Surveys of state environmental officials confirm that they have a more positive relationship with regional rather than central agency staff.[49] Regional offices have played a key role in many of the most promising state-level innovations, including those in Minnesota and New Jersey. Their involvement may include formal advocacy on behalf of the state with central headquarters, direct collaboration on meshing state initiatives with federal requirements, and special grant support or technical assistance. This cooperation appears to be particularly common when regional office heads have prior state experience, as demonstrated in a number of instances in the Clinton, Bush, and Obama administrations.

The Interstate Environmental Balance of Trade

States may be structurally ill equipped to handle a large range of environmental concerns. In particular, they may be reluctant to invest significant energies to tackle problems that might literally migrate to another state or nation in the absence of intervention. The days of state agencies being captured securely in the hip pockets of major industries are probably long gone, reflecting fundamental changes in state government.[50] Nonetheless, state regulatory dynamism may diminish when cross-boundary transfer is likely.

The state imperative of economic development clearly contributes to this phenomenon. As states increasingly devise economic development strategies that resemble the industrial policies of European Union nations, a range of research has concluded they are far more deeply committed to strategies that promote investment or development than to those that involve social service provision or public health promotion.[51] A number of states offer incentives in excess of $50,000 per new job to prospective developers and have intensified efforts to retain jobs in the struggling manufacturing sector. Environmental protection can be eminently compatible with economic development goals, promoting overall quality of life and general environmental attractiveness that entices private investment. In many states, the tourism industry has played an active role in seeking strong environmental programs designed to maintain natural assets. In some instances, states may be keen to take actions that could produce internal environmental benefits as long as these actions do not have much near-term localized economic impact. California and other states that have formally endorsed setting strict emissions standards from vehicles, for example, have very few jobs to lose in the vehicle manufacturing sector and also see potential economic advantages if they can take a lead role nationally in developing alternative transportation technologies. At times, states may be judged by federal courts to have gone too far in trying to extend the reach of their policies to reshape the economies of their neighbors, as Minnesota found in being forced to dial back some of its clean air and climate goals after federal court review.

But much of what a state might undertake in environmental policy may largely benefit other states or regions, thereby reducing an individual state's incentive to take meaningful action. In fact, in many instances, states continue to pursue a "we make it, you take it" strategy. As political scientist William T. Gormley Jr. notes, sometimes "states can readily export their problems to other states," resulting in potentially serious environmental "balance of trade" problems.[52] In such situations, states may be inclined to export environmental contaminants to other states while enjoying any economic benefits to be derived from the activity that generated the contamination. One careful study of state air quality enforcement found no evidence of reduced effort along state borders but a measurable decline in effort along state borders with Mexican states or Canadian provinces.[53] Such cross-boundary transfers take many forms and may be particularly prevalent in environmental policy areas in which long-distance migration of pollutants is most likely. Air quality policy has long fit this pattern. States such as Ohio and Pennsylvania, for example, have depended heavily on burning massive quantities of coal to meet energy demands. Prevailing winds invariably transfer pollutants from this activity to other regions, particularly New England, leading to serious concern about acid deposition and related contamination threats. At times, states throughout the nation have utilized so-called dispersion enhancement as one approach to improve local air quality. Average industrial stack height in the United States soared from 243 feet in 1960 to 730 feet in 1980.[54] Although this increase resulted in significant air quality improvement in many areas near elevated stacks, it generally served to disperse air pollution problems elsewhere. It also contributed to the growing problem of airborne toxics that ultimately pollute water or land in other regions. Between 80 and 90 percent of many of the most dangerous toxic substances found in Lake Superior, for example, stem from air deposition, much of which is generated outside of the Great Lakes Basin.

Interstate conflicts, often becoming protracted battles in the federal courts, have endured in recent decades as states allege they are recipients of such unwanted "imports." In April 2014, the Supreme Court voted decisively to reinstate the EPA's Cross-State Air Pollution Rule, the agency's "good neighbor" provision that restricts cross-border exports of nitrogen oxides and sulfur dioxide emissions from twenty-eight midwestern and southern states into the Northeast. No region of the nation or environmental media appears immune from this kind of conflict. Prolonged battles between Alabama, Florida, and Georgia over access to waters from Lake Lanier and six rivers that cross their borders, for example, reached new intensity in recent years, resulting in extended mediation, litigation, and uncertainty about long-term approaches. Growing water scarcity linked to increased demand for water and extended drought in many regions has only exacerbated these conflicts.

Perhaps nowhere is the problem of interstate transfer more evident than in the disposal of solid, hazardous, and nuclear wastes. States have generally retained enormous latitude to devise their own systems of waste management and facility siting, working either independently or in concert with neighbors. Many states, including a number of those usually deemed among the most innovative and committed environmentally, continue to generate substantial quantities of waste and have struggled to establish comprehensive treatment, storage, and disposal capacity. Instead, out-of-state (and -region) export has been an increasingly common pattern, with a system that often resembles a shell game in which waste is ultimately deposited in the least resistant state or facility at any given moment. This pattern is repeated in emerging areas of waste management, such as the disposal of wastes generated by hydraulic fracturing procedures, and it is perhaps best illustrated in the migration of wastes generated in western Pennsylvania to deep-injection wells in eastern Ohio. This policy has triggered considerable controversy in Ohio, especially following a significant expansion of earthquake activity in areas near wells that accept large amounts of out-of-state fracking wastes.

No area of waste management, however, is as contentious as nuclear waste disposal. In the case of so-called high-level wastes, intensely contaminated materials from nuclear power plants that require between ten thousand and a hundred thousand years of isolation, the federal government and the vast majority of states have supported a thirty-year effort to transfer all of these wastes to a geological repository in Nevada where more than $10 billion has been invested in site development. Ferocious resistance by Nevada officials and concerns among states who would host transfer shipments have continued to scuttle this approach, leaving each of the 99 nuclear reactors spread across thirty-one states a de facto storage site. In the case of "low level" wastes, greater in volume but posing a less severe threat, states received considerable latitude from Washington in the early 1980s to develop a strategy for creating a series of regional sites, as well as access to funds to develop facilities. But subsequent siting efforts were riddled with conflict, and the growing reality is that increasing amounts of such waste must be stored near its point of generation.[55] One facility established for hazardous waste in western Texas has volunteered as a potential "host" for such waste, though it was not designed for nuclear waste and is remote, actually closest to settled communities across the New Mexico border and thousands of miles away from the bulk of generated waste. In turn, the Trump administration proposed reopening active exploration of the Nevada disposal option in 2017, triggering renewed opposition from that state.

Rethinking Environmental Federalism

Federalism scholars and some political officials have explored models for the constructive sharing of authority in the American federal system, many of which attempt to build on the respective strengths of varied governmental levels and create a more functional intergovernmental partnership.[56] But it has generally proven difficult to translate these ideas into actual policy, particularly in the area of environmental policy. Perhaps the most ambitious effort to reallocate intergovernmental functions in environmental protection took place in the 1990s during the Clinton administration, under the National Environmental Performance Partnership System (NEPPS). This effort was linked to Clinton's attempts to "reinvent government," heralded by proponents as a way to give states substantially greater administrative flexibility over many federal environmental programs if they could demonstrate innovation and actual performance that improved environmental outcomes.[57] NEPPS also offered Performance Partnership Grants that would allow participating states to concentrate resources on innovative projects that promised environmental performance improvements.

More than forty states elected to participate in the NEPPS program, which required extensive negotiations between state and federal agency counterparts. Although a few promising examples of innovation can be noted, this initiative failed to approach its ambitious goals, and in the words of two scholarly analysts, "there have been few real gains."[58] NEPPS stemmed from an administrative action by a single president and thereby lacked the clout of legislation or resilient political support. In response, federal authorities often resisted altering established practices and failed to assume the innovative role anticipated by NEPPS proponents. In turn, states proved considerably less amenable to innovation than expected. They tended to balk at any possibility that the federal government might establish—and publicize—serious performance measures that would evaluate their effectiveness and environmental outcomes.

Ultimately, many NEPPS agreements were signed, especially in the waning years of the Clinton administration, and these generally remain in place. But the Bush administration never pursued NEPPS with enthusiasm, and the Obama administration made little effort to revitalize this program. It thereby remains a very modest test of the viability of accountable decentralization, whereby state autonomy is increased formally in exchange for demonstrable performance. As we shall see, one prominent Obama-era initiative proposed a new form of federal and state collaboration in climate change, but this faced evisceration under President Trump.

Challenges to State Routines

The future role of states in environmental policy may be further shaped by three additional developments. First, despite considerable national recovery from the Great Recession, it remains increasingly unclear whether states will have sufficient fiscal resources to maintain core environmental protection functions and continue to consider new initiatives. Industrial states such as Illinois struggled with severe fiscal problems, and many states with significant emphases on oil, gas, and coal production, such as Alaska and Louisiana, faced major budget deficits. Overall, revenue grew unevenly during the mid-2010s across states and more slowly than after any of the prior three recessions.[59] In turn, pressures for expanded spending in certain domains, such as unfunded pensions and benefits for state employees and the state share of the Medicaid program, further threatened any restoration of state fiscal support for environmental protection as the economic recovery accelerated.

Second, a sequence of elections from 2010 through 2016 reversed a long-standing pattern of divided, joint-party control of most state governments in favor of sweeping control by one party, with particularly strong gains among Republicans. As of 2017, Republicans held "trifectas," controlling both legislative chambers and the governorship in 25 states. Of the remaining states, only 6 featured exclusive Democratic control of the legislative and executive branches, 17 had divided partisan control, and the remaining 2 included either an independent governor or nonpartisan legislature. In 2017, 68 of the 99 legislative chambers with partisan representation were in Republican hands, the largest margin for that party since the 1920s. This represented the greatest Republican domination over state government in generations and also the most unified period in which one party controlled all state functions in many decades—and it raised the possibility of major shifts in state environmental policy.

Third, one early testing ground for potential environmental policy shifts was reflected in a flurry of new legislative proposals between 2010 and 2017 to either downsize or repeal many established state policies. Many of these focused on climate change and reflected standardized legislative templates produced by the conservative American Legislative Exchange Council (ALEC), which offers luxurious conference venues and detailed policy advice for state legislators. One early theme in ALEC-supported repeal bills involved the reversal of state renewable portfolio standards, although only one state, Kansas in 2015, formally adopted such legislation through mid-2017. Vermont established such a standard in that same year, leaving the national total at 29 states, many of which explored expansion as noted above. In 2017, one emerging theme in such bills was placing a tax on wind turbines, advanced by supporters of fossil fuel interests to slow the pace of wind adoption. These taxes faced intense opposition from wind-producing districts in states such as Montana, Wyoming, and North Dakota, although Oklahoma created a 0.5 cent per kilowatt-hour tax on wind and also repealed its tax credit for wind farm developers. Other state climate policies proved less durable, however. While RGGI and California remained steadfast in their commitment to carbon cap-and-trade policies, 13 other states abandoned such initiatives after 2010, including Arizona, New Jersey, New Mexico, and Oregon, along with three Canadian provinces. These reversals were frequently linked to shifts in partisan control of state governments and collapses in interstate collaboration efforts.

Looking Ahead

Amid the continued squabbling over the proper role of the federal government vis-à-vis the states in environmental policy, remarkably little effort has been made to sort out which functions might best be concentrated in Washington and which ones ought to be transferred to state capitals. Some former governors and federal legislators of both parties offered useful proposals during the 1990s that might allocate such responsibilities more constructively than at present. These proposals have been supplemented by thoughtful scholarly works by think tanks, political scientists, economists, and other policy analysts. Interestingly, many of these experts concur that environmental protection policy defies easy designation as warranting extreme centralization or decentralization. Instead, many observers endorse a process of selective decentralization, one leading to an appropriately balanced set of responsibilities across governmental levels. It might be particularly useful to revisit these options before taking major new environmental policy steps, including any far-reaching effort to retract state policy commitments.

Different presidents have attempted to advance a more functional form of environmental federalism that allowed for intergovernmental collaboration and played to the respective strengths of both federal and state partners. The NEPPS experiment in the Bill Clinton administration was one such example, as was an effort under George W. Bush to create more flexible state compliance paths for some contaminants under the Clean Air Act. In 2015, the Obama administration followed in this arena with the launch of the Clean Power Plan that established a national cap on carbon emissions from the electricity sector but offered states considerable latitude in achieving reduction targets. This drew on an EPA reinterpretation of Section 111(d) of the Clean Air Act that requires each state to develop an "implementation plan" to reach required emission reductions. EPA approval of such a plan places the state's environmental agency in the lead role to ensure compliance, supported in part by federal funding and technical expertise. If a state failed to comply, the EPA could impose a "federal implementation plan," but this has only occurred rarely over the many decades of Clean Air Act operations. The Clean Power

Plan was designed to extend that process to carbon emissions, which were expected to decline over time to achieve a 32 percent reduction from 2005 levels by 2030, although individual states received different reduction targets based on their unique circumstances. The EPA also presented a menu of options whereby a state might achieve these goals, though it encouraged states to adopt some "trading ready" form of the cap-and-trade system operational in RGGI states and California to minimize costs and maximize flexibility.

EPA administrator Gina McCarthy conducted extensive outreach to states and described the Clean Power Plan as a bold new step in advancing environmental goals through an intergovernmental partnership. But states were quite divided in their response, and more than two dozen states, led by attorneys general in West Virginia, Oklahoma, and Texas, challenged the plan in federal court as an illegal expansion of federal power. Other states countered this opposition and embraced the federal program, including most states that had already established active climate mitigation policies. Implementation was stayed by federal courts, with the expectation that the plan's fate would eventually be decided by the Supreme Court and the 2016 election. That election featured a pair of major party candidates, Hillary Clinton and Donald Trump, with substantial differences on many environmental issues, as is explored elsewhere in this volume. Federalism did not figure prominently in most campaign pronouncements, although Clinton was clearly inclined to pursue Clean Power Plan implementation and also support continued use of the California waiver process to promote further emission reductions in the transportation sector. But she also designated as a lead campaign spokesperson on environmental and energy issues a former governor, Michigan's Jennifer Granholm, who spoke extensively about using federal funds for an incentive program whereby states would compete for revenue on the basis of their commitment to innovative policy ideas. Granholm first discussed this approach in a 2013 TED talk when she asked, "What if we decided to create a challenge to the governors of this country, and the price to enter into this competition [was that] you'd have to get 80 percent of your energy from clean sources by the year 2030?"

This talk went viral and ultimately took the form of a Clinton proposal to create a $60 billion fund that would be allocated to the states on the basis of their proposals on clean energy transition. This "race-to-the-top" approach resembled what the Obama administration undertook in public education funding under the No Child Left Behind Act. Granholm was widely expected to play a central role in a Clinton administration, likely including oversight of such a state incentive program.

The 45th president would indeed turn to former state officials to lead environmental and energy programs, but this would involve Donald Trump selecting Oklahoma Attorney General Pruitt to head the EPA and former Texas governor Rick Perry to serve as secretary of energy. Pruitt would gain particular prominence in the early stages of the Trump administration, given the direct EPA role in overseeing key environmental statutes and controversial decisions about the future direction of climate policy. Pruitt had faced widespread criticism for his work in Oklahoma, including for his lax response to major water pollution problems in the Illinois River, his reluctance to address a staggering increase in earthquakes as well as other concerns related to widespread fracking, the closure of the environmental enforcement division in his office, and his heavy historic reliance on oil and gas sector campaign funds in his many previous races for state legislative and executive offices. "Cooperative federalism" became his mantra leading up to his 2017 confirmation, which he revisited in his opening address to EPA staff, when he pleaded with them to give him a chance to demonstrate his commitment to secure a federal and state relationship as "partners" rather than "adversaries." "I seek to ensure that we engender the trust of those at the state level," he said.[60]

It soon became evident, however, that this new intergovernmental partnership would be defined by not only constraining federal authority but also weakening state capacity. Pruitt looked on favorably as President Trump signed a series of executive orders in March 2017 that began the elimination of the Clean Power Plan. In turn, Pruitt began to explore ways to reverse or scale back the long-standing California waiver process for vehicle emissions, including an unprecedented possible step of reconsidering waivers that EPA had previously granted. Moreover, he ultimately backed far-reaching EPA budget cuts, many of which were targeted on intergovernmental funding to support state implementation capacity and regional programs such as the Great Lakes Restoration Initiative. Additional executive actions in the early stages of the Trump administration would dramatically scale back federal efforts in fracking regulatory oversight, including regulations to reduce methane releases during drilling. Pruitt also emerged as a prominent figure in promoting the administration's withdrawal from the Paris climate accord.

These steps represented far less of an approach toward intergovernmental cooperation than an effort to reduce both federal and state capacity, perhaps suggesting a new model of "inoperative federalism," whereby no governmental level could remain effective, rather than a collaborative partnership. However, this policy thrust at least initially reflected only executive actions by an incoming president rather than new legislation or budgets backed by Congress. There was immediate and strong criticism of these steps in many environmental policy circles and from many state officials. Attorneys general from states with strong environmental and climate records, primarily from the Democratic Party, began to take near-immediate aim at the Trump-Pruitt model of federalism, exploring numerous ways to bring legal challenges to slow or reverse new executive actions. Attorneys general Eric Schneiderman (New York), Maura Healey (Massachusetts), Brian Frosh (Maryland), Lisa Madigan (Illinois), and Bob Ferguson (Washington) emerged as early leaders in this effort.[61]

California, however, began to explore even more expansive efforts to offer a vigorous counterbalance to the Trump administration in numerous areas of climate and environmental protection, particularly following the president's June 1, 2017, decision to withdraw the United States from the Paris Agreement. The state quickly assembled the United States Climate

Alliance with New York and Washington State, ultimately bringing together six additional governors who pledged to honor their own Paris emission reduction commitments and explore new climate protection efforts. Governor Jerry Brown traveled to China to meet leaders and discuss ways that the largest American state might expand cooperation with the world's largest national greenhouse gas emitter. Brown also continued to explore aggressive California responses to any potential constraint on unilateral state or multistate action on climate change and promised a particularly fierce intergovernmental reaction to any Trump administration effort to dial back its long-standing waiver authority over vehicle emissions. Brown and a legislature with Democratic supermajorities in each chamber began to consider major expansions of existing climate legislation and stepped up efforts to find partners among other states and governments. Xavier Becerra resigned a safe seat in Congress and a leadership role among House Democrats to accept appointment as California's attorney general, and he pledged to join forces with other like-minded states to lead an aggressive legal attack on anticipated Trump administration environmental policies. Governor Brown further bolstered his legal response team by taking the unique step of hiring former attorney general Eric Holder, who served during much of the Obama administration, to assist the state with future litigation challenges to the incoming administration in areas that included immigration and environmental policy.

All of this left open the question of how best to position federal and state governments for effective roles in environmental protection going forward, including how these governments might best cooperate on challenging issues such as climate change, and it raised the possibility of increasingly partisan divides whereby state authority might be subject to severe shifts with each change in partisan control of the presidency. The Founding Fathers envisioned such risks but designed the U.S. Constitution to mitigate against these kinds of volatile shifts.[62] Looking ahead, a more discerning environmental federalism might also begin by concentrating federal regulatory energies on problems that are clearly national in character. Many air and water pollution problems, for example, are by definition cross-boundary concerns unlikely to be resolved by a series of unilateral state actions. In contrast, problems such as protecting indoor air quality and cleanup of abandoned hazardous waste dumps may present more geographically confinable challenges; they are perhaps best handled through substantial delegation of authority to states. As policy analyst John D. Donahue notes, "Most waste sites are situated within a single state, and stay there," yet they are governed by highly centralized Superfund legislation, in direct contrast to more decentralized programs in environmental areas in which cross-boundary transfers are prevalent.[63] Under a more rational system, the federal regulatory presence might intensify as the likelihood of cross-boundary contaminant transfer escalates. Emerging issues, such as environmental protection in the wake of expanded shale gas and oil drilling, present an opportunity to test this approach because they involve the combination of a highly decentralized system of relatively small and localized drilling operations with considerable cross-border movement of wastes and chemicals, as well as the transport of natural gas and oil via rail and pipelines. Such an initial attempt to sort out functions might be reinforced by federal policy efforts to encourage states or regions to take responsibility for internally generated environmental problems rather than tacitly allowing exportation to occur. In the area of waste management, for example, federal per-mile fees on waste shipments would provide a disincentive for long-distance transfer, instead encouraging states, regions, and waste generators to either develop their own capacity or pursue waste reduction options more aggressively.

In many areas, shared federal and state roles likely remain appropriate, reflecting the inherent complexity of many environmental problems. Effective intergovernmental partnerships are already well established in certain areas. But even if essentially sound, these partnerships could clearly benefit from further maturation and development. Alongside the sorting-out activities discussed earlier in this section, both federal and state governments could do much more to promote the creative sharing of policy ideas and environmental data, ultimately developing a system informed by "best practices" and evidence of actual performance that reduces environmental risks. Such information has received remarkably limited dissemination across state and regional boundaries, and potentially considerable advantage is to be gained from an active process of intergovernmental policy learning. More broadly, the federal government might explore other ways to encourage states to work cooperatively, especially on common boundary problems. As we have discussed, state capacity to find creative solutions to pressing environmental problems has generally been on the ascendance. However, as Lord Bryce concluded many decades ago, cooperation among states does not arise automatically, although at times it can, in the words of California Air Resources Board Chair Mary Nichols, "produce a very lovely and effective patchwork quilt."[64]

Suggested Websites

Environmental Council of the States (www.ecos.org) The Environmental Council of the States represents the lead environmental protection agencies of all fifty states. The site contains access to state environmental data and periodic "Green Reports" on major issues.

Center for Local, State, and Urban Policy (www.closup.umich.edu) The Center for Local, State, and Urban Policy's Energy and Environmental Policy Initiative places a strong emphasis on state and local policy issues. It also features results from National Surveys on Energy and Environment, public opinion surveys that emphasize state and intergovernmental questions in collaboration with the Muhlenberg Institute of Public Opinion.

Governing Institute (www.governing.com/gov-institute) The Governing Institute provides in-depth coverage of a range of issues involving state and local governments, with a strong emphasis on environmental issues. It publishes a prominent monthly magazine (www.governing.com), offers feature stories and regular updates on its website, and is particularly strong in examining the performance of public management at the state and local levels.

National Conference of State Legislatures (www.ncsl.org) The National Conference of State Legislatures conducts extensive research on a wide range of environmental, energy, and natural resource issues for its primary constituency of state legislators, as well as for the general citizenry. The organization offers an extensive set of publications, including specialized reports and an excellent monthly magazine on state and federal energy policy, *Plugged In.*

National Governors Association (www.nga.org) The National Governors Association maintains an active research program concerning state environmental protection, natural resources, and energy concerns. It has placed special emphasis on maintaining a database on state "best practices," which it uses to promote diffusion of promising innovations and to demonstrate state government capacity in federal policy deliberations.

Notes

1. John Kincaid and Richard L. Cole, "Citizen Attitudes toward Issues of Federalism in Canada, Mexico, and the United States," *Publius: The Journal of Federalism* 41 (January 2011): 53–75.
2. Paul Teske, *Regulation in the States* (Washington, DC: Brookings Institution Press, 2004), 9.
3. R. Steven Brown, *State Environmental Expenditures* (Washington, DC: Environmental Council of the States, 2008).
4. Martha Derthick, "Compensatory Federalism," in *Greenhouse Governance*, ed. Barry Rabe (Washington, DC: Brookings Institution Press, 2010), 66.
5. Christopher McGrory Klyza and David Sousa, *American Environmental Policy: Beyond Gridlock*, updated and expanded edition (Cambridge, MA: MIT Press, 2013), 247.
6. Stephen Goldsmith and Donald F. Kettl, eds., *Unlocking the Power of Networks* (Washington, DC: Brookings Institution Press, 2009).
7. Elinor Ostrom, *Governing the Commons: The Evolution of Institutions for Collective Action* (New York: Cambridge University Press, 1990); Elinor Ostrom, *A Polycentric Approach to Climate Change* (Washington, DC: World Bank, 2009).
8. Barry G. Rabe, *Statehouse and Greenhouse: The Emerging Politics of American Climate Change Policy* (Washington, DC: Brookings Institution Press, 2004).
9. Michelle Pautz and Sara Rinfret, *The Lilliputians of Environmental Regulation: The Perspective of State Regulators* (New York: Routledge, 2013).
10. Andrew Karch, *Democratic Laboratories: Policy Diffusion among the American States* (Ann Arbor: University of Michigan Press, 2007).
11. American Council for an Energy-Efficient Economy, *2016 State Energy Efficiency Scorecard* (Washington, DC: ACEEE, 2016).
12. Evan J. Ringquist, *Environmental Protection at the State Level: Politics and Progress in Controlling Pollution* (Armonk, NY: M. E. Sharpe, 1993).
13. Daniel Fiorino and Riordan Frost, "The Pilot Eco-Efficiency Index: A New State Environmental Ranking for Researchers and Government" (paper presented at the Association for Public Policy Analysis and Management's fall research conference, Washington, DC, November 4, 2016), www.researchgate.net/publication/315736703_The_Pilot_Eco-Efficiency_Index_A_New_State_Environmental_Ranking_for_Researchers_and_Government.

14. Kathy Kinsey, "Neither of These Bills Address the Law's Failings," *Environmental Forum* 31 (May–June 2014): 48.

15. Linda Breggin, "Broad State Efforts on Toxic Controls," *Environmental Forum* 28 (March–April 2011): 10.

16. Andy Kim, "Time to Ban BPA?" *Governing* (March 2011): 13.

17. Christopher Bosso, ed., *Governing Uncertainty: Environmental Regulation in the Age of Nanotechnology* (Washington, DC: Resources for the Future, 2010), 105–30.

18. Andrew Kear, "Natural Gas Path—Built to Boom," *Journal of Policy History* (in press).

19. Jonathan M. Fisk, The Fracking Debate: Intergovernmental Politics of the Oil and Gas Renaissance (New York: Routledge, 2018).

20. Barry G. Rabe and Christopher Borick, "Carbon Taxation and Policy Labeling: Experience from American States and Canadian Provinces," *Review of Policy Research* 29 (May 2012): 358–82.

21. R. Steven Brown, *Status of State Environmental Agency Budgets: 2011–2013* (Washington, DC: Environmental Council of the States, 2012).

22. Samantha McBride, *Recycling Reconsidered: The Present Failure and Future Promise of Environmental Action in the United States* (Cambridge, MA: MIT Press, 2012).

23. Leigh Raymond, *Reclaiming the Atmospheric Commons: The Regional Greenhouse Gas Initiative and a New Model of Emissions Trading* (Cambridge, MA: MIT Press, 2016).

24. Barry G. Rabe, *Can We Price Carbon?* (Cambridge, MA: MIT Press, 2018).

25. Devashree Saha and Mark Muro, *Cleantech Venture Capital* (Washington, DC: Brookings Institution, 2017).

26. Roger Karapin, *Political Opportunities for Climate Policy: California, New York, and the Federal Government* (New York: Cambridge University Press, 2016).

27. Vivian E. Thomson, *Sophisticated Interdependence in Climate Policy: Federalism in the United States, Brazil, and Germany* (London: Anthem Press, 2014).

28. Neil Craik, Isabel Studer, and Debora Van Nijnatten, *Climate Change Policy in North America* (Toronto, ON: University of Toronto Press, 2013).

29. Linda Breggin, "Hawaii's New 100% Portfolio Standard," *Environmental Forum* 32, no. 5 (September–October 2015): 10.

30. American Council for an Energy-Efficient Economy, *2016 State Energy Efficiency Score Card*, Research Report U1606 (Washington, DC: ACEEE, 2016).

31. David Vogel, How The Golden State Became Green (Princeton: Princeton University Press, 2018).

32. Barry G. Rabe, "Leveraged Federalism and the Clean Air Act: The Case of Vehicle Emissions Control," in The Future of U.S. Energy Policy: Lessons from the Clean Air Act. ed. Ann Carlson and Dallas Burtraw (Cambridge: Cambridge University Press, 2018).

33. Paul Nolette, *Federalism on Trial: State Attorneys General and National Policymaking in Contemporary America* (Lawrence, KS: University Press of Kansas, 2015).

34. William R. Lowry, *The Dimensions of Federalism: State Governments and Pollution Control Policies*, rev. ed. (Durham, NC: Duke University Press, 1997), 125.

35. In Wisconsin, for example, Governor Scott Walker has overseen significant reductions in state environmental staff and research capacity, with a primary focus on accelerating approval time for proposed development. See Steven Verberg, "DNR to Alter Handling of Pollution, Parks, Enforcement," *Wisconsin State Journal*, December 1, 2016; Evan Osnos, "Chemical Valley," *New Yorker*, April 7, 2014, 38–49; Keith Matheny, "Did State Agency Lobby to Bend Rules on Pollutants at Steel Mill?" *Detroit Free Press*, May 5, 2014; and Trip Gabriel, "Ash Spill Shows How Watchdog Was Defanged," *New York Times*, February 28, 2014.

36. Brown, *Status of State Environmental Agency Budgets*.

37. Linda K. Breggin, "Stringency Laws Widely Adopted," *Environmental Forum* 32, no. 3 (May–June 2015): 18.

38. John A. Hoornbeek, "The Promise and Pitfalls of Devolution: Water Pollution Policies in the American States," *Publius: The Journal of Federalism* 35 (Winter 2005): 87–114.

39. Shama Ghamkar and J. Mitchell Pickerill, "The State of American Federalism 2011–2012," *Publius: The Journal of Federalism* 42 (Summer 2012): 357–86.

40. Sheldon Kamieniecki, *Corporate America and Environmental Policy* (Palo Alto, CA: Stanford University Press, 2006), 253.

41. William Lowry, *Repairing Paradise: The Restoration of Nature in America's National Parks* (Washington, DC: Brookings Institution Press, 2010), Chapter 4.

42. Bridge Magazine, *Poison on Tap: How Government Failed Flint, and the Heroes Who Fought Back* (Traverse City, MI: Mission Point Press, 2016).

43. Benjamin Y. Clark and Andrew B. Whitford, "Does More Federal Environmental Funding Increase or Decrease States' Efforts?" *Journal of Policy Analysis and Management* 30 (Winter 2010): 136–52.

44. Environmental Council of the States, *Priority Areas in a Time of Political Transition, 2016–2017* (Washington, DC: ECOS, 2016).

45. Michael E. Kraft, Mark Stephan, and Troy D. Abel, *Coming Clean: Information Disclosure and Environmental Performance* (Cambridge, MA: MIT Press, 2011).

46. Matthew J. Hoffmann, *Climate Governance at the Crossroads* (New York: Oxford University Press, 2011); Michael E. Kraft, *Using Information Disclosure to Achieve Policy Goals: How Experience with the Toxics Release Inventory Can Inform Action on Natural Gas Fracturing*, Issues in Energy and Environmental Policy No. 6 (Ann Arbor, MI: Center for Local, State, and Urban Policy, March 2014).

47. Paul Posner, "Networks in the Shadow of Government: The Chesapeake Bay Program," in *Unlocking the Power of Networks*, ed. Stephen Goldsmith and Donald F. Kettl (Washington, DC: Brookings Institution Press, 2009), Chapter 4; Barry G. Rabe and Marc Gaden, "Sustainability in a Regional Context: The Case of the Great Lakes Basin," in *Toward Sustainable Communities: Transition and Transformations in Environmental Policy*, ed. Daniel A. Mazmanian and Michael E. Kraft, 2nd ed. (Cambridge, MA: MIT Press, 2009), 266–69.

48. Denise Scheberle, *Federalism and Environmental Policy: Trust and the Politics of Implementation*, rev. ed. (Washington, DC: Georgetown University Press, 2004), Chapter 7.

49. Michelle Pautz and Sarah Rinfret, *The Lilliputians of Environmental Regulations*, 50–51.

50. Paul Teske, *Regulation in the States*; Pautz and Rinfret, *The Lilliputians of Environmental Regulation*.

51. John D. Donahue, *Disunited States: What's at Stake as Washington Fades and the States Take the Lead* (New York: Basic Books, 1997); Paul E. Peterson, *The Price of Federalism* (Washington, DC: Brookings Institution Press, 1995), Chapter 4.

52. William T. Gormley Jr., "Intergovernmental Conflict on Environmental Policy: The Attitudinal Connection," *Western Political Quarterly* 40 (1987): 298–99.

53. David M. Konisky and Neal D. Woods, "Exporting Air Pollution? Regulatory Enforcement and Environmental Free Riding in the United States," *Political Research Quarterly* 63 (2010): 771–82.

54. Lowry, *The Dimensions of Federalism*, 45.

55. Daniel J. Sherman, *Not Here, Not There, Not Anywhere* (Washington, DC: Resources for the Future, 2011).

56. Alice Rivlin, "Rethinking Federalism for More Effective Governance," *Publius: The Journal of Federalism* 42 (Summer 2012): 357–86; Jenna Bednar, *The Robust Federation* (New York: Cambridge University Press, 2008); R. Daniel Keleman, *The Rules of Federalism* (Cambridge, MA: Harvard University Press, 2004).

57. John Buntin, "25 Years Later, What Happened to 'Reinventing Government'?" *Governing* (September 2016).

58. Klyza and Sousa, *American Environmental Policy, 1990–2006*, 253.

59. PEW Charitable Trusts, *Fiscal 50: State Trends and Analysis* [interactive online resource], accessed February 2017, http://www.pewtrusts.org/en/research-and-analysis/collections/2014/05/19/fiscal-50-state-trends-and-analysis; Liz Farmer, "Purchase Power: A Special Report on State Procurement," *Governing*, February 17, 2016.

60. Robin Bravender and Kevin Bogardus, "Pruitt's Pitch to Staff: Give Me a Chance," *E&E News*, February 27, 2017.

61. Amanda Reilly, "Tables Are Turned as State AGs Set Their Sights on Pruitt," *E&E News*, March 1, 2017.

62. Alexander Hamilton, James Madison, and John Jay, *The Federalist: The Famous Papers on the Principles of American Government*, ed. Benjamin Fletcher Wright (Cambridge, MA: Harvard University Press, 1961). The complete Federalist Papers (published from 1787 to 1788) are available online from the Library of Congress.

63. Donahue, *Disunited States*, 65.

64. Mary D. Nichols, "Policymaking Is a Patchwork Quilt" (presentation at the CAPCOA Climate Change Forum, San Francisco, CA, August 30, 2010).

Chapter 3

Environmental Advocacy at the
Dawn of the Trump Era
Assessing Strategies for the Preservation of Progress
Luis E. Hestres and Matthew C. Nisbet

On November 6, 2015, environmental activists celebrated what they considered a major victory in the fight against fossil fuel extraction and for the mitigation of climate change. On that day, President Barack Obama announced his State Department's decision that the Keystone XL pipeline, a controversial project intended to link the Alberta oil sands in Canada with Gulf of Mexico refineries and distribution centers in the United States, would not be approved. The president agreed with his State Department's determination that building the pipeline "would not serve the national interest of the United States," although he made it clear that he believed the pipeline would "neither be a silver bullet for the economy, as was promised by some, nor the express lane to climate disaster proclaimed by others."[1] For climate and environmental activists, this announcement was the culmination of a multiyear campaign to stop construction of the pipeline, a campaign that generated hundreds of thousands of e-mails to the White House and Congress, mobilized thousands of activists who participated in sit-ins and rallies, and even occasioned more than a thousand civil disobedience arrests.[2]

Activists had even more reason for celebration six weeks later, when the 21st Conference of the Parties of the United Nations Framework Convention on Climate Change (COP21 of the UNFCCC) reached a far-reaching agreement in Paris to curtail greenhouse gas emissions around the world.[3] These events, along with the Environmental Protection Agency's (EPA's) rules limiting emissions from coal-fired power plants and the potential election to the presidency of former secretary of state Hillary Clinton, who was running on a platform of continuing her predecessor's climate policies,[4] gave climate and environmental activists reasonable cause for optimism heading into the 2016 presidential election. That optimism suffered a severe blow on November 8, 2016—just over a year after the Keystone pipeline decision—when real estate magnate Donald Trump, defying the forecasts of nearly all election prognosticators, won the presidential election by capturing 304 electoral votes.[5] Trump ran on a platform that professed skepticism about climate change as a scientific phenomenon and promised to roll back virtually all of his predecessor's climate and environmental policies.

After years of pushing and prodding a generally sympathetic president in a policy direction with which he broadly agreed, climate and environmental activists found themselves in a completely different situation after Trump's inauguration, facing a president and Congress that appear almost uniformly hostile to their goals. Activists have altered their playbook according to this strategic assumption. Grassroots-oriented advocacy groups such as 350.org have adopted a defiant posture toward the new administration, declaring their ongoing opposition to the Keystone pipeline and similar fossil fuel extraction projects. Meanwhile, legacy environmental organizations are taking the Trump administration to court to prevent his proposed rollback of the EPA's climate pollution regulations. A broad array of climate and environmental groups has also opposed Trump's proposed rollback of President Obama's carbon emission rules, cuts to the EPA's budget, and other proposals.

This chapter briefly chronicles the activities that environmental advocates undertook during the Obama administration and how they became involved in the 2016 presidential election. It lays out the challenges they face under the new Trump administration, and it discusses how they are responding to these challenges so far.

Activism in the Obama Era

The Obama era of environmental activism is bifurcated by Congress's failure to pass a cap-and-trade bill in 2010. This failure has been blamed on many different factors. The economic recession, the heavy focus on the health care debate, a perceived lack of leadership by the White House, the country's intense political polarization, the rise of the Tea Party movement, the difficulty in passing legislation that strongly challenged the political status quo, and miscalculations by key leaders in the Senate all contributed to the bill's demise.[6] In the cap-and-trade fight, environmental leaders acknowledged that they had lacked the capacity for grassroots mobilization in key House districts and in states where Senate seats were at stake. According to some critiques, the campaign to pass cap-and-trade legislation had focused too much on a "big fix," communicating about the technical details of the policy rather than showing the public how climate change action might personally benefit people and their communities.

Environmental groups had conducted a "policy" campaign rather than a "cultural" campaign, and they lacked the ability to punish or reward members of Congress.[7] In a much debated assessment of the bill's failure, Harvard University political scientist Theda Skocpol argued that groups such as the Environmental Defense Fund (EDF) and the Natural Resources Defense Council (NRDC) had relied too heavily on traditional inside-the-Beltway strategies of coalition building and lobbying and had not done enough to rally grassroots support for cap-and-trade legislation. The design of the policy itself, argued Skocpol, was confusing to the public, focusing too heavily on providing giveaways to corporations rather than on direct benefits to the public. The bill also generated skepticism from more activist-minded environmental groups and progressive leaders who either threw their support behind the bill reluctantly or remained quietly on the sidelines.[8] After the demise of cap-and-trade legislation, the coordinated alliance among the EDF, the NRDC, and other big-budget environmental groups lobbying on behalf of congressional action split apart. With Republicans winning control of the House in 2010, there was little chance of a major climate bill passing, leaving this coalition without a defining goal to align around. Instead, the NRDC focused on passing a federal clean energy standard, increasing fuel efficiency for cars, and promoting new rules by the EPA to limit greenhouse gas emissions from power plants.

At the state and local levels, other groups led by the Sierra Club and the League of Conservation Voters took legal action against coal-fired power plants, marshaled grassroots pressure to shut them down, and funded electoral campaigns to elect Democrats supportive of action on climate change. "The national environmental groups said, 'We need to do more in-your-face activism,'" Gene Karpinski, president of the League of Conservation Voters, told the *New York Times*. "You can't just lobby members of Congress with a poll that says people support you."[9] Most significantly, the period 2011–2014 is notable for the rise to prominence of a new form of environmental advocacy group, much smaller in size and budget and focused specifically on climate change. These groups specialize in a sophisticated form of Internet-enabled grassroots activism designed to pressure political leaders, institutions, and industry members by rallying a liberal base of activists around issues such as the Keystone XL pipeline and divestment from fossil fuel industries. It took the failure of the national environmental organizations to pass cap and trade, the search among funders and advocates for new grassroots strategies and leaders, and the cultural, media, and economic factors that converged in the wake of the 2010 elections to help push environmental activists and writer Bill McKibben and the activist group he cofounded, 350.org, into national prominence.[10] In February 2005, as a scholar in residence at Middlebury College, McKibben began meeting informally with students to discuss strategies for mobilizing political action on climate change, which led in 2006 to a thousand-person, five-day hike to call attention to climate change. The perceived success of the event prompted McKibben and his collaborators in 2007 to organize national "Step It Up" days of action, which they coordinated by way of the Step It Up website.[11]

To share insight about their new model for organizing, McKibben and his five co-organizers published in 2007 *Fight Global Warming Now: The Handbook for Taking Action in Your Community*.[12] In 2008, McKibben and his collaborators from Middlebury College launched 350.org. The name of the organization was derived from climate scientist James Hansen's declaration that 350 parts per million was the "safe" level for the stabilization of atmospheric carbon dioxide levels, a goal required to avoid the worst effects of climate change. In comparison to the EDF or NRDC, each of which boasts a budget greater than $100 million and hundreds of highly credentialed staff,[13] as of 2015, 350.org employed 120 staff in the United States and abroad—but spent only $7.6 million on campaign work and grassroots field organizing.[14]

The main goal of 350.org was to use Internet-enabled organizing strategies to increase the intensity of political activity among those members of the public already alarmed about climate change. In targeting this segment, McKibben was appealing directly to the base of readers and fans he had built up over the past twenty years as a best-selling author. Yet despite an avid interest in climate change and a shared worldview, these people had a historically low level of activism, as was evident in the cap-and-trade debate. As May Boeve, executive director of 350.org, said in a 2011 interview, "Our most consistent audience is the community of people who care about climate change and see it as a problem and are committed to do something about it. The metaphor we like to use is, yes, there's an issue of preaching to the choir, but imagine if you could have the choir all singing from the same song sheet."[15]

Sparking a National Pipeline Controversy

Following the demise of cap-and-trade legislation and with international negotiations stalled, McKibben and 350.org began the search for a new political target to mobilize a movement around. In early 2011, McKibben learned of the proposed Keystone XL pipeline and the pending approval by the U.S. State Department. Most experts had predicted that the Obama administration would approve the Keystone XL pipeline. Yet McKibben and 350.org have played a central role in delaying its approval by morally dramatizing the stakes involved and rallying a small, yet intense, base of opposition.

To be approved, the pipeline had to be judged in the "national interest" by the Obama administration and U.S. State Department. McKibben realized not only that the pipeline was a potent symbol to rally activists against but also that rejecting the pipeline was an action by which Obama could demonstrate his commitment to climate change, bypassing a gridlocked Congress. Turning again to James Hansen to muster rhetorical authority, McKibben cited Hansen's (contested) conclusion that by speeding up the development of the oil sands, approval of the pipeline would mean "[e]ssentially, it's game over for the planet."[16]

Using Hansen's dramatic assessment as a rallying cry, in August 2011, 350.org and its allies mobilized thousands to protest in front of the White House, with more than twelve hundred participants arrested. They followed in November by turning out an estimated fifteen thousand activists who encircled the White House in a last push to convince President Obama to reject the pipeline. Later, in February 2012, after Obama had delayed the decision on the pipeline until 2013, the Senate took up legislation revisiting the pipeline. In response, McKibben and 350.org joined with other environmental groups to generate more than eight hundred thousand messages to senators, an effort that aided the defeat of the bill. In February 2013, an estimated thirty thousand gathered on the National Mall to once again pressure the president as they waited on a decision.[17]

The staged protests, arrests, and related strategies were the first in an ongoing series that, for a second time, pressured the Obama administration into delaying a decision on the Keystone pipeline until at least 2015. Protests occurred not only in Washington, DC, but were coordinated across other cities and states. In Nebraska, environmentalists joined with ranchers, farmers, and Native Americans to oppose the pipeline. This self-described "Cowboy Indian Alliance" has cited risks from pipeline spills to local groundwater contamination and threats to public safety. Activists have also challenged the Nebraska governor's authority to approve the construction of the pipeline within the state, taking the case to the state supreme court. Local spin-offs of the national 350.org effort, such as 350 Maine and 350 Massachusetts, have applied similar protest strategies in opposing regional oil pipeline projects, coal-fired power plants, and natural gas development.[18] Major environmental groups joining with 350.org in opposing the Keystone pipeline include the NRDC, the League of Conservation Voters, Friends of the Earth, and the Sierra Club. Along with supporting protest actions, the Sierra Club and Friends of the Earth have also used freedom of information requests to call attention to what they allege are corrupting ties between the State Department, the consulting firm hired to assess environmental impacts, and related industry members.[19]

Delaying a decision on the Keystone pipeline seemed prudent. Obama and his advisers feared that a decision to reject the pipeline might hurt the 2014 electoral chances of Democrats in swing states and districts by giving Republicans a ready-made issue to intensify support and turnout among their own grassroots base. Alternatively, if Obama were to approve the pipeline, the decision would risk provoking a rebellion among a network of major liberal donors and depress electoral support among progressive activists and voters.[20] At his influential Dot Earth blog at the *New York Times*, environmental writer Andrew Revkin was critical of McKibben's effort to block the Keystone XL pipeline, arguing that the controversy was a "distraction from core issues and opportunities on energy and largely insignificant if your concern is averting a disruptive buildup of carbon dioxide in the atmosphere."[21] The Editorial Board at the *Washington Post* and the editors of the journal *Nature* offered similar lines of criticism. [22] As the *Nature* editors wrote, "The pipeline is not going to determine whether the Canadian tar sands are developed or not. Only a broader—and much more important—shift in energy policy will do that." A more comprehensive action, according to the *Nature* editors, would be the implementation of pending EPA regulations for power plants that would "send a message to the coal industry: clean up or fade away."[23]

The 2016 Democratic Primary

Environmental activists could justifiably look back on the Obama years with a sense that some progress had been achieved, especially on the climate change front: The Keystone pipeline had been rejected, new EPA regulations on the biggest climate polluters had been enacted, millions had been spent on energy efficiency and clean energy technology research, and a sweeping agreement to curb carbon emissions had been adopted in Paris. At the same time, they could point to several disappointments, such as Obama's stance on offshore drilling. Looking beyond the Obama presidency, activist groups wanted to consolidate the gains made over the previous years while ensuring prospects for more progress. Grassroots climate groups in particular wanted the next administration to be even more aggressive on climate change than the Obama administration had been; in their estimation, Obama-era policy had fallen short on the issue in several ways.

With these goals in mind, environmental and climate groups of all stripes threw themselves into the struggle within the Democratic Party to find a successor to Obama. In the leading Democratic presidential contenders, former secretary of state Hillary Clinton and Vermont senator Bernie Sanders, activists had candidates they could support, as both pledged to at least continue, or even improve upon, many of President Obama's environmental policies. Climate and environmental advocacy groups split their support between Clinton and Sanders, with larger, well-established environmental groups usually endorsing Clinton and smaller, climate-focused groups endorsing Sanders.[24]

The NRDC issued its first-ever endorsement of a candidate during a presidential primary by endorsing Hillary Clinton, extolling her as "an environmental champion with the passion, experience and savvy to build on President Obama's environmental legacy."[25] In its endorsement of Clinton, the League of Conservation Voters (LCV) called her "without a doubt the most effective leader to stand up to Big Polluters and push forward an aggressive plan to tackle climate change and get it done."[26] Meanwhile, Friends of the Earth, widely considered more left leaning than most major environmental groups, endorsed Sen. Sanders, citing his "bold ideas and real solutions to addressing climate change, inequality and promoting a transformative economy that prioritizes public health and the environment over corporate profits."[27] Environmental writer and 350.org cofounder Bill McKibben became deeply involved in the Sanders campaign, going so far as to serve as a party platform delegate for the Vermont senator.[28]

Despite some victories, McKibben mostly expressed disappointment at the party's platform committee and accused the Clinton campaign of being "unwilling to commit to delivering specifics about fundamental change in America."[29] McKibben was particularly disappointed at the Clinton campaign's decision to block several climate change–related planks sponsored by the Sanders campaign, such as a carbon tax, a ban on fracking, an effort to keep fossil fuels in the ground on federal land, and mandating that federal agencies weigh the climate impacts of their decisions.[30] Fracking—the process of extracting oil or gas from the ground by injecting pressurized liquid into rock—was one of the most prominent environmental issues during the Democratic presidential primary. Climate change activism and anti-fracking campaigns have been increasingly coinciding in recent years, with activists drawing connections between the local impacts of fracking and its global impact on climate change.[31] This pattern continued throughout the Democratic primaries. For example, Josh Fox, the director of *Gasland*, a documentary about fracking, rallied around Sen. Sanders, who proposed a national ban on the practice and also advocated an ambitious plan to curb climate change.[32]

Secretary Clinton, meanwhile, supported fracking as a way to fight climate change, encourage American energy independence, and undercut petro-states such as Russia, but she also supported "smart regulations" on fracking.[33]

Taking on Donald Trump

Despite their differences during the primary campaign, environmental activists mostly coalesced around Secretary Clinton's candidacy as a way to prevent a Donald Trump presidency. As a candidate, Trump repeatedly denied the scientific consensus on climate change, calling it a "hoax" that helped China undercut the United States in manufacturing.[34] During the presidential campaign, Trump called for more fossil fuel extraction and pledged to rescind environmental regulations promulgated by the Obama administration to curb climate pollution, to pull the United States out of the Paris Agreement, to revive the coal economy, and to restart the Keystone XL pipeline project that the Obama State Department refused to approve in 2015.[35] Trump also often spoke derisively of President Obama's climate and energy policies. During a major energy policy speech in Bismarck, North Dakota, he said, "Regulations that shut down hundreds of coal-fired power plants and block the construction of new ones—how stupid is that?"[36]

Environmental activists saw a Trump presidency as a dire threat to gains made during the Obama administration, as well as to their ability to address issues like climate change more aggressively in the future. While endorsing Secretary Clinton, NRDC Action Fund president Rhea Suh sharply criticized Trump's environmental agenda: "His plan for his first 100 days would take us back 100 years, and America cannot afford to indulge his climate conspiracy theories."[37] EDF issued a point-by-point refutation of Trump's most controversial environmental claims, including that climate change is a hoax and that "there is no drought" in California.[38] LCV used the spotlight of the Democratic National Convention to name Donald Trump to its "Dirty Dozen"—a collection of the candidates who, in its judgment, most consistently side against the environment. During the convention, LCV president Gene Karpinski declared about the so-designated Trump, "I can't imagine anyone more deserving."[39] After Trump's Republican presidential nomination became a foregone conclusion, the Sierra Club issued a report stating that, if elected, Trump would be "the only world leader to deny the science and dangers of climate change."[40] Large environmental organizations, along with billionaire Tom Steyer's NextGen Climate organization, backed up their opposition to Trump with large campaign expenditures. Together, these groups spent more than $100 million during the 2016 election cycle, much of it focused on the presidential election. LCV spent $40 million in its campaign to defeat Donald Trump, while NextGen Climate reportedly spent $55 million.[41]

Climate advocacy groups such as 350.org also supported Clinton, but they did so in a more subdued tone. Power Shift, a climate advocacy group that focuses on millennials, did not even send a preelection mobilization e-mail to its supporters, focusing instead on the Dakota Access pipeline. In a mass e-mail to supporters, 350.org's Duncan Meisel wrote, "Hillary Clinton, after much pressure, says she opposes Keystone XL. If she's President, we have a shot at pressuring her into doing the right thing on fracking, Dakota Access, and more." It also accused Donald Trump of personally investing "up to $1 million into the company behind the Dakota Access pipeline" and said he would "doom international efforts to stop climate change, making the world hotter, poorer, and more dangerous."[42] One of the tactics 350.org used to influence the election's outcome was trying to influence the agenda of the presidential debates. The group directed its supporters to vote online for one of three questions related to climate change that might be included in the second debate—the town hall version—if they garnered enough votes.[43] Ultimately, none of the questions about climate change were included in the debate, although Clinton mentioned the issue once.[44]

In the end, all the money and manpower that environmental activists invested in electing Secretary Clinton president were for naught. On November 8, 2016, Donald Trump was elected president of the United States after amassing 304 electoral votes, even as he lost the popular vote to Hillary Clinton by more than 2.8 million votes.[45] Given that nearly all election prognosticators had predicted a Clinton win,[46] Trump's victory came as a shock to many election observers—including environmental activists.

The Trump Victory: Shock, Grief, and Defiance

Reactions from environmental activist groups ranged from shock and grief to defiance and resolve. Fred Krupp, the president of EDF, which is considered a moderate environmental organization, emphasized in his post-election statement the group's ability for "finding opportunity where others see impasse . . . while always sticking to our core principles."[47] NRDC's Rhea Suh expressed "shock and disappointment" and said that "[f]eeling shell-shocked is an appropriate response," but she also declared that the "NRDC will fight for our environment, for our climate, and for our shared clean energy future—harder than we ever have fought before."[48] Michael Brune, executive director of the Sierra Club, said the following during remarks at the National Press Club: "For people all over the country, the pain, anger, and fear at the prospect of a Trump presidency are very real." But he also declared, "We aren't defeated. We are determined."[49] Greenpeace USA's Annie Leonard wrote that the "election of Donald Trump as President of the United States has been devastating" but also pledged that "Greenpeace is not going anywhere, and we are committed to continue building a movement that fights for environmental, social, racial, and economic justice. We are going to get through this—together."[50] Friends of the Earth U.S. Climate and Energy Director Benjamin Schreiber claimed the entire American climate movement was "stunned" by Trump's victory, declared the United States would now likely be a "rogue state on climate change," and gave up any notions of progress during a Trump administration, even calling on the world to "use economic and diplomatic pressure to compel U.S. leaders to act" on climate change.[51]

Climate change advocacy groups were equally grief stricken but also defiant. The Climate Reality Project, led by former vice president Al Gore, struck a moderate tone, cautioning against giving in to despair and telling its supporters that "this challenge is too important and too pressing to ignore, so we must face the truth in front of us and commit to fighting harder than ever before to protect our precious home."[52] In a mass e-mail, Power Shift executive director Lydia Avila told supporters that the country's "darkest, ugliest impulses celebrated an enormous victory last night" but also made "a commitment to you, and to everyone I love, that we will not let this kill our spirit." She called on fellow activists to "fight and organize harder than many of us ever have."[53] As May Boeve, executive director of 350.org, wrote, "The hardest thing to do right now is to hold on to hope, but it's what we must do. . . . [W]e are in this together, and when we mobilize, we are capable of the unimaginable. No one man—no matter how cruel or powerful—can take that away."[54] Her e-mail, which was available as a blog post, also included an invitation to supporters to participate in a national organizing call taking place two days later.

With these and other statements, environmental groups across the spectrum declared their virtually unanimous opposition to the Trump administration. In the months following the election, this opposition would take various forms, including Internet-mediated offline events such as marches and rallies, as well as insider-type tactics such as lawsuits.

Activism at the Dawn of the Trump Era

The months between the election and the presidential inauguration seemed to confirm all the fears that activists had about a Trump administration. As president-elect, Trump signaled that he was looking for the quickest possible way to withdraw the United States from the Paris Agreement.[55] He also appointed Myron Ebell to head the EPA's transition team. Ebell, a leading contrarian of the scientific consensus on global warming, is head of environmental and energy policy at the Competitive Enterprise Institute, a libertarian advocacy group financed in part by the fossil fuel industry.[56] Ebell's appointment was widely believed to be a preamble for the undoing of many of President Obama's environmental policies, including his Clean Power Plan, which aimed to reduce carbon emissions from coal-fired power plants, emissions that fuel climate change.

President-elect Trump's appointments to his cabinet did not inspire confidence among environmental activists either. Trump appointed ExxonMobil chairman and CEO Rex Tillerson as secretary of state, former Texas governor Rick Perry as secretary of energy, and Oklahoma Attorney General Scott Pruitt as EPA administrator. Activists objected to the incoming cabinet's ties to the fossil fuel industry, and they especially condemned Pruitt's appointment, given that as attorney general of Oklahoma he had sued the EPA fourteen times.[57] Several environmental groups, including the Sierra Club and the LCV, ran online petitions urging the Senate to reject Pruitt's nomination.[58] Although these petitions failed to keep Pruitt from becoming EPA administrator, they likely served to grow the supporter lists of various environmental advocacy groups and to keep these groups engaged in preparation for battles to come.

Women's March on Washington

Environmental activism's first major effort to register opposition to the Trump administration came during the Women's March on Washington that took place on January 21, 2017—the day after President Trump's inauguration. The stated purpose of the Women's March, according to its organizers, was to "stand together in solidarity with our partners and children for the protection of our rights, our safety, our health, and our families—recognizing that our vibrant and diverse communities are the strength of our country."[59] The march became a focal point for a wide range of grievances against the incoming president, including his treatment of women, minorities, the disabled, and other underprivileged groups, as well as his climate change denialism and other environmental stances. In fact, "environmental justice" was one of the "unity principles" of the march.[60]

Many environmental advocacy groups, including the Sierra Club, NRDC, and 350.org, declared solidarity with the march. Their participation often emphasized the concept of *intersectionality*—the notion that multiple identities intersect to create a whole that is different from its constituent parts. As sociologist Patricia Hill Collins defines the term, "race, class, gender, sexuality, ethnicity, nation, ability, and age operate not as unitary, mutually exclusive entities, but rather as reciprocally constructing phenomena."[61] The Sierra Club's characterization of its participation in the march is a good example of this phenomenon. In *Sierra*, the organization's magazine, Wendy Becktold opens an article about the Women's March this way:

> Cindy Wiesner is queer, Latina, and the daughter of an immigrant. She also lives in Miami, which she points out will eventually be under water because of rising sea levels. Like many people participating in the Women's March on Washington this Saturday, she won't be marching just for women's rights, racial equality, or environmental justice. She'll be marching for all three, because she lives the struggle for each.[62]

In a similar vein, 350.org's May Boeve wrote in a mass e-mail to the group's supporters on Inauguration Day about the Women's March, emphasizing the intersectionality between the different communities that were scheduled to meet in Washington, DC, the following day:

> Every one of the problems posed by the next President has, at its core, the same solution: people speaking the truth, without apology, in every way available to them. The Women's March is open to all people who recognize the violence of the next Administration, and wish to speak out about it. It will be a history-making day—here's where to go to be a part of it.[63]

The Women's March on Washington spawned a global movement, with 161 sister marches occurring in 61 countries and all seven continents, including Antarctica.[64] It is estimated that between 470,000 to 680,000 people marched in Washington, DC, while between 3.3 million and 4.6 million marched throughout the United States.[65]

The success of the Women's March suggested renewed interest in progressive activism, including environmental activism, centered on opposition to President Trump and his conservative agenda. Other signs, such as monthly donations, also pointed to a surge of interest in anti-Trump environmental activism. Several environmental organizations, including the Sierra Club, Greenpeace, and Friends of the Earth, saw surges in their numbers of monthly donors. The Sierra Club's chief advancement officer said, "We've never seen the volume like this and we've never seen it around monthly donors. . . . [T]hat people are joining monthly, so being committed to the cause over time, is something that is truly unprecedented."[66] Greenpeace and Friends of the Earth also reported major increases in their monthly donors. Another sign of renewed interest in environmentally centered political participation was a spike in individuals (especially women) interested in running for public office on explicitly environmental platforms. In another example of intersectionality, a collection of women's and environmental groups, including EMILY's List, NextGen Climate, ROSA PAC, EDF, Rachel's Network, the Sierra Club, and others, cosponsored the training for women interested in running for office called "Running to Win 101." More than 300 women applied for the training, but only 150 were allowed to participate due to space constraints. The training emphasized the political benefits of touting clean energy jobs.[67]

March for Science

Environmentalists had a second opportunity to participate in a high-profile march against the Trump administration during the March for Science, which took place in Washington, DC, and satellite locations on Earth Day, April 22, 2017. The original idea for the march sprang from the success of the Women's March, when a Reddit commenter, during a discussion of President Trump's science policies, suggested a "Scientists' March on Washington." Shortly thereafter, the march had a Facebook page, a Twitter handle, a website, two cochairs, and a Google form through which interested scientists could sign up to help.[68]

By the time the march took place, major scientific organizations such as the American Association for the Advancement of Science, the Paleontological Society, the Genetics Society of America, and others, as well as environmental organizations, such as the Nature Conservancy, NextGen Climate, Friends of the Earth, Green for All, and 350.org, had become partners of the march.[69] As with the March for Women, intersectionality was at the core of the March for Science. Through their "Diversity Principles," march organizers fully embraced the language of intersectionality:

Inclusion, diversity, equity, and accessibility are central to the mission and princi-
ples of the March for Science [emphasis in original]. Scientists and people who
care about science are an intersectional group, embodying a diverse range of
races, sexual orientations, gender identities, abilities, religions, ages, socioeconomic and immigration statuses. We, the march organizers, represent and
stand in solidarity with historically underrepresented scientists and science
advocates. We are united by our passion to pursue and share knowledge.[70]

Also, like the Women's March, the March for Science spawned satellite marches around the United States and other countries. It is estimated
that 40,000 people attended marches in both Washington, DC, and Chicago;
20,000 attended in New York City; and 10,000 attended marches in both
Philadelphia and London.[71] Despite its relatively broad support among the
scientific community, the march was not without detractors. For example,
University of Maryland physics professor Sylvester James Gates worried that
"such a politically charged event might send a message to the public that scientists are driven by ideology more than by evidence."[72] Representing science
as a political faction or interest group, Gates told reporters at a gathering of
the American Association for the Advancement of Science, is "extraordinarily
dangerous."

People's Climate March

To date, the People's Climate March has been the environmental
movement's most direct contribution to the proliferation of marches and
demonstrations following Donald Trump's election. Its history goes back to
the first People's Climate March, which took place in New York City on
September 21, 2014, two days before the UN Climate Summit. That first
march attracted approximately 300,000 people, making it at the time the
biggest climate change march in history.[73]

The 2017 People's Climate March was announced soon after the
Women's March, by the same organizing coalition behind the 2014 march.
Organizers declared that the April 29, 2017, march

comes in response to widespread outrage against President Trump's disastrous anti-climate agenda—including his executive orders yesterday
advancing the Keystone and Dakota Access pipelines—as well as his
attacks on healthcare, immigrants, and programs and policies that improve
the lives of all Americans.[74]

The march's steering committee consisted of more than 50 organizations.
They ranged from well-established environmental organizations, such as the
LCV, the Natural Resources Defense Council, Oceana, and the Sierra Club,
to newer, climate-focused groups, such as 350.org, Power Shift, and Green for
All. Also included were nonenvironmental groups such as Public Citizen, the
American Postal Workers Union, the Center for Community Change, and
others.[75] As with the preceding marches, the People's Climate March echoed

in its organizing principles the language of intersectionality. Its organizers aimed to "[p]rioritize leadership of front-line communities, communities of color, low-income communities, workers and others impacted by climate, economic and racial inequity" and to "[d]evelop opportunities for a range of organizations and social movements to work together, and to use our joint efforts to give greater visibility to our common struggle."[76] The main march in Washington, DC, and its sister marches in the United States and around the world were heavily promoted via social media, using hashtags such as #climatemarch. The main march was also broadcast live online via the website peoplesclimate.org/live. Attendance at the march in Washington, DC, has been estimated at around 200,000.[77]

Despite its success in rallying hundreds of thousands under the banner of climate action and justice, the march has had some detractors. For example, journalism professor Jill Hopke argues that the march's messaging was too narrow and would not help grow the climate movement beyond its natural constituencies.[78] Relying on research from the Yale Program on Climate Change Communication,[79] Hopke notes that only 18 percent of the U.S. population can be classified as being "alarmed" about climate change while a plurality is only concerned about it. She then argues that the messages that march organizers spread through social media would appeal only to the "alarmed" public, thus limiting the march's appeal and ability to grow the climate movement as a whole. "As a first step," says Hopke, "it will be critical for climate activists to reach beyond core supporters after the march. It is time to disassociate climate action in the United States from the political left and climate denialism from conservatives."[80]

Taking Trump to Court

Although marches and similar grassroots efforts featured prominently among the tactics used by environmentalists during the first 100 days of the Trump administration, they were far from the only ones. Taking the administration to court over various energy and environmental policies has been another prominent insider tactic used by several environmental groups. A major focus of environmental activists at the dawn of the Trump presidency has been defending President Obama's Clean Power Plan. This initiative, which was finalized by the Obama administration in August 2015, would cut carbon emissions 32 percent below 2005 levels by 2030 by having states achieve specific levels or rates of reduction. States would choose the mix of natural gas, renewable energy, and energy savings they would deploy to achieve their reduction targets. The plan immediately came under attack in the courts, where nearly 150 opponents, including 27 states, filed more than fifty lawsuits against it.[81] The plan was put on hold by the U.S. Supreme Court in 2016 pending litigation by states and business groups.[82]

President Trump issued an executive order on March 28, 2017, ordering the EPA to review the Clean Power Plan. The order directed all executive departments and agencies to immediately review existing regulations that potentially burden the development or use of domestically produced energy resources and appropriately suspend, revise, or rescind those that unduly burden the development of domestic energy resources beyond the degree necessary to protect the public interest or otherwise comply with the law.[83]

Environmental activists and advocacy groups, including EDF and the Sierra Club, immediately took the Trump administration to court in an attempt to save the Clean Power Plan. As of this writing, however, the U.S. Court of Appeals for the District of Columbia had issued a stay on litigation against the EPA rule for sixty days. Although opponents of the Clean Power Plan hailed the decision as a "death knell" for the plan, EDF's general counsel said that the EPA has "a duty to protect Americans from dangerous climate pollution under our nation's clean air laws, and Environmental Defense Fund will take swift action to ensure that EPA carries out its responsibilities under the law."[84] The quotation refers to the *Massachusetts v. EPA* Supreme Court decision that holds the EPA accountable for reducing carbon pollution.[85]

The legal wrangling over the Clean Power Plan is just one of several legal battles that environmentalists are waging against the Trump administration. For example, the Sierra Club, the Center for Biological Diversity, and Earthjustice have joined forces with the Northern Cheyenne Tribe to block President Trump's March 28 order because it lifts restrictions on coal sales from federal lands. An attorney for Earthjustice characterized the lifting of the moratorium as "a hail Mary to a dying industry."[86] Another prominent legal battle being waged by environmentalists against the Trump administration revolves around the Keystone XL project. Groups that include the Center for Biological Diversity, the Sierra Club, and the Northern Plains Resource Council argued that the Trump administration used an "outdated and incomplete environmental impact statement" when making its decision to revive the project that the Obama administration had rejected, and that by approving the pipeline without public input and an up-to-date environmental assessment, the administration violated the National Environmental Policy Act (the case was still under litigation as of this writing).[87] Environmental activists have even used the courts to take on some of President Trump's most controversial nonenvironmental policies. For example, the Center for Biological Diversity and Representative Raúl M. Grijalva (D-Arizona) sued the Trump administration over construction of the border wall between Mexico and the United States that candidate Trump promised during the campaign. The center and Grijalva alleged in court that the Trump administration had failed to study the wall's environmental impact before gearing up for its construction.[88] If this pattern holds, the rest of President Trump's four-year term promises to be one of never-ending environmental litigation.

Conclusion

This chapter has chronicled some of the most important instances of environmental activism during the last years of the Obama administration and the beginning of the Trump presidency. There are important similarities and differences to note. Although some of the tactics deployed by activists during both periods may be similar, such as marches and rallies, the intensity of vitriol directed toward the targets make for a stark contrast. President Obama was treated by activists as essentially a reluctant ally who had to be pushed and prodded into doing the right thing from the activists' point of view. President Trump, on the other hand, has been treated so far as an implacable enemy of the environment and climate action who must be opposed vociferously at every turn. But the Trump administration's positions on climate and the environment are not as uniformly opposed to the preferences of activists as they might appear at first sight. There appears to be some support within the administration for keeping the United States within the Paris Agreement, and there is even support in some quarters for a carbon tax.[89] These climate-friendly positions are deeply embedded in struggles within the administration among top aides seeking to influence the president, and it is too early as of this writing to predict which faction will win. Despite these divisions, activists show no obvious signs of seeking to exploit them.

Another theme that emerges throughout the most recent instances of activism against the incipient Trump administration is the widespread embrace of the concept of intersectionality. Activists have not only embraced the idea that individuals can have distinct yet intersecting identities and also be the victims of distinct yet intersecting systems of oppression, such as racism, sexism, homophobia, and others,[90] but also incorporated this idea into their organizing. Although there may be strong moral reasons for this embrace, from a strategic angle, intersectionality can be a double-edged sword for environmental activists. Intersectionality has the potential to expand environmental activism's public by appealing to individuals who have traditionally not been part of it, such as minorities. Yet intersectionality also holds the potential to consume environmental actions in internecine battles over the proper representation of various identities. Activists will have to balance carefully their wish to be more inclusive with the environmental movement's strategic priorities.

A third theme that emerges from this chapter is the communication strategies that environmental advocates have deployed so far vis-à-vis the Trump administration. Environmental activists (and progressives, more broadly) have been remarkably successful at repeatedly mobilizing hundreds of thousands of people into the streets to protest the new president. Yet Jill Hopke's critique poses a question: Can environmental and climate activists move public opinion significantly with their current communication strategies? Using these strategies, argues Hopke, climate and environmental activists only appeal to the "alarmed" segment of the public (which comprises 18 percent of the public, at least on climate change). To expand their base of support and heighten the urgency of climate and related issues, activists would have to appeal more effectively to the "concerned" segment of the public, which comprises 34 percent, and move them into the alarmed category. It remains to be seen whether highly partisan and polarizing attacks on the Trump administration can help accomplish this. Given the escalating polarization of the country after the election of Donald Trump,[91] however, it is difficult to see how this communication strategy will help change public opinion in the direction that activists would like to see it move.

Suggested Websites

350.org (www.350.org) An advocacy group specializing in grassroots mobilization and industry pressure campaigns, 350.org was cofounded by environmental writer Bill McKibben. The site features multimedia campaign updates, backgrounders, blogs, and videos.

Ensia (www.ensia.com) Web magazine *Ensia* features news and commentary about environmental science and policy with a focus on identifying new ideas, voices, and opportunities for collaboration in support of policy solutions and actions.

The Breakthrough Institute (www.thebreakthrough.org) The Breakthrough Institute is a San Francisco–based progressive think tank focused on an "eco-modernist," pragmatic approach to environmental problems and advocacy. The website features commentary, articles, analysis, and reports from experts and journalists analyzing trends and directions related to climate change and energy policy.

Inside Climate News (insideclimatenews.org) This Pulitzer Prize–winning advocacy news site features coverage and analysis of the debate over the Keystone XL pipeline, the fossil fuel divestment movement, and climate change–related electoral politics.

Dot Earth: *New York Times* **Blog** (www.nytimes.com/dotearth) Dot Earth features commentary and analysis of trends in climate science, politics, and policy ideas by veteran environmental writer Andrew Revkin.

Notes

1. Barack H. Obama, "Statement by the President on the Keystone XL Pipeline," *The White House Briefing Room: Statements & Releases*, November 6, 2015, http://obamawhitehouse .archives.gov/the-press-office/2015/11/06/statement-president-keystone-xl-pipeline.

2. Ben Adler, "The Inside Story of How the Keystone Fight Was Won," *Grist*, November 6, 2015, http://grist.org/climate-energy/the-inside-story-of-how-the-keystone-fight-was-won/.

3. United Nations Framework Convention on Climate Change, *Paris Agreement* (Bonn, Germany: UNFCCC, 2005), http://unfccc.int/files/essential_background/convention/ application/pdf/english_paris_agreement.pdf.

4. "Climate Change," *Hillary for America*, http://www.hillaryclinton.com/issues/climate/.

5. "2016 Presidential Election Forecasts," *270toWin.com*, http://www.270towin.com/ 2016-election-forecast-predictions/.

6. Theda Skocpol, *Naming the Problem: What It Will Take to Counter Extremism and Engage Americans in the Fight against Global Warming* (Cambridge, MA: Scholars Strategy Network, 2013), http://www.scholarsstrategynetwork.org/sites/default/files/skocpol_ captrade_report_january_2013y.pdf; Petra Bartosiewicz and Miley Marissa, *The Too*

Polite Revolution: Why the Recent Campaign to Pass Comprehensive Climate Legislation in the United States Failed (Cambridge, MA: Scholars Strategy Network, 2013), http://www .scholarsstrategynetwork.org/sites/default/files/rff_final_report_bartosiewicz_miley.pdf.

7. EcoAmerica, *America the Best: Social Solutions for Climate* (Washington, DC: EcoAmerica, 2010), http://ecoamerica.org/wp-content/uploads/2013/02/America_ The_Best.pdf.

8. Theda Skocpol, "You Can't Change the Climate from Inside Washington," *Foreign Policy*, January 24, 2013.

9. Michael Wines, "Environmental Groups Focus on Change by Strengthening Their Political Operations," *New York Times*, May 31, 2014.

10. Matthew C. Nisbet, *Nature's Prophet: Bill McKibben as Journalist, Public Intellectual, and Advocate*, Discussion Paper Series No. D-78 (Cambridge, MA: Kennedy School of Government, Harvard University, March 2012), http://shorensteincenter.org/ natures-prophet-bill-mckibben-as-journalist-public-intellectual-and-activist/.

11. Dana R. Fisher and Marije Boekkooi, "Mobilizing Friends and Strangers," *Information, Communication & Society* 13, no. 2 (2010): 193–208.

12. Bill McKibben, *Fight Global Warming Now: The Handbook for Taking Action in Your Community* (New York: St. Martin's Griffin, 2007).

13. Matthew C. Nisbet, *Climate Shift: Clear Vision for the Next Decade of Public Debate* (Washington, DC: American University, 2011), http://climateshiftproject.org/ report/climate-shift-clear-vision-for-the-next-decade-of-public-debate/.

14. 350.org, *350.org Annual Report, 2015*, accessed May 1, 2017, https://350.org/2015-annual-report/.

15. Luis Hestres, "Preaching to the Choir: Internet-Mediated Advocacy, Issue Public Mobilization, and Climate Change," *New Media & Society* 16, no. 2 (2014): 323–39.

16. Hestres, "Preaching to the Choir."

17. Matthew C. Nisbet, "How Bill McKibben Changed Environmental Politics and Took On the Oil Patch," *Policy Options*, May 1, 2013, http://policyoptions.irpp.org/ issues/arctic-visions/nisbet/.

18. Saul Elbein, "Jan Kleeb vs. the Keystone Pipeline," *New York Times Magazine*, May 16, 2014.

19. Lauren Barron-Lopez, "Greens Demand State Hand over Keystone Docs," *The Hill*, August 14, 2014.

20. Andrew Restuccia and Darren Goode, "Keystone Decision Delayed Yet Again," *Politico*, April 14, 2014.

21. Andrew Revkin, "Can Obama Escape the Alberta Tar Pit?" *New York Times*, September 5, 2011.

22. "Keystone XL Is Coming Back," *Washington Post*, January 23, 2013.

23. "Change for Good: The US Must Boost Its Spending on Clean Energy to Make Its Mark on the Climate Debate," editorial, *Nature*, January 29, 2013.

24. Emily Atkin, "Big Green Groups Line up Behind Clinton, While Smaller Ones Stick to Sanders," *Think Progress*, June 10, 2016, https://thinkprogress.org/big-green-groups-line-up-behind-clinton-while-smaller-ones-stick-to-sanders-9ff97dd6ebd.

25. Abby Phillip, "Major Environmental Group Backs Hillary Clinton in Its First Presidential Endorsement," *Washington Post*, May 31, 2016, https://www.washingtonpost .com/news/post-politics/wp/2016/05/31/major-environmental-group-makes-first-ever-endorsement-of-hillary-clinton/.

26. Samantha Page, "Hillary Clinton Wins the Support of a Major Environmental Group," *ThinkProgress*, November 9, 2015, https://thinkprogress.org/hillary-clinton-wins-the-support-of-a-major-environmental-group-de85cad053f3.

27. "Friends of the Earth Action Endorses Bernie Sanders for President," *Friends of the Earth Action* [press release], August 1, 2015, https://foeaction.org/news-release/foea-endorses-bernie-sanders-for-president/.

28. Amy Goodman, "Climate Leader Bill McKibben Named by Sanders to DNC Platform Committee," *Alternet*, May 26, 2016, http://www.alternet.org/election-2016/bill-mckibben-named-bernie-sanders-dnc-platform-committee.

29. Bill McKibben, "The Clinton Campaign Is Obstructing Change to the Democratic Platform," *Politico Magazine*, June 27, 2016, http://politi.co/28YuxZK.

30. McKibben, "The Clinton Campaign Is Obstructing."

31. Jill E. Hopke, "Translocal Anti-Fracking Activism: An Exploration of Network Structure and Tie Content," *Environmental Communication* 10, no. 3 (May 3, 2016): 380–94, http://dx.doi.org/10.1080/17524032.2016.1147474.

32. Dave Weigel, "Sanders Calls for National Fracking Ban, with Eye on Clinton," *Washington Post*, April 11, 2016, https://www.washingtonpost.com/news/post-politics/wp/2016/04/11/sanders-and-activist-go-after-clinton-on-fracking/.

33. Linda Qiu, "Does Hillary Clinton Support Fracking?" *PolitiFact*, April 13, 2016, http://www.politifact.com/truth-o-meter/statements/2016/apr/13/bernie-s/does-hillary-clinton-support-fracking/.

34. Louis Jacobson. "Yes, Donald Trump Did Call Climate Change a Chinese Hoax," *PolitiFact*, June 3, 2016, http://www.politifact.com/truth-o-meter/statements/2016/jun/03/hillary-clinton/yes-donald-trump-did-call-climate-change-chinese-h/.

35. Ashley Parker and Coral Davenport, "Donald Trump's Energy Plan: More Fossil Fuels and Fewer Rules," *New York Times*, May 26, 2016. https://www.nytimes.com/2016/05/27/us/politics/donald-trump-global-warming-energy-policy.html.

36. Parker and Davenport, "Donald Trump's Energy Plan."

37. Phillip, "Major Environmental Group Backs Hillary Clinton in Its First Presidential Endorsement."

38. Environmental Defense Fund, "EDF Action Statement on the Presidential Race," *EDF Action*, July 26, 2016, http://www.edfaction.org/media/edf-action-statement-presidential-race.

39. "LCV Names Donald Trump to Signature 'Dirty Dozen' List," *League of Conservation Voters*, July 28, 2016, http://www.lcv.org/article/lcv-names-donald-trump-to-signature-dirty-dozen-list/.

40. "Report: Trump Would Be Only World Leader to Deny Climate Science," *Sierra Club National*, July 12, 2016, http://content.sierraclub.org/press-releases/2016/07/report-trump-would-be-only-world-leader-deny-climate-science.

41. Juliet Eilperin, "Top Green Group to Spend at Least $40 Million This Election, Shattering Past Records," *Washington Post*, October 10, 2016, https://www.washingtonpost.com/news/energy-environment/wp/2016/10/10/top-green-group-to-spend-at-least-40-million-this-election-shattering-past-records/.

42. Duncan Meisel, "We Stopped Keystone XL. Now Let's Stop Trump," *350.org*, November 6, 2016.

43. May Boeve, "Put a Question about Climate in the next Presidential Debate," *350.org*, October 5, 2016, https://350.org/put-a-question-about-climate-in-the-next-presidential-debate/.

44. *Politico* staff, "Full Transcript: Second 2016 Presidential Debate," *Politico*, October 10, 2016, http://politi.co/2d661FN.

45. "Official 2016 Presidential General Election Results," *Federal Election Commission*, January 30, 2017, http://www.fec.gov/pubrec/fe2016/2016presgeresults.pdf.

46. "2016 Presidential Election Forecasts," *270toWin.com*.

47. Fred Krupp, "Donald Trump Elected, but Our Resolve Is Unbroken," *Environmental Defense Fund*, November 9, 2016, https://www.edf.org/blog/2016/11/09/donald-trump-elected-our-resolve-unbroken.

48. Rhea Suh, "The Election Is Over. Our Resolve Isn't," *NRDC*, November 10, 2016, https://www.nrdc.org/experts/rhea-suh/election-over-our-resolve-isnt.

49. Michael Brune, "Determined, Not Defeated," *Sierra Club*, November 10, 2016, http://www.sierraclub.org/michael-brune/2016/11/trump.

50. Annie Leonard, "Trump as President: Here's How We Get Through This," *Greenpeace USA*, November 9, 2016, http://www.greenpeace.org/usa/trump-president-heres-get/.

51. "U.S. Election Is a Gut Punch to the Planet," *Friends of the Earth*, November 9, 2016, http://www.foe.org/news/archives/2016-11-us-election-is-a-gut-punch-to-the-planet.

52. "What the Election Results Mean for the Climate Crisis," *Climate Reality Project*, November 10, 2016, https://www.climaterealityproject.org/blog/what-election-results-mean-climate-change.

53. Lydia Avila, "Mourn, Then Organize," *Power Shift Network*, November 9, 2016.

54. May Boeve, "Deep Breaths. Now Let's Plan the Fight Ahead," *350.org*, November 9, 2016, https://350.org/deep-breaths-now-lets-plan-the-fight-ahead/.

55. "Trump Seeking Quickest Way to Quit Paris Climate Agreement, Says Report," *The Guardian*, November 13, 2016, https://www.theguardian.com/us-news/2016/nov/13/trump-looking-at-quickest-way-to-quit-paris-climate-agreement-says-report.

56. Priyanka Boghani, "Meet Myron Ebell, the Climate Contrarian Leading Trump's EPA Transition," *Frontline*, November 14, 2016, http://www.pbs.org/wgbh/frontline/article/meet-myron-ebell-the-climate-contrarian-leading-trumps-epa-transition/.

57. Dominique Mosbergen, "Scott Pruitt Has Sued the Environmental Protection Agency 13 Times. Now He Wants to Lead It," *Huffington Post*, January 17, 2017, http://www.huffingtonpost.com/entry/scott-pruitt-environmental-protection-agency_us_5878ad15e4b0b3c7a7b0c29c.

58. "Sign the Petition: Don't Let Big Polluters Run the EPA," *League of Conservation Voters*, accessed April 29, 2017, https://secure3.convio.net/lcv/site/Advocacy?cmd=display&page=UserAction&id=3657; "Take Action: Tell Your Senators to Oppose Scott Pruitt's Nomination to Head EPA," *Sierra Club*, accessed April 29, 2017, https://sierra.secure.force.com/actions/National?actionId=AR0062590&id=70131000001Lp1FAAS.

59. "Mission & Vision," *Women's March on Washington*, accessed April 29, 2017, https://www.womensmarch.com/mission/. Note that the mission statement has since changed, but the older version is available from Google's cache at https://www.womensmarch.com/mission2/.

60. "Unity Principles," *Women's March on Washington*, accessed April 29, 2017. https://www.womensmarch.com/principles/.

61. Patricia Hill Collins, "Intersectionality's Definitional Dilemmas," *Annual Review of Sociology* 41 (2015): 1–20.

62. Wendy Becktold, "Climate Activists Bring It All to the Women's March on Washington," *Sierra Club*, January 19, 2017, https://sierraclub.org/sierra/green-life/climate-activists-bring-it-all-women-s-march-washington.

63. May Boeve, "Women's March," *350.org*, January 20, 2017.

64. Noël Bakhtian, "Women's Marches, Occurring across Seven Continents, Include a Focus on Environment," *Grist*, January 19, 2017, https://grist.org/opinion/womens-marches-occurring-across-seven-continents-include-a-focus-on-environment/.

65. Kaveh Waddell, "The Exhausting Work of Tallying America's Largest Protest," *The Atlantic*, January 23, 2017, https://www.theatlantic.com/technology/archive/2017/01/womens-march-protest-count/514166/.

66. Karl Mathiesen, "Green Groups Get 'Unprecedented' Trump Bump in Donations," *Climate Home*, December 13, 2016, http://www.climatechangenews.com/2016/12/13/green-groups-get-unprecedented-trump-bump-in-donations/.

67. Mark Hand, "New Effort Aims to Inspire the next Generation of pro-Environment Women Candidates," *ThinkProgress*, April 28, 2017, https://thinkprogress.org/women-candidates-to-protect-the-planet-57d2d197ec80.

68. Sarah Kaplan, "Are Scientists Going to March on Washington?" *Washington Post*, January 25, 2017, https://www.washingtonpost.com/news/speaking-of-science/wp/2017/01/24/are-scientists-going-to-march-on-washington/.

69. "Our Partners," *March for Science*, accessed April 30, 2017, https://www.marchforscience.com/partners/.

70. "Diversity Principles," *March for Science*, accessed April 30, 2017, https://www.marchforscience.com/diversity-principles/.

71. Lorenzo Tanos, "March for Science Attendance: Rallies Draw Solid Crowds, Inspire the Cleverest Signs," *The Inquisitr*, April 23, 2017, http://www.inquisitr.com/4166885/march-for-science-attendance-rallies-signs/.

72. Faye Flam, "Why Some Scientists Won't March for Science," *Bloomberg View*, March 7, 2017, https://www.bloomberg.com/view/articles/2017-03-07/why-some-scientists-won-t-march-for-science.

73. Lisa W. Foderaro, "Taking a Call for Climate Change to the Streets," *New York Times*, September 21, 2014, https://www.nytimes.com/2014/09/22/nyregion/new-york-city-climate-change-march.html.

74. "Activists Announce Major Climate March in DC & Nationwide on April 29th," *Sierra Club National*, January 25, 2017, http://content.sierraclub.org/press-releases/2017/01/activists-announce-major-climate-march-dc-nationwide-april-29th.

75. "Partner Organizations," *Peoples Climate Movement 2017*, accessed April 30, 2017, https://peoplesclimate.org/partners/.

76. "PCM History," *Peoples Climate Movement 2017*, accessed April 30, 2017, https://peoplesclimate.org/history/.

77. Samantha Page, "People's Climate March Draws 200,000 Protesters as Trump Flees to Coal Country," *ThinkProgress*, April 29, 2017, https://thinkprogress.org/climate-march-2017-48815ae47ba1.

78. Jill E. Hopke, "To Have Impact, the People's Climate March Needs to Reach beyond Activists," *The Conversation*, April 25, 2017, http://theconversation.com/to-have-impact-the-peoples-climate-march-needs-to-reach-beyond-activists-75974.

79. "Global Warming's Six Americas," *Yale Program on Climate Change Communication*, accessed May 1, 2017, http://climatecommunication.yale.edu/about/projects/global-warmings-six-americas/. See also Anthony Leiserowitz, Edward Maibach, Connie Roser-Renouf, Seth Rosenthal, and Matthew Cutler, *Climate Change in the American Mind: May 2017* (New Haven, CT: Yale Program on Climate Change Communication, 2017).

80. Hopke, "To Have Impact."

81. "E&E's Power Plan Hub: Battle Lines," *E&E News*, accessed April 30, 2017, https://www.eenews.net/interactive/clean_power_plan/fact_sheets/legal_battle_lines.

82. "E&E's Power Plan Hub: How Did We Get Here?" *E&E News*, accessed April 30, 2017, https://www.eenews.net/interactive/clean_power_plan/fact_sheets/rule.

83. Donald J. Trump, "Presidential Executive Order on Promoting Energy Independence and Economic Growth," *White House Briefing Room: Presidential Actions—Executive Orders*, March 28, 2017, https://www.whitehouse.gov/the-press-office/2017/03/28/presidential-executive-order-promoting-energy-independence-and-economi-1.

84. Juliet Eilperin and Brady Dennis, "Court Freezes Clean Power Plan Lawsuit, Signaling Likely End to Obama's Signature Climate Policy," *Washington Post*, April 28, 2017, https://www.washingtonpost.com/news/energy-environment/wp/2017/04/28/court-freezes-clean-power-plan-lawsuit-signaling-likely-end-to-obamas-signature-climate-policy/.

85. *Massachusetts v. EPA*, 127 S. Ct. 1438 (2007).

86. Tammy Webber and Matthew Brown, "Environmental Groups File Lawsuit Over Trump Climate Order," *AP News*, March 29, 2017, https://apnews.com/23000549831 849e494b26b0b9d861b3e/environmental-groups-vowing-fight-trump-climate-actions.

87. Valerie Volcovici, "Environmental Groups Sue Trump Administration for Approving Keystone Pipeline," *Reuters*, March 30, 2017, http://www.reuters.com/article/us-usa-pipeline-keystone-lawsuit-idUSKBN1712DZ.

88. Fernanda Santos, "No Environmental Impact Study? No Border Wall, Lawsuit Says," *New York Times*, April 13, 2017, https://www.nytimes.com/2017/04/13/us/no-environmental-impact-study-no-border-wall-lawsuit-says.html.

89. Laura Koran and Kevin Liptak, "Trump Team to Debate Future of Paris Agreement," *CNN*, April 17, 2017, http://www.cnn.com/2017/04/17/politics/trump-advisers-climate-change/index.html.

90. Collins, "Intersectionality's Definitional Dilemmas."

91. Pew Research Center, "In First Month, Views of Trump Are Already Strongly Felt, Deeply Polarized," *U.S. Politics*, February 16, 2017, http://www.people-press.org/2017/02/16/in-first-month-views-of-trump-are-already-strongly-felt-deeply-polarized/.

Part II

Federal Institutions and Policy Change

Chapter 4

Presidential Powers and Environmental Policy

Norman J. Vig

I don't believe in climate change.

Donald Trump, CNN Interview,
September 24, 2015

*We cannot risk putting a climate denier in the White House. . . .
We need a president who believes in science and who has a plan.*

Hillary Clinton, Speech in Miami,
October 11, 2016

Elections have consequences, especially presidential elections. This was starkly evident in the 2016 presidential election between Hillary Clinton and Donald Trump. They disagreed on virtually every issue, none more sharply than the environment. While Mrs. Clinton pledged to continue and strengthen President Barack Obama's strong environmental legacy, particularly on actions to stem climate change, Mr. Trump repeatedly called climate change a "hoax" and threatened to reverse Obama's policies. He promised to repeal Obama's Clean Power Plan and other climate change regulations; to "cancel" the Paris Agreement on climate; to dismantle much of the Environmental Protection Agency (EPA); and to remove barriers to the rapid expansion of oil, gas, and coal production as part of his "America First" energy plan.[1] Although Trump later indicated that he had an open mind on some issues, his early actions suggested that he would attempt to alter the nation's environmental policies drastically.[2]

Presidents of both parties have utilized their powers to shape natural resource and environmental policies throughout our history. But ever since the 1970s, when most of our current environmental laws were enacted (see Chapter 1 and Appendix 1), environmental policies have oscillated back and forth depending on which party controlled the presidency. With some exceptions, Republican presidents since Richard Nixon have opposed new legislation and have sought to weaken or roll back environmental regulations that they consider burdensome to business and industry. Democratic presidents, on the other hand, have attempted to strengthen and extend environmental protections, culminating in Barack Obama's climate change initiatives. The partisan divide over environmental science and policy now appears wider than at any time in history.[3]

Given this polarization, and consequent gridlock in Congress (see Chapter 5), presidents have increasingly utilized executive powers to promote their environmental and natural resource agendas.[4] President Obama began his first term with a majority in both houses of Congress, but he was unable to convince the Senate to pass climate change legislation in 2010. Facing implacable opposition after Republicans gained control of the House of Representatives later that year, he relied increasingly on unilateral presidential powers. During his second term, he promoted an impressive national and international regime to address climate change through executive actions. Obama's policies thus raised the question of how much a president can accomplish without the support of Congress. President Trump has set out to reverse many of these executive actions while also enjoying majorities in both houses of Congress, but he too has expanded the powers of the presidency.[5]

Nevertheless, presidents operate within a system of constitutional, legal, and political constraints that limit their authority. I will compare the environmental records of recent presidents, as well as Trump's early efforts to change national priorities, later in this chapter. But first it is necessary to take a closer look at the powers of the presidency and the criteria for comparing presidents' environmental policies.

Presidential Powers and Constraints

The formal *roles* of the president have been summarized as commander in chief of the armed forces, chief diplomat, chief executive, legislative leader, and opinion/party leader.[6] If we look only at environmental policy, the president's role as chief executive has probably been most important.[7] But some presidents, including Teddy Roosevelt, Franklin Roosevelt, and Richard Nixon, have played a leading role in enacting environmental legislation and in using the "bully pulpit" to rally public opinion behind new environmental policies. The role of chief diplomat has also become more important as many environmental problems have required international solutions; for example, Ronald Reagan supported and signed the landmark Montreal Protocol on Substances that Deplete the Ozone Layer in 1987, and Barack Obama played a leading role in negotiating the Paris Agreement of 2015. Finally, as commander in chief of the armed forces, the president also deals with a growing range of environmental issues, including the destabilization of regions and governments affected by climate change.[8]

Some of the president's *powers* are "contextual"; that is, they shape the general context of policymaking and the broad directions of the administration. Presidents can draw attention to issues and frame the political agenda through speeches, press conferences, and other types of media; they can propose legislation and budgets; they nominate and appoint cabinet members and other key officials; and they can reorganize their staffs and departments to better implement their policies. Other powers of the president are more "unilateral" and allow the president to influence policy decisions directly.

These include the power to veto legislation; to issue executive orders, directives, and proclamations; to make executive agreements; and to monitor and control regulatory processes.[9] One unique power is the authority to designate national monuments to protect areas of exceptional scenic, scientific, cultural, or historical value under the Antiquities Act of 1906.[10]

Article II of the Constitution directs the president to "faithfully execute the laws." Most legislation passed by Congress is quite broad, however, and leaves much to the discretion of the president and the implementing agencies. The EPA, for example, is charged by the Clean Air Act to formulate and issue detailed standards, rules, and regulations to control the emission of pollutants so as to ensure healthy air quality (see Chapter 7). These rules and regulations are adopted through lengthy administrative proceedings, and once finalized, they have the full force of law. Presidents therefore try to centralize and control rulemaking to ensure that it reflects their policy agendas. All presidents since Nixon have required that important regulations be cleared by the Office of Management and Budget (OMB) before they are proposed by the EPA and other regulatory agencies. Presidents can thus have a major impact on policy decisions through controlling the bureaucracy rather than passing new legislation.[11]

Ultimately, however, presidents cannot govern alone; they are part of a government of "separated powers."[12] Their policies must be grounded in statutes passed by Congress, and Congress also determines the budgets and spending limits of all executive agencies. The Senate can refuse to confirm the president's nominees for office and deny the ratification of treaties. Even with a majority in both houses, the president may not be able to get sufficient support to pass new legislation (as in the case of climate change legislation in 2010). Without such legislation, executive actions may be difficult to carry out. There can be considerable resistance to policy change within the bureaucracy itself.[13] Moreover, most major rules and regulations, as well as many executive orders and other presidential actions, are challenged in the courts by affected parties, often tying up policies in litigation for years (see Chapter 6). Executive orders can also be modified or rescinded by subsequent presidents, so they are rarely permanent. Finally, in our federal system, most environmental laws depend heavily on the states for implementation (see Chapters 2 and 7). In some cases, as with President Obama's Clean Power Plan to control carbon emissions from coal-fired power plants, many states have refused to implement national policies.

Comparing Environmental Presidencies

Presidential leadership on environmental policy can be analyzed and compared in different ways. We can examine how each president performs the five basic *roles* noted in the previous section as they pertain to the environment.[14] Two of the political scientists who developed this approach to presidents' environmental records have extended their analysis to twelve past presidents, focusing on four differentiating factors: *political communication, legislative leadership, administrative actions,* and *environmental diplomacy.*[15] Presidents were then ranked according to their positive or negative impacts on the environment, yielding a "continuum of greenness." Seven presidents are classified as having had a positive impact (Franklin Roosevelt, Harry Truman, John Kennedy, Lyndon Johnson, Richard Nixon, Jimmy Carter, and Bill Clinton), three as having mixed impacts (Dwight Eisenhower, Gerald Ford, and George H. W. Bush), and two as having negative impacts (Ronald Reagan and George W. Bush). Roosevelt and Nixon rank as the "greenest" by these criteria.[16] Roosevelt greatly expanded the conservation programs pioneered by his cousin, Teddy Roosevelt; and Nixon proclaimed the 1970s the "environmental decade," created the EPA by executive action, and signed most of the landmark environmental legislation of our era.[17]

We can also look at how presidents have influenced longer-term *policy cycles* (as discussed in Chapter 1): what role have they played in *agenda setting, policy formulation, policy legitimation, policy implementation, policy evaluation,* and *policy change?* From this perspective, we can trace how individual policies have been initiated and modified over time and how effectively they have been implemented. Some presidents (for example, Nixon and Obama) launch new policy cycles, while others (such as Reagan and George W. Bush) attempt to modify them in favor of different priorities. This raises the question of to what extent a president like Donald Trump can fundamentally alter policy and bureaucratic structures that have become institutionalized over decades. But it also points to the difficulties of implementing policies that are not fully legitimated (for example, by Congress) such as Barack Obama's climate change initiatives.

For our purposes, a president's overall environmental performance can be evaluated by examining a few basic indicators: (1) the president's environmental *agenda* as expressed in campaign statements, policy documents, and other pronouncements; (2) presidential *appointments* to key positions in government departments and agencies and to the White House staff; (3) the relative priority given to environmental programs in the president's proposed *budgets*; (4) presidential *legislative success*; (5) *executive orders and other unilateral actions* by the president; and (6) presidential support for or opposition to *international environmental agreements*. By these criteria, some presidents have been much more favorable to the environment than others.

Space does not allow a full comparison of all recent administrations. I will briefly summarize the environmental records of four presidents since 1980: Reagan, G.H.W. Bush, Clinton, and G.W. Bush. We can see many contrasts in presidential leadership from these case studies—as well as some of the dynamics of policy cycles over time. Fuller attention will be paid to the Obama presidency's environmental policy and the early initiatives of the Trump administration to undo it. The conclusion to the chapter will attempt a preliminary assessment of the extent of likely policy change under President Trump.

The Reagan Revolution: Environmental Backlash

The "environmental decade" of the 1970s came to an abrupt halt with Reagan's victory in 1980. Although the environment was not a major issue in the election, Reagan was the first president to come to office with an avowedly antienvironmental agenda. Influenced by the Sagebrush Rebellion—an attempt by several western states to claim ownership of federal lands—as well as by his long years of public relations work for corporate and conservative causes, Reagan viewed environmental conservation as fundamentally at odds with economic growth and prosperity. He saw environmental regulation as a barrier to "supply side" economics and sought to reverse or weaken many of the policies of the previous decade.[18] Although only partially successful, Reagan's agenda laid the groundwork for renewed attacks on environmental policy in later decades.

Because it came after a period of economic decline, Reagan's landslide victory appeared to reflect a strong mandate for policy change. And with a new Republican majority in the Senate, he was able to gain congressional support for the Economic Recovery Tax Act of 1981, which embodied much of his program. He reduced income taxes by nearly 25 percent and deeply cut spending for environmental and social programs. Despite this initial victory, however, Reagan faced a Congress that was divided on most issues and did not support his broader environmental goals. On the contrary, the bipartisan majority that had enacted most of the environmental legislation of the 1970s remained largely intact.

Faced with this situation, Reagan turned to what has been termed an "administrative presidency."[19] Essentially, this involved an attempt to change federal policies by maximizing control of policy implementation within the executive branch. The administrative strategy initially had four major components: (1) careful screening of all appointees to environmental and other agencies to ensure compliance with Reagan's ideological goals, (2) tight policy coordination through cabinet councils and White House staff, (3) deep cuts in the budgets of environmental agencies and programs, and (4) an enhanced form of regulatory oversight to eliminate or revise regulations considered burdensome by industry.

Reagan's appointment of officials who were overtly hostile to the mission of their agencies aroused strong opposition from the environmental community. In particular, his selection of Anne Gorsuch (later Burford) to head the EPA and James Watt as secretary of the interior provoked controversy from the beginning because both were attorneys who had spent long years litigating against environmental regulation. Both made it clear that they intended to rewrite the rules and procedures of their agencies to accommodate industries such as mining, logging, and oil and gas. Watt was also designated head of the new cabinet council to coordinate policies in all of the environmental and natural resource agencies, and to bring these policies in line with the president's agenda.

In the White House, Reagan lost no time in changing the policy machinery to accomplish the same goal. He all but eliminated his environmental advisers and instead appointed Vice President George H. W. Bush to head a new Task Force on Regulatory Relief, to identify and modify or rescind regulations targeted by business and industry. More important, in February 1981 Reagan issued Executive Order 12291, which carried White House control of the regulatory process to a new level. All major regulations (costing over $100 million) were now to undergo prepublication review by the Office of Information and Regulatory Affairs (OIRA) in the OMB. They were to be accompanied by rigorous benefit-cost analyses demonstrating that benefits exceeded costs, and they had to include evaluation of alternatives to ensure that net social benefits were maximized. OIRA consequently held up, reviewed, and revised hundreds of EPA and other regulations to reduce their effect on industry. The number of new environmental rules thus declined sharply in the Reagan years.[20] At the same time, Reagan's budget cuts had major effects on the capacity of environmental agencies to implement their growing policy mandates. The EPA lost approximately one-third of its operating budget and one-fifth of its personnel in the early 1980s. The White House Council on Environmental Quality (CEQ) lost most of its staff and barely continued to function. In the Interior Department and elsewhere, funds were shifted from environmental to development programs.[21]

Not surprisingly, Congress responded by investigating OIRA procedures and other activities of Reagan appointees, especially Burford and Watt. Burford came under heavy attack for confidential dealings with business and political interests that allegedly led to sweetheart deals on matters such as Superfund cleanups. After refusing to disclose documents, she was found in contempt of Congress and forced to resign (along with twenty other high-level EPA officials) in March 1983. Watt was pilloried in Congress for his efforts to open virtually all public lands (including wilderness areas) and off-shore coastal areas to mining and oil and gas development, and he left office later in 1983.[22] William Ruckelshaus, the original EPA administrator, was brought back in to run the EPA.

Because of these embarrassments and widespread public and congressional opposition to weakening environmental protection, Reagan's deregulatory campaign was largely spent by the end of his first term. Recognizing that his policies had backfired, the president took few new initiatives during his second term. His appointees to the EPA and the Interior Department diffused some of the political conflict generated by Watt and Burford and partially restored their agencies' budgets and staffs. But Congress passed a series of amendments to existing laws such as Superfund, the Safe Drinking Water Act, and the Clean Water Act (see Appendix 1). These laws mandated stricter regulatory timetables and enforcement and were intended to reduce the discretionary authority of the EPA and other executive agencies. Indeed, the backlash *against* Reagan *strengthened* rather than weakened key environmental statutes, thus reinforcing these policy cycles.

Reagan deserves credit for supporting and signing the Montreal Protocol on Substances that Deplete the Ozone Layer in 1987. This treaty, which banned the use of chlorofluorocarbons (CFCs) and other chemicals that were destroying the atmospheric ozone layer, has proven to be one of the most effective international environmental agreements.[23] However, Reagan continued to oppose actions on other air pollution issues such as acid rain. By the end of his presidency, public opinion clearly demanded stronger environmental measures.[24]

President George H. W. Bush: Clean Air Legislation

George H. W. Bush's presidency thus returned to a more moderate tradition of Republican leadership, particularly in the first two years. While promising to "stay the course" on Reagan's economic policies, Bush also pledged a "kinder and gentler" America. Although his domestic policy agenda was the most limited of any recent president, it included action on the environment. Indeed, during the campaign, Bush declared himself a "conservationist" in the tradition of Teddy Roosevelt and promised to be an "environmental president."

If Bush surprised almost everyone by seizing the initiative on what most assumed was a strong issue for the Democrats, he impressed environmentalists even more by soliciting their advice and by appointing a number of environmental leaders to his administration. William Reilly, the highly respected president of the World Wildlife Fund and the Conservation Foundation, became EPA administrator; and Michael Deland, formerly New England director of the EPA, became chairman of the CEQ. Bush promised to restore the CEQ to an influential role and made it clear that he intended to work closely with the Democratic Congress to strengthen the Clean Air Act early in his administration.

Yet Bush's nominees to head the public lands and natural resource agencies were not much different from those of the Reagan administration. In particular, his choice of Manuel Lujan Jr., a ten-term retired congressman from New Mexico, to serve as secretary of the interior indicated that no major departures would be made in western land policies. The president's top White House advisers were also much more conservative on environmental matters than were Reilly and Deland. This was especially true of his chief of staff, John Sununu. Nevertheless, Bush increased funding for the EPA and other environmental agencies and largely restored their credibility.

Bush also pursued a bipartisan strategy in passing the Clean Air Act Amendments of 1990, arguably the single most important legislative achievement of his presidency. His draft bill, sent to Congress on July 21, 1989, had three major goals: to control acid rain by reducing by nearly half sulfur dioxide emissions from coal-burning power plants by 2000, to reduce air pollution in eighty urban areas that still had not met 1977 air quality standards, and to lower emissions of nearly two hundred airborne toxic chemicals by 75 to 90 percent by 2000. To reach the acid precipitation goals—to which the White House devoted most of its attention—Bush proposed a cap-and-trade system rather than command-and-control regulation, so as to achieve emissions reductions more efficiently (see Chapter 10).[25] The act also prohibited the use of CFCs and other ozone-depleting chemicals by 2000.

However, during his reelection campaign, Bush declared a moratorium on further environmental regulation and retreated to a more traditional Republican stance. He also threatened to boycott the UN Conference on Environment and Development (the Earth Summit) in June 1992 until he had ensured that the climate change convention to be signed would contain no binding targets for carbon dioxide reduction. He further alienated the environmental community by refusing to sign the Convention on Biological Diversity, despite efforts by his delegation chief, William Reilly, to seek a last-minute compromise.[26] Thus, despite Bush's other foreign policy accomplishments, the United States failed to lead in environmental diplomacy (see Chapter 13).

The Clinton Presidency: Frustrated Ambitions

President Bill Clinton entered office in 1993 with high expectations from environmentalists. His campaign promises included many environmental pledges: to raise the Corporate Average Fuel Economy (CAFE) standard for automobiles, encourage mass transit programs, support renewable energy research and development, limit U.S. carbon dioxide emissions to 1990 levels by 2000, create a new solid waste reduction program and provide other incentives for recycling, pass a new Clean Water Act with standards for nonpoint sources, reform the Superfund program and tighten the enforcement of toxic waste laws, protect ancient forests and wetlands, preserve the Arctic National Wildlife Refuge, sign the biodiversity convention, and restore funding to UN population programs.[27]

Clinton's early actions indicated that he intended to deliver on his environmental agenda. The environmental community largely applauded his appointments to key environmental positions. Perhaps most important, Vice President Al Gore was given the lead responsibility for formulating and coordinating environmental policy in the White House. Several of his former Senate aides were also appointed to high positions, including EPA administrator Carol Browner. Other appointments to the cabinet and executive office staffs were largely pro-environmental. The most notable environmental leader was Bruce Babbitt, a former Arizona governor and president of the League of Conservation Voters, who became secretary of the interior. In contrast to his predecessors in the Reagan and Bush administrations, Babbitt came to office with a strong reform agenda for western public lands management.[28]

Although Clinton entered office with an expansive agenda and Democratic majorities in both houses of Congress, his environmental agenda quickly got bogged down. Two events early in the term gave the administration an appearance of environmental policy failure. Babbitt promptly launched a campaign to "revolutionize" western land use policies; it included a proposal in Clinton's first budget to raise grazing fees on public lands closer to private market levels (something natural resource economists had advocated for many years). The predictable result was a furious outcry from cattle ranchers and their representatives in Congress. After meeting with several western Democratic senators, Clinton backed down and removed the proposal from the bill. Much the same thing happened on the so-called BTU tax. This was a proposal to levy a broad-based tax on the energy content of fuels as a means of promoting energy conservation and addressing climate change. Originally included in the president's budget package at Gore's request, it was eventually dropped in favor of a much smaller gasoline tax (4.3 cents per gallon) in the face of fierce opposition from members of both parties in Congress.

These and other failures (including Clinton's proposed health care reform) contributed to a Republican takeover of Congress after the 1994 elections. Claiming a mandate for the "Contract with America," the new House Speaker, Newt Gingrich, R-Georgia, vowed "to begin decisively changing the shape of the government." With the help of industry lobbyists, the new congressional leaders unleashed a massive effort to rewrite the environmental legislation of the past quarter-century.[29] Although Clinton derailed most of these initiatives, he followed a more centrist course thereafter. Fights with Congress over the budget, including a partial government shutdown in 1995–1996, reduced environmental spending below previous levels in real terms. Clinton was, however, able to get bipartisan support for the passage of two relatively uncontroversial bills in 1996, the Food Quality Protection Act, which established a new basis for regulating pesticide uses, and the Safe Drinking Water Act Amendments (discussed in Chapter 7).

Clinton also relied heavily on his executive powers to pursue his environmental agenda. A "reinventing environmental regulation" initiative launched in 1995 created some fifty new EPA programs to encourage voluntary pollution reduction and to reward states and companies that exceeded regulatory requirements.[30] EPA administrator Browner also strengthened existing regulations and enforcement. For example, in 1997, she issued tighter ambient air quality standards for ozone and small particulate matter. In the final year of the Clinton administration, the EPA proposed a series of new regulations tightening standards on other forms of pollution, including diesel emissions from trucks and buses and arsenic in drinking water.

In addition to strengthening EPA regulations, the Clinton administration took numerous executive actions to protect public lands and endangered species. For example, it helped to broker agreements to protect old-growth forests in the Pacific Northwest, the Florida Everglades, and Yellowstone National Park. The White House actively promoted voluntary agreements to establish habitat conservation plans to protect wildlife throughout the country.[31] Clinton also used his authority under the Antiquities Act to establish or enlarge twenty-two national monuments covering more than six million acres. Finally, in January 2001, Clinton issued a long-awaited executive order protecting nearly sixty million acres of "roadless" areas in national forests from future road construction and hence from logging and development. He could thus claim to have preserved more public land in the contiguous United States than any president since Theodore Roosevelt.[32]

However, the Clinton administration largely failed to develop an effective response to perhaps the greatest challenge of the new century: climate change. After defeat of the BTU tax in 1993, Clinton's climate change proposals called for only voluntary actions; and the administration refused to commit the United States to binding reductions prior to the Kyoto treaty negotiations in December 1997. By then, the Senate had gone on record opposing any agreement limiting U.S. emissions.[33] Ultimately, Clinton authorized Vice President Gore to break the deadlock at Kyoto with an offer to reduce U.S. emissions to 7 percent below 1990 levels by 2008–2012, and the United States signed the treaty in 1998. However, Congress made it clear that it would not ratify the agreement and prohibited all efforts to implement it.

President George W. Bush: Regulatory Stalemate

George W. Bush took office in 2001 with a weak mandate to govern. He had lost the popular vote to Al Gore and had been declared the Electoral College winner only after several weeks of wrangling over contested Florida ballots, a dispute culminating in the Supreme Court's intervention. However, in the wake of the September 11, 2001, terrorist attacks on New York City and Washington, DC, his powers were greatly enlarged. Like Reagan, Bush used the executive powers of the presidency to advance an antiregulatory, pro-business agenda, though not to the same degree. He exercised the powers of appointment, budget, regulatory oversight, and rulemaking to weaken environmental policies.[34] Vice President Dick Cheney played a leading role in selecting cabinet appointees and, like previous vice presidents, in shaping energy and environmental policies.[35]

With the exception of Christine Todd Whitman, the former governor of New Jersey who was picked to head the EPA, Bush's initial appointments to environmental and natural resource agencies were largely drawn from business corporations or from conservative interest groups, law firms, and think tanks. Among the more controversial of these appointees were Secretary of the Interior Gale Norton, a protégée of James Watt and a strong advocate of resource development; J. Steven Griles, her deputy secretary and a longtime coal and oil industry lobbyist; Julie MacDonald, deputy assistant secretary of interior for fish and wildlife (responsible for the Endangered Species Act); and Mark Rey, a timber industry lobbyist, as undersecretary of agriculture for natural resources and environment (including the U.S. Forest Service). All of these officials left office under a cloud of investigation after ignoring numerous statutory and regulatory limits on resource exploitation.

Some of Bush's other environmental appointees were less controversial, if not less partisan. When Whitman resigned in 2003 after being undercut on climate change and clean air standards by the vice president and other cabinet members, Bush appointed Michael Leavitt, the conservative governor of Utah, as EPA administrator. Leavitt moved on to become secretary of health and human services in 2005, and Stephen L. Johnson was named EPA administrator. Although a career scientist at the EPA, Johnson had little influence in the White House.[36] The former governor and senator from Idaho, Dirk Kempthorne, succeeded Norton as secretary of the interior in 2006 and largely continued her policies.

President Bush's first budget proposal, for fiscal year 2002, called for a modest 4 percent increase in overall domestic discretionary spending, but an 8 percent reduction in funding for natural resource and environmental programs (the largest cut for any sector). The EPA's budget was to be slashed by nearly $500 million, or 6.4 percent, and the Interior Department budget was slated for a 3.5 percent cut.[37] Congress, however, did not approve these budget cuts; in fact, the EPA's budget was increased to $7.9 billion, $600 million more than the president had requested. Total EPA spending remained near $8 billion through 2008 but declined somewhat when adjusted for inflation. On the other hand, federal outlays for the Departments of Energy and the Interior increased significantly, and overall spending for natural resources and the environment rose by about 25 percent between 2001 and 2008.[38] Thus, environmental agencies did not suffer the deep budget cuts they did during the Reagan administration.

After suspending or rejecting many of Clinton's last-minute regulations, the Bush White House reestablished the Reagan-era rules for regulatory review. OIRA carried out an extensive analysis of proposed regulations, demanding that agencies justify all new rules on the basis of strict benefit-cost analysis. At the behest of business groups, existing rules were also reviewed in order to reduce the burden of regulation wherever possible.[39] Going one better than Reagan, in January 2007, the president issued a new executive order requiring that each agency must have a regulatory policy office run by a political appointee to manage the regulatory review process.[40] The order also granted OIRA new authority to review and edit "agency guidance documents," including scientific reports and memoranda, and to hold up proposed regulations indefinitely. The result was a highly politicized form of administration in which the political interests of the president and his supporters frequently overrode scientific and technical considerations in the bureaucracy.[41]

President Bush's energy and environmental agenda was quickly shaped after he took office. During spring 2001, a national energy plan was drafted in secrecy by a task force appointed by Vice President Cheney.[42] By all accounts, virtually all of the outside experts consulted were from energy producers and related industries, and many of the report's recommendations directly reflected these interests.[43] The plan called for major increases in future energy supplies, including domestic oil, gas, nuclear, and "clean coal" development, and for streamlining environmental regulations to accelerate new energy production. A bill incorporating these and other aspects of the Bush-Cheney plan, together with additional tax breaks for the energy industries, quickly passed the House of Representatives in 2001 but later stalled in the Senate when authorization to drill in the Arctic National Wildlife Refuge was defeated. Eventually, an energy bill was passed in 2005 providing large subsidies, loan guarantees, and other incentives to conventional energy producers (see Appendix 1), but by then, many of the original plan's recommendations had already been implemented by administrative actions. For example, coal, oil, and gas leasing had already been greatly expanded in the West. President Bush also set aside or rewrote many of the Clinton administration's last-minute resource conservation rules, including the Roadless Area Conservation Rule.[44]

The administration's "Clear Skies" bill, introduced in Congress in 2002, incorporated many of industries' suggestions for scaling back the pollution control requirements of the Clean Air Act. When this legislation went nowhere, Bush proceeded to issue executive orders that, in effect, implemented similar rules. For example, one of the more controversial rules relaxed requirements for the installation of new pollution equipment when power plants and oil refineries expanded or increased production (see Chapter 7). A broader Clean Air Interstate Rule issued in 2005 set standards for conventional air pollutants such as sulfur dioxide and ozone in twenty-eight eastern states, while another rule regulated mercury emissions from coal-fired power plants. These rules raised current standards but were less rigorous than those recommended by EPA scientists and, in most cases, were overturned by the courts (Chapter 6).[45]

Perhaps President Bush's most significant executive action was his rejection of the Kyoto Protocol on climate change in 2001. Calling the treaty "fatally flawed," the president officially withdrew United States participation in the international regime for regulating greenhouse gases. This was part of a larger shift away from international treaty obligations in the Bush administration, but it presaged an eight-year effort to block any mandatory requirements for controlling greenhouse gases (despite Bush's campaign promises to regulate carbon dioxide). During his first term, Bush refused to acknowledge the growing scientific consensus on global warming and opposed all efforts to limit greenhouse gas emissions. Instead, he supported continuing research programs on climate science and technological development, including new efforts to develop hydrogen energy and other alternative fuels.[46] The Energy Independence and Security Act of 2007 incorporated many of these proposals and also modestly raised fuel efficiency standards for the first time in twenty years.[47] But despite a landmark U.S. Supreme Court decision in April 2007 holding that the EPA could regulate greenhouse gases under the Clean Air Act, the White House refused to allow the agency to develop a regulatory strategy for climate change or to grant California a waiver to regulate carbon dioxide emissions from vehicles (see Chapter 7).

On the more positive side, President Bush used his executive authority to create several national monuments in the Pacific Ocean. In 2006, he established the world's largest marine reserve covering 140,000 square miles in the Northwestern Hawaiian Islands. Then, just before leaving office in January 2009, he designated three more monuments over large tracts of ocean in the western Pacific near American Samoa. These sparsely inhabited areas of reefs, atolls, and undersea mountains will be protected from commercial fishing, drilling, and mineral extraction, thereby preserving their unique ecological features.[48]

President Barack Obama: Climate Breakthrough

Barack Obama took office in January 2009 with what appeared to be a strong electoral mandate. Although he inherited the multiple economic and foreign policy crises left by the Bush administration, his campaign based on messages of "hope" and "change we can believe in" seemed to provide an opening for far-reaching reforms. Obama had also endorsed a strong environmental agenda. Among other things, he promised to create a cap-and-trade program for reducing U.S. greenhouse gas emissions, to make massive investments in renewable energy to create millions of new jobs, to double auto fuel economy standards by 2025, to tighten air pollution standards for mercury and other pollutants from power plants, to make major improvements in energy efficiency standards for buildings and in the national electricity grid, and to reverse Bush administration policies on mining and the protection of roadless areas.[49] The Democratic Party also gained the largest majorities in Congress in decades, making a legislative strategy appear feasible.

However, as noted earlier in this chapter, the climate change bill failed in the Senate, and after the Republicans regained a majority in the House of Representatives in 2010, it became impossible to enact any environmental legislation (Chapter 5). Thus, like his predecessors Ronald Reagan, Bill Clinton, and George W. Bush, Obama turned increasingly to an administrative strategy to carry out his agenda. Although he had criticized Bush during the 2008 campaign for misusing his executive powers, by 2012, Obama saw no alternative other than to utilize these same powers—but to strengthen rather than weaken environmental protection.[50] After his reelection, the president made it clear that he would act with or without the support of Congress.[51]

President Obama's choices for cabinet and top White House staff positions were well regarded by environmentalists. His first-term "green team" included Carol Browner, EPA head in the Clinton administration, as White House coordinator of energy and climate policy (a new position); Lisa Jackson, a chemical engineer who had served in the EPA and as commissioner of the New Jersey Department of Environmental Protection, as EPA administrator; Steven Chu, a Nobel Prize–winning physicist who directed the Lawrence Berkeley National Laboratory, as energy secretary; and Sen. Ken Salazar, D-Colorado, as interior secretary.[52] Obama also appointed a number of other top scientists to the administration. In addition to Chu, he chose John Holdren as White House science adviser, director of the Office of Science and Technology Policy, and chair of the President's Council of Advisors on Science and Technology. Holdren, a physics professor at Harvard, is a leading expert on energy and an advocate for action on climate change.[53]

Obama's second-term appointments were considered strong environmentalists but pragmatic administrators as well. Gina McCarthy, the assistant administrator in charge of air and radiation at the EPA, became the new EPA head; Ernest J. Moniz, a distinguished physicist from the Massachusetts Institute of Technology, replaced Steven Chu at the Energy Department; and Sally Jewell, an oil geologist, banker, and president of REI, an outdoor equipment company, became secretary of the interior. Finally, in December 2013, President Obama made a dramatic move to strengthen White House capabilities by bringing John Podesta in as special adviser. Podesta, former chief of staff in the Clinton administration and founder of the Center for American Progress, was given management and oversight responsibilities for implementing the EPA's new power plant regulations, and he played a key role in negotiating international climate change agreements (see below).[54]

Despite taking office amidst the worst recession since the 1930s and strong opposition from Republicans to raising the national debt, President Obama presided over a significant increase in federal spending on energy, natural resources, and the environment. Many of his goals for developing new energy technologies were incorporated into his emergency "stimulus bill" (the American Recovery and Reinvestment Act of 2009), which included some $80 billion in new spending, tax incentives, and loan guarantees to promote energy efficiency, renewable energy sources, fuel-efficient cars, mass transit, and cleaner fuel technologies. He also called for large increases in the budget of the EPA and in the budgets of other environmental agencies. His first budget (for fiscal year 2010) requested $10.5 billion for the EPA (48 percent more than requested by President Bush in his final budget), and Congress approved $10.2 billion. Actual EPA spending rose from $8 billion in 2009 to over $12.7 billion in 2012 and then fell back to an estimated $8.3 billion in 2016 (about the same as in the Bush administration, but less in real terms). Energy Department spending rose from $23.7 billion in 2009 to a peak of $32.4 billion in 2012 before retreating to $27.4 billion in 2016. And overall spending for natural resources and the environment increased from $35.5 billion in 2009 to a peak of $45.9 billion in 2011 before settling back to an estimated $39.5 billion in 2016.[55] Some of the later reductions were the result of across-the-board budget cuts (the "sequester") that the administration was forced to accept after Republicans threatened to default on the national debt in 2011 and forced a partial shutdown of the government in 2013.

Given his experience as a senator, his criticism of George W. Bush's style of leadership, and his preference for legislative solutions, it is not surprising that President Obama was slower to develop an administrative presidency. Nevertheless, he utilized some executive powers from the beginning. Upon taking office, he suspended or revoked a number of Bush's executive orders and regulations, including those on California's request for a waiver to regulate greenhouse gas emissions from automobiles, oil and gas leasing in potential wilderness areas, and the political direction of regulatory review. In March 2009, he issued a "Presidential Memorandum on Scientific Integrity" to heads of agencies and departments to prevent political misuse of scientific research and information such as was alleged to have occurred during his predecessor's tenure.[56]

In general, however, Obama took a relatively cautious approach to the use of unilateral powers during his first term. He issued a total of 147 executive orders (compared to 173 by Bush in his first term), but only 7 of these dealt with environmental or energy policy.[57] Nevertheless, among other regulations, the EPA issued ones to control mercury and other toxic emissions from industrial boilers, incinerators, and power plants; to tighten standards for the emission of sulfur dioxide, nitrogen oxides, and particulates that drift downwind from twenty-eight eastern states and the District of Columbia (the Cross-State Air Pollution Rule); and to limit some carbon emissions from large industries. More significantly, in 2010, President Obama raised the CAFE standards for automobile fuel efficiency to 35.5 miles per gallon in

2016 (roughly equal to the California standard the Bush administration had rejected) and, in August 2012, following negotiations with the auto industry, environmentalists, and energy experts, to 54.5 miles per gallon by 2025.[58] In October 2010, the government also proposed mileage standards for heavy trucks and buses (the final rule was issued in August 2016).[59] These and other measures laid the basis for a more comprehensive attack on climate change in Obama's second term.

At the Copenhagen climate change conference in December 2009, President Obama pledged to reduce U.S. greenhouse gas emissions by 17 percent from 2005 levels by 2020, roughly the reduction expected from passage of the climate change bill then pending in Congress. Despite the failure of the bill, Obama continued to espouse this goal and in his second term made its achievement a top priority.[60]

Obama outlined his strategy for climate change in a speech at Georgetown University in June 2013.[61] The plan, which contained some seventy-five specific proposals, relied heavily on executive action and expansive interpretations of existing law. It included the regulation of carbon dioxide emissions from new and existing power plants and a continuing shift to cleaner fuels such as natural gas; a redoubling of wind and solar energy production (which had doubled in the previous four years) and opening public lands and military bases to renewable energy construction; a new goal for the federal government to consume 20 percent of its electricity from renewable sources by 2020; increased preparedness for the impacts of climate change through support of infrastructure improvements such as seawalls and hardened power, water, and fuel supply systems; and the reassertion of American international leadership on climate change. As part of reclaiming global environmental leadership, the United States would negotiate cooperative agreements with rapidly developing countries such as China, end U.S. aid and support for the construction of coal-fired power plants abroad, and seek a new global treaty to cut carbon pollution.[62]

The first of these policies—especially regulating carbon emissions from more than five hundred coal-fired power plants—was the most important departure from past policies because these plants were the largest single source of greenhouse gases in the nation. Here the president relied heavily on the statutory authority conferred on the EPA by the Clean Air Act, as affirmed by the U.S. Supreme Court's *Massachusetts v. EPA* decision in 2007 (see Chapter 6). Whereas the Bush administration had refused to act on the basis of the court decision, Obama saw it as an opportunity to carry out much of his climate change agenda through the executive branch (see Chapter 7). His administration first issued mobile source regulations for automobiles and trucks, as mentioned above, and then extended greenhouse gas regulation to power plants and other large stationary sources for the first time. In September 2013, the EPA proposed a carbon emission standard for all *new* electric power plants that would make future construction of coal-fired plants prohibitively expensive; and in June 2014, it issued a draft rule that would require *existing* coal plants to reduce their carbon emissions by approximately 30 percent from 2005 levels by 2030.[63] After a year of public comment and negotiation, the Clean Power Plan rule was finalized in August 2015.[64] The regulations would give considerable flexibility to the states in designing their implementation plans and allowed states up to 15 years to comply, but it was nevertheless denounced by the Republican Party—and some Democrats—as a "war on coal" during the 2014 congressional elections.

Despite losing the Senate in the election, President Obama followed through on his promise to pursue a new international climate change agreement. He announced a landmark executive agreement with China a week after the elections. Under the agreement, China made a commitment to limit its use of fossil fuels for the first time by pledging that its carbon emissions will peak no later than 2030. China also agreed to produce 20 percent of its total energy consumption from clean sources by the same year. On its side, the United States pledged to reduce its carbon emissions by 26 to 28 percent by 2025, compared to 2005.[65] This joint leadership by the United States and China, as well as the Clean Power Plan to limit domestic emissions, paved the way for the landmark Paris Agreement in December 2015 (see Chapter 13).[66] The United States and China also brokered a historic international agreement in 2016 to phase out use of hydrofluorocarbons (HFCs), which are widely used as refrigerants throughout the world but are potent greenhouse gases.[67]

However, Republican majorities in Congress continued to oppose all actions to limit climate change (Chapter 5). The Senate voted to block the power plant regulations after Senate majority leader Mitch McConnell urged states not to comply with them.[68] Attorneys general from twenty-nine Republican states together with dozens of corporations and industry groups eventually filed suit in the District of Columbia Circuit Court to block them. After the court refused to grant a preliminary injunction, the U.S. Supreme Court, in an unusual move, intervened in early 2016 to order an indefinite stay pending full review by the appellate court.[69] Several other rules, including EPA regulations limiting emissions of mercury and other toxic pollutants from power plants and regulations to control oil and gas fracking on public lands, were also held up or struck down by the courts.[70]

President Obama continued to battle Congress on other fronts as well. He delayed a decision on the controversial Keystone XL oil pipeline, vetoed a bill passed by Congress to approve it, and finally rejected the pipeline entirely on grounds that it would contribute disproportionately to carbon emissions.[71] After weeks of protests by Native American and environmental groups, he also held up the Dakota Access pipeline, which would transport oil from North Dakota to Illinois. In the closing months of his administration, several other important environmental decisions were promulgated as well, including EPA rules to reduce carbon emissions from heavy-duty trucks and tractor-trailers and to reaffirm fuel economy standards for cars and light trucks through 2025 models; Interior Department regulations to limit methane emissions from oil and gas operations on public lands and to protect streams from mountain coal-mining discharges; and a presidential order under the 1953 Outer Continental Shelf Lands Act to permanently ban oil drilling along the Atlantic Seaboard and in much of the Arctic Ocean.[72] Republicans in Congress vowed to reverse most if not all of these new regulations.

Finally, President Obama left a strong legacy of public lands conservation by designating 29 new national monuments and expanding several others, including the vast marine sanctuaries in the Pacific Ocean created by his predecessor, George W. Bush. Among the most significant of the new protected areas are the 1.35-million-acre Bears Ears National Monument in Utah and the Gold Butte National Monument in the Mojave Desert in Nevada. Altogether, Obama designated more monuments and protected more land and waters under the Antiquities Act of 1906 than any previous president.[73]

President Donald J. Trump: Policy Reversal

Donald Trump came to the presidency with the most antienvironmental agenda since Ronald Reagan. During the election campaign, he had repeatedly attacked Barack Obama's environmental initiatives, especially Obama's actions to limit climate change, which Trump referred to as an "expensive hoax." He promised to roll back these policies, to withdraw from the Paris Agreement on climate change, and to dismantle the EPA "in almost every form."[74] Echoing Reagan—and most Republicans—he argued that environmental regulations were "job-killers" impeding economic growth and declared that he would remove all rules and regulations deemed "unnecessary" and impose a temporary moratorium on new ones. He called for the repeal of Obama's "war on coal," stating that he would end restrictions on America's "untapped energy—some $50 trillion . . . in shale energy, oil reserves and natural gas on federal lands, in addition to hundreds of years of coal energy reserves."[75] Rarely has a presidential candidate called for such total repudiation of his predecessor's legacy.

Trump's appointments reflected these views. Scott Pruitt, the new EPA administrator, had filed 14 major lawsuits against the agency as attorney general of Oklahoma. With the support of fossil fuel interests, he had played a leading role in the multistate legal challenge to the Clean Power Plan, the suit that had resulted in a Supreme Court stay of the plan in early 2016.[76] He denied any scientific consensus on climate change and indicated that he would seek to halt all EPA and other agency actions directed toward limiting greenhouse gas emissions. Pruitt also hired several high-level aides from the staff of Sen. James Inhofe (R-Oklahoma), the leading critic of climate science in Congress, and called for the EPA to return to its "core functions" of protecting clean air and water. He also suggested that many of these responsibilities could be transferred to the states.[77]

Trump's other environmental and energy appointments were somewhat less controversial. Ryan Zinke, a little-known congressman and outdoorsman from Montana, was named secretary of the interior. Calling himself a "conservative conservationist" in the Teddy Roosevelt tradition, he called for the continuing protection of federal lands and increased funding for department programs, including the National Park Service and the Land and Water Conservation Fund.[78] He also departed from administration orthodoxy in stating during his confirmation hearing that he accepted the reality of climate change. On the other hand, he also supported increased mining, drilling, and lumbering on federal lands and indicated that he would review all Obama-era rules.[79] The agriculture secretary, former Georgia governor Sonny Perdue, is a climate change denier who has long had close ties to corporate agriculture and timbering interests. The new energy secretary, former Texas governor Rick Perry, was a stranger fit. Long known for his ties to the oil and gas industry, he had previously called for abolishing the department he would now lead. As he had little knowledge of the agency's mission, and no scientific background, it was unclear what his policies would be.[80] Many of the new White House staff members, however, were former lawyers and lobbyists for the energy industries. Unlike previous presidents, Trump appointed no science advisers early in his term.[81]

Trump's initial budget proposal called for massive cuts in virtually all environmental and science programs.[82] The EPA was singled out for the steepest funding cuts of all; its budget would be reduced from about $8.3 billion to $5.7 billion, or by about 31 percent, and, if Congress approves, the agency could lose more than 20 percent of its employees.[83] A total of 56 EPA programs could be eliminated, including many state and regional water programs such as those to clean up the Great Lakes and Chesapeake Bay.[84] Other agencies supporting research related to climate change were also cut sharply: spending by the National Oceanic and Atmospheric Administration (NOAA) was to be cut 18 percent, with the largest reductions in the agency's environmental satellite programs; and the Energy Department's nonnuclear programs were to be reduced by about the same amount, including its national laboratories and Office of Science. The Advanced Research Projects Agency-Energy (ARPA-E), which supports high-risk, high-reward research on new energy technologies, research that might not otherwise be pursued, was slated for elimination along with other renewable energy programs. The National Aeronautics and Space Administration (NASA) would be cut less but would lose its climate monitoring capabilities.[85] "As to climate change," Trump's budget director, Mick Mulvaney, stated bluntly, "I think the president was fairly straightforward: We're not spending money on that anymore."[86] Although Congress refused to accept the proposed cuts in its initial negotiations to avoid a government shutdown through September 2017, the president's budget proposal for 2018 contained similar cuts.[87]

As if to dramatize these changes, the climate change page was removed from the White House website within an hour after Trump took the oath of office.[88] Like previous presidents, Trump quickly utilized his authority to revoke several of Obama's executive orders and to issue new directives of his own. He issued 30 executive orders during his first 100 days in office, almost all of them calling for deregulation. All new regulations not yet in effect were frozen, as were all pending EPA contracts and awards.[89] The president then issued a series of executive orders on regulatory reform: Executive Order (EO) 13771 required that any new regulation be offset by repeal of at least two other regulations that would reduce compliance costs by at least the same amount, with a "net-zero cost" cap for the year; and EO 13777 required the appointment of "regulatory reform officers" and "regulatory reform task forces" in all agencies to "evaluate existing regulations . . . and make recommendations to the agency head regarding their repeal, replacement, or modification, consistent with applicable law."[90] A further memorandum instructed the Commerce Department to solicit comments from manufacturing industries on which regulations to target. These mandates were similar to those imposed by Ronald Reagan, but they appeared to go even further in focusing on regulatory costs regardless of benefits.[91] A third order, EO 13781, directed the Office of Management and Budget to propose a plan for reorganizing the executive branch so as to eliminate unnecessary agencies, components of agencies, and programs.

EO 13783 on "Promoting Energy Independence and Economic Growth," issued on March 28, 2017, took direct aim at President Obama's climate change policies. It required federal departments and agencies to "immediately review all existing regulations that potentially burden the development or use of domestically produced energy resources and appropriately suspend, revise, or rescind" any that are unnecessary; instructed the EPA administrator to begin the process of withdrawing the Clean Power Plan; revoked all other presidential directives related to the consideration of greenhouse gas emissions, including environmental reviews under the National Environmental Policy Act and calculation of the "social costs of carbon"; ended the moratorium on coal leasing on federal lands; and ordered the review of Obama-era rules regarding the control of methane emissions and of hydraulic fracturing (fracking) on public lands. It also directed the attorney general to request that all pending court cases be suspended or delayed in light of the new administration policies.[92]

Trump took several other high-profile actions in his first months to erase Obama's environmental legacy: he approved the Keystone XL and Dakota Access pipelines; announced that he would seek to relax the fuel economy standards for cars and trucks that had been negotiated with the auto industry for 2022–2025 models; proposed repeal of Obama's Clean Water Rule (Waters of the United States); and signed a series of Congressional Review Act bills, including one that repealed the stream protection rule to limit the dumping of coal-mining wastes into adjacent streams and rivers (these legislative issues are discussed further in Chapter 5).[93] The president indicated that he would review the ambient ozone standard and restrictions on methane emissions set by Obama.[94] Trump also ordered the Interior Department to review all regulations on offshore oil drilling—including those imposed after the Deepwater Horizon Oil Spill of 2010—with a view toward opening large areas of the Atlantic, Pacific, and Arctic Oceans to offshore oil and gas leasing.[95] He also issued EO 13792, which required the department to (1) review all national monument designations since 1996—including

Utah's Grand-Staircase Escalante and Bears Ears National Monuments and the large marine sanctuaries created by Presidents Bush and Obama—and (2) suggest ways of modifying or canceling previous monument proclamations under the 1906 Antiquities Act. No president has ever attempted to rescind a monument designation, but it is possible that some monuments will be reduced in size or opened to more commercial activities.[96]

Finally, at a Rose Garden ceremony on June 1, 2017, Trump announced that the United States would withdraw from the Paris Agreement on climate change. Displaying little understanding of climate science, he called for "renegotiation" of the agreement to allow our "reentry" or negotiation of an entirely new "deal" that is "fairer" to the American economy and workers. The United States will also halt all contributions to the Green Climate Fund, which assists developing countries in meeting their pledges under the accords.[97] Leaders of other nations, as well as many governors, mayors, and corporate executives in this country, condemned the decision and pledged to continue their efforts to meet the agreement's emission reduction goals. Nevertheless, withdrawal of all support from Washington will make achievement of the Paris goals much more difficult.[98] And, as in the case of George W. Bush rejecting the Kyoto Protocol sixteen years earlier, the withdrawal is again likely to isolate the United States in global environmental diplomacy.[99]

This pace of deregulation was unprecedented—surpassing even that of the Reagan era—and was indicative of what former White House strategist Stephen Bannon called the "deconstruction of the administrative state."[100] EPA administrator Scott Pruitt and interior secretary Ryan Zinke are pursuing this goal with breakneck speed, often in secrecy with little input from career staff and scientists. By one count, the administration has identified nearly 300 regulations related to energy production and environmental protection that it plans to rescind, review, or delay.[101] Even some allies in the oil and gas industry feared that the administration was proceeding too quickly, inviting an inevitable political backlash.[102]

However, undoing rules and regulations that have been adopted by formal administrative procedures is difficult and time consuming, often taking years. Major decisions will be subjected to court challenges and continuing resistance from cities and states, environmental and other interest groups, businesses, and citizens. Economic forces are also likely to limit markets for coal and other fossil fuels and further the global trend toward cleaner energy. We discuss these issues in greater detail in Chapter 15.

Conclusion

The Obama and Trump presidencies make it clear that the president has become the most significant actor in national environmental policymaking. The powers of the presidency have continued to expand in the current era of ideological polarization and congressional gridlock. The result is violent pendulum swings between liberal and conservative policies, which reflect fundamentally different views on the role of government, the nature and place of science in designing environmental policies, and global economic forces and trends. Obama's reliance on executive powers alone to impose climate policies was clearly a weakness, albeit a necessary one given the opposition he faced in Congress. Donald Trump is now using the same executive authority in an attempt to erase his predecessor's entire environmental legacy. The uncertainty and division that are likely to result could permanently weaken the nation's commitment to environmental goals, as discussed in Chapter 1. However, environmental policy cycles proved resilient during the Reagan years and may well survive the Trump era as well.

Suggested Websites

Competitive Enterprise Institute (www.cei.org) This libertarian think tank was influential in shaping Donald Trump's environmental policies.

Department of the Interior (www.interior.gov) This is the official website for the department and bureaus within it.

Environmental Protection Agency (www.epa.gov) This official website for the EPA offers information on environmental topics and U.S. environmental policy, laws, and regulations.

The Heritage Foundation (www.heritage.org) The website of this nonprofit think tank offers research and analysis on energy and environmental issues from a conservative perspective.

Natural Resources Defense Council (www.nrdc.org) The website of this leading environmental organization provides analysis and criticism; it includes a "Trump Watch."

Center for Climate and Energy Solutions (www.C2ES.org) This site provides research from a leading think tank on climate change policies.

The White House (www.whitehouse.gov) The president's official website provides information on presidential actions, including executive orders, and pending, signed, and vetoed legislation.

Notes

1. Coral Davenport, "Clinton's Climate Change Plan Avoids Mention of Carbon Tax," *New York Times*, July 3, 2016; Davenport, "Climate Policy Faces Reversal by New Leader," *New York Times*, November 11, 2016; Julie Hirschfield Davis and Michael D. Shear, "Donald Trump, in Louisiana, Says He Will End Energy Regulations," *New York Times*, December 9, 2016.
2. For a summary of Trump's statements regarding climate change, see John Schwartz, "Combative, Conflicting and Confusing," *New York Times*, March 11, 2017.
3. Coral Davenport, "Parties' Divide Over Climate Change Bursts into Forefront of Campaign," *New York Times*, August 2, 2016; Tatiana Schlossberg, "Party Lines Inform Split Over Climate, Poll Shows," *New York Times*, October 5, 2016; and Davenport and Eric Lipton, "How G.O.P. Shifted on Climate Science," *New York Times*, June 4, 2017.

4. See Norman J. Vig, "The American Presidency and Environmental Policy," in *The Oxford Handbook of U.S. Environmental Policy*, ed. Sheldon Kamieniecki and Michael E. Kraft (Oxford: Oxford University Press, 2013), 306–28; and Christopher McGrory Klyza and David Sousa, *American Environmental Policy: Beyond Gridlock*, updated and expanded ed. (Cambridge, MA: MIT Press, 2013).

5. Marc Fisher, "Donald Trump and the Expanding Powers of the Presidency," *Washington Post*, July 30, 2016; Darla Cameron, "What President Obama's Executive Actions Mean for President Trump," *Washington Post*, December 6, 2016.

6. Dennis L. Soden, ed., *The Environmental Presidency* (Albany: State University of New York Press, 1999), 3.

7. Soden, *The Environmental Presidency*, 346.

8. See, for example, Coral Davenport, "Climate Change Deemed Growing Security Threat by Military Researchers," *New York Times*, May 14, 2014; and Davenport, "Pentagon Signals Security Risks of Climate Change," *New York Times*, October 14, 2014.

9. Kenneth R. Mayer, "Going Alone: The Presidential Power of Unilateral Action," in *The Oxford Handbook of the American Presidency*, ed. George C. Edwards III and William G. Howell (Oxford: Oxford University Press, 2009), 427–54. There are nearly thirty different types of presidential executive actions; see Cameron, "What President Obama's Executive Actions Mean for President Trump."

10. For a list of national monuments, see National Parks Conservation Association, "Monuments Protected Under the Antiquities Act," updated January 13, 2017, npca .org/resources/2658-monuments-protected-under-the-antiquities-act#sm.000c9py5 21124cnd103ia72cijzvk.

11. David E. Lewis and Terry M. Moe, "The Presidency and the Bureaucracy: The Levers of Presidential Control," in *The Presidency and the Political System*, 9th ed., ed. Michael Nelson (Washington, DC: CQ Press, 2010), 367–400.

12. Charles O. Jones, *The Presidency in a Separated System* (Washington, DC: Brookings Institution Press, 1994); Charles O. Jones, *Separate but Equal Branches: Congress and the Presidency* (Chatham, NJ: Chatham House, 1995).

13. Robert F. Durant and William G. Resh, "Presidential Agendas, Administrative Strategies, and the Bureaucracy," in *The Oxford Handbook of the American Presidency*, ed. George C. Edwards III and William G. Howell (Oxford: Oxford University Press, 2009), 577–600.

14. Soden, *The Environmental Presidency*, 346.

15. Byron W. Daynes and Glen Sussman, *White House Politics and the Environment: Franklin D. Roosevelt to George W. Bush* (College City: Texas A&M University Press, 2010).

16. Daynes and Sussman, *White House Politics*, 210–15.

17. See Douglas Brinkley, *Rightful Heritage: Franklin D. Roosevelt and the Land of America* (New York: HarperCollins, 2016); and Russell E. Train, "The Environmental Record of the Nixon Administration," *Presidential Studies Quarterly* 26, no. 1 (Winter 1996): 185–96.

18. For a more detailed analysis of Reagan's environmental record, see Michael E. Kraft and Norman J. Vig, "Environmental Policy in the Reagan Presidency," *Political Science Quarterly* 99, no. 3 (Fall 1984): 414–39; Norman J. Vig and Michael E. Kraft, eds., *Environmental Policy in the 1980s: Reagan's New Agenda* (Washington, DC: CQ Press, 1984).

19. Richard P. Nathan, *The Administrative Presidency* (New York: Wiley, 1983).

20. Lewis and Moe, "The Presidency and the Bureaucracy," 390; and Marc Allen Eisner, *Governing the Environment: The Transformation of Environmental Regulation* (Boulder, CO: Lynne Rienner, 2007), 80–85.

21. On the impact of the Reagan budget cuts, see especially two chapters in *Environmental Policy in the 1980s: Reagan's New Agenda*: Robert V. Bartlett, "The Budgetary Process and Environmental Policy," 121–42; and J. Clarence Davies, "Environmental Institutions and the Reagan Administration," 143–60.
22. For a detailed summary of Watt's policies, see Paul J. Culhane, "Sagebrush Rebels in Office: Jim Watt's Land and Water Policies," in *Environmental Policy in the 1980s: Reagan's New Agenda*, 293–317.
23. Cass R. Sunstein, "Climate Change: Lessons from Ronald Reagan," *New York Times*, November 11, 2012; Justin Gillis, "The Little Treaty That Could," *New York Times*, December 10, 2013.
24. See Robert Cameron Mitchell, "Public Opinion and the Green Lobby," in *Environmental Policy in the 1990s*, ed. Norman J. Vig and Michael E. Kraft (Washington, DC: CQ Press, 1990), 81–99.
25. See Gary C. Bryner, *Blue Skies, Green Politics: The Clean Air Act of 1990 and Its Implementation*, 2nd ed. (Washington, DC: CQ Press, 1995).
26. Keith Schneider, "White House Snubs U.S. Envoy's Plea to Sign Rio Treaty," *New York Times*, June 5, 1992.
27. Bill Clinton and Al Gore, *Putting People First* (New York: Times Books, 1992), 89–99.
28. Timothy Egan, "Sweeping Reversal of U.S. Land Policy Sought by Clinton," *New York Times*, February 24, 1993.
29. For a summary of the Republican agenda and responses to it, see "GOP Sets the 104th Congress on New Regulatory Course," *Congressional Quarterly Weekly Report*, June 17, 1995, 1693–1701. For Gingrich quotation, see "Republican Conference: Taking Speaker's Mantle, Gingrich Vows 'Profound Transformation,'" *CQ Weekly*, December 10, 1994, 3522–24.
30. On the "reinvention" effort, see Daniel J. Fiorino, *The New Environmental Regulation* (Cambridge, MA: MIT Press, 2006), Chapter 5.
31. As an alternative way of implementing the Endangered Species Act, the Clinton administration supported completion of more than 250 habitat conservation plans protecting some 170 endangered plant and animal species while allowing controlled development on twenty million acres of private land. William Booth, "A Slow Start Built to an Environmental End-Run," *Washington Post*, January 13, 2001.
32. Bill Clinton, *My Life* (New York: Knopf, 2004), 948.
33. In particular, the Byrd-Hagel resolution (passed 95–0 on June 12, 1997) opposed any agreement that would harm the U.S. economy or that did not require control of greenhouse gas emissions by developing countries.
34. Douglas Jehl, "On Rules for Environment, Bush Sees a Balance, Critics a Threat," *New York Times*, February 23, 2003; Jonathan Weisman, "In 2003, It's Reagan Revolution Redux," *Washington Post*, February 4, 2003; Bill Keller, "Reagan's Son," *New York Times Magazine*, January 26, 2003.
35. On Cheney's role, see Jo Becker and Barton Gellman, "Leaving No Tracks," *Washington Post*, June 27, 2007; and Barton Gellman, *Angler: The Cheney Vice Presidency* (New York: Penguin, 2008).
36. See Margaret Kriz, "Vanishing Act," *National Journal*, April 12, 2008. On Christine Whitman's resignation, see Whitman, *It's My Party, Too* (New York: Penguin, 2005).
37. "Bush's Budget: The Losers," *Washington Post*, April 10, 2001; "Who Gets What Slice of the President's First Federal Budget Pie," *New York Times*, April 10, 2001.
38. Budgets for the EPA and other agencies since 1976 can be found at www.whitehouse.gov/omb/budget/Historicals.

39. Joel Brinkley, "Out of Spotlight, Bush Overhauls U.S. Regulations," *New York Times*, August 16, 2004; Bruce Barcott, "Changing All the Rules," *New York Times Magazine*, April 4, 2004; and Christopher Klyza and David Sousa, *American Environmental Policy, 1990–2006* (Cambridge, MA: MIT Press, 2008), 135–52.

40. Robert Pear, "Bush Directive Increases Sway on Regulation," *New York Times*, January 30, 2007; C. W. Copeland, "The Law: Executive Order 13422: An Expansion of Presidential Influence in the Rulemaking Process," *Presidential Studies Quarterly* 37 (2007): 531–44.

41. Union of Concerned Scientists, *Interference at the EPA: Science and Politics at the U.S. Environmental Protection Agency* (Cambridge, MA: Union of Concerned Scientists, April 2008), http://www.ucsusa.org/sites/default/files/legacy/assets/documents/scientific_integrity/interference-at-the-epa.pdf.

42. See also David E. Sanger and Joseph Kahn, "Bush, Pushing Energy Plan, Offers Scores of Proposals to Find New Power Sources," *New York Times*, May 18, 2001; "Energy Report Highlights," *Washington Post*, May 18, 2001.

43. Neela Banerjee, "Documents Show Energy Official Met Only with Industry Leaders," *New York Times*, March 26, 2002.

44. Klyza and Sousa, *American Environmental Policy: Beyond Gridlock*, 2008, 112–23.

45. For details on these actions and their outcomes, see Klyza and Sousa, *American Environmental Policy: Beyond Gridlock*, 2008 Chapters 4 and 9.

46. In his 2007 State of the Union address, Bush called for mandatory standards requiring that 35 million gallons of renewable and alternative fuels be produced by 2017, nearly a fivefold increase.

47. See John M. Broder, "Bush Signs Broad Energy Bill," *New York Times*, December 19, 2007.

48. John M. Broder, "Bush to Protect Vast New Pacific Tracts," *New York Times*, January 6, 2009; "Mr. Bush's Monument," editorial, *New York Times*, January 7, 2009.

49. "Barack Obama and Joe Biden: Promoting a Healthy Environment" (https://energy.gov/sites/prod/files/edg/media/Obama_Cap_and_Trade_0512.pdf) and "Barack Obama and Joe Biden: New Energy for America" (https://energy.gov/sites/prod/files/edg/media/Obama_New_Energy_0804.pdf).

50. Binyamin Appelbaum and Michael D. Shear, "How the President Came to Embrace Executive Power," *New York Times*, August 14, 2016; Andrew Rudalevige, "The Obama Administrative Presidency: Some Late-Term Patterns," *Presidential Studies Quarterly* 46, no. 4 (December 2016), 868–90.

51. Emmarie Huetteman, "Aides Say Obama Is Willing to Work with or without Congress to Meet Goals," *New York Times*, January 26, 2014; Charles M. Blow, "A Pen, a Phone and a Meme," *New York Times*, February 7, 2014.

52. John M. Broder, "Obama Team Set on Environment," *New York Times*, December 11, 2008; Broder, "Title, but Unclear Power, for a New Climate Czar," *New York Times*, December 12, 2008; Broder, "Praise and Criticism for Proposed Interior Secretary," *New York Times*, December 18, 2008.

53. Gardiner Harris, "4 Top Science Advisers Are Named by Obama," *New York Times*, December 21, 2008; "A New Respect for Science," editorial, *New York Times*, December 22, 2008.

54. John M. Broder and Matthew L. Wald, "Cabinet Picks Could Take on Climate Policy," *New York Times*, March 4, 2013; "Two Enlistees in the Climate Wars," editorial, *New York Times*, March 6, 2013; Bruce Barcott, "Sizing Up Sally Jewell," *Outside*, November 12, 2013; Robert B. Semple Jr., "The Return of John Podesta," *New York Times*, December 14, 2013; Darren Goode, "John Podesta Will Dig into Energy and

Climate Policy," *Politico*, December 12, 2013; Mark Landler, "U.S. and China Reach Deal on Climate Change in Secret Talks," *New York Times*, November 11, 2014.

55. See Note 38. These numbers refer to budget outlays rather than budget authority.

56. "Memorandum for the Heads of Executive Departments and Agencies—Subject: Scientific Integrity [called Presidential Memorandum on Scientific Integrity]," March 9, 2009, https://obamawhitehouse.archives.gov/the-press-office/memorandum-heads-executive-departments-and-agencies-3-9-09.

57. Presidential executive orders are available online at www.federalregister.gov/executive-orders/.

58. John M. Broder, "Obama Seeking a Steep Increase in Auto Mileage," *New York Times*, July 4, 2011. These rules were also converted to greenhouse gas emission limits; see Bill Vlasic, "U.S. Sets High Long-Term Fuel Efficiency Goals for Automakers," *New York Times*, August 29, 2012.

59. Matthew L. Wald, "Heavy Trucks to Be Subject to New Rules for Mileage," *New York Times*, August 10, 2011; Peter Baker and Coral Davenport, "Obama Orders New Efficiency for Big Trucks," *New York Times*, February 19, 2014.

60. See Julie Hirschfeld Davis, Mark Landler, and Coral Davenport, "'Terrifying' Path of Climate Crisis Weighs on Obama," *New York Times*, September 8, 2016.

61. See "Remarks by the President on Climate Change," June 25, 2013, www.whitehouse.gov/the-press-office/2013/06/25/remarks-president-climate-change; and "At Last, an Action Plan on Climate," editorial, *New York Times*, June 26, 2013.

62. See Center for Climate and Energy Solutions, "President Obama's Climate Action Plan: One Year Later," June 2014, https://www.c2es.org/publications/president-obamas-climate-action-plan-one-year-later, for a list of proposals and actions taken.

63. Michael D. Shear, "Administration Presses Ahead with Limits on Emissions from Power Plants," *New York Times*, September 20, 2013; Coral Davenport, "E.P.A. Staff Struggling to Create Pollution Rule," *New York Times*, February 5, 2014; Davenport, "E.P.A. to Seek 30 Percent Cut in Carbon Emissions," *New York Times*, June 2, 2014; Davenport and Peter Baker, "Taking Page from Health Care Act, Obama Climate Plan Relies on States," *New York Times*, June 3, 2014.

64. Julie Hirschfeld Davis, "Obama Unveils Plan to Sharply Limit Greenhouse Gas Emissions," *New York Times*, August 3, 2015; Richard L. Revesz and Jack Lienke, "Obama Takes a Crucial Step on Climate Change," *New York Times*, August 3, 2015.

65. Mark Landler, "U.S. and China Reach Deal on Climate Change in Secret Talks," *New York Times*, November 11, 2014; "Climate Change Breakthrough in Beijing," editorial, *New York Times*, November 12, 2014; Henry Fountain and John Schwartz, "Climate Accord Relies on Environmental Policies Now in Place," *New York Times*, November 12, 2014; Edward Wong, "In Step to Lower Carbon Emissions, China Will Place a Limit on Coal Use in 2020," *New York Times*, November 20, 2014.

66. Coral Davenport, "Deal on Carbon Emissions by Obama and Xi Jinping Raises Hopes for Upcoming Paris Climate Talks," *New York Times*, November 12, 2014; Davenport, "Nations Approve Landmark Climate Accord in Paris," *New York Times*, December 12, 2015; Davenport, "A Climate Deal, 6 Fateful Years in the Making," *New York Times*, December 14, 2015; Mark Landler and Jane Perlez, "U.S. and China Set Aside Rifts for Climate Accord," *New York Times*, September 4, 2016.

67. Alexander Ovodenka, "140 Countries Will Phase Out HFCs. What Are These and Why Do They Matter?" *Washington Post*, November 3, 2016.

68. Coral Davenport, "McConnell Urges States to Defy U.S. Plan to Cut Greenhouse Gas," *New York Times*, March 5, 2015; Davenport, "McConnell Urges States to Help Thwart Obama's 'War on Coal,'" *New York Times*, March 20, 2015; Davenport, "Senate Rejects Obama Plan to Cut Emissions at Coal-Burning Plants," *New York Times*,

November 18, 2015; David M. Herszenhorn, "As Obama Pushes Climate Deal, Republicans Move to Block Emissions Rules," *New York Times*, December 1, 2015.

69. Coral Davenport, "Numerous States Will Sue to Stop New Climate Rules," *New York Times*, October 22, 2015; Davenport, "Appeals Court Hears Challenges to Obama's Climate Change Regulations," *New York Times*, September 28, 2016; Adam Liptak and Coral Davenport, "Supreme Court Deals Blow to Obama's Efforts to Regulate Coal Emissions," *New York Times*, February 9, 2016. The 5–4 decision was unusual, as the Supreme Court rarely blocks a regulation prior to review by a federal appeals court.

70. Adam Liptak and Coral Davenport, "Justices Block the Obama Administration's Limits on Power Plant Emissions," *New York Times*, June 30, 2015; Davenport, "Obama Rule on Fracking Is Struck Down by Court," *New York Times*, June 23, 2016.

71. Coral Davenport and Michael D. Shear, "Obama Vetoes Keystone XL Pipeline Bill," *New York Times*, February 24, 2015; Davenport, "President Rejects Keystone Pipeline to Transport Oil," *New York Times*, November 7, 2015.

72. Brady Dennis, "Obama Administration Will Keep Tough Fuel Standards in Place," *Washington Post*, November 30, 2016; Coral Davenport, "Obama Leans On a 1953 Law to Ban Drilling," *New York Times*, December 21, 2016; Juliet Eilperin, "In a Race to the Finish, Obama Administration Presses Ahead with Ambitious Rules," *Washington Post*, December 1, 2016.

73. See note 10 above and Juliet Eilperin and Brady Dennis, "With New Monuments in Nevada, Utah, Obama Adds to His Environmental Legacy," *Washington Post*, December 28, 2016.

74. Davenport, "Climate Policy Faces Reversal by New Leader" (note 1).

75. John W. Miller, "Donald Trump Promises Deregulation of Energy Production," *Wall Street Journal*, September 22, 2016. See also Ashley Parker and Coral Davenport, "Trump Urges More Drilling and Few Rules," *New York Times*, May 27, 2016; Coral Davenport, "Trump Goes to Pittsburgh to Pledge the Impossible: A Boom for Coal and Gas," *New York Times*, September 23, 2016.

76. Chris Mooney, Brady Dennis, and Steven Mufson, "Trump to Name Scott Pruitt, Oklahoma Attorney General Suing EPA on Climate Change, to Head the EPA," *Washington Post*, December 7, 2016; Coral Davenport and Eric Lipton, "Choice for E.P.A. has Led Battles to Constrain It," *New York Times*, December 8, 2016; "An Enemy of the E.P.A. to Head It," editorial, *New York Times*, December 8, 2016; Eric Lipton and Coral Davenport, "Choice for E.P.A. a Frequent Ally of the Regulated," *New York Times*, January 15, 2017; Davenport and Lipton, "E.P.A. Chief was Cozy with Energy Industry, Trove of Emails Shows," *New York Times*, February 23, 2017; Coral Davenport and Brady Dennis, "Trump to Tap Longtime Coal Lobbyist for EPA's No. 2 Spot," *Washington Post*, July 21, 2017.

77. Coral Davenport, "E.P.A. Nominee Criticizes Rules to Protect Climate," *New York Times*, January 19, 2017; Davenport, "Scott Pruitt is Seen Cutting the E.P.A. with a Scalpel, Not a Cleaver," *New York Times*, February 5, 2017; Davenport, "E.P.A. Chief Doubts Consensus View of Climate Change," *New York Times*, March 9, 2017; Davenport, "New Administrator Stacks the E.P.A. with Climate Change Skeptics," *New York Times*, March 8, 2017; Juliet Eilperin and Brady Dennis, "How James Inhofe is Upending the Nation's Energy and Environmental Policies," *Washington Post*, March 14, 2017.

78. Juliet Eilperin, "Trump Taps Montana Congressman Ryan Zinke as Interior Secretary," *Washington Post*, December 13, 2016; Emmarie Huetteman, "Vowing to Preserve, and Develop, Federal Lands," *New York Times*, January 18, 2017; Juliet Turkewitz, "He Controls a Fifth of the Nation. Meet Ryan Zinke," *New York Times*, March 2, 2017.

79. Matthew Daly, "Interior Nominee Zinke Disputes Trump on Climate Change," *AP News*, January 17, 2017, https://apnews.com/6b5cb558094c43e186fcb58a405 99b1e; Valerie Volcovici, "New Interior Chief Vows Review of Obama-era Rules, 'Bold' Restructuring," *Reuters*, March 3, 2017, http://www.reuters.com/article/us-usa-trump-budget-debt-idUSKCN1B41WM.

80. Chris Mooney and John Wagner, "Trump Picks Sonny Perdue for Agriculture Secretary, *Washington Post*, January 19, 2017; Georgina Gustin, "Sonny Perdue, Trump's Agriculture Pick, Could Roll Back Forest Protections," *InsideClimate News*, February 7, 2017; Juliet Eilperin and Steven Mufson, "Trump Taps Former Texas Gov. Rick Perry to Head Energy Department He Once Vowed to Abolish," *Washington Post*, December 13, 2016; Mufson, "Rick Perry Just Denied that Humans are the Main Cause of Climate Change," *Washington Post*, June 19, 2017.

81. Eric Lipton, Ben Protess, and Andrew W. Lehren, "Raft of Potential Conflicts in President's Appointments," *New York Times*, April 16, 2017; Cecelia Kang and Michael D. Shear, "Trump Leaves Science Jobs Vacant, Troubling Critics," *New York Times*, March 30, 2017; Stuart Leavenworth, "Science Takes a Back Seat in Early Trump Administration," *Sacramento Bee*, April 25, 2017; Chris Mooney, "Trump Has Filled Just 15 Percent of the Government's Top Science Jobs," *Washington Post*, June 6, 2017. As this book went to press, Trump nominated Kathleen Hartnett-White, former chair of the Texas Commission on Environmental Quality, to head the White House Council on Environmental Quality (CEQ). Hartnett-White is an outspoken critic of climate science, but has no evident scientific credentials herself. See Brady Dennis and Chris Mooney, "Trump Taps Climate Skeptic for Top White House Environmental Post," *Washington Post*, October 13, 2017."

82. Kim Soffen and Denise Lu, "Trump Federal Budget 2018: Massive Cuts to the Arts, Science and the Poor," *Washington Post*, March 16, 2017; Gregory Korte, "The 62 Agencies and Programs Trump Wants to Eliminate," *USA Today*, March 16, 2017.

83. Brady Dennis and Juliet Eilperin, "Trump's Budget Takes a Sledgehammer to the EPA," *Washington Post*, March 16, 2017; Timothy Gardner and Valerie Volcovici, "Trump's EPA Budget Proposal Targets Climate, Clean Water Programs," *Reuters*, March 16, 2017, http://www.reuters.com/article/usa-trump-epa-budget-idUSL2N1GF1NC; Juliet Eilperin, Chris Mooney, and Steven Mufson, "New EPA Documents Reveal Even Deeper Proposed Cuts to Staff and Programs," *Washington Post*, March 31, 2017.

84. Denise Lu and Tim Meko, "How Eliminating Two EPA Programs Could Affect Large Parts of America," *Washington Post*, March 24, 2017; Denise Lu and Armand Emamdjomeh, "Local Programs Get the Biggest Hit in Proposed EPA Budget," *Washington* Post, April 11, 2017.

85. Joel Achenbach, "Trump's Budget Calls for Seismic Disruption in Medical and Science Research," *Washington Post*, March 16, 2017; Steven Mufson, Jason Samenow, and Brady Dennis, "White House Proposes Steep Budget Cut to Leading Climate Science Agency," *Washington Post*, March 3, 2017; Henry Fountain, "Fearing a Climate Data Gap," *New York Times*, April 11, 2017.

86. Henry Fountain and John Schwartz, "Researchers Bristle at Extent of Cuts," *New York Times*, March 17, 2017.

87. Coral Davenport, "Budget Seeks Cuts at E.P.A. to Regulators and Cleanups," *New York Times*, May 19, 2017.

88. Coral Davenport, "Climate Change References are Purged from the White House Website," *New York Times*, January 21, 2017.

89. White House, "Memorandum: Implementation of Regulatory Freeze," January 24, 2017, https://www.whitehouse.gov/the-press-office/2017/01/24/implementation-regulatory-freeze; Environmental Protection Agency, "Delay of Effective Date for 30 Final Regulations Published by the Environmental Protection Agency between October 28, 2016 and January 17, 2017," *Federal Register*, January 26, 2017.

90. See White House, "Presidential Executive Order on Reducing Regulation and Controlling Regulatory Costs," January 30, 2017; and "Presidential Executive Order on Enforcing the Regulatory Agenda," February 24, 2017. These and other executive orders (not archived) are available from https://www.whitehouse.gov/briefing-room/presidential-actions/executive-orders.

91. Juliet Eilperin, "Trump Undertakes Most Ambitious Regulatory Rollback Since Reagan," *Washington Post*, February 12, 2017; Eilperin, "Why Trump's Order to Cut Government Regulation is Even Bolder Than it Seems," *Washington Post*, February 13, 2017; Eilperin, "EPA Emerges as Major Target after Trump Solicits Policy Advice from Industry," *Washington Post*, April 16, 2017; Danielle Ivory and Robert Faturechi, "Secrecy and Suspicion Surround Administration's Deregulation Teams," *New York Times*, August 8, 2017.

92. White House, "Presidential Executive Order on Promoting Energy Independence and Economic Growth," March 28, 2017. For further summary and commentary see Juliet Eilperin and Brady Dennis, "Trump Moves Decisively to Wipe Out Obama's Climate-Change Record," *Washington* Post, March 28, 2017; Coral Davenport and Alissa J. Rubin, "Trump Signs Rule to Block Efforts on Aiding Climate," *New York Times*, March 29, 2017; Lisa Freedman, "Trump Takes a First Step Toward Scrapping Obama's Global Warming Policy," *New York Times*, October 4, 2017.

93. Peter Baker, "Trump Revives Pipelines Thwarted Under Obama, " *New York Times*, January 25, 3017; Clifford Krauss, "U.S., in Reversal, Issues Permit for Keystone Oil Pipeline," *New York Times*, March 25, 2017; Steven Overly, "Trump to Pull Back EPA's Fuel Efficiency Determination, Opening the Door for Reduced Standards," *Washington Post*, March 15, 2017; Bill Vlasic, "Trump, Easing Emissions Rule, Vows to Expand Auto Jobs," *New York Times*, March 15, 2017; Hiroko Tabuchi, "G.O.P. Reverses Obama-Era Rule to Protect Streams from Coal Mining," *New York Times*, February 3, 2017; Juliet Eilperin and Steven Mufson, "Trump Administration to Propose Repealing Rule Giving EPA Broad Authority over Water Pollution," *Washington Post*, June 27, 2017.

94. Timothy Cama, "EPA May Seek to Repeal Obama Ozone Pollution Rule," *The Hill*, April 7, 2017; Timothy Gardner, "Trump's EPA to Reconsider Oil and Gas Emissions Rules," *Reuters*, April 19, 2017, http://www.reuters.com/article/us-usa-epa-idUSKBN17L215.

95. Juliet Eilperin and Steven Mufson, "Trump Moves to Open Atlantic Coast to Oil Drilling for First Time in More Than 30 Years," *Washington Post*, April 7, 2017; Coral Davenport, "Trump Orders Review of Drilling Rules," *New York Times*, April 29, 2017; Kurtis Alexander, "Proposal for Drilling Could Affect California," *San Francisco Chronicle*, April 30, 2017. The federal government has not issued a new lease for drilling off the California coast since 1984.

96. Juliet Eilperin, "Trump to Issue New Order Calling into Question Two Decades of National Monument Designations," *Washington Post*, April 1, 2017; Lisa Freedman, Nadja Popovich and Matt McCann, "Monuments of Nature Get a Second Look," *New York Times*, August 12, 2017; Julie Turkewitz and Lisa Freedman, "4 National Monuments Proposed for Contraction," *New York Times*, August 25, 2017.

97. Michael D. Shear, "Trump Abandoning Global Climate Accord," *New York Times*, June 2, 2017; Philip Rucker and Jenna Johnson, "Trump Announces U.S. Will Exit Paris Climate Deal, Sparking Criticism at Home and Abroad," *Washington Post*, June 2, 2017.

98. Michael D. Shear and Alison Smale, "Foreign Leaders Lament U.S. Withdrawal, but Say It Won't Stop Climate Effort," *New York Times*, June 3, 2017; Brad Plumer, "Meeting Climate Goals Was Always Hard. Without the U.S. It's Far Harder," *New York Times*, June 3, 2017; Jonathan Watts and Kate Connolly, "World Leaders Reject Trump's Claim Paris Climate Deal Can Be Renegotiated," *The Guardian*, June 2, 2017.

99. Peter Baker, "16 Years Later, Bush's Climate Pact Exit Held Lessons for Trump," *New York Times*, June 4, 2017. The U.S. may still participate in some United Nations climate negotiations; see Lisa Freedman, "U.S. to Join Climate Talks Despite Withdrawal from Paris Accord," *New York Times*, August 4, 2017.

100. Philip Rucker, "Bannon: Trump Administration Is in Unending Battle for 'Deconstruction of the Administrative State,'" *Washington Post*, February 23, 2017.

101. Coral Davenport, "E.P.A. Chief Voids Obama Era Rules in Blazing Start," *New York Times*, July 2, 2017; Nadia Popovich and Livia Albeck-Ripka, "48 Environmental Rules on the Way Out Under Trump," *New York Times*, October 5, 2017; Davenport and Nicholas Fandos, "Strolling Through Parks, Rolling Back Regulations," *New York Times*, July 25, 2017; David Shepardson and Valerie Volcovici, "White House Deregulation Push Clears Hundreds of Proposed Rules," *Reuters*, July 21, 2017, https://www.reuters.com/article/us-usa-trump-regulation-idUSKBN1A51O1.

102. Ben Lefebvre, "Oil and Gas Allies to Trump: Slow Down," *Politico*, August 25, 2017, http://www.politico.com/story/2017/08/25/oil-and-gas-allies-want-trump-to-slow-down-242008.

Chapter 5

Environmental Policy in Congress

Michael E. Kraft

The days of "trust me" science are over. . . . This bill ensures that the EPA is not promoting a one-sided ideological agenda.

Rep. Lamar Smith, R-Texas, chairman, House Science, Space, and Technology Committee, March 2017

[This bill] is a Pandora's Box which could have untold consequences for the EPA, industry and the general public. . . . In reality, this bill isn't about science. It's about undermining public health and the environment."

Rep. Eddie Bernice Johnson, D-Texas, ranking Democrat, House Science, Space, and Technology Committee, March 2017[1]

In March 2017, the U.S. House voted largely along party lines to approve legislation that could sharply alter how the Environmental Protection Agency (EPA) makes regulatory decisions. It was the latest attempt by House Republicans to rein in what they saw as the EPA's overly zealous actions on climate change, air pollution, and other environmental and public health issues. The Republican majority's position, captured in Rep. Smith's comment above, prevailed, while the Democratic minority, whose views are represented by Rep. Johnson's criticism, lost. The House Rules Committee sent the brief (four-page) measure to the floor on a party-line vote, and the House approved it by a margin of 228 to 194, with only seven Republicans voting no and three Democrats voting yes.

Two years previously, the House had passed similar legislation, the Secret Science Reform Act, only to see it die in the Senate. The 2017 act once again sought to ensure that new regulations are based on science that is "transparent or reproducible," and not on what Rep. Smith and his supporters refer to as "secret science." Hence the formal title of the legislation, the "Honest and Open New EPA Science Treatment Act," or the HONEST Act. In a committee hearing on the measure, Smith justified the new legislation by restating his long-held skepticism about climate science: "[M]uch of climate science today appears to be based more on exaggerations, personal agendas and questionable predictions than on the scientific method."[2]

Critics argued that, if enacted, the measure could prohibit the EPA from basing its regulations on peer-reviewed scientific studies of the health effects of pollutants. They also said the chief impact of the proposed law would be to weaken the EPA's reliance on professional expertise and to amplify the voice of industry in regulatory decision making. Paul Billings, senior vice president for advocacy at the American Lung Association's Washington, DC, office, put it this way: "The concern is that a lot of this looks like a clever, stealth attempt to create new legal and administrative pathways for slowing agencies down and tying them up in court."[3]

This latest controversy over the connection between science and public policy reflects a decades-long effort by congressional Republicans to pare back environmental regulations, which they see as excessive, costly, and harmful to economic growth and job creation.[4] Most Democrats fall on the other side of this debate and are equally intent on blocking what they see as political interference in a regulatory process that they believe should be rooted in well-established administrative law, credible science, and professional judgment by experienced agency staff. Republicans gained the majority in the House after the 2010 elections and in the following three elections, and thus they had the votes to enact measures like the HONEST Act. The Senate was captured by Republicans in the 2014 and 2016 elections, but the party lacked the votes to follow the House on such measures. As noted in Chapters 1 and 4, President Donald Trump shared the Republican Party's views on the negative economic impacts of environmental regulations such as tighter controls on urban air pollution, new restrictions on coal-fired power plants, and the recently approved Clean Water Rule (also called the Waters of the United States Rule) that affects smaller bodies of water that flow into streams, rivers, and lakes. This homogeneity of attitude within the Republican Party ensures continued partisan conflict over the issues.[5]

Environmental Challenges and Political Constraints

The battles over environmental science, the EPA, and regulatory decision making in 2017, as well as over the past two decades, say much about the way Congress deals with environmental, energy, and natural resource issues today, and the many obstacles it will face in trying to chart new policy directions to better address the twenty-first-century challenges described in Chapter 1, such as climate change.[6] The capacity of the 115th Congress to act, like that of many Congresses before it, was deeply affected by what analysts have called an "era of partisan warfare" on Capitol Hill. Increasingly, each party had appealed to its core constituency through a continuous political campaign that emphasized an ideological "message politics" that was more about taking positions on the issues than crafting good policies. In this context, compromise between the parties was never easy, as each often sought to deny the other any semblance of victory, even at the cost of stalemate in dealing with pressing national environmental problems.[7]

Whichever party dominates Congress in the years ahead, it will not be easy to regain the broad bipartisan support for environmental policies that prevailed during the 1970s and even through the 1980s. This is particularly the case for major policy actions, such as rewriting the basic environmental laws, most of which were adopted almost fifty years ago. It was not always so. For nearly three decades, from the late 1960s to the mid-1990s, Congress enacted—and over time strengthened—an extraordinary range of environmental policies, typified by the 1970 Clean Air Act, the 1972 Clean Water Act, the 1973 Endangered Species Act, and the 1976 Resource Conservation and Recovery Act (see Chapter 1 and Appendix 1). In doing so, members within both political parties recognized and responded to rising public concern about environmental degradation and its impacts on public health. For the same reasons, they stoutly defended and even expanded those policies during the 1980s when environmental legislation was assailed by Ronald Reagan's White House.[8]

This pattern of bipartisan cooperation and compromise changed dramatically with the election of the 104th Congress in 1994, as the new Republican majority brought to the Hill a very different position on the environment. It was far more critical of regulatory bureaucracies, such as the EPA, and of the environmental and public health policies they are charged with implementing.[9] On energy and natural resource issues—from drilling for oil in the Arctic National Wildlife Refuge (ANWR) or on offshore public lands to, more recently, the Keystone XL pipeline controversy, oil and gas drilling on public land, and especially actions to mitigate climate change—Republicans have tended to lean heavily toward increasing resource use and economic development rather than conservation or environmental protection.

As party leaders pursued these goals from 1995 through 2017, they invariably faced intense opposition from Democrats who were just as determined to block what they characterized as ill-advised attempts to roll back years of progress in protecting public health and the environment.[10] The 2006 election put Democrats in control of Congress once again, giving them substantial opportunities to challenge President George W. Bush on environmental and energy issues, and they did so frequently. But the short-term effect of political conflict over many of President Bush's proposals, from drilling for oil in ANWR to his Clear Skies initiative, was partisan polarization and policy stalemate. As noted at the chapter's opening, building consensus on environmental issues, with very few exceptions, has proven to be exceptionally difficult. As a result, Congress has been unable to approve either the sweeping changes sought by Republicans or the moderate policy reforms preferred by most Democrats.

The ongoing partisan fights in Congress mean that existing policies—with their many acknowledged flaws—have largely continued in force. State and local governments have fostered innovative policy actions that help to fill this void (see Chapter 2), and progress also can be seen in administrative proceedings and judicial decisions that help to compensate for congressional gridlock (see Chapters 6 and 7).[11] Yet, only Congress can redesign environmental policy for the twenty-first century. For that reason, it is important to understand how it makes decisions on environmental issues and why members adopt the positions and take the actions they do. In the sections below, I examine efforts at policy change on Capitol Hill and compare them with the way Congress dealt previously with environmental issues. I give special consideration to the phenomenon of policy stalemate or gridlock, which at times, including during the 2010s, has been a defining characteristic of congressional involvement with environmental policy.

Congressional Authority and Environmental Policy

Under the Constitution, Congress shares authority with the president for federal policymaking on the environment. In most years, members of Congress make critical decisions on hundreds of measures that affect environmental policy broadly defined. These range from funding the operations of the EPA, the Department of the Interior, and other agencies to supporting highways, mass transit, forestry, farming, oil and gas exploration, energy research and development, the protection of wilderness areas, and international population and development assistance programs. These actions are rarely front-page news, and the public may hear little about them.[12]

As discussed in Chapter 1, we can distinguish congressional actions in several different stages of the policy process: agenda setting, formulation and adoption of policies, and implementation of them in executive agencies. Presidents have greater opportunities than does Congress to set the political agenda, that is, to call attention to specific problems and define or frame the terms of debate. Yet members of Congress can have a major impact on the agenda through legislative and oversight hearings as well as through the abundant opportunities they have for introducing legislation, requesting and publicizing studies and reports, making speeches, taking positions, voting, and campaigning for reelection.

All of these actions can assist them in framing issues in a way that promotes their preferred solutions, as was evident in the House debate over the HONEST Act in March 2017 and, particularly, in the arguments of Republicans against what they see as EPA rulemaking they believe is both unjustifiable and too costly. In a similar effort to shape debate, in June 2014, Senate Democrats invited former EPA heads under Republican presidents Richard Nixon, Ronald Reagan, George H. W. Bush, and George W. Bush to testify at a well-publicized committee hearing. They sought to demonstrate bipartisan support for climate change policy despite the prevailing skepticism toward climate science among Republican members of Congress.[13]

Because of their extensive executive powers, presidents also can dominate the process of policy implementation in the agencies (see Chapters 4 and 7). Here too, however, Congress can significantly affect agency actions, particularly through its budgetary decisions. For example, shortly after he took office, President Trump proposed exceptionally deep budgetary and staffing cuts for the EPA and for environmental science and energy technology research at the EPA, Department of Energy, National Aeronautics and Space Administration (NASA), and National Oceanic and Atmospheric Administration (NOAA). However, Congress will have the final say on funding, and thus on the agencies' capacity to engage in scientific research and to implement existing laws and programs.[14]

These congressional powers translate into an influential and continuing role of overseeing, and often criticizing, actions in executive agencies as varied as the EPA, Department of Energy, U.S. Geological Survey, Fish and Wildlife Service, Bureau of Land Management, and Forest Service. As one example of such congressional oversight, the chair of the House Science Committee, Rep. Smith, frequently used his influential position to criticize government scientists and their research. In one set of hearings, he tried to debunk the findings of NOAA scientists on climate change, saying they had intentionally doctored data to refute the widely held belief of climate denialists that warming had paused in the late 1990s and early 2000s, and therefore was not caused by human activities. Even after the scientific report was published in the peer-reviewed and prestigious journal *Science*, Smith assailed the scientists for advancing what he termed Obama's "extreme climate agenda"; later scientific studies confirmed NOAA's findings.[15] Under the committee's authority, Smith also subpoenaed e-mails and draft papers of government climate scientists to try to show what he considered to be their political bias. He used the same committee powers to compel the EPA administrator under Obama, Gina McCarthy, to turn over text messages and phone records related to the agency's proposed tougher limits on ozone pollution, which Smith opposed.[16]

In one unusual instance in 2017, when the head of the EPA's Board of Scientific Counselors, representing scientists outside the agency who advise it, was to testify before the Science Committee on state environmental policymaking, Scott Pruitt's political staff at the agency pressured her to change her previously submitted written testimony. The EPA's chief of staff sought to limit criticism that the agency was dismissing scientific advisers even though such actions already had been reported by leading newspapers. Agency efforts of this kind demonstrate the importance the EPA attaches to congressional hearings and testimony.[17]

In addition to committee oversight authority, the Senate plays a major role in choosing who will fill critical positions through its constitutional power to advise and consent on presidential nominations to the agencies and the courts. The Senate almost always approves presidential nominees when the same party controls both institutions, although when a president faces a Congress controlled by the other party, approval is far less certain. For example, President Trump's nomination of Scott Pruitt to head the EPA was among the most controversial of his appointments in 2017, and it drew widespread media coverage and condemnation from Senate Democrats and environmental, scientific, and public health organizations. Hundreds of current and former EPA employees also urged the Senate to reject his nomination. Democrats on the Senate Committee on Environment and Public Works, chaired by Sen. John Barrasso

(R-Wyoming), even chose to boycott the committee meeting to slow Pruitt's approval and force him to answer more of their questions. Republican members responded by suspending the rules and approving Pruitt's nomination by a vote of 11–0 when Democrats were absent. They then sent the nomination to the full Senate where it was approved on a largely party-line vote of 52 to 46.[18] In contrast, the Senate approved Ryan Zinke as Trump's Interior Department secretary with a bipartisan vote of 68 to 31.

Even if it cannot compete on an equal footing with the president in some of these policymaking activities and personnel decisions, in many ways, Congress has been more influential than the White House in the formulation and adoption of environmental policies.[19] Yet the way in which Congress exercises its formidable policymaking powers at any given time is shaped by several key variables, such as its institutional structure and norms, public opinion on the environment, whether the president's party also controls Congress—and by what margins—and members' willingness to defer to the president's recommendations.

Congress's actions on the environment also invariably reflect its dual mission to be deeply engaged with both lawmaking and representation. In addition to serving as a national legislative body, the House and Senate are assemblies of elected officials who represent politically disparate districts and states. It is hardly surprising that members are politically motivated to try to represent local, state, and regional concerns and interests, such as coal mining, oil and gas development, or vehicle manufacturing, which can put them at odds with the president or their own party leaders. Indeed, powerful electoral incentives continually induce members of Congress to think at least as much about local and regional impacts of environmental policies as they do about the larger national interest.[20] Such political pressures led members in the early 2000s, for example, to drive up the cost of President Bush's energy proposals with what one journalist called an "abundance of pet projects, subsidies and tax breaks" to specific industries in their districts and states.[21]

Another distinctive institutional characteristic is the system of House and Senate standing committees, where most significant policy decisions take place, as illustrated by the previous discussion of the House Science Committee. Dozens of committees and subcommittees have jurisdiction over environmental policy (see Table 1-1 in Chapter 1), which tends to fragment decisions and erect barriers to integrated or holistic approaches to energy, the environment, and sustainable development. Such a committee structure also means that the outcomes of specific legislative battles often turn on which members sit on and control those committees. For example, in the Senate, James Inhofe used his positions on the Senate Environment and Public Works Committee (variously, chair and ranking Republican member) to question the science of climate change. Some half dozen of Inhofe's former aides on the committee were later hired for high-level positions at the EPA under Scott Pruitt or at President Trump's White House.[22]

Taken together, these congressional characteristics have important implications for environmental policy. First, building policy consensus in

Congress is rarely easy because of the diversity of interests and of members whose concerns need to be met and because of the conflicts that can arise among committees and leaders. Second, policy compromises invariably reflect members' preoccupation with the local and regional impacts of environmental decisions, for example, how climate change policy will affect industries and homeowners in coal-producing states and those heavily dependent on coal-fired power plants, such as West Virginia, Kentucky, Ohio, and Indiana. Third, the White House matters a great deal in how the issues are defined and whether policy decisions can be made acceptable to all concerned, but the president's influence is nevertheless limited by independent political calculations made on Capitol Hill. President Obama's relatively low standing in the polls in 2014 doubtless played a role in congressional opposition to his climate change actions, and President Trump's historically low approval ratings in 2017 likely will encourage more congressional opposition to his budgetary and legislative proposals than otherwise would be the case with Republican control of the House, Senate, and White House.

Given these constraints, Congress frequently finds itself unable to make crucial decisions on environmental policy. The U.S. public may see a "do-nothing Congress," or as one pundit put it describing the paucity of legislation enacted in 2013 and 2014, a "do-even-less Congress."[23] Inaction on a range of environmental and energy issues was just as prevalent in 2015 and 2016. Yet the reality is that all too often members can find no way to reconcile the conflicting views of multiple interests and constituencies. It remains to be seen if this pattern will change in 2018 and beyond. Through 2017, though, Congress remained as divided as ever.

However, there are some important exceptions to this common pattern of policy stalemate. A brief examination of the way Congress has dealt with environmental issues since the early 1970s helps to explain this seeming anomaly. Such a review also provides a useful context in which to examine and assess the actions of recent Congresses and the outlook for environmental policymaking for the early twenty-first century.

Causes and Consequences of Environmental Gridlock

Policy gridlock refers to an inability to resolve conflicts in a policymaking body such as Congress, which results in government inaction in the face of important public problems. There is no consensus on *what* to do, and therefore no movement occurs in any direction. Present policies, or slight revisions of them, continue until agreement is reached on the direction and magnitude of change. Sometimes environmental or other programs officially expire but continue to be funded by Congress through a waiver of the rules governing the annual appropriations process. The failure to renew the programs, however, contributes to administrative and public policy drift, ineffectual congressional oversight, and a propensity for members to use the appropriations process to achieve what cannot be gained through statutory change.[24] While usually seen as a negative characteristic, policy gridlock in

Congress also has had what environmentalists would see as positive effects. For example, it has stimulated environmental policy change at the state and local levels, which in turn may illustrate the political feasibility or effectiveness of new policy directions (see Chapter 2). It has pushed executive agencies to alter administrative decision making in creative ways to compensate for the lack of new congressional directives (see Chapter 7). It also means that multiple parties in policy disputes are more likely to turn to the courts to resolve disagreements, which may lead to decisions that facilitate environmental policy reforms even in the face of intense partisan conflicts (see Chapter 6).[25]

Why does policy gridlock occur so frequently in Congress? There is no one answer that fits every situation, but among the major reasons are the sharply divergent policy views of Democrats and Republicans, the influence of organized interest groups in both elections and policymaking, and the inherent complexity of environmental problems. The lack of public consensus on the issues or unclear public preferences, the constitutionally mandated structure of U.S. government (especially the separation of powers between the presidency and Congress), and weak or ineffectual political leadership also make a difference.[26]

Most of these factors are easy to understand. For example, Republicans and Democrats bring very different political philosophies and beliefs to the table, and those views are reinforced by the nature of congressional elections today. Most members come from relatively safe districts or states that lean strongly toward one party or the other. For the House, district safety often is a consequence of strong partisan gerrymandering that is intended to expand the party's political power. In recent elections, only about two to three dozen House seats out of 435 have been competitive between the major parties. One result is that the electoral system gives exceptional clout to the majority party's base or core voters, particularly in low-turnout, off-year elections. Members are forced to appeal more to these voters (such as the Tea Party forces within the Republican Party in the 2010s or to Trump's base of voters in 2017) than to those in the political center or in the other party. That in turn tends to promote ideological rigidity among members and also to discourage the kind of compromise and consensus building in policymaking that long prevailed in Congress until recent years.[27]

It is also understandable that when a given issue sparks involvement by diverse and opposing interests (such as oil and gas companies, renewable energy companies, electric utilities, the coal industry, the automobile industry, labor unions, and environmentalists), finding politically acceptable solutions can be exceptionally difficult. Similarly, public opinion polls may show a strong public preference for certain actions on the environment, energy, or climate change, but the public tends not to be very well informed on the issues, and these issues also typically are low in salience for most people. Both factors limit the extent to which members of Congress are likely to give public preferences much weight in their voting decisions.[28] These conditions significantly diminish the public's political influence. Absent a clear and forceful public voice, members of Congress look elsewhere when deciding how to vote on measures before them, and most people are not likely to notice how their representatives are voting.[29] It is for that reason that some groups, such as the Citizens' Climate Lobby, try to change the political calculus. They organize grassroots campaigns on climate change in congressional districts nationwide that are designed to convince members of Congress from both parties that their constituents do desire strong policies and that they are watching the votes.[30]

The notable differences in policy preferences between Republicans and Democrats on environmental and energy issues today reflect a striking trend toward ideological polarization that has developed over the past several decades. The shift has been well documented by scholars, and it can be seen in public opinion surveys as well as rankings of members' voting on environmental issues.[31] For example, based on rankings by the League of Conservation Voters (LCV), the parties showed increasing divergence from the early 1970s through the early 2000s. On average, they differed by nearly 25 points on a 100-point scale, and those differences grew much wider over time.[32] The gap is exceptionally large today. In 2016, for example, Senate Democrats voted 96 percent of the time in support of the positions endorsed by the LCV and the environmental community whereas Senate Republicans averaged only 14 percent. Partisan differences in the House were even greater. Democrats averaged 94 percent scores while Republicans stood at only 5 percent, with many members scoring zero.[33] Smaller but still significant differences appear in surveys of the general public, with Republicans generally less supportive of environmental policy action than Democrats. Environmental policies have become at least as polarizing as any other issue in the late 2010s, a striking shift from the public consensus and bipartisanship that prevailed in the 1970s.[34]

Despite these disagreements on the issues, members of Congress come together on occasion to form bipartisan caucuses or congressional member organizations that seek practical solutions with broad public appeal. One illustration is the new House Climate Solutions Caucus, designed to have equal Republican and Democratic membership. Some of the caucuses and coalitions, however, attract most or all of their members from one party. This is the case, for example, for the House Sustainable Energy and Environment Coalition, whose fifty members in 2017 were all Democrats.

From Consensus in the Environmental Decade to Deadlock in the 1990s

As Chapter 1 makes clear, the legislative record for the environmental decade of the 1970s is remarkable. The National Environmental Policy Act, Clean Air Act, Clean Water Act, Endangered Species Act, and Resource Conservation and Recovery Act, among others, were all signed into law in that decade, and most of them were enacted in a six-year period: 1970 to 1976. We can debate the merits of these early statutes with the clarity of hindsight and in light of contemporary criticism of them. Yet their adoption demonstrates vividly that the U.S. political system is capable of developing major environmental policies in fairly short order under the right conditions.

Consensus on environmental policy could prevail in the 1970s, in part, because the issues were new and politically popular, and attention was focused on broadly supported program goals such as cleaning up the nation's air and water rather than on the means used (command-and-control regulation) or the costs to achieve them. At that time, there was also little overt and sustained opposition to these measures.

Environmental Gridlock Emerges

The pattern of the 1970s did not last. Congress's enthusiasm for environmental policy gradually gave way to apprehension about its impacts on the economy, and policy stalemate became the norm in the early 1980s. Ronald Reagan's election as president in 1980 also altered the political climate and threw Congress into a defensive posture. It was forced to react to the Reagan administration's aggressive policy actions. Rather than proposing new programs or expanding old ones, Congress focused its resources on oversight and criticism of the administration's policies, and bipartisan agreement became more difficult. Members were increasingly cross-pressured by environmental and industry groups, partisanship on these issues increased, and Congress and President Reagan battled repeatedly over budget and program priorities.[35] The cumulative effect of these developments in the early 1980s was that Congress was unable to agree on new environmental policy directions.

Gridlock Eases: 1984–1990

The legislative logjam began breaking up in late 1983, as the U.S. public and Congress repudiated Reagan's antienvironmental agenda (see Chapter 4). The new pattern was evident by 1984 when, after several years of deliberation, Congress approved major amendments to the 1976 Resource Conservation and Recovery Act; these strengthened the program and set tight new deadlines for EPA rulemaking on control of hazardous chemical wastes. The 99th Congress (1985–1987) compiled a record very much at odds with the deferral politics of the 97th and 98th Congresses (1981–1985). In 1986, the Safe Drinking Water Act was strengthened and expanded, and Congress approved the Superfund Amendments and Reauthorization Act, adding a separate Title III, the Emergency Planning and Community Right-to-Know Act (EPCRA), which created the Toxics Release Inventory. Democrats regained control of the Senate following the 1986 election, and Congress reauthorized the Clean Water Act over a presidential veto. Still, Congress could renew neither the Clean Air Act nor the Federal Insecticide, Fungicide, and Rodenticide Act—the nation's key pesticide control act—nor could it pass new legislation to control acid rain.

However, with the election of George H. W. Bush in 1988, Congress and the White House were able to agree on enactment of the innovative and stringent Clean Air Act Amendments of 1990 and the Energy Policy Act of 1992. The latter was an important, if modest, advancement in promoting energy conservation, and it restructured the electric utility industry to promote greater competition and efficiency. Success on the Clean Air Act was particularly important because for years it was a stark symbol of Congress's inability to reauthorize controversial environmental programs. Passage was possible in 1990 because of improved scientific research that clarified the risks of dirty air, reports of worsening ozone in urban areas, and President Bush's leadership. He had vowed to "break the gridlock" and support renewal of the Clean Air Act, and Sen. George Mitchell, D-Maine, newly elected as Senate majority leader, was equally determined to enact a bill.[36] Unsurprisingly, the Senate approved the act by a vote of 89 to 10 and the House by 401 to 25.

Policy Stalemate Returns

Unfortunately, approval of the 1990 Clean Air Act Amendments was no signal that a new era of cooperative and bipartisan policymaking on the environment was about to begin. Nor was the election of Bill Clinton and Al Gore in 1992, even as Democrats regained control of both houses of Congress. Most of the major environmental laws were once again up for renewal. Yet despite an emerging consensus on many of the laws, in the end, the 103rd Congress (1993–1995) remained far too divided to act. Coalitions of environmental groups and business interests clashed regularly on all of these initiatives, and congressional leaders and the Clinton White House were unsuccessful in resolving the disputes.

The 104th Congress:
Revolutionary Fervor Meets Political Reality

Few analysts had predicted the astonishing outcomes of the 1994 mid-term elections, even after one of the most expensive, negative, and anti-Washington campaigns in modern times. Republicans captured both houses of Congress, picking up an additional fifty-two seats in the House and eight in the Senate. They also did well in other elections throughout the country, contributing to their belief that voters had endorsed the Contract with America, which symbolized the new Republican agenda.[37] The contract had promised a rolling back of government regulations and a shrinking of the federal government's role. There was no specific mention of environmental policy, however, and the document's language was carefully constructed for broad appeal to a disgruntled electorate. It drew heavily from the work of conservative and pro-business think tanks, which for years had waged a multifaceted campaign to discredit environmentalist thinking and policies.[38] In recent years, much the same kind of effort can be seen in the reports of the Heritage Foundation, the Competitive Enterprise Institute, the CATO Institute, and the Heartland Institute. These reports have influenced the environmental policy agenda of the Trump administration and the EPA under its new administrator, Scott Pruitt (see Chapters 4 and 7).[39]

The preponderance of evidence suggests that the Republican victory in November of 1994 conveyed no public mandate to roll back environmental protection.[40] Yet the political result was clear enough. It put Republicans in charge of the House for the first time in four decades and initiated an extraordinary period of legislative action on environmental policy characterized by bitter relations between the two parties, setting the stage for a similar confrontation that emerged following the 2010 elections and again after the 2016 elections.

The environmental policy deadlock in the mid-1990s should have come as no surprise. With several notable exceptions, consensus on the issues simply could not be built, and the Republican revolution under Speaker Newt Gingrich failed for the most part. The lesson seemed to be that a direct and well-publicized attack on popular environmental programs could not work because it would provoke a political backlash. Those who supported a new conservative policy agenda turned instead to a strategy of evolutionary or incremental environmental policy change through a subtler and far less visible exercise of Congress's appropriations and oversight powers. This strategy included what is usually termed "regulatory reform." Here they were more successful.[41] The George W. Bush administration relied on a similar strategy from 2001 to early 2009, the quiet pursuit of a deregulatory agenda, and there is evidence of a similar strategy in the 115th Congress in 2017 and in the Trump administration's emphasis on environmental deregulation and defunding instead of statutory reforms.

Environmental Policy Actions in Recent Congresses

As discussed earlier, Congress influences nearly every environmental and resource policy through exercise of its powers to legislate, oversee executive agencies, advise and consent on nominations, and appropriate funds. Sometimes these activities take place largely within the specialized committees and subcommittees, and sometimes they reach the floor of the House and Senate, where they may attract greater media attention. Some of the decisions are made routinely and are relatively free of controversy (for example, appropriations for the national parks) whereas others stimulate more political conflict, as was the case with George W. Bush's Clear Skies bill, the long-running dispute over drilling for oil in ANWR, and debates over the Keystone XL pipeline, energy legislation, and climate change.

The capacity of members of Congress to cooperate in the search for environmental policy reforms became even more problematic by 2017 as political polarization in both the media and the nation increased. Adding to the challenge was the adoption by the Trump administration of a largely uncompromising posture on major environmental, energy, and natural resource issues, most notably EPA regulation, oil and gas development on public lands, and climate change. To put the current policy debates into a useful historical context, I briefly review in this section some of the most notable congressional actions from 1995 to 2017. These actions are presented within three broad categories: regulatory reform initiatives (directed at the way agencies make decisions), appropriations (funding levels and use of budgetary riders), and proposals for changing the substance of environmental policy.

Regulatory Reform: Changing Agency Procedures

Regulatory reform has long been of concern in U.S. environmental policy (see Chapters 1, 4, and 7). There is no real dispute about the need to reform that part of agency rulemaking, which has been widely faulted for being too inflexible, intrusive, cumbersome, and adversarial, and sometimes based on insufficient consideration of science and economics.[42] However, much disagreement exists over precisely what elements of the regulatory process need to be reformed and how best to ensure that the changes are both fair and effective.

Beginning in 1995 and continuing for several Congresses, the Republican Party and conservative Democrats favored omnibus regulatory reform legislation that would affect all environmental policies by imposing broad and stringent mandates on executive agencies, particularly the EPA. Those mandates were especially directed at the use of benefit-cost analysis and risk assessment in proposing new regulations. As discussed early in the chapter, proponents of such legislation also sought to open agency technical studies and rulemaking to additional legal challenges to help protect the business community against what they viewed as unjustifiable regulatory action. Opponents of both kinds of measures argued that such impositions and opportunities for lawsuits were not reform in any meaningful sense and would wreak havoc within agencies that already faced daunting procedural hurdles and frequent legal disputes as they developed regulations (see Chapters 6 and 7).[43]

Ultimately, Congress did approve several bills in 1995 and 1996 that Republicans characterized as regulatory reform, including the Unfunded Mandates Reform Act (1995) and the Small Business Regulatory Enforcement Fairness Act (1996). As part of the latter, the separately named Congressional Review Act gives Congress the ability to reject a newly approved agency rule if within sixty legislative working days a simple majority in each house approves a "resolution of disapproval" that is also signed by the president.

With the election of George W. Bush in 2000, the regulatory reform agenda shifted from imposing these kinds of congressional mandates on Clinton administration agencies to direct intervention by the White House. Bush appointed conservative and pro-business officials to nearly all environmental and natural resource agencies, and rulemaking shifted decisively toward the interests of the business community (see Chapter 4).[44] Bush and his supporters saw less need for congressional involvement in regulatory reform.

Barack Obama's election coincided with another shift in regulatory philosophy. In light of the financial meltdown on Wall Street in 2008 and reports of ineffective federal regulation of banking institutions and of food, drugs, consumer products, and the environment, public sentiment at least temporarily shifted back in favor of strong, or at least "smart," regulation that achieves its purposes without imposing unreasonable burdens.[45] However, following the 2010 elections, Republicans once again controlled the House, and antiregulatory sentiment returned as members sought to reduce perceived burdens on the business community in a slowly recovering economy and to limit or repeal regulations that they believed were hindering job creation. These efforts had limited impact beyond helping to set a regulatory reform agenda for the future because President Obama, of course, was unlikely to sign any legislation that would weaken his own policy initiatives or the major regulatory actions taken by his appointees in the agencies.

By 2017, however, the political alignment changed radically with the election of President Trump. This shift was evident in Rep. Lamar Smith's efforts, described earlier, to block the EPA from using scientific studies in regulatory processes if those studies were not fully public or transparent. It was equally apparent in a broad Regulatory Accountability Act Congress considered in 2017 and in a measure that the House passed on a largely party-line vote in May of 2017: the Reducing Regulatory Burdens Act of 2017, a measure intended to weaken regulation of pesticides under the Clean Water Act.[46] It was even more palpable in the unprecedented use of the Congressional Review Act to overturn recently approved regulations and in the appointment of Scott Pruitt as administrator of the EPA, as well as in his recruitment of top-level political staff to the agency who were dedicated to the same deregulatory agenda.

Until 2017, the Congressional Review Act was not a useful tool for regulatory reform, and it was employed only once by Congress, in March 2001, to overturn a Clinton-era workplace ergonomics rule. With the election of President Trump and Republican majorities in both the House and Senate, the act became a convenient way to roll back Obama-era environmental rules, among others, and to do so quickly. Less than one month into the new administration, the House had used the review act to nullify eight rules, as it considered dozens more. Some quickly cleared Congress and were sent to the president for approval. These included an EPA rule intended to prevent coal mining waste from contaminating streams (the stream protection rule) and a Fish and Wildlife rule that forbade the baiting, trapping, and killing of bears and wolfs in their winter dens in Alaska's national wildlife refuges.[47] By May 1, the president had signed thirteen such bills to erase new rules, leading one journalist to describe his use of the act as a "regulatory wrecking ball."[48] The Senate narrowly rejected one of the proposed rule changes, aimed at overturning a Bureau of Land Management regulation that set standards for limiting release of methane (a potent greenhouse gas) by oil and gas drillers on federal land; three Republicans joined all Democrats in opposing the measure.

Beyond the review act, congressional interest in deregulation at environmental agencies was aided by a Trump executive order in late February 2017 that required each agency to designate a "Regulatory Reform Officer" and a Regulatory Reform Task Force to examine existing regulations that eliminate jobs, are unnecessary or ineffective, impose costs that exceed benefits, or are inconsistent with other regulatory reform initiatives. It seems very likely that sympathetic members of Congress will keep a close eye on how agencies comply with the order.

Scott Pruitt's appointment as EPA administrator should reduce the extent to which a Republican Congress will need to pursue a regulatory reform agenda similar to the one it has pursued in the past. This is because members are confident that Pruitt and the other political appointees at the agency will aggressively pursue such an agenda without congressional prodding. The biggest constraint that Pruitt will face in rolling back major Obama-era regulations, such as the Clean Power Plan and the Clean Water Rule, is that he must begin the full regulatory process anew, so he will need to base any subsequent regulations on science and economics that are sufficient to pass muster with the courts.

Appropriation Politics: Budgets and Riders

The implementation of environmental policies depends heavily on the funds that Congress appropriates each year. Thus, if certain policy goals cannot be achieved through changing the governing statutes or altering the rulemaking process through regulatory reform, attention may turn instead to the appropriations process. This was the case during the Reagan administration in the 1980s, which severely cut environmental budgets. Limiting such budgets became a major element of the Republican strategy in Congress from 1995 to 2006, as well as in the George W. Bush administration. The importance of budgetary politics depends in part on which party controls Congress and the White House. Democrats tend to favor increased spending on the environment, and Republicans generally favor decreased spending. Regardless of which party controls Congress, however, the appropriations process has been used in two distinct ways to achieve policy change. One is through reliance on riders, loosely related legislative stipulations attached to appropriations bills; they ride along with the bill, hence the name. The other is through changes in the level of funding, either a cut in spending for programs that are not favored or an increase for those that are endorsed.

Appropriation Riders. The use of riders became a common strategy following the 1994 election. For example, in the 104th Congress, more than fifty antienvironmental riders were included in seven different appropriations bills, largely with the purpose of slowing or halting enforcement of laws by the EPA, the Interior Department, and other agencies until Congress could revise them.[49]

The use of riders continued in subsequent years, as has opposition to the strategy by environmental groups. In 2011, a rider attached to the fiscal year 2012 spending bill would have kept the Obama administration EPA from issuing any proposed regulations on emissions of greenhouse gases from power plants or industrial facilities. Another would have prevented the Interior Department from using any federal funds to limit oil, gas, or other commercial development on public lands that might qualify in the future for wilderness designation.[50]

Why use budgetary riders to achieve policy change rather than introducing freestanding legislation to pursue the same goals? Such a strategy is attractive to its proponents because appropriations bills, unlike authorizing legislation, typically move quickly, and Congress must enact them each year to keep the government operating. Many Republicans and business lobbyists also argue that the use of riders is one of the few ways they have to rope in a bureaucracy that they believe needs additional constraints. They argue that they are unable to address their concerns through changing the authorizing statutes themselves, a far more controversial and uncertain path to follow.[51] Even if members fail, their efforts on such riders help to assure critical constituency groups that their representatives are determined to meet their needs.

Critics of the process, however, say that relying on riders is an inappropriate way to institute policy change because the process provides little opportunity to debate the issues openly, and there are no public hearings or public votes. For example, the provisions of the Data Quality Act of 2000, a rider designed to ensure the accuracy of data on which agencies base their rulemaking, were written largely by an industry lobbyist and were enacted quietly as twenty-seven lines of text buried in a massive budget bill that President Clinton had ·to sign.[52] In a retrospective review in 2001, the Natural Resources Defense Council (NRDC) counted hundreds of antienvironmental riders attached to appropriations bills since 1995. Clinton blocked more than seventy-five of them, but many became law, including the Data Quality Act.[53]

Cutting Environmental Budgets. The history of congressional funding for environmental programs was discussed in Chapter 1, and it is set out in Appendix 2 for selected agencies and in Appendix 4 for overall federal spending on natural resources and the environment. These budgets have been the focus of continuing conflict within Congress since the 1980s. For example, in the 104th Congress in the mid-1990s, GOP leaders enacted deep cuts in environmental spending only to face President Clinton's veto of the budget bill. Those conflicts led eventually to a temporary shutdown of the federal government, with the Republicans receiving the brunt of the public's wrath for the budget wars. Most of the environmental cuts were reversed, but disagreements over program priorities have continued since that time.[54]

George W. Bush regularly sought to cut the EPA's budget but was rebuffed by Congress until 2004, after which it tended to go along with the president. Since then, overall appropriations for the environment and natural resources have increased, although only slightly in real terms, while spending on pollution control (by the EPA, for example) has declined markedly after adjusting for inflation.

As reviewed in Chapter 1, President Obama initially increased environmental spending, but the level of funding was reduced over time because of overall budgetary constraints. It remains to be seen how Congress will respond to the Trump administration's proposal of deep spending cuts to environmental agencies, particularly the EPA, and to scientific research. As was evident in a short-term funding measure in late April of 2017 (in which the EPA's budget was reduced by only 1 percent, not Trump's recommended 30 percent), members of Congress seem likely to decline to go along fully with the president's sharp departure from previous spending levels, in part because their states and districts benefit directly from that spending.[55]

Legislating Policy Change

As noted earlier, in most years, Congress makes decisions that affect nearly all environmental or resource programs. In this section, I highlight selective actions in recent Congresses that demonstrate both the ability of members to reach across party lines to find common ground and the continuing ideological and partisan fights that often prevent legislative action.

Pesticides and Drinking Water. Among the most notable achievements of the otherwise antienvironmental 104th and 105th Congresses are two conspicuous success stories involving control of pesticides and agricultural chemicals and drinking water. Years of legislative gridlock were overcome as Republicans and Democrats uncharacteristically reached agreement on new policy directions.

The Food Quality Protection Act of 1996 was a major revision of the nation's pesticide law, long a prime example of policy gridlock as environmentalists battled with the agricultural, chemical, and food industries. The act required the EPA to develop a new, uniform, reasonable-risk approach to regulating pesticides used on food, fiber, and other crops, and it required that special attention be given to the diverse ways in which both children and adults are exposed to such chemicals. The act sped through Congress in record time without a single dissenting vote because the food industry was desperate to get the new law enacted after court rulings that would have adversely affected it without the legislation. In addition, after the bruising battles of 1995, GOP lawmakers were eager to adopt an election year environmental measure.[56]

The 1996 rewrite and reauthorization of the Safe Drinking Water Act sought to address many long-standing problems with the nation's drinking water program. It dealt more realistically with regulating contaminants based on their risk to public health and authorized $7 billion for state-administered loan and grant funds to help localities with compliance costs. It also created a new right-to-know provision that requires large water systems to provide their customers with annual reports on the safety of local water supplies. Bipartisan cooperation on the bill was made easier because it aided financially pressed state and local governments and, like the pesticide bill, allowed Republicans to score some election-year points with environmentalists.[57]

Brownfields, Healthy Forests, and Wilderness. Congress also completed action on a number of somewhat less visible issues that demonstrated its potential to fashion bipartisan compromises. In 2001, President Bush gained congressional approval of important legislation to reclaim so-called urban brownfields. House Republicans sought to reduce liability for small businesses under the Superfund program, and Democrats wanted to see contaminated and abandoned industrial sites in urban areas cleaned up.[58]

In a somewhat similar action in 2003, the 108th Congress approved the Healthy Forests Initiative over the objections of environmental groups. The measure was designed to permit increased logging in national forests, allegedly to lessen the risk of wildfires. Bipartisan concern over communities at risk from wildfires was sufficient for enactment. Wildfires struck Southern California only days before the Senate voted 80–14 to approve the bill.[59]

Finally, throughout 2007 and 2008, Congress considered a dozen proposals for setting aside large parcels of federal land for wilderness protection, totaling about two million acres in eight states, largely without significant media coverage. The measures were broadly supported within both parties, in part because environmentalists helped to build public support by working with opposing interests at the local level. Progress like this was also possible because of Democratic victories in the 2006 election, which switched control of the House Natural Resources Committee from Republican Richard Pombo of California to Democrat Nick J. Rahall of West Virginia. Pombo was a fierce opponent of such wilderness protection, and Rahall strongly favored it. Congress couldn't approve the wilderness bills in 2008, but by March 2009, in a more favorable political climate, they were approved as part of an Omnibus Public Land Management Act.[60]

National Energy Policy and Chemical Safety. In 2005, Congress finally enacted one of the Bush administration's priorities that the president had sought since 2001: the Energy Policy Act of 2005. It was the first major overhaul of U.S. energy policy since 1992. The original Bush energy plan, formulated in 2001 by a task force headed by Vice President Dick Cheney, called for an increase in the production and use of fossil fuels and nuclear energy, gave modest attention to the role of energy conservation, and sparked intense debate on Capitol Hill because of its emphasis on oil and gas drilling in ANWR. The Republican House quickly approved the measure in 2001, after what the press called "aggressive lobbying by the Bush administration, labor unions and the oil, gas, and coal industries."[61] The vote largely followed party lines.

Competing energy bills were debated on the Hill through mid-2005 without resolution and served as another prominent example of legislative gridlock. Neither side was prepared to compromise as lobbying by car manufacturers, labor unions, the oil and gas industry, and environmentalists continued. As one writer put it in 2002, the "debate between energy and the environment is important to core constituencies of both parties, the kind of loyal followers vital in a congressional election year."[62] Finally, the House and Senate reached agreement on an energy package, and the president signed the 1,700-page bill on August 8, 2005.[63] The thrust of the legislation remained largely what Bush and Cheney had sought in 2001, although the final measure included significant funding for energy research and development and other measures that Democrats had supported, such as new energy efficiency standards for federal office buildings and short-term tax credits for the purchase of hybrid vehicles.[64]

In 2007, Congress also approved the Energy Independence and Security Act of 2007, which set a national automobile fuel economy standard of 35 miles per gallon by 2020. In one of his most consequential acts, President Obama later negotiated with automakers to raise the fuel economy standard to 54.5 miles per gallon by 2025. However, the Trump administration announced in early 2017 that it would seek to revisit that rule with the aim of lowering the standards at the behest of the automakers who wanted to sell more trucks and SUVs, which were once again popular with buyers as gasoline prices remained low.

President Obama's economic stimulus measure, which Congress approved in February 2009, contained about $80 billion in spending, tax incentives, and loan guarantees, including funds for energy efficiency, renewable energy sources, mass transit, and technologies for the capture and storage of greenhouse gases produced by coal-fired power plants. Had these energy components been a stand-alone measure, the *New York Times* observed, they would have amounted to "the biggest energy bill in history." In this case, however, bipartisan cooperation was largely absent. In the end, only three Republicans in Congress, all in the Senate, voted for the bill.[65]

Similarly, after several years of partisan gridlock, in April 2016, the Senate approved a modest but bipartisan energy efficiency and electrical grid infrastructure measure, the Energy Policy Modernization Act, by a vote of 85 to 12. Republican Lisa Murkowski of Alaska and Democrat Maria Cantwell of Washington State had worked together for several years on the legislation. Nearly five months earlier, in December of 2015, the House had approved a companion bill. However, House Republicans attached a number of unrelated and controversial environmental policy provisions that eroded almost all Democratic support for the measure. As a result, the final House vote was 249 to 174, with only nine Democrats voting in favor. The Senate and House measures were so at odds that no compromise legislation could clear the 114th Congress. Murkowski vowed to reintroduce the bipartisan Senate bill in the 115th Congress.[66]

Successful bipartisanship was more in evidence during a significant reform of the widely criticized Toxic Substances Control Act (TSCA) of 1976. After years of unsuccessful efforts to modernize and strengthen the act, in 2016, Congress approved the Frank R. Lautenberg Chemical Safety for the 21st Century Act, a major revision of TSCA. The new act mandated that the EPA evaluate existing chemicals with a new risk-based safety standard, that it do so with clear and enforceable deadlines, with increased transparency for chemical information, and with assurances that the agency would have the budgetary resources to carry out its responsibilities for chemical safety.[67]

Continuing Partisan Conflict and Stalemate. The examples discussed previously and many more that could be cited, such as approval of a historic Great Lakes Compact in 2008 to prevent water diversion from the lakes and a new Higher Education Sustainability Act in 2008, show that over the past decade Congress has been able to move ahead on a wide range of environmental and natural resource policies.[68] Yet continuing partisan conflict has blocked action on key federal laws such as the Superfund program, the Endangered Species Act, the Clean Water Act, and the Clean Air Act, as well as on legislation to address climate change.

The Superfund program, for example, has not been reauthorized for well over two decades, and except for the brownfields measure discussed earlier, congressional agreement has not been forthcoming. The Endangered Species Act presents a similar level of conflict and lack of resolution. In 2001, then House Resources Committee chair James V. Hansen, R-Utah, captured the dilemma well: "We haven't reauthorized it because no one could agree on how to reform and modernize the law. Everyone agrees there are problems with the Act, but no one can agree on how to fix them."[69]

Climate change policy, of course, is something of a poster child for legislative gridlock. In 2009, the House approved a cap-and-trade bill, the American Clean Energy and Security Act of 2009, after extensive and prolonged negotiations and major concessions for the various industries likely to be affected by it. These included automakers, steel companies, natural gas drillers, oil refiners, utilities, and farmers, among others. The final vote was 219 to 212, with all but eight Republicans voting in opposition, along with forty-four Democrats. However, the Senate failed to pass comparable legislation, and Republicans won control of Congress in the 2010 elections, ending any prospect of a legislative solution to climate change. President Obama then had little choice but to pursue administrative solutions, such as the auto fuel economy rules and the EPA's Clean Power Plan.

Conclusion

The political struggles on Capitol Hill over the last several decades reveal sharply contrasting visions for environmental policy. The revolutionary rhetoric of the 104th Congress had dissipated by the 2000s, but it was replaced in the 2010s by similar views held by Tea Party Republicans, especially in the House Freedom Caucus, and then by a solidly conservative Republican majority in both houses following Donald Trump's election in 2016. From the mid-1990s through 2017, Congress was able to revise several major statutes in an uncommon display of bipartisan cooperation. Nonetheless, for many other environmental programs, policy gridlock continued to frustrate all participants, and deep partisan differences prevented emerging issues such as climate change from being addressed seriously and directly.

The election of President Obama did little to alter legislative prospects on the Hill, particularly after Republican gains in the 2010 and 2012 elections. The electoral success of Tea Party activists within the Republican Party led to heightened levels of ideological polarization and political conflict between the White House and Congress on both economic and environmental issues. The election of President Trump in 2016 solidified these political barriers to action. If anything, environmental policy debate became even more polarized, and partisan conflict largely prevented legislative action beyond congressional regulatory pullback and the defunding of agency programs.

Under these conditions, it is no surprise that, by 2017, public ratings of Congress remained near historic lows, with strong public disapproval of both parties. Moreover, Congress ranked at the very bottom in the public's confidence in American institutions, well below big business, newspapers, and television news, and far below the presidency and the courts.[70] The constitutional divisions between the House and Senate, and between Congress and the White House, guarantee that newly emergent forces, whether on the left or the right of the political spectrum, cannot easily push a particular legislative agenda. The 2016 elections did not change this outlook, and it is likely that the 2018 elections will not do so either, even if Democrats regain a majority in the House or Senate. Nor will it be easy for the next several Congresses to address the remaining environmental and energy challenges facing the nation and world, most notably climate change and the imperative of fostering sustainable development (see Chapter 15).

Yet the environmental policy battles of the past decade remind us that in the U.S. political system, effective policymaking will always require cooperation between the two branches and leadership within both to advance sensible policies and secure public approval for them. The public also has a role to play in these deliberations, and the history of congressional policymaking on the environment strongly suggests the power of public beliefs and action. Public disillusionment with government and politics today creates significant barriers to policy change that would serve the public's interest. However, at the same time, it facilitates the power of special interests to secure the changes that they desire, which may differ greatly from public preferences. Ultimately, the solution can be found only in a heightened awareness of the problems and active participation by the American public in the political process.

Suggested Websites

Environmental Protection Agency (www.epa.gov/epahome/rule.html) The EPA site for laws, rules, and regulations includes the full text of the dozen key laws administered by the EPA. It also has a link to current legislation before Congress.

League of Conservation Voters (www.lcv.org) The LCV compiles environmental voting records for all members of Congress.

Congress.gov (www.congress.gov) This site is one of the most comprehensive public sites available for legislative searches. See also www.house.gov and www.senate.gov for portals to the House and Senate and to the committee and individual member websites.

National Association of Manufacturers (www.nam.org) This leading business organization offers policy news, studies, and position statements on environmental issues, as well as extensive resources for public action on the issues.

Heritage Foundation (www.heritage.org) One of the most prominent and influential conservative think tanks, Heritage has strong ties to Republican members of Congress and issues frequent reports on a range of environmental, energy, and natural resource issues.

Natural Resources Defense Council (www.nrdc.org) The NRDC is perhaps the most active and influential of the national environmental groups that lobby Congress.

Sierra Club (www.sierraclub.org) The Sierra Club is one of the leading national environmental groups that track congressional legislative battles.

U.S. Chamber of Commerce (www.uschamber.com) The U.S. Chamber of Commerce is one of the nation's leading business organizations, and it frequently challenges legislative proposals that it believes may harm business interests.

Notes

1. Chairman Smith's remarks are from his statement to his House colleagues and can be found in full in his press release, "Statement of Chairman Lamar Smith (R-Texas), H.R. 1430, Honest and Open New EPA Science Treatment Act of 2017, March 9, 2017." Rep. Johnson's statement comes from Timothy Cama, "House Votes to Restrict EPA's Use of Science," *The Hill*, March 29, 2017.

2. Quoted in Marianna Brady, "House Votes to Restrict EPA's Use of Scientific Studies," *U.S. News and World Report*, March 29, 2017. At about the same time, the House also enacted the Regulatory Accountability Act of 2017, designed to streamline the regulatory process. Its fate in the Senate is as much in doubt as that of the HONEST Act. See Michael Grunwald, "The Coming GOP Assault on Regulations," *Politico*, March 10, 2017. On the overwhelming scientific consensus on climate change, see John Cook, Naomi Oreskes, Peter T. Doran, William R. L. Anderegg, Bart Verheggen, Ed W. Maibach, J. Stuart Carlton, et al., "Consensus on Consensus: A Synthesis of Consensus Estimates on Human-Caused Global Warming," *Environmental Research Letters* 11, no. 4 (2016): 1–7.

3. See David Malakoff, "A Battle over the 'Best Science,'" *Science*, March 17, 2017, 1108–9.

4. See, for example, Leslie Kaufman, "Republicans Seek Big Cuts in Environmental Rules," *New York Times*, July 27, 2011; Robert B. Semple Jr., "Concealed Weapons against the Environment," *New York Times*, July 31, 2011; and Paul Kane, "House GOP Revs Up a Repeal, Reduce and Rein-in Agenda for the Fall," *Washington Post*, August 28, 2011.

5. See, for example, Juliet Eilperin and Abby Phillip, "Trump to Direct Rollback of Obama-Era Water Rule Tuesday," *Washington Post*, February 27, 2017; Michelle Ye Hee Lee, "Trump's Claim that Waters of the United States Rule Cost 'Hundreds of Thousands' of Jobs," *New York Times*, March 2, 2017; and Coral Davenport, "Trump Lays Plans to Reverse Obama's Climate Change Legacy," *New York Times*, March 21, 2017.

6. See Daniel J. Fiorino, *The New Environmental Regulation* (Cambridge, MA: MIT Press, 2006); Marc Allen Eisner, *Governing the Environment: The Transformation of Environmental Regulation* (Boulder, CO: Lynne Rienner, 2007); and Daniel A. Mazmanian and Michael E. Kraft, eds., *Toward Sustainable Communities: Transition and Transformation in Environmental Policy*, 2nd ed. (Cambridge, MA: MIT Press, 2009).

7. See Eric Schickler and Kathryn Pearson, "The House Leadership in an Era of Partisan Warfare," in *Congress Reconsidered*, 8th ed., ed. Lawrence C. Dodd and Bruce I. Oppenheimer (Washington, DC: CQ Press, 2005), 207–26. See also Thomas E. Mann and Norman J. Ornstein, *The Broken Branch: How Congress Is Failing America and How to Get It Back on Track* (New York: Oxford University Press, 2006).

8. See Chapter 1 in this volume and Michael E. Kraft, "Congress and Environmental Policy," in *The Oxford Handbook of U.S. Environmental Policy*, ed. Sheldon Kamieniecki and Michael E. Kraft (New York: Oxford University Press, 2013), 280–305.

9. Ed Gillespie and Bob Schellhas, eds., *Contract with America* (New York: Times Books/Random House, 1994); Bob Benenson, "GOP Sets the 104th Congress on New Regulatory Course," *Congressional Quarterly Weekly Report*, June 17, 1995, 1693–705.

10. For a general review of much of this period, see Lawrence C. Dodd and Bruce I. Oppenheimer, "A Decade of Republican Control: The House of Representatives, 1995–2005," in *Congress Reconsidered*, 8th ed., ed. Lawrence C. Dodd and Bruce I. Oppenheimer (Washington, DC: CQ Press, 2005), 23–54.

11. See Mazmanian and Kraft, *Toward Sustainable Communities*; Eisner, *Governing the Environment*; Christopher McGrory Klyza and David Sousa, *American Environmental Policy: Beyond Gridlock*, updated and expanded edition (Cambridge, MA: MIT Press, 2013); and Robert F. Durant, Daniel J. Fiorino, and Rosemary O'Leary, eds., *Environmental Governance Reconsidered: Challenges, Choices, and Opportunities*, 2nd ed. (Cambridge, MA: MIT Press, 2017).

12. For a general analysis of roles that Congress plays in the U.S. political system, see Roger H. Davidson, Walter J. Oleszek, Frances E. Lee, and Eric Schickler, *Congress and Its Members*, 15th ed. (Thousand Oaks, CA: CQ Press, 2016).

13. "Republican EPA Chiefs to Congress: Act on Climate," Associated Press, June 18, 2014. See also William D. Ruckelshaus, Lee M. Thomas, William K. Reilly, and Christine Todd Whitman, "A Republican Case for Climate Action," *New York Times*, August 1, 2013.

14. See Juliet Eilperin, Chris Mooney, and Steven Mufson, "New EPA Documents Reveal Even Deeper Proposed Cuts to Staff and Programs," *Washington Post*, March 31, 2017; Oliver Milman, "Trump Budget Would Gut EPA Programs Tackling Climate Change and Pollution," *The Guardian*, U.S. Edition, March 16, 2017; and David Malakoff and Warren Cornwall, "Trump Targets Environmental Science for Cuts," *Science* 355, March 10, 2017, 1000–1001. On the congressional decision not to cut the EPA's budget as Trump proposed, see James Hohmann, "The Daily 202: Eight Ways Trump Got Rolled in His First Budget Negotiation," *Washington Post*, May 1, 2017.

15. Chris Mooney, "NOAA Challenged the Global Warming 'Pause.' Now New Research Says the Agency Was Right," *Washington Post*, January 4, 2017; Lisa Rein, "Meet the House Science Chairman Who's Trying to Put Global Warming Research on Ice," *Washington Post*, December 22, 2015.

16. Rein, "Meet the House Science Chairman."

17. See Coral Davenport, "E.P.A. Official Pressured Scientist on Congressional Testimony, Emails Show," *New York Times*, June 26, 2017.

18. See Brady Dennis and Chris Mooney, "Senate Republicans Suspend Committee Rules to Approve Scott Pruitt, Trump's EPA Nominee, *Washington Post*, February 2, 2017; Coral Davenport, "Scott Pruitt, Trump's E.P.A. Pick, Is Approved by Senate Committee," *New York Times*, February 2, 2017; and Brady Dennis and Juliet Eilperin, "Hundreds of Current, Former EPA Employees Urge Senate to Reject Trump's Nominee for the Agency," *Washington Post*, February 6, 2017.

19. Kraft, "Congress and Environmental Policy."

20. Davidson, Oleszek, Lee, and Schickler, *Congress and Its Members*. See also Gary C. Jacobson, *The Politics of Congressional Elections*, 9th ed. (New York: Rowman and Littlefield, 2016).

21. Carl Hulse, "Consensus on Energy Bill Arose One Project at a Time," *New York Times*, November 19, 2003. The energy bill, which ultimately was approved as the Energy Policy Act of 2005, is summarized in Michael E. Kraft, *Environmental Policy and Politics*, 7th ed. (New York: Routledge, 2018), Chapter 6.

140   Michael E. Kraft

22. See John M. Broder, "At House E.P.A. Hearing, Both Sides Claim Science," *New York Times*, March 8, 2011; and Juliet Eilperin and Brady Dennis, "How James Inhofe Is Upending the Nation's Energy and Environmental Policies," *Washington Post*, March 14, 2017.

23. Charles M. Blow, "The Do-Even-Less Congress," *New York Times*, August 3, 2014.

24. On the general idea of policy drift and failure to reform key public policies, see Jacob S. Hacker and Paul Pierson, *Winner-Take-All Politics: How Washington Made the Rich Richer—and Turned Its Back on the Middle Class* (New York: Simon and Schuster, 2010).

25. On the role of administrative agencies and the courts in policy change, see Klyza and Sousa, *American Environmental Policy*.

26. One of the few scholarly analyses of the subject is Sarah A. Binder, *Stalemate: Causes and Consequences of Legislative Gridlock* (Washington, DC: Brookings Institution Press, 2003). Aside from what the chapter covers, other factors also affect legislative gridlock today. Among them are the constitutional specification that the Senate be composed of two senators for each state (thus giving small and often conservative states an oversized representation in that body), the effects of legislative redistricting or gerrymandering that can distort the public's partisan preferences, and the weak national laws on campaign financing in the wake of the Supreme Court's *Citizens United v. FEC* decision. Even the filibuster in the Senate plays a role; it prevents the majority party from taking action without the sixty votes needed to overcome frequent filibusters by the minority party.

27. See, for example, several of the chapters on the electoral foundation of congressional gridlock in Nathaniel Persily, ed., *Solutions to Political Polarization in America* (New York: Cambridge University Press, 2015). See also James A. Thurber and Antoine Yoshinaka, eds., *American Gridlock: The Sources, Character, and Impact of Political Polarization* (New York: Cambridge University Press, 2015); and Jeffery A. Jenkins and Eric M. Patashnik, eds., *Congress and Policy Making in the 21st Century* (New York: Cambridge University Press, 2016).

28. This was one of the more important conclusions about constituency influence on congressional voting John Kingdon reached in his influential *Congressmen's Voting Decisions*, 3rd ed. (Ann Arbor: University of Michigan Press, 1989). For one of the most thorough studies of public opinion on the environment, see David P. Daniels, Jon A. Krosnick, Michael P. Tichy, and Trevor Tompson, "Public Opinion on Environmental Policy in the United States," in *The Oxford Handbook of U.S. Environmental Policy*, ed. Sheldon Kamieniecki and Michael E. Kraft (New York: Oxford University Press, 2013), 461–86.

29. Studies show that members of Congress generally do vote in a way that is consistent with their campaign promises on environmental issues but that Republicans are "far more likely to break their campaign promises" and that pro-environmental campaign promises are more likely to be broken than are others. See Evan J. Ringquist and Carl Dasse, "Lies, Damned Lies, and Campaign Promises? Environmental Legislation in the 105th Congress," *Social Science Quarterly* 85 (June 2004): 400–19. The quotation is from p. 417. See also Evan J. Ringquist, Milena I. Neshkova, and Joseph Aamidor, "Campaign Promises, Democratic Governance, and Environmental Policy in the U.S. Congress," *Policy Studies Journal* 41, no. 2 (2013): 365–87.

30. See David Bornstein, "Cracking Washington's Gridlock to Save the Planet," *New York Times*, May 19, 2017. Recent polls document the continued low saliency of environmental issues, including climate change, even though the public favors many policy actions on climate change and has for several years, according to both the Gallup poll and the Yale Project on Climate Change Communication. For example, a survey that the Yale center

conducted with George Mason University just after the November 2016 election found that 78 percent of the public supported taxing global warming pollution, regulating it, or using both approaches. Only one in ten was opposed. Some 70 percent of registered voters supported setting strict carbon dioxide emission limits on existing coal-fired power plants, even if the cost of electricity increased. Even 62 percent of Trump voters supported taxing and/or regulating pollution that causes global warming. See Anthony Leiserowitz, Edward Maibach, Connie Roser-Renouf, Seth Rosenthal and Matthew Cutler, *Politics & Global Warming, November 2016.* (New Haven, CT: Yale Program on Climate Change Communication, 2016). The report is available at http://climatecommunication.yale.edu/publications/politics-global-warming-november-2016/2/.

31. See, for example, Nolan McCarty, Keith Poole, and Howard Rosenthal, *Polarized America: The Dance of Ideology and Unequal Riches* (Cambridge, MA: MIT Press, 2008); and Persily, *Solutions to Political Polarization in America.*

32. See Charles R. Shipan and William R. Lowry, "Environmental Policy and Party Divergence in Congress," *Political Research Quarterly* 54 (June 2001): 245–63. See also Amy Below, "Parties, Campaigns, and Elections," in *The Oxford Handbook of U.S. Environmental Policy*, ed. Sheldon Kamieniecki and Michael E. Kraft (New York: Oxford University Press, 2013), 525–49.

33. See the League of Conservation Voters (LCV), *National Environmental Scorecard* (Washington, DC: LCV, 2016). The scorecard is published annually at the league's website (www.lcv.org); the party averages are taken from Marianne Lavelle, "Partisan Divide in Congress Wider Than Ever on Environmental Issues, Group Says," *Inside-Climate News*, February 23, 2017. For a detailed examination of these patterns over time, see Riley E. Dunlap, Aaron M. McCright, and Jerrod H. Yarosh, "The Political Divide on Climate Change: Partisan Polarization Widens in the U.S." *Environment* 58, no. 5 (September/October 2016): 4–22.

34. See Aaron M. McCright, Chenyang Xiao, and Riley E. Dunlap, "Political Polarization on Support for Government Spending on Environmental Protection in the USA, 1974–2012," *Social Science Research* 48 (2014): 251–60.

35. Mary Etta Cook and Roger H. Davidson, "Deferral Politics: Congressional Decision Making on Environmental Issues in the 1980s," in *Public Policy and the Natural Environment*, ed. Helen M. Ingram and R. Kenneth Godwin (Greenwich, CT: JAI, 1985). See also Norman J. Vig and Michael E. Kraft, eds., *Environmental Policy in the 1980s: Reagan's New Agenda* (Washington, DC: CQ Press, 1984); and Michael E. Kraft and Norman J. Vig, "Environmental Policy in the Reagan Presidency," *Political Science Quarterly* 99, no. 3 (Fall 1984): 415–39.

36. For a fuller discussion of the gridlock over clean air legislation, see Gary C. Bryner, *Blue Skies, Green Politics: The Clean Air Act of 1990 and Its Implementation* (Washington, DC: CQ Press, 1995).

37. Rhodes Cook, "Rare Combination of Forces May Make History of '94," *Congressional Quarterly Weekly Report*, April 15, 1995, 1076–81.

38. Katharine Q. Seelye, "Files Show How Gingrich Laid a Grand G.O.P. Plan," *New York Times*, December 3, 1995. On the broader history of conservative and business campaigns against environmental policy, see Judith A. Layzer, *Open for Business: Conservatives' Opposition to Environmental Regulation* (Cambridge, MA: MIT Press, 2012). For a somewhat parallel development in recent years to discredit climate change, see Riley E. Dunlap and Aaron M. McCright, "Challenging Climate Change: The Denial Countermovement," in *Climate Change and Society: Sociological Perspectives*, ed. R. E. Dunlap and R. J. Brulle (New York: Oxford University Press, 2015), 300–32.

39. Groups such as Americans for Prosperity, part of what is often termed the "Koch Network," have been influential as well as major contributors to congressional campaigns, and they have emphasized an antienvironmental and pro-fossil fuels agenda at odds with public preferences for environmental protection and action on climate change. See Eric Lipton, "G.O.P. Hurries to Slash Oil and Gas Rules, Ending Industries' 8-Year Wait," *New York Times*, February 4, 2017; and Theda Skocpol and Alexander Hertel-Fernandez, "The Koch Network and Republican Party Extremism," *Perspectives on Politics*, 14, no. 3 (September 2016): 681–99.

40. Everett Carll Ladd, "The 1994 Congressional Elections: The Postindustrial Realignment Continues," *Political Science Quarterly* 110 (Spring 1995): 1–23; Alfred J. Tuchfarber, Stephen E. Bennett, Andrew E. Smith, and Eric W. Rademacher, "The Republican Tidal Wave of 1994: Testing Hypotheses about Realignment, Restructuring, and Rebellion," *PS: Political Science and Politics* 28 (December 1995): 689–96.

41. Allan Freedman, "GOP's Secret Weapon against Regulations: Finesse," *CQ Weekly*, September 5, 1998, 2314–20; and Charles Pope, "Environmental Bills Hitch a Ride through the Legislative Gantlet," *CQ Weekly*, April 4, 1998, 872–75.

42. See Fiorino, *The New Environmental Regulation*; and Eisner, *Governing the Environment*.

43. See Sara R. Rinfret and Scott R. Furlong, "Defining Environmental Rulemaking," in *The Oxford Handbook of Environmental Policy*, ed. Sheldon Kamieniecki and Michael E. Kraft (New York: Oxford University, 2013), 372–94.

44. See Michael E. Kraft and Sheldon Kamieniecki, eds., *Business and Environmental Policy: Corporate Interests in the American Political System* (Cambridge, MA: MIT Press, 2007).

45. See Jackie Calmes, "Both Sides of the Aisle Say More Regulation, and Not Just of Banks," *New York Times*, October 14, 2008.

46. On the broad regulatory reform actions in Congress in 2017, see William W. Buzbee, "Regulatory 'Reform' That Is Anything But," *New York Times*, June 15, 2017.

47. David Malakoff, "Republicans Ready a Regulatory Rollback," *Science* 354 (November 25, 2016): 951; and Philip A. Wallach and Nicholas W. Zeppos, "Is the Congressional Review Act About to Supercharge Deregulation?" *FIXGOV* [blog of Brookings Institution], April 4, 2017. The quotation is from Juliette Eilperin, "Trump Undertakes Most Ambitious Regulatory Rollback Since Reagan," *Washington Post*, February 12, 2017. See also Michael Grunwald, "Trump's Secret Weapon Against Obama's Legacy," *Politico*, April 10, 2017.

48. Michael D. Shear, "Trump Discards Obama Legacy, One Rule at a Time," *New York Times*, May 1, 2017.

49. John H. Cushman Jr., "G.O.P.'s Plan for Environment Is Facing a Big Test in Congress," *New York Times*, July 17, 1995.

50. Semple, "Concealed Weapons against the Environment."

51. Pope, "Environmental Bills Hitch a Ride."

52. Andrew Revkin, "Law Revises Standards for Scientific Study," *New York Times*, March 21, 2002. See also Rick Weiss, "'Data Quality' Law Is Nemesis of Regulation," *Washington Post*, August 16, 2004; and Paul Raeburn, "A Regulation on Regulations," *Scientific American*, July 2006, 18–19. Raeburn reported that by 2006, perhaps one hundred Data Quality Act petitions had been filed with dozens of different government agencies, most of them by industry groups.

53. Susan Zakin, "Riders from Hell," *Amicus Journal* (Spring 2001): 20–22.

54. Carroll J. Doherty and the staff of *CQ Weekly*, "Congress Compiles a Modest Record in a Session Sidetracked by Scandal: Appropriations," *CQ Weekly*, November 14, 1998, 3086–87 and 3090–91.

55. Jeffrey Mervis and the *Science* News Staff, "Congress Trumps President in Backing Science," *Science* 356 (May 5, 2017): 470–71. See also Lewis M. Milford and Mark Muro, "A Senate Panel Speaks for Sound Clean Energy Policy—and Rebukes Trump," Brookings Institution, August 8, 2017, available at www.brookings.edu/blog/the-avenue/2017/08/08/a-senate-rebukes-trump/.

56. David Hosansky, "Rewrite of Laws on Pesticides on Way to President's Desk," *Congressional Quarterly Weekly Report*, July 27, 1996, 2101–03; Hosansky, "Provisions: Pesticide, Food Safety Law," *Congressional Quarterly Weekly Report*, September 7, 1996, 2546–50.

57. David Hosansky, "Drinking Water Bill Clears; Clinton Expected to Sign," *Congressional Quarterly Weekly Report*, August 3, 1996, 2179–80; Allan Freedman, "Provisions: Safe Drinking Water Act Amendments," *Congressional Quarterly Weekly Report*, September 14, 1996, 2622–27.

58. Rebecca Adams, "Pressure from White House and Hastert Pries Brownfields Bill from Committee," *CQ Weekly*, September 8, 2001, 2065–66.

59. Mary Clare Jalonick, "Healthy Forests Initiative Provisions," *CQ Weekly*, January 24, 2004, 246–47.

60. Juliet Eilperin, "Keeping the Wilderness Untamed: Bills in Congress Could Add as Much as Two Million Acres of Unspoiled Land to Federal Control," *Washington Post* (National edition), June 23–July 6, 2008, 35; and Avery Palmer, "Long-Stalled Lands Bill Gets Nod from Senate," *CQ Weekly*, January 19, 2009, 128.

61. Chuck McCutcheon, "House Passage of Bush Energy Plan Sets Up Clash with Senate," *CQ Weekly*, August 4, 2001, 1915–17.

62. Rebecca Adams, "Politics Stokes Energy Debate," *CQ Weekly*, January 12, 2002, 108.

63. Carl Hulse, "House Votes to Approve Broad Energy Legislation," *New York Times*, April 22, 2005.

64. See Ben Evans and Joseph J. Schatz, "Details of Energy Policy Law," *CQ Weekly*, September 5, 2005, 2337–45.

65. Editorial, "An $80 Billion Start," *New York Times*, February 18, 2009.

66. See Editorial Board, "An Energy Bill in Need of Fixes, *New York Times*, April 20, 2016.

67. See Coral Davenport and Emmarie Huetteman, "Lawmakers Reach Deal to Expand Regulation of Toxic Chemicals," *New York Times*, May 19, 2016.

68. The education act was part of the Higher Education Opportunity Act of 2008. It authorized competitive grants to institutions and associations in higher education to promote the development of sustainability curricula, programs, and practices. It was the first new federal environmental education program in eighteen years.

69. Cited in *Science and Environmental Policy Update*, the Ecological Society of America online newsletter, April 20, 2001.

70. The Gallup poll reports regularly on the public's approval of Congress and its trust and confidence in governmental and other institutions. In mid-2017, only 20 percent approved of "the job that Congress is doing," while 74 percent disapproved. See "Congress and the Public," at www.gallup.com/poll/1600/congress-public.aspx, and "Confidence in Institutions," at www.gallup.com/poll/1597/confidence-institutions.aspx.

Chapter 6

Environmental Policy in the Courts

Rosemary O'Leary

In 1966, on one of her frequent trips to a family cabin in rural upstate New York, Carol Yannacone was shocked to find hundreds of dead fish floating on the surface of Yaphank Lake, where she had spent her summers as a child. After discovering that the county had sprayed the foliage surrounding the lake with DDT to kill mosquitoes immediately prior to the fish kill, Yannacone persuaded her lawyer husband to file suit on her behalf against the county mosquito control commission. The suit requested an injunction to halt the spraying of pesticides containing DDT around the lake.

Although Carol Yannacone and her husband initially were able to win only a one-year injunction, they set into motion a chain of events that would permanently change environmental policy in the courts. It was through this lawsuit that a group of environmentalists and scientists formed the Environmental Defense Fund (EDF), a nonprofit group dedicated to promoting change in environmental policy through legal action. After eight years of protracted litigation, the EDF won a court battle against the U.S. Environmental Protection Agency (EPA) that Judge David Bazelon heralded as the beginning of "a new era in the . . . long and fruitful collaboration of administrative agencies and reviewing courts."[1] That judicial decision triggered a permanent suspension in the United States of the registration of pesticides containing DDT.

Fast forward to 2017. Newly elected President Donald Trump quickly became fully aware of the concept of environmental policymaking in the courts as these headlines portray:

Environmental Groups Sue Trump Administration Over Offshore Drilling[2]

The Battle Against Trump's Assault on Climate Is Moving to the Courts[3]

Environmental Groups Sue Trump Administration for Approving Keystone Pipeline[4]

Trump's Environmental Assault Met with Immediate Legal Challenges[5]

Donald Trump Is Fueling an Explosion of New Lawsuits[6]

Environmentalists Flood the Courts with Lawsuits to Stop Trump's Agenda[7]

The Court Standing Between Trump and Environmental Deregulation[8]

At the same time, the Trump administration itself has been a savvy user of courts to change environmental policy. For example, in 2017, in response to a request by the Trump administration, the U.S. Court of Appeals for the District of Columbia deferred ruling on litigation challenging the Clean Power Plan developed by the Obama administration, legislation aimed at combating climate change. In 2016, the Supreme Court, in a 5 to 4 decision, had ordered the EPA to halt enforcement of the plan until a lower court ruled in the lawsuit against the plan.[9] By stalling the decision of the lower court for 60 days, the Trump administration was given an easier road toward dismantling the policy.

Both in legal analyses and in "dicta" (remarks or observations made by a judge in a decision), courts are an integral part of environmental policy-making. An important aspect of environmental conflicts, however, is that multiple forums exist for decision making. Litigation is by no means the only way to resolve environmental disputes. Most environmental conflicts never reach a court, and an estimated 50 to 90 percent of those that do are settled out of court. Discussion and debate are informal ways of resolving environmental conflict. Enacting legislation is another way to deal with such conflict. Environmental conflict resolution approaches, ranging from collaborative problem solving to mediation, are becoming more common in environmental policy.

The focus of this chapter, however, is environmental policy in the courts. First, a profile of the U.S. court system and a primer on the judicial review of agency actions are offered. Next, the focus changes to how courts shape environmental policy, with several in-depth case analyses provided. The chapter concludes with a view to the future.

The Organization and Operation of the U.S. Court System

If we are to understand environmental policy in the courts, a brief profile of the U.S. court system is essential. The United States has a dual court system, with different cases starting either in federal court or in state or county court. This section describes the organization of the U.S. court system (Figure 6-1). As you read it, keep in mind that most legal disputes never go to court (they are resolved through one of the informal methods mentioned in the introduction to this chapter).

When legal disputes do go to court, most are resolved in state courts. Many of these disputes are criminal or domestic controversies. They usually start in trial courts and are heard by a judge and sometimes a jury. If the case is lost at the trial court level, appeal to an intermediate court of appeals is possible. At this level, the appeals court usually reviews only questions of law, not fact. If a party to a case is not satisfied with the outcome at the intermediate level, then the party may appeal to the state supreme court. In cases involving federal questions, final appeal to the U.S. Supreme Court is possible, but the court has wide discretion as to which cases it will review.

Most of the environmental cases discussed in this chapter began in the federal court system because they concerned interpretations of federal statutes or the Constitution. Cases that begin in the federal court system usually begin

Figure 6-1   The Dual Court System

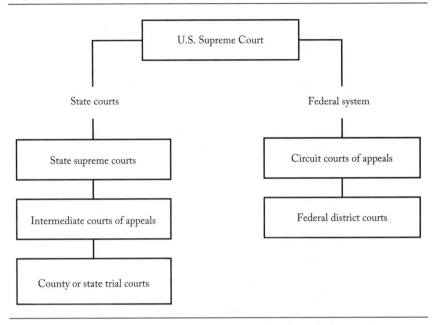

in the federal district courts. There are ninety-four federal district courts staffed by approximately 677 active judges. (There are also so-called specialty courts such as the U.S. bankruptcy courts, the U.S. Court of Appeals for the Armed Forces, and the U.S. Court of Federal Claims. There are also tribal courts.)

Some statutes, however, provide for an appeal of the decisions of federal regulatory agencies directly to the federal courts of appeals rather than through district courts. These cases, coupled with appeals from federal district courts, make for a full docket for the federal courts of appeals. There are thirteen federal circuit courts of appeals with about 179 active judges in total. Here, judges sit in groups of three when deciding cases. When there are conflicting opinions among the lower federal district courts within a circuit, all the judges of the circuit will sit together and hear a case. An unsatisfactory outcome in a circuit court can be appealed to the U.S. Supreme Court. Usually, less than 10 percent of the requests for Supreme Court review are granted.

Sources of Law

The decisions of appellate courts are considered precedent. Precedent is judge-made law that guides and informs subsequent court decisions involving similar or analogous situations. But precedent is only one of several sources of environmental law. The major sources of environmental law are as follows:

- Constitutions (federal and state)
- Statutes (federal, state, and local)
- Administrative regulations (promulgated by administrative agencies)
- Treaties (signed by the president and ratified by the Senate)
- Executive orders (proclamations issued by presidents or governors)
- Appellate court decisions

Judicial Review of Agency Actions

One of the pivotal issues in environmental law today is the scope of judicial review of an agency's action. The purpose of judicial review of administrative decision making generally is to ensure at least minimum levels of fairness. It has been said that the scope of review for a specific administrative decision may range from 0 to 100 percent, meaning that depending on the issue in question, a reviewing court may have broad or narrow powers to decide a case—or authority somewhere in between.

When an agency makes a decision, it usually does three things. First, it interprets the law in question. Second, it collects facts concerning a particular situation. Third, it uses its discretionary power to apply the law to the facts. A court's review of an agency's actions in each of these three steps is very different. (At the same time, it must be acknowledged that separating an agency's actions into three categories can be difficult, as in instances when there are mixed questions of law and fact.)

An agency's *interpretation of the law* usually demands a strong examination by a reviewing court. When constitutional issues are of concern, judges will rarely defer to administrative interpretations. However, when an agency's interpretation of its own regulation is at issue, it is said that deference is "even more clearly in order."[10] The general practice is that a court will give less deference to an agency's legal conclusions than to its factual or discretionary decisions.

At the same time, courts have shown deference to administrative interpretations of the law. The signature case that illustrates this point is *Chevron U.S.A., Inc. v. Natural Resources Defense Council*,[11] which concerned the EPA's "bubble concept" pursuant to the Clean Air Act. Under the bubble concept, the EPA allows states to adopt a plant-wide definition of the term *stationary source*. Under this definition, an existing plant that contained several pollution-emitting devices could install or modify one piece of equipment without meeting the permit conditions, if the alteration did not increase the total emissions from the plant. This allowed a state to treat all of the pollution-emitting sources within the same industrial group as if they were encased in a single bubble. Environmentalists sued the EPA, asserting that this definition of a stationary source violated the Clean Air Act. In a unanimous decision, the Supreme Court held that the EPA's plant-wide definition was permissible. The Supreme Court's opinion is now referred to as the *Chevron* doctrine. It holds that, when Congress has spoken clearly to the precise question at issue, the rule of law demands agency adherence to its intent. However, if Congress has not addressed the matter precisely, then an agency may adopt any reasonable interpretation—regardless of whether a reviewing court may consider some other interpretation more reasonable or sensible. As such, the *Chevron* doctrine is often thought of as making it more difficult for courts to overrule agency interpretations.

In 2017, newly appointed Supreme Court Justice Neil Gorsuch argued in his confirmation hearings that *Chevron* was decided incorrectly. Judge Gorsuch had previously denounced *Chevron* deference in a 2016 court of appeals decision as "a judge-made doctrine for the abdication of the judicial duty."[12] His rationale centered on Article III of the U.S. Constitution, which gives the judiciary the power to decide "all cases, in law and equity, arising under this Constitution, the laws of the United States, and treaties made, or which shall be made, under their authority." Nowhere in the Constitution is it written that courts should defer to administrative agencies, Gorsuch argued. To date, *Chevron* is still good law, but many are fearful that it will be overturned. Ironically, some anti-Trump advocates want *Chevron* to be overturned, arguing that stronger judicial scrutiny of Trump administration actions is needed.

An agency's *fact finding* usually demands less scrutiny by reviewing courts than do legal issues. Although an agency's decision may be reversed if it is unwarranted by the facts, courts generally acknowledge that agencies are in a better position to ascertain facts than is a reviewing court.

Judicial review of an agency's *discretionary powers* is usually deferential to a point, while maintaining an important oversight role for the courts. A court usually will make sure the agency has done a careful job of collecting and analyzing information, taking a hard look at the important issues and facts.

Even if a reviewing court decides that the agency correctly understood the law involved and concludes that the agency's view of the facts was reasonable, it may still negate the decision if the agency's activity is found to be "arbitrary, capricious, an abuse of discretion, or otherwise not in accordance with the law."[13] This can involve legal, factual, or discretionary issues. This type of review has been called several things: a rational basis review, an arbitrariness review, and an abuse of discretion review.

How Courts Shape Environmental Policy

As they decide environmental cases to ensure minimum levels of fairness, courts shape environmental policy in many ways. First, the courts determine who does or does not have standing, or the right, to sue. Although many environmental statutes give citizens, broadly defined, the right to sue polluters or regulators,[14] procedural hurdles must still be cleared in order for individuals or groups to gain access to the courts. Plaintiffs usually must demonstrate injury in fact, which is often not clear-cut and is subject to interpretation by judges. By controlling who may sue, courts affect the environmental policy agenda.

Second, and related to the first power, courts shape environmental policy by deciding which cases are ripe, or ready, for review. For a case to be justiciable, an actual controversy must exist. The alleged wrong must be more than merely anticipated. To decide whether an issue is ripe for judicial review, courts will examine both the fitness of the issue for judicial decision and the hardship on the parties if a court withholds consideration. Deciding which cases are ripe and which are not makes the courts powerful gatekeepers.

A third way in which courts shape environmental policy is by their choice of standard of review. Will the court, for example, take a hard look at the actions of public environmental officials in this particular case, or will it defer to the administrative expertise of the agency? Under what conditions will government environmental experts be deemed to have exceeded their legislative or constitutional authority? To what standards will polluters be held?

A fourth way in which courts shape environmental policy is by interpreting environmental laws. Courts interpret statutes, administrative rules and regulations, executive orders, treaties, constitutions, and prior court decisions. Often these laws are ambiguous and vague. Situations may arise that the laws' drafters did not anticipate. Hence, judicial interpretation becomes of paramount importance. And given the precedent-setting nature of court orders, a judicial interpretation made today may determine not only current environmental policy but also that of the future.

A final major way in which courts shape environmental policy is through the remedies they choose. Will the court, for example, order a punitive fine for polluters or probation? Judges generally have great discretion in their choice of remedy, thus affecting environmental policy.

The Supreme Court, the final arbiter of many precedent-setting environmental cases, shapes environmental policy primarily through the selection of cases it chooses to hear, the limits it places on other branches of government, and the limits it places on the states. Justices' values, ideological backgrounds, and policy preferences at times influence the outcome of environmental court decisions. Thus the implications of courts shaping environmental policy are formidable, and one may easily see why environmental advocates, concerned citizens, and big businesses often use lawsuits as tools to force policy changes in public environment and natural resource agencies. The cases discussed in the sections that follow paint a vivid portrait of environmental policymaking in the courts.

Standing to Sue: The Case of Global Warming

On October 12, 2007, Al Gore was awarded the Nobel Peace Prize for his campaign to curb global climate change. Gore shared the prize with the UN Intergovernmental Panel on Climate Change, whose head, Rajendra Pachauri, told leaders at a climate conference in Indonesia that a well-documented rise in global temperatures has coincided with a significant increase in the concentration of carbon dioxide in the atmosphere. "Heed the wisdom of science,"

Pachauri told conference participants on behalf of the UN, as scientists believe the two trends are related. When carbon dioxide is released into the atmosphere, it acts like the ceiling of a greenhouse, trapping solar energy and retarding the escape of reflected heat.

In 1999, eight years before Gore received the Nobel Peace Prize, the International Center for Technology Assessment joined other parties in petitioning the EPA to set standards for four greenhouse gases emitted by new motor vehicles: carbon dioxide, methane, nitrous oxide, and hydrofluorocarbons. The petition argued that these greenhouse gases are air pollutants and that scientists had concluded that global warming will endanger public health and the environment. Hence, the petition argued, the EPA is obligated to regulate greenhouse gas emissions from new mobile sources.

The EPA refused to regulate greenhouse gases, citing several reasons: First, the EPA said that the Clean Air Act "does not authorize regulation to address global climate change."[15] Tied in with this, the agency maintained that air pollutants associated with climate change "are not air pollutants under the [act's] regulatory provisions."[16] Moreover, the EPA stated that it disagreed with the regulatory approach urged by the petitioners and that it would not be "effective or appropriate for EPA to establish [greenhouse gas] standards for motor vehicles" at this time.[17] Instead, the EPA chose to encourage voluntary actions to curb emissions through incentives for more technological development.

The agency noted that "the science of climate change is extraordinarily complex and still evolving."[18] The agency also said that since many sources of air pollutants were associated with global climate change, to regulate only pollutants emitted by new motor vehicles would "result in an inefficient, piecemeal approach to addressing the climate change issue."[19] The agency concluded that it is the president's prerogative to address global climate change as an important foreign policy issue.

The petitioners appealed the EPA's decision to the U.S. Court of Appeals for the District of Columbia Circuit. That court split three different ways, with the majority ruling in favor of the EPA.[20] In 2006, the Supreme Court agreed to review the case, *Massachusetts v. Environmental Protection Agency*,[21] focusing on whether the EPA had authority to regulate greenhouse gases under the Clean Air Act and whether it could decline to exercise that authority based on policy considerations not mentioned in the statute.[22] One of the pivotal issues the Supreme Court had to grapple with in the case was whether the plaintiffs—the state of Massachusetts as well as other states, local governments, and nonprofit environmental advocacy groups—had standing to sue. The Supreme Court has ruled consistently that, to have standing to sue, a party must demonstrate injury—in fact, "a concrete and particularized, actual or imminent invasion of a legally protected interest."[23] In federal cases, this requirement arises out of the U.S. Constitution's "case or controversy" requirement.[24] In response, the EPA, supported by another group of states paired with six trade associations, countered that the plaintiffs did not have standing to sue. The EPA and its supporters maintained that because greenhouse gas emissions inflict widespread harm, the doctrine of standing presents an insurmountable obstacle. They argued that those who filed the lawsuit did not have a personal stake in the outcome of the controversy; specifically, they could not demonstrate a particularized injury, actual or imminent, traceable to the defendant, as precedent requires. They also argued that the EPA's decision not to regulate greenhouse gas emissions from new motor vehicles contributed so insignificantly to any alleged injuries that the agency could not be made to answer for them.

On April 2, 2007, the Supreme Court disagreed with the EPA, siding with the state of Massachusetts, its partner states and local governments, and environmental advocates. Only one plaintiff needs to show standing, the court said, and the state of Massachusetts clearly demonstrated a stake in the outcome of the controversy, given the projected rise in sea levels predicted to come from global warming. Calling the harms associated with climate change serious and well recognized, the court found the risk of catastrophic harm, though remote, to be real. That risk would be reduced to some extent if the plaintiffs received the relief they requested in their lawsuit. Therefore, the court found that the plaintiffs had standing to challenge the EPA.

After affirming the standing of the plaintiffs, the Supreme Court went on to issue a remarkable decision in which five of the nine justices chastised the Bush administration for its inaction on global warming. The court declared that carbon dioxide and other greenhouse gases are air pollutants and must be regulated by the EPA under the Clean Air Act. The court rebuked the administration's argument that, even if it did have authority to act, it would be unwise to regulate those pollutants at the current time. Rejecting rulemaking based on these impermissible considerations was arbitrary, capricious, and otherwise not in accordance with law, the court said. The court ordered the EPA to decide, pursuant to the mandates of the Clean Air Act, whether greenhouse gases may reasonably be anticipated to endanger public health or welfare.

This landmark case illustrates how courts shape environmental policy by determining who has standing. Without a finding by the Supreme Court that the state of Massachusetts had standing, it would not have had the legal authority to sue. Without the legal authority to sue, Massachusetts and the other parties would have been blocked—and the case never would have come to court. Calling the decision "a watershed moment in the fight against global warming," a spokesperson for the Sierra Club environmental group said, "This is a total repudiation of the refusal of the Bush administration to use the authority he has to meet the challenge of global warming."[25] Legal scholars pointed out that the EPA would no longer have any excuse to refuse to regulate pollutants from other sources, such as power plants, that are governed by the same Clean Air Act sections.

In June 2011, the Supreme Court added another interesting twist to the issue of regulating carbon emissions. In *American Electric Power Company, Inc. et al. v. Connecticut et al.*,[26] the court considered whether the lower courts could still hear cases against four private power companies and the federal

Tennessee Valley Authority. These cases were brought by several states, the city of New York, and three private land trusts and were initiated prior to *Massachusetts v. EPA*. The plaintiffs were asking for judicial decrees setting carbon dioxide emissions for each defendant pursuant to the federal common law of interstate nuisance, as well as state tort law. Reversing a lower court decision, the Supreme Court held that Congress clearly delegated to the EPA the decision as to whether and how to regulate carbon dioxide emissions from power plants. That delegation, the court said, displaces federal common law, even if the EPA's regulations were still being developed. In addition, Congress's scheme outlined in the Clean Air Act prescribes a specific order of decision making that must be followed, first by the experts at the EPA and then by federal judges. In response to this Supreme Court case, there have been attempts in Congress (unsuccessful to date) to repeal the EPA's authority to regulate carbon emissions.

A more recent decision, the 2014 Supreme Court case *Utility Air Group v. EPA*,[27] examined whether the EPA permissibly determined that its regulation of greenhouse gas emissions from new motor vehicles under the Clean Air Act also triggered permit requirements for stationary sources of greenhouse gas emissions. In a complex decision that split the court, the justices voted 5–4 to reject the EPA's broadest view of its power over greenhouse gas emissions, but it also voted 7–2 to allow the EPA to impose its air pollution control strategy on 83 percent of the power plants and other fixed sources of greenhouse gases in the United States.

On the one hand, the court chastised the agency for exceeding its statutory mandates by attempting to regulate all forms of greenhouse gas emissions as well as changing the limits enacted by Congress in order to make the implementation of the law more manageable, saying that "an agency may not rewrite clear statutory terms to suit its own sense of how the statute should operate. We are not willing to stand on the dock and wave goodbye as EPA embarks on a multiyear voyage of discovery" about how it wants to regulate greenhouse gases. On the other hand, the court held that the EPA does have the power, if it is already regulating a specific source because it emits other kinds of air pollution, to require that source to use the best available technology also to control greenhouse gases. Overall, the case was heralded as a victory for environmentalists. "E.P.A. is getting almost everything it wanted in this case," Justice Antonin Scalia wrote.

As mentioned previously, in 2016 the Supreme Court issued a blow to the Obama administration's climate policy. In the case of *West Virginia v. EPA*, twenty-nine states asked the Court to issue a stay blocking the Obama administration's Clean Power Plan until all litigation concerning it is complete, and the majority of the justices agreed to do so. The plan would have, among other things, forced states to dismantle old coal-burning power plants, and it was intricately linked with U.S. policy on the Paris Agreement, the first international climate accord, which President Trump plans to pull out of.

In 2017, twenty-one children brought suit in federal court in Oregon against the Trump administration for failing to protect future generations against the harms associated with climate change. They previously sued President Obama for the same reason, arguing that their rights to life, liberty, and property are being violated by climate change. Since their generation will be the most affected by climate change, they also maintain that they are being discriminated as a class.[28] This will surely remain an area of contention for decades.

Ripeness and Standard of Review:
The Case of Timber Cutting

The U.S. National Forest System is vast. It includes 155 national forests, 20 national grasslands, 8 land utilization projects, and other lands that together occupy nearly three hundred thousand square miles of land located in forty-four states, Puerto Rico, and the Virgin Islands. To manage those lands, the U.S. Forest Service, housed in the U.S. Department of Agriculture, develops land and resource management plans, as mandated by the National Forest Management Act of 1976. In developing the plans, the Forest Service must take into account both environmental and commercial goals.

In the late 1980s, the Forest Service developed a plan for the Wayne National Forest located in southern Ohio. When the plan was proposed, several environmental groups, including the Sierra Club and the Citizens Council on Conservation and Environmental Control, protested in administrative hearings that the plan was unlawful in part because it allowed below-cost timber sales and so encouraged clear-cutting. Opposing the environmental groups was the Ohio Forestry Association.

When the plan was not changed, the Sierra Club brought suit in federal court against the Forest Service and the secretary of agriculture. Among its requests to the district court, the Sierra Club asked for a declaration that the plan was unlawful because it authorized below-cost timber cutting. The Sierra Club also asked for an injunction to halt below-cost timber harvesting.

After many twists and turns,[29] the Supreme Court eventually ruled in favor of the Ohio Forestry Association in the 1998 case *Ohio Forestry Association, Inc. v. Sierra Club*.[30] Among the many arguments cited in its rationale, the Court said that the case was not ripe for review because it concerned abstract disagreements over administrative policies. The Court said that immediate judicial intervention would require it to second-guess thousands of technical decisions made by scientists and other forestry experts and might hinder the Forest Service's efforts to refine its policies. Further, delayed judicial review would not cause significant hardship for the parties. (The forest plan for the Wayne National Forest, which was at issue in *Ohio Forestry*, was again challenged unsuccessfully by environmental advocates in 2005, in *Buckeye Forest Council v. U.S. Forest Service*,[31] which concerned the Endangered Species Act.)

The *Ohio Forestry* case is still good law today and is an example of how courts shape environmental policy by applying the concepts of standard of review and ripeness. Notable is the court's reluctance to second-guess the judgments of government scientists and other technical analysts. In a case in which there is no showing of arbitrary or capricious government action, the court will give great deference to experts in its review. Also notable is the court's reluctance to review a plan that had not yet been implemented. Because no clear-cutting or timber sales had occurred, there was not yet a case or controversy, and so the case was not ripe for review. Regrettably, however, the interpretation is that concrete damage to the environment is needed before the court will act.

Though wise from a legal perspective, this approach is shortsighted from an environmental perspective. Two legal scholars called for Congress to respond to this case by changing the law.[32] The scholars concluded that the case, coupled with other cases, created significant roadblocks in the path of those wishing to challenge federal government planning decisions. In addition, these cases have encouraged land management agencies to change their uses of land management plans to "paperwork that makes no commitments about land suitability and sets few, if any, standards for governing future activities."[33]

Standard of Review: The Case of Air Quality

The Clean Air Act mandates that the EPA administrator promulgate National Ambient Air Quality Standards for each air pollutant for which air quality criteria have been issued. Once a standard has been promulgated, the administrator must review the standard and the criteria on which it is based every five years, and revise the standard if necessary. On July 18, 1997, the EPA administrator revised the standards for particulate matter and ozone. Because ozone and particulate matter are both nonthreshold pollutants—that is, any amount harms the public health—the EPA set stringent standards that would cost hundreds of millions of dollars to implement nationwide.

The American Trucking Associations, as well as other business groups and the states of Michigan, Ohio, and West Virginia, challenged the new standards in the U.S. Court of Appeals for the District of Columbia Circuit and then in the U.S. Supreme Court. Among other things, the plaintiffs argued that the statute that delegated the authority to the EPA to set the standards was unconstitutionally vague. They also argued that the EPA, in order to keep costs in check, should perform a benefit-cost analysis when setting national air quality standards.

In 2001, in a unanimous decision in the case of *Whitman v. American Trucking Associations*,[34] the Supreme Court mostly upheld the EPA and its new regulations. The court wrote that the statute, while ambiguous, was not overly vague and reversed the court of appeals. Furthermore, no benefit-cost analysis was needed. The EPA, based on the information about health effects contained in the technical documents it compiled, is to identify the maximum airborne concentration of a pollutant that the public health can tolerate, decrease the concentration to provide an adequate margin of safety, and set the standard at that level. Nowhere are the costs of achieving such a standard made part of that initial calculation, according to the court.

Concerning the appropriate standard of review, the Supreme Court invoked the rule that if a statute is silent or ambiguous with respect to an issue, then a court must defer to a reasonable interpretation made by the agency administrator. The key words for understanding the concept of standard of review are *ambiguous*, *reasonable*, and *defer*. The statute must be silent or ambiguous, the agency's actions must be judged by the court to be reasonable, and the court will then defer to the agency.

The key word for understanding the essence of this specific case is *reasonable*, for in one ambiguous instance in this case the court found the EPA's actions reasonable, whereas in another ambiguous instance in the same case, the court found the EPA's actions unreasonable. Specifically, the EPA's actions concerning benefit-cost analysis were found to be reasonable. Contrasted to this, the EPA's interpretation concerning the implementation of the act in another ambiguous section was found to be unreasonable. In the second instance, the EPA read the statute in a way that completely nullified text meant to limit the agency's discretion. This, the court said, was unlawful.

Once again, we have a case that is a clear example of how courts shape environmental policy—here by choosing and applying a standard of review. An appropriate standard of review can, and should, change from case to case. In addition, reasonable judges can differ on what constitutes an appropriate standard of review. Further, once a standard of review is selected, the application of that standard becomes important. Crucial in this case were judgments concerning whether the EPA administrator acted reasonably. Hence, when judges are selected, an examination of their judicial philosophies and predispositions becomes important.

Interpretation of Environmental Laws

Judges shape environmental policy in how they interpret laws. Environmental laws are often broad and vague. Circumstances arise that the drafters of the laws did not foresee. Environmental statutes sometimes conflict with each other. Different stakeholders interpret mandates contrarily. The cases analyzed in this section exemplify how courts shape environmental policy through judicial interpretation of laws.

Interpreting Statutes: Two Cases
Concerning the Endangered Species Act

The Endangered Species Act of 1973 contains a variety of protections designed to save from extinction selected species that the secretary of the interior designates as endangered or threatened.[35] Section 9 of the act makes it unlawful for any person to "take" any endangered or threatened species. *Taking* is defined by the law as "harassing, harming, pursuing, hunting, shooting, wounding, killing, trapping, capturing or collecting any of the protected wildlife."[36] In the early 1990s, the secretary promulgated a regulation that defined the statute's prohibition on takings to include "significant habitat modification or degradation where it actually kills or injures wildlife."[37] A group calling itself the Sweet Home Chapter of Communities for a Great Oregon filed suit alleging that the secretary of the interior exceeded his authority under the Endangered Species Act by promulgating that regulation. The plaintiff group comprised small landowners, logging companies, and families dependent on the forest products industries of the Pacific Northwest. They argued that the legislative history of the act demonstrated that Congress considered, and rejected, such a broad definition. Further, they argued that the regulation, as applied to the habitat of the northern spotted owl and the red-cockaded woodpecker, had injured them economically because there were now vast areas of land that could not be logged. If the secretary wanted to protect the habitat of these endangered species, they maintained, the secretary would have to buy their land.

The district court entered summary judgment for the secretary of the interior, finding that the regulation was a reasonable interpretation of congressional intent.[38] In the U.S. Court of Appeals for the District of Columbia, a divided panel first affirmed the judgment of the lower court. After granting a rehearing, however, the panel reversed the lower court's ruling. The confusion, and final decision, centered on how to interpret the word *harm* in the Endangered Species Act, looking at the totality of the act.

The secretary of the interior appealed to the U.S. Supreme Court. In a 6–3 decision, in the case of *Babbitt v. Sweet Home Chapter of Communities for a Great Oregon* (1995),[39] the Supreme Court reversed the decision of the court of appeals and upheld the Department of the Interior's regulation. Examining the legislative history of the Endangered Species Act, and applying rules of statutory construction, the majority of the court concluded that the secretary's definition of *harm* was reasonable. Further, the court concluded that the writing of this technical and science-based regulation involved a complex policy choice. Congress entrusted the secretary with broad discretion in these matters, and the court expressed a reluctance to substitute its views of wise policy for those of the secretary.

This pathbreaking endangered species case demonstrates how courts shape environmental policy by the way they interpret statutes. Different judges at different stages of review in this case interpreted the statutory word *harm* differently. The protection of endangered species hinged on these interpretations. Tied in with this is the important notion of which rules of statutory construction courts choose to apply and how they apply them. Further, this case is another example of how courts are hesitant to substitute their views for the views of experts in scientific and technical matters, absent a showing of arbitrary or capricious action, or obvious error. The final Supreme Court decision set a precedent that strengthened endangered species policy throughout the United States.

Twelve years later, in 2007, the Supreme Court decided a case that concerned "dueling statutes," resulting in a *weakening* of the Endangered Species Act. In its interesting rationale, the court juxtaposed the reasoning of the *Babbitt* decision with the reasoning of the *Chevron* decision.

Under the Clean Water Act (CWA), the EPA initially administers each state's National Pollutant Discharge Elimination System (NPDES) permitting program. Once a state meets nine criteria, the EPA must transfer authority for the NPDES program to the state.

At the same time, the Endangered Species Act requires federal agencies to consult with agencies designated by the secretaries of commerce and the interior to ensure that a proposed agency action is unlikely to jeopardize an endangered or a threatened species. The Fish and Wildlife Service and the National Marine Fisheries Service administer the Endangered Species Act. Once a consultation process is complete, a written biological opinion is issued, which may suggest alternative actions to protect a jeopardized species or its critical habitat.

When Arizona officials sought EPA authorization to administer the state's NPDES program, the EPA initiated consultation with the Fish and Wildlife Service to determine whether the transfer would adversely affect any listed species. The Fish and Wildlife Service regional office wanted potential impacts taken into account, but the EPA disagreed, finding that the Clean Water Act's mandatory language stripped the EPA of authority to disapprove a transfer based on any other considerations. The dispute was referred to the agencies' national offices for resolution.

The Fish and Wildlife Service's biological opinion concluded that the requested transfer would not jeopardize listed species. The EPA concluded that Arizona had met each of the Clean Water Act's nine criteria and approved the transfer, noting that the biological opinion had fulfilled the consultation mandate of the Endangered Species Act.

Defenders of Wildlife, an environmental advocacy group, filed a lawsuit against the EPA in the Ninth Circuit Court of Appeals. The National Association of Home Builders intervened to support the EPA. The Court of Appeals held in favor of Defenders of Wildlife, stating that the EPA's transfer to the state of Arizona of the authority to run its own NPDES program was arbitrary and capricious. It did not dispute that Arizona had met the Clean Water Act's nine criteria but instead concluded that the Endangered Species Act required the EPA to determine whether its transfer decision would jeopardize listed endangered species.

The National Association of Home Builders appealed the court of appeals decision to the U.S. Supreme Court. On June 25, 2007, in a 5–4 decision, *National Association of Home Builders v. Defenders of Wildlife*,[40] the Supreme Court reversed the decision of the court of appeals, noting that this case entailed a conflict of statutes.

Among its conclusions, the Supreme Court found that the Ninth Circuit's determination that the EPA's action was arbitrary and capricious was not supported by the record. The EPA is mandated by the Clean Water Act to turn over the operation of an NPDES program to a state if that state meets all nine criteria enumerated in the statute. The state of Arizona met all nine criteria; therefore, the EPA had no choice but to turn over the program to the state, the majority of the court said.

As to the Endangered Species Act, the court said that the statute's mandate applies only to discretionary agency actions. It does not apply to actions like the NPDES permitting transfer authorization that an agency is *required* by statute to undertake once certain specified triggering events have occurred. To decide otherwise would be to add a tenth criterion to the Clean Water Act.

The court emphasized that while a later-enacted statute such as the Endangered Species Act can sometimes operate to amend or even repeal an earlier statutory provision such as that of the Clean Water Act, Congress did not expressly override the Clean Water Act in this case. The Supreme Court acknowledged that it owes "some degree of deference" to the secretary of the interior's reasonable interpretation of the Endangered Species Act under the *Babbitt* decision. At the same time, the Supreme Court, citing the *Chevron* case, said that deference is not due if Congress has made its intent clear in a statute, but "if the statute is silent or ambiguous . . . the question . . . is whether the agency's answer is based on a permissible construction of the statute."[41] In this case, the EPA's interpretation was a reasonable construction of the Clean Water Act, and so the EPA was entitled to "*Chevron* deference."

Justice John Paul Stevens, joined by Justices David Hackett Souter, Ruth Bader Ginsburg, and Stephen Breyer, wrote a twenty-seven-page dissenting opinion, in which they argued that, when faced with competing statutory mandates, the U.S. Supreme Court should balance both laws instead of choosing one over the other. In the dissenting justices' view, the EPA acted arbitrarily and capriciously by choosing the Clean Water Act over the Endangered Species Act. Citing the famous 1978 snail darter case, in which the discovery of the endangered snail darter halted the construction of a dam, the justices proclaimed that Congress had already given endangered species priority over the primary missions of federal agencies.

This fascinating case, which is still good law, demonstrates how courts shape environmental policy by the way judges interpret "dueling" statutes and "dueling" precedents governing "dueling" federal agencies. The majority of justices chose the rationale of *Chevron* over the rationale of *Babbitt*. In addition, different judges interpreted the mandate of the Endangered Species Act differently, with the result being a general weakening of the act.

Interpreting Statutes and the Constitution: Regulatory Takings and Land Use

In 1986, David H. Lucas purchased two vacant oceanfront lots on the Isle of Palms in Charleston County, South Carolina, for $975,000. He intended to build single-family residences on the lots, but in 1988, the South Carolina Legislature enacted the Beachfront Management Act.[42] In Lucas's case, this act prohibited him from constructing any permanent structure (including a dwelling) except for a small deck or walkway on the property. Lucas filed suit in the court of common pleas, asserting that the restrictions on the use of his lots amounted to the government taking his property without justly compensating him, a so-called *regulatory taking*. The lower court agreed with Lucas, maintaining that the act rendered the land value-less, and awarded him over $1.2 million for the regulatory taking. Upon appeal, the Supreme Court of South Carolina reversed the lower court's decision. The judges maintained that the regulation under attack prevented a use seriously harming the public. Consequently, they argued, no regulatory taking occurred.[43]

On June 29, 1992, however, the U.S. Supreme Court, in a 6–3 decision, reversed the holding of the highest court in South Carolina and remanded the case to it for further action.[44] In its decision, the court articulated several pivotal principles that constitute a test for regulatory takings. First, the justices emphasized that regulations denying a property owner all "economically viable use of his land" require compensation, regardless of the public interest advanced in support of the restraint. Consequently, even when a regulation addresses or prevents a "harmful or noxious use," government must compensate owners when their property is rendered economically useless to them.

At the same time, however, the court threw back to the South Carolina courts the issue of whether a taking occurred in Lucas's case. The lower courts had to examine the context of the state's power over the "bundle of rights" Lucas acquired when he took title to his property. Put differently, the pivotal question for all state regulators today is this: Do state environmental regulations merely make explicit what already was implicit in any property title (that is, the right to regulate its use), or are they decisions that come after a person acquires a title that were not originally implied? In the latter case, they are takings that governments must compensate.

Equally important in *Lucas* was what the court did *not* discuss in its narrowly worded opinion. First, the court did not say that Lucas was entitled to compensation. Rather, it implied that the South Carolina Supreme Court was hasty in concluding that Lucas was not entitled to recompense. Second, the court did not address the issue of property that is merely diminished in value—a far more common occurrence. Instead, it addressed only the issue of property that was rendered totally valueless. Finally, in pushing the regulatory takings issue back onto the state, the court did not say that state laws may never change. Indeed, the majority held that "changed circumstances or new knowledge may make what was previously permissible no longer so." Hence, the court left the door open for some regulation of newly discovered environmental harms after title to a property changes hands. Still, Lucas did prevail. Upon remand, the South Carolina Supreme Court reversed its earlier decision and awarded Lucas over $1.5 million.

A few years later, the Supreme Court continued to develop the area of regulatory takings in a local government planning and zoning case that also is having profound effects on environmental policy. In *Dolan v. Tigard* (1994),[45] the owner of a plumbing and electrical supply store applied to the City of Tigard, Oregon, for a permit to redevelop a site. The plaintiff wanted to expand the size of her store and to pave the parking lot.

The city, pursuant to a state-required land use program, had adopted a comprehensive plan, a plan for pedestrian-and-bicycle pathways, and a master drainage plan. So the city's planning commission conditioned Dolan's permit on her doing two things. First, she had to dedicate (that is, convey title) to the city the portion of her property lying within a hundred-year floodplain so that the city could improve a storm drainage system for the area. Second, she had to dedicate an additional fifteen-foot strip of land adjacent to the floodplain as a pedestrian-and-bicycle pathway. The planning commission argued that its conditions regarding the floodplain were "reasonably related" to the owner's request to intensify use of the site, given its impervious surface. Likewise, the commission claimed that creating the pedestrian-and-bicycle pathway system could lessen or offset the increased traffic congestion that the permit would cause.

In a previous case, *Nollan v. California Coastal Commission* (1987),[46] the court had ruled that an agency needs to show that an "essential nexus" exists between the "end advanced" (that is, the enunciated purpose of the regulation) and the "condition imposed" by applying the regulation. The "essential nexus" requirement is still good law today. The *Nollan* court also held that a government must be prepared to prove in court that a "legitimate state interest" is "substantially advanced" by any regulation affecting property rights. In 2005, the Supreme Court removed the "substantially advanced" requirement as improper in a nonenvironmental case, *Lingle v. Chevron*,[47] because it did not address the effect of a regulation on property but rather was concerned solely with whether the underlying regulation itself was valid.

After reviewing various doctrines that state courts had used to guide such analyses, the court in *Dolan* enunciated its own test of "rough proportionality" that is still valid today. It stated that "no precise mathematical calculation is required, but the city must make some sort of individualized determination that the required dedication is related both in nature and extent to the impact of the proposed development." If there is rough proportionality, then there is no taking. In this instance, the court decided that the city had not made any such determination and concluded that the city's findings did not show a relationship between the floodplain easement and the owner's proposed new building. Furthermore, the city had failed to quantify precisely how much the pedestrian-and-bicycle pathway would proportionately offset some of the demand generated.

The implications of the court's decision in this case are profound. The facts are hardly unique and represent the types of zoning challenges that local governments face daily. What is more, the court's logic potentially extends to all local government regulatory activities. Finally, the decision means that the courts can become even more involved than they had been in reviewing and judging the adequacy of local regulatory decisions—the dissent in *Dolan* called this "micromanaging."

These and other cases together indicate that with the burden of proof in takings cases falling on the government, considerable litigation is inevitable. Thus, local governments will have to do more individualized analysis of the expected impacts of land use changes and the conditions they impose on these changes. Not only will this be more costly, but it will likely have a chilling effect on regulatory activity at that level. Finally, because no clear guidance exists concerning how to operationalize concepts such as *rough proportionality*, local regulators should expect continuing litigation in different regulatory contexts. Lower and appellate courts have been busy trying to clarify this test for them.

There have been hundreds of takings cases in the courts since *Dolan* and *Nollan*. One of the most important current decisions is *Koontz v. St. Johns River Water Management District*.[48] Coy Koontz Sr. sought permits to develop a section of his property from the St. Johns River Water Management District, which, consistent with Florida law, requires permit applicants wishing to build on wetlands to offset the resulting environmental damage. Koontz offered to mitigate the environmental effects of his development proposal by deeding to the district a conservation easement on nearly three-quarters of his property. The district rejected Koontz's proposal and informed him that it would approve construction only if he either reduced the size of his development and, among other things, deeded to the district a conservation easement on the resulting larger remainder of his property or hired contractors to make improvements to district-owned wetlands several miles away. Believing the district's demands to be excessive in light of the environmental effects his proposal would have caused, Koontz filed suit under a state law that provides money damages for agency action that is an "unreasonable exercise of the state's police power constituting a taking without just compensation."

In a case with many twists and turns, Koontz won at the trial level, won again at the district court of appeals level, but lost at the state supreme court level. In a 5–4 decision, the U.S. Supreme Court reversed the Florida Supreme Court and ruled in favor of Koontz, writing that, when a government engages in land use regulation, including by denying a permit or demanding payment as a condition for a permit, the government must show that there is a nexus and rough proportionality between its demand on the landowner and the effects of the proposed land use, and that was not done here. In essence, the Supreme Court clarified that the *Nollan* and *Dolan* nexus and proportionality requirements apply in the context of permit denials, not just approvals. It also held that these requirements apply to demands for money (or actions that cost money) and not just to demands for an interest in land. The case is likely to trigger even more takings lawsuits.

These cases are still good law, and subsequent lawsuits have further developed takings law. Environmental advocates charge that if takings suits are successful, the trend will destroy years of hard-fought incremental progress in protecting the environment. Government regulators agree, adding that the trend could devastate already ailing government budgets. This will be true especially if proposed federal legislation is enacted that would take compensation payments from the coffers of the agency that issued such regulations. These are excellent examples of how courts help shape environmental policy.

Choice of Remedy

A final way in which courts affect environmental policy is through their choice of remedies. When a recalcitrant polluter is taken to court, the two most common actions ordered by a court are mandatory compliance with environmental law and punitive monetary penalties to deter future violations. As an example, consider the Clean Water Act case *Friends of the Earth, Inc. v. Laidlaw Environmental Services*,[49] which concerned a company that repeatedly violated the conditions of its permit by discharging pollutants such as mercury numerous times into a river. The settlement decree ordered Laidlaw to comply with the Clean Water Act, and the district court assessed punitive monetary penalties. In a case involving criminal violations of environmental law, the penalty might involve jail time or probation. In each of these scenarios, considerable judicial discretion is involved.

The Clean Air Act, the Clean Water Act, the Resource Conservation and Recovery Act, and the Emergency Planning and Community Right-to-Know Act also allow those who win citizen suits to seek monetary penalties, which go to the U.S. Treasury rather than to the plaintiff. In these circumstances, again, a judge has immense discretion. Most often, the only curbs on judges in these circumstances are statutorily set maximum amounts, as well as lists of factors that judges must weigh.

A relatively new remedy being used more often in both judicial decrees and administrative orders is a supplemental environmental project (SEP). The EPA updated its SEP policy in 2015 and now defines SEPs as

> an environmentally beneficial project or activity that is not required by law, but that a defendant agrees to undertake as part of the settlement of an enforcement action. SEPs are projects or activities that go beyond what could legally be required in order for the defendant to return to compliance, and secure environmental and/or public health benefits in addition to those achieved by compliance with applicable laws.[50]

In 2015, the EPA clarified seven categories of projects that might qualify as SEPs. The seven categories areas are public health, pollution prevention, pollution reduction, environmental restoration and protection, assessments and audits, environmental compliance promotion, and emergency planning and preparedness. There is an eighth category of "other" that allows parties to suggest SEPs not on this list.

To award SEPs, judges must have the statutory authority to do so or at least be assured that the statute does not forbid them to do so. Although the EPA has included SEPs in its orders in various forms and under various names since the late 1970s, they became more widely accepted in the 1990s. For example, in February 1994, President Clinton issued Executive Order 12898, which directed federal agencies to integrate environmental justice issues into agency policy. The EPA seized this opportunity by incorporating SEPs into many consent decrees that address environmental challenges in minority and low-income neighborhoods.

An example of an early SEP is the case in which the EPA's Region 1 received an anonymous tip to check out properties of the Massachusetts Highway Department (MHD). There they found nearly two hundred barrels of illegally stored hazardous wastes in 149 MHD facilities. The resulting settlement, negotiated in less than a year and approved by a court, included over $20 million in cleanup costs and $5 million in SEPs.[51] A relatively small penalty of $100,000 also was ordered to be paid to federal government coffers. The SEPs undertaken by the MHD made a concrete difference in a way that traditional penalties often do not. They ranged from the development of an environmental education program for MHD personnel and the public to the cleanup of environmentally contaminated minority neighborhoods throughout Massachusetts.

Recent SEPs have branched into other areas. In 2014, the DeKalb County, Georgia, Department of Watershed Management's Capital Improvement Projects Division announced a one-time SEP involving the removal of trash and debris from the banks and streambeds of South River, South Fork Peachtree Creek, and Snapfinger Creek as part of a Clean Water Act settlement with the EPA. Also in 2014, the Town of Canaan, Vermont, agreed to fund a diversified agriculture vocational program at Canaan High School that included many units of study about water quality. The program was part of a settlement involving multiple violations of a Clean Water Act discharge permit. Since the new 2015 SEP policy was issued by the EPA, SEPs have included the use of safer chemicals at water treatment facilities, lead paint abatement, the repair or replacement of defective sewer lines in low-income neighborhoods, and local government household hazardous waste disposal programs. The EPA is also encouraging SEPS to use new and innovative technologies.

These are just a few examples from the hundreds of SEPs ordered annually. Although mandatory compliance with environmental laws and monetary penalties remain the most often court-ordered remedies, the use of SEPs in the future is promising. The EPA has a special website on SEPs,[52] as does Colorado.[53] The choice of remedy is yet another way in which courts shape environmental policy.

Conclusion: A View to the Future

Judge Bazelon was right: Since 1971, administrative agencies and reviewing courts have collaborated fruitfully, especially in the area of environmental policy. An early study examining the impact of over two thousand federal court decisions on the EPA's policies and administration in its first two decades found that, from an agency-wide perspective, compliance with court orders has become one of the EPA's top priorities, at times overtaking congressional mandates.[54] A more recent study predicts that the courts will become an increasingly important pathway for revising policies because Congress has been legislatively gridlocked for decades.[55] Many predict that

Donald Trump will be the most sued president in the history of the United States, especially by those challenging his environmental policies.

The courts in the United States have become permanent players in environmental policymaking. Supporting this conclusion are dozens of websites concerning environmental policy in the courts. The most useful of these sites are listed at the end of this chapter. Although the extent of judicial involvement in environmental cases will ebb and flow over the years, the courts will always be involved in environmental policy to some degree.

As this chapter has demonstrated, courts have a major influence in how environmental laws work in practice. Courts shape environmental policy in many ways. The most significant ways are by determining who has standing to sue, by deciding which cases are ripe for review, by the court's choice of a standard of review, by interpreting statutes and the Constitution, by the remedies judges choose, and simply by resolving environmental conflicts.

Environmental court decisions are influenced by the state of the law, such as precedent and rules for interpreting statutes. They are also influenced by the courts' environment, such as mass public opinion, litigants and interest groups, congressional expansion or perhaps narrowing of jurisdiction, and presidential appointments. Environmental court decisions are influenced as well by justices' values: liberal, moderate, conservative, or somewhere in between. In addition, environmental court decisions are affected by group interaction on the bench, with individual justices at times influencing others.

The importance of judicial appointments cannot be overemphasized. Federal judges are appointed for life, barring illegal or unethical behavior. As of the writing of this chapter, President Trump has over 100 federal court vacancies to fill, nearly twice the number President Obama inherited from his predecessor. It remains to be seen how President Trump's judicial appointments will affect environmental policy and the role of the courts in making it, but most are predicting a diminution of environmental protections.

The environmental policies that are developed, expanded, narrowed, and clarified in our courts will continue to affect the air we breathe, the water we drink, and the food we eat. The United States is the most litigious country in the world. Clearly, environmental policy in the courts—at least in the United States—is here to stay.

Suggested Websites

Council on Environmental Quality (www.whitehouse.gov/ceq) This council coordinates federal environmental efforts; its website provides links to important environmental and natural resource agencies, as well as to reports. Especially helpful is the CEQ National Environmental Policy Act (NEPA) link (www.nepa.gov).

Environmental Law Institute (www.eli.org) The website of this research and education center provides objective, nonpartisan analysis of current environmental law issues.

Lexis and Westlaw (www.lexis.com; www.westlaw.com) These excellent commercial websites provide basic materials concerning domestic environmental law.

Natural Resources Defense Council (www.nrdc.org) The NRDC site provides expert analyses of issues and reports that are relevant to ongoing legal decisions.

U.S. Department of the Interior (www.doi.gov) This site lists laws and regulations for the major agencies within the department.

U.S. Environmental Protection Agency (www.epa.gov/epahome/law-regs.htm) This section of the EPA site offers links to laws, regulations, the U.S. Code, and pending legislation in Congress concerning the EPA.

U.S. Forest Service (www.fs.fed.us/publications) This page gives access to laws, regulations, and publications concerning federal forests.

U.S. Institute for Environmental Conflict Resolution (www.ecr.gov) This website provides a primer on environmental conflict resolution with an emphasis on evaluating its effectiveness.

Notes

1. *Environmental Defense Fund v. Ruckelshaus*, 439 F. 2d 584 (1971).
2. Brady Dennis, "Environmental Groups Sue Trump Administration Over Offshore Drilling," *Washington Post*, May 3, 2017, https://www.washingtonpost.com/news/energy-environment/wp/2017/05/03/environmental-groups-sue-trump-administration-over-offshore-drilling/?utm_term=.5b8976c09053.
3. Michael Burger, "The Battle Against Trump's Assault on Climate Is Moving to the Courts," *YaleEnvironment360*, May 2, 2017, https://e360.yale.edu/features/stopping-trump-the-battle-to-thwart-the-assault-on-climate-moves-to-the-courts.
4. Valerie Volcovici, "Environmental Groups Sue Trump Administration for Approving Keystone Pipeline," *Reuters*, March 30, 2017, http://www.reuters.com/article/us-usa-pipeline-keystone-lawsuit-idUSKBN1712DZ.
5. Natasha Geiling, "Trump's Environmental Assault Met with Immediate Legal Challenges," *ThinkProgress*, March 31, 2017, https://thinkprogress.org/trump-environmental-legal-challenges-1360b60417.
6. Tina Nguyen, "Donald Trump Is Fueling an Explosion of New Lawsuits," *Vanity Fair*, March 30, 2017, http://www.vanityfair.com/news/2017/03/donald-trump-new-lawsuits.
7. Michael Bastasch, "Environmentalists Flood the Courts with Lawsuits to Stop Trump's Agenda," *The Daily Caller*, May 4, 2017, http://dailycaller.com/2017/05/04/environmentalists-flood-the-courts-with-lawsuits-to-stop-trumps-agenda/.
8. Kyle Dickman, "The Court Standing Between Trump and Environmental Deregulation," *Outside*, February 2017, https://www.outsideonline.com/2154956/undo-environmental-regulations-republicans-will-have-get-through-dc-circuit-court-appeals-first.
9. *West Virginia v. EPA*, 577 U.S. ____ (2016).
10. *Udall v. Tallman*, 380 U.S. 1 (1965).
11. *Chevron U.S.A., Inc. v. Natural Resources Defense Council*, 467 U.S. 837 (1984).
12. *Gutierrez-Brizuela v. Lynch*, 834 F.3d 1142 (2016).
13. Administrative Procedure Act, Section 706[2][A].

14. Six of the EPA's seven major environmental statutes have citizen suit provisions.
15. "Control of Emissions from New Highway Vehicles and Engines," 68 Fed. Reg. at 52,930 (September 8, 2003).
16. Ibid. at 52,928.
17. Ibid. at 52,929.
18. Ibid. at 52,930.
19. Ibid. at 52,931.
20. *Massachusetts v. Environmental Protection Agency*, 415 F. 3d 50 (DC Cir. 2005).
21. *Massachusetts v. Environmental Protection Agency*, 127 S. Ct. 1438 (2007).
22. *Massachusetts v. Environmental Protection Agency*, 126 S. Ct. 2960 (2006).
23. For a good discussion of this requirement, see *Lujan, Secretary of the Interior v. Defenders of Wildlife et al.*, 504 U.S. 555 (1992).
24. See U.S. Constitution, Article III, Section 2.
25. Fanny Carrier, "Environmentalists Hail 'Watershed' US Supreme Court Ruling," *Agence France Presse*, April 3, 2007.
26. *American Electric Power Company, Inc. et al. v. Connecticut et al.*, 131 S. Ct. 2527 (2011).
27. *Utility Air Regulatory Group v. Environmental Protection Agency*, 573 U.S. ___ (2014).
28. *Juliana et al., v. United States of America et al.*, No. 6:15-cv-01517 (Oregon).
29. *Sierra Club v. Thomas*, 105 F. 3d 248 (1997).
30. *Ohio Forestry Association, Inc. v. Sierra Club*, 523 U.S. 726 (1998).
31. *Buckeye Forest Council v. U.S. Forest Service*, 378 F. Supp. 2d 835 (2005).
32. Michael C. Blumm and Sherry L. Bosse, "*Norton v. SUWA* and the Unraveling of Federal Public Land Planning," *Duke Environmental Law and Policy Forum* 18 (Fall 2007): 105–61.
33. Blumm and Bosse, "*Norton v. SUWA*," 111.
34. *Whitman v. American Trucking Associations*, 531 U.S. 457 (2001).
35. Endangered Species Act, 16 U.S.C. Section 1531 et seq.
36. 16 U.S.C. Section 1538 (a)(1).
37. 50 C.F.R. Section 17.3 (1994).
38. *Sweet Home Chapter of Communities for a Great Oregon v. Lujan*, 806 F. Supp. 279 (1992); 1 F. 3d 1 (1993); 17 F. 3d 1463 (1994).
39. *Babbitt v. Sweet Home Chapter of Communities for a Great Oregon*, 515 U.S. 687 (1995).
40. *National Association of Home Builders v. Defenders of Wildlife*, 551 U.S. 644 (2007).
41. *Chevron U.S.A., Inc. v. Natural Resources Defense Council, Inc.*, 467 U.S. 837 (1984).
42. S.C. Code Ann. (1989) Sections 48-39-10 et seq.
43. *Lucas v. South Carolina Coastal Council*, 304 S. C. 376 (1991).
44. *Lucas v. South Carolina Coastal Council*, 505 U.S. 1003 (1992).
45. *Dolan v. Tigard*, 512 U.S. 374 (1994); *Dura Pharmaceuticals, Inc. v. Broudo*, 544 U.S. 2974 (2005).
46. *Nollan v. California Coastal Commission*, 483 U.S. 825 (1987).
47. *Lingle v. Chevron*, 544 U.S. 528 (2005).
48. *Koontz v. St. Johns River Water Management District*, 133 S. Ct 2586 (2013).
49. *Friends of the Earth, Inc. v. Laidlaw Environmental Services*, 528 U.S. 167 (2000).
50. EPA, *U.S. Environmental Protection Agency Supplemental Environmental Projects Policy 2015 Update* (Washington, DC: EPA, 2015), 1, https://www.epa.gov/sites/production/files/2015-04/documents/sepupdatedpolicy15.pdf.
51. In the Matter of: The Commonwealth of Massachusetts, Massachusetts Highway Department, EPA Docket No. RCRA-I-94-1071, Consent Agreement and Order, October 3, 1994.

52. EPA, "Enforcement: 2015 Update to the 1998 U.S. EPA Supplemental Environmental Projects Policy," https://www.epa.gov/enforcement/2015-update-1998-us-epa-supplemental-environmental-projects-policy.

53. Colorado Department of Public Health & Environment, "Supplemental Environmental Projects," https://www.colorado.gov/pacific/cdphe/supplemental-environmental-projects.

54. Rosemary O'Leary, *Environmental Change: Federal Courts and the EPA* (Philadelphia, PA: Temple University Press, 1993).

55. Christopher McGrory Klyza and David Sousa, *American Environmental Policy: Beyond Gridlock*, updated and expanded edition (Cambridge, MA: MIT Press, 2013), Chapter 5.

Chapter 7

The Environmental Protection Agency

Richard N. L. Andrews

The Environmental Protection Agency (EPA) is the lead U.S. agency responsible for protecting the environment from air and water pollution and for protecting people from the health hazards of pollution and toxic chemicals in the environment. Created in 1970, just a few months after the first Earth Day and before most of today's major pollution control laws were enacted, it regulates air pollution from cars and smokestacks, water pollution from urban sewers and industrial outfalls, hazardous wastes and municipal landfills, drinking water contaminants, and pesticides and toxic chemicals; and under President Obama, it also began to impose regulations to reduce carbon emissions from motor vehicles as well as power plants and other industries that contribute to global climate change. Environmental and public health advocates see it as the government's champion for those widely shared values. Some critics, however, accuse it of imposing excessive red tape and unjustified costs on businesses, property owners, and state and local governments; and others accuse it at least of not using the most economically efficient and effective policy tools to achieve its goals.

The EPA itself pioneered the development of innovative new policy tools beyond traditional regulations, to try to reduce environmental risks in the most cost-effective ways. Examples include "market-oriented" incentives, such as tradable emission allowances; information disclosure requirements, such as those for radon and for chemicals covered by the Toxics Release Inventory Program; and elaborate procedures for risk assessment. The EPA also provides subsidized loans for drinking water and wastewater treatment facilities, conducts research to reduce pollution, and provides extensive technical assistance and enforcement cooperation to support state environmental protection programs (see also Chapter 2 on state environmental policymaking).

An unavoidable challenge for the EPA is that the primary tools it has been given by Congress are regulations, and regulations inherently place new restrictions and costs on influential businesses and state and local governments. This chapter discusses how the EPA makes decisions in the face of constant pressures, not only from advocates of environmental protection and the news media but also from businesses, the president, members of Congress, state and local officials, and the courts.

Background[1]

The EPA was created in 1970 by President Richard Nixon, in the midst of a widespread public outcry for the federal government to "do something" about pollution.[2] The EPA was created not by an act of Congress but through a presidential reorganization plan that pulled together a number of separate programs into a single new agency. Air pollution and waste management programs were transferred from the Department of Health, Education, and Welfare, water pollution programs from the Department of the Interior, pesticide programs from the Department of Agriculture, and some radiation protection programs from the Atomic Energy Commission.

The EPA, or any federal administrative agency, for that matter, can act only under the authority of laws passed by Congress, known as statutes. In approving a new statute, Congress authorizes or prohibits certain kinds of actions, including authorizing the EPA to implement and enforce the statute's requirements. Appropriations statutes also authorize how much money the agency can spend each year to implement and enforce each of its statutes. A regulation, in contrast, is a standard or rule written by the agency to interpret a statute, apply it in particular situations, and enforce it. In short, Congress directs the EPA to issue regulations to solve a problem, and the EPA must then write the necessary details of the regulations to do so, a process that is often challenging, contentious, and politicized by those who are affected by the regulations. If someone challenges a regulation, decisions by the courts can either confirm or overrule the agency's interpretation. Statutes, regulations, and judicial decisions all have the force of law.

Beginning in 1970, Congress passed a series of far-reaching new statutes to address pollution and other environmental health hazards and assigned them to the EPA to carry out. These included the Clean Air Act, the Federal Water Pollution Control Act, the Safe Drinking Water Act, and laws regulating pesticides, toxic substances, and solid and hazardous wastes (see Chapter 1 and Appendix 1). Since EPA itself was created only by a presidential reorganization plan rather than by an act of Congress, it functions largely as an umbrella organization managing separate programs to implement each of these laws, plus crosscutting units for enforcement, legal counsel, research and development, and more recently information and financial management. Its administrator has only limited authority to integrate, coordinate, or set priorities among its separate program units except through its annual budget requests. And Congress often does not grant its requests: in recent years, a gridlocked Congress has often passed only continuing resolutions to maintain specified levels of its existing funding, not new appropriations bills, let alone new environmental laws.

One of the main tools Congress gave to the EPA to carry out these laws was the authority to issue regulations. In addition, Congress authorized the EPA to provide technical and compliance assistance to state governments, through ten regional offices; to provide grants to state and local governments to implement federal air and water quality standards, monitor public water supplies, and clean up hazardous wastes; and to provide low-interest loans to local governments to build new drinking-water and wastewater-treatment facilities. Many of these tools thus rely heavily on environmental federalism, discussed in Chapter 2.[3] In 2016, the EPA had a budget of $8 billion, just two-tenths of 1 percent of the overall federal budget; but only 22 percent of this was used to pay its fifteen thousand staff members, while nearly half was spent on state and tribal assistance agreements.[4]

To reduce air pollution, for instance, Congress directed the EPA to set National Ambient Air Quality Standards (NAAQS) specifying how clean the air around us must be in order to protect public health; and it required states to produce state implementation plans (SIPs) for achieving these standards. The law also required all new sources of air pollution to have EPA permits and to use the "best available control technology" to minimize their emissions. Important amendments in 1990 set caps on total emissions of sulfur from all large power plants and allowed polluters to buy and sell their shares of that total—their "emission allowances"—so that companies that do better than the requirements could sell their allowances to companies that found it cheaper to buy more allowances and keep polluting. The law also ordered the EPA to set tailpipe emission standards for cars and trucks that all manufacturers must meet on average across the "fleet" of new vehicles they sell each year.

The Federal Water Pollution Control Act authorizes the EPA to regulate *all* "point sources" of water pollution (such as factory outfalls and municipal wastewater treatment plants), not just new sources as in the case of air pollution. All point sources of water pollution must get permits from the EPA (or in practice, from the state agency administering the EPA permit program) and must use the "best available technology." The EPA also provides low-interest loans to fund construction of new publicly owned wastewater treatment plants. However, the EPA was not authorized to regulate pollution from "nonpoint" sources such as farm runoff, due to the influence of the farm lobby. All treatment, storage, and disposal facilities for hazardous wastes also must have EPA permits, as must municipal landfills and incinerators; and all shipments of hazardous wastes must be documented, from the factory where they were generated as waste to their ultimate disposal in a permitted facility.

Each of these statutes addressed a particular environmental problem, but many of them affected the same industries, often with conflicting consequences. Many electric companies complied with air pollution regulations in the 1970s, for instance, by building taller smokestacks to disperse their pollutants so that they would reduce health effects immediately downwind; but this simply caused the pollutants to rain out further away as acid rain, damaging forests and fisheries.[5] More recently, the EPA tightened regulations on sulfur dioxide and mercury emissions to protect public health, and to comply, electric utilities put expensive "wet scrubbers" on their stacks to capture these pollutants before they were released into the air; but these materials then were piped into coal ash ponds, some of which later leaked and caused serious water pollution.[6] Similarly, sewage treatment improves water quality by removing contaminants from wastewater, but these materials then must themselves be managed, often by landfilling, incineration, or spraying them on farmlands where they may cause new hazards.

In an ideal world, the EPA would design an integrated set of policy incentives to promote pollution *prevention*, minimizing the use of polluting materials and energy all the way from the initial extraction of resources through production, consumer use, reuse and recycling, and eventual disposal. In practice, however, the EPA must use limited and sometimes expensive tools aimed at separate problems—such as technology-based standards for air and water pollution—to try to solve complex environmental problems whose outcomes are often environmentally interconnected. More recently, Congress has sometimes allowed the EPA to adopt more flexible tools to reduce pollutants, such as cap-and-trade requirements, but these options are available only for a few specific uses approved by Congress, such as limiting sulfur emissions from power plants.

The EPA also regulates individual substances that have environmental health risks, such as pesticides, drinking water contaminants, and toxic chemicals used in manufacturing. Before doing so, however, it must undertake an elaborate process of "risk assessment" to determine how serious a hazard a substance is and how many people might be exposed to it, and the agency must then balance its risk against the economic benefits and costs of restricting it.

The EPA and the laws it administers were created with broad bipartisan support, and the agency itself and most of its laws were even approved by Republican presidents. Supporters of the agency argue that the EPA has made valuable and cost-effective contributions, given the tools, funds, and limitations Congress has given it, toward cleaning up air and water pollution and hazardous wastes and preventing toxic chemicals from endangering public health and the environment.[7] Critics argue, however, that its regulations are burdensome to the industries, small businesses, and state and local governments that must comply with them, even though most have been documented as having greater overall benefits to society than their costs. They also charge that these regulations hurt jobs and profits; that the EPA sometimes fails to do its job effectively (for example, when it failed to protect drinking water in Flint, Michigan, from lead contamination); and that the agency should therefore be reined in or even abolished.[8]

Consider, therefore, three examples of EPA regulations and how they were developed. How can the EPA reduce air pollution from coal-fired power plants? How can it reduce human exposure to toxic chemicals such as arsenic? And how can it reduce emissions of greenhouse gases (GHGs) such as carbon dioxide, which contribute to global climate change but were not considered when Congress passed the Clean Air Act?

Air Pollution from Electric Power Plants

Coal-fired power plants are one of the most significant sources of air pollution, including particularly sulfur dioxide (SO_2), nitrogen oxides (NO_x), particulates, and mercury (as well as GHGs, discussed later). As of 2008, the United States had 1,466 coal-fired generating units, most of them built before 1990; 58 percent of them were built even before the landmark Clean Air Act requirements of 1970.[9]

When Congress passed the Clean Air Act in 1970, it directed the EPA to set air pollution emission standards for all *new* facilities. Each of these must meet "new source performance standards," based on "the best emission reduction technology that had been adequately demonstrated, taking into account its cost." However, it exempted *existing* power plants so long as they were not modified. Retrofitting existing plants would have been far more expensive, and some state economies were heavily dependent on coal mining and use, so Congress preferred to assume that these old sources would gradually be phased out anyway. If an existing facility underwent "any" physical change or change in method of operation that would increase emissions, however, it would become subject to the new source standards as well.[10] The 1977 amendments to the Clean Air Act added a specific permit requirement, New Source Review (NSR), before construction of any new or modified facility that might increase air pollution.[11]

The EPA faced the question, therefore, of how to interpret this mandate. Did Congress really intend it to require costly new pollution controls for literally "any" physical or operational change in an existing facility? Or did Congress really mean to leave existing facilities alone so long as changes to them did not cause significant increases in air pollution? The EPA's initial regulations tried to strike this balance by setting a threshold: "any," it said, meant only a modification that would increase emissions by more than fifty tons of emissions per year. But it was immediately sued, both by environmental groups and by electric utility companies, and the court rejected this interpretation, holding that the "plain language" of the law meant "any" modification that results in more than a minimal increase in emissions.[12]

The EPA then revised its regulations to exempt "routine maintenance, repair, and replacements," as well as modifications that added only minimal amounts of pollutants. But once new power plants were more strictly controlled than existing ones, the utilities had a greater incentive to keep the old plants operating longer, and also to upgrade them as much as they could without triggering the NSR process. They did this by "spreading out" upgrades to the facilities over multiple years, integrating these upgrades into their operating and maintenance schedules, and then arguing that this was all part of "routine" maintenance for plant "rehabilitation"—even though the intended effect was to keep these old facilities operating longer, and sometimes at higher levels of emissions.[13]

These practices were tolerated by the EPA under Presidents Ronald Reagan and George H. W. Bush during the 1980s, but President Bush also introduced an innovative new solution by creating a "cap-and-trade" system, capping *total* emissions of sulfur from *all* large power plants and allowing the utilities to trade emission allowances among both existing and new plants to stay within the cap. This allowance market was highly effective in reducing total emissions, but it did not protect downwind communities from the emissions of particular facilities that bought the allowances and kept on polluting.

President Bill Clinton's EPA administrator, Carol Browner, therefore began an aggressive investigation into evasion of the NSR requirements by old coal-fired power plants, and filed suit against thirteen electric utilities for violations at fifty-one plants in thirteen states.[14] The utilities fought back, arguing that the EPA was now trying to enforce a more restrictive definition of "routine maintenance" than in the past; and they also spent heavily to support George W. Bush's successful presidential campaign over Clinton's vice president, Al Gore.

Once Bush was elected, the utilities lobbied vigorously to loosen the NSR rules, and in 2003, Bush's EPA officials proposed a new NSR rule that redefined "routine maintenance" as any upgrades that did not cost more than 20 percent of the plant's value—a huge loophole—and announced a weaker enforcement policy, dropping some seventy-five NSR enforcement investigations.[15] Environmental and public health groups objected strenuously, and fourteen states sued to block the rule changes. In 2003, a court ruled that one of the utilities had indeed violated the NSR rules eleven times at one of its plants; and in 2005 and 2006, the U.S. Court of Appeals for the District of Columbia rejected the Bush EPA's changes to the rules, holding that when Congress had originally applied NSR to "any" physical or operational changes that would increase pollution, it did indeed mean "any," not just those costing more than 20 percent of the facility's value.[16]

In the closing months of the Bush administration, his EPA officials tried once more to weaken NSR by substituting more discretionary (and thus less enforceable) criteria for review. Once President Obama took office, however, an environmental advocacy group immediately petitioned the new EPA administrator to reverse this change, and she did. After a decade and a half of litigation and a reaffirmation of support for NSR by a new president, the EPA ultimately took enforcement actions against some 45 percent of the country's electricity generating units, leading to 22 major settlements covering 263 units.[17]

What lessons does this case offer about how the EPA makes decisions? First, the issues involved are rarely simple and straightforward. The Clinton and Obama administrations, as well as the courts, generally supported the "plain language" of the NSR requirement—ironically, a position more often advocated by the most conservative judges. In contrast, some independent critics—not just the utilities—have argued that the NSR requirement itself prolongs the problem, by perpetuating the difference in cost that motivates power companies to keep using old coal-fired power plants rather than new ones with expensive end-of-pipe controls.[18] In these critics' view, a strict cap on overall emissions of both new and old power plants, combined with tradable permits, would achieve far greater pollution reduction. Others support a trading program, but one with safeguards to prevent regional "hot spots" of continued pollution downwind of the plants that choose to buy permits and keep polluting: a good example is the EPA's more recent Cross-State Air Pollution Rule (the "good neighbor rule"), which limits upwind states' overall emissions that interfere with downwind states' compliance.[19] Still others have argued that the EPA should simply phase out the "routine repair and maintenance" exemption.[20]

Second, the EPA itself is rarely the final decision maker. Almost any significant EPA decision will be challenged in lawsuits, either by the regulated businesses or by environmental advocacy groups or both. The courts thus play an essential role in EPA decision making, often supporting protective interpretations of the environmental laws, but not always (see also Chapter 6 on environmental policy in the courts).

Finally, the EPA's decisions rarely remain settled. Its decisions change economic outcomes for businesses that are regulated, thus creating ongoing incentives for companies to challenge regulations rather than comply. These challenges include not only petitions and lawsuits but also attempts to reverse EPA policies by congressional legislation or budget provisions and by electing presidents with different philosophies.

Toxic Chemicals: Arsenic in Drinking Water

In addition to pollutant emissions and other wastes, the EPA is responsible for protecting public health from toxic chemicals in drinking water, pesticides, and other products. These include thousands of substances, far too many to address individually in laws. Many have not been well studied, and many are not wastes but have profitable economic uses. How should the EPA decide which ones even to study, let alone to regulate, and how tightly should it regulate them? And to what extent should those decisions be based on documented public health risks, on the economic costs and anticipated benefits of restricting contaminants, and on expert opinions about risks that appear possible or even likely but remain uncertain?

To control toxic chemicals, Congress enacted "risk-based" and "risk-balancing" statutes. The air and water emission standards had required the EPA only to show that the "best available technology" they required was already being used by the best firms in each industry. In contrast, for risk-based regulation, the EPA must present "substantial evidence" to prove that a chemical poses an "unreasonable risk" to public health and that this risk outweighs the economic costs of restricting it.[21] And the agency must continually update all the scientific and economic evidence for each chemical. This places a heavy and costly burden of proof on the agency, especially with a limited budget and staff and the fact that scientific knowledge about many chemicals is limited, uncertain, contested, and constantly changing.

An example is the risk of arsenic contamination in drinking water.[22] Arsenic can cause nausea, diarrhea, numbness, blindness, paralysis, and even death, and it has been linked with several lethal kinds of cancer. As one member of Congress commented, "Anyone who has read an Agatha Christie novel knows that arsenic is a poison."[23] Yet it can be found in many Americans' drinking water, sometimes due to industrial wastes or agricultural use but often also as a natural contaminant. How then should the EPA decide how much to protect people from a health risk, when that decision also imposes costs on them to do so?

Under the Safe Drinking Water Act of 1974 (SDWA), the EPA became responsible for setting maximum contaminant levels (MCLs) for contaminants in public water supplies. These water suppliers included not only large cities and towns but also rural communities serving as few as fifteen households or twenty-five people, for which even testing regularly for contaminants would be a major expense, let alone removing them, since the costs were spread across so few households. In 1996, Congress amended the SDWA by creating a Drinking Water State Revolving Fund to provide low-interest loans for local water-supply improvements, and it also required the EPA to determine that the health benefits of its proposed MCLs exceeded their economic costs; if they did not, the EPA was to impose an MCL that "maximizes the benefits of health risk reduction only to the extent that the cost is justified by the benefits." For small water systems, the EPA administrator also was allowed to require a technology that did not fully meet the MCL but was considered affordable and provided some public health benefits.

The EPA adopted an initial MCL for arsenic in 1975, set at 50 micrograms per liter (equivalent to 50 parts per billion, or ppb). This MCL was based on a standard set by the Public Health Service in 1942, with the limited scientific knowledge available at the time. From the outset, however, many EPA scientists as well as public health and environmental advocacy groups questioned whether that level adequately protected public health. As early as 1962, the Public Health Service recommended that "the concentration of arsenic in drinking water should not exceed 0.01 mg/l and concentrations in excess of 0.05 mg/l are grounds for rejection of the supply" (that is, 10 and 50 ppb, respectively).[24] In 1988, an EPA risk assessment concluded that based on three recent epidemiological studies conducted in other countries, arsenic in drinking water should be considered a potential carcinogen as well as a poison.

In 1993, the World Health Organization adopted the 10 ppb limit, as did the European Union. Local U.S. water suppliers, however, continued to resist requirements that they provide costly water treatment, and there was still enough controversy over scientific uncertainties that the EPA did not tighten the standard. For instance, how similar were U.S. populations to those exposed to arsenic in other countries, how accurately could the EPA measure arsenic at levels of 3 ppb, and how much was it really worth to require very small water systems to pay to prevent small numbers of statistical cancer risks? A citizen group sued the EPA to demand that it tighten its regulations, however, and the EPA signed a consent decree promising to do so, but the agency then repeatedly requested extensions of the court's deadlines. Finally, in 1996, even a conservative-led Congress passed amendments to the SDWA that ordered the EPA to issue a revised draft MCL for arsenic by 2000 and a final rule by 2001. The EPA's appropriations bill in 2000 also ordered it to issue a final arsenic standard no later than June 22, 2001.

Beginning in 1996, the EPA responded by commissioning an independent scientific review by the National Research Council (NRC) and also by conducting extensive meetings with state, local, and tribal governments; water supply utilities; and other stakeholder groups. In 1999, the NRC concluded that based on both the earlier studies and more recent scientific information, arsenic should be considered a serious carcinogen. It also concluded that arsenic could cause non-cancer health effects at as little as 1 ppb exposure and that it could be reliably measured down to a level of at least 4 ppb. It recommended, therefore, that the 50 ppb standard should be significantly tightened.[25] On the basis of these studies, the EPA set an MCL goal of zero and considered setting an actual MCL of 3 ppb. But in June 2000, recognizing the cost burden this might impose on small water systems as well as the measurement challenges at such low levels, it proposed an MCL of 5 ppb as the level that "maximizes health risk reduction at a level where costs and benefits are balanced." It also conducted a "regulatory impact assessment"—a benefit-cost analysis—which concluded that if one based a decision solely on the costs and benefits of reducing bladder cancer, an MCL of 3, 5, 10, or even 20 ppb would have economic costs greater than its benefits, but that reducing arsenic exposure to these levels would also provide many other health benefits, although data did not exist to quantify them.[26]

The EPA then requested comment on the draft regulation from the public and from its Science Advisory Board, and the agency was sued by an environmental group pressing for the 3 ppb standard. In January 2001, it finally issued a regulation reducing the arsenic MCL from 50 to 10 (rather than 5 or 3) ppb.

In short, it took nearly forty years from the Public Health Service's recommendation of 10 ppb in 1962, and twenty-seven years from the time the EPA was given responsibility to regulate drinking water contaminants under the SDWA, before the EPA finally limited arsenic in drinking water to 10 ppb. Despite all the scientific reviews and risk assessments, the EPA's decision ultimately was still a discretionary administrative judgment that sought to "balance" assumptions about the effects of arsenic on cancer and other health risks, the economic benefits of preventing these effects, the practical costs of doing so, the relevance and persuasiveness of the scientific studies available, and other factors. EPA data also suggest that another reason for choosing 10 ppb may have been simply the number of water utilities that would have to comply: in the twenty-five states for which data were then available, fewer than 1,300 water systems would have to reduce their arsenic to reach 10 ppb but more than twice as many would require action to reach 5 ppb and nearly 2,000 more to reach 3 ppb.[27]

This "final" rule was not the end of the story, however. In late January 2001, the Clinton administration departed, and in March, President Bush's new EPA administrator, Christine Todd Whitman, suspended the rule for further review, claiming that she wanted to "replace sound-bite rule making with sound-science rule making" and to be "sure that the conclusions about arsenic in the rule are supported by the best available science." The implied message was that despite nearly forty years of study since the Public Health Service's recommendation in 1962 and the nine years that had passed since the World Health Organization adopted the same recommendation, the Clinton administration had somehow rushed the rule to completion before its term ended based on poor science.

The administrator's decision was applauded by westerners concerned about the rule's cost for communities with naturally occurring arsenic in their water, by the industries that produced and used arsenic, by antiregulatory conservatives more generally, and by some economists who argued that the EPA's benefit estimates were overstated. However, a firestorm of public opposition and media criticism followed. The decision to suspend the arsenic rule came just a week after Bush had reversed his commitment to reduce greenhouse gas emissions and withdrawn the United States from the Kyoto Protocol on global climate change. Suspension of the arsenic rule as well seemed to prove the Bush administration's hostility to environmental regulation. An environmental group sued the EPA again, demanding that it implement the regulation. Even the House of Representatives, with significant Republican support, proposed legislation to require a standard no less stringent than 10 ppb. Administrator Whitman commissioned several reviews of the rule, both within the EPA and by the NRC, and the NRC reconfirmed its 1999 findings, adding that new information might justify an even stronger standard.[28] In October, Whitman finally reconfirmed the new rule at the 10 ppb level, acknowledging that whatever the scientific and economic uncertainties, her suspension of the rule had been a political and public relations disaster.[29]

The arsenic MCL was thus finally confirmed at 10 ppb, and the EPA then had to implement it. According to the EPA, only 4,100 of the nation's 74,000 water systems would have to reduce arsenic contamination to comply with the rule, but the vast majority of these were very small systems: 73 percent served fewer than one thousand people, and 30 percent served fewer than one hundred. For many of these water systems, the arsenic rule required the first water treatment of any kind that they had been required to provide.[30] Many of these systems might therefore be given exceptions or waivers, which in turn would reduce the rule's effectiveness in protecting public health.

What lessons does this case teach? First, substance-by-substance regulation of contaminants is a far slower and more difficult process than technology-based or cap-and-trade regulation of air or water pollution. Despite decades of precedents by the Public Health Service and the World Health Organization, sustained lobbying and lawsuits by public health and environmental advocacy organizations, and even congressional mandates and deadlines, in the face of resistance from water utilities and their public officials, it required an outgoing presidential administration that was determined to leave a strong environmental legacy and had relatively few political debts to most of the states most affected, as well as a major public outcry in the media, to force the EPA finally to issue the regulation in 2001.

Second, a key reason for the EPA's slow regulatory process is that risk-based, substance-by-substance regulation imposes a heavy burden of proof on the agency. The EPA relies on independent external scientific organizations, such as its Science Advisory Board and the NRC, to validate its justifications; but despite the best science and economics available, significant uncertainties remain, as well as budget and staff constraints.[31] The agency's decisions therefore remain discretionary administrative "balancing" judgments, relying on assumptions about the remaining uncertainties, and the agency knows that these assumptions will always be attacked by opposing interests in the courts and the Congress. One could even argue that the EPA regulates most effectively when it has *least* discretion: when Congress sets a specific criterion by statute, for instance, as it did for motor vehicle emissions (95 percent reduction of average new car emissions by 1975) and new air pollution sources (requiring best available technology for new or modified emissions sources).

Finally, the EPA's decisions are deeply influenced by their anticipated impacts on small businesses and local governments, and these impacts pose significant challenges for the EPA in designing effective policies. As of 2012, an estimated six hundred water systems were still out of compliance with the 10 ppb standard.[32] One could argue, therefore, that a 10 ppb national standard was too stringent to be achieved by the very small systems yet not as stringent as would be justifiable for larger ones. Some economists argued that since drinking water quality was an inherently local issue, the EPA should simply require disclosure of contaminant levels and their associated risks and leave regulation to local choice.[33] However, this approach would run contrary to the EPA's mandate to protect all Americans and to a substantial literature showing that people often make bad choices in such situations and that the resulting burdens of ill health often fall on others (such as children and taxpayers who must pay for extra health care costs).[34]

Greenhouse Gas Emissions and Climate Change

A final case raises this question: How can the EPA deal with a newly identified environmental problem that was not fully anticipated when its regulatory statutes were enacted?

Climate change has been an important public policy issue since the late 1970s, when scientists proposed that global warming was increasing beyond its historic range due to carbon dioxide emissions from human activities: in particular, fossil fuel combustion in power plants, other industries, and motor vehicles. In 1987, Congress directed the EPA to develop a coordinated national policy on climate change, but most early policymaking focused on crafting an international agreement—the 1992 Framework Convention on Climate Change, which the United States adopted, and the 1997 Kyoto Protocol, which it did not—rather than on policies to control domestic emissions.

The Kyoto Protocol included binding targets for GHG emission reductions, which President Clinton agreed to but the U.S. Senate in 1997 voted overwhelmingly to reject unless industrializing countries such as China were also held to them. With Clinton's support, therefore, the EPA began to assert a more active policy role. In 1998, its legal office issued an opinion that EPA had the authority to regulate GHG emissions under the Clean Air Act even though it had not previously done so. In 1999, a group of environmental organizations and renewable energy businesses, citing this opinion, petitioned the EPA to regulate GHG emissions from new motor vehicles under the

Clean Air Act; and in January 2001, just as the Clinton administration left office, the EPA invited public comments on this petition, which produced nearly fifty thousand responses during the first five months of the incoming Bush administration.

While Bush was campaigning for the presidency against Al Gore in September 2000, he pledged that "[w]e will require all power plants to meet clean-air standards in order to reduce emissions of carbon dioxide within a reasonable period of time."[35] Once elected, however, he renounced this pledge and ended U.S. participation in the Kyoto Protocol negotiations; and his new appointee as the EPA's legal counsel issued a reinterpretation arguing that, contrary to the agency's previously issued opinion, the EPA did *not* have authority to regulate GHGs as air pollutants under the Clean Air Act. Bush's EPA officials also rejected the petition that had called on the EPA to regulate GHG emissions from motor vehicles. Unlike other regulated air pollutants, they argued, GHGs were only significant at a global scale and therefore were not amenable to the national- and state-level regulations provided by the Clean Air Act. Moreover, they argued that such a far-reaching new regulatory initiative should only be undertaken with explicit direction by Congress and after more extensive research, and that in the 1990 Clean Air Act amendments, Congress itself had only directed the EPA to pursue research and non-regulatory solutions for GHG emissions.[36]

Led by the state of Massachusetts, however, a group of states, cities, and environmental groups challenged this reinterpretation and asked the courts to require the EPA to regulate GHG emissions from motor vehicles. In 2005, the initial court upheld the Bush EPA's interpretation, but in 2007, the Supreme Court ruled that GHGs *did* fall within the Clean Air Act's definition of air pollutants and that the EPA therefore did have authority to regulate them. Given that authority, the court said, the EPA also had a legal *responsibility* to determine whether they "cause, or contribute to, air pollution which may reasonably be anticipated to endanger public health or welfare" (an "endangerment finding").[37] An affirmative endangerment finding, in turn, would automatically trigger an EPA obligation to set GHG emission standards.

In 2009, following the election of President Barack Obama, a bipartisan group of congressional leaders tried but ultimately failed to enact new legislation that would have created a cap-and-trade regime to reduce GHG emissions. Given the Supreme Court's *Massachusetts* decision as a mandate and President Obama's commitment to address the problem, the EPA thus became the lead agency to try to reduce GHG emissions. The new administrator issued an endangerment finding in 2009, concluding that GHGs did indeed contribute to risks to public health and welfare and that emissions from new cars and trucks contributed to these effects. President Obama then announced a joint initiative by the EPA and the Department of Transportation to coordinate the regulation of GHG emissions and of motor vehicle fuel efficiency, and several of the major car manufacturers and other major corporations announced their support. The motor vehicle standards (the "Tailpipe Rule") were finalized in 2010 and tightened further in 2012.[38]

An additional implication of the endangerment finding, however, was that once an emission is regulated as an air pollutant under *any* part of the Clean Air Act (motor vehicle emissions, in this case), all major *stationary* sources automatically became subject to regulation as well.[39] This principle empowered EPA to regulate GHGs from stationary as well as mobile sources, but it also had unintended consequences: "major" stationary sources had been defined as those emitting more than one hundred tons per year of traditional air pollutants, which meant only large industrial facilities and power plants; but far more facilities might emit that amount of carbon dioxide, including many hospitals, schools, restaurants, office buildings, farm buildings, and other establishments. The number of sources required to have permits thus could potentially increase from fewer than fifteen thousand to over six million, even though most of them were relatively small contributors to total GHG emissions. Annual administrative costs would increase from $62 million to $21 billion, and the newly regulated sources would face permitting costs estimated at $147 billion.[40] In 2010, the EPA therefore issued a rule requiring permits for new or modified GHG sources but "tailoring" these regulations to focus only on the largest sources—the power plants and other industrial facilities that emitted more than one hundred *thousand* tons of GHGs per year—while excluding the many smaller and nonindustrial facilities.[41] In 2012, the EPA also proposed performance standards requiring that all new or modified power plants use the "best system of emission reduction" (BSER) for GHGs, and in 2013, it issued a revised version of this standard.[42]

These standards relied on a crucial assumption: that carbon capture and storage (CCS) technologies had been "adequately demonstrated" as a "best system of emission reduction," even though only a handful of CCS facilities were actually operating so far, or that other options such as energy efficiency improvements could be used to achieve the reductions. The EPA's rationale was that few new coal-fired power plants were planned before 2020 and that new plants after that were already being designed to include CCS technology. Businesses and states opposed to the rule argued, however, that these technologies had not yet been adequately demonstrated at a commercial scale.

Two further complications also followed. First, issuing a performance standard for *new* power plants also triggered a requirement for the EPA to develop guidelines that *states* must use to reduce emissions from *existing* facilities, as part of their required "state implementation plans" for complying with the Clean Air Act. In June 2014, the EPA issued the Obama administration's "Clean Power Plan" (CPP), a proposed rule that set state-specific goals based on each state's power-plant GHG emission rates.[43] The goal of the rule was to reduce overall power-plant GHG emissions by 30 percent from 2005 levels, while allowing each state to adopt flexible strategies for doing so that best suited its circumstances. If a state did not submit a plan that satisfied the EPA's guidelines, EPA could write a plan for the state itself. The final CPP rule was issued in October 2015; initial state plans were to be completed by September 2016, and final ones by September 2018.

Second, because only some of the necessary emission reductions would likely be achieved by the existing power plants, the states would have to use additional measures to achieve the goals, such as increasing the substitution of natural gas and renewable energy for coal, avoiding the retirement of existing nuclear plants, increasing energy efficiency, adopting market-based incentives, and perhaps joining multistate cap-and-trade programs. Critics immediately argued that the CPP stretched the EPA's use of planning guidelines under environmental federalism beyond previous precedents and without legal authority.

In 2013 a group of utilities, other carbon-intensive industries, and some states and public officials (the "Utility Air Regulatory Group," or UARG) petitioned the Supreme Court to overrule the EPA's regulation of GHG emissions from stationary sources, arguing that CCS technology had not yet been adequately demonstrated and that trying to regulate GHG emissions from stationary sources would thus expand EPA regulation far beyond what Congress had intended in the Clean Air Act (the *Massachusetts* decision had only addressed motor vehicle emissions, not the effects of this decision in triggering the regulation of other sources as well). In its decision in this case in June 2014, the Supreme Court confirmed that the EPA had the authority to regulate GHG emissions from stationary sources that also emitted other pollutants specifically covered by the Clean Air Act. It also ruled, however, that the EPA could not regulate other sources solely for GHGs without congressional approval, nor did it have administrative discretion to change the specific tonnage triggers in the law (from one hundred to one hundred thousand tons per year) to solve the awkwardness of trying to "tailor" these provisions to "major" GHG sources. In effect, under this ruling the Supreme Court confirmed the EPA's authority to regulate sources of 83 percent of GHG emissions but protected many other smaller sources from becoming newly subject to EPA regulation without congressional action.[44]

In the same month as the court's *UARG* decision, the EPA announced its proposed Clean Power Plan rule, and the coal industry, along with twenty-six state governments and hundreds of other businesses and business organizations, immediately sued the EPA again to try to block it. The EPA, they argued, was trying to force the states to reduce GHGs by taking actions far beyond the actual performance of the regulated power plants themselves, using the Clean Air Act not just to reduce the power plants' own emissions but to try to create a whole new low-carbon energy economy. The EPA responded—supported by eighteen other states, many local governments, businesses, and environmental groups—by arguing that the flexibility it was offering to the states was in fact a classic case of cooperative environmental federalism: consistent with the original Clean Air Act and similar to previous environmental regulations, it set a national goal to reduce emissions endangering public health and welfare and allowed states broad flexibility to develop plans to achieve it.

The rule was finalized in August 2015, but in February 2016, a 5–4 majority of the Supreme Court put the rule on hold until the court case was decided, and in September 2016, the U.S. Court of Appeals for the District of Columbia Circuit heard oral arguments on the case.[45] In November 2016, meanwhile, Donald Trump was elected president, and on taking office he immediately issued an executive order directing the EPA to review the Clean Power Plan rule with the expectation of rescinding it. His new EPA administrator—the former attorney general of Oklahoma, and an outspoken opponent of climate-change regulations—then sent a letter to state governors declaring that "the days of coercive federalism are over" and telling them that they had no obligation to comply with the rule while it was on hold.[46]

This case thus offers several further lessons. First, as in both the previous cases, the EPA's decisions are driven by both internal and external forces, including its own staff, environmental and business advocacy groups, presidential policy preferences, and court decisions. Key decision points in this case included a memo from the EPA's legal staff under a supportive Clinton administration; a petition by environmental groups, based on this memo, asking the EPA to regulate carbon emissions from motor vehicles; a contrary memo by President Bush's EPA officials, disavowing that interpretation and rejecting the petition; a Supreme Court decision reaffirming the previous interpretation; a series of subsequent EPA rules under the Obama administration implementing that interpretation; a further Supreme Court decision affirming the EPA's authority to regulate but specifying more clearly the rationale and limits of that authority; an EPA rule implementing that authority but delayed by the Supreme Court pending final judicial review; and, following the 2016 election, a presidential executive order directing the EPA to review and presumably rescind the rule.

Second, as in the previous two cases, the EPA's policies clearly are influenced by presidential politics. Its first administrator, William Ruckelshaus, sought vigorously to establish its independence as a regulatory agency responsible first and foremost to faithfully execute the laws, based on the best science and economics available, even when that mission conflicted with President Nixon's business supporters. Beginning with the Reagan administration in the 1980s, however, the agency's policies became much more subject to change based on presidential politics, though those changes remained constrained by judicial oversight. The EPA's position on regulating GHG emissions changed significantly from the Clinton to the Bush administration and again under Obama, and yet again under President Trump; a critical question still unanswered is the extent to which President Trump's appointees will be upheld by the courts in their initiatives to change regulations put in place by their predecessors.

Third, what may appear to be relatively straightforward choices, such as whether the EPA should protect the environment by regulating GHG emissions from cars and trucks, can trigger far more complex consequences. In this case, it triggered regulatory consequences for thousands of stationary sources as well. If the CPP is upheld and not rescinded, there will be consequences also for state governments, which must develop state implementation plans to meet the EPA's compliance targets. Many observers believe that a broad-based carbon tax or cap-and-trade system would be more effective and more workable, whether or not they support that goal; but either of those tools would require new legislation, which Congress so far has been unable to pass. State cap-and-trade programs may be another option, but a more effective national solution would require congressional action (see also Chapter 2 on state environmental policymaking).

Achievements and Limitations

Overall, using the regulatory tools it has been given, the EPA has accomplished a great deal in making the environment cleaner (see Chapter 1). Air pollution has been dramatically reduced, and regulations for cars and trucks have produced major improvements in motor vehicle design to reduce air pollution and increase fuel efficiency. The EPA's permit requirements also have greatly reduced water pollution from wastewater treatment plants and industrial discharges, although runoff from farms, construction sites, and other nonpoint sources continues to cause serious problems. Solid and hazardous wastes are now managed far more safely: the EPA's regulations closed more than five thousand open-burning dumps in the 1970s, and municipal and commercial landfills are now far better managed by professionals under permit standards set by the EPA.[47] The EPA itself has pioneered some of the most important innovations in environmental policy, such as emissions trading and information disclosure requirements.

The EPA's risk-based, substance-by-substance regulations of hazardous chemicals have had far more limited success. They have banned or restricted a few highly visible and controversial toxic chemicals, but due to scientific uncertainties, limited staff and resources, political and legal resistance, and the heavy burden of proof it must sustain, the EPA has actually studied and regulated very few. One small ray of hope for the future was a rare bipartisan vote by Congress in 2016 to pass the Lautenberg Chemical Safety Act. The new law reformed the EPA's least effective mandate—the Toxic Substances Control Act—by making all commercial chemicals subject to EPA review, prioritizing those that posed the greatest risks, and giving the EPA broader options to manage these risks and to require more safety testing.

Both business advocates and policy scholars have sometimes criticized the EPA's regulations. Businesses often criticize them because of the additional costs of compliance, sometimes disregarding the "external" costs of the health effects and other economic damage that their own pollution imposes on others. Policy scholars often criticize the regulations as economically inefficient and discouraging of innovation: technology-based permit requirements, they argue, sometimes impose extra costs on firms that could reduce pollution more cheaply in other ways, and "best available technology" requirements tend to "lock in" the best existing technology rather than encouraging the discovery of more innovative solutions. Policy scholars have repeatedly recommended the use of markets, environmental taxes, information disclosure, and other innovative policy tools to achieve environmental protection more efficiently and effectively (see Chapter 10).[48]

In reality, however, the EPA can use only the tools that Congress has authorized, which often do not yet include innovative solutions that have been proposed.[49] It therefore has tried to use the regulatory powers it does have to address new problems, such as allowing trading of emission allowances, redefining animal feedlots as point sources, regulating genetically modified organisms as pesticides, and regulating greenhouse gases as dangers to public health and welfare. These are sometimes awkward substitutes, however, for designing more effective policies by statute.

The EPA's Future

Donald Trump was elected president in November 2016, after a campaign that included promises to revitalize the coal industry, get rid of "burdensome" environmental regulations—especially those addressing climate change—and drastically reduce or even abolish the EPA. He immediately rescinded all of President Obama's presidential directives on climate change and ordered the EPA to review and potentially rescind the Clean Power Plan, GHG emission standards for cars and trucks, and several other major EPA regulations. He also issued an executive order requiring that the agency must rescind at least two existing regulations before approving any new one, and that it should focus only on reducing compliance costs rather than on the benefits of regulations. And he appointed as EPA administrator the attorney general of Oklahoma, Scott Pruitt, who had declared himself skeptical of human effects on climate change and who had sued the EPA 14 times—in most cases, in collaboration with regulated industries, and so far unsuccessfully—to try to block the Clean Power Plan, the Cross-State Air Pollution Rule, and other EPA regulations, as examples of "federal overreach."[50]

In an initial "budget blueprint," Trump proposed narrowing the EPA's scope to focus on its "core legal requirements," leaving many of its responsibilities to the states and "easing the burden of unnecessary regulations that impose significant costs on workers and consumers without justifiable environmental benefits." To do this, he proposed cutting the EPA's budget by 31 percent, and its staff by 3,200 people. Under the proposal, support would continue for locally popular drinking-water and wastewater-treatment grants programs, but the agency's research funds would be cut by nearly half, its enforcement budget by nearly a quarter, and its hazardous waste cleanup funds by 30 percent. Trump also proposed eliminating funds for the EPA's climate change programs, its cleanup programs for major multistate resources such as the Great Lakes and Chesapeake Bay, and more than 50 other programs. Even as EPA administrator Pruitt praised environmental federalism and talked up closer EPA partnerships with the states, the budget blueprint proposed leaving many more responsibilities to the states while cutting the EPA's categorical grants—which support the state and tribal environmental agencies—by 44 percent.[51]

Congress responded with a bipartisan funding bill for the rest of 2017 that rejected nearly all these cuts, and Trump signed it. In May 2017, however, he sent Congress a proposed budget for 2018 that would cut the EPA's budget by nearly one-third and its workforce by 20 percent, the largest cuts for any federal agency. They included a 40 percent cut in its enforcement budget, 45 percent cuts in its research budget and its implementation and enforcement grants to states, a 50 percent cut in funds for setting drinking water standards, and a 25 percent cut in hazardous waste cleanup funds. Once again, he proposed eliminating the funding of all EPA's cleanup programs for geographic regions such as the Great Lakes, Chesapeake Bay, Puget Sound, and others, and abolishing the widely popular Energy Star program that provides energy-efficiency ratings for appliances. And he proposed severe cuts in funding for climate science research and monitoring. These reductions would affect not only the EPA but also NASA's Earth monitoring satellites, NOAA's climate-related studies, and even the National Science Foundation's basic climate research, as well as most of the Department of Energy's clean-energy programs.

What then is the likely future of the EPA? One outcome could indeed be the radical diminution of the agency that Trump has proposed. During the initial months of the Trump administration, Congress revoked proposed EPA rules to protect streams from mining debris, and Trump's EPA administrator revoked proposed rules that would require the reporting of methane emissions and ban a widely used insecticide that scientists had found to cause damage to fetal brains and nervous systems. In addition to the Clean Power Plan review, the EPA administrator also announced reviews of rules that protect wetlands (the Waters of the United States [WOTUS] rule), require greater fuel efficiency by cars and trucks, and limit toxic wastewater discharges from power plants, among others.[52] He declined to reappoint many of the members of several of the EPA's major scientific review boards, and he removed information about climate change from several of the EPA's websites. And even before congressional action on Trump's proposed budget cuts, Administrator Pruitt imposed a hiring freeze and began a process for the buy-out or early retirement of more than 1,200 of the EPA's staff, about 8 percent of its workforce.[53] A study of EPA's enforcement actions during Trump's first six months found that both the number of enforcement cases and the civil penalties collected were significantly lower than during the same period under Presidents Clinton and Obama and even under George W. Bush.[54]

President Reagan tried once before to "deregulate, defund, and delegate" the EPA's responsibilities, but it did not end well for him: the public and many members of Congress mobilized to "save EPA," he was forced to retreat and replace most of the agency's leadership, and, in the next elections, the public voted in congressional majorities supportive of the agency. The second President Bush also tried to weaken environmental regulations by reinterpreting them, but he too was then confronted with a more environmentally supportive Congress during his second term.

Trump could perhaps be more successful. First, his appointees to the EPA are more politically experienced, and the present congressional majorities are both more conservative and perhaps safer in their seats than those in the 1980s. However, the extent to which he will ultimately succeed in weakening the EPA is by no means certain. He was easily able to cancel rules that had not yet been finalized, but once rules have been adopted, they cannot be rescinded simply by the stroke of the president's or administrator's pen. They can only be replaced through the full process that was required to approve them in the first place, and proposed changes can be overturned by the courts, as was shown repeatedly in the three policy examples discussed in this chapter; several of Pruitt's initial rule changes also were overturned by the courts, and others are under challenge. Rewriting the EPA rules requires convincing new evidence to justify changing rules that were previously justified. It also is a labor- and science-intensive process, which will be even more challenging if the EPA receives severe cuts to its science budget and its personnel.

Second, EPA Administrator Pruitt's claim of a return to a "back to basics" form of environmental federalism is misleading. The EPA was founded, and its basic statutes were enacted, to create a stronger federal role in environmental protection, not a weaker one: it would set national minimum standards using science that was beyond the expertise of 50 separate states, and the states would then implement these with technical and financial assistance from the EPA. The EPA also served as a convenient "gorilla in the closet" whom the states could blame when they were compelled to regulate pollution from influential industries. Pruitt's proposal to reduce or even eliminate the agency's responsibilities for many environmental issues and leave them to the states, while simultaneously reducing the EPA's financial support to the states, is a far more radical notion of federalism: it would return many issues not to the period of the EPA's original mission but to the era before the EPA was created, when many states lacked the resources and the political will to address environmental problems themselves. Some conservative and fossil-fuel-dependent state governments may support such a change, but many other states do not, and will both lobby and sue to prevent it.

Finally, a serious attempt to gut the agency could well rekindle a backlash of public and even business opposition. Environmental protection often is not a major issue in elections, but frequently becomes one in the face of any serious threat to it. Congress routinely rewrites every president's budget proposals, either maintaining (or even increasing) existing funding levels or cutting them even more deeply; and it could, of course, even change the basic statutes that authorize its regulations and other programs. However, the EPA's mission and many of its programs are still popular with the public, with some influential businesses, and with many members of Congress, including even some Republicans; and even with full Republican support, the current Senate majority is less than would be needed to override a filibuster. Some business interests support radically weakening the EPA's regulations, but others benefit from them: they provide a single set of national standards rather than different ones in each state, they protect companies' reputations and compliance investments against less principled competitors, and they provide predictable requirements consistent with global as well as domestic expectations. And more than a few members of Congress may have second thoughts about defunding federal science research programs, which provide the factual evidence necessary to justify both legislative and administrative decisions. For all these reasons, many of Trump's proposed cuts may not be approved.

The most likely outcomes, therefore, are that during the Trump administration, the EPA will issue few if any new regulations but will make some attempts to revise and weaken existing ones. It probably will not succeed in actually rescinding many of the existing regulations, but it appears likely to try to undermine them by cutting budgets and staff for enforcement and by taking administrative decisions not to enforce them, though these tactics could be vulnerable to lawsuits and court orders requiring enforcement. One of the most serious long-term dangers is probably the attempt to radically defund the scientific research activities that are needed to understand the problems the agency is charged with addressing. A particular danger, for instance, is the attempt to eliminate nearly every trace of federal capacity to address climate change, including not simply the EPA's regulations but also climate science research, mitigation, and adaptation capacities throughout the federal agencies. These changes, if successful, could do serious damage to both America's and the world's understanding of important environmental forces and trends, and significantly hinder our ability to respond to them.

Rays of Hope

Despite attacks by some businesses and other critics, the basic frameworks and scientific foundations of the EPA's decisions remain largely intact so far. Even during unsupportive presidencies, the courts have frequently upheld the EPA's statutory responsibilities to protect the environment and have overruled attempts to reinterpret them in less protective ways. Both environmental advocacy groups and some state governments—and even some supportive businesses—have played key roles in bringing such lawsuits.

There is additional hope in the recent proliferation of state-level policy innovations (see Chapter 2). California and New Jersey led in developing hazardous chemical "right-to-know" laws in the 1980s, which led to the EPA's nationwide Toxics Release Inventory. More than half the states have passed renewable energy mandates, and twenty-four have passed tax credits for renewable energy. North Carolina passed a Clean Smokestacks Act in 2001, a state-level cap-and-trade requirement that forced its electric utilities to clean up or close down old coal-fired power plants that had been "grandfathered" under federal law. The act reduced sulfur emissions by more than

80 percent.[55] More recently, California and a coalition of northeastern states (the Regional Greenhouse Gas Initiative, or RGGI) are now becoming leading voices in climate-change policy both within the United States and in cooperation with other countries, with California in particular passing strong policies to reduce GHG emissions and promote energy efficiency and renewable energy (see Chapters 2 and 13). Other states have also moved aggressively to promote renewable energy, including even "deep red" states such as Texas and Iowa. At the same time, however, polluting industries and wealthy individuals opposed to regulation have begun pouring money into state election campaigns, as well as national ones, and proposing "model" state legislation to try to block strong environmental policy initiatives at the state level as well.[56]

There is also hope in coalitions between environmental advocacy groups and businesses that would prosper in a greener economy. Many leading businesses have identified ways in which good environmental management can be good business and, in cooperation with some environmental organizations, are positioning themselves to prosper in a more environmentally sustainable economy (see Chapter 11). Market forces favoring greener outcomes, such as the rapidly decreasing prices of natural gas and solar and wind energy and global expectations demanding mitigation of climate change, also have become important drivers of business decisions, and these influences will continue whether or not Trump's deregulation agenda succeeds. But the EPA's regulations remain an important motivator for other businesses, many of which are still polluting either because they lack the will to modernize old facilities or because it is inherently more expensive for them to control pollution than to pay for lawyers, lobbyists, and politicians to resist regulation.

The EPA thus remains an essential institution and—so far, at least—an important force within the limits of its authority, resources, and politically unstable leadership. The limits and imperfections of its policy tools are real, but more often than not, they result not from any unwillingness by the EPA to use more effective ones but from the inability of Congress—hamstrung by partisan and ideological gridlock and by the power of entrenched interests—to authorize better alternatives. Any hope of truly fundamental policy improvement must lie with broader political reforms and in broader coalitions of environmental and public health advocates with those businesses and state governments that are supportive of environmental protection.

Suggested Websites

U.S. Environmental Protection Agency (www.epa.gov) There are numerous links on this site that provide access to all major activities and issues of concern at the EPA, including environmental laws and regulations.

U.S. Environmental Protection Agency—EPA History (www2.epa .gov/aboutepa/epa-history) This section of the EPA site explores the agency's history and the significant changes over time in environmental laws and regulations.

U.S. Environmental Protection Agency New Source Review (www .epa.gov/nsr) This part of the EPA site is dedicated to explaining the New Source Review provisions under the Clean Air Act.

U.S. Environmental Protection Agency Arsenic Rule (https://www .epa.gov/dwreginfo/drinking-water-arsenic-rule-history) This part of the EPA site explains arsenic regulations under the Safe Drinking Water Act.

U.S. Environmental Protection Agency Carbon Pollution Standards and Clean Power Plan (https://19january2017snapshot.epa.gov/cleanpower-plan_.html)) This was the major EPA website for developments under the Clean Power Plan and other EPA actions to address carbon pollution under the Obama administration; it was replaced in 2017 by one showing current Trump administration initiatives to revise or rescind these rules (https:// www.epa.gov/energy-independence).

Notes

1. For a more detailed history of the EPA, see Richard Andrews, "The EPA at 40: An Historical Perspective," *Duke Environmental Law and Policy Forum* 21 (2011): 223–58.
2. Russell Train, "The Environmental Record of the Nixon Administration," *Presidential Studies Quarterly* 26 (1996): 185–96.
3. For more detail on EPA budgets and staffing, see Chapter 1 and Appendixes 2 and 3.
4. U.S. Environmental Protection Agency, *Fiscal Year 2016 Agency Financial Report* (Washington, DC: EPA, 2016), https://www.epa.gov/sites/production/files/2016-11/documents/epa_fy_2016_afr_2.pdf.
5. Philip Shabecoff, "E.P.A. Aims to Curb Tall Smokestacks," *New York Times*, June 28, 1985.
6. See, for instance, Trip Gabriel, "Utility Cited for Violating Pollution Law in North Carolina," *New York Times*, March 3, 2014.
7. Brian Clark Howard and Robert Kunzig, "5 Reasons to Like the U.S. Environmental Protection Agency," *National Geographic*, December 9, 2016, http://news.nationalgeographic .com/2016/12/environmental-protection-agency-epa-history-pruitt/.
8. Coral Davenport, "E.P.A. Faces Bigger Tasks, Smaller Budgets and Louder Critics," *New York Times*, March 18, 2016.
9. "Existing U.S. Coal Plants, Age Comparison," *SourceWatch,* http://www.sourcewatch .org/index.php/Existing_U.S._Coal_Plants#cite_note-14; U.S. Energy Information Administration, "Most Coal Plants in the United States Were Built Before 1990," *Today in Energy,* April 17, 2017, https://www.eia.gov/todayinenergy/detail .php?id=30812.
10. Clean Air Act of 1970, Public Law 91-604, Section 111.
11. U.S. Environmental Protection Agency, *New Source Review*, www.epa.gov/nsr.
12. *Alabama Power Co. v. Costle*, 636 F.2d 323, 400 (D.C. Cir. 1979).
13. Larry Parker, *Clean Air: New Source Review Policies and Proposals*, CRS Report No. RL31757 (Washington, DC: Congressional Research Service, 2003); *Clean Air and New Source Review: Defining Routine Maintenance*, CRS Report No. RS21608 (Washington, DC: Congressional Research Service, 2005).

14. James E. McCarthy, "Clean Air Act: A Summary of the Act and Its Major Requirements," in *Clean Air Act: Interpretation and Analysis*, ed. James P. Lipton (New York: Nova Science, 2006), Chapter 1. See pages 41–43 on New Source Review.

15. Christopher Drew and Richard Oppel Jr., "Air War—Remaking Energy Policy: How Power Lobby Won Battle of Pollution Control at E.P.A.," *New York Times Magazine*, March 6, 2004.

16. John Shiffman and John Sullivan, "EPA's Court Follies Sow Doubt, Delay," *Philadelphia Inquirer*, December 8, 2008; *New York v. EPA*, 413 F. 3d 3 (D.C. Cir. 2005); *New York v. EPA*, 443 F. 3d 880 (D.C. Cir. 2006).

17. Thomas McGarity, "When Strong Enforcement Works Better Than Weak Regulation," *Maryland Law Review* 72 (2013): 1204–94.

18. Howard Gruenspecht and Robert Stavins, "New Source Review under the Clean Air Act: Ripe for Reform," *Resources* 147 (2002): 19–23.

19. Laura Barron-Lopez, "Court Upholds Cross-State Air Pollution Rule," *The Hill*, April 29, 2014, http://thehill.com/regulation/energy-environment/204658-supreme-court-upholds-epa-cross-state-air-pollution-rule.

20. Victor Flatt and Kim Diana Connolly, "'Grandfathered' Air Pollution Sources and Pollution Control: New Source Review under the Clean Air Act," Center for Progressive Regulation White Paper (March 2005), www.progressivereform.org/articles/NSR_504.pdf.

21. John Applegate, "The Perils of Unreasonable Risk," *Columbia Law Review* 91 (1991): 261–333, www.repository.law.indiana.edu/cgi/viewcontent.cgi?article=1715&context=facpub.

22. Mary Tiemann, *Arsenic in Drinking Water: Regulatory Developments and Issues*, CRS Report No. RS20672 (Washington, DC: Congressional Research Service, May 1, 2007).

23. Rep. Anna Eshoo, 147 Cong. Rec. H4751 (July 27, 2001).

24. U.S. Public Health Service, *Public Health Service Drinking Water Standards* (Washington, DC: Department of Health, Education, and Welfare, 1962), 26, https://archive.org/stream/gov.law.usphs.956.1962/usphs.956.1962.

25. National Research Council, *Arsenic in Drinking Water* (Washington, DC: National Academy Press, 1999).

26. U.S. EPA, *Proposed Arsenic in Drinking Water Rule: Regulatory Impact Analysis*, EPA 815-R-00-013 (Washington, DC: EPA, 2000), 113.

27. Natural Resources Defense Council, *Arsenic and Old Laws* (New York: NRDC, 2000), http://www.fluoride-class-action.com/wp-content/uploads/nrdc-arsenic-and-old-laws-nrdc.org_.water_.drinking.arsenic.exesum.asp_.doc, Table 1.

28. Katherine Seelye, "EPA to Adopt Clinton Arsenic Rule," *New York Times*, November 1, 2001.

29. Greg Easterbrook, "Hostile Environment," *New York Times Magazine*, August 19, 2001.

30. U.S. EPA, *Arsenic Rule: Small Systems Implementation Strategy & Exemptions* (2002), https://www.epa.gov/sites/production/files/2015-09/documents/train3-implementation.pdf.

31. Cass Sunstein, "The Arithmetic of Arsenic," *Georgetown Law Journal* 90 (2001–2002): 2255–309.

32. U.S. EPA, Arsenic Small Systems Working Group, *Synthesis of Individual Participant Input* (2012), www.ruralwater.org/arsenicreportdraft.pdf.

33. Wallace Oates, "The Arsenic Rule: A Case for Decentralized Standard Setting?" *Resources* 147 (2002): 16–18.

34. Tom Gorman, "Nevada Town's Residents Unperturbed about Arsenic in Its Drinking Water," *Los Angeles Times*, April 9, 2001.
35. Seth Borenstein, "Bush Changes Pledge on Emissions," *Philadelphia Inquirer*, March 14, 2001.
36. Robert Fabricant (EPA General Counsel), "EPA's Authority to Impose Mandatory Controls to Address Global Climate Change under the Clean Air Act" (August 29, 2003), cited in *Federal Register* 68(173): 52922–32 at page 52925.
37. *Massachusetts v. EPA*, 549 U.S. 497 (2007).
38. James McCarthy, *Cars, Trucks, and Climate: EPA Regulation of Greenhouse Gases from Mobile Sources*, CRS Report No. R40506 (Washington, DC: Congressional Research Service, 2014).
39. The "timing rule" (also known as the "PSD Triggering Rule") was issued in 1980; it made any source emitting more than one hundred tons of any regulated air pollutant subject to requirements for an EPA permit for "prevention of significant deterioration" of air quality (PSD). The Supreme Court unanimously reconfirmed the EPA's authority to regulate GHGs from power plants in *American Electric Power Co. v. Connecticut*, 564 U.S. 410 (2011).
40. *Utility Air Regulatory Group v. EPA*, 134 S. Ct. 2427 (June 23, 2014).
41. *Federal Register* 75: 31514, June 3, 2010; Robin Bravender, "EPA Issues Final 'Tailoring' Rule for Greenhouse Gas Emissions," *New York Times*, May 13, 2010.
42. *Federal Register* 77 (2012): 22392; James McCarthy, *EPA Standards for Greenhouse Gas Emissions from Power Plants: Many Questions, Some Answers*, CRS Report No. R43127 (Washington, DC: Congressional Research Service, 2013).
43. Environmental Protection Agency, *Carbon Pollution Emission Guidelines for Existing Stationary Sources: Electric Utility Generating Units*, 40 *CFR* Part 60, *Fed. Reg.* 79: 34830 (2014).
44. *Utility Air Regulatory Group v. EPA*, 134 S. Ct. 2427 (June 23, 2014).
45. Linda Tsang and Alexandra Wyatt, *Clean Power Plan: Legal Background and Pending Litigation in West Virginia v. EPA*. CRS Report No. R44480 (Washington, DC: Congressional Research Service, March 8, 2017).
46. Letter, Scott Pruitt to the Honorable Matt Bevin, March 30, 2017, accessed September 4, 2017, https://www.epa.gov/sites/production/files/2017-03/documents/ky_bevin.pdf.
47. Richard Andrews, *Managing the Environment, Managing Ourselves: A History of American Environmental Policy* (New Haven, CT: Yale University Press, 2006), 245–49.
48. At least one scholar, however, has argued that this conventional wisdom is overstated and often wrong and that "there are solid reasons to suspect that an emissions trading program does a poorer job of stimulating innovation than a comparably designed traditional regulation." See David Driesen, "Does Emissions Trading Encourage Innovation?" *Environmental Law Reporter* 33 (2003): 10094–108.
49. Andrews, "The EPA at 40," 229–34.
50. "Pruitt v. EPA: 14 Challenges of EPA Rules by the Oklahoma Attorney General," *New York Times*, January 14, 2017.
51. U.S. Office of Management and Budget, *America First: A Budget Blueprint to Make American Great Again* (March 2017).
52. Nadja Popovich and Tatiana Schlossberg, "23 Environmental Rules Rolled Back in Trump's First 100 Days," *New York Times*, May 2, 2017, https://www.nytimes.com/interactive/2017/05/02/climate/environmental-rules-reversed-trump-100-days.html?mcubz=0&_r=0.

53. Brady Dennis, "EPA Plans to Buy Out More Than 1,200 Employees This Summer," *Washington Post*, June 20, 2017, https://www.washingtonpost.com/news/energy-environment/wp/2017/06/20/epa-plans-to-buy-out-more-than-1200-employees-by-the-end-of-summer/?utm_term=.a7a9c9ba72ef.

54. Eric Schaeffer, *Environmental Enforcement Under Trump* (Washington, DC: Environmental Integrity Project, August 10, 2017), http://www.environmentalintegrity.org/wp-content/uploads/2017/08/Enforcement-Report.pdf.

55. Richard Andrews, "State Environmental Policy Innovations: North Carolina's Clean Smokestacks Act," *Environmental Law* 43 (2013): 881–940.

56. Suzanne Goldenberg, "Conservative Lobby Group Alec Plans Anti-Environmental Onslaught," *The Guardian*, December 2, 2014, https://www.theguardian.com/us-news/2014/dec/02/alec-environmental-protection-agency-climate-change.

Part III

Public Policy Dilemmas

Chapter 8

Energy Policy
Fracking, Coal, and the Water-Energy Nexus

Edward P. Weber, David Bernell, Hilary S. Boudet,
and Patricia Fernandez-Guajardo

E nergy is a core component of modern economies. A functioning economy requires not only labor and capital but also energy, for manufacturing processes, transportation, communication, agriculture, and more. Access to energy is also critical for basic social needs, such as lighting, heating, cooking, and health care. As a result, the price of energy has a direct effect on jobs, economic productivity and business competitiveness, and the cost of goods and services. For example, sustained increases in the price of oil were a key contributor to the economic recessions of 1974, 1979, and the early 1990s. On the other hand, recent declines in the price of natural gas in the United States have led to lower operating costs at manufacturing facilities, spurring new facilities and jobs, while lowering home heating and cooling costs, which leaves more money in consumers' pockets.

Providing the energy needed for economic growth is rife with challenges. Heavy reliance on fossil fuel, or carbon-based, energy sources—oil, coal, and natural gas—is responsible for releasing massive amounts of greenhouse gases (GHGs), particularly carbon dioxide, into the atmosphere and contributing significantly to global warming and climate change (see Chapter 13). The production and transportation of oil and gas through pipelines and oceangoing tankers risks disastrous spills, as highlighted by the 2010 Deepwater Horizon accident in the Gulf of Mexico. Coal extraction poses its own set of risks, including serious health problems from coal dust, safety issues associated with underground working conditions, and pollution from mining wastes. As well, the human health and ecological risks associated with nuclear energy are illustrated by accidents at Three Mile Island (United States, 1979), Chernobyl (Ukraine, 1986), and Fukushima (Japan, 2011). Even wind and solar energy, often cited as a panacea for our energy challenges, present environmental risks to endangered species, can result in habitat degradation, and require water resources in arid areas.

The many technical, economic, and environmental challenges associated with energy resources inevitably means that controversy and conflict are all too common in the U.S. energy policy arena. The classic NIMBY, or not in my backyard, resistance applies to energy development, whether it is fossil fuels or renewables. There are serious internal disagreements within the broader environmental movement as some groups, for example, promote "green" priorities such as endangered species protection, water conservation in arid areas, and forest and grassland protection that directly interfere with renewable energy siting and development. There are organized and massive protests against major fossil fuel projects such as the Dakota Access pipeline from North Dakota to the Midwest and in support of policies to combat climate change (Chapter 3). There are legislative- and voter-approved bans or restrictions on hydraulic fracturing (fracking) in states as varied as Colorado, Pennsylvania, California, and New York. And there is stiff resistance from political conservatives to government policies subsidizing and otherwise facilitating renewable energy development.

The conflict often translates into a partisan divide, with each presidential administration bringing different sets of values and priorities for how to address these challenges (see Chapter 4). With Republican president George W. Bush, oil, gas, and nuclear energy all received strong rhetorical and policy support, including a push for additional oil and gas drilling on public lands and in offshore (near ocean) zones, as well as large government subsidies for new nuclear plants. However, President Barack Obama, a Democrat, charted a different direction. The Department of the Interior (DOI) reduced new oil and gas leases for federal public lands and offshore areas while also aggressively promoting the development of renewable energy. Moreover, the Obama administration used the 2007 Supreme Court ruling allowing the Environmental Protection Agency (EPA) to regulate greenhouse gases as the rationale for the EPA's new, stricter regulations on power-plant pollution; many believe this policy signaled the "end of coal" in the U.S. power industry (see Chapter 7). President Donald Trump's rhetoric and early executive decisions are designed to reverse major Obama administration energy initiatives, such as the Clean Power Plan and the decision *not* to build the Keystone XL pipeline, while also promoting coal and oil and gas development, including offshore drilling on the southeast coast of the United States and Alaska.

These partisan differences between presidents, and between Democrats and Republicans, have become ever more important, given congressional gridlock on environmental and energy issues and the increasing willingness of presidents to use their executive powers to pursue policy goals unilaterally. Such developments place even greater pressure on each government agency involved in energy issues, from the EPA to the Department of Energy (DOE) and DOI agencies, as they struggle to balance competing needs and priorities in the face of intensive lobbying by energy interests. They also place greater pressure on state legislatures, governors, and energy-policy-oriented regulatory officials at that level, given the lack of an overall national energy policy and the fact that they make many of the nation's critical energy development decisions.

These issues—the technical, economic, and environmental challenges of energy; the contemporary conflict and controversies; and the partisan divide over energy—frame much of the analysis in this chapter. We also provide a glimpse into the intricate connections between water and energy, along with some policy solutions to the dilemma of the water-energy nexus that strike a different, more bipartisan tone. To bring these issues to light, we use three case studies important to contemporary energy politics and policy in the United States:

- The emergence and growth of hydraulic fracturing to exploit previously inaccessible shale gas and "tight" oil
- The challenges facing coal
- The emerging recognition of, and some solutions to, the complex problem set known as the water-energy nexus

Prior to these cases, the chapter dissects the dynamic underlying the politics of energy.

U.S. Energy Policy and Politics Today

Currently, the major issues in U.S. energy policy revolve around the rapidly growing production of domestic and other North American energy resources. Technological advances in hydraulic fracturing and horizontal drilling have allowed access to oil and natural gas in shale rock formations. The development of renewable, or "green," energies such as solar, wind, bio-mass, and geothermal has greatly expanded due to new policies and growing concern over climate change. In fact, in 2015, wind power accounted for 4.7 percent of U.S. electricity generation, a figure 20 percent higher than in 2013 and up from less than 1 percent fifteen years earlier. Colorado, Texas, Idaho, Oregon, Minnesota, Vermont, Iowa, and Maine now receive more than 10 percent of their electricity from wind power.[1] Iowa is the leader with more than 35 percent of its electricity generated by wind. The explosion in U.S. supplies of natural gas due to hydraulic fracturing since 2000, and consequent low prices, has increased natural gas's share of the national energy portfolio from 16 percent of all electricity generated in 2000 to 33 percent in 2016. By contrast, coal use has dropped from 51 percent to 32 percent over the same time frame.[2] Taken together, these developments suggest that the United States could soon achieve energy independence.

However, the U.S. drive toward energy independence and less reliance on oil and coal is fraught with partisan conflict because these issues revolve around how best to balance both competing values, such as environmental protection and economic growth, and the demands of rival organized interests, such as those of the fossil fuel industry and of the newer renewable energy businesses. Just as importantly, many of these disputes directly involve the executive branch agencies responsible for writing regulations.

In order to better understand U.S. energy politics and policy today, we first describe the technical, economic, and environmental elements of energy policy using a four-part lens—supply expansion, demand management and reduction, cost analysis, and reliability of supply. The analysis then turns to the contours of contemporary U.S. energy politics.

Supply Expansion

This approach seeks to determine the extent to which policy measures impact the expansion of different forms of energy supplies. Analyzing policy through this lens tends to be based upon an understanding that the ever-growing demands for energy need to be met. Energy shortages are not the problem—there are a wide variety of resources available—but converting these resources into usable energy is. The focus thus is on the existing barriers to such a goal, be they technical, policy (statutory or regulatory), economic, environmental, geographical, or political, and how to overcome them through policy solutions (financing, tax incentives, direct appropriations, demonstration projects, regulatory mandates). And the key to determining the value of a policy is its ability to expand energy supplies.

Demand Management and Reduction

This approach takes the opposite tack; the key to determining the value of a policy is the extent to which its measures reduce energy demand—in other words, how well a policy promotes and achieves efficiency and conservation. Analyzing policy through this lens acknowledges that energy needs are growing and that new supplies are necessary but suggests that new supplies are not sufficient. Because so much energy is wasted through overconsumption and inefficiency, one of the best ways to become more energy secure is to reduce demand. The policy focus here has been on incentives (tax credits and rebates for energy-efficient equipment), consumer education (energy rating information on appliances), technological development, mandates (Corporate Average Fuel Economy [CAFE] standards, building codes), and reducing barriers to lifestyle changes that would result in reduced energy usage (city planning that would encourage walking and biking over driving). This type of analysis seeks to determine the value of policy by measuring its ability to reduce energy demand.

Cost Analysis

A cost analysis approach seeks to capture the expected and unintended costs of energy resources and associated policies. This approach reflects an understanding that the best energy resources (and this includes efficiency and conservation) are those that minimize the costs associated with their production and use. Costs can be defined narrowly—in terms of the financial costs to consumers (the price of a kilowatt-hour of electricity or a gallon of gasoline) or taxpayers (government appropriations and tax expenditures)—or broadly, in terms of environmental, national security, and social costs. Broadly defined costs can include the health and environmental impacts of coal (mining, transportation, pollution from combustion, hazardous waste disposal) or the costs incurred by military operations securing access to oil (for example, in the Persian Gulf region).

Reliability of Supply

Another key consideration for energy policy is reliability of supply. Every energy source has inherent limitations on its reliability. When supply falls short of demand, fuel prices are likely to rise steeply and cause economic disruptions, particularly in countries dependent on a single fuel type or supplier. Historically, the reliability problem for oil and natural gas stems from a mismatch between the locations of major supplies and the locations of major demand centers—a problem that becomes more acute when supplies are located in politically volatile regions of the world such as the Middle East and Russia.

Reliability of supply is also critically important to electricity production and delivery. A key reason electric systems rely heavily on coal, oil, natural gas, and nuclear power is that these energy sources can be managed to generate electrical outputs that match widely varying demands, including peaks in energy demand by households and industry. The push to produce more electricity from solar and wind power has brought the reliability question into sharper relief because solar and wind are intermittent sources of energy: they produce electricity only when the sun shines or the wind blows. Intermittent renewable energy sources thus require backup sources of generation to produce a more predictable flow of electricity to match demand. As a result, these renewable systems are often paired with traditional energy sources, such as coal, gas, nuclear, or hydropower.

Politics and Energy

Understanding U.S. energy policy also requires an analysis of politics and the conflict behind policy choices, particularly the changing values of the American public, the emergence of climate change on the policy agenda, and partisan battles over whether and how much government intervention is warranted in support of a particular type of energy. Other fault lines include the level of government in charge of energy development and the value-based disagreements over the costs and benefits associated with different energy types.

The first piece in the energy politics puzzle involves the level of public support for different energy types and the issues associated with energy development and use. For example, prior to the emergence of the contemporary environmental movement in the 1960s, policies promoting the aggressive exploitation of fossil fuels were not controversial; rather, fossil fuels were widely supported as engines for economic growth. Key to this support were the narrow and largely invisible policy subgovernments of congressional committees, federal agencies, and organized industry interests favorable to oil and gas leasing on public lands, nuclear power, and coal development. However, as more citizens came to understand the social costs of pollution and as concerns over climate change grew, public opinion shifted to be less supportive of fossil fuels and more supportive of green energy sources.

A second component of energy politics involves the conflict over whether and how much government intervention is warranted in support of a particular type of energy. For example, considerable disagreement exists over the role government should play in the transition toward a green energy economy, with conservatives and Republicans in staunch opposition to both the premise that green energy is necessary and that government has a major role to play in promoting the development of green energy sources. Despite the resistance, the trend is toward more government promotion of renewable energies, which finds strong support among Democrats, their "green energy" industry allies, and environmentalists. The Obama administration, in particular, supported many green energy initiatives, especially when compared to the Trump and George W. Bush administrations. These federal and state policies have taken four general forms:

Corporate Subsidies for Energy Development and New Energy Technologies. More than a dozen states refund up to half of wind energy development costs, with Oregon willing to pay up to $10 million per site. The U.S. Energy Policy Act of 2005 offered grants, loans, and tax credits to firms developing renewable energy and green technologies such as solar panels, zero emission vehicles, and hybrid cars. In addition, the Energy Policy Act of 1992 provided a tax credit of 2.3 cents per kilowatt-hour to renewable energy generators in order to make renewables more competitive with natural gas and coal. The Obama administration dramatically expanded government subsidies for renewable energy development in 2009 when, under the auspices of the American Recovery and Reinvestment Act, it created the Section 1603 U.S. Treasury grant program. Over three years, the Treasury awarded $9 billion in "1603" grants to small and startup green energy companies, which accounted for 50 percent of the total nonhydropower renewables capacity added between 2009 and 2011.[3]

Regulatory Incentives to Lower Carbon Emissions. These policies are designed to either raise the costs of nonrenewables, thus discouraging their use, or lower the costs of preferred green energy and related technologies. The three primary types are carbon taxes, emissions trading (for carbon), and tax credits for individual consumers (e.g., for rooftop solar panels or hybrid vehicles). President Obama and congressional Democrats made clear in 2009, in their unsuccessful push for national climate change legislation, that a carbon emissions trading, or cap-and-trade, program was their preferred approach. At the state level, emissions trading programs have also found political support. Major efforts have included the Regional Greenhouse Gas Initiative (RGGI) to cap and reduce carbon dioxide emissions from the power sector in nine northeastern and Atlantic region states and California's statewide cap-and-trade program for GHGs, implemented by Democratic governor Jerry Brown in 2012 (see Chapter 2). The possible withdrawal from the 2015 Paris Agreement on climate change by President Trump and his early stance against incentives (e.g., tax credits) for renewables suggest that if these regulatory incentives are to continue in a significant way for the near future, it will be states leading the charge.

Leniency in Regulatory and Permitting Processes for Green Energy. A growing number of state and federal agencies, such as the Bureau of Land Management (BLM), now practice streamlining, or "fast-track" permitting, for green energy development projects. At the same time, shortly after President Obama took office, the DOI relaxed the long-standing "strict liability" approach to the Migratory Bird Treaty Act (MBTA) of 1918 as one way of protecting wind energy projects from legal liability. The MBTA prohibited the taking or killing of migratory birds, including eagles, even if preventative measures were taken and even if the activity was not directed against wildlife. In 2010, the DOI's Fish and Wildlife Service designed a specific program— the Bird and Bat Conservation Strategy (BBCS)—that allows for takes of migratory birds at wind energy installations.[4] Critics such as the National Audubon Society called the rule "a blank check" for the wind power industry.[5] And although the Trump administration's approach in this area is not fully formed, it is reasonable to expect less favoritism for green energy projects.

Renewable Portfolio Standards (RPS). Employed by thirty states, RPS set a minimum standard, or share of electricity, to be provided from renewable resources, including wind, solar, geothermal, biomass, landfill gas, and solid waste. A leading example is California, where electric utilities must derive 25 percent of their retail sales from renewables by the end of 2016 and 50 percent by 2030 (see Chapter 2).

There also is political conflict over which level of government should be in charge. Currently, a large number of agencies have energy policy responsibilities at the federal level, including but not limited to the DOE, Federal Energy Regulatory Commission (FERC), Nuclear Regulatory Commission (NRC), and EPA. Moreover, with federally controlled offshore zones and public lands in the western United States amenable to all types of energy development, federal agencies such as the Bureau of Ocean Energy Management (BOEM) and BLM will likely continue to play an important, and perhaps decisive, role in many projects. And it is often in these federal bureaucracies where the differences in partisan preferences for different types of energy, approaches to regulation, and values are on full display. An important example involves the significant differences in the EPA's approach to power industry regulation under Presidents Bush and Obama. Despite some momentum for reducing carbon dioxide emissions from power plants at the end of the Clinton administration, the Bush administration decided against EPA rules for capping carbon dioxide emissions and actively sought to delay their implementation despite a 2007 Supreme Court ruling (Massachusetts v. EPA) that carbon dioxide was a covered pollutant under the Clean Air Act (CAA). Bush also promoted his 2002 Clear Skies Initiative calling for a market-based approach to CAA goals, which necessarily would weaken the requirement that coal-fired plants reduce mercury emissions. President Obama, on the other hand, took a top-down, command-and-control approach to air pollution and viewed the EPA as one of his most powerful tools for fighting climate change. His administration took the 2007 Massachusetts v. EPA ruling and retailored the CAA "major source" rule to cover over 86 percent of industrial GHG emissions (see Chapter 7). President Trump's appointments to the EPA and the DOI, Oklahoma Attorney General Scott Pruitt and U.S. Rep. Ryan Zinke (R-Montana), respectively, along with Trump's strong push for deregulation, suggest a return to a more conservative approach that favors market forces and state-level control of energy-related decisions. Trump's EPA is also highly unlikely to take many, if any, initiatives on behalf of mitigating climate change.

At the same time, federal policy gridlock over climate change and the lack of an overall strategic national energy policy has created opportunities for states to take the lead in battling climate change and forging the transition to new types of energy.[6] Complicating the issue further are the strong private property and mineral rights in the United States that give individual citizens significant control over whether energy development will take place in a specific area. In fact, the United States is the only country in which surface property rights also include the rights to subsurface mineral deposits, including hydrocarbons. When these property rights are considered together with the fact that energy development of any type is disruptive, visible, and highly impactful, with benefits and externalities directly affecting the local "place" of development, one sees that local governments have a genuine stake in energy policy, too.

A full understanding of the politics of energy also requires attention to costs and benefits. Political opposition to new alternative energy forms often focuses on its higher *economic* cost relative to fossil fuels such as coal or natural gas, although, as the numbers below demonstrate, this cost difference between fuels is changing rapidly. Chief opponents include economic conservatives and Republicans, energy-intensive heavy industries, and labor unions involved in energy infrastructure and energy-intensive manufacturing enterprises. Such differences at present are significant if the focus is on kilowatt-hour costs of electricity. For example, the average per-kilowatt-hour cost of household electricity in Germany, a world leader in installing solar and wind capacity, was 28.8 cents in 2016 compared to the U.S. average of 12.43 cents. Another comparative measure is the *unsubsidized* levelized cost of electricity, which represents the per-kilowatt-hour cost of building and operating a generating plant over the full life of the facility. This measure shows that onshore wind (5.58 cents) and solar PV (7.37 cents) are now significantly less expensive than coal (10.0 cents) and advanced nuclear (9.77 cents), but both are still higher than advanced combined cycle natural gas (5.38 cents).[7]

Proponents of green energy, on the other hand, typically include environmental and climate change advocates, industries with low energy needs, public sector unions, political liberals, and Democrats. Their focus is on the negative "social," or health and environmental, costs of fossil fuels (which are largely externalized), the long-term benefits from weaning society off carbon-based fuels, and the expectation that green energy costs will eventually become competitively priced, particularly as technological innovation continues apace and once the true social costs of carbon are factored into the equation. In fact, the cost of onshore wind energy declined 51.2 percent between

2009 and 2016, while the price of solar panels has dropped over 99 percent since the 1970s.[8] Moreover, according to three prominent economists, the "social" cost of six major air pollutants emitted by coal power plants add 2.8 cents per kilowatt-hour to coal's cost, while a relatively conservative estimate of $27 per ton for the social cost of carbon adds another 0.8 cent per kilowatt-hour. With this adjustment, the levelized cost of new conventional coal plants increases to almost double that of onshore wind and to roughly 46 percent more than the cost of photovoltaic solar energy.[9] These comparative costs may change, however, given the Trump administration's skepticism about the need to force energy producers to factor a "social cost" for carbon into their decisions. If this change occurs, then renewable energy sources, by definition, would lose some of their current cost competitiveness with fossil fuel sources.

Yet, in many cases, it can be the geographical distribution of costs and benefits that determines where the political battle lines will be drawn around a specific energy facility proposal. Although specific local economies do benefit from more jobs and tax revenues from energy development, many of the negative costs are also direct and localized. In contrast, actual energy usage and many, if not most, of the economic benefits of a particular facility are dispersed to users and corporations in other places. This geographic mismatch of costs and benefits can explain, for example, why many stakeholders in rural areas may be against a particular renewable energy project that creates localized costs in terms of blighted landscapes but benefits neighboring states and faraway cities in terms of a green energy supply. It can also explain why coal-producing and heavy coal-use states such as West Virginia, Ohio, and Indiana tend to oppose climate change regulations that negatively affect the price and demand for coal.

Values and Priorities: Conflict and Common Ground

The technical, economic, and environmental challenges of energy have translated into a conflict over values and priorities, and this conflict is often expressed as a political divide over energy types, development, and use. Yet there is also movement in the complex and interdependent world of water and energy toward positive sum, or mutual gain, solutions—solutions bringing together groups and interests that cut across traditional partisan lines. Three cases—fracking, the challenges to coal, and the water-energy nexus—illustrate the challenges and political landscape associated with contemporary U.S. energy policy.

The World of Fracking: New Technologies for Old Fuels

Hydraulic fracturing (or "fracking") is a technique for tapping unconventional oil and natural gas reserves that are otherwise inaccessible. In the late 1990s and early 2000s, energy companies began combining horizontal (or directional) drilling with hydraulic fracturing to tap these reserves. The process involves drilling horizontally through a rock layer and injecting a pressurized mixture of water, sand, and other chemicals that fractures the rock and facilitates the flow of oil and gas. These combined methods have allowed for expanded development in shale and other formations in the United States, Europe, Asia, Australia, and elsewhere. The rapid expansion of fracking, although slowed by a recent global supply glut, is projected to make the United States a net exporter of natural gas by 2017 and potentially a net energy exporter by the 2020s.[10] Production from hydraulically fractured wells now comprises about two-thirds of total natural gas production and about half of crude oil production in the United States.[11]

Hydraulic fracturing is just one part of the unconventional oil and gas development process, which also includes clearing land for well pads, constructing access roads and associated infrastructure (e.g., pipelines, compressor stations), transporting and processing extracted fossil fuels, transporting millions of gallons of water and wastewater for treatment and disposal, and bringing large (and often transient) populations to a community. These activities involve potential economic, environmental, social, and health impacts.

At the local level, potential economic benefits include job creation, increased income and wealth for individuals who sign gas leases on private lands, expanded local business opportunities for those who either directly or indirectly service the energy industry (e.g., in the construction or hospitality industries), and rising tax revenue for communities.[12] At a national level, the potential for U.S. energy self-sufficiency created by the fracking boom may decrease national security concerns associated with securing and protecting energy supplies overseas and has led to a resurgence of U.S. manufacturing industries dependent on natural gas as a fuel stock.[13] If the natural gas produced from hydraulic fracturing replaces more carbon-intensive fuels like coal, it could lower GHG emissions.[14] Yet if, as some research suggests and as many environmentalists have argued, the emissions from methane leakage negate other GHG reductions achieved because of a transition to natural gas, such a transition might essentially serve as a "bridge to nowhere" as opposed to a "bridge to renewable energy."[15]

A major environmental impact of hydraulic fracturing relates to water availability and quality. Hydraulic fracturing requires two to twenty million gallons of water per well, which raises concerns about the depletion of water resources, although there is a trend toward wastewater recycling for hydraulic fracturing to reduce freshwater requirements.[16] Also, contamination of subterranean and surface water can occur because of the release into rivers and streams of inadequately treated drilling wastewater with potentially toxic materials, surface spills of chemicals, and methane migration from gas wells into aquifers.[17] Social impacts are a third area of concern and relate to a community's ability to accommodate the frenzied activity associated with an energy development boom.[18] And, more recently, concerns have arisen about the potential link between fracking and increased seismic, or earthquake, activity, particularly resulting from the pressure created by the injection wells used to dispose of wastewater but also from the fracking process itself.[19]

For all of the controversy and hype, national surveys have found Americans, until recently, to be relatively uninformed about fracking.[20] Among those who have made a decision, Americans have been equally divided in their support and opposition, with evidence of growing opposition.[21] Like other emerging technologies, women, individuals with egalitarian worldviews, and those who associated fracking with environmental issues have been more likely to oppose fracking. Older, more conservative individuals and those who associated fracking with economic issues have been more likely to support it.[22] Moreover, as for many energy issues, public support and opposition largely fall along party lines, with Republicans in support and Democrats in opposition.[23] Yet early in his tenure, President Obama did little to limit fracking's expansion—which was also supported strongly by the Bush administration. In fact, the Obama administration made the case for increased domestic oil and gas production as part of its "All-of-the-Above Energy Strategy."[24] At the end of Obama's second term, federal agencies did make moves to regulate the more controversial aspects of the process, as described below. However, as many of these actions were taken using executive powers,[25] President Trump has promised to undo much of this regulation and has already made moves to do so.[26]

As with developing rules to govern many emerging energy technologies, the regulation of fracking and its impacts in the United States has been a fragmented process, likely resulting from fracking's numerous technical, economic, and environmental challenges, which feed into conflict over values and priorities. The Safe Drinking Water Act (SDWA) of 1974 required the EPA to regulate underground fluid injection and banned the injection of hazardous materials, but it exempted hydraulic fracturing. In 1997, after a fracking operation in Alabama contaminated drinking water supplies, the Legal Environmental Assistance Foundation sued to regulate fracking under the SDWA and won.[27] After a three-year investigation, the EPA determined that fracking posed no serious threat to drinking water supplies and needed no further regulation under the SDWA. However, in December 2016, the EPA changed its conclusion in part, acknowledging that fracking had contaminated drinking water in some circumstances.[28] The Energy Policy Act of 2005 sealed the exemption under the SDWA into law via the "Halliburton loophole"—so named because Halliburton engineers invented the fracking process.[29]

Surface water discharge, a common practice in fracking operations, is also regulated under the 1972 Clean Water Act, while the 1970 National Environmental Policy Act requires the preparation of environmental impact assessments prior to drilling on federal lands. Hazardous chemicals are regulated under the Comprehensive Environmental Response, Compensation, and Liability Act of 1980 ("Superfund"), but oil and gas operations are exempt. In January 2015, the EPA proposed programs to reduce methane emissions from oil and gas operations on federal land. In March 2015, the BLM released regulations on fracking on public lands. These efforts did little to appease either side in the fracking debate, were quickly challenged in court, and are unlikely to survive Trump's tenure.[30] As one indication, in May 2017, the Senate rejected an attempt through the Congressional Review Act procedure to repeal the Obama methane rule, with three Republicans voting against it (Chapter 5). Rewriting the rule itself will be difficult.

As with much of the oversight of oil and gas development, the regulation of fracking has largely been left to the states, resulting in significant heterogeneity.[31] The most comprehensive study to date of fracking policy in the twenty-seven states with significant shale gas development found considerable variation in the use of twenty different regulatory elements related to site selection and preparation, well drilling, hydraulic fracturing, wastewater storage and disposal, excess gas disposal, and plugging and abandonment.[32] In general, researchers found that states tend to prefer command-and-control regulations (e.g., requiring wells to be cased and cemented to a specific depth below the water table) as opposed to performance standards (e.g., requiring wells to be cased and cemented to a level sufficient to protect all "freshwater bearing zones").

Some states have taken a leadership role in regulating fracking. For example, New York, Vermont, and Maryland have all banned the practice, as have many local governments. In 2010, Wyoming became the first state to require disclosure of fracking chemicals.[33] In 2014, Ohio released new permitting conditions to regulate fracking near known active faults,[34] while Colorado became the first state to regulate methane emissions. Some of these policy efforts have created strange bedfellows. For example, Colorado's regulations were developed collaboratively by the Environmental Defense Fund and three oil and gas companies under the watch of Democratic governor John Hickenlooper.[35] Further, an increasing number of local governments have sought to ban fracking. However, some states, such as Pennsylvania and Texas, have reacted strongly to quash these efforts.

Local regulation can also be found in the leases that private landowners sign with oil and gas companies. These leases establish not only financial terms but also other conditions that may impact drilling operations. These leases provide a critical piece of the policy puzzle because, in the absence of comprehensive state or federal policies, leases offer immediate protection to landowners seeking to control what happens on their property.

The Challenges to Coal

Coal is an abundant domestic energy source, with more than 257 billion tons of reserves in the United States; this is 25 percent of the total reserves in the entire world.[36] In 2016, coal was used in 427 domestic power plants to generate 1.3 trillion kilowatt-hours, about 32 percent of all electricity consumed in the country.[37] Coal offers numerous benefits. It is plentiful and affordable, the supply chain is secure, and reliance upon coal does not pose risks to U.S. national security in the way that oil does; more than 40 percent of all the coal mined in the United Sates comes from Wyoming alone.[38] Despite these advantages, the amount of coal used in the American electricity sector has fallen due to a number of market pressures and policy changes.

The economic forces affecting the use of coal include, first and foremost, the growing availability and low price of natural gas. At the same time, wind and solar energy have seen high levels of adoption due to their falling costs, which has been aided in many states by the enactment of renewable portfolio standards—legal requirements for utilities to provide specified levels of renewable energy to their customers. These developments have prompted utilities and independent power producers to prefer natural gas, wind, and solar energy facilities as opposed to coal plants when adding capacity or replacing aging equipment.

Amidst these developments, a number of regulations have been adopted to diminish the environmental impacts of coal and to reduce its use. The combination of these changes makes alternatives to coal financially attractive at a time when its regulatory environment has become more challenging. Thus there has been a rapid reduction in the use of coal. Although coal accounted for 30 percent of U.S. electricity generation in 2016—a significant share of the market—it accounted for as much as 50 percent as recently as 2007.[39] The newly installed Trump administration has expressed its intention to reverse this market trend by providing greater support for coal in federal policy.

Regulating Coal

The coal industry is one of the most heavily regulated in the United States. Surface mining, which provides 70 percent of the country's coal, is governed by the Surface Mining Control and Reclamation Act of 1977, and the U.S. Department of the Interior is responsible for implementing this law. Underground mining is regulated by the Mine Safety and Health Administration in the Department of Labor, under the authority of the Mine Safety and Health Act of 1977. Coal mining operations are also covered by the Clean Air Act, the Clean Water Act, the Toxic Substances Control Act, the Safe Drinking Water Act, and the Emergency Planning and Community Right to Know Act, to name a few of the most relevant statutes.

The regulation of power plants is largely the work of the EPA, which enforces the Clean Air Act to manage air pollution throughout the country. Under the Clean Air Act, the EPA has implemented several regulations placing limits on pollution emissions, while also requiring the use of pollution control technologies. This regulatory framework has been one of the most contentious parts of the political debate over environmental regulation.

One of the EPA's key tools in regulating power plants has been the Clean Air Act's New Source Review (NSR) permitting program (see Chapter 7). Adopted in 1977, NSR requires pre-construction approval for new power plants, and for major modifications to existing plants, to ensure that air pollution standards are met, particularly with regard to the levels of sulfur dioxide (SO_2), nitrogen oxides (NOx), and fine particle matter. The EPA can require the use of "scrubbers" to trap pollutants, specify smokestack heights, and determine the type and level of pollutants that can be emitted.[40] One contentious issue involves defining what types of modifications trigger compliance with higher standards. A provision in the Clean Air Act exempts power plants built before the NSR program from using certain pollution controls. These plants are only subject to NSR standards at the time they make major upgrades or modifications. As a result, many coal-fired plants in the United States do not use the most effective pollution control technologies, and they can account for high levels of air pollution. In 2010, coal plants without desulfurization scrubbers produced 42 percent of coal-fired electricity, but they contributed 73 percent of coal's SO_2 emissions.[41]

Regulatory standards expanded during the Obama administration. The Cross-State Air Pollution Rule, finalized in 2011, is designed to cut emissions of SO_2 and NOx that carry across state lines. These pollutants can prevent cities and regions downwind from maintaining air quality standards, thereby contributing to adverse public health impacts.[42] This regulation faced legal challenges, but the Supreme Court ruled in 2014 that the EPA does have the authority to implement it. The Mercury and Air Toxics Standards (MATS) are another 2011 addition to the regulatory framework governing coal power plants. The MATS are the first federal standards requiring power plants to limit emissions of mercury, lead, arsenic, nickel, cobalt, and other toxic gases.[43] These rules were also challenged in court, and in this case, the Supreme Court placed a hold on their enforcement. The court did not invalidate MATS, but it ruled that the EPA did not properly consider the costs of implementing these standards. To comply with the ruling, EPA assessed several cost metrics and concluded in 2015 that industry can comply with these regulations and deliver affordable electricity to consumers.[44]

The EPA and Carbon Dioxide

As climate change has gained greater political saliency, the EPA has become involved in the process of regulating carbon dioxide (CO_2) as an air pollutant. After a battle pitting several states against the federal government, the Supreme Court ruled in 2007 that the EPA had not only the authority to regulate carbon dioxide under the Clean Air Act but also the obligation to do so, as CO_2 could be expected to endanger public health. Based on this "endangerment" ruling, and following the election of President Obama in 2009, the EPA began the effort to regulate CO_2 emissions from power plants, both new and existing.

Starting with new power plants, the EPA proposed a rule in 2012 to establish a carbon emissions standard allowing 1,000 pounds of CO_2 emissions per megawatt-hour (MWh) of electricity generated. This would apply to both coal and natural gas plants. A controversy erupted because this standard is feasible *only* in natural gas plants. The carbon capture and storage technology that would be required for coal plants to meet the standard is so new, expensive, and untested, that compliance would effectively mean an end to new coal plant construction until the technology could be proven. The opposition from the coal and utility industries to this proposal was quick and forceful, and it prompted an EPA revision. The final rule adopted in 2015 limited carbon dioxide emissions from coal-fired plants to 1,400 pounds per MWh and natural gas plants to 1,000 pounds.[45]

The EPA also created a CO_2 standard for existing power plants. In 2015, it issued the Clean Power Plan to cut CO_2 emissions nationally by 30 percent over a fifteen-year period.[46] The rule provides options for states to achieve compliance: energy efficiency, demand reduction, and increased use of renewable energy. Each state's carbon dioxide target is different based on its starting point with regard to the overall fuel mix, the level of renewables in use, and the policies already adopted. For example, in Oregon, the closure of the state's only coal-fired plant in 2020 will bring the state into full compliance. States such as Kentucky and West Virginia, however, have more modest targets because their power generation systems rely heavily on coal and have less potential for major reductions. The Clean Power Plan was hailed by supporters as one of the most significant actions the U.S. government has ever taken to address global warming, and decried by opponents as a major threat to the U.S. economy. Neither side got the opportunity to see if its prediction would come true. In early 2016, the Supreme Court halted implementation of the plan until legal challenges were resolved. Then in January 2017, the Trump administration came into office promising that it would withdraw the Clean Power Plan and promote the use of coal.

The Trump Administration—Changing Course

The election of Donald Trump is expected to bring significant changes to energy and environmental regulation. President Trump and many other Republicans argue that the new regulations described in the previous section were not merely attempts to reduce the environmental and health impacts of using coal but constituted a "war on coal" that would depress the economy in coal mining states, cause electricity prices to rise, and do little to improve the environment. Trump promised to reverse regulations that harmed the coal industry and to put coal miners back to work. Soon after taking office, he began to act. In March 2017, President Trump issued an executive order on energy signaling this reversal: "The heads of agencies shall review all existing regulations, orders, guidance documents, policies, and any other similar agency actions (collectively, agency actions) that potentially burden the development or use of domestically produced energy resources, with particular attention to oil, natural gas, coal, and nuclear energy resources."[47] As a start, Trump announced the reversal of the Clean Power Plan. He also lifted the Obama era moratorium on coal leasing on federal public lands and announced that the United States would withdraw from the Paris climate agreement, while halting a U.S. government study on the health impacts of "mountaintop removal" coal mining. At the same time, congressional Republicans used the Congressional Review Act in March 2017 to repeal the "stream protection rule," which was designed to stop the dumping of coal mine wastes into areas in and around adjacent waterways.

The EPA will play an important role in reversing or revising energy and environmental regulations, and Scott Pruitt, the administrator that Trump appointed, is expected to pursue regulatory changes more favorable to coal usage. While serving as the attorney general of Oklahoma, Pruitt filed suit against the EPA over the Clean Power Plan and MATS, arguing that the agency's actions constituted federal overreach into constitutionally protected state affairs. He also has questioned the science documenting climate change and expressed doubts about whether the EPA should regulate carbon dioxide emissions as per the Supreme Court's endangerment finding. Under Pruitt, the EPA has started the process of eliminating the Clean Power Plan, along with regulations to limit water pollution from coal-fired power plants.

Although few changes in energy policy have been fully implemented several months into Trump's presidency, it is clear that the ground is being prepared to engage in major departures from the Obama administration's policies regarding coal use and regulation. The political battle surrounding this issue will remain intense because the stakes are high and the two opposing views—characterized as either a "war on coal" conducted through "job-killing regulations" or "protecting public health and the environment" by cutting "carbon pollution" and other "toxins"—will remain salient in the political realm.

Coal mining and exports rose in the first months of the Trump administration, and President Trump touted his policies as the reason for this.[48] However, despite the policy changes that can be anticipated, the long-term outlook is that the market share for coal-fired power will continue to decline and will not be easily reversed. The low price of natural gas and technological advances in fracking techniques, along with renewable portfolio standards in many states, have made new coal plants a difficult, low-return investment; hence few new plants are being constructed. At the same time, coal plant closures nationwide have increased, accounting for 80 percent of retired generating capacity in 2015.[49] Even if the EPA is able to provide a more favorable regulatory climate for coal power, it may be the case that ongoing market trends will continue to favor natural gas, wind, and solar power.

The Water-Energy Nexus

Water and energy are essential resources for human life and health, and for practically all economic and social activities. They also are interconnected and mutually dependent, as one is needed for generating or providing the other.[50] This means that solving a problem in one domain without considering the other often aggravates problems in the second domain, suggesting that the best strategy for achieving a more sustainable and efficient use of both resources is the integrated management approach now being called the water-energy nexus. Moreover, the task of managing this nexus is exacerbated by projected increases in human population and the corresponding increase in demand for water and energy; the challenge of climate change, which is leading to water supply constraints via shifting precipitation patterns and enhanced droughts; and significantly higher energy costs related to renewable energy, at least in the short term.

The recognition of this interdependence has led to significant growth in policymaking efforts in recent years to treat both energy and water together. A U.S. Department of Energy report in 2006 alerted Congress about the "interdependency of energy and water," while the water-energy nexus was a major topic at the 2011 Davos World Economic Forum and at Rio+20, the United Nations Conference on Sustainable Development held in June 2012.[51] Major reports in 2012 from the American Geophysical Union (AGU) and the U.S. Government Accountability Office (GAO) examined this nexus and recommended measures to address it. Then, in 2013, Congress passed the Bureau of Reclamation Small Conduit Hydropower Development and Rural Jobs Act and the Hydropower Regulatory Efficiency Act (HREA) in order to create more efficient, sustainable marriages between energy and water being used for irrigated farmlands.[52] There have also been innovations in repurposing existing power plants to assist with renewable energy development and in transforming irrigation systems into integrated hydro-irrigation-restoration systems (see cases below).

Energy Development and Generation

Energy generation, which relies primarily on coal, natural gas, and oil, accounts for around 8 percent of all global water withdrawals. Yet in Europe, energy generation demands account for over 45 percent of the total water withdrawn, and in the United States, water use for electricity generation takes about 40 percent of withdrawals.[53]

Most of this water is used in traditional thermoelectric power plant cooling systems. They generate electricity by burning a fuel source to boil water (fresh, saline, or treated) and produce steam to drive turbine generators. The steam is then cooled before being discharged. A typical U.S. thermoelectric plant uses 25 gallons of water per kWh, or over 200 billion gallons per day for all U.S. plants.[54] And although most of this water is technically not consumed, the "cooled" water typically enters surrounding water bodies 10 to 20 degrees (Fahrenheit) higher than when it was withdrawn, thus damaging adjacent ecological systems. Further, most of these plants were coal fired historically. In 2010, 45 percent of the total U.S. electricity demand was filled by coal-fired plants, although plants using natural gas surpassed those using coal in 2016, supplying 33 percent of total demand compared to 32 percent for coal.[55] The mining of coal is also water intensive; the American Geophysical Union estimates that coal mining in the United States consumes between 70 and 260 million gallons of water per day.[56]

The fracking techniques used to extract shale oil and natural gas deposits also are water intensive. For shale oil, the U.S. Bureau of Land Management (BLM) estimates that one to three barrels of water are needed for each barrel of oil produced by in-situ extraction, and 2.6 to 4 barrels of water are required per barrel for what is called the "mining and surface retort method."[57] For natural gas, the fluids pumped into shale formations to fracture the rock and release natural gas are composed mainly of water (about 90 percent), and large amounts of water are required as part of the accompanying drilling process. When these water needs are combined, each well requires an estimated 2.9 to 5.0 million gallons of water. With an estimated 300,000 fracking rigs in place as of early 2016, this equals a range of 8.7 to 15 trillion gallons each year.[58]

Yet it is perhaps the renewable energy option that best exemplifies the water-energy dilemma. Biofuels, especially ethanol, are significantly more water-intensive to produce and use than fossil fuels, by several orders of magnitude. It takes approximately 1,100 gallons of water to produce one gallon of ethanol from corn, and this is in addition to the large amounts of water used in the fermentation, distillation, and cooling processes that convert the feedstock into biofuel.[59] Hydropower, which accounts for 86 percent of global renewable energy, tends to suffer massive water losses from evaporation at an estimated rate of 4,500 gallons for every MWh produced. This means that water hydropower losses equal over 6 billion gallons per day in the United States.[60]

Energy for Water

Water systems require a significant amount of energy for moving, pumping, distributing, and treating water. In fact, electricity represents about 75 percent of the cost of municipal water and, in many cities, water supply systems represent between 30 percent and 50 percent of total annual municipal energy budgets. Approximately 80 percent of the energy used in water systems is used to move and pump water, with most of the rest devoted to treatment. Further, 18 percent of home energy use, and costs, is attributable to water heaters.[61]

The energy intensity of water supplies is often related to the fact that water sources are not always close to human population centers. For example, the Southern Delivery System in Colorado is designed to pump 52,900 acre-feet of water, or 17.25 billion gallons per year, from Pueblo Reservoir to Colorado Springs, lifting the water 2,100 feet higher over a distance of 62 miles. This project has an estimated energy intensity of 4,630 kilowatt-hours per acre-foot, or 245 million kilowatt-hours per year.[62] In California, 20 percent of the electricity supply is devoted to moving water, with a major project being the 242-mile Colorado River Aqueduct, which transfers and lifts (pumps) 900 million gallons per day up 1,617 feet in elevation along the route. The costs for these projects are going up rapidly, with the dual challenge of relying on renewables instead of coal and meeting the requirements of the state's greenhouse gas cap-and-trade program predicted to increase power costs by 80 percent in the next ten years. Likewise, California's 444-mile State Water Project expects to see electricity costs increase by $20 million per year over the next decade for similar reasons, which leads some to this conclusion:

> The twin forces of energy prices and climate-change regulations are threatening Southern California's long love affair with imported water, increasing the allure of local sources such as groundwater, rain and recycled supplies.[63]

Yet if water availability decreases as projected due to climate change, the future energy demands of water systems will also increase because of the need to pump water from lower depths in aquifers or transport it from sources farther away.

Another strategy for improving water supply quantities and reliability is desalination, a process through which salt is removed from seawater or brackish water. The two primary methods of desalination are distillation (thermal evaporation) and reverse osmosis, which employs membranes and filters to remove the salt ions. However, both are economically costly and require significant amounts of energy to work. Seawater distillation requires between 11,000 and 27,000 kWh per million gallons of water produced, while brackish water distillation requires 1,900 to 11,000 kWh for the same amount of water. The reverse osmosis technology uses between 12,000 and 25,000 kWh per million gallons of water.[64]

Using Water to Speed the Transition to Renewables

A key problem for solar and wind energy is reliability because the sun and wind are intermittent sources of power that often (1) do not provide enough power during peak demands for electricity and (2) provide excess energy when demand is low. This dilemma means that these renewables must either be backed up with additional base-load energy sources, such as fossil fuels or nuclear power, or that peak solar and wind energy supplies must be captured and stored for later use. New storage technologies—high-tech batteries, compressed air and ice—are under development and may be key in the future. But an old technology, the pumped-storage "battery pack," is finding political support in a growing number of regions from energy companies, environmentalists, elected officials, and public utility officials. With pumped storage, existing nuclear and coal-fired plants move large volumes of water uphill into existing onsite reservoirs when there is surplus electricity. The water is banked until needed during peak energy times, and then it is released through hydroelectric turbines or plants to help keep electric grids running smoothly. Although expensive to build, the pumped-storage facility is still the cheapest form of large-scale electricity storage, which is why 99 percent of all "stored" energy in the world is pumped storage. Currently, there are forty-two pumped-storage plants in the United States with a capacity of 23,000 megawatts (about twenty nuclear reactors). And, as of summer 2016, there were proposals before the Federal Energy Regulatory Commission for an additional 18,000 megawatts of pumped storage.[65]

Off the Grid: Integrated Hydro-Irrigation-Restoration Systems

Population growth, increasing energy demands, and the climate change challenge for arid to semiarid areas are likely to create an unsustainable trajectory for water consumption. When the increasing demand for environmental and species protection and the larger instream flows that leave more water in rivers are added to this mix, many rural, irrigated farming communities in the West are at risk, especially those farmers with less reliable junior water rights. Increasingly, however, communities in Washington, Montana, Oregon, Colorado, California, and elsewhere are turning to innovative solutions that combine small, run-of-river hydroelectric plants with upgraded, enclosed, and pressurized conduit irrigation systems and stronger environmental protections for fish, insects, water quality, and riparian zones.

The Whychus Creek watershed of the Deschutes River Basin in Oregon provides an example. Annually, 50 percent of irrigation water was "lost" in canals and on fields due to evaporation and the "leaky basalt" geology. A new fifty-mile, $50 million, pressurized and piped water delivery system captured the "lost" water and created reliability for even junior water users in dry years. It also saved five million kWh ($490,000) in pumping costs annually, and with the new "surplus" water from efficiency gains, fully 25 percent of the river's flow was turned into permanent instream rights for threatened fish and stream restoration. Moreover, the Three Sisters Irrigation District took advantage of the new conduit system to build two small carbon-free hydropower plants (1,050 kWh total). These plants allow many farms to go off grid, while the extra hydropower revenue and water sales help to pay off the principal and interest on the conduit system construction loans.[66]

Conclusion

The cases of hydraulic fracturing, the challenges to coal, and the water-energy nexus show that the quest for the energy required to power modern economies and meet basic social needs is a critical public policy issue beset with major challenges as well as sharp political and partisan conflicts. These challenges have been made more explicit by the U.S. drive to seek greater energy independence using an amalgamation of policies and new technologies that not only support oil and natural gas development but also renewable energy development and conservation through energy efficiency measures. Complicating the picture is the specter of climate change, and the consequent pressure to lessen carbon emissions. Yet, as the water-energy nexus section shows, sometimes these challenges are bringing people with different political views and goals together in support of approaches with broad, crosscutting political support.

Taken together, these developments make it clear that modern societies, the United States included, want energy to do more things than ever before: support and grow the economy while minimizing or eliminating environmental and national security impacts. Put differently, we want energy that is abundant, reliable, affordable, clean, and diversified (in terms of both fuel sources and the countries that supply it). Yet precisely because no single energy source gives us all of these things, we inevitably end up with policies that support some of these goals at the cost of others.

Another key lesson is the fragmented nature of U.S. energy policy and the seeming lack of national priorities, which in turn reflects the sharp partisan divisions over energy policy. There is no agreement in Congress on what to do, and different presidents can, and do, have dramatically different energy priorities. The climate change debate—and gridlock in Congress—as much as anything, illustrates the disagreement over contemporary and future energy policy (see Chapter 5). Each side of the debate claims to be fighting for the public interest, but neither side appears willing to explore the "radical middle" upon which a national climate change policy, much less a national energy policy, is likely to be built. The election of President Trump is unlikely to change this reality and, in fact, may exacerbate it. This fragmentation also results from shared policy control by multiple federal and state authorities, and from democratic processes that allow vocal and well-funded interest groups to influence policy choices. In addition, the distinctive property (mineral) rights system of the United States grants significant power to individual landowners. Seen from this perspective, and as evidenced by two of the three cases outlined above, the conflict and cacophony that define contemporary U.S. energy politics seem unlikely to change anytime soon, although the potential for innovative solutions to the water-energy puzzle might well challenge this narrative from going forward.

Suggested Websites

U.S. Energy Information Administration (EIA) *Total Energy* **website** (www.eia.gov/totalenergy) This site contains independent energy statistics and analysis across energy types, trends, and more. It's a great basic source of information.

The State Energy Data System (www.eia.gov/state/seds/?src=email& src=Total-f4) This is the source of the EIA's comprehensive state energy statistics. The EIA's goal in maintaining the system is to create historical time series of energy production, consumption, prices, and expenditures by state that are defined as consistently as possible over time and across sectors for analysis and forecasting purposes.

Global Statistical Energy Yearbook 2016 (http://yearbook.enerdata .net) This comprehensive database on energy supply, demand, prices, and GHG emissions for 186 countries is produced by Enerdata, an energy intelligence and consulting company.

Database of State Incentives (and Policies) for Renewables and Efficiency (www.dsireusa.org) The U.S. Department of Energy funds this source of information on incentives and policies that support renewables and energy efficiency in the United States. It is operated by the N.C. Clean Energy Technology Center at N.C. State University.

Notes

1. "Pricing Sunshine," *The Economist*, December 28, 2012; American Wind Energy Association, "U.S. Number One in the World in Wind Energy Production," *Wind in the News* [press releases], February 29, 2016, http://www.awea.org/MediaCenter/pressrelease.aspx?ItemNumber=8463.
2. U.S. Energy Information Administration, *Monthly Energy Review, March 2016* (Washington, DC: EIA, 2016).
3. Daniel Steinberg, Gian Porro, and Marshall Goldberg, *Preliminary Analysis of the Jobs and Economic Impacts of the Renewable Energy Projects Supported by the 1603 Treasury Grant Program*, Document No. NREL/TP-6A20-52739 (Golden, CO: National Renewable Energy Laboratory, April 2012).
4. Brian Ferrasci-O'Malley, "Recent Developments Regarding Avian Take at Wind Farms," *Marten Law Newsletter*, January 27, 2014, http://www.martenlaw.com/newsletter/20140127-avian-take-wind-farms.
5. National Audubon Society, "Interior Dept. Rule Greenlights Eagle Slaughter at Wind Farms, Says Audubon CEO," *Press Room* [press release], December 5, 2013, http://www.audubon.org/news/interior-dept-rule-greenlights-eagle-slaughter-wind-farms-says-audubon-ceo.
6. Barry Rabe, *Statehouse and Greenhouse: The Emerging Politics of American Climate Change Policy* (Washington, DC: Brookings, 2004).
7. For plants coming online in year 2012, see Energy Information Administration, *Levelized Costs: Annual Energy Outlook* (Washington, DC: U.S. Department of Energy, April 2017), https://www.eia.gov/outlooks/aeo/pdf/electricity_generation.pdf.
8. U.S. Energy Information Administration, *Levelized Costs*.
9. Nicholas Z. Muller, Robert Mendelsohn, and William Nordhaus, "Environmental Accounting for Pollution in the United States Economy," *American Economic Review* 101, no. 5 (2011): 1649–75.
10. U.S. Department of Energy, *Annual Energy Outlook, 2017* (Washington, DC: U.S. Department of Energy, 2017).
11. Energy Information Administration, "Hydraulically Fractured Wells Provide Two-Thirds of U.S. Natural Gas Production," *Today in Energy*, May 5, 2016, https://www.eia.gov/todayinenergy/detail.php?id=26112#.
12. Joseph Marchand and Jeremy Weber, "Local Labor Markets and Natural Resources: A Synthesis of the Literature," *Journal of Economic Surveys* (forthcoming), http://onlinelibrary.wiley.com/doi/10.1111/joes.12199/abstract.
13. Benjamin K. Sovacool, "Cornucopia or Curse? Reviewing the Costs and Benefits of Shale Gas Hydraulic Fracturing (Fracking)," *Renewable and Sustainable Energy Reviews* 37 (2014): 249–64, https://doi.org/10.1016/j.rser.2014.04.068.
14. Robert B. Jackson, Avner Vengosh, J. William Carey, Richard J. Davies, Thomas H. Darrah, Francis O'Sullivan, and Gabrielle Pétron, "The Environmental Costs and Benefits of Fracking," *Annual Review of Environment and Resources* 39 (2014): 327–62, https://doi.org/10.1146/annurev-environ-031113-144051.
15. Robert W. Howarth, "A Bridge to Nowhere: Methane Emissions and the Greenhouse Gas Footprint of Natural Gas," *Energy Science & Engineering* 2, no. 2 (2014): 47–60, http://dx.doi.org/10.1002/ese3.35. See also Adam R. Brandt, G. A. Heath, E. A. Kort, F. O'Sullivan, G. Pétron, S. M. Jordaan, P. Tans et al., "Methane Leaks from North American Natural Gas Systems," *Science* 343, no. 6172 (2014): 733–35.
16. Robert B. Jackson et al., "The Environmental Costs and Benefits of Fracking."
17. Robert B. Jackson et al., "The Environmental Costs and Benefits of Fracking."

18. Jeffrey B. Jacquet, "Review of Risks to Communities from Shale Energy Development," *Environmental Science & Technology* 48 (2014): 8321–33, https://doi.org/10.1021/es404647x.

19. Katie M. Keranen, M. Weingarten, G. A. Abers, B. A. Bekins, and S. Ge, "Sharp Increase in Central Oklahoma Seismicity Since 2008 Induced by Massive Wastewater Injection," *Science* 345, no. 6195 (2014): 448–51, https://doi.org/10.1126/science.1255802.

20. Hilary Boudet, Christopher Clarke, Dylan Bugden, Edward Maibach, Connie Roser-Renouf, and Anthony Leiserowitz, "'Fracking' Controversy and Communication: Using National Survey Data to Understand Public Perceptions of Hydraulic Fracturing," *Energy Policy* 65 (2013): 57–67.

21. Art Swift, "Opposition to Fracking Mounts in the U.S.," *Gallup Politics*, March 30, 2016, http://www.gallup.com/poll/190355/opposition-fracking-mounts.aspx.

22. Hilary Boudet et al., "'Fracking' Controversy and Communication."

23. Hilary Boudet et al., "'Fracking' Controversy and Communication."

24. Executive Office of the President of the United States, *The All-of-the-Above Energy Strategy as a Path to Sustainable Economic Growth* (Washington, DC: White House, May 2014), 5, https://obamawhitehouse.archives.gov/sites/default/files/docs/aota_energy_strategy_as_a_path_to_sustainable_economic_growth.pdf.

25. David M. Konisky and Neal D. Woods, "Environmental Policy, Federalism, and the Obama Presidency," *Publius: The Journal of Federalism* 46, no. 3 (2016): 366–91, https://doi.org/10.1093/publius/pjw004.

26. Juliet Eilperin, "Interior Department to Withdraw Obama-Era Fracking Rule, Filing Reveal," *Washington Post*, March 15, 2017.

27. Lisa Sumi, *Our Drinking Water at Risk: What EPA and the Oil and Gas Industry Don't Want Us to Know about Hydraulic Fracturing* (Durango, CO: Oil and Gas Accountability Project, 2005), https://www.earthworksaction.org/files/publications/DrinkingWaterAtRisk.pdf.

28. U.S. Environmental Protection Agency, *Evaluation of Impacts to Underground Sources of Drinking Water by Hydraulic Fracturing of Coalbed Methane Reservoirs*, 816-R-01-003 (Washington, DC: Environmental Protection Agency, 2004). A 2016 study by the EPA found that "hydraulic fracturing activities can impact drinking water resources under some circumstances," but also that data gaps and uncertainties limit its ability to characterize the severity of the impacts. See U.S. Environmental Protection Agency, *Hydraulic Fracturing for Oil and Gas: Impacts from the Hydraulic Fracturing Water Cycle on Drinking Water Resources in the United States, Final Report*, EPA/600/R-16/236F (Washington, DC: EPA, 2016), https://www.epa.gov/hfstudy.

29. Dianne Rahm, "Regulating Hydraulic Fracturing in Shale Gas Plays: The Case of Texas," *Energy Policy* 39, no. 5 (2011): 2974–81.

30. David M. Konisky and Neal D. Woods, "Environmental Policy, Federalism, and the Obama Presidency."

31. Nathan Richardson, Madeline Gottlieb, Alan Krupnick, and Hannah Wiseman, *The State of State Shale Gas Regulation* (Washington, DC: Resources for the Future, 2013).

32. Richardson et al., *The State of State Shale Gas Regulation.*

33. Mead Gruver, "Wyoming High Court Remands Fracking Secrets Case," *Daily Mail Online* [Wires AP], March 12, 2014, http://www.dailymail.co.uk/wires/ap/article-2579422/Wyoming-high-court-remands-fracking-secrets-case.html.

34. Julie C. Smyth, "Ohio Geologists Link Small Quakes to Fracking," *Associated Press*, April 11, 2014, https://finance.yahoo.com/news/ohio-geologists-small-quakes-fracking-182904257.html.

35. Stephanie Paige Ogburn and ClimateWire, "Colorado First State to Limit Methane Pollution from Oil and Gas Wells," *Scientific American*, February 25, 2014.

36. The National Academy of Sciences, "Our Energy Sources—Fossil Fuels: Coal," *What You Need to Know about Energy*, accessed April 26, 2017, http://needtoknow.nas.edu/energy/energy-sources/fossil-fuels/coal/.

37. U.S. Energy Information Administration (EIA), *Electric Power Annual 2015* (Washington, DC: U.S. Department of Energy, November 2016).

38. The National Academy of Sciences, "Our Energy Sources."

39. EIA, *Electric Power Monthly*, March 24, 2015.

40. U.S. Environmental Protection Agency (EPA), "New Source Review (NSR) Permitting," accessed April 26, 2017, http://www.epa.gov/nsr/.

41. EIA, "Coal Plants without Scrubbers Account for a Majority of U.S. SO_2 Emissions," *Today in Energy*, December 21, 2011.

42. EPA, *Cross-State Air Pollution Rule*, accessed April 26, 2017, https://www.epa.gov/csapr.

43. EPA, *Mercury and Air Toxics Standards*, accessed April 26, 2017, https://www.epa.gov/mats.

44. EPA, "Fact Sheet: Final Consideration of Cost in the Appropriate and Necessary Finding for the Mercury and Air Toxics Standards for Power Plants," accessed April 26, 2017, https://www.epa.gov/sites/production/files/2016-05/documents/20160414_mats_ff_fr_fs.pdf.

45. EPA, "Final Limits on Carbon Pollution from New, Modified and Reconstructed Power Plants," *EPA Fact Sheet*, accessed April 26, 2017, https://archive.epa.gov/epa/sites/production/files/2015-11/documents/fs-cps-overview.pdf.

46. EPA, "Carbon Pollution Emission Guidelines for Existing Stationary Sources: Electric Utility Generating Units [final rule]," *Federal Register*, October 23, 2015, https://www.federalregister.gov/documents/2015/10/23/2015-22842/carbon-pollution-emission-guidelines-for-existing-stationary-sources-electric-utility-generating.

47. Donald Trump, "Presidential Executive Order on Promoting Energy Independence and Economic Growth," White House, Office of the Press Secretary, March 28, 2017.

48. U.S. Energy Information Administration (EIA), "Weekly U.S. Coal Production," August 31, 2017, https://www.eia.gov/coal/production/weekly/tables/weekly_production.php; EIA, *Quarterly Coal Report, January–March 2017*, June 2017.

49. EIA, "Planned US Electric Generating Unit Additions," *Electric Power Monthly*, April 25, 2017; EIA, "Coal Made Up More than 80% of Retired Generation Capacity in 2015," *Today in Energy*, March 8, 2016.

50. C. A. Scott, S. A. Pierce, M. J. Pasqualetti, A. L. Jones, B. E. Montz, and J. H. Hoover, "Policy and Institutional Dimensions of the Water-Energy Nexus," *Energy Policy* 39, no. 10 (2011): 6622–30.

51. U.S. Department of Energy, *Energy Demands on Water Resources: Report to Congress on the Interdependency of Energy and Water* (Washington, DC: U.S. Department of Energy, December 2006), 3.

52. C. Krause, E. Koziol, and M. Merrill, "Incorporating Small-Scale Hydropower Projects into Our Energy Future," *Natural Resources & Environment: ABA Section of Environment, Energy, and Resources* 30, no. 4 (Spring 2016), 3–7.

53. H. Hoff, *Understanding the Nexus*, Background Paper for the Bonn2011 Conference: The Water, Energy, and Food Security Nexus (Stockholm: Stockholm Environment Institute, 2011); D. S. Kenney and R. Wilkinson, eds., *The Water-Energy Nexus in the American West* (Cheltenham, UK: Edward Elgar Publishing, 2011).

54. One solution to minimize the water requirements for power-station cooling is to employ dry recirculating methods, which rely on air as a coolant instead of water. However, dry cooling has been proved to be less efficient and to increase CO_2 emissions. See B. K. Sovacool, "Running on Empty: The Electricity-Water Nexus and the U.S. Electric Utility Sector," *Energy Law Journal* 30 (2009): 11.

55. U.S. Energy Information Administration, *Monthly Energy Review, March 2016*.

56. American Geophysical Union, *Water-Energy Nexus: Solutions to Meet a Growing Demand* (Washington, DC: American Geophysical Union, 2012).

57. Kenney and Wilkinson, *The Water-Energy Nexus in the American West*, 46.

58. Javier H. Estrada, *Desarrollo del gas lutita (shale gas) y su impacto en el mercado energético de México: Reflexiones para Centroamérica* (Santiago de Chile: Naciones Unidas, 2013), http://www.cepal.org/publicaciones/xml/8/51438/desarrollodelgaslutita.pdf.

59. Government Accountability Office, *Energy-Water Nexus: Coordinated Federal Approach Needed to Better Manage Energy and Water Tradeoffs* (Washington, DC: GAO, 2012).

60. Kenney and Wilkinson, *The Water-Energy Nexus in the American West*.

61. Kenney and Wilkinson, *The Water-Energy Nexus in the American West*.

62. Kenney and Wilkinson, *The Water-Energy Nexus in the American West*.

63. Bettina Boxall, "Water's Energy—and Expense," *Los Angeles Times*, November 14, 2011, http://articles.latimes.com/2011/nov/14/local/la-me-water-power-20111114.

64. Kenney and Wilkinson, *The Water-Energy Nexus in the American West*.

65. Rebecca Smith, "Pumped Up: Renewables Growth Revives Old Energy-Storage Method," *Wall Street Journal*, July 22, 2016.

66. Edward P. Weber, "Integrated Hydro-Irrigation-Restoration Systems: Resolving a Wicked Problem in the Whychus Creek Watershed," *Journal of Sustainable Development* 10, no. 2 (2017): 104–15, https://doi.org/10.5539/jsd.v10n2p104.

Chapter 9

Eating and the Environment
Ecological Tensions in Food Production

Christopher Bosso and Nicole E. Tichenor

Some facts are not in dispute. In 2013, Wyoming rancher Andy Johnson, after obtaining local and state permits, piled earth and rocks across a creek running through his land to create a stock pond for his cattle. What happened next was federal overreach, or justifiable punishment for breaking federal law. Or both.

Johnson's pond caught the attention of the Environmental Protection Agency (EPA), which with the U.S. Army Corps of Engineers administers the federal Clean Water Act (CWA). EPA officials ruled that while stock ponds are exempt from federal oversight, the Six Mile Creek impeded by Johnson's dam was a tributary of the Black Fork River, which in turn ran into the Green River, a "navigable, interstate water of the United States." By extension, the creek fell under Section 404 of the CWA, which gives the federal government authority to regulate discharges into or obstructions of the Waters of the United States (WOTUS). The EPA charged Johnson with damming a federal waterway without a federal permit and threatened heavy fines until he restored the creek to its previous state.[1]

Not surprisingly, Johnson became a cause célèbre for antigovernment activists, land developers and builders, and, especially, key sectors of the nation's agricultural establishment, for which control of water is always a contentious issue. A libertarian legal group took up his case and countersued the EPA for regulatory overreach.

The problem was that in devising the Clean Water Act of 1972 Congress had left unclear what qualified as the "waters of the United States." That ambiguity sparked a decades-long battle. On one side were environmentalists, wildlife advocates, and urban water users, for whom federal oversight was a counterweight to powerful local interests, particularly extractive and agricultural industries whose activities affected water quality. For example, the public water supply operator for Des Moines, Iowa, sought federal action after state officials limited its ability to compel agricultural producers to reduce the flow of nutrients from fertilizers and cattle manure into waters tapped for residential consumption.[2] On the other side were ideological conservatives supportive of Johnson's private property rights along with a myriad of business and agricultural interests, including pesticide and fertilizer manufacturers, cattle and dairy operations, and a range of crop producers who saw federal regulators as insensitive to local economic needs and intruding into state and local authority.

The Supreme Court only muddied the waters. In *Rapanos v. United States* (547 U.S. 715, 2006), four justices ruled that the EPA over several administrations overstepped its authority in applying the WOTUS rule when developers filled in non-navigable wetlands. Four other justices voted to support the EPA view. But Justice Anthony Kennedy, in a concurring opinion, suggested that federal authorities *could* intervene when there was a "significant nexus" between larger and smaller water bodies, including intermittent ones such as wetlands.[3] Absent a majority, the case went back to the lower federal courts, which applied varying interpretations.

The Obama administration sought to resolve the issue with a rule that would interpret Section 404 to apply to more than 60 percent of the nation's streams and millions of acres of wetlands not clearly protected under previous interpretations. After more than 400 public hearings, its final rule was announced in May 2015.[4] It met with furious opposition, and in June 2015, thirteen states sued the EPA, arguing that the rule unconstitutionally violated their Tenth Amendment prerogatives. A federal court in October 2015 issued a temporary injunction, a stay later extended nationally by a U.S. court of appeals. Meanwhile, in May 2016, Johnson and the EPA came to a settlement: he would limit the number of cattle using the pond and plant trees to lessen runoff; the EPA would drop all charges and fines.[5] But the settlement did nothing to resolve the war over WOTUS that roiled much of rural America but that few in the nation's urban centers even knew about.

That asymmetry in passion, even knowledge, was an apt reflection of deeper tensions between agriculture and environment. It also helped to explain the antipathy between rural America and the Obama EPA. This chapter examines those tensions by describing key traits of the current food system, its ecological impacts, the U.S. environmental laws relevant to (if not always addressing) those impacts, and ideas for reducing the food system's negative externalities even as it continues to focus on feeding the greatest number at the lowest possible direct cost.

The Food System

Eating is an agricultural act.

—Wendell Berry[6]

Americans are accustomed to food that is plentiful, diverse, convenient, and inexpensive. Or, to put it plainly, for most Americans, the food system gives us what we want, when we want it, at a price we're willing to pay. Indeed, the average American family now spends around 6 percent of disposable income on food consumed at home (10 percent when you include food consumed away from it), the lowest direct cost anywhere—and likely in human history.[7] This is no trivial achievement. While the United States started out with advantages in arable land and conducive growing conditions, much of today's abundance is due to key characteristics of the dominant food system, many of them promoted by U.S. agricultural policy.[8]

Industrial Scale

Despite the lingering agrarian ideal of small scale, self-sufficient farms that the U.S. Department of Agriculture (USDA) is always eager to promote, the core of American agricultural production is industrial in scale. In 1935, some 6.5 million farms dotted the landscape, averaging 155 acres. That number plummeted to 2.7 million by 1975, with average size growing to 391 acres. Despite a modest uptick in the number of smaller farms (fewer than 10 acres) due to rising demand for local food, the overall number continued to fall, to about 2.1 million by 2012, the year of the most recent Census of Agriculture. Average farm size was 434 acres.[9] More telling, by 2012, 3.8 percent of farms accounted for 66 percent of the market value of all agricultural products.[10] In this instance, scale matters. While 1,000 acres devoted to strawberries would be a large and profitable operation, a 1,000-acre corn farm is considered small or mid-scale, and economically marginal.[11] As one USDA study put it, "An economically viable crop/livestock operation in the Corn Belt would have between 2,000 and 3,000 acres of row crops and between 500 and 600 sows."[12]

Emphasis on Efficiency

The system is efficient in classical industrial terms. For example, in 1970, approximately 67 million acres were dedicated to field corn (versus sweet corn, which is less than 1 percent of all corn produced), with each acre yielding 72 bushels on average. By 2016, due partly to federal farm policies stressing production and mandates supporting ethanol (see Box 9-1), land devoted to corn had gone up to 94 million acres. More important, production per acre more than *doubled*, to 175 bushels—about 15 billion bushels overall. Put in perspective, the United States produces about 2 bushels (or 112 pounds) of field corn for each of the 7.4 billion persons now alive in the world. About 40 percent of that output goes to ethanol, another 40 percent into animal feed.[13] What writer Michael Pollan vividly describes as a "river of corn"[14] thus enables the United States to produce around 44 billion pounds of poultry, 26 billion pounds of beef, and 23 billion pounds of pork each year— 290 pounds per American.[15]

Or take dairy. From 1970 to 2012, the number of dairy cows in the United States dropped from 12 million to just over 9 million, and the number of dairy operations from 650,000 to about 90,000, due in part to federal policies favoring larger and more efficient operations. At the same time, average herd sizes went from 20 to 100 cows and per-cow milk output from 9,700 to 21,700 pounds per year. The result was a near *doubling* of dairy production from 117 billion pounds in 1970 to over 200 billion pounds in 2012.[16] Fewer farms, fewer cows—more milk than ever.

Box 9-1   Debating Corn Ethanol

By law, most regular gasoline in the United States contains at least 10 percent ethanol, an oxygenated biofuel derived from various feedstocks, including sugarcane, certain grasses, and field corn. Ethanol in the United States largely is derived from corn, with annual production escalating from 175 million gallons in the early 1980s to 15 billion gallons in 2016.[1]

The merits of corn ethanol are contested. To supporters, which include midwestern corn growers and ethanol producers and the members of Congress, governors, state legislatures, and communities throughout the Corn Belt, it is renewable, lessens U.S. dependence on imported oil, reduces greenhouse gas emissions, and supports American farmers.[2] To critics, which include environmental groups, alternative energy advocates, and free market economists, it depends on billions in government subsidies and encourages overproduction of corn, with attendant commodity market distortions and ecological harms. Moreover, fermenting corn into ethanol requires massive amounts of water and energy—more net energy than ethanol generates—via a process that itself emits greenhouse gases.[3] Despite severe criticism, corn ethanol survives, nurtured by its political support in the nation's Corn Belt.

---

1. Renewable Fuels Association, *Annual U.S. Fuel Ethanol Production* (Washington, DC: RFA, 2017), http://ethanolrfa.org/resources/industry/stat istics/#1454099788442-e48b2782-ea53.
2. Renewable Fuels Association, *Building Partnerships/Growing Markets: 2017 Ethanol Industry Outlook* (Washington, DC: RFA, 2017), http://www.ethanolrfa .org/wp-content/uploads/2017/02/Ethanol-Industry-Outlook-2017.pdf.
3. Gary Libecap, "Agricultural Programs with Dubious Environmental Benefits: The Political Economy of Ethanol," in *Agricultural Policy and the Environment*, ed. Roger Meiners and Bruce Yandle (Lanham, MD: Rowman and Littlefield, 2003), 89–106.

Specialized

Imperatives of scale and efficiency drive specialization. Where most American farmers once practiced some version of *polyculture*—such as rotating two or three row crops annually while also raising some cattle and hogs—today's "factory in the field" stresses *monoculture*—devoting all acreage to one crop, such as corn or soybeans.[17] Farmers may alternate years of corn with soy depending on market demand, but it is typically *all* corn or *all* soy. Specialization extends to animals, notably in concentrated animal feeding operations (CAFOs) in which thousands of cattle or hogs, and tens of thousands of chickens or turkeys, are fattened for market in controlled environments on calibrated and nutritionally augmented corn- or soy-based feed.[18] In Iowa, for example, the percentage of farms raising hogs fell from 70 percent in 1964 to 11 percent by 2000, yet *total* hog production remained stable.[19] Nationally, the number of hog producers dropped from 700,000 in 1980 to 68,300 in 2012, and facilities of more than 5,000 head now account for 62 percent of all the hogs brought to market.[20] Similar trends are seen for beef and poultry.

Technologized

Agriculture is a temple to technology, from global positioning system–guided seeders (to ensure straight rows) and drones (to better monitor production over large expanses) to the computer-calibrated application of fertilizers, adoption of animal and seed hybrids (including genetically modified ones), and widespread application of animal growth hormones and antibiotics and synthetic chemical herbicides, pesticides, and fungicides. Except in fresh fruit and vegetable sectors where migrant workers still pick crops, capital-intensive technologies have largely replaced people, enabling the few who farm to get greater yields on more land with less labor. In 1940, nearly 31 million Americans, 25 percent of the population, worked the farm. In 2012, it was 3.1 million—a farming 1 percent feeding everyone else.[21]

Energy Dependent

Industrial-scale, mechanized, technologized agriculture runs on energy—a lot of it. Not including the largely carbon-based fuels that power the nation's electrical grid and move food from processing facilities to consumers, contemporary agriculture depends on natural gas to produce the ammonium nitrate that is the building block of synthetic nitrogen fertilizers, petroleum to catalyze a wide range of chemical pesticides, and gasoline and diesel fuel to power tractors, combines, trucks, irrigation pumps, and on-site processing facilities. Total energy use in agriculture comes to about 1.6 trillion British thermal units (BTUs) per year, compared to the 8 trillion BTUs used annually by all U.S. households.[22] While agriculture has made efficiency gains in terms of gallons of oil per bushel of crops produced, the economic health of this sector, as of the nation overall, is affected by the availability and cost of oil and natural gas.[23]

Globalized

Finally, the food system is inextricably global. U.S. farmers produce far more food than Americans can possibly eat, and agricultural exports come to more than $144 billion a year, about 9 percent of total U.S. exports by value.[24] Yet Americans also import large shares of their seafood, fresh fruits, and vegetables.[25] If you live in Green Bay and want fresh raspberries in February, you can get them, shipped in by air from South America. What you want, when you want it, at a price you're willing to pay.

Ecological Impacts of Food Production

It also bears reminding that agriculture, *however* practiced, always has ecological impacts. As plant geneticist Nina Fedoroff put it, with perhaps a little hyperbole, "agriculture is more devastating ecologically than anything else we could do except pouring concrete on the land."[26] And, as just noted, the reality of contemporary food production is industrial. As a result, it is necessary to take a "life cycle" perspective on the ecological impacts of food production. Such a perspective, by widening the lens of analysis to encompass the entire life cycle of foods from raw material extraction to final disposal, provides a holistic accounting of how the foods we produce and eat affect the environment. Examining foods from a "cradle-to-grave" perspective gives us a better understanding of the true cost of what is served up on Americans' plates.

Land and Water

The United States devotes approximately 45 percent of its total land to agriculture, as compared to 78 percent for Nigeria, for example.[27] However, unlike Nigeria, that 45 percent is typically farmed in highly intensive ways. The large-scale, mechanized monoculture encouraged by long-standing U.S. agricultural policy, combined with global commodity markets that place a premium on volume and price, has resulted in the literal application of former USDA secretary Earl Butz's oft-cited exhortation to plant "fencepost to fencepost." Those growing crops such as corn and soy have every incentive to maximize production: little land is either left fallow to refresh the soil or set aside for woodlands. The result, critics argue, is a tragic loss of topsoil to degraded fertility through overuse or to erosion from wind and water. In the Midwest grain belt, for example, topsoil loss from erosion is estimated to be 343 million tons per year, much of it eventually washing down the Mississippi River into the Gulf of Mexico.[28] While erosion can be lessened through "no till" methods that disturb the soil as little as possible, doing so may require greater use of herbicides to combat weeds and maintain production levels, a telling example of the trade-offs in the nexus between agriculture and the environment.[29]

Intensive agricultural land use by itself harms wildlife. For example, farmers working under the aegis of federal "swamp reclamation" programs have drained millions of acres of wetlands to expand tillable acreage. This practice so diminished wildlife habitats by the late 1920s that concerned anglers and hunters established groups like the National Wildlife Federation (1935) and Ducks Unlimited (1937) to preserve what wetlands remained.[30] These early disputes about water put current debates over WOTUS into perspective. Intensive cultivation has also reduced the number and diversity of native honeybees essential to producing foods such as almonds, apples, and peaches. Large-scale farms now depend on commercial bee operations that transport hives from field to field to pollinate crops, but the survival of these managed bee colonies is threatened by pesticides and disease, calling into question the future viability of this system.[31]

Agriculture also depends on sufficient and predictable supplies of water, especially in regions where rainfall is irregular. For example, crop production in much of the lower Great Plains relies on water drawn from the Ogallala Aquifer, an ancient water table running from South Dakota to Texas that also provides drinking water to the region's cities. Heavy reliance on the Ogallala in recent decades, combined with low natural recharge rates, has degraded the water table and forced many to return to dryland farming, with consequent impacts on crop yields. The situation inspired proposals to pipe in water from the Great Lakes that, in turn, led to a federally approved compact among Great Lakes states to prohibit any such schemes.[32] The picture is starker in Arizona and in California's Imperial Valley, key fruit- and vegetable-producing areas whose existence depends on water supplied from sources hundreds of miles away and according to complex permitting rights set decades ago, under far different demand and climactic conditions.[33] The reservoirs on which the West depends are also controversial for their impacts on fish populations, in particular, on migratory species such as salmon whose spawning grounds were cut off by dams built for water and hydropower.

Chemicals

Conventional agriculture depends on chemicals derived from petroleum or natural gas. The list starts with inorganic fertilizers, which, along with hybrid seeds and synthetic pesticides, were key to the "Green Revolution" of the 1960s that enabled countries like India to become more food self-sufficient.[34] However, overuse of fertilizer adds significant and harmful amounts of nitrogen and phosphorus to terrestrial and aquatic ecosystems. In the United States, 97 percent of acres devoted to corn are treated with synthetic nitrogen fertilizer, the application-per-acre rate of which has gone from 112 pounds in 1970 to 144 in 2014.[35] Such increases helped to boost corn production but are subject to the law of diminishing returns: as yields increase, each additional bushel produced requires even more fertilizer than the one before.

Next come a broad array of compounds used to decrease crop loss at various stages of production, processing, or shipment; these include insecticides, herbicides, fungicides, fumigants, nematicides (for soil-borne nematodes, microscopic plant parasites), and rodenticides. Agriculture accounts for about 80 percent of all U.S. pesticide use, with 877 million pounds of pesticide active ingredients applied in 2008 alone (the most recently available data), nearly two-thirds of which went to five crops: corn, cotton, potatoes, soybeans, and wheat.[36] Leading the way is glyphosate, a broad-spectrum herbicide (i.e., effective on many types of plants) that is the most widely applied pesticide in the United States, with about 140 million pounds applied annually, on average, to the top five pesticide-receiving crops.[37] Its popularity is due to the wide adoption of Monsanto's Roundup Ready seeds, which allow farmers to spray the herbicide over entire fields, wiping out weeds while sparing their genetically modified (GM) corn, soy, cotton, alfalfa, canola, or sugar beet plants. This technological breakthrough, brought to market in 1996, was heralded as an economic and ecological achievement. Farmers would save time and effort in herbicide application, and it was projected that herbicide use and toxicity would decrease as farmers would only need to spray Roundup (or its generic equivalents), a chemical with lower toxicity and residence time in the environment than older formulations (e.g., atrazine). Such hopes were important given the known and potential negative health effects of heavy pesticide use on nontarget species, including humans.[38]

Although use of glyphosate led to lower herbicide use early on, the logic of monoculture soon imposed itself. That is, applying the same chemical repeatedly on the same land over time breeds resistance. Weeds evolve and adapt. Agrichemical firms responded to new "superweeds" by "stacking" multiple resistance traits in seeds' genetic code, which over time made the plant resistant to applications of multiple types of pesticides.[39] The trade-off, then, for producing a simplified but technology-dependent pest management system means that farmers came to apply greater quantities and potentially more toxic formulations. Indeed, it is estimated that reliance on herbicide-resistant packages such as Roundup Ready led to an *increase* of 527 million pounds in U.S. herbicide application between 1996 and 2011.[40] Additional research is needed to understand the extent to which this shift has influenced human and ecosystem toxicity risks.[41]

Genetically Modified Variants

Beyond intensifying the use of chemical inputs (e.g., via use of Roundup Ready seed), GM crops also raise concerns about impacts on organic agriculture (see Box 9-2) and about the acceleration of overall reliance on a few variants. In this regard, the proliferation of GM technology in commodity crop production has dramatically shaped the landscape and business of farming. One company, Monsanto, owns or has legally enforceable control of over 87 percent of GM seed planted worldwide.[42] In the United States, about 90 percent of corn, soybean, and cotton acres are planted with GM seed to resist pests or herbicides.[43] As a result, in some areas, there are few non-GM seed choices for farmers, thereby reducing the biodiversity of planted acreage and farmers' choices because they cannot opt out of using GM technology if they continue to farm conventionally.

Waste

Industrial-scale agriculture produces a lot of waste. About 60 percent of the nitrogen fertilizer applied ends up in surface and ground waters, contributing to eutrophication (excessive plant growth) and compromised drinking water supplies.[44] Fertilizer is a significant contributor to stream loads of nitrogen and phosphorus throughout the central United States.[45] As noted, because each incremental increase in fertilizer use comes with diminishing gains in crop yields, farmers tend to apply more than is needed just to maintain production. Farmers often also over-apply because of their uncertainty about existing nutrients in the soil and their desire to mitigate potential

---

Box 9-2   GM and Organic: The Case of Bt

Regulations based on the Organic Foods Production Act of 1990 define genetically modified (GM) variants as "synthetic" and not legal in organic production.[1] Yet, questions arise over what is "natural," and whether genetic modification can contribute to reducing the harmful impacts of synthetic pesticides in agriculture.

Take *Bacillus thuringiensis* (Bt). In its "natural" state, it is a soil bacterium with insecticidal properties widely used in organic agriculture. As with *any* pesticide, the more Bt is used, the more resistance to it pests develop. To compensate, firms developed GM variants expressing Bt genes. By one study, use of Bt corn and cotton reduced synthetic insecticide use by 123 million pounds between 1996 and 2011.[2]

Proponents see no genetic difference between "natural" and GM Bt. Critics retort that Bt sprayed *on* plants can be washed off but toxins *in* GM variants remain, with uncertain effects. To genetic modification's proponents, the legal definition of "organic" rests on a mistaken notion of "natural." To critics, genetic modification is an agribusiness assault on organic agriculture. As the Bt case suggests, this debate is not easily resolved.

---

1. Miles McEvoy, "Organic 101: Can GMOs Be Used in Organic Production?" USDA blog, May 17, 2013, https://www.usda.gov/media/blog/2013/05/17/organic-101-can-gmos-be-used-organic-products.
2. Charles Benbrook, "Impacts of Genetically Engineered Crops on Pesticide Use in the U.S.: The First Sixteen Years," *Environmental Sciences Europe* 24 (2012), https://doi.org/10.1186/2190-4715-24-24.

---

economic losses from suboptimal production. Additionally, much of the Corn Belt uses tile drainage to remove excess water from the soil and foster crop growth. These subsurface tubes (which are "nonpoint" sources under the Clean Water Act and thus not regulated by the federal government) sluice water, often highly polluted with nitrate, directly into surface waters and other catchments. Concerns over nitrate in drinking water were at the center of the dispute between Iowa agriculture and the Des Moines Water Works, in which state and federal courts ultimately sided with agricultural producers.[46] Many of these waters ultimately drain into the Gulf of Mexico, where algae feed on the nutrients and create an oxygen-poor "dead zone" the size of Connecticut. Similar conditions occur off the delta of the San Joaquin and Sacramento Rivers, which drains California's fertile Central Valley.[47] In addition to killing fish and producing foul odors, such dead zones can emit nitrous oxide, a greenhouse gas 300 times more powerful than carbon dioxide.[48]

Animal Waste. Almost 10 billion animals are raised and slaughtered for food in the United States each year. While the increasing specialization and concentration of meat production in large-scale CAFOs made economic sense, the shift challenged the capacity of surrounding environments to handle nutrients from animals' liquid and solid manure. Despite decreases in nitrogen and phosphorus excretion per unit of meat, increased production and low nutrient recovery in crop and livestock systems concentrated nutrients beyond the capacity of the soil to absorb and filter them.[49] Manure that enters local soil or escapes from CAFO containment lagoons—also nonpoint sources of water pollution—adds to the eutrophication problem in even far-off waters.

Chemical Runoff. A significant but still undetermined portion of the hundreds of millions of pounds of pesticides used annually in agriculture also ends up in water—as does a significant but undetermined amount applied to residential lawns, golf courses, and other nonagricultural spaces.[50] Atrazine, the second most widely applied pesticide in the United States, has been detected in surface and drinking waters throughout the Midwest. The herbicide has documented carcinogenic and endocrine-disrupting activities in animals, and concerns about its ubiquity in groundwater led to its ban in the European Union in 2003. The EPA spent years reviewing the pesticide registration for atrazine, which includes assessments of ecological and human health risks. Its ecological assessment, released for public comment in 2016, found worrisome levels of potential risk to mammals, birds, and plants.[51] Although the health risk assessment has not yet been released, EPA's most recent review deemed as safe the current levels of human exposure to triazine herbicides (the most common of which is atrazine).[52] Atrazine's regulatory fate remains unclear, but the Trump administration's focus on deregulation suggests that no new restrictions will be placed on the chemical anytime soon.

Antibiotics. Almost 80 percent of all antibiotics sold in the United States are used in livestock and poultry production, an unknown amount of which also ends up in water.[53] Farmers can purchase these drugs without veterinary oversight and use them for animal growth promotion, disease prevention, and treatment. Prophylactic use of antibiotics is central to the CAFO system, where large numbers of animals are packed into confined spaces that are ideal conditions for the spread of disease. Such unregulated use also facilitates antibiotic resistance, with potential human health effects. Bacteria have the ability to share genes, so once a resistance gene evolves in one bacterium, it binds to another. Then, when producers use an antibiotic, all nonresistant bacteria are exterminated, leaving the resistance gene to spread to other bacteria. Resistant pathogens, such as *E. coli*, thus can be spread on the landscape in manure, can be transported to communities via workers and equipment, and can eventually make their way into the supermarket meat case.[54]

Greenhouse Gas Emissions

Industrial-scale agriculture generates significant greenhouse gas emissions, calculated at approximately 7 percent of the nation's total by economic sector.[55] For the average American household, about 83 percent of its food consumption carbon footprint stems from agricultural production.[56] A large portion of its impact—not including land use change—is due to large-scale animal production, particularly of ruminants (e.g., beef cattle), which emit greenhouse gases such as methane.[57] Red meat is the most greenhouse gas–intensive part of the American diet, leading some to argue that the average American family could reduce its carbon footprint more by going without red meat once a week than by buying all food from local sources.[58]

Agriculture and U.S. Environmental Law

Despite these often serious externalities, U.S. environmental laws typically do not apply to or carve out exemptions for agricultural production. In part, such differential treatment reflects the iconography of the small family farm in American culture. In part, it reflects the still potent (if waning) political clout of the farm sector in Congress. At minimum, as Megan Stubbs observes, "environmental policies have focused on large industrial sources such as factories and power plants, because attempting to regulate numerous individual crop and livestock operations can be a challenge for government regulators." Therefore, despite popular portrayals of overbearing federal regulators, "current federal farm policy addressing environmental concerns is in large part voluntary; that is, it seeks to encourage agricultural producers to adopt conservation practices through economic incentives."[59]

Although incentives have always been part of the EPA's tool kit, in this instance, its reliance on them reflects a long-standing *realpolitik* by a perpetually beleaguered regulatory agency facing strong congressional support for farmers as local small businesses, regardless (or because) of their actual size and economic clout. Take, for example, the Obama EPA's consideration of having large CAFOs voluntarily report methane emissions, based on a directive by Congress in its fiscal year 2008 appropriations requiring "mandatory reporting of greenhouse gas (GHG) emissions above appropriate thresholds in all sectors of the economy of the United States." Two years later, a new Republican-led Congress explicitly *barred* the EPA from using its budget to apply GHG reporting rules to CAFOs, even on a voluntary basis.[60] This rider has been extended in subsequent appropriations, reflecting an overall pattern of congressional intervention in federal environmental policy as it applies to agriculture.

Table 9-1 lays out elements of major U.S. environmental laws that can apply to agriculture. Most were enacted in the 1970s, the "golden age" of environmental policy formation in the United States. While few have been formally updated by Congress, how they are implemented varies by presidential administration and has been shaped by countless legal battles.[61] These laws also typically set threshold limits that exempt small farm operations (variously defined) and, in many instances, as with the Clean Air Act, leave implementation to the states, raising concerns about variability in monitoring and enforcement.

Table 9-1   U.S. Environmental Laws Affecting Agriculture

	Applies to	*Requirements*
Endangered Species Act		
Pesticide use (via FIFRA)	All operations	Possible limits on pesticide use
Forests and other habitats	All operations	Restrict activities that could adversely affect habitat of listed species
Clean Water Act		
National Pollutant Discharge Elimination System (NPDES)	Concentrated animal feeding operations	Federal permit if discharging into waterways
	Pesticide application on or near irrigation ditches, other water bodies	No federal permit required
	Application of biosolids to land	No federal permit required, but farms must meet regulatory requirements
Wetlands	Discharges of dredged or fill material into "waters of the United States"	Federal permit for nonexempt activities
Clean Air Act		
Particulates	Some operations in specified areas	Varies based on state implementation plans
Ozone (nitrogen oxides, volatile organic compounds)	Some operations in specified areas	
Federal Insecticide, Fungicide, and Rodenticide Act		
	All practices that involve pest control	Follow label instructions
	Restricted use applicators	Certain training requirements
Resource Conservation and Recovery Act		
Waste pesticides	All operations	Proper disposal of unused pesticides
Underground storage tanks	Farms with fuel storage tanks > 1,100 gallons	Meet design and tech requirements

	Applies to	*Requirements*
Emergency Planning and Right to Know Act		
Hazardous chemicals	Operations storing above-threshold amounts ("routine agricultural operations") excluded	Report inventory to state and local authorities

Source: Adapted from *Major Existing EPA Laws and Programs That Could Affect Agricultural Producers,* EPA, 2007, https://nepis.epa.gov/Exe/ZyPDF.cgi/P1003E7I.PDF?Dockey=P1003E7I.PDF.

Endangered Species

Agriculture's impact on the land includes effects on wildlife, whether as a result of "swamp" clearance, woodlands loss, or the externalities of practices ranging from extensive fertilizer and chemical use to the size and density of CAFOs.[62] While land use issues are for the most part state and local matters, the Endangered Species Act (ESA) comes into play when agriculture threatens a listed species. The law's "incidental takings" provision protects farmers and ranchers in instances where "routine" activities (e.g., proper use of authorized rodenticides) lead inadvertently to deaths of otherwise protected species. Even so, complaints about the ESA's purported negative impacts on farming and ranching are a perennial feature of attacks on the law, which in many instances hearkens back to decades-old battles over Interior Department "predator control" efforts. For example, grazing interests, backed by conservative activists seeking local control over federal rangelands, have pushed the U.S. Fish and Wildlife Service to "delist" the gray wolf and leave its management to the states, a move opposed by wildlife groups.[63] Conflicts over the ESA also reflect broader tensions over the Fifth Amendment's "takings" clause when it comes to framing environmental policy that balances private property rights with the needs of the commons, including nonhuman species.[64] The Trump administration has signaled its support for delisting the gray wolf, and for a more robust defense of property rights more generally.

Air Pollution

The Clean Air Act authorizes the EPA to set National Ambient Air Quality Standards (NAAQS) for pollutants that "may reasonably be anticipated to endanger public health or welfare," and then it assigns to the states a significant duty to implement those standards.[65] The act applies to agricultural activities as they generate specific pollutants, such as particulates from CAFOs (e.g., feedlot dust), nitrogen oxides from fertilizers, and various GHG emissions. To date, the EPA has been reluctant to treat large-scale agriculture in the same manner as other industries, and instead it grants states flexibility in doing so within their respective state implementation plans (SIPs). For their part, states with large farm sectors tend to treat food production and processing activities with care, leaving critics to argue that industrial farming gets off too easily.

The EPA also has authority to regulate "hazardous" air pollutants (HAPs), those known or reasonably anticipated to pose serious health risks, including cancer, neurological disorders, and reproductive dysfunction. While the agency has promulgated standards on manufacturers of agriculture-related products such as pesticides, it has been reluctant to extend oversight directly to agricultural activities. For example, CAFOs can emit significant amounts of hydrogen sulfide, which at low doses is a respiratory irritant and at high doses can be fatal. The substance was "inadvertently" included on the list of HAPs to be regulated under the 1990 amendments to the Clean Air Act, but it was removed from the list a year later by a joint resolution of Congress, signed by President George H. W. Bush, at the behest of farming interests.[66] Despite intensified lobbying by environmental and public health advocates, spurred on by new releases of hydrogen sulfide in hydraulic fracturing processes, the EPA to date has declined to add the substance to the HAP list.[67]

Water Pollution

As suggested earlier, the Clean Water Act's differential treatment of *point* and *nonpoint* sources exempts most agricultural practices from direct EPA oversight. CAFOs that discharge animal waste directly into waterways may be required to obtain a National Pollutant Discharge Elimination System (NPDES) permit, so most store it in large manure lagoons, which are considered nonpoint. That distinction is controversial given the size of many such containment structures and the chance of accidental spills. In 2001, the EPA proposed to require that large CAFOs obtain permits unless they demonstrated that they had no potential to discharge waste. The proposed rule provoked considerable criticism, with livestock producers opposing it as too stringent and environmental groups as too lenient. The controversy went to federal court, and in *Waterkeeper Alliance v. EPA* (2005), the Second Circuit Court of Appeals ruled that the EPA could only regulate *actual* discharge and thus had exceeded its statutory authority in requiring mandatory permitting of all CAFOs.[68] The EPA issued a new rule in 2008, requiring an NPDES permit only if facilities discharge or propose to discharge into local waters; the rule does not cover application of manure onto fields that may leach into those waters. Today, only 30 percent of the 19,496 operations defined as CAFOs by the Clean Water Act require such a permit.[69]

Chemicals

Given the centrality of synthetic pesticides to conventional agriculture, it is no surprise that the Federal Insecticide, Fungicide, and Rodenticide Act (FIFRA) is at the center of some of the nation's most charged environmental battles, including over Rachel Carson's *Silent Spring* in 1962, the EPA's suspension of the growth regulator Alar on apples in 1989, and the use of atrazine today.[70] In each, the conflict is between those defending chemicals as key to food production and those for whom chemical use, or overuse, poses unacceptable ecological and human health risks. This said, most of FIFRA's focus is on chemical manufacturers and their products, not on applicators, and farmers who apply pesticides as directed are generally exempt from oversight. Controversies over pesticides tend to focus on chemical efficacy, toxicity, and chronic effects, and in such instances, farmers fearful about losing any tool in their fight against crop loss tend to side with chemical makers against regulators and nonfarm interests when environmental and health concerns are raised. In the case of atrazine, for example, midwestern corn growers have opposed tighter restrictions on the herbicide even after it was found in the region's public drinking water supplies.[71]

Making Agriculture More Ecologically Sustainable

The food system's central players—including the USDA and state departments of agriculture, agribusinesses, agricultural research centers at land grant universities, and members of Congress concerned about farming's future—have not remained complacent as these externalities accrued and, in many instances, threatened the system's capacity to maintain production. They also have been pushed by critics, ranging from environmental and animal rights activists to nutritionists and proponents of "alternative" agriculture, to make the food system more transparent and sustainable.

Moving toward sustainability first requires articulating its meaning. Sustainability clearly encompasses multiple dimensions but can often seem vague or difficult to define. Across many definitions, as Kent Portney points out in Chapter 12 of this volume, the concept is operationalized in context-specific ways with a core focus on the environment. Within the U.S. context, the USDA defines "sustainable agriculture" as including the broad objectives of long-term profitability, quality of life for producers and rural communities, and stewardship of the country's land, air, and water.[72] Improving the ecological sustainability of agriculture will require shifting practices and systems and balancing trade-offs between environmental, social, and economic outcomes.

Improving Conventional Production

Such innovations begin with new, or reintroduced, methods of planting. Conservation tillage (reduced or no till) reduces soil exposure to wind or water erosion.[73] Cover cropping, or planting a crop such as alfalfa or rye in the off season, can add fertility, reduce soil erosion, and suppress pests.[74] Using legumes as a cover crop in a rotation with other crops fixes nitrogen in soils, thereby reducing the need for synthetic fertilizer and resultant nutrient loss.[75] Many of these once common practices had been abandoned as farmers opted for monoculture and synthetic fertilizers. In some cases, the integrated use of conservation practices in conventional farming can be as effective as organic approaches in reducing negative impacts.[76] Despite their potential, such practices are not the norm, particularly among growers of major commodity crops pushed by economic imperatives to maximize production.[77] Though the USDA offers support to farmers who adopt conservation practices, less than 12 percent of corn- and soybean-planted acres are enrolled in such programs, in part due to limits on funding.[78]

Expanding Organic

Organic production is seen as an ecologically preferable alternative to conventional systems, and, done well, it results in increased soil organic matter and biodiversity, less energy use, and lower nutrient loss across the landscape.[79] At the same time, going organic requires more land—84 percent more, in one analysis—to produce the same amount of a crop or livestock product as a conventional system due to 25 percent lower average yield per acre, lower animal productivity, and more land in rotation for soil fertility.[80] The implications of higher land needs are important in debates over addressing imbalances in federal supports for conventional versus organic farming. Moreover, those concerned about global food security see high-yield conventional systems as key to saving forests and grasslands from conversion to agriculture of any kind—which would result in large biodiversity losses and carbon fluxes into the atmosphere.

Opportunities to increase organic yields exist, and such systems offer other benefits that must be considered. For example, given their emphasis on maintaining healthy soils, organic systems may offer increased resilience to ecological stressors such as drought, an important factor as agriculture feels the impacts of climate change (see Box 9-3).[81] Furthermore, organic farms tend to be smaller and multifunctional and to have higher productivity in terms of overall output of multiple crops per acre compared to larger, industrialized systems.[82] Not surprisingly, there is real interest in the metrics to be used to conceptualize and assess the future sustainability of agricultural systems, conventional or organic.

Bolstering Local and Regional Food Systems

Many consumers are looking to purchase food more locally to lessen the ecological impacts of their food consumption. The definition of "local" varies and is generally marked by a set distance between farm production and consumption. Local food largely is sold to consumers via farmers' markets, farm stands, and community-supported agriculture (CSA) shares, with an expanding share going to restaurants, institutions like universities, food service providers, and supermarkets. Buying food locally, even when its ecological advantages aren't clear, also can restore transparency in the food system and the relationships that people once had to agriculture through "knowing their farmer." Finally, local food is seen as a mechanism for economic development, with a documented ability to increase employment and income in communities.

Box 9-3   Climate Change and Food

The nation's farm sector likely noted that the 2014 *National Climate Assessment* opens as follows:

> Climate change, once considered an issue for a distant future, has moved firmly into the present. Corn producers in Iowa, oyster growers in Washington State, and maple syrup producers in Vermont are all observing climate-related changes that are outside of recent experience.[1]

Among its findings, the assessment lays out specific implications of climate change for the U.S. food system:

- **Climate disruptions to agricultural production**, ranging from more frequent heavy rains to longer and more serious droughts;
- **Declines in crop and livestock production** due to weeds, diseases, insect pests, and other stresses induced by climate change; and
- **Loss and degradation of critical agricultural soil and water** assets due to increasing extremes in precipitation.

Add to this picture climate-induced stresses on the world's oceans, the primary source of food for at least one billion people,[2] and implications are clear. As the assessment warns, climate change will "alter the stability of food supplies and create new food security challenges for the United States as the world seeks to feed nine billion people by 2050."[3]

---

1. Jerry Melillo, Terese Richmond, and Gary Yohe, eds., *Climate Change Impacts in the United States: The Third National Climate Assessment* (Washington, DC: U.S. Global Change Research Program, 2014), 1, doi:10.7930/J0Z31WJ2.
2. Melillo, Richmond, and Yohe, *Climate Change Impacts*, 49.
3. Jerry Hatfield, Gene Takle, Richard Grotjahn, Patrick Holden, R. Cesar Izaurralde, Terry Mader, Elizabeth Marshall et al., "Chapter 6: Agriculture," in *Climate Change Impacts in the United States: The Third National Climate Assessment*, 150–74, see page 151.

However, focusing on local food is limiting in terms of scale, price, and variety. Perhaps more useful is the notion of a *regional* food system that includes local products and is nested within national and global systems.[83] Although Congress defined a local or regional food product as one that is sold no more than 400 miles from its origin or within the state where it was produced,[84] Clancy and Ruhf argue that the optimal regional system would be "self-reliant" insofar as it leverages a geographic area's productive, economic, and social resources to meet as much of its food needs as possible in a sustainable way.[85] At the regional level, more opportunities exist to aggregate food from multiple farms for sale at lower prices through traditional venues like supermarkets. Larger volumes of food shipped could lead to efficiency increases in transportation, reducing per-unit GHG emissions, and lowering per-unit costs for processing (e.g., freezing and canning), although obtaining such gains would depend on rebuilding much of the regional processing infrastructure that has disappeared in the recent decades of industry consolidation. Moreover, from an agronomic perspective, regional systems inherently include multiple climates and growing zones, enabling greater diversity and resilience of production than is possible within a strictly localized system.

Perhaps most relevant to this discussion is what local and regional foods are *not*. While consumers understandably look to nearby sources as a solution to the ills brought about by the globalized, industrialized paradigm, the mere fact that a product is local conveys only information about the locus and scale of the supply chain. Local and regional are *not* inherently more ecologically benign, fair, or equitable, just as "global" need not connote "exploitative" and "destructive."[86] Increasing overall food system sustainability and resilience will require nesting systems at different scales—local, regional, national, and global—and identifying the goals such a nested system should achieve.[87]

Reducing Food Waste

A promising approach to improving the sustainability of agriculture lies not in changing how or where farming occurs but the fate of the food that is produced. Approximately 40 percent of food produced annually in the United States is wasted.[88] The overwhelming majority of this waste occurs at the point of sale (e.g., grocery stores, institutions, restaurants) or within households.[89] In 2010, 133 billion pounds of food were lost at the retail and household stages of the U.S. food supply chain.[90] Discarding this much food represents a tremendous waste not only of nourishment but also of the inputs required to produce the food (e.g., fertilizers, land, fuel, labor, water) and the emissions generated in its journey from farm to store or plate. In addition to these embedded emissions, food is the largest component of municipal solid waste (21 percent) that ends up in landfills.[91] Landfills are responsible for 20 percent of U.S. emissions of methane,[92] a greenhouse gas 25 times more powerful than carbon dioxide. Reducing food waste would clearly have myriad benefits, including that less food would need to be produced to feed the same number of people.

In a national call to action, the EPA and USDA under the Obama administration announced a national food waste reduction goal of 50 percent by 2030.[93] This is an ambitious goal that will require collaboration, innovation, and action across multiple sectors within the food system and beyond. A primary policy tool to help meet this objective exists at the state and municipal levels: banning food and other organic materials from landfills. California and the New England states, save New Hampshire and Maine, have implemented such bans to date.[94] Three of the five cities Portney identifies as "taking sustainability seriously"—Portland, San Francisco, and Seattle—have also gone down this road.[95] Emerging evidence indicates that landfill bans are making positive impacts on both the food supply and economic development. Vermont has seen donations to the Vermont Food Bank increase by 60 percent over one year.[96] In Massachusetts, organizations that recover and redistribute edible food (i.e., food rescue operations) and that haul and process food waste have grown economically in the two-year period after the state's ban was implemented.[97]

Steps Back?

It is such a horrible, horrible rule. Has sort of a nice name, but everything else is bad.

—President Donald Trump[98]

Rural voters went big for Donald Trump, who during the 2016 campaign promised to eliminate federal regulations seen as burdensome to agriculture. On February 27, 2017, the new president delivered, at least symbolically. Surrounded by a phalanx of farmers, home builders, and county commissioners, Trump signed an executive order mandating a review of the still-unimplemented Obama WOTUS rule, saying that it should have applied only to "navigable waters" affecting "interstate commerce." The president called the Obama EPA's WOTUS rule "one of the worst examples of federal regulation" and added that "it has truly run amok, and is one of the rules most strongly opposed by farmers, ranchers and agricultural workers all across our land. It's prohibiting them from being allowed to do what they're supposed to be doing. It's been a disaster."[99]

Any new WOTUS rule would take months, even years, to wend its way through the formal approval process, not to mention the expected gauntlet of legal challenges, but the imagery conveyed by Trump's signing ceremony sent a clear signal: in conflicts between food production and the environment, he would favor food. New EPA administrator Scott Pruitt underscored the point a month later when he overruled agency science experts and refused to ban the insecticide chlorpyrifos in agricultural use. Environmental groups had long called for such a ban, citing the chemical's health effects on farm workers and on children exposed to it through contaminated drinking water, arguments contested by agricultural producers and the chemical's makers. The EPA under Obama had neared such a ban. Pruitt, in reversing direction, argued that the science on chlorpyrifos was still unsettled and that farmers needed "regulatory certainty" until "sound science" determined whether the chemical posed unreasonable risks.[100]

Overall, then, the political pendulum has swung in favor of producer priorities. Even so, agriculture is not guaranteed to get all that it wants, if only because ever more Americans, few who ever farmed, express evident concerns about where their food comes from, the conditions under which it is produced, and the impacts of food production on their health and environment. It must mean something that Walmart, not Whole Foods, is the largest retail source for organic produce.[101] It must mean something that McDonald's now requires its egg suppliers to provide hens with larger enclosures and its pork suppliers to phase out "gestation crates" for pregnant sows,[102] actions the iconic American fast-food chain is taking to please its mass customer base, not "elitist" animal rights activists. Consumer concerns, however expressed, also induced major dairy producers to keep their milk free of artificial growth hormones despite Food and Drug Administration rulings of no health risk from such stimulants, in turn leading Monsanto to sell off its dairy hormone business.[103] More Americans now purchase some of their food from an ever-increasing number and range of local sources, many created and run by a new generation of activist-entrepreneurs. More consumers want food that is local, community based, ecologically sustainable, fairly traded, and humane—whatever those terms mean in actual implementation.

In short, more Americans care about how their food is produced. At one level, their concerns have had real effects on the food system, with consequent impacts on the relationship between food production and the environment. *However*, we still want what we want, when we want it, at a price we're willing to pay. Although many consumers seek food that is more local and more organic, most merely want it to be plentiful, diverse, and inexpensive. Moreover, demands on the food system will get more complicated with the expected need to feed an estimated nine billion people by 2050 amidst the effects of climate change. "One way or another," as agricultural economist Parke Wilde bluntly puts it, "there will be a reckoning between human food needs and the natural environment."[104] The Trump administration may seek to tilt that balance in one direction, and is likely to achieve some goals, but, on food at least, it will encounter a political landscape where agricultural interests will not always dominate. Eaters are also paying attention.

Suggested Websites

Harvard Food Law and Policy Clinic (http://www.chlpi.org/food-law-and-policy/about/) This Harvard Law School clinic offers legal research on a range of food issues, particularly food waste.

Food Tank (https://foodtank.com) This think tank for food is a useful source for news and commentary on a range of agricultural issues, with a focus on sustainability, food security, and urban agriculture.

National Sustainable Agriculture Coalition (http://sustainableagriculture.net) The coalition is an alliance of organizations seeking to make U.S. agriculture more ecologically sustainable, among other goals.

U.S. EPA National Agriculture Center (www.epa.gov/oecaagct/index.html) The website is the EPA's official source for information, guidelines, and regulations pertaining to agriculture.

Notes

1. Jack Healy, "Family Pond Boils at Center of a 'Regulatory War' in Wyoming," *New York Times*, September 19, 2015.

2. Jonathan Coppess, "Dead Zones and Drinking Water," *farmdoc daily* (6): 37, Department of Agricultural and Consumer Economics, University of Illinois at Urbana-Champaign, February 25, 2016, http://farmdocdaily.illinois.edu/2016/02/dead-zones-drinking-water-part1.html

3. Juliet Eilperin and Abby Phillip, "Trump Directs Rollback of Obama-Era Water Rule He Calls 'Destructive and Horrible,'" *Washington Post*, February 28, 2017.

4. Clean Water Rule: Definition of "Waters of the United States," 80 *Fed. Reg.* 37054 (June 29, 2015).

5. Valerie Richardson, "Wyoming Rancher Facing $20M in EPA Fines Claims Victory, Keeps Cash, Stock Pond," *Washington Times*, May 9, 2016.

6. Wendell Berry, "The Pleasures of Eating," in *What Are People For?* (New York: North Point Press, 1990), 145–52.

7. USDA, "Table 8: Food Expenditures by Families and Individual as a Share of Disposable Personal Income," *Food Expenditures*, January 2016, https://www.ers.usda.gov/data-products/food-expenditures.aspx.

8. See Christopher Bosso, *Framing the Farm Bill: Interests, Ideology, and the Agricultural Act of 2014* (Lawrence, University Press of Kansas, 2017).

9. USDA Census of Agriculture Historical Archive, *Farms, Acreage, and Value*, http://usda.mannlib.cornell.edu/usda/AgCensusImages/1935/03/01/1522/Table-01.pdf; USDA National Agricultural Statistics Service, *Acreage*, www.nass.usda.gov/index.asp; USDA, *2012 Census of Agriculture*, www.agcensus.usda.gov/Publications/2012/Preliminary_Report/Full_Report.pdf.

10. USDA, "Table 2: Market Value of Agricultural Products Sold Including Landlord's Share and Direct Sales: 2012 and 2007," *2012 Census of Agriculture*, www.agcensus.usda.gov/Publications/2012/Full_Report/Volume_1,_Chapter_1_US/st99_1_002_002.pdf. The next Census is in 2017.

11. Robert Hoppe and James McDonald, "Classifying U.S. Farms to Reflect Today's Agriculture," *Amber Waves*, May 6, 2013, www.ers.usda.gov/amber-waves/2013-may/the-revised-ers-farm-typology-classifying-us-farms-to-reflect-todays-agriculture.aspx.

12. EPA, "Demographics," *Ag 101*, https://www.epa.gov/sites/production/files/2015-07/documents/ag_101_agriculture_us_epa_0.pdf.

13. USDA, "Feed Grains Data—Recent Years," *Feed Grains: Yearbook Tables*, accessed August 25, 2017, https://www.ers.usda.gov/data-products/feed-grains-database/feed-grains-yearbook-tables/; USDA Economic Research Service, *Corn and Other Feed Grains—Background*, www.ers.usda.gov/topics/crops/corn/background.aspx#.U3Tpr17rVa8.

14. Michael Pollan, *The Omnivore's Dilemma: A Natural History of Four Meals* (New York: Penguin, 2006), 63.

15. American Meat Institute, *The United States Meat Industry at a Glance*, https://www.meatinstitute.org/index.php?ht=d/sp/i/47465/pid/47465; USDA Economic Research Service, *Livestock and Meat Domestic Data*, www.ers.usda.gov/data-products/livestock-meat-domestic-data.aspx#.U3Yb817rVa8.

16. USDA Economic Research Service, *Dairy: Overview*, https://www.ers.usda.gov/topics/animal-products/dairy/; USDA National Agricultural Statistics Service, *Milk Production per Cow by Year*, www.nass.usda.gov/Charts_and_Maps/Milk_Production_and_Milk_Cows/cowrates.php.

17. See Bruce L. Gardner, *American Agriculture in the Twentieth Century: How It Flour-ished and What It Cost* (Cambridge, MA: Harvard University Press, 2002).

18. James McDonald and William McBride, *The Transformation of U.S. Livestock Agricul-ture: Scale, Efficiency, and Risks*, Electronic Information Bulletin No. 43 (Washington, DC: USDA Economic Research Service, 2009), www.ers.usda.gov/publications/eib-economic-information-bulletin/eib43.aspx#.U3tToV7rVa8.

19. Stuart Melvin, John Mabry, Wendy Power, James Kliebenstein, Kelley Donham, and Carol Hodne, "Industry Structure and Trends in Iowa," *Iowa Concentrated Animal Feeding Operations Air Quality Study* (Iowa City, IA: University of Iowa, 2003), 18–34, https://www.public-health.uiowa.edu/ehsrc/CAFOstudy/CAFO_final2-14.pdf.

20. USDA Economic Research Service, *Hogs & Pork: Overview*, http://www.ers.usda .gov/topics/animal-products/hogs-pork.aspx.

21. USDA, "Table 55: Selected Operator Characteristics for Principal, Second, and Third Operator," *2012 Census of Agriculture*, www.agcensus.usda.gov/Publications/2012/ Full_Report/Volume_1,_Chapter_1_US/st99_1_055_055.pdf.

22. This is the amount of energy needed to heat or cool one pound of water by one degree Fahrenheit. Jayson Beckman, Allison Borchers, and Carol A. Jones, *Agri-culture's Supply and Demand for Energy and Energy Products*, Economic Informa-tion Bulletin No. 112 (Washington, DC: USDA, 2013), https://www.ers.usda.gov/ webdocs/publications/43756/37427_eib112.pdf?v=41407.

23. Patrick Westhoff, *The Economics of Food: How Feeding and Fueling the Planet Affects Food Prices* (Upper Saddle River, NJ: Pearson, 2010).

24. USDA Economic Research Service, *Interactive Chart: The Evolution of U.S. Agri-cultural Exports Over the Last Two Decades*, https://www.ers.usda.gov/topics/ international-markets-trade/us-agricultural-trade/interactive-chart-the-evolution-of-us-agricultural-exports-over-the-last-two-decades/.

25. USDA Economic Research Service, *Imports*, https://www.ers.usda.gov/topics/ international-markets-trade/us-agricultural-trade/imports/.

26. Quoted in James McWilliams, *Just Food: Where Locavores Get It Wrong and How We Can Truly Eat Responsibly* (Boston: Little Brown, 2009), 7.

27. World Bank, *Agricultural Land as Percent of Land Area*, data.worldbank.org/indicator/ AG.LND.AGRI.ZS?order=wbapi_data_value_2011+wbapi_data_value+wbapi_data_ value-last&sort=asc.

28. USDA, "National Soil Erosion Results Tables," *Natural Resources Inventory, 2007*, www .nrcs.usda.gov/wps/portal/nrcs/detailfull/national/technical/nra/nri/?cid=nrcs143_ 013656.

29. Parke Wilde, *Food Policy in the United States: An Introduction* (New York: Routledge, 2013), 46.

30. Christopher Bosso, *Environment, Inc.: From Grassroots to Beltway* (Lawrence, University Press of Kansas, 2005), 27–33.

31. Chensheng Lu, Kenneth M. Warchol, and Richard A. Callahan, "Sub-lethal Expo-sure to Neonicotinoids Impaired Honey Bees Winterization before Proceeding to Colony Collapse Disorder," *Bulletin of Insectology* 67, no. 1 (2014): 125–30.

32. Michael Wines, "Wells Dry, Fertile Plains Turn to Dust," *New York Times*, May 19, 2013.

33. Marc Reisner, *Cadillac Desert: The American West and Its Disappearing Water*, 2nd ed. (New York: Penguin, 1993).

34. Robert Paarlberg, *Food Politics: What Everyone Needs to Know* (New York: Oxford University Press, 2010), Chapter 6.

35. USDA, Economic Research Service, *Fertilizer Use and Price*, https://www.ers.usda .gov/data-products/fertilizer-use-and-price/.

36. USDA Economic Research Service, *Pesticide Use and Markets*, www.ers.usda.gov/topics/farm-practices-management/chemical-inputs/pesticide-use-markets.aspx.

37. See the 2014 and 2015 statistics from the NASS surveys: USDA, *Agricultural Chemical Use Program*, www.nass.usda.gov/Surveys/Guide_to_NASS_Surveys/Chemical_Use/.

38. Rachel Carson, *Silent Spring* (Boston: Houghton Mifflin, 1962); Christopher Bosso, *Pesticides and Politics: The Life Cycle of a Public Issue* (Pittsburgh, PA: University of Pittsburgh Press, 1987).

39. Union of Concerned Scientists, *The Rise of Superweeds—and What to Do About It*, Policy Brief (Cambridge, MA: Union of Concerned Scientists, 2013), www.ucsusa.org/assets/documents/food_and_agriculture/rise-of-superweeds.pdf.

40. Charles Benbrook, "Impacts of Genetically Engineered Crops on Pesticide Use in the U.S.—The First Sixteen Years," *Environmental Sciences Europe* 24, no. 1 (2012): 1–13.

41. National Academies of Sciences, Engineering and Medicine. *Genetically Engineered Crops: Experiences and Prospects* (Washington, DC: NAS Press, 2016).

42. ETC Group, *Who Owns Nature? Corporate Power and the Final Frontier in the Commodification of Life*, Communiqué No. 100 (Ottawa, ON: ETC Group, 2008), www.etcgroup.org/content/who-owns-nature.

43. "GM Crops: A Story in Numbers," *Nature* 497 (2013): 22–23.

44. Jan Willem Erisman, Mark A. Sutton, James Galloway, Zbigniew Klimont, and Wilfried Winiwarter, "How a Century of Ammonia Synthesis Changed the World," *Nature Geoscience* 1 (2008): 636–39.

45. Stephen Preston, R. B. Alexander, G. E. Schwarz, and C. G. Crawford, "Factors Affecting Stream Nutrient Loads: A Synthesis of Regional SPARROW Model Results for the Continental United States," *Journal of the American Water Resources Association* 47, no. 5 (2011): 891–915.

46. Coppess, "Dead Zones and Drinking Water."

47. Ellen Hanak, Jay Lund, Ariel Dinar, Brian Gray, Richard Howitt, Jeffrey Mount, Peter Moyle, and Barton "Buzz" Thompson, *Managing California's Water: From Conflict to Reconciliation* (San Francisco: Public Policy Institute of California, 2011).

48. Liang Dong and David Nedwell, "Sources of Nitrogen Used for Denitrification and Nitrous Oxide Formation in Sediments of the Hypernutrified Colne, the Nitrified Humber, and the Oligotrophic Conwy Estuaries, United Kingdom," *Limnology and Oceanography* 51, no. 1 (2006): 545–57.

49. Lex Bouwman, Kees Klein Goldewijk, Klaas W. Van Der Hoek, Arthur H. W. Beusen, Detlef P. Van Vuuren, Jaap Willems, Mariana C. Rufino, and Elke Stehfest, "Exploring Global Changes in Nitrogen and Phosphorus Cycles in Agriculture Induced by Livestock Production over the 1900–2050 Period," *Proceedings of the National Academy of Sciences* 110, no. 52 (December 24, 2013): 20882–87.

50. Robert Kellogg, Arthur Grube, Don W. Goss, and Steve Plotkin, *Environmental Indicators of Pesticide Leaching and Runoff from Farm Fields* (Washington, DC: USDA, 2000), www.nrcs.usda.gov/wps/portal/nrcs/detail/national/technical/?cid=nrcs143_014053.

51. Frank T. Farruggia, Colleen M. Rossmeisl, James A. Hetrick, and Melanie Biscoe, *Refined Ecological Risk Assessment for Atrazine* (Washington, DC: EPA, 2016), https://www.regulations.gov/document?D=EPA-HQ-OPP-2013-0266-0315.

52. EPA Office of Pesticide Programs, *Cumulative Risk from Triazine Pesticides* (Washington, DC: EPA, 2006), https://www.regulations.gov/document?D=EPA-HQ-OPP-2005-0481-0003.

53. Johns Hopkins Center for a Livable Future, *Industrial Food Animal Production in America: Examining the Impact of the Pew Commission's Priority Recommendations*

(Baltimore, MD: Johns Hopkins Bloomberg School of Public Health, 2013), http://www.jhsph.edu/research/centers-and-institutes/johns-hopkins-center-for-a-livable-future/_pdf/research/clf_reports/CLF-PEW-for Web.pdf.

54. Jeff Benedict, *Poisoned: The True Story of the Deadly E. Coli Outbreak That Changed the Way Americans Eat* (Buena Vista, VA: Inspire Books, 2011).

55. Based on 2009 totals. EPA, Greenhouse Gas Inventory Report, as reported in Wilde, *Food Policy in the United States*, 48.

56. Christopher Weber and H. Scott Matthews, "Food-Miles and the Relative Climate Impacts of Food Choices in the United States," *Environmental Science & Technology* 42 (2008): 3508–13.

57. United Nations Food and Agriculture Organization, *Emissions—Agriculture, 1990–2011 Average*, data are available from the FAOSTAT portal at http://www.fao.org/faostat/en/.

58. Weber and Matthews, "Food-Miles and the Relative Climate Impacts."

59. Megan Stubbs, *Environmental Regulation and Agriculture*, CRS Report R41622 (Washington, DC: Congressional Research Service, U.S. Congress, 2014): 1.

60. Stubbs, *Environmental Regulation and Agriculture*, 6–7.

61. Christopher Klyza and David Sousa, *American Environmental Policy, 1990–2006: Beyond Gridlock* (Cambridge, MA: MIT Press, 2008).

62. David Wilcove, *The Condor's Shadow: The Loss and Recovery of Wildlife in America* (New York: Anchor Books, 1999).

63. Felicity Berringer, "Federal Protection of Gray Wolves May Be Lifted, Agency Says," *New York Times*, June 7, 2013; Associated Press, "Midwest Wolves May Find Themselves in the Crosshairs Again," *New York Times*, May 7, 2017.

64. Jacqueline Vaughn Switzer, *Green Backlash: The History and Politics of Environmental Opposition in the U.S.* (Boulder, CO: Lynne Rienner, 1997).

65. Teresa Clemer, "Agriculture and the Clean Air Act," in *Food, Agriculture, and Environmental Law*, ed. Mary Jane Angelo (Washington, DC: Environmental Law Institute, 2013), 163–84.

66. EPA, *Modification to the 112(b)1: Hazardous Air Pollutants*, www.epa.gov/ttn/atw/pollutants/atwsmod.html.

67. Sierra Club, letter to EPA Commissioner Lisa Jackson, March 30, 2009, https://www.earthworksaction.org/files/publications/H2SLetterToEPA.pdf.

68. *Waterkeeper Alliance v. EPA*, 399 F.3d 486 (2nd Cir. 2005); Ryan A. Mohr, "*Waterkeeper Alliance v. EPA*: A Demonstration in Regulating the Regulators," *Great Plains Natural Resources Journal* 10 (2006): 17–41.

69. EPA, *NPDES CAFO Rule Implementation Status—National Summary, Endyear 2016*, available from https://www.epa.gov/npdes/npdes-cafo-regulations-implementation-status-reports.

70. Stubbs, *Environmental Regulation and Agriculture*, 43–44.

71. Charles Duhigg, "Debating How Much Weed Killer Is Safe in Your Drinking Water," *New York Times*, August 22, 2009.

72. U.S. Department of Agriculture, Sustainable Agriculture Research and Education program (USDA SARE), *What is Sustainable Agriculture?* (College Park, SARE Outreach, University of Maryland, 2010), http://www.sare.org/Learning-Center/SARE-Program-Materials/National-Program-Materials/What-is-Sustainable-Agriculture.

73. *National Resources Inventory: Soil Erosion on Cropland*, www.nrcs.usda.gov/wps/portal/nrcs/main/national/technical/nra/nri/results/.

74. Jorge Delgado, Merlin A. Dillon, Richard T. Sparks, and Samuel Y. C. Essah, "A Decade of Advances in Cover Crops," *Journal of Soil and Water Conservation* 62, no. 5 (2007): 110A–17A.

75. Christina Tonitto, M. B. David, L. E. Drinkwater, "Replacing Bare Fallows with Cover Crops in Fertilizer-Intensive Cropping Systems: A Meta-Analysis of Crop Yield and N Dynamics," *Agriculture, Ecosystems & Environment*, 112, no. 1 (2006): 58–72.

76. Gunnar Torstensson, Helena Aronsson, and Lars Bergström, "Nutrient Use Efficiencies and Leaching of Organic and Conventional Cropping Systems in Sweden," *Agronomy Journal* 98, no. 3 (2006): 603–15.

77. Robert Buman, B. A. Alesii, J. L. Hatfield, and D. L. Karlen, "Profit, Yield, and Soil Quality Effects of Tillage Systems in Corn-Soybean Rotations," *Journal of Soil and Water Conservation* 59, no. 6 (2004): 260–71.

78. USDA, Economic Research Services, "Crop and Livestock Practices," *ARMS Data*, https://www.ers.usda.gov/data-products/arms-farm-financial-and-crop-production-practices/arms-data/.

79. Hanna Tuomisto, I. D. Hodge, P. Riordan, and D. W. Macdonald, "Does Organic Farming Reduce Environmental Impacts? A Meta-Analysis of European Research," *Journal of Environmental Management* 112 (2012): 309–20.

80. Verena Seufert, Navin Ramankutty, and Jonathan A. Foley, "Comparing the Yields of Organic and Conventional Agriculture," *Nature* 485, no. 7397 (2012): 229–32.

81. Rodale Institute, *The Farming Systems Trial: Celebrating 30 Years* (Kutztown, PA: Rodale Institute, 2011), rodaleinstitute.org/our-work/farming-systems-trial/farming-systems-trial-30-year-report/.

82. Ivette Perfecto and John Vandermeer, "The Agroecological Matrix as Alternative to the Land-Sparing/Agriculture Intensification Model," *Proceedings of the National Academy of Sciences* 107, no. 13 (2010): 5786–91.

83. Brian Donahue, Joanne Burke, Molly Anderson, Amanda Beal, Tom Kelly, Mark Lapping, Hannah Ramer, Russell Libby, and Linda Berlin, *A New England Food Vision* (Durham, NH: Food Solutions New England, 2014), www.foodsolutionsne.org/new-england-food-vision.

84. Stephen Martinez, Michael S. Hand, Michelle Da Pra, Susan Pollack, Katherine Ralston, Travis Smith, Stephen Vogel et al., *Local Food Systems: Concepts, Impacts, and Issues*, Economic Research Report No. 97 (Washington; DC, USDA Economic Research Service, May 2010), https://www.ers.usda.gov/publications/pub-details/?pubid=46395.

85. Kate Clancy and Kathy Ruhf, "Is Local Enough? Some Arguments for Regional Food Systems," *Choices: The Magazine of Farm, Food, and Resource Issues* 25, no. 1 (2010).

86. See James McWilliams, *Just Food*.

87. Committee on Twenty-First Century Systems Agriculture, *Toward Sustainable Agricultural Systems in the 21st Century* (Washington, DC: National Research Council, 2010).

88. Emily Broad Leib, Christina Rice, and Jill Mahoney, "Fresh Look at Organics Bans and Waste Recycling Laws" *BioCycle* 57, no. 10 (2016): 16.

89. ReThink Food Waste, *A Roadmap to Reduce U.S. Food Waste by 20 Percent* (New York: ReFED, 2016), refed.com/downloads/ReFED_Report_2016.

90. Jean Buzby, Hodan Wells, and Jeffrey Hyman, *The Estimated Amount, Value, and Calories of Postharvest Food Losses at the Retail and Consumer Levels in the United States*, EIB-121 (Washington, DC: U.S. Department of Agriculture, Economic Research Service, February 2014).

91. EPA, "United States 2030 Food Loss and Waste Reduction Goal," *Sustainable Management of Food*, 2017, https://www.epa.gov/sustainable-management-food/united-states-2030-food-loss-and-waste-reduction-goal.

92. EPA, "United States 2030 Food Loss and Waste Reduction Goal."
93. EPA, "United States 2030 Food Loss and Waste Reduction Goal."
94. Broad Leib et al., "Fresh Look."
95. Keith Hodge, James W. Levis, Joseph F. DeCarolis, and Morton A. Bariaz, "Systematic Evaluation of Industrial, Commercial, and Institutional Food Waste Management Strategies in the United States," *Environmental Science and Technology* 50, no. 16 (2016): 8444–52.
96. Broad Leib et al., "Fresh Look."
97. ICF-International, *Massachusetts Commercial Food Waste Ban Economic Impact Analysis* (Cambridge, MA: ICF, 2016), http://www.mass.gov/eea/docs/dep/recycle/priorities/orgecon-study.pdf.
98. White House, "Remarks by President Trump at Signing of Waters of the United States (WOTUS) Executive Order," Speeches & Remarks, February 28, 2017, https://www.whitehouse.gov/the-press-office/2017/02/28/remarks-president-trump-signing-waters-united-states-wotus-executive.
99. White House, "Remarks by President Trump," February 28, 2017; see also Eilperin and Phillip, "Trump Directs Rollback."
100. Eric Lipton, "E.P.A. Chief, Rejecting Agency's Science, Chooses Not to Ban Insecticide," *New York Times*, March 30, 2017, A21.
101. Elizabeth Harris and Stephanie Strom, "Walmart to Sell Organic Food, Undercutting Big Brands," *New York Times*, April 10, 2014.
102. Mark Bittman, "OMG: McDonald's Does the Right Thing," *New York Times*, February 13, 2012.
103. Andrew Martin and Andrew Pollack, "Monsanto Looks to Sell Dairy Hormone Business," *New York Times*, August 7, 2008.
104. Wilde, *Food Policy in the United States*, 36.

Chapter 10

Applying Market Principles to Environmental Policy

Sheila M. Olmstead[1]

E ach day, you make decisions that require trade-offs. Should you walk to work or drive? Walking takes more time; driving costs money for gasoline and parking. You might also consider the benefits of exercise if you walk, or the costs to the environment of the emissions if you drive. In considering this question, you need to determine how to allocate important scarce resources—your time and money—to achieve a particular goal.

Economics is the study of the allocation of scarce resources, and economists typically apply two simple concepts, efficiency and cost-effectiveness, for systematically making decisions. Let's take a concrete environmental policy example. The Snake River in the Pacific Northwest provides water for drinking, agricultural irrigation, transportation, industrial production, and hydroelectricity generation. It also supports rapidly dwindling populations of endangered salmon species. If there is not enough water to provide each of these services and to satisfy everyone, we must trade off one good thing for another.

Some scientific evidence indicates that removing hydroelectric dams on the upper Snake River may assist in the recovery of salmon populations. Salmon declines may also be caused by too little water in the river, which might be addressed by reducing agricultural or urban water withdrawals. Each of these measures could be implemented at some cost. Benefit-cost analysis would compare the benefits of each measure (the expected increase in salmon populations) to its costs. An *efficient* policy choice would maximize net benefits; we would choose the policy that offered the greatest difference between benefits and costs.

What if the Endangered Species Act requires that a specific level of salmon recovery be achieved? In this case, the benefits of salmon recovery may never be monetized. But economics can still play a role in choosing policies to achieve salmon recovery. Cost-effectiveness analysis would compare the costs of each potential policy intervention that could achieve the mandated salmon recovery goal. Decision makers would then choose the least costly or most *cost-effective* policy option.

This discussion is highly simplified. Explaining the causes of Snake River salmon decline and forecasting the impact of policy changes on salmon populations are complex scientific tasks, and different experts have different models that produce different results.[2] The trade-offs can also be multidimensional. Removing dams may sound like a great environmental idea, but hydroelectric power is an important source of clean energy in the Pacific Northwest. Would the dams' hydroelectricity be replaced by coal- or gas-fired power plants? What would be the impacts of the increased emissions of local and global air pollutants? In this chapter, we discuss some simple economic tools for examining such trade-offs. The basic intuition we develop to assess these issues functions well even in complex settings.

Economic Concepts and Environmental Policy

Economic Efficiency and Benefit-Cost Analysis of Environmental Policy

Many countries regulate emissions of sulfur dioxide (SO_2), an air pollutant that can damage human health and also causes acid rain, which harms forest and aquatic ecosystems. In the United States, power plants are a major source of SO_2 emissions, regulated under the Clean Air Act (CAA). As evidence accumulated in the 1980s regarding the damages from acid rain in the northeastern United States, Congress considered updating the CAA so that it would cover many old power plants not regulated by the original legislation. This process culminated in the 1990 CAA Amendments, which set a new goal for SO_2 emissions reductions from older power plants. Assume that it is 1989, and you have been asked to tell the U.S. Congress, from an economic perspective, how much SO_2 emissions should be reduced.

First, consider the costs of reducing SO_2 emissions. Economic costs are *opportunity costs*—what we must give up by abating each ton of emissions rather than spending that money on other important things. Emissions abatement can be achieved by removing SO_2 emissions from power plant smokestack gases using a "scrubber," which requires an up-front investment, as well as labor and materials for routine operation. Power plants can also change the fuels they use to generate electricity, switching from high-sulfur to more expensive low-sulfur coal or from coal to natural gas. Spending this money on pollution control leaves less to spend to improve a plant's operations or increase output. These costs are passed on by the firm to its employees (in the form of reduced wages), stockholders (in terms of lower share prices), consumers (in the form of higher prices), and other stakeholders.

If required to reduce emissions, firms will accomplish the cheapest abatement first, and resort to more and more expensive options as the amount of required abatement increases. The cost of abating each ton of pollution tends to rise slowly at first, as we abate the first tons of SO_2 emissions, and then more quickly. This typical pattern of costs is represented by the lower, convex curve in Figure 10-1, labeled total costs, or $C(Q)$.

The value of reducing emissions declines as we abate more and more tons of SO_2. At high levels of SO_2 emissions (low abatement), this pollutant causes acid rain as well as respiratory and cardiovascular ailments in populated areas. But as the air gets cleaner, low SO_2 concentrations cause fewer problems. Thus, while the total benefits of reducing SO_2 may always increase as we

Figure 10-1   Comparing the Total Benefits and Costs of Pollution Abatement

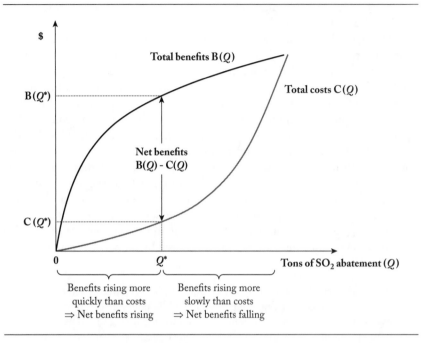

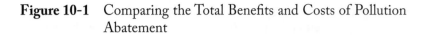

reduce emissions, the benefit of each additional ton of abatement will go down. This typical pattern of benefits is represented by the upper, concave curve in Figure 10-1, labeled total benefits, or B(Q).[3]

Economic efficiency requires that we find the policy that will give us the greatest net benefits—the biggest difference between total benefits and total costs. In Figure 10-1, the efficient amount of SO_2 emissions abatement is marked as Q^*, where the vertical distance between the benefit and cost curves is biggest. Why would it be inefficient to abate more or less than Q^* tons of SO_2 emissions? To the right of Q^*, the total benefits of reducing pollution are still positive and still rising. But costs are rising faster than benefits. So for every dollar in benefit we gain by eliminating a ton of emissions, we incur greater costs. To the left of Q^*, the benefits of each ton of abatement are rising more quickly than costs, so if we move to the left, we will also reduce the policy's net benefits.

Note that we have emphasized the costs and benefits of reducing each individual ton of pollution. Where total benefits increase quickly, at low levels of abatement, the benefit of an additional ton is very high. Where the total benefits curve flattens out, the benefit of an additional ton is low. This concept of the decreasing "benefit of an additional ton" defines the economic concept of *marginal benefit*. On the cost side, where total costs are almost flat, at low levels of abatement, the cost of adding an additional ton is very low. As total costs get very steep, the cost of abating an additional ton is high.

This concept of the increasing "cost of an additional ton" defines the concept of *marginal cost*. The efficient quantity of pollution abatement is the number of tons at which the marginal benefit of abating an additional ton is exactly equal to the marginal cost.[4]

What we have just done is a benefit-cost analysis of a potential SO_2 emissions reduction policy. If you had completed the analysis to advise Congress, the information amassed on benefits, costs, and the efficient quantity of pollution to abate would illuminate the trade-offs involved in improving air quality. When Congress passed the CAA Amendments of 1990, it eventually required 10 million tons of SO_2 emissions abatement, roughly a 50 percent reduction in power plant emissions of this pollutant. Was this the efficient level of pollution control? Subsequent analysis (particularly of the human health benefits of avoided SO_2 emissions) suggests that the efficient amount of SO_2 abatement would have been higher than the 10-million-ton goal.[5] But economic efficiency is one of many criteria considered in the making of environmental policy, some others of which are detailed elsewhere in this book. An excellent summary of how economists see the role of benefit-cost analysis in public decision making is offered by Nobel Laureate Kenneth Arrow and coauthors:

> Although formal benefit-cost analysis should not be viewed as either necessary or sufficient for designing sensible public policy, it can provide an exceptionally useful framework for consistently organizing disparate information, and in this way, it can greatly improve the process and, hence, the outcome of policy analysis.[6]

There are many critiques of benefit-cost analysis.[7] A common critique is that basing environmental policy decisions on whether benefits outweigh costs ignores important political and ethical considerations. As is clear from the preceding quotation, most economists reject the idea that policy should be designed using strict benefit-cost tests. Even when citizens and their governments design policy based on concerns other than efficiency, however, collecting information about benefits and costs can be extremely useful. Some critics of benefit-cost analysis object to placing a dollar value on environmental goods and services, suggesting that these "priceless" resources are devalued when treated in monetary terms.[8] But benefit-cost analysis simply makes explicit the trade-offs represented by a policy choice—it does not create the trade-offs themselves. When environmental policy is made, we establish how much we are willing to spend to protect endangered species or avoid the human health impacts of pollution exposure. Whether we estimate the value of such things in advance and use these numbers to guide policy or set policy first based on other criteria and then back out our implied values for such things, we have still made the same trade-off. No economic argument can suggest whether explicit or implicit consideration of benefits and costs is *ethically* preferable. But the choice does not affect the outcome that a trade-off has been made. Used as one of many inputs to the consideration of policy choices, benefit-cost analysis is a powerful and illuminating tool.

Figure 10-2   Marginal Costs of Protecting the California Condor

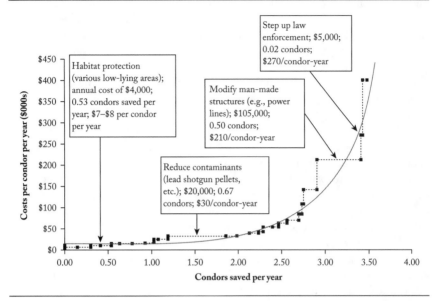

Source: From *Markets and the Environment* (2nd ed.), by Nathaniel O. Keohane and Sheila M. Olmstead. Published by Island Press. Copyright © 2016 by the authors.

The Measurement of Environmental Benefits and Costs

Thus far, we have discussed benefits and costs abstractly. In an actual economic analysis, benefits and costs would be measured, so that the horizontal and vertical axes of Figure 10-1 would take on specific numerical units. Quantifying the costs of environmental policies can require rough approximations. For example, one study has estimated the costs of protecting California condors, designated an endangered species following the near extinction of these enormous birds and their later reintroduction into the wild from a captive breeding program.[9] Figure 10-2 describes the costs of each potential step that policymakers might take to protect the condor population; when the number of condors saved per year is graphed against the cost of each potential step taken to save them, a marginal cost curve results that is upward sloping like those we discussed for pollution abatement.

Economists measure the benefits of an environmental policy as the sum of individuals' willingness to pay for the changes it may induce. This notion is clearly anthropocentric—the changes induced by an environmental policy are economically beneficial only to the extent that human beings value them. This does not suggest that improvements in ecosystem function or other "nonhuman" effects of a policy have no value. Many people value open space, endangered species preservation, and biodiversity and have shown through their memberships in environmental advocacy groups, votes in local referenda, and lobbying activities on global environmental issues that they are willing to sacrifice much for these causes. The economic value of an environmental amenity (such as clean air or water or open space) comprises the value that people experience from using it, and the so-called nonuse value. Nonuse value captures the value people have for simply knowing that an endangered species (like the grizzly bear) or a pristine area (like the Arctic National Wildlife Refuge) exists, even if they never plan to see or use such resources. To carry out a benefit-cost analysis, however, we must know more than that people have some value for a policy's goal; we must measure that value to compare it to the policy's costs.

An in-depth discussion of environmental benefit estimation methods is beyond the scope of this chapter.[10] But we can sketch out the basic intuition behind the major approaches. Some benefits of environmental policies can be measured straightforwardly through their impacts on actual markets. For example, if we are considering a policy to reduce water pollution that may increase commercial fish populations, estimates of the increased market value of the total catch would be included in an estimate of the policy's total benefits.

For most environmental goods and services, however, measuring benefits is much trickier. The values that people have for using environmental amenities can often be measured indirectly through their behavior in markets. For example, many people spend money on wilderness vacations. While they are not purchasing wilderness, per se, when they do this, economists can estimate the recreational value of wilderness sites from travelers' expenditures. Travel-cost models are a class of statistical methods that economists use for this purpose.

Another method, the hedonic housing price model, is based on the idea that what people are willing to pay for a home reflects, in part, the environmental attributes of its neighborhood. Economists use statistical techniques to estimate what portion of a home's price is determined by environmental attributes, such as the surrounding air quality, controlling for other price determinants, for example, the home's physical characteristics, school district quality, and proximity to jobs and transportation. To estimate the value of human health impacts of an environmental policy, economists primarily use hedonic wage studies. These models estimate people's willingness to pay for small decreases in risks to life and health by examining the differences in wages for jobs with different levels of risk. As in the hedonic housing price model, statistical methods must be used to control for the many other determinants of wages (for example, how skilled or educated a worker must be to take a particular job).

Travel-cost and hedonic models are *revealed preference* models—they estimate how people value a particular aspect of an environmental amenity from their actual behavior, revealed in markets. But if we were to stop with values expressed in markets, the benefits we could estimate for things like wilderness areas and species preservation would be incomplete. Nonuse value leaves no footprint in any market. Thus a *stated preference* approach must be used to quantify nonuse values. Economists design carefully structured surveys to ask people how much they are willing to pay for a specific improvement in environmental quality or a natural resource amenity, and they sum across individuals to assess a society's willingness to pay.

The Environmental Protection Agency's (EPA's) 1985 benefit-cost analysis of reducing the lead content of gasoline offers an example of what each side of such an analysis might include. The analysis quantified the main benefits from phasing out leaded gas: reduced human health damages from lead exposure (retardation of children's cognitive and physiological development and exacerbation of high blood pressure in adult males), reduction in other local air pollutants from vehicle emissions (since leaded gas destroyed catalytic converters, designed to reduce emissions), and lower costs of engine maintenance and related increases in fuel economy. The costs were primarily the installation of new refinery equipment and the production of alternative fuel additives. The study found that the lead phasedown policy had projected annual net benefits of $7 billion (in 1983 dollars), even though only a portion of benefits were actually monetized. The health benefits of the regulation that the EPA estimated included the avoided costs of medical care and of remedial education for affected children. Americans, if surveyed, would likely have had significant willingness to pay to avoid the lasting health and cognitive impacts of childhood lead exposure, but these benefits were never monetized. Even with these gaps, acknowledged by the study's authors, this analysis helped to "sell" the regulation; a few years earlier, the EPA had decided on a much weaker rule, citing potential costs to refineries.[11]

The fact that the EPA did not monetize some benefits of the U.S. lead phasedown brings us to an important point. In some cases, existing estimation methods may be sufficient to evaluate the benefits of an environmental policy but are too complex and expensive to implement. In the lead case, this was immaterial. The benefits of the policy exceeded the costs by a large margin, even excluding those (presumably large) unmonetized benefits, so the eventual policy decision was not affected by this choice. In other cases, when benefits are hard to monetize, doing so may matter for the ultimate policy outcome.

In some cases, economic tools simply prove insufficient to estimate the benefits (or avoided damages) from environmental policy. For example, climate science suggests that sudden, catastrophic events (like the reversal of thermohaline circulations or sudden collapse of the Greenland or West Antarctic ice sheets) are possible outcomes of the current warming trend. The probabilities of such disastrous events may be very small. When these low probabilities are combined with the fact that important climate change impacts may occur in the distant future, estimating the benefits of current climate change policy becomes a challenging and controversial task.[12] Some analysts have attempted, incorrectly, to estimate the benefits of avoiding the elimination of vital ecosystem services, such as pollination and nutrient cycling, using economic benefit estimation tools.[13] Used correctly, these tools measure our collective willingness to pay for small changes in the status quo. The elimination of Earth's vital ecosystem services would cause dramatic shifts in human and market activity of all kinds. While the benefit estimation techniques we have discussed are well suited to assessing the net effect of specific policies, like reducing air pollutant concentrations or setting aside land to preserve open space, they are inadequate to the task of measuring the value of drastic changes in global ecosystems—efforts to use them for this purpose have resulted in, as one economist quipped, a "serious underestimate of infinity."[14] Estimation of the benefits from environmental policy is the subject of a great deal of economic research, and much progress has been made. But, in some situations, the limits of these tools remain a significant challenge to comprehensive benefit-cost analysis.

Cost-Effective Environmental Policy

The economists' goal of maximizing net benefits is one of many competing goals in the policy process. Even when an environmental standard is inefficient (too stringent or not stringent enough), economic analysis can still help to select the particular policy instruments used to achieve that goal. Earlier we defined the concept of cost-effectiveness as choosing the policy that can achieve a given environmental standard at least cost. Let's return to our SO_2 example to see how this works in practice.

Imagine that you are a policy analyst at the EPA, given the job of figuring out how U.S. power plants will meet the 10-million-ton reduction in SO_2 emissions required under the 1990 CAA Amendments. One important issue to consider is how much the policy will cost. All else equal, you would like to attain the new standard as cheaply as possible. We can reduce this problem to a simple case to demonstrate how an economist would answer this question. Assume that the entire 10-million-ton reduction will be achieved by two power plants, firms A and B. Each has a set of SO_2 abatement technologies, and the sequence of technologies for each firm and their associated costs determine the marginal cost curves in Figure 10-3, labeled MC_A and MC_B. Notice that abatement increases from left to right for firm A, and from right to left for firm B. At any point along the horizontal axis, the sum of the two firms' emissions reductions will always equal 10 million tons, as the CAA Amendments require.

Let's begin with one simple solution that seems like a fair approach: divide the total required reduction in half and ask each firm to abate 5 million tons of SO_2. This allocation of pollution control is represented by the leftmost dotted vertical line in Figure 10-3 and is often referred to as a "uniform pollution control standard," because the abatement requirement is uniform across firms. Is this the cheapest way to reduce pollution by 10 million tons? Suppose we require firm A to reduce one extra ton and require firm B to reduce one ton less? We would still achieve a 10-million-ton reduction, but that last ton would cost less than it did before. Firm B's cost curve lies above A's at the uniform standard, so when we shift responsibility for abating that ton from B to A, we reduce the total cost of achieving the new standard. How long can we move to the right along the horizontal axis and continue to lower total costs? Until the marginal costs of abatement for the two firms are exactly equal: where the two curves intersect, when firm A abates 6 million tons and B abates 4 million tons.

Figure 10-3   Cost-Effective Pollution Abatement by Two Firms

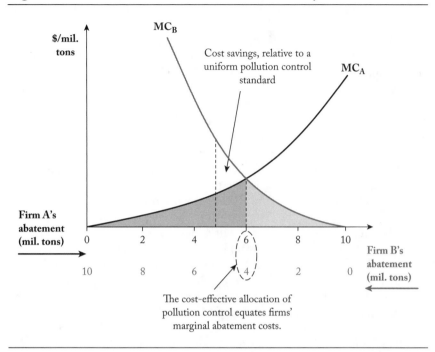

The cost-effective allocation of
pollution control equates firms'
marginal abatement costs.

The cost savings from allocating abatement in this way rather than using the uniform standard is equivalent to the difference in costs between firm A and firm B for the last million tons of abatement. On Figure 10-3, that is equal to the area between the two firms' marginal cost curves (the cost to firm B minus the cost to firm A), bounded by the dotted lines marking the uniform standard and the cost-effective allocation. In a two-dimensional representation such as Figure 10-3, we cannot easily demonstrate how this principle works for more firms. But the rule of thumb for a cost-effective environmental policy instrument is the same for a large number of firms as it is in this simple example: a pollution control policy minimizes costs if the marginal abatement costs of all firms reducing pollution under the policy are equal.

You may have noticed that, in order to identify the cost-effective pollution control allocation in this simple case, we needed a lot of information about each firm's abatement costs—we used their marginal cost curves to accomplish the task. As an EPA policy analyst, you would not likely have this information, and having it would be even less likely if you were to move from considering two power plants to looking at the thousands eventually covered by the CAA Amendments of 1990. In a competitive market, the structure of firms' costs is proprietary information that they will not likely share with regulators. So how can a cost-effective pollution control policy be designed?

One class of environmental policy instruments, often called "market-based" or "incentive-based" approaches, does not require regulators to have specific information about individual firms' marginal abatement costs in order to attain a particular pollution control standard at least cost. In the case of the SO_2 emissions reduction required by the CAA Amendments of 1990, regulators chose one of these approaches, a system of tradable pollution permits, to achieve this goal.

A market for tradable pollution permits works quite simply. Return to the world of two firms and assume that you have advised the EPA administrator to allocate responsibility for 5 million tons of SO_2 emissions abatement to each of the two firms. You add, however, the provision that the firms should be able to trade their allocations, so long as the aggregate reduction of 10 million tons is achieved. If we begin at the (5 million, 5 million) allocation in Figure 10-3, we can imagine the incentives for the two firms under this trading policy.

The last ton abated by firm B costs much more than the last ton abated by A if each sticks to the 5-million-ton abatement requirement. Firm B would be willing to pay A to increase its own abatement, so that B could abate fewer tons of SO_2. In fact, B would pay any price that lies below its own marginal abatement cost. Firm A would be willing to make such a deal, so long as B paid more than A's own marginal abatement cost. So the vertical distance between the two cost curves at (5 million, 5 million) represents the potential gain from trading for that last ton of abatement. The same is true of the next ton, and the next, all the way to the point at which B is abating 4 million tons and A is abating 6 million. Notice that the firms will trade permits until exactly the point at which the total costs of reducing 10 million tons of SO_2 are minimized.[15] The bigger the differences in abatement costs across regulated firms, the larger the potential cost savings from trading.

How much of a difference did this make in the SO_2 emissions abatement regulation we have been discussing? While it operated, the U.S. SO_2 trading program produced cost savings of about $1.8 billion annually, compared with the most likely alternative policy considered during deliberations over the 1990 CAA Amendments (which would have required each firm to install the same technology to reduce emissions).[16] In fact, the Environmental Defense Fund, an environmental advocacy organization, agreed to endorse and help write the legislation proposed by the George H. W. Bush administration to amend the CAA if the administration would increase the required emissions reduction (from 8 million tons, which it was proposing) to the eventual 10 million tons of SO_2, based on the potential cost savings of the tradable permit approach. In this case, the tradable permit policy was not only cost-effective, but it allowed political actors to take a step closer to the efficient level of abatement, with significant benefits for human and ecosystem health.[17]

Principles of Market-Based Environmental Policy

You may have noticed that the notion that firms A and B are inherently doing something wrong when they produce SO_2 emissions along with electricity has been conspicuously lacking from our discussion. In economic terms, pollution is the result of a simple set of incentives facing firms and consumers that is "stacked against" environmental protection. The consumption and production decisions that result can be changed if we alter the relevant incentives. The social problem of pollution results from what economists call market failure. The three types of market failure most relevant to environmental policy are externalities, public goods, and the "tragedy of the commons."[18]

Let's consider externalities first. If you have driven a car, checked e-mail, or turned on a light today, you have contributed to the problem of global climate change. With near unanimity, the scientific community agrees that the accumulation of carbon dioxide (CO_2) and other heat-trapping gases in Earth's upper atmosphere has increased global mean surface temperatures by about 1 degree Fahrenheit since the start of the twentieth century, with consequences including sea level rise, regional changes in precipitation, increased frequency of extreme weather events, species migration and extinction, and spatial shifts in the prevalence of disease. Ask an economist, however, and he or she will suggest that the roots of the problem are not only in the complex dynamics of Earth's atmosphere but also in the incentives facing individuals and firms when they choose to consume and produce energy. Each such decision imposes a small cost in terms of its contribution to future atmospheric carbon concentrations. However, the individuals making these decisions do not bear these costs. Your electricity bill does include the cost of producing electricity and moving it from the plant to your home, but (in most countries) it does not include the cost of the carbon emissions from electricity production. Carbon emissions are an *externality*—their costs are external to the transaction between the buyer and the seller of electricity. The market for energy is incomplete, since its price does not reflect the full cost of its provision.[19]

You also may have noticed that bringing nations together to negotiate a solution to the problem of global climate change seems to be difficult. Clean air and a stable global climate are *public goods*: everyone benefits from their provision, whether or not they have contributed, and we can all enjoy these goods without interfering with the ability of others to enjoy them. Other public goods include national defense, weather forecasting, and public parks. If you have ever listened to public radio or watched public television without contributing money to these institutions, then you have been a free rider. Free riding is a rational response to the incentives created by a public good: many beneficiaries will pay nothing for its provision, and those who do pay will generally pay less than what, in their heart of hearts, they would be willing to pay. Markets for public goods are incomplete. Left to their own devices, markets will underprovide these valuable goods and services.

The third category of market failure most relevant to environmental policy is the tragedy of the commons.[20] A group of individuals sharing access to a common resource (a pasture for grazing cattle, a fishery, or a busy highway) will tend to overexploit it. The "tragedy" is that, if individuals could self-regulate and reduce their collective use of the resource, the productivity of the resource would increase to everyone's benefit. But the actions of single individuals are not enough to make a difference. Individuals restricting their own use only bear the costs of this activity, with no benefits. The resulting spiral of overexploitation can destroy the resource entirely. A prominent example of the tragedy of the commons is the collapse of many deep-sea fisheries over the past few decades. But climate change is also an example of this type of market failure. The global upper atmosphere is a resource shared by everyone and owned by no one. The incentive for individual citizens to reduce carbon emissions (their exploitation of this resource) is small; thus the resource is overexploited.

When markets fail in these three ways and environmental damages result, government intervention may be required to fix the situation. Governments can correct externalities, provide public goods, and avert the tragedy of the commons. From an economic perspective, market principles should be used to correct these market failures.

Using Market Principles to Solve Environmental Problems

Like the global damages from carbon emissions, the local and regional damages from SO_2 emissions (for example, human health problems and acid rain) are external to power plants' production decisions and their consumers' decisions about how much energy to use. The tradable permit program described earlier is an excellent example of using market principles to correct market failures. The government distributed permits to power plants and allowed them to trade. Plants made these trades by deciding how to minimize the costs of producing power—for each ton of SO_2 that they produced before the regulation was passed, they now faced a choice. Either a plant could continue to emit that ton, and use one of its permits, or it could spend money to abate that ton, freeing up a permit to sell to another power plant (and earning the permit price as a reward). The result was an active market for SO_2 emissions permits. In June 2008 alone, 250,000 tons of emissions were traded in this market, at an end-of-month price of $325 per ton. By putting a price on pollution, the government internalized its cost, represented by the price of a permit to emit one ton of SO_2, a cost that firms took into account when they decided how much electricity to produce.

Unfortunately, regulatory and judicial actions in 2008 to 2010 effectively dismantled the U.S. SO_2 allowance market, one of the most significant experiments with a market-based approach to pollution control.[21] Since the late 1990s, scientific evidence regarding the health effects of fine particulate matter associated with SO_2 emissions had suggested that further reductions would be required under the CAA. The initial approach of the EPA during the George W. Bush administration was to tighten the SO_2 emissions cap, requiring midwestern states contributing to violations of CAA fine particulate standards on the East Coast to surrender three permits for every one ton of SO_2 emissions. A legal challenge by states and electric utilities resulted in a 2008 federal court decision vacating this new approach, on the grounds that the EPA could not modify the existing interstate SO_2 market to meet stricter standards in the absence of legislation from Congress. After further revisions and an additional court challenge under the Obama administration, the SO_2 market was replaced by state-level and source-level emissions constraints by 2012. When governments create environmental markets, even well-functioning markets that dramatically reduce the costs of pollution control, they can also dismantle them.

Another way to use market principles to reduce pollution is to impose a tax. Rather than imposing a cap on the quantity of pollution, and allowing regulated firms to trade emissions permits to establish a market price for pollution, a tax imposes a specific price on pollution and allows firms to decide how much to pollute in response. A tax has an effect on firms' decisions that is essentially identical to the effect of the permit price created by a cap-and-trade policy; polluters decide, for each ton of emissions, whether to abate that ton (incurring the resulting abatement costs) or to pay the tax and continue to emit that ton.

Taxes on air and water pollution are quite common, though existing environmental taxes tend to be lower than efficient levels.[22] British Columbia's carbon tax, established in 2008, may be an exception; the current tax of about $27.50 per ton is in the range of current economic estimates of the marginal damages from carbon emissions.[23] Australia's carbon tax was levied at a similar level beginning in 2012 but repealed in July 2014, after an election in which debate over the carbon tax played an important role. Developing countries such as China, Malaysia, and Colombia have also experimented with environmental taxes.

Some important differences exist between taxes and tradable permits. First, a cap-and-trade system pins down a total quantity of allowable pollution. The trade among firms that results establishes the permit price. Before any trading has taken place, we know exactly how much pollution the policy is going to allow, but we are uncertain how much it will cost society to achieve that goal. In setting a tax, regulators pin down the price of pollution instead, creating some degree of certainty about how much a regulation may cost. As under the permit policy, firms make private choices about how much pollution to emit, comparing their abatement costs to the tax. But the total quantity of pollution that will result is uncertain. To be certain about how much pollution will result after the tax is imposed, regulators need to have good information about the cost of reducing pollution in the regulated industry. Both the total quantity of allowable pollution and the total cost of pollution reduction are important pieces of information to consider in designing environmental policy. Each of the two primary market-based approaches to internalizing the cost of pollution, taxes and permits, offers certainty over one, but not both, of these important variables.[24]

Taxes and tradable permits can also differ in their costs to regulated firms. Under a pollution tax, a firm must pay the tax for every ton of pollution it emits. Under a permit system, permits are typically given to firms for free, at least initially. So a permit system requires a firm to pay only for pollution in excess of its permit allocation. For this reason, complying with a tax can be more expensive for firms than complying with a permit system.[25] The political opposition that results may be one reason that there are few significant environmental taxes in the United States. Taxes may be preferable to tradable permits along many dimensions as a policy to address climate change, but serious discussion of a global carbon tax is lacking.[26] If taxes and tradable permits are fundamentally equivalent pollution regulations from an economic perspective, what about those extra compliance costs? Taxes create revenues for the government agency that collects them, exactly equal to the aggregate tax bill for all firms, whereas tradable permits distributed for free do not. The net impact of this difference between the two policies depends on how tax revenues are spent. From the standpoint of efficiency, the best thing to do with environmental tax revenues may be to use them to reduce other taxes in the economy that tend to distort consumers' and firms' decisions—taxes on income, sales, and capital gains, for example.[27] Society may benefit to a smaller degree if governments use tax revenues to provide additional goods and services.

Taxes on pollution may also be imposed indirectly. For example, many countries tax gasoline. In the United States, the revenues from most state gasoline taxes are used to maintain and expand transportation infrastructure; U.S. gas taxes are not explicit pollution control policies. However, economists have estimated the optimal U.S. gasoline tax, taking into account the most significant externalities: emissions of local pollutants (particulate matter and nitrous oxides), CO_2 emissions (which contribute to global climate change), traffic congestion, and the costs of accidents not borne by drivers.[28] In their estimation, the efficient tax would be $0.83 per gallon. A more recent study suggests potential regional heterogeneity in the optimal gas tax; California's efficient tax may be about $1.37 per gallon (including oil security externalities, as well as the others).[29] However, most of these externalities depend on the number of miles driven, not the amount of gasoline consumed (only a proxy for miles driven); taxing miles driven rather than gasoline would be better from an economic perspective. This highlights the important fact that the choice of what to tax may be as important as the level of a tax.

Notice that as we have discussed the virtues of market-based approaches to environmental policy, all of the options we have mentioned require some role for government intervention, setting a tax, for example, or enforcing a cap on pollution. This is a critical point. Market-based approaches should not be conflated with voluntary (nonregulatory) environmental policies, which would not be expected to have a strong impact on environmental quality.

Market-Based Environmental Policy Instruments in Practice

Using Markets to Reduce Air Pollution

Market-based approaches have reduced air pollutants other than SO_2. In the 1980s, the EPA implemented a lead-trading policy to enforce a regulation reducing the allowable lead content of U.S. gasoline by 90 percent. Earlier in this chapter, we discussed the benefit-cost analysis of this policy, which suggested that the benefits of eliminating lead in gasoline exceeded its costs. The policy the EPA chose to implement the lead phasedown had something to do with this; it lowered costs relative to a more prescriptive approach. Refiners producing gasoline with a lower lead content than was required earned credits that could be traded and banked. In each year of the program, more than 60 percent of the lead added to gasoline was associated with traded lead credits.[30] This policy successfully met its environmental goal, and the EPA estimated cost savings from the lead trading program of approximately $250 million per year until the phasedown was completed in 1987.[31]

The Kyoto Protocol, the 1997 international climate change treaty ratified by 191 countries and the European Union, included emissions trading as a mechanism for achieving national emissions reduction targets. Among industrialized countries that took on emissions reduction targets under the Kyoto Protocol, the countries of the EU opted to use an emissions trading system (ETS), established in 2005, to meet their emissions reduction targets. The protocol sets a cap on CO_2 emissions for the EU as a whole, allocated by the EU to member countries. Member countries then divide emissions allotments among the following industries: electric power generation; refineries; iron and steel; cement, glass, and ceramics; and pulp and paper.

The EU ETS is the world's largest emissions trading system, covering almost twelve thousand facilities in twenty-seven countries in 2014 (as well as intra-EU airline flights), and accounting for about 45 percent of EU CO_2 emissions.[32] The Kyoto Protocol's emissions caps did not begin to bind until 2008, so the pilot phase of the EU ETS (2005–2007) was designed to set up the institutional and operating structures necessary for trading. The cap in the EU system in this pilot phase was a small reduction (a few percentage points) below expected emissions in the absence of the policy, though in retrospect permits in the pilot phase were overallocated.[33] A more stringent cap was introduced in 2008. Determining the impact of the EU ETS on emissions in the pilot phase is difficult, in part because the binding of caps beginning in 2008 coincided with a global economic recession (resulting in falling CO_2 emissions). However, several studies suggest that the ETS has decreased emissions, independent of reductions from the recession, by 2–5 percent below "business as usual" in the pilot phase and by about 8 percent in 2008–2009.[34] Going forward, the aggregate emissions target under the EU ETS in phase 3 (2013–2020) will decline by almost 2 percent per year. No studies have estimated the cost savings from this approach relative to those that counterfactual policies offering the same level of aggregate emissions reduction might have achieved.

The United States did not ratify the Kyoto Protocol, though the Obama administration set a national goal of reducing carbon emissions by 17 percent over 2005 levels by 2020 largely through prescriptive regulations (discussed further in Chapters 7 and 13).[35] However, support for action on climate change has led some states to enact market-based policies to reduce greenhouse gas (GHG) emissions. California's Global Warming Solutions Act of 2006 (AB 32) seeks to reduce GHG emissions to 1990 levels by 2020, with a cap-and-trade policy as its centerpiece; the program's first allowance auction took place in November 2012, and the cap began to bind in January 2013. In 2015, California's market covered 85 percent of GHG emissions (from power plants, industrial sources, natural gas, and the transportation sector). It is too early to measure the impact of California's cap-and-trade system on GHG emissions, or the system's abatement costs relative to alternative approaches. Another U.S. market-based initiative is the Regional Greenhouse Gas Initiative (RGGI), a cap-and-trade system among electricity generators in nine northeastern states. The RGGI began in 2009, but the combination of reduced electricity demand due to the economic recession of 2008–2009 and lower natural gas prices (due to increased U.S. supplies of shale gas) resulted in the RGGI emissions cap being nonbinding in early years.[36] A more stringent 2014 cap, scheduled to decline by 2.5 percent per year from 2015 to 2020, may bode well for the RGGI's future.

Individual Tradable Quotas for Fishing

Thus far, we have talked about cap-and-trade policies as if they applied only to pollution problems. But a common application is to fisheries management, to avert the tragedy of the commons. The world's largest market for tradable individual fishing quotas (IFQs), created in 1986, is in New Zealand.[37] By 2004, it covered seventy different fish species, and the government of New Zealand had divided coastal waters into "species-regions," generating 275 separate markets that covered more than 85 percent of the commercial catch in the area extending two hundred miles from New Zealand's coast. In the United States, Pacific halibut and sablefish off the coast of Alaska, mid-Atlantic surf clams and ocean quahogs, South Atlantic wreckfish, and red snapper in the Gulf of Mexico are all regulated using IFQ markets. Iceland manages stocks of twenty fish and shellfish species using IFQ markets, in a system established in 1990.

A market for fishing quotas works similarly to a market for pollution permits. The government establishes a total allowable catch (TAC), distributing shares to individual fishers. Fishers can trade their assigned quotas, which represent a percentage of the TAC for a particular species-region. An analysis of catch statistics from 11,315 global fisheries between 1950 and 2003 provides the first large-scale empirical evidence for the effectiveness of these approaches in halting, and even reversing, the global trend toward fisheries collapse. The authors empirically estimate the relative advantage of IFQ fisheries over non-IFQ fisheries in terms of a lower probability of collapse, and estimate that, had all non-IFQ global fisheries switched to management through tradable quotas in 1970, the percentage of collapsed global fisheries by 2003 could have been reduced from more than 25 percent to about 9 percent.[38]

Waste Management Policies

Market-based approaches have also been used to manage solid waste. Some waste products have high recycling value. If you live in a community with curbside recycling, you may have seen low-income residents of the community picking aluminum cans out of recycling bins at the curb; they do this because it is much less costly to produce aluminum from scrap metal than from virgin ore, and as a result, those cans are quite valuable. But most household waste ends up as trash, disposed of legally in landfills or incinerators or illegally dumped. The marginal cost of public garbage collection and disposal for an American household has been estimated at $1.03 per trash bag, but until recently, the marginal cost of disposal borne by households was approximately zero.[39] An increasingly common waste management policy is the "pay-as-you-throw" system, a volume-based waste disposal charge often assessed as a requirement for the purchase of official garbage bags, stickers to attach to bags of specific volume, periodic disposal charges for official city trash cans of particular sizes, and (rarely) charges based on the measured weight of curbside trash. These systems function like an environmental tax, internalizing the costs of disposing of household waste. In 2006, more than seven thousand U.S. communities had some form of pay-as-you-throw disposal.[40] A comprehensive study of a pay-as-you-throw policy was performed in Charlottesville, Virginia, which imposed a charge of 80 cents per trash bag.[41] This tax was estimated to have reduced the number of bags households threw out by about 37 percent. However, the effect was offset by two factors that have proven to be common problems with such programs. First, the reduction in the total weight of trash thrown away was much smaller (about a 14 percent reduction), since consumers compacted their trash in order to reduce the number of bags they used. Second, illegal disposal increased. As noted earlier in the discussion of the gasoline tax, Charlottesville's experience suggests that the decision of *what* to tax may be as important as (or more important than) how high the tax should be. A more recent study of two hundred towns in New Hampshire (31 percent of which had adopted pay-as-you-throw policies) suggests that the introduction of such policies reduces municipal solid waste generation very significantly, with an additional marginal effect of increasing the disposal cost per bag.[42]

Habitat and Land Management Policies

Tradable development rights (TDRs) have been applied to solve problems as diverse as deforestation in the Brazilian Amazon and the development of former farmland in the Maryland suburbs of Washington, DC.[43] About 140 U.S. communities have implemented TDRs, with many other potential programs in the pipeline.[44] The program in Calvert County, Maryland, preserved an estimated thirteen thousand acres of farmland between 1978 and 2005. In Brazil since 1998, TDRs have been used to slow the conversion of ecologically valuable lands to agriculture; each parcel of private property that is developed must be offset by preserving a forested parcel elsewhere (within the same ecosystem and with land of greater or equal ecological value). Simulations of the Brazilian policy for the state of Minas Gerais suggest that

TDRs lower the cost to landowners of protecting a unit of forested land. Landowners can develop the most profitable land and preserve less profitable land. But this highlights two of the chief problems with TDRs. First, how can land developers prove (and regulators ensure) that a preserved parcel is really additional—that it would not have remained in forest without the developer's efforts? Second, how can we measure the ecological equivalence of two land parcels? In the case of carbon emissions, each ton of emissions has essentially the same impact on our ultimate concern—atmospheric carbon concentrations—no matter where it is emitted. The same cannot be said of land preservation.

A related policy, wetlands mitigation banking, holds similar promise and faces similar challenges. Wetlands are classic public goods. They provide a rich set of ecosystem services, for which there are no markets and from which everyone benefits, regardless of who pays for their preservation. Wetlands have been depleted rapidly in the United States and other parts of the world by conversion to agricultural and urban use. The externalities to wetlands conversion—such as increased flood risk; loss of habitat for birds, fish, and mammals; and reduced groundwater recharge—are taken into account only when governments intervene to require it.

Since the early 1990s, the United States has experimented with mitigation banking, a policy under which land developers compensate for any lost wetlands by preserving, expanding, or creating wetlands elsewhere.[45] Wetlands banks serve as central brokers, allowing developers to purchase credits and to fulfill credits through the physical process of wetlands preservation, creation, and management. In 2005, there were 405 approved U.S. wetland banks in operation. We can think of mitigation banking as a market-based approach in two different ways. First, it is a tax on land development, internalizing some of the externalities of wetlands depletion. Second, given that the U.S. federal government has purported to enforce a "no net loss" policy with regard to the national stock of wetlands since 1989, we can think of mitigation banking as a cap-and-trade policy in which the cap on acres of wetlands lost is zero.

As in the case of TDRs, wetlands mitigation banking reduces the costs of preserving wetlands acreage but faces significant challenges. A wetland in a particular location provides a specific portfolio of biophysical services. For example, coastal wetlands support shellfish nurseries and may reduce damages from storm-related flooding. Inland wetlands may filter contaminants and provide islands of habitat for migratory bird species in overland flight. If development pressures in coastal cities create incentives for landowners to develop wetlands in these locations, and to pay for wetlands creation inland, the net effect of these kinds of trades must be considered. This is a significant change from the simple ton-for-ton trading that occurs for some air pollutants.

This section offered a handful of examples of the many applications of market principles to environmental policy.[46] We emphasized the strong arguments in favor of taxes, tradable permits, and other market-based approaches, especially given that these policies can achieve environmental policy goals at less cost than more prescriptive approaches. But they are not appropriate solutions to all environmental problems. The issues we raised in our discussion of market-based land management policies arise in other contexts, as well. Market-based policies can be designed for situations in which the location of pollution emissions or natural resource amenities matters for the benefits of pollution control or resource management. But they are not workable in extreme cases. For example, the impacts of a toxic waste dump are highly localized. Economists would not advise setting a national limit on toxic waste disposal, allowing firms to trade disposal permits, and letting the waste end up where it may. Environmental problems at this end of the spectrum—the opposite end from a problem like carbon emissions, which can be reduced anywhere with essentially the same net effect—may be better addressed through prescriptive approaches.

Conclusion

Economics offers a powerful pair of tools—efficiency and cost-effectiveness—with which to consider environmental policy trade-offs. Efficiency has to do with the setting of environmental policy goals: how much pollution should we reduce, or how many acres of wetlands should be preserved? An efficient pollution control policy equalizes the monetized benefits and costs of the last ton of pollution eliminated. The process used to determine whether an environmental policy is efficient is benefit-cost analysis. If a strict benefit-cost test were applied to the decision of how much SO_2 pollution to eliminate from power plant smokestacks in the 1990s, additional reductions would have been required. Benefit-cost analysis would also have suggested that lead be eliminated from U.S. gasoline sooner than it was. In other cases, applying the rule of efficiency suggests that environmental standards should be weakened.

However, efficiency is not the only potential input to good environmental policy. The treatment of benefit-cost analysis in the major U.S. environmental statutes is a good indication of our ambivalence toward analyzing environmental trade-offs in this systematic way; the statutes alternately "forbid, inhibit, tolerate, allow, invite, or require the use of economic analysis in environmental decision making."[47] For example, the CAA forbids the consideration of costs in setting the National Ambient Air Quality Standards, and the U.S. Safe Drinking Water Act requires benefit-cost analysis of all new drinking water contaminant standards. Environmental regulatory agencies are not economic agencies. While laying out the trade-offs involved in setting environmental standards is critically important from an economic perspective, political, social, and ethical concerns may hold more influence than benefit-cost analysis in this process.

Even when environmental standards are inefficient, however, policymakers can choose policies to achieve those standards at least cost. The billions of dollars saved by policies like SO_2 trading, paired with their proven environmental effectiveness, have made market-based approaches such as tradable permits and taxes appealing policy instruments for solving environmental problems. Ironically, as the theoretical and empirical evidence of the cost savings and environmental effectiveness of these policies has stacked up, U.S. political support for them has not only eroded during the recent economic recession but also been thoroughly demonized, and especially so by Republicans in Congress,[48] in direct conflict with their support for markets in most other contexts. This political shift may make it much harder in the future to implement market-based policies, unnecessarily raising the cost of environmental regulation to firms and consumers. Market-based environmental policy approaches are not appropriate for all situations. But where market incentives create environmental problems, market principles should be harnessed to solve them.

Suggested Websites

EPA National Center for Environmental Economics (www.epa.gov/environmental-economics) This page provides access to research reports, regulatory impact analyses, and other EPA publications.

Center for Effective Government (www.foreffectivegov.org) This center follows budgets and regulatory policies.

Resources for the Future (www.rff.org) This nonprofit research organization is devoted to environmental and resource economics and policy.

Notes

1. This chapter is reprinted from the 9th edition of the text with the permission of the author and with minimal alterations except for a new Figure 10-2. At the time of production, Sheila Olmstead was serving on the Council of Economic Advisers and thus was unable to revise the chapter. However, the editors believe that the 2016 chapter remains current and is not in need of any substantive changes.
2. For competing scientific opinions about Snake River salmon decline, see Charles C. Mann and Mark L. Plummer, "Can Science Rescue Salmon?" *Science* 298 (2000): 716–19, with letters and responses. See also David L. Halsing and Michael R. Moore, "Cost-Effective Management Alternatives for Snake River Chinook Salmon: A Biological-Economic Synthesis," *Conservation Biology* 22, no. 2 (2000): 338–50.
3. In reality, each ton of emissions is not equivalent. SO_2 emissions in urban areas or those upwind of critical ecosystems may cause relatively greater harm. In addition, costs and benefits may not follow the smooth, continuous functions we depict in Figure 10-1. The simple curves help us to develop intuition that carries through even in more complex situations.
4. Since marginal benefits and costs represent the rate at which benefits and costs change when we add an additional ton of emissions reduction, they are also measured by

the slope of the total benefit and cost curves; notice that net benefits are largest in Figure 10-1 (at Q^*) when the slopes of $B(Q)$ and $C(Q)$ are equal.

5. Dallas Burtraw, Alan Krupnick, Erin Mansur, David Austin, and Deirdre Farrell, "The Costs and Benefits of Reducing Air Pollutants Related to Acid Rain," *Contemporary Economic Policy* 16 (1998): 379–400.

6. Kenneth J. Arrow, Maureen L. Cropper, George C. Eads, Robert W. Hahn, Lester B. Lave, Roger G. Noll, Paul R. Portney, Milton Russell, Richard Schmalensee, V. Kerry Smith, and Robert N. Stavins, "Is There a Role for Benefit-Cost Analysis in Environmental, Health, and Safety Regulation?" *Science* (April 12, 1996): 221–22.

7. Stephen Kelman, "Cost-Benefit Analysis: An Ethical Critique," with replies, *AEI Journal on Government and Social Regulation* 5, no. 1 (January/February 1981): 33–40.

8. Frank Ackerman and Lisa Heinzerling, *Priceless: On Knowing the Price of Everything and the Value of Nothing* (New York: New Press, 2004).

9. This discussion is based on Nathaniel O. Keohane, Benjamin Van Roy, and Richard J. Zeckhauser, "Managing the Quality of a Resource with Stock and Flow Controls," *Journal of Public Economics* 91 (2007): 541–69.

10. See A. Myrick Freeman III, *The Measurement of Environmental and Resource Values*, 2nd ed. (Washington, DC: Resources for the Future, 2003).

11. Albert L. Nichols, "Lead in Gasoline," in *Economic Analyses at EPA: Assessing Regulatory Impact*, ed. Richard D. Morgenstern (Washington, DC: Resources for the Future, 1997), 49–86.

12. See Martin L. Weitzman, "A Review of the *Stern Review on the Economics of Climate Change*," *Journal of Economic Literature* 45, no. 3 (2007): 703–24.

13. Robert Costanza, Ralph d'Arge, Rudolf de Groot, Stephen Farber, Monica Grasso, Bruce Hannon, Karin Limburg, Shahid Naeem, Robert V. O'Neill, Jose Paruelo, Robert G. Raskin, Paul Sutton, and Marjan van den Belt, "The Value of the World's Ecosystem Services and Natural Capital," *Nature* 387 (1997): 253–60.

14. Michael Toman, "Why Not to Calculate the Value of the World's Ecosystem Services and Natural Capital," *Ecological Economics* 25 (1998): 57–60.

15. We emphasize the cost-effectiveness of market-based approaches to environmental policy in the short run, a critical concept and one that is relatively easy to develop at an intuitive level. However, the greatest potential cost savings from these types of environmental policies may be achieved in the long run. Because they require firms to pay to pollute, market-based policies provide strong incentives for regulated firms to invest in technologies that reduce pollution abatement costs over time, either developing these technologies themselves or adopting cheaper pollution control technologies developed elsewhere.

16. Nathaniel O. Keohane, "Cost Savings from Allowance Trading in the 1990 Clean Air Act," in *Moving to Markets in Environmental Regulation: Lessons from Twenty Years of Experience*, ed. Charles E. Kolstad and Jody Freeman (New York: Oxford University Press, 2007).

17. The definitive overview of the SO_2 permit-trading program is found in A. Denny Ellerman, Richard Schmalensee, Elizabeth M. Bailey, Paul L. Joskow, and Juan-Pablo Montero, *Markets for Clean Air: The U.S. Acid Rain Program* (New York: Cambridge University Press, 2000).

18. These concepts are described in much greater detail in Nathaniel O. Keohane and Sheila M. Olmstead, *Markets and the Environment* (Washington, DC: Island Press, 2007), Chapter 5.

19. Pollution is a negative externality, but externalities can also be positive. For example, a child vaccinated against measles benefits because she is unlikely to contract that disease. But a vaccinated child in turn benefits her family, neighbors, and schoolmates, as she is less likely to expose them to disease.

20. Garrett Hardin, "The Tragedy of the Commons," *Science* 162 (1968): 1243–48.

21. Richard Schmalensee and Robert N. Stavins, "The SO_2 Allowance Trading System: The Ironic History of a Grand Policy Experiment," *Journal of Economic Perspectives* 27 (2013): 103–22.

22. Robert N. Stavins, "Experience with Market-Based Environmental Policy Instruments," in *Handbook of Environmental Economics*, vol. 1, ed. Karl-Göran Mäler and Jeffrey Vincent (Amsterdam: Elsevier Science, 2003), 355–435.

23. Interagency Working Group on Social Cost of Carbon, United States Government, *Technical Support Document: Technical Update of the Social Cost of Carbon for Regulatory Impact Analysis under Executive Order 12866*, May 2013.

24. This difference between the two approaches—taxes and permits—can cause one approach to be more efficient than the other; see Martin L. Weitzman, "Prices v. Quantities," *Review of Economic Studies* 41 (1974): 477–91.

25. This distinction disappears if permits are auctioned rather than given away. But auctioned permit systems are rare. Even the biggest existing tradable permit systems, including the U.S. SO_2 trading program and the European Union Emissions Trading System (EU ETS), auction only a very small percentage of permits.

26. The EU tried to implement a carbon tax in the early 1990s but failed to achieve unanimous approval of its (then) fifteen member states; the ETS faced much less opposition. Some European countries, including Norway, implemented carbon taxes prior to the establishment of the ETS. On the potential advantages of a carbon tax over permits, see William D. Nordhaus, "To Tax or Not to Tax: Alternative Approaches to Slowing Global Warming," *Review of Environmental Economics and Policy* 1, no. 1 (2007): 26–44.

27. This decision of how best to use the revenues from an environmental tax is actually more complicated because environmental taxes can exacerbate the distortions introduced by other taxes. For a straightforward discussion of this problem and for other comparisons between taxes and permits, see Lawrence H. Goulder and Ian W. H. Parry, "Instrument Choice in Environmental Policy," *Review of Environmental Economics and Policy* 2, no. 2 (2007): 152–74.

28. Ian Parry and Kenneth Small, "Does Britain or the United States Have the Right Gasoline Tax?" *American Economic Review* 95 (2005): 1276–89.

29. C.-Y. Cynthia Lin and Lea Prince, "The Optimal Gas Tax for California," *Energy Policy* 37, no. 12 (2009): 5173–83.

30. Robert W. Hahn and G. L. Hester, "Marketable Permits: Lessons for Theory and Practice," *Ecology Law Quarterly* 16 (1989): 361–406.

31. EPA, Office of Policy Analysis, *Costs and Benefits of Reducing Lead in Gasoline, Final Regulatory Impact Analysis* (Washington, DC: EPA, 1985).

32. See A. Denny Ellerman and Barbara K. Buchner, "The European Union Emissions Trading Scheme: Origins, Allocation, and Early Results," *Review of Environmental Economics and Policy* 1, no. 1 (2007): 66–87; A. Denny Ellerman and Paul L. Joskow, *The European Union's Emissions Trading System in Perspective* (Washington, DC: Pew Center on Global Climate Change, 2008); Frank J. Convery and Luke Redmond, "Market and Price Developments in the European Union Emissions Trading Scheme," *Review of Environmental Economics and Policy* 1, no. 1 (2007): 88–111; European Commission, *The EU Emissions Trading System (EU ETS)*, http://ec.europa.eu/clima/policies/ets/index_en.htm.

33. A. Denny Ellerman, Barbara Buchner, and Carlo Carraro, *Allocation in the European Emissions Trading Scheme: Rights, Rents and Fairness* (Cambridge: Cambridge University Press, 2007).

34. Christian Egenhofer, Monica Alessi, Anton Georgiev, and Noriko Fujiwara, *The EU Emissions Trading System and Climate Policy towards 2050: Real Incentives to Reduce Emissions and Drive Innovation?* CEPS Special Report (Brussels: Centre for European Policy Studies, 2011).

35. In June 2009, the U.S. federal government appeared to be taking significant steps toward setting up an economy-wide cap-and-trade system to reduce CO_2 emissions, with the passage in the House of Representatives of the American Clean Energy and Security Act, also known as the Waxman-Markey bill. In July 2010, the U.S. Senate abandoned its effort to draft companion legislation (see Chapter 5).

36. While small effects of the RGGI on emissions have been estimated, the effects of the (low) carbon price from the cap-and-trade system cannot be separated from the effects of the RGGI's other components. In addition, some or all of those declines may have been offset by increased emissions in surrounding states. See Brian C. Murray, Peter T. Maniloff, and Evan M. Murray, "Why Have Greenhouse Emissions in RGGI States Declined? An Econometric Attribution to Economic, Energy Market and Policy Factors," *Energy Economics* 51 (September 2015): 581–89.

37. See Suzanne Iudicello, Michael Weber, and Robert Wieland, *Fish, Markets and Fishermen: The Economics of Overfishing* (Washington, DC: Island Press, 1999). For assessments of New Zealand's policy, see John H. Annala, "New Zealand's ITQ System: Have the First Eight Years Been a Success or a Failure?" *Reviews in Fish Biology and Fisheries* 6 (1996): 43–62; Richard G. Newell, James N. Sanchirico, and Suzi Kerr, "Fishing Quota Markets," *Journal of Environmental Economics and Management* 49, no. 3 (2005): 437–62.

38. Christopher Costello, Stephen D. Gaines, and John Lynham, "Can Catch Shares Prevent Fisheries Collapse?" *Science* 321 (2008): 1678–81.

39. See Robert Repetto, Roger C. Dower, Robin Jenkins, and Jacqueline Geoghegan, *Green Fees: How a Tax Shift Can Work for the Environment and the Economy* (Washington, DC: World Resources Institute, 1992).

40. Skumatz Economic Research Associates, Inc., "Pay as You Throw (PAYT) in the U.S.: 2006 Update and Analyses," Final report to the EPA Office of Solid Waste, December 30, 2006, Superior, CO. See https://archive.epa.gov/wastes/conserve/tools/payt/web/pdf/sera06.pdf.

41. Don Fullerton and Thomas C. Kinnaman, "Household Responses to Pricing Garbage by the Bag," *American Economic Review* 86, no. 4 (1996): 971–84.

42. Ju-Chin Huang, John M. Halstead, and Shanna B. Saunders, "Managing Municipal Solid Waste with Unit-Based Pricing: Policy Effects and Responsiveness to Pricing," *Land Economics* 87, no. 4 (2011): 645–60.

43. On Brazil, see Kenneth M. Chomitz, "Transferable Development Rights and Forest Protection: An Exploratory Analysis," *International Regional Science Review* 27, no. 3 (2004): 348–73. On Calvert County, Maryland, see Virginia McConnell, Margaret Walls, and Elizabeth Kopits, "Zoning, Transferable Development Rights and the Density of Development," *Journal of Urban Economics* 59 (2006): 440–57.

44. Virginia McConnell and Margaret Walls, "U.S. Experience with Transferable Development Rights," *Review of Environmental Economics and Policy* 3, no. 2 (2009): 288–303.

45. National Research Council, *Compensating for Wetland Losses under the Clean Water Act* (Washington, DC: National Academies Press, 2001); David Salvesen, Lindell L. Marsh,

and Douglas R. Porter, eds., *Mitigation Banking: Theory and Practice* (Washington, DC: Island Press, 1996).

46. For surveys of these approaches, see Stavins, "Experience with Market-Based Environmental Policy Instruments"; Thomas Sterner and Jessica Coria, *Policy Instruments for Environmental and Natural Resource Management*, 2nd ed. (Washington, DC: Resources for the Future, 2011); and Theodore Panayotou, *Instruments of Change: Motivating and Financing Sustainable Development* (London: Earthscan, 1998).

47. Richard D. Morgenstern, "Decision Making at EPA: Economics, Incentives and Efficiency," draft conference paper in *EPA at Thirty: Evaluating and Improving the Environmental Protection Agency* (Durham, NC: Duke University Press, 2000), 36–38.

48. Richard Schmalensee and Robert N. Stavins, "The SO_2 Allowance Trading System: The Ironic History of a Grand Policy Experiment," *Journal of Economic Perspectives* 27 (2013): 103–22.

Chapter 11

Toward Sustainable Production
Finding Workable Strategies for Government and Industry

Daniel Press and Daniel A. Mazmanian

The greening of industry emerged as an important topic among business, environmental, and government leaders in the mid-1980s. It has since evolved through several transitional stages benefiting from the experience of especially leading firms, of trying out different public policy drivers under different political administrations in Washington, and of a growing appreciation in society of the significant changes required to place us on a more viable path, that is, to a more sustainable world. Today, most standard corporate messaging espouses some or many aspects of environmental sustainability. Major firms employ sustainability officers at senior levels, devote website space to their corporate environmental responsibilities, and garner accolades from state or federal environmental agencies. Each year, more firms earn some form of sustainability certification for their products, whether these firms sell goods from organic farms, sustainable fisheries, or forests; use recycled materials in their products; or invest in more efficient or renewable energy.

Most recently, the focus of sustainability advocates among the public as well as among business and government leaders has been on fostering sustainable production, which reaches well beyond the attention to waste reduction and pollution prevention of the previous decades. Every indication is that it will require a transformation, not simply a transition, in public policy and business practices for sustainable production to be realized. The effort has been and continues to be challenged by a significant sector of business and industrial actors and their political representatives, which raises strategic questions for the United States: With the needed long-term transformation in mind, which business and industry practices are most in need of change and to what extent can those firms or industrial sectors unable to transform themselves be accommodated while the transformation moves forward? We also face tactical choices. Is policy intervention best applied at the stage of waste management, air and water pollution control, or energy usage? Can the most change be realized in production methods, product design, or the end products themselves? Will the strongest drive for change come at the stage of consumption and usage of products? Perhaps most important, what information will tell us whether the greening being promoted is transformative or mainly a matter of greenwashing?

Equally debated is the best position for society to adopt in order to promote the most comprehensive and cost-effective transformation.[1] Four broad approaches to this question illustrate the differences of opinion about the best way to achieve sustainable business and industry. The first and most traditional approach, reaching back to the 1970s and 1980s, involves government imposing on business and industry prescribed environmental protection technologies and methods of emissions reduction. A second, more flexible approach that emerged in the 1980s and 1990s allows businesses to select their own cost-effective strategies for reducing emissions, under the watchful eye of government. A third approach, introduced out of recognition of the enormity of the challenge of transforming business and industry, uses market-based incentives that provide bottom-line rewards for environmentally friendly business behavior, leaving change to the natural workings of the marketplace. The fourth approach relies largely on volunteerism, wherein businesses commit to environmental and sustainability goals that match or exceed those required in exchange for relief from the prescribed technology and command-and-control regulations that would otherwise be imposed. This is more of a hybrid of the prior approaches, attempting to find a viable balance between the overly restrictive regulatory approach and the free market.

The range and extent of research on these approaches has expanded appreciably, and heated debate has ensued about which approach or which mix of approaches to utilize. Some experts focus their attention mainly on the shortcomings of the nation's long-standing environmental pollution policies— variously referred to as "command-and-control," "top-down," and "deterrence-based" policies for air, water, land use, noise, and endangered species protection—and the need to loosen the strictures of these policies appreciably. Others focus on the growing importance of the corporate responsibility and quality management movements within and across industries that emerged in the 1990s—domestically and internationally—and how this shift is moving many businesses toward a greener path. Most recently, attention has turned to the need for firms, individually and working within their business and industry sectors, to contribute to society's environmental goals that extend beyond their business or industry, such as reducing greenhouse gas emissions that contribute to global climate change.[2] All reformers want to know how best to accelerate their preferred strategy through various flexible governmental and voluntary policies, particularly in light of the unrelenting challenges to the environment posed by modern technological society, our ever-expanding global population, and the growing recognition of the serious challenges posed by climate change, challenges that will be with us for decades to come.

In assessing the contending positions and approaches, we can reasonably assume that, all else being equal, everyone involved in business and industry policymaking—business and industry owners, managers, and workers; government officials; environmental and health advocates; and citizens—would prefer to live and work in a cleaner, more environmentally sustainable world. Yet seldom is all else equal. The market economy in which businesses operate today has a long history of freely using natural resources and nature's goods (such as clean air, water, and soil, as well as food and fodder) and shielding both producers and consumers from the environmental pollution and resource degradation associated with the extraction of these goods, their use in production, and their consumption. This is the very same market economy that nurtures consumer tastes and expectations and, ultimately, consumer demand for ever more goods and services, resulting in the extraordinary material consumption of today's American lifestyle.[3]

Consequently, and despite a few very laudable exceptions,[4] sustainable production can be understood not as a private business matter or a minor marketplace imperfection so much as a serious "public" policy problem, in need of a public policy solution. Because significant costs can be associated with the transformation to a green economy, we cannot expect businesses to assume these costs automatically or enthusiastically.[5] Indeed, it is typically in a firm's best interest to minimize if not avoid the additional near-term costs of transformation to the extent that such investments do not demonstrably improve its near-term market position. Collectively, of course, the near-term cost of not reducing greenhouse gases or of not cleaning the water or the air over a city can be substantial. This is precisely why the first generation of environmental laws, starting in the 1970s in the United States, was compulsory for all business, creating the command-and-control regulatory regime of the first environmental epoch. As this chapter and the one introducing this volume both show, a good deal of progress resulted but at great expense; arguably, many burdensome costs were incurred by business and government, costs that might be avoided under a different approach. During the early 2000s, it seemed that the challenge was no longer about persuading many individual enterprises or even business or industrial sectors but about how to move the entire society toward a sustainable economy. But business and industry continue to push back today. Thus, a combination of corporate greenwashing and continuing resistance calls into question how society can achieve a more sustainable economy. It is also still unclear how to outflank or convert those who in business and industry object to the necessity of greening.

The Dilemma of Collective Action for Environmental Protection

How to bring about significant changes that are in the best health and environmental interest of all can be understood as one of a category of problems known as "collective action problems" or "collective action dilemmas."[6] These occur when individuals, firms, or governments would be better off if they cooperated in the pursuit of a common goal, but, for one reason or another, one or more of those involved choose a less optimal course of action—one that typically satisfies some other highly important goal. The challenge to policymakers when facing collective action problems is to devise an approach that anticipates and counteracts the normal (in the language of game theory, the "rational") tendency of actors to forgo the better *joint* gain for a nearer-term assured and secure, but lesser, *individual* gain, with the resultant higher societal cost to everyone.

Figure 11-1   Green Industry as a Collective Action Dilemma

<table>
<tr><th></th><th></th><th colspan="2">Firm's choice</th></tr>
<tr><th></th><th></th><th>Evasion</th><th>Self-policing</th></tr>
<tr><td rowspan="4">Government's choice</td><td>Flexible regulation</td><td>**Cell A**
Government as potential "sucker"</td><td>**Cell B**
Win–win: superior outcomes for government and industry</td></tr>
<tr><td>Deterrence (through command-and-control)</td><td>**Cell C**
Suboptimal for both government and business but a typical outcome</td><td>**Cell D**
Green industry initiatives of the 1980s to today, with industry as potential "sucker"</td></tr>
</table>

Source: Based on Matthew Potoski and Aseem Prakash, "The Regulation Dilemma: Cooperation and Conflict in Environmental Governance," *Public Administration Review* 64 (March/April 2004): 137–48.

The collective action dilemma in the case of sustainable production has been portrayed by Matthew Potoski and Aseem Prakash as a two-dimensional game-theoretic problem, which we have adapted in Figure 11-1. The vertical and horizontal labels show the options available to each player, and the four cells represent the payoff (or benefits) and risk (or costs) to each of the actors based on the combinations of each option. For example, should government and industry decide to cooperate to maximize the gains to each (Cell B)? Or should they not cooperate in order to avoid the possibility of being taken advantage of by the other or of incurring some other cost (Cell C)? For the government, one cost might be the loss of public confidence and trust, while a firm might lose market share and profitability.

Although simplified, the game situation approximates closely the real world of the relations between business and society. Consequently, if left to its own devices, industry would choose to have little or no governmental requirement placed on it to protect the environment. This would be only reasonable (rational) for a business trying to maximize its profits in a market economy with little or no cost imposed for adversely affecting health and the environment. This option is represented by the "Evasion" position on the horizontal dimension, on the "Firm's choice" axis. However, if compelled by law to provide environmental and health protection and safeguards, and possibly to go even further to transform itself into a green industry, firms would prefer an approach that allowed for self-policing and regulatory flexibility. They would find this superior to being heavily regulated by a command-and-control government bureaucracy.

Government, in turn, has the choice of opting for a policy of "deterrence," which experience has shown to be workable based on the command-and-control regulatory approach taken to environmental protection since 1970 in air, water, and toxic chemical pollution. The downside, as experience has also shown, is that this approach has required the growth and support of a large government bureaucracy to carry out the oversight and regulation of businesses and has resulted in the suppression of creativity on the part of firms to develop their own green business strategies. Ultimately, industries transformed themselves far less than lawmakers and environmentalists had hoped. Conversely, government could choose to be more flexible and lenient on industry, relying instead on a modest amount of monitoring combined with market forces, consumer demands, and new technology to ensure greater protection of public health and the environment. There is risk in this approach for the government. It embraces the promise of an eventually large payoff, but as market forces and modest oversight combine to bring about the desired green transformation of business in the short term, some, if not most, businesses will not change their behavior or will do so insufficiently or slowly, absent stringent regulation. In the language of game theory, this raises the dual problems of "free riding" (not paying one's share of the costs) and "shirking" (paying less than one's share of the costs).

This is the dilemma: As the logic of game theory suggests and a fair amount of experience affirms, under flexible regulatory systems that rely on market forces to bring about changed behavior, market forces are insufficient, and many businesses do not change or do so only minimally. When firms know that they are unlikely to be detected or penalized even when caught, they too often opt for evasion over committing the capital required to transform. The result is that government (and thus the public) ends up being betrayed, realizing even less movement toward the green transformation than under a command-and-control approach: government finds itself in the position of the "sucker," which is the worst possible outcome in a collective action game.

Armed with the insights of game theory, we can logically expect that, left to their own resources and absent compulsion, most businesses and industries will choose evasion or minimal action over transformative greening. Government, in turn, will choose command-and-control over flexibility, not because it is optimal but to avoid the risk of ending up the sucker. Thus, game theory tells us that most of the activity surrounding environmental protection can be expected to take place in the lower-left cell of Figure 11-1, Cell C, the zone in which government regulates with a heavy hand to prevent business from evading environmental protection laws and regulations. This is precisely where the action took place throughout the first environmental epoch, which began in the 1970s and remains with us today.[7] A second epoch began in the 1980s and continues today, characterized by recognition of the collective action dilemma and efforts to extricate government and business from its grasp. The challenge is how to combine flexible regulatory strategies with market forces to move the central theater of action out of the lower-left Cell C to the upper-right Cell B.

A number of pilot and experimental programs by government and business have been initiated and are reviewed in this chapter. The experience underscores how difficult it has been to dislodge the players from their long-standing positions. This should come as no surprise in light of the dilemma they face and the amount of time they have spent living and working under the command-and-control approach. The crux of the matter remains that, by and large, government is usually loath to relinquish its reliance on deterrence, and most businesses can be expected to evade when circumstances allow.

Yet the need for society to find a win-win solution—a more optimal mix of flexibility and self-policing—continues and has motivated the ongoing search for the needed policy breakthrough. A growing body of research on strategies that appear to work is guiding these efforts among self-motivated businesses, at least on an experimental basis.[8] Thus, devising a new hybrid public policy approach seems feasible, at least in principle, within a game-theoretic framework. Of course, the direction of public policy is set by the politics of policymaking, not simply by the logic of policy analysis, so this too will be considered in our final assessment.

What follows is an overview of the efforts made since 1970 to address the problems of environmental pollution and the degradation of our natural resources base by greening the practices of business and industry. This overview moves through the strict command-and-control environmental policy epoch, located schematically in Cell C, and then turns to the market-oriented and flexible regulatory strategies that reflected a significant change in the understanding of the problem. In actuality, the debate and center of activity has moved only part way, with innovative action taking place "under the shadow of regulation" (in Cell D).

We examine several impressive examples of corporate self-regulation and the voluntary green approaches of some individual firms, often encouraged by government officials, as illustrative of how change has occurred and how it can occur. These accomplishments need to be juxtaposed against political efforts to slow down, if not derail, the greening of America's economy, efforts that have existed from the outset of the 1970s and that are reflected, most recently, in current actions to undermine the authority and capacity of the nation's Environmental Protection Agency under the Trump administration (see Chapter 7). The chapter ends with an assessment of how we can best accomplish the much-needed green transformation of America's business and industry as we look to the future, determined to meet the ever-increasing threats to our environment and natural resources at home and around the world, to accomplish the needed revitalization of the nation's economy, and to maintain the quality of life most Americans strive for and have come to expect.

The Accomplishments of Command-and-Control since 1970

Although the needed green transformation of the economy and society is actively being discussed and dominates the policy debate today, largely because of concerns about climate change and energy pricing, command-and-control regulation remains the most widespread policy approach in practice. In a number of important respects, the approach has worked and continues to work to clean up the environment, in some instances quite admirably.[9] Moreover, evidence indicates that the nation's strict environmental regulations have spurred innovation in businesses, which ultimately provides them a source of competitive advantage in the market economy.[10] Also, one can point to the creation of jobs in the pollution control technology sector as a source of the economic growth and employment that has resulted from this traditional form of environmental regulation.[11]

Since the 1970s, government rules and regulations have spurred reductions throughout the nation in air, water, and soil contamination; these reductions are noted at numerous points throughout this book (see especially Chapter 1). Nationwide, air emissions trends from all industrial sources (including electricity-generating power plants) show that air emissions reached a peak in the early to mid-1970s, declined sharply, and then plateaued by the mid-1980s, after which, year after year, they diminished decisively. Official records for all environmental data are often unavailable for the same years (here we present ranges for the closest years); however, all of these figures should be viewed as rough approximations. Although the U.S. Environmental Protection Agency (EPA) officially reports impressive emissions reductions in its annual inventories, the agency admits, when pressed, that "estimates for the non-utility manufacturing sector are some of the most unreliable data we have in the national emission inventory."[12] Between 1990 and 2014, emissions of sulfur oxides declined consistently (by as much as 83 percent), very likely as a consequence of the 1990 Clean Air Act's Acid Rain Program.[13]

Between 1970 and 2016, volatile organic compound (VOC) emissions declined by 54 percent. Other air pollutants exhibit some worrisome trends. While overall carbon monoxide (CO) emissions plummeted in the last 50 years, CO releases from industrial fuel combustion fluctuated over the years, probably as a function of economic conditions, but factories burning fuel emitted about as much CO in 2016 as they did a decade earlier, in 2006. Industrial nitrogen oxides decreased overall during the same time period, thanks to much cleaner fuel combustion. However, in recent years NOx emissions have increased in some industries, including pulp and paper, petroleum refining, oil and gas production, and the merchant marine. Emissions of particulate matter 2.5 microns or smaller (referred to as "$PM_{2.5}$"), widely considered to be some of the most threatening to public health, have persistently increased since the early 2000s. Nearly one in ten Americans currently lives in a county out of attainment with the $PM_{2.5}$ standard.[14] Even more worrisome, 40 percent of Americans live in areas with unacceptable ozone levels.[15] Water quality is even harder to assess reliably but has also improved somewhat, thanks largely to the thousands of municipal wastewater treatment plants built with financing from the federal government since 1970.[16] Although most Americans can expect drinkable water as a matter of course, with regular monitoring for quality and reasonably rapid responses to contamination threats, infrastructure water delivery and sewage treatment systems are showing their age and failing with alarming regularity. It is less clear, however, how industry's overall contribution to water quality protection has changed over the years, because such data are not routinely collected or centrally distributed.

Energy consumption also presents some progress. Manufacturing firms slowly reduced their annual primary energy consumption between the 1970s and 2000s, going from a high of 24.7 quads (quadrillion British thermal units, or BTUs) in 1973 to 19 quads in 2014.[17] This roughly 24 percent overall (or total) decrease in primary energy consumption from 1973 to 2014 occurred while manufacturing output more than doubled during the same time period.[18] Looking at more recent trends, total energy consumption in the manufacturing sector fell by 15 percent between 2002 and 2014, while manufacturing output dipped during the Great Recession but had resumed its overall growth by 2014, signaling that factories reduced their energy intensity (the amount of energy it takes to manufacture a product).[19] In one high-energy sector, iron and steel, energy intensity decreased between 2002 and 2010, whether measured as the energy it took to produce a ton of steel or the energy it took to produce a dollar of value added.[20] This was probably a result of the industry's greater reliance on cleaner electric arc furnaces than on the old basic oxygen furnaces, which consume enormous quantities of coal.

A great deal of money has been spent to accomplish these results, in terms of total dollars and as a percentage of the gross national product, and over time, the costs borne by industry have increased. This is reflected in the increasing level of expenditures by industry. In 1973, U.S. industries spent about $4.8 billion on pollution abatement, split almost equally between capital and operating costs. By 1994, American manufacturing was spending $10 billion on capital costs, but these costs dropped to just under $6 billion by 2005 (both in 2005 dollars). Operating costs dropped in the same decade, from $24.7 billion to $20.7 billion.[21] Chemical, coal, and petroleum companies spent the most in capital and operating costs, about $12 billion among them. Perhaps most significantly, today's operating costs represent steadily smaller proportions of industry's total economic output—this finding suggests either that new pollution abatement equipment can run more efficiently (and thus at less cost) or that industry is cutting corners.[22] Both explanations may be true.

Is the news about industrial pollution good, bad, or uncertain? Undeniably, the country's air would have been far worse if industry had not been installing abatement equipment since 1970. Moreover, it is remarkable that, thus far, air pollution seems to rise at a smaller rate than economic growth. The bad news is that, globally, industry is consuming as much or more energy and raw materials, which in turn creates serious pollution and resource degradation and is burdening air, land, and water with larger pollutant loads each year, in both the United States and in other nations. Thus, even if the rate of increase is small, the overall burden grows, which is not the right direction for protecting public and environmental health.

Regulatory Experiments in Industrial Greening

Command-and-control approaches have clearly resulted in both better environmental practices in business and industry and a significant curbing of traditional patterns of environmental pollution, but they ultimately fall short of the fundamental transformation needed in business and industry. The best end-of-pipe pollution management has not sufficiently reduced the overall pollution load generated by an economy that is always expanding to satisfy the needs of a global population projected to grow by 50 percent over the next fifty years.

Therefore, attention has begun to shift from pollution reduction to pollution prevention, and to doing so by devising incentive-based, self-regulatory, and voluntary policy approaches (see Chapter 10). Building on the successes and limitations of command-and-control regulation, U.S. industry and government moved on a limited basis toward an industrial greening approach (see Figure 11-1, Cell D). Characterized by industry self-policing and government deterrence, this approach has achieved some successes but is clearly suboptimal—from economic and environmental perspectives—to the relationship that could exist if the situation in Cell B were the case (across-the-board cooperation by both business and industry).

A first phase in the movement toward greening has used market incentives, self-reporting, and environmental management systems to improve corporate environmental performance. More recently, bolder experiments in self-regulation have advanced industry closer to the cooperative zone.

Phase I: Market Incentives, Self-Reporting, and Environmental Management Systems

As indicated in Chapter 10, incentive-based approaches to environmental policy, such as emissions taxes, tradable permit systems, and deposit-refund programs, can be both effective at preventing pollution and more economically efficient. The EPA and many states have experimented with a wide range of market incentives, mostly since the 1980s, many of which have demonstrated promising results.[23] Experimentation with these "efficiency-based regulatory reforms" characterizes the second epoch of the environmental movement.[24]

Two of the most well-known experiments with market incentives include the Acid Rain Program of the 1990 Clean Air Act and the tradable permits program in the Los Angeles basin, known as the Regional Clean Air Incentives Market (RECLAIM). By most accounts, the Acid Rain Program made good on economists' predictions: emissions decreased, and industry spent less money overall.[25] The Los Angeles program has also worked reasonably well in reducing emissions overall and in keeping down pollution control costs. However, it has been faulted for failing to address effectively the serious pollution "hot spots" existing within the overall region.[26] Another significant second-epoch regulatory experiment consisted of self-reporting, auditing, and disclosure requirements, beginning in 1986 with the Superfund Amendments and Reauthorization Act. This legislation created the Toxics Release Inventory (TRI), the first major federal environmental program that moved away from the traditional command-and-control approach (characterized by heavy fines, specified emissions levels, and mandatory pollution abatement technologies) toward a "softer, gentler" self-reporting and cooperative framework. The TRI requires companies that have ten or more employees and that use significant amounts of any one of the hundreds of listed chemicals to report annual releases and transfers of these chemicals to the EPA, which then makes these data available to the public through an annual report.[27]

The TRI requires companies to report their activities but does not require that they change their behavior. To view such policies as "all study and no action," however, would be to miss their contribution to what David Morell calls "regulation by embarrassment."[28] Indeed, environmental groups such as Communities for a Better Environment, INFORM, Inc. (a national nonprofit active in the 1980s and '90s that produced short films designed to educate the public about the effects of human activity on the environment and human health), and Greenpeace have seized on TRI data to publicize particularly heavy polluters. Some organizations make TRI data easily available over the Internet, allowing communities to view local toxic releases in map form.[29] Moreover, many state environmental agencies are basing their rulemaking on the TRI reports for industries in their states. Some industries have called for an end to the TRI reporting process because of these new regulatory uses.

In 2015, U.S. industry generated about 1.6 million tons of toxic waste—or about 10.5 pounds per American—most of which was released to air, land, and water as treated or untreated waste rather than recycled or reused.[30] Making year-to-year comparisons in toxic releases is difficult because the EPA has expanded the kinds of facilities required to report releases as well as added to the list of chemicals to report. But if we limit ourselves to the three hundred or so core chemicals from the original reporting industries, total on- and off-site releases decreased 67 percent from 1989 to 2015.[31] Unfortunately, not all parts of the country enjoyed the same toxic release reductions. As the authors of *Coming Clean*, a comprehensive study of the TRI, point out, there is substantial variation in releases across regions, industrial sectors, and individual firms themselves.[32]

Although the EPA and industry applaud declines in toxic releases with every new TRI report, critics of the program have raised serious doubts about the validity of TRI data. For example, the Environmental Integrity Project (EIP) challenged the TRI results in a 2004 report titled *Who's Counting? The Systematic Underreporting of Toxic Air Emissions*. The EIP compared TRI reports for refineries and chemical facilities in Texas with actual smokestack emissions, in some cases using infrared scanners aboard aerial surveys. The EIP and the Texas Commission on Environmental Quality found that, for ten of the most common hydrocarbons, the EPA's reports underestimated actual emissions by 25 percent to 440 percent, raising serious concerns about outdated or inaccurate estimation methods that never actually measure releases themselves.[33] It's very unlikely that TRI releases continue their decades-old decline primarily because industries simply move offshore—there were about as many facilities reporting releases to the TRI in 2015 (21,884) as in 1999 (23,424).[34] The TRI only reports on a subset of the nation's dangerous wastes. Hazardous wastes—as defined by the Resource Conservation and Recovery Act (RCRA) and its amendments—comprise a much larger set. Some of these wastes are not nearly as dangerous as those on the TRI list (e.g., oily water), but many are quite toxic. All are required by law to receive some kind of treatment before disposal. In stark contrast to the TRI reports, RCRA waste totals have barely changed since the late 1990s, fluctuating from thirty million to forty million tons per year, depending largely on the state of the national economy.[35] If the TRI faithfully represented American pollution prevention trends, why wouldn't these trends mirror the RCRA totals?

The TRI is the most widely known and used database of self-reported information, but it is not unique. Thousands of companies around the world implement corporate environmental reports (CERs) every year and submit annual documents similar to their financial reports. These include "management policies and systems; input/output inventor[ies] of environmental impacts; financial implications of environmental actions; relationships with stakeholders; and the [company's] sustainable development agenda."[36] Despite the appealing logic of self-reporting and auditing, it is exceedingly difficult to tell what such information achieves. Firms may be reluctant to disclose accurately potential problems with their facilities, fearing that regulators or third-party organizations (such as environmental litigants) might seize on the data to impose fines, facility changes in equipment and operation, or both.[37]

The relatively small amount of research done on self-reporting suggests that, at best, CER systems improve company data collection and internal management, while possibly rendering environmental issues more transparent to government and the public.[38] More critical research shows that self-audits overwhelmingly reveal inventory and reporting violations (for example, of hazardous materials) rather than the much more serious unlawful emissions releases that the EPA discovers during its standard enforcement procedures.[39]

The third innovation of industrial greening actually modifies company management philosophies and practices. To implement green strategies, firms have adopted environmental management systems (EMSs) that include corporate environmental pledges, internal training programs, environmental education programs, and the use of cradle-to-grave systems of management control such as full-cost accounting and total quality management.[40] EMSs vary enormously, but the basic idea is to (1) track a firm's environmental footprint, (2) assign management responsibility for company-wide environmental performance, (3) establish environmental improvement goals, and (4) establish a means to assess whether a company is meeting its environmental targets.

Given their interest in avoiding environmental protection costs, why do firms adopt EMSs? After all, they are costly—in terms of both money and staff time—and they open private firms to external scrutiny that might not be welcome. Prakash and Potoski report that annual third-party audits for ISO 14001 certification (an international environmental management system discussed later in this chapter) can cost a small firm from $25,000 to $100,000, and much, much more for larger firms.[41] Based on a survey of over two hundred U.S. manufacturing plants, Richard Florida and Derek Davison identify the three most important reasons given for adopting such systems: management "commitment to environmental improvement . . . corporate goals and objectives . . . and business performance." Compliance with state and federal regulations and improved community relations were other frequently cited reasons.[42]

Firms that go green can also be rewarded by the financial markets. Some investment brokers offer socially responsible environmental investment portfolios, although they are only a small (but growing) part of the investments market. By the mid-1990s, about forty mutual funds were managing $3 billion of green investments.[43] In 2016, the Forum for Sustainable and Responsible Investment reported that socially responsible investment portfolios—those that select companies through a wide range of social screens, including shareholder advocacy and investment in communities—had reached $8.72 trillion in assets, or about a fifth of the total investment assets under U.S. management. Moreover, socially responsible investment (SRI) assets performed better during the recent financial crisis. From 1995 to 2012, SRI assets grew at a compound annual rate of 11 percent, about 1.2 percent faster than all professionally managed U.S. investments.[44] Managers of green mutual funds are constantly updating their social ratings of industries worthy of investment. Indeed, a number of studies now suggest a strong correlation between profitability and greening, although researchers are quick to point out that just how a company's profits are tied to its investments in pollution prevention or abatement is not clear.[45]

Do environmental management systems make a difference? Because of the difficulty linking management changes to verifiable, objective environmental outcomes—and because EMSs are all so different[46]—the jury is still out on that question.[47] Some researchers conclude that such systems are effective when they have strong support from top management, who in turn rely on the systems to greatly improve company environmental awareness and to better track the flow of raw materials, energy, labor, quality, and costs throughout the firm's operations.[48] And adopters of environmental management systems report that they recycle more; release fewer air, water, and waste emissions; and use less electricity than do nonadopters, but such findings are not based on third-party audits.[49]

Phase II: Self-Regulation

More recently, greening includes businesses and industries coming together in voluntary self-regulatory associations, at home and around the world. Some of these efforts are "invited" by regulators, whereas others are initiated and implemented by corporate leaders themselves or, in a few cases, by nongovernmental organizations. The primary attractions of self-regulating voluntary associations are that they reduce the compliance costs that can come with the avoidance of command-and-control regulation, they signal a company's green intent to consumers and those up- and downstream in the production chain (green branding), and they help companies to establish greater rapport with regulators and policymakers.[50] From a public policy perspective, voluntary self-regulation also reduces the cost to government that comes with regulating many thousands of firms throughout the nation, and it fills a void if, for whatever reason, regulations do not exist.

Nonetheless, critics raise several objections to self-regulation. It may be nothing more than "greenwashing" by firms wishing to improve their public image without fundamentally changing their production practices, although some companies address this charge by subjecting their environmental practices to third-party audits and then reporting the results using widely accepted indicators.[51] By their very nature, which involves adopting changes internal to a firm, self-regulation policies and their exact effects may be exceedingly difficult to assess; regulators and the public, in effect, must trust that firms are honest when reporting on their voluntary activities. Also, cleaner manufacturing often requires management, labor, equipment, or process changes, usually up front, before potential savings can be realized. As a result, these initial costs of self-regulation can seriously discourage participation. Finally, it can be argued that voluntary environmental management may lead to lower productivity if new practices are cleaner but less efficient than old ones.[52] Since the mid-1980s, the EPA has launched more than fifty voluntary programs, emanating mostly from its office specific to air regulations, followed by its office for toxics and pollution prevention, and then its waste, water, policy, and research offices.[53] Performance Track was the most comprehensive of the EPA's voluntary program initiatives before President Barack Obama's first EPA administrator, Lisa P. Jackson, scrapped the program just weeks after assuming her duties. Begun in 2000, it encouraged companies to adopt management practices that would lead to emissions reductions beyond those legally required.[54] Participants had to commit to measurable improvements in environmental performance, implement an environmental management system, and demonstrate their compliance. In turn, the EPA could grant regulatory flexibility or a reduction in other reporting requirements. According to a survey of program participants, the primary reasons for participation were the resulting positive rapport with the EPA and the public recognition accruing to those enrolled in the program for their environmental care and responsibility. Since the program's inception in 2000, membership grew at 12 percent a year and, by mid-2008, was approaching 550 companies.[55]

So why did the new EPA administrator cancel a program launched under the Bill Clinton administration? A deteriorating reputation may explain her decision. The EPA's own independent inspector general, Nikki Tinsley, issued a very critical report in 2007, faulting the program for not connecting clear goals to measurable activities and also for including members whose environmental performance was not necessarily above average.[56] Shortly thereafter, at the end of 2008, three *Philadelphia Inquirer* reporters, John Sullivan, John Shiffman, and Tom Avril, published a very critical four-part series on the EPA titled *Smoke and Mirrors: The Subversion of the EPA*.[57] Their third story, "Green Club an EPA Charade," argued that too many Performance Track members continued to violate their permit limits while receiving less scrutiny by virtue of their "club" membership.[58] Doing away with the Performance Track also signaled a shift from the George W. Bush-era focus on voluntary initiatives, which, in turn, was seen by environmentalists as a justification for lax regulatory enforcement and negligible rule development.[59] After its demise, many Performance Track members formed a new "Stewardship Action Council" (SAC), ostensibly to continue publicizing their excellent environmental programs and performance. Although the SAC comprises several large environmental organizations, it arguably asks even less of its members than did the Performance Track.[60]

In a thoroughgoing postmortem of Performance Track, Cary Coglianese and Jennifer Nash made the environmental performance comparisons that EPA was never willing or able to carry out. Combining case studies of five sets of matching industry pairs, including Performance Track facilities and nonenrolled facilities, plus a large-scale survey, Coglianese and Nash could not distinguish between firms that were in the program and those that were not. Participating facilities did not outperform similar facilities in their industrial sectors; rather, Performance Track facilities simply appeared to be the ones most aggressively seeking government recognition and community engagement. Although both are laudable goals, Coglianese and Nash found no evidence that such goals resulted in better environmental performance.[61]

The EPA is not alone in its efforts to promote green management. In 1996, the International Organization for Standardization (ISO) released its ISO 14001 environmental management standards. A company registering for ISO 14001 certification must (1) develop an environmental management system, (2) demonstrate compliance with all local environmental laws, and (3) demonstrate a commitment to continuous improvement.[62] By 2016, almost 350,000 firms had been ISO 14001-certified worldwide, but the North American countries—with 8,438 certified firms—lagged dramatically behind Europe (with 120,595 firms).[63]

Increasingly, large manufacturers require that their suppliers become ISO 14001-certified as well.[64] Ford Motor Company led the way in the mid-1990s but was soon followed by all the major automakers.[65] Prakash and Potoski analyzed ISO 14001-certified firms in the United States, asking whether their air emissions were significantly lower than those of noncertified firms, and indeed they were. Their explanation is that, on the spectrum of voluntary measures, ISO 14001 represents a "weak sword" because it requires only third-party audits. A "strong sword" system (what the EPA's Performance Track program was supposed to be) requires third-party monitoring, public disclosure of audit information, and sanctions by program sponsors.[66]

Ultimately, only high-quality data will tell us whether greening or green-washing is the outcome. Currently, one of the most widespread forms of corporate environmental and social responsibility activity involves information. Increasingly, companies disclose some aspect of their activity (e.g., reporting carbon dioxide emissions to the Carbon Disclosure Project[67]) or promise to clean up their supply chain. To boost their credibility, firms employ third parties, such as the Forest Trust,[68] to verify their claims. Third-party certifiers are only as good as their reputation, and their work raises the question of who will guard the guardians. Our ability to verify certified claims is next to nil, especially when emissions are not directly measured or the verifiers themselves do not disclose their own contracts or data.[69]

Win-Win as a Business Proposition

Overall, the national effort, under the Clean Air Act, to reduce the air pollution emitted by business and industry, particularly in major urban areas across the United States, has been reasonably successful. Significantly helping this effort since 1970 has been the dramatic reduction of emissions per automobile on the road. Many of our most polluted waterways have been cleaned up over this period as well.

Balanced against this record are some countervailing observations. Automobiles burning gasoline are approaching hard limits in their per-mile emissions reductions, while U.S. ridership (officially measured as "vehicle miles traveled") in 2014 reached a *trillion* miles per year, almost three hundred billion miles more than in 2000.[70] And there is little evidence indicating that either the automobile emissions reduction or the waterways cleanup was accomplished in the most cost-effective manner. Possibly more important in looking forward, more than three decades of experience did not result in any visible commitment by a majority of businesses in the United States to a comprehensive, green transition.

As a result, we cannot be certain about the continuation of abating large-scale pollution or that the aggregate of emissions from American industry will remain below previous levels. That is, businesses have made little commitment to moving beyond the long-standing command-and-control regulatory approach to a life-cycle environmental analysis of their products. We are even less likely to see widespread closed-system toxics management in manufacturing or product use or sustained attention to more global and growing problems such as greenhouse gas emissions, destruction of natural habitats, or depletion of ocean resources. Equally important, no national policy goals or mandated regulations exist in the United States to move industry toward addressing these global, potentially catastrophic trends.

An instructive lesson from the voluntary programs established since 1991 is that, when businesses form an alliance within their sector, either voluntarily or under the pressure of government policy, significant reductions can be realized, especially in high-profile sectors such as the chemical industry. Yet this very example suggests that chemicals may be the proverbial exception to the rule because the change in that industry was due to the extraordinary public pressure brought to bear in the early 1990s as a result of the few colossal environmental disasters experienced in the United States and abroad and the fact that the industry is fairly well concentrated. Thus, cooperation was brought about among a relatively few number of actors. In effect, the conditions for moving into a win-win game position for both government and the chemical industry existed, in that flexible regulation and volunteerism could be achieved, and the action moved into Cell B of Figure 11-1. Today, few other such examples can be found within major business and industrial sectors.[71]

How might this situation be changed? After a thorough review of the pilots and experiments in flexible regulation, self-regulation, and voluntary approaches since the mid-1990s, Marc Eisner has woven together the best components from each into a promising synthesis.[72] His approach is designed to overcome the natural (that is, rational) reticence of business and industry and move the greening agenda beyond Cell D and into Cell B. He focuses on bridging the gap between business and government, on "harnessing the market and industrial associations to achieve superior results by creating a system of government supervised self-regulation."[73] The central propositions of his policy synthesis are as follows:

- Market rewards should be the primary motivator; these place emphasis on the "carrot" while retaining in reserve the traditional regulatory "stick."
- Reliance should be placed on trade and business associations; these sectoral and quasi-governmental organizations can serve as the central implementers of greening policy (they are "quasi" in that they are nonprofit organizations, although they would be imbued with governing authority).
- Emphasis should be placed on disclosure and "sunshine" provisions over government-prescribed techniques of emissions reduction and on-site government inspection.
- Sectoral associations would serve as intermediary entities, both to implement policy and to assure the government that policy would be carried out as intended.

The proposal does not require significant new public laws or the creation of new government bureaucracy because its policies can be woven together from existing programs and authority.

The critical virtue of this approach is that, if adopted as the overall framework for greening, it would mitigate, on the one hand, the businesses' fear of an overbearing regulatory regime and the government's fear of becoming a "sucker" and, on the other hand, the concern that other businesses will evade their responsibilities to go green. In short, we have in Eisner's proposal a game-theoretic and pragmatically attractive approach to moving government and business into Cell B. As we mentioned at the outset, policy is set by the politics of policymaking and not simply by the logic of policy analysis, as attractive as that logic may be. We will now turn to the politics of sustainable production policy.

Another instructive lesson comes from those who are reengineering to compete in the worldwide economy of the twenty-first century, and doing so in ways that are beginning to anticipate when green production will be the norm, not the exception, in the economic marketplace. Box 11-1 illustrates how some firms are implementing this strategy.[74]

Box 11-1   Three Industries, Three Companies,
One Industrial-Ecological Strategy

In an era of global trade dominated by Chinese manufacturing, it's easy to wonder how American manufacturers can remain in business, much less whether they will pursue greening strategies. On the one hand, companies in the Global South enjoy access to large pools of low-wage workers and structure their manufacturing at very high outputs. On the other hand, many American facilities are old, employ a mature and higher-paid workforce, face very high cultural and legal expectations when it comes to environmental and health considerations, and enjoy few protections from America's open trade access policies. Combined, these factors reasonably suggest that the downward spiral in American manufacturing of the past several decades should end in complete collapse.

But there is a new and promising *industrial-ecological* manufacturing paradigm imaginable for mature industrial nations like the United States, one that takes advantage of very short supply and distribution chains. The idea is simple. Raw materials and energy have become so expensive that recycling often appears more attractive than making commodities (such as steel, paper, aluminum, glass, and plastic containers) from virgin materials. In most heavy industries, recycled raw materials require far less energy than do new inputs to be converted to usable products. The United States also produces enormous amounts of high-quality recyclables every year, some of which find their way to reprocessors overseas.

Asian exporters put a high value on recyclables, too. They send full container ships to U.S. ports but have relatively little to fill them with for the return voyage, so scrap metals, paper, and plastics fit the bill nicely. While it may seem sensible to ship recyclables to any country willing or able to reprocess them, the fuel demand for transporting, say, a load of scrap metal from the American Midwest to an inland Chinese mill—*and back to the United States*—is enormous.

Increasingly, American firms find ways to capitalize on their local or regional advantages: very highly productive labor, sophisticated

(Continued)

(Continued)

automation, a weak dollar (which makes U.S. exports possible, but fluctuates considerably over time), steady supplies of recyclables, and nearby markets for finished products. Three Midwestern companies provide very good examples of how manufacturers can be green and competitive.

- *SSAB, Iowa, Inc., Davenport, Iowa* This relatively new (1996) steel mill on the banks of the Mississippi uses exclusively old steel from scrap yards, brokers, and pipe makers within a couple of hours of the plant. SSAB bought 1.4 million tons of scrap steel in 2007 (for $250–$500 per ton, depending on the quality). Using an electric arc furnace, the plant's five hundred highly paid (but nonunion) employees produced about 1.2 million tons of high-strength steel plate and coil, worth nearly $1 billion. In recent years, SSAB's heavy plate steel became bulldozer buckets and other parts of heavy equipment manufactured in the many Caterpillar and John Deere facilities located nearby. Interestingly, 20 percent of SSAB's sales now go to makers of wind turbines, most of which also are manufactured and sold regionally.
- *Jupiter Aluminum Corporation, Hammond, Indiana* Nearly every American driver knows what his or her license plates look and feel like. Most people don't know that one company in the gritty, northern Indiana town of Hammond makes almost all of the aluminum used for license plates in the United States. Jupiter Aluminum produces the aluminum for license plates as well as gutters and downspouts entirely from recycled aluminum. Most recently, the company produced about 150 million tons of aluminum coil, drawing on 160 million tons of scrap that it purchases for about $1 per pound from scores of sellers in the Midwest. Jupiter's 268 employees shipped about $250 million worth of aluminum products in recent years, making its workforce tremendously productive (in terms of dollars of product per worker).
- *Corenso North America, Wisconsin Rapids, Wisconsin* Situated close to the banks of the Wisconsin River, Corenso produces the corrugated cardboard cores (tubes) on which many other companies wind their papers, sheet metals, fabrics, and ribbons. Employing about 170 union workers, Corenso uses exclusively scrap cardboard from the upper Midwest to make the cardboard strips the company then winds and glues into tubular cores. In recent years, Corenso bought over 45,000 tons of scrap cardboard for $100–$125 per ton, relying on

three to five regional scrap brokers and distributors as well as cardboard drop-off locations for local residents. Corenso turns that scrap into some 35,000 tons of coreboard valued at about $18 million.

Each of these facilities faces strong command-and-control regulations requiring it to keep air emissions and wastewater low. But they all went much further than this regulatory "floor." Under pressure by a very tough Iowa Department of Natural Resources, SSAB steel meets some of the most stringent particulate matter requirements faced by any steel mill anywhere in the world. Jupiter Aluminum installed an "oxy-fuel"–fired furnace, allowing it to burn natural gas in a pure oxygen environment, thereby eliminating all of its nitrogen oxide emissions. And Corenso's reliance on recycling means that the company can repulp scrap cardboard with no chemicals, thereby releasing almost no waste to the city sewage treatment plant or to the Wisconsin River.

Two Steps Forward, One Step Back: Mixed Signals from Industry and Washington

Despite the effort by President Obama to update and make more efficient environmental regulations and procedures, especially in his second administration, and the concomitant good image nurtured by corporate public relations officers, many industry lobbyists continued to work assiduously at blocking or rolling back environmental mandates.[75] With respect to the former, in response to Obama's executive order to all federal agencies to undertake a thorough review of their practices and procedures (see Chapter 4), in the summer of 2011, the EPA developed a plan focused on four goals: introducing greater electronic reporting, improving agency transparency, working with affected parties to develop innovative compliance approaches, and developing integrated problem-solving and systems approaches to replace its segmented and disparate activities that had grown by accretion over four decades.[76] Some three dozen initiatives were launched between 2011 and 2014, in areas ranging from the technical updating of water quality standards to introducing electronic industry reporting and integrated research and compliance procedures; half or more of these initiatives have been completed.[77]

While working with the EPA on the retrospective review on one hand, on the other hand, industry political action committees kept up a steady stream of campaign contributions to antienvironmentalist legislators, as they have done for years.[78] In fact, industry opposition to new or strengthened environmental initiatives with respect to climate change intensified as Obama's term was coming to an end. For example, the EPA's Clean Air Scientific Advisory Committee recommended lowering the ozone standard from 75 to 60 parts per billion. What should have been fairly routine revisions to air quality standards were met with staunch opposition; for example, the American Petroleum Institute asserted that the new rule would pose "massive and disruptive" challenges to states and factories.[79] And as one of the arguably most important environmental issues of our time, climate change should be an area most benefiting from the greening of industry. Despite some first movers, the top American industrial emitters put on a full court press to block the Obama administration's implementation of curbs on power plant carbon dioxide emissions in 2014 and to urge approval of the Keystone XL pipeline from the tar sand fields of Canada.

The interests opposing Obama's environmental agenda moved to the forefront in President Trump's election campaign promises to roll back domestic environmental regulations on business and industry in pursuit of near-term economic growth and to reverse the national and international efforts championed by Obama that would address the dire implications of global climate change. Although more than campaign rhetoric is needed to change the basic direction toward environmental protection prescribed in the congressionally enacted clean air and water policies of the nation over the course of four decades, President Trump's intention of doing so was made clear in his cabinet appointments in environmental protection, energy, and natural resources. Additionally, a set of executive orders enacted early in his presidency called for the lessening if not elimination of federal regulations protecting the environment (see Chapters 4 and 7).

Given the steps toward greening over the past several decades and especially the prevalence of green corporate rhetoric and company sustainability plans, not to mention the growth of environmental consumerism, one might conclude that American business and industry had embraced the environmental agenda, quibbling only over timelines for change and the details of implementation. Unfortunately, absent strong pressure from national political leaders, a different side of industry is being revealed. Indeed, industry positions on environmental rules, big and small, offer the strongest indication that the sustainability transition is stalled, at best, or perhaps taking one step backward.

The largest and most polluting American industrial sectors—for example, petrochemicals, power generation, and oil, gas, and mining interests—all voiced their opposition to the details of cleaner regulations during President Obama's administration, but then they revealed a deeper opposition to the important environmental and climate change policies aimed at them as soon as President Trump took office.

Several actions by Congress and President Trump early in his presidency stand out in particular. First, the new administration took aim at a deal President Obama negotiated with thirteen automakers, which obtained their approval for an increase in the Corporate Average Fuel Economy (CAFE) standards. These would rise to 54.5 miles per gallon by the 2025 model year. Within weeks of Donald Trump taking office, automakers clamored to scrap the CAFE target.

Second, acting on campaign promises, the Trump administration moved quickly to rescind support for two major Obama-era rules working their ways through court challenges: the Waters of the United States (WOTUS) rule and the Clean Power Plan. Third, the Republican-controlled Congress quickly set to work relaxing environmental regulation, using the Congressional Review Act to repeal EPA rulemaking completed late in President Obama's last term (see Chapter 5). President Trump's third major break with the Obama administration came when he announced that he would pull the United States out of the Paris Agreement, an international accord designed to reduce greenhouse gas emissions. These three major actions, along with numerous smaller reversals on federal environmental policy, make it far more likely that collective action involving pollution- and energy-intensive industries will move the United States toward Cell A (firm evasion and flexible regulation). Moving toward Cell A could increase the potential for government to play the role of "sucker" in game-theoretic terms. We could expect some industry actors to cut corners or engage in outright violations despite the country's many watchdogs and monitoring systems.

The most spectacular environmental regulation scandal in recent years comes from an unlikely source: Volkswagen, the huge German auto manufacturer. In a story breaking from 2015 through 2017, university engineers and environmental agency staff discovered that VW had installed "defeat devices" on millions of diesel-engine light-duty vehicles.

In recent years, VW made modest sales of diesel-powered passenger vehicles in the United States, but diesels account for about 60 percent of cars in some European countries. That's because the Europeans found they could achieve their energy efficiency and greenhouse gas reduction goals by pushing diesel engines, which get significantly better gas mileage than their gasoline-powered counterparts.

Unfortunately, diesel engines pollute more NOx than gas engines, thus requiring complex pollution control equipment, which can rob the diesel vehicles of power and pickup. To make good on its claim that its diesel vehicles offered both power and efficiency, VW engineers programmed the cars to detect when emissions tests were being conducted. During such tests, the NOx emissions controls worked well, but under normal driving conditions, the equipment was turned off, resulting in more power but in up to 40 times more NOx emissions than allowed by law. When confronted with on-road emissions tests, Volkswagen officials obfuscated, lied, and fabricated data for over a year until the company admitted it had installed "defeat devices" in its diesel engine emissions control systems. Volkswagen will have to pay about $15 billion to buy back vehicles in the United States alone; plus it has settlement costs totaling at least $4.3 billion. Included in the settlement is a $2.8 billion criminal penalty, the largest an automaker has ever paid the U.S. government. Ironically, if Volkswagen had simply acknowledged its wrongdoing from the very start, the company could have paid fines 100 times less than the ones currently levied.[80]

Reaching beyond Win-Win

We assume that devising ways to improve protection of the environment will need to build on the several generations of existing or enhanced law and public policy, that any thought of disregarding or abandoning these and starting anew is unrealistic. For this reason, the synthetic approach conceived by Eisner, designed to harness the core self-interested impulses of business and government on behalf of protection of the natural environment, is even more appealing today than when it was first envisioned. To be effective, environmental and sustainability policies have always required and will continue to require business to improve the production of material goods and services while reducing to a minimum adverse impacts on the natural environment. Indeed, this is not only the win-win of game theory but also industrial ecology's "double bottom-line" aspiration of achieving both economic development and environmental protection. As a blueprint for politically realistic, near and long-term policy goals, we believe Eisner provides an ambitious while realizable approach to environmental protection and the greening of industry.

Not even the best policy ideas succeed in the real world, of course. With this in mind, we know that should the Eisner approach fail due to either resistance from industry or a lack of leadership from the national government, in other words, should it become necessary to look for more ambitious though over-the-horizon approaches, they do exist. We can suggest two options in particular to underscore the point. These are the "theory of the economic dynamics of environmental law," articulated by David Driesen,[81] and steady-state, or "true cost economics," long advocated by Herman Daly.[82] In a recent treatise on law and the environment, Driesen argues that dramatic greening is unlikely until the priority given to efficiency and benefit-cost thinking in neoclassical microeconomic behavior is replaced by the goal of encouraging "dynamic technology change" and adaptation, in a world of growing natural resource scarcity.

A second and similarly ambitious and transformative approach consists of efforts to refocus attention at the macroeconomic level away from the exclusive attention on production of material goods and human services to balancing production with the costs to natural assets and the environment, a movement led by Daly and a small but growing number of "ecological economists" around the world.

In the effort to deal with climate change, many new policy ideas are being introduced that will address the range of environmental and resource issues raised throughout the first and second environmental epochs, issues that have been addressed piecemeal by the EPA and the federal policy it reflects. Today, these issues are being tackled with new vigor and in a more comprehensive manner and, in many ways, not simply as public policy that government imposes on business and industry but from myriad business concerns. These concerns motivate business and industry to think more in the longer term and strategically. On the one hand, both will anticipate enormous market opportunities at home and abroad. On the other hand, they will feel strong government pressure as the world begins to experience the unprecedented and challenging effects of climate change.

Market opportunities or challenges such as the meltdown in the financial services sector in 2008 may shape industrial greening as much as or more than new policy programs. The relatively low energy prices that American companies enjoyed throughout the 1990s and early 2000s came back with the hydraulic fracturing (or fracking) boom. Fracking has meant less reliance on coal for energy production, but also a glut of cheap domestic oil, keeping gas prices low. And for the first time in perhaps a generation, many large companies view green tech as the next high-growth frontier for the United States. Despite a sputtering economic recovery, the second decade of the 2000s saw venture capitalists pouring money into solar power, battery and fuel cell technology, biofuels research, and other clean energy research and development projects.[83] How rapidly and extensively green industry will grow may depend not only on energy and materials prices but also on whether state and federal policymakers connect environmental policy to trade, development, labor, and tax policies.

Suggested Websites

Independent Analysis of Corporate Environmental and Social Performance

The Forest Trust (www.tft-forests.org) This third-party group focuses on products and supply chains to bring about sustainable development, especially in land-based forest and extractive industries.

Global Reporting Initiative (www.globalreporting.org) GRI is an independent nongovernmental organization charged with developing and disseminating globally applicable sustainability reporting guidelines.

Greening of Industry Network (www.greeningofindustry.org) This independent network of professionals is focused on aligning industrial development strategies with sustainable development practices.

Six Sigma (www.isixsigma.com) The organization promotes in business the adoption, advancement, and integration of Six Sigma, a management and auditing methodology to identify errors or defects in manufacturing and service.

Business Sustainability Councils

World Business Council for Sustainable Development (www.wbcsd.ch) WBCSD is a global green industry clearinghouse.

World Resources Institute (www.wri.org) This global research organization is an environmental clearinghouse with programs tying industry to development.

Leading Business and Environment Journals

Business Strategy and the Environment (http://onlinelibrary.wiley.com/journal/10.1002/(ISSN)1099-0836) The journal publishes scholarship on business responses to improving environmental performance.

Corporate Social Responsibility and Environmental Management (http://onlinelibrary.wiley.com/journal/10.1002/(ISSN)1535-3966) This journal specializes in research related to the development of tools and techniques for improving corporate performance and accountability on social and environmental dimensions.

Environmental Quality Management (http://onlinelibrary.wiley.com/journal/10.1002/(ISSN)1520-6483) This applied and practice-oriented journal demonstrates how to improve environmental performance and exceed new voluntary standards such as ISO 14000.

The Green Business Letter (www.greenbiz.com) This monthly online newsletter provides information for businesses and universities wishing to integrate environmental thinking throughout their organizations in profitable ways.

U.S. Environmental Protection Agency Sites

Energy Star (www.energystar.gov) This is a good site for learning about energy efficiency programs and efficient equipment, lighting, and buildings.

Toxics Release Inventory (https://iaspub.epa.gov/triexplorer/tri) The nation's list of toxic chemical releases from manufacturing, power generation, and mining facilities is available here.

Notes

1. Robert B. Gibson, ed., *Voluntary Initiatives: The New Politics of Corporate Greening* (Peterborough, ON: Broadview Press, 1999).
2. Charles A. Jones and David L. Levy, "Business Strategies and Climate Change," in *Changing Climates in North American Politics*, ed. Henrik Selin and Stacy VanDeveer (Cambridge, MA: MIT Press, 2010), 219–40.
3. Thomas Princen, Michael Maniates, and Ken Conca, eds., *Confronting Consumption* (Cambridge, MA: MIT Press, 2002).
4. Richard Kashmanian, Cheryl Keenan, and Richard Wells, "Corporate Environmental Leadership: Drivers, Characteristics, and Examples," *Environmental Quality Management* 19, no. 4 (Summer 2010): 1–20.
5. Tobias Hahn, Frank Figge, Jonatan Pinkse, and Lutz Preuss, "Trade-Offs in Corporate Sustainability: You Can't Have Your Cake and Eat It," *Business Strategy and the Environment* 19 (2010): 217–29.
6. Huib Pellikaan and Robert J. van der Veen, *Environmental Dilemmas and Policy Design* (New York: Cambridge University Press, 2002); Nives Dolšak and Elinor Ostrom, eds., *The Commons in the New Millennium: Challenges and Adaptation* (Cambridge, MA: MIT Press, 2003).
7. Daniel A. Mazmanian and Michael E. Kraft, "The Three Epochs of the Environmental Movement," in *Toward Sustainable Communities: Transition and Transformations in Environmental Policy*, 2nd ed., ed. Daniel A. Mazmanian and Michael E. Kraft (Cambridge, MA: MIT Press, 2009), 3–32.
8. Daniel C. Esty and Andrew S. Winston, *Green to Gold: How Smart Companies Use Environmental Strategy to Innovate, Create Value, and Build Competitive Advantage* (New Haven, CT: Yale University Press 2006); Matthew Potoski and Aseem Prakash, eds., *Voluntary Programs: A Club Theory Perspective* (Cambridge, MA: MIT Press, 2009).

9. U.S. Environmental Protection Agency, *Planning, Budget, and Results* (Washington, DC: EPA, 2014). The most recent and historical budgets are accessible from http://www2.epa.gov/planandbudget.

10. Michael E. Porter and Claas van der Linde, "Green and Competitive: Ending the Stalemate," *Harvard Business Review* 73 (September/October 1995): 120–34; Esty and Winston, *Green to Gold.*

11. Doris Fuchs and Daniel A. Mazmanian, "The Greening of Industry: Needs of the Field," *Business Strategy and Environment* 7 (1998): 193–203; Daniel Press, "Industry, Environmental Policy, and Environmental Outcomes," *Annual Review of Environment and Resources* 32 (2007): 317–44.

12. Roy Huntley, Environmental Engineer, Emission Factor and Inventory Group, EPA, personal communication, August 26, 2004.

13. U.S. EPA, *Clean Air Markets Progress Report: Emission Reductions*, last updated August 30, 2017, https://www3.epa.gov/airmarkets/progress/reports/emissions_reductions.html.

14. U.S. EPA, Clearinghouse for Inventories & Emissions Factors, *National Emissions Inventory (NEI) Air Pollutant Emissions Trends Data, 1970–2016*, https://www.epa.gov/air-emissions-inventories/air-pollutant-emissions-trends-data; U.S. EPA, *Summary Nonattainment Area Population Exposure Report*, last updated June 20, 2017, www.epa.gov/airquality/greenbook/popexp.html.

15. U.S. EPA, *Summary Nonattainment Area Population Exposure Report.*

16. Cary Coglianese and Jennifer Nash, eds., *Regulating from the Inside: Can Environmental Management Systems Achieve Policy Goals?* (Washington, DC: Resources for the Future, 2001).

17. Energy Information Administration, *Manufacturing Energy Consumption Survey (MECS)* (Washington, DC: U.S. Department of Energy, 2017), https://www.eia.gov/consumption/manufacturing/. See in particular EIA, "Preliminary Estimates Show That U.S. Manufacturing Energy Consumption Increased between 2010 and 2014," *MECS 2010 and 2014*, October 13, 2016, https://www.eia.gov/consumption/manufacturing/reports/2014/pre_estimates/?src=‹ Consumption Manufacturing Energy Consumption Survey (MECS)-f1.

18. U.S. Census Bureau, *Annual Survey of Manufactures*, http://www.census.gov/manufacturing/asm.

19. EIA, "Preliminary Estimates Show That U.S. Manufacturing Energy Consumption Increased."

20. Energy Information Administration, *Manufacturing Energy Consumption Survey (MECS)* (Washington, DC: U.S. Department of Energy, 2002 and 2010). See the data available from https://www.eia.gov/consumption/.

21. U.S. Department of Commerce, *Pollution Abatement Costs and Expenditures*, MA-200(80)-1 and MA-200(05) (Washington, DC: U.S. Department of Commerce, Bureau of the Census, 1980, 1985, 1993, 1994, 2005).

22. U.S. EPA, National Center for Environmental Economics, *Pollution Abatement Costs and Expenditures: 2005 Survey*, https://www.epa.gov/environmental-economics/pollution-abatement-costs-and-expenditures-2005-survey.

23. Walter A. Rosenbaum, *Environmental Politics and Policy*, 6th ed. (Washington, DC: CQ Press, 2005), 163.

24. Mazmanian and Kraft, "The Three Epochs of the Environmental Movement."

25. U.S. EPA, *The EPA Acid Rain Program 2009 Progress Report* (Washington, DC: EPA, August 2010). Historical reports for the Acid Rain Program and other Clean Air Markets programs are available from https://www.epa.gov/airmarkets/historical-reports.

26. Daniel A. Mazmanian, "Los Angeles's Clean Air Saga: Spanning Three Decades," in *Toward Sustainable Communities*, 2nd ed. (Cambridge, MA: MIT Press, 2009), Chapter 4.

27. To see the *Toxic Release Inventory National Analysis*, go to https://www.epa.gov/trinationalanalysis.

28. David Morell, STC Environmental, personal communication, 1995.

29. For an example, see the Right-to-Know Network (www.rtknet.org) or GoodGuide's Scorecard website (www.scorecard.org).

30. U.S. EPA, *2015 Toxics Release Inventory Public Data Release*, https://iaspub.epa.gov/triexplorer/tri_release.chemical.

31. U.S. EPA, *2015 Toxics Release Inventory Public Data Release*.

32. Michael E. Kraft, Mark Stephan, and Troy D. Abel, *Coming Clean: Information Disclosure and Environmental Performance* (Cambridge, MA: MIT Press, 2011).

33. Environmental Integrity Project and Galveston-Houston Association for Smog Prevention, *Who's Counting? The Systematic Underreporting of Toxic Air Emissions* (Washington, DC: Environmental Integrity Project, June 22, 2004), http://environmentalintegrity.org/pdf/publications/TRIFINALJune_22.pdf.

34. U.S.EPA, *TRI Basic Data Files: Calendar Years 1987–2015* (Washington, DC: EPA, 2017), www2.epa.gov/toxics-release-inventory-tri-program/tri-basic-data-files-calendar-years-1987-2015.

35. Solid Waste and Emergency Response, *The National Biennial RCRA Hazardous Waste Report*, EPA530-R-10-014A (Washington, DC: EPA, 1997, 1999, 2001, 2003, 2005, 2007, 2009, 2011).

36. David Annandale, Angus Morrison-Saunders, and George Bouma, "The Impact of Voluntary Environmental Protection Instruments on Company Environmental Performance," *Business Strategy and the Environment* 13 (2004): 1–12.

37. Alexander Pfaff and Chris William Sanchirico, "Big Field, Small Potatoes: An Empirical Assessment of EPA's Self-Audit Policy," *Journal of Policy Analysis and Management* 23 (Summer 2004): 415–32.

38. Annandale, Morrison-Saunders, and Bouma, "The Impact of Voluntary Environmental Protection Instruments."

39. Pfaff and Sanchirico, "Big Field, Small Potatoes."

40. John T. Willig, ed., *Environmental TQM*, 2nd ed. (New York: McGraw-Hill, 1994); Coglianese and Nash, *Regulating from the Inside;* Marc Allen Eisner, "Corporate Environmentalism, Regulatory Reform, and Industry Self-Regulation: Toward Genuine Regulatory Reinvention in the United States," *Governance: An International Journal of Policy, Administration, and Institutions* 17 (April 2004): 145–67.

41. Aseem Prakash and Matthew Potoski, *The Voluntary Environmentalists: Green Clubs, ISO 14001, and Voluntary Environmental Regulations* (Cambridge: Cambridge University Press, 2006), 92.

42. Richard Florida and Derek Davison, "Why Do Firms Adopt Advanced Environmental Practices (and Do They Make a Difference)?" in *Regulating from the Inside: Can Environmental Management Systems Achieve Policy Goals?* ed. Cary Coglianese and Jennifer Nash (Washington, DC: Resources for the Future, 2001), 82–104, see page 87.

43. Ricardo Sandoval, "How Green Are the Green Funds?" *Amicus Journal* 17 (Spring 1995): 29–33. One widely respected eco-rating of Fortune 500 companies is provided by the Investor Responsibility Research Center in Washington, DC, http://www.irrcinstitute.org.

44. Social Investment Forum, *2016 Report on US Sustainable, Responsible and Impact Investing Trends* (Washington, DC: US SIF, 2017), http://ussif.org.

45. David Austin, "The Green and the Gold: How a Firm's Clean Quotient Affects Its Value," *Resources* 132 (Summer 1998): 15–17.
46. Dagmara Nawrocka and Thomas Parker, "Finding the Connection: Environmental Management Systems and Environmental Performance," *Journal of Cleaner Production* 17 (2009): 601–07.
47. Press, "Industry, Environmental Policy, and Environmental Outcomes."
48. Annandale, Morrison-Saunders, and Bouma, "The Impact of Voluntary Environmental Protection Instruments"; Bruce Smart, ed., *Beyond Compliance: A New Industry View of the Environment* (Washington, DC: World Resources Institute, 1992).
49. Florida and Davison, "Why Do Firms Adopt Advanced Environmental Practices?"
50. Potoski and Prakash, *Voluntary Programs.*
51. Jan Mazurek, "Third-Party Auditing of Environmental Management Systems," in *Environmental Governance Reconsidered*, ed. Robert Durant, Daniel Fiorino, and Rosemary O'Leary (Cambridge, MA: MIT Press, 2004), Chapter 13; Eisner, "Corporate Environmentalism." For a study of selective environmental disclosure, see Eun-Hee Kim and Thomas P. Lyon, "Strategic Environmental Disclosure: Evidence from the DOE's Voluntary Greenhouse Gas Registry," *Journal of Environmental Economics and Management* 61 (2011): 311–26.
52. Natalie Stoeckl, "The Private Costs and Benefits of Environmental Self-Regulation: Which Firms Have Most to Gain?" *Business Strategy and the Environment* 13 (2004): 135–55.
53. Daniel J. Fiorino, *The New Environmental Regulation* (Cambridge, MA: MIT Press, 2006); Daniel J. Fiorino, "Green Clubs: A New Tool for Government," in *Voluntary Programs: A Club Theory Perspective*, ed. Matthew Potoski and Aseem Prakash (Cambridge, MA: MIT Press, 2009), Chapter 7.
54. Cary Coglianese and Jennifer Nash, *Beyond Compliance: Business Decision Making and the U.S. EPA's Performance Track Program* (Cambridge, MA: Regulatory Policy Program, Kennedy School of Government, Harvard University, 2006).
55. Cary Coglianese and Jennifer Nash, "Government Clubs: Theory and Evidence from Environmental Programs," in *Voluntary Programs: A Club Theory Perspective*, ed. Matthew Potoski and Aseem Prakash (Cambridge, MA: MIT Press, 2009), Chapter 8.
56. Office of Inspector General, *Performance Track Could Improve Program Design and Management to Ensure Value*, 2007-P-00013 (Washington, DC: EPA, 2007).
57. The "Smoke and Mirrors" stories ran in the *Philadelphia Inquirer* on December 7, 8, 9, and 10, 2008: http://www.philly.com/philly/news/special_packages/inquirer/36110664.html.
58. John Sullivan and John Shiffman, "Green Club an EPA Charade: The EPA Touts the Perk-Filled Program, but Has Recruited Some Firms with Dismal Environmental Records," *Philadelphia Inquirer*, December 9, 2008.
59. Robin Bravender, "EPA: Voluntary Programs under Scrutiny as Regulatory Obligations Rise," *EE News*, February 5, 2010.
60. See the National Stewardship Action Council at https://nsaction.us/.
61. Cary Coglianese and Jennifer Nash, "Performance Track's Postmortem: Lessons from the Rise and Fall of EPA's 'Flagship' Voluntary Program," *Harvard Environmental Law Review* 38, no. 1 (2014): 1–86.
62. Information on ISO 14001 is available at https://www.iso.org/iso-14001-environmental-management.html.
63. International Organization for Standardization (ISO), *The ISO Survey, 2016* (Geneva: ISO, 2017). The most recent survey is available at https://www.iso.org/the-iso-survey.html.

64. Toshi H. Arimura, Nicole Darnall, and Hajime Katayama, "Is ISO 14001 a Gateway to More Advanced Voluntary Action? The Case of Green Supply Chain Management," *Journal of Environmental Economics and Management* 61 (2011): 170–82.
65. Eisner, "Corporate Environmentalism," 150.
66. Prakash and Potoski, *The Voluntary Environmentalists.*
67. See the Carbon Disclosure Project, www.cdp.net/en.
68. See The Forest Trust, www.tft-forests.org/.
69. Fred Pearce, "Monitoring Corporate Behavior: Greening or Merely Greenwash?" *YaleEnvironment360*, January 27, 2014, http://e360.yale.edu/feature/monitoring_corporate_behavior_greening_or_merely_greenwash/2732/.
70. U.S. Federal Highway Transportation Administration, "Quick Find: Vehicle Miles of Travel," *Highway Statistics Series*, https://www.fhwa.dot.gov/policyinformation/quickfinddata/qftravel.cfm.
71. Hahn, Figge, Pinkse, and Preuss, "Trade-Offs in Corporate Sustainability."
72. Eisner, "Corporate Environmentalism." See also Marc Allen Eisner, *Governing the Environment: The Transformation of Environmental Regulation* (Boulder, CO: Lynne Rienner, 2007).
73. Eisner, "Corporate Environmentalism," 145.
74. For many more examples of innovative industrial greening, see Esty and Winston, *Green to Gold*; Aseem Prakash, *Greening the Firm: The Politics of Corporate Environmentalism* (Cambridge: Cambridge University Press, 2000); Roy Lewicki, Barbara Gray, and Michael Elliott, eds., *Making Sense of Intractable Environmental Conflicts: Concepts and Cases* (Washington, DC: Island Press, 2003); and Andrew Hoffman, *Carbon Strategies: How Leading Companies Are Reducing Their Climate Change Footprint* (Ann Arbor: University of Michigan Press, 2007).
75. Marc S. Reisch, "Twenty Years after Bhopal: Smokescreen or True Reform? Has the Chemical Industry Changed Enough to Make Another Massive Accident Unlikely?" *Chemical and Engineering News*, June 7, 2004, 19–23.
76. Environmental Protection Agency, *Improving Our Regulations: A Preliminary Plan for Periodic Retrospective Review of Existing Regulations* (Washington, DC: EPA, May 24, 2011).
77. Environmental Protection Agency, "Retrospective Review History," *Laws and Regulations*, https://www.epa.gov/laws-regulations/retrospective-review-history.
78. Larry Makinson and Joshua Goldstein, *The Cash Constituents of Congress* (Washington, DC: Center for Responsive Politics, 1994).
79. Amanda Peterka, "Oil Industry Warns against 'Massive and Disruptive' Tightening of Ozone Standard," *EE News PM*, May 27, 2014.
80. Jack Ewing, "Inside VW's Campaign of Trickery," *New York Times*, May 7, 2017.
81. David M. Driesen, *The Economic Dynamics of Environmental Law* (Cambridge, MA: MIT Press, 2003).
82. Herman Daly, *Beyond Growth: The Economics of Sustainable Development* (Boston: Beacon Press, 1996). For a discussion of true cost economics, see Brendan Themes, "True Cost Economics: The Current Economic Model Has Failed Us," *Utne Reader*, August 26, 2004, http://www.utne.com/community/truecosteconomics.
83. Tiffany Hsu, "Venture Capital Sweeps into Clean-Tech Industry," *Los Angeles Times*, May 2, 2011; Charles Fleming, "Tesla Motors Picks Nevada for Planned $5-Billion Factory Site," *Los Angeles Times*, August 4, 2014.

Chapter 12

Taking Sustainable Cities Seriously
What Cities Are Doing
Kent E. Portney

I f the "sustainability epoch" of environmental policy described by Daniel Mazmanian and Michael Kraft seems completely foreign to national policymakers in Washington, DC, it has nonetheless taken hold in many of the world's cities, including in numerous cities in the United States.[1] This chapter takes a close look at what cities in the United States are doing in order to try to become more sustainable. The focus here is on local public policies and programs that are designed to make progress toward protecting and improving cities' biophysical environments while still seeking to grow municipal economies. Over the last twenty years or more, many U.S. cities have made significant commitments to achieving these goals. They have enacted and implemented many different types of programs and policies, and have sought to do this with an eye toward becoming more livable and sustainable places.

Of course, cities vary in how seriously they pursue these goals, and they vary in what kinds of programs and policies they create. After briefly discussing the idea and origins of city sustainability, this chapter will review the wide array of local policies and programs that major U.S. cities have adopted and implemented in the pursuit of sustainability, providing examples from a range of cities that have made significant commitments. The chapter ends with a look at some of the challenges that cities face as they try to do more and then suggests some strategies to facilitate these efforts.

The Idea of Sustainability in Cities

Sustainability is a very broad, and sometimes misunderstood, concept that has evolved over the last 30 years or so.[2] The core of the concept of sustainability, as articulated in the 1987 report of the United Nations' World Commission on Environment and Development, refers to economic development activity that "meets the needs of the present without compromising the ability of future generations to meet their own needs."[3] This means that sustainability does not readily accept a trade-off between protecting the environment and growing the economy; rather, the two go hand in hand to support and improve human well-being. Sustainability has become an important principle in a variety of contexts, including the private sector (as discussed by Press and Mazmanian in Chapter 11), state government (as discussed by Rabe in Chapter 2), and others.

297

Over the more than twenty years since U.S. cities started developing sustainability programs, experience and research have painted a fairly clear picture of what cities can do if they wish to try to become more sustainable places. One aspect of sustainability that seems to be constant across nearly all definitions is the fact that the environment is at the core of what it means to be, or become more, sustainable. Today, as will be elaborated below, cities' efforts to try to become more sustainable have included policies and programs on mass transit and transit-oriented development, smart growth, energy efficiency, housing densification, water conservation and protection, climate protection (climate mitigation and adaptation), carbon footprint reduction, and urban agriculture and food systems. Although early research argued that such sustainability programs only were found in wealthy places, places with a well-educated population, or cities on the West Coast, subsequent analysis has firmly established that communities of all sorts have successfully pursued sustainability policies. The fact is, many U.S. cities—indeed, cities around the world—have come to understand that to grow and thrive, they need to pay close attention to the quality of life offered to current and prospective residents. Cities may embark on sustainability policies because they wish to be responsive to demands placed by residents through local environmental and other nonprofit groups, but they quickly learn that these policies represent a new and effective way to engage in economic development.

City Sustainability Policies and Programs

What can a city do to try to become more sustainable? In fact, based on the efforts of cities all around the United States, cities can do a lot. What have cities done as a matter of local public policy in order to try to become more sustainable? By 2016, at least forty-nine of the fifty-five largest cities in the United States had created significant sustainability programs, and only five seem to have made no effort to try explicitly to become more sustainable as a matter of public policy.[4] Sustainability programs take many different forms and include many different programmatic elements. In Seattle, the heart of the program is found in the city's comprehensive plan "Toward a Sustainable Seattle." In New York City, sustainability represents the core of its OneNYC. In Philadelphia, the program is encapsulated in its Greenworks Philadelphia program. In Denver, the sustainability program got its start in the Greenprint Denver program. After more than twenty years of experience, cities have tended to settle on several dozen specific types of programs and policies. Of course, not all cities are the same. Some take a much more comprehensive approach to their policies than others. After this chapter reviews an array of municipal sustainability policies and programs, variations across the fifty-five largest U.S. cities will become evident.

The content of cities' sustainability efforts spans a wide range of programs and environmental results. The policies and programs include general statements of sustainability policy as reflected in city comprehensive plans, planning documents, and resolutions of chief executives and legislative bodies. They also include specific programs designed to address climate protection (climate change mitigation and adaptation), energy efficiency, smart growth, and the reduction of metropolitan sprawl. Many other initiatives are pursued as well, such as developing transit-oriented housing, housing densification, and the protection of environmentally sensitive lands. We can think of thirty-eight categories of these kinds of actions, and they focus on programs and policies that include the following: household and industrial recycling, hazardous waste recycling, brownfield redevelopment, hazardous waste site remediation, tax incentives for environmentally friendly development, alternatively fueled city vehicles, car pool lanes, the operation of public transportation, eco-industrial projects, the use of zoning to protect environmentally vulnerable land, air emissions (greenhouse gas) reduction and climate mitigation and adaptation, bicycle ridership, asbestos and lead abatement, green building, urban infill and transit-oriented housing development, energy efficiency, renewable energy for city and general residential customers, water conservation and water quality protection, recycling wastewater and reduction in stormwater runoff, creating a citywide comprehensive sustainability plan, having a single city agency responsible for managing sustainability, green city purchasing, and initiating a sustainability indicators or performance management program.

Table 12-1 shows the results of an assessment designed to determine how many different program elements each of the largest U.S. cities had adopted and implemented as of July 2012. This assessment is based on a comprehensive effort to examine cities' policies and programs by considering materials available on each city's respective website, by consulting independent surveys of city officials, and by talking to selected city administrators. In order for a city's program to be counted, there must be tangible evidence that it has actually been implemented in some way. A program that exists only on paper would not be counted in this assessment. The evidence to support the assessments is found in the context of city sustainability and comprehensive plans, and from the programs that are operated by a variety of different city departments.

The results show that three cities have adopted and implemented thirty-five of the thirty-eight different policies and programs—Portland, Oregon; San Francisco, California; and Seattle, Washington. Denver, Colorado, has adopted thirty-three programs. Oakland, California; Charlotte, North Carolina; and Albuquerque, New Mexico, have adopted thirty-two; and six cities have adopted thirty-one each. At the lower end, Virginia Beach, Virginia, and Detroit, Michigan, have adopted seventeen; Santa Ana, California, and Pittsburgh, Pennsylvania, have adopted sixteen each; and Wichita, Kansas, has adopted only seven. The exact content of these efforts may well vary considerably. Although Portland, San Francisco, and Seattle reside at the top of the list, the character of any one particular type of program could very well differ. All three cities have energy efficiency programs, yet the programs differ in how they have gone about trying to achieve greater efficiency. These latter differences are not captured in the sustainability scores presented in Table 12-1.

Table 12-1   2012 Sustainability Scores for the Fifty-Five Largest
U.S. Cities

City	Sustainability Score	City	Sustainability Score
Portland	**35**	Louisville	26
San Francisco	**35**	Miami	26
Seattle	**35**	Raleigh	26
Denver	**33**	San Antonio	26
Albuquerque	32	Baltimore	25
Charlotte	32	El Paso	25
Oakland	32	Cleveland	24
Chicago	**31**	Milwaukee	24
Columbus	31	Atlanta	23
Minneapolis	31	Jacksonville	23
Philadelphia	**31**	Honolulu	22
Phoenix	31	Houston	22
Sacramento	31	Long Beach	22
New York City	**30**	Mesa	22
San Diego	30	Arlington, TX	20
San Jose	30	Memphis	20
Austin	**29**	Tampa	20
Dallas	29	Tulsa	20
Fort Worth	29	Colorado Springs	19
Nashville	29	Omaha	19
Tucson	29	St. Louis	19
Washington, DC	29	Oklahoma City	18
Boston	28	Detroit	17
Kansas City	28	Virginia Beach	17
Los Angeles	**28**	Pittsburgh	16
Indianapolis	27	Santa Ana	16
Fresno	26	Wichita	7
Las Vegas	26		

Source: Drawn from Kent E. Portney, *Taking Sustainable Cities Seriously: Economic Development, the Environment, and Quality of Life in American Cities,* 2nd ed. (Cambridge, MA: MIT Press, 2013), 23–24, updated. The sustainability score in the table refers to the number of sustainability programs enacted and implemented out of a maximum of thirty-eight.

Note: Cities profiled in this chapter are in bold.

It should also be noted that this chapter focuses on cities' policies and programs—the programs that they have adopted and implemented in their efforts to try to become more sustainable. It is perhaps natural to want to know what these programs have achieved—what their results are. Yet assessing the "outcomes" of these programs is no small task, and indeed, there are no comprehensive data available to allow such assessments to be conducted. As cities push forward with their programs, our understanding of the efficacy of these programs will improve. At this moment, however, it is not possible to know with any degree of accuracy whether these programs have improved the quality of the air, the water, and the environment broadly.

City Sustainability Programs: A Closer Look

One way to get a sense of the character of cities' sustainability programs is to look at them as individual cases and to describe in detail what they are doing. This chapter provides at least a glimpse into what a number of U.S. cities are doing in their efforts to try to become more sustainable. We will first look at four large cities—New York City, Los Angeles, Chicago, and Philadelphia. These cities are very similar in terms of the numbers of specific programs they have implemented, having adopted and implemented between twenty-eight and thirty-one of the programs. After discussing these four cities, our attention will turn to a group of five cities with populations of between 450,000 and 800,000 people according to the 2010 U.S. Census. This group represents the cities that are the most aggressive in trying to become more sustainable. All of these cities have adopted between twenty-nine and thirty-five of the programs, with Seattle, San Francisco, and Portland at the top of the list, in terms of their sustainability scores, of the cities considered in Table 12-1. Finally, we will take a look at two smaller cities within this group—Denver and Austin—chosen to illustrate how much even smaller cities can accomplish. What these cities also tend to have in common is that they have been able to pursue sustainability and grow their local economies by protecting the environment.

Sustainability in Four Large Cities

Although four of the five largest cities in the United States, New York City, Los Angeles, Chicago, and Philadelphia, came to the pursuit of sustainability somewhat later than many other cities, they nonetheless have gotten very serious about enacting and implementing programs. Because of their population sizes, and perhaps their geographic sizes as well, these four cities face a somewhat more formidable set of challenges than do other cities, and that is perhaps why these cities did not stand out as early adopters of sustainability programs and policies.

New York City. New York City's sustainability effort is summarized in its OneNYC plan, an updated version of the earlier PlaNYC, a comprehensive plan first released in 2007 during the administration of Mayor Michael Bloomberg. PlaNYC addressed ten different sustainability-related policy areas and involved at least twenty-five major city departments and agencies,[5] all geared toward the city's effort to create jobs while protecting the environment and becoming more resilient in the face of rising sea levels and increasingly severe storms. The 2011 update of PlaNYC contained 132 specific program initiatives with over four hundred "milestones" or goals to be achieved between 2013 and 2030, and it addressed sustainability issues related to the city's housing and neighborhoods, parks and public spaces, brownfield redevelopment, waterways and water resources, transportation, energy, air quality and climate action, and solid waste, as well as "crosscutting" issues such as public health, food, natural systems, green building, waterfront development, economic development, and public engagement. The 2011 plan update provided a comprehensive implementation plan and assessment, showing each milestone or goal, its timeline, what had been accomplished, who was responsible for accomplishing it, where the funding was supposed to come from, and what progress had been made to date.[6] It also presented the city's sustainability indicators report, with annual progress report assessments of accomplishments in twenty-nine broad indicators. The explicit inclusion and treatment of public health as part of its sustainability plan stands out, as very few other cities make this connection.[7]

OneNYC, released in 2015 under the administration of Mayor Bill de Blasio, represents an expansion of PlaNYC, adding goals related to making the city more resilient and increasing emphasis on issues of environmental equity. It is organized around four broad "visions": to promote economic growth and development, to achieve greater equity in public services and public well-being, to become more sustainable and aggressive in fighting climate change, and to adapt to the realities of climate change by becoming more resilient. So what does OneNYC prescribe for programs and goals related to the environment and environmental sustainability? Most of the goals associated with the biophysical environment are incorporated in Vision 3, referred to as "Our Sustainability City," and address climate protection, energy, air quality, water, hazardous and solid waste, and many other areas. The city's climate plan contains dozens of different initiatives with associated milestones, including conducting and releasing an annual inventory of greenhouse gas emissions, assessing opportunities to further reduce greenhouse gas emissions by 80 percent by 2050, regularly assessing climate change projections, partnering with the Federal Emergency Management Agency to update flood insurance rate maps, developing tools to measure the city's current and future climate exposure, updating regulations to increase the resilience of buildings, working with the insurance industry to develop strategies to encourage the use of flood protection in buildings, protecting New York City's critical infrastructure, identifying and evaluating citywide coastal protective measures, mitigating the urban heat island effect, and enhancing the city's understanding of the impacts of climate change on public health.

Ostensibly, all of the programs and projects outlined in the sustainability vision, along with many of those associated with the fourth vision, "Our Resilient City," represent a full statement of the city's policy and planning around the environment. A few of the pertinent policies outlined in

Vision 4 include the effort to integrate climate change projections into emergency management and preparedness, working with communities and neighborhoods to increase their climate resilience, and improving the city's critical infrastructure.[8]

OneNYC is designed to be used, in part, as an implementation tool, as it specifies performance metrics or measures, along with goals and milestones for each action area. Even so, some of the action areas and milestones do not seem terribly well tailored to serve this purpose, particularly when the milestone is just a restatement of the action area. OneNYC provides assessments of progress on each milestone, although, unlike many other sustainability plans, it has no clear-cut interventions prescribed when milestones are not met. Presumably, the designation of funding sources, while typically not very specific, does provide some sense that internal funding decisions may well be tied to these action areas, milestones, and goals. And, of course, there is always the question as to whether any of the specific programs, when implemented, will have their intended effects on the environment or resiliency. For example, although there are no serious assessments available, Brian Paul argued that the NYC approach to transit-oriented development would actually increase the city's greenhouse gas emissions by putting many more motor vehicles on the streets.[9]

Los Angeles. Although Los Angeles had developed elements of a sustainability plan earlier, its sustainability policy became official in 2007 when the then mayor Antonio Villaraigosa issued Executive Directive 10, instructing all city departments to create sustainability plans. The city's Department of Environmental Affairs had primary responsibility for managing and coordinating these plans. Much of this sustainability effort focused on the environment. Programs such as the "Mayor's Green Agenda" and green infrastructure, air quality and climate change, green building, energy, solid and hazardous waste, brownfield redevelopment, water, and urban habitats initiatives were all placed under the auspices of the Environmental Affairs Office. Los Angeles has not worked from a single comprehensive sustainability plan; instead, it defined specific programs, which, taken together, make up its initiative. Sustainability plans in many cities change when the political leadership changes, and this is true in Los Angeles. With the election of Eric Garcetti as mayor in 2013, only time will tell whether these initiatives will continue, get stronger, or take a back seat to others. It is already clear that sustainability is not particularly important to Garcetti, as reflected in his elimination of the Department of Environmental Affairs, whose functions have been distributed to numerous other agencies, and in his message of "back to basics," which apparently do not place a high priority on sustainability.

Over the last decade, one of the key components of the Los Angeles sustainability program has been the city's Green LA climate change initiative. The program is complemented by a Clean Air Action Plan, which calls for the city to reduce its greenhouse gas emissions 35 percent below 1990 levels by 2030 and to increase the city's use of renewable energy to 40 percent by

2020. The plan includes about fifty specific initiatives designed to produce the targeted carbon reduction levels, such as the increased use of energy-efficient lighting, extensive plans for green building, and the hallmark creation of an extensive wind turbine farm. In 2009, Los Angeles completed the construction of the Pine Tree Wind Power Project, consisting of eighty municipally owned wind turbines producing about 120 megawatts of electricity to serve about 56,000 households in the city. The Los Angeles Department of Water and Power operates this facility, along with numerous other energy efficiency and alternative energy programs, and claims to be on track to generate 20 percent of the city's energy from renewable sources by 2020.

The Los Angeles sustainability program also includes efforts to convert the city's fleet vehicles to ones using alternative fuels, a bicycle ridership program, a significant brownfield redevelopment effort, and extensive tree and native planting efforts. Two specific initiatives deserve special mention. The first, a major initiative on water conservation, is important because of the limited supplies available to the city. The second, a commitment to public transit, focuses its attention on the city's relatively new subway system. Operated by the Los Angeles County Metropolitan Transportation Authority (Metro), the regional transit authority, the subway system is much smaller than those in other major cities, including New York, Boston, Philadelphia, San Francisco, and Washington, DC. About 150,000 people ride the subway daily, with estimated ridership per mile of track making it the ninth busiest subway in the United States. The system has received extensive criticism, primarily for its cost and, because the population of Los Angeles is so widely dispersed, for "not going anywhere" that people want to go. Yet one of the purposes of the system was to influence the patterns of new development, encouraging more transit-oriented development and nudging people back toward the "downtown" of the city. Whether and to what extent this has started to happen is still unclear.

Chicago. By the time Mayor Richard M. Daley declared that Chicago would become the greenest city in America, he had already made a commitment to improving the biophysical environment of the city. Particularly over the last five or so years of his twenty-two-year tenure as mayor, Daley and his administration made significant commitments to sustainability. Although making substantial changes to the way the people operate in a city is fraught with challenges and obstacles, the city created a Department of Environment, headed by a commissioner, with four offices each headed by a deputy commissioner. These offices, Energy and Sustainable Business, Permitting and Enforcement, Natural Resources and Water Quality, and Urban Management and Brownfield Redevelopment, combine a number of traditional city functions, such as permitting, with a broader environmental mandate. Additionally, the city's Department of Planning and Development has a division of Sustainable Development with responsibility for applying sustainable design to all of the city's economic and housing development projects. Together, these made up the heart of the administrative apparatus responsible for sustainability until 2012 when the city released a comprehensive sustainability plan. Under Mayor Rahm Emanuel, a Sustainability Council, composed of numerous department heads, was established, as was the office of "Chief Sustainability Officer."

Unlike New York City or Philadelphia, Chicago did not have a unified, comprehensive sustainability plan until 2012. Previously, "greening" efforts were defined fairly piecemeal, with many different departments developing a part of the overall effort. For example, the Sustainable Development division worked with a guide for encouraging, and sometimes requiring, green urban design in new construction. This plan, *Adding Green to Urban Design*, was probably the closest thing to a full sustainability plan in the city until the release of the 2015 Sustainable Chicago Action Plan.[10] The primary purpose of the earlier document was to provide all city departments, the city council, and the city Plan Commission with some guidance as to what constitutes sustainable development, so they could apply sustainability principles when it was time to review and approve specific development projects. The guide provided a rationale for why each proposed project needed to take into consideration a wide array of environmental impacts on the land, the air, the water, and ultimately the quality of life in the city. Presumably, the intent behind this effort was to encourage the disapproval of projects that did not meet the implied standards of what constitutes sustainable development.

But certainly not all of the programs and policies that make up Chicago's sustainability activities are contained in this, or any other, single document. For example, the Sustainable Development division also has responsibility for the Eat Local, Live Healthy program, outlined in a separate document.[11] This program seeks to coordinate Chicago's sustainable food system in order to support local and regional agriculture while improving human nutrition and health. Another program not represented in any comprehensive plan is the Department of Aviation's Sustainable Airport Initiatives, designed to encourage the airports in the city to adopt a variety of practices that are consistent with sustainability in construction, renovation, and daily operations.[12] The city's Department of Transportation has responsibility for traffic management, including a bicycle ridership program, but the mass transit system is managed by the Chicago Transit Authority, an independent agency. Climate action has been tackled by a task force appointed by the mayor and operating as a nonprofit organization called the Chicago Climate Action Plan. This group, which works with the Chicago Department of the Environment and Sustainability and many other city agencies, has responsibility for the city's greenhouse gas inventory, and for the plan to reduce the city's carbon footprint.[13] The city still operates under the 2015 Action Plan, which incorporates and consolidates the various elements developed previously.[14]

Philadelphia. Although there were rumblings of interest in sustainability during the latter part of the term of former mayor John F. Street, it wasn't until the beginning of Mayor Michael Nutter's administration in 2008 that the city seemingly started to get interested in sustainability issues. Nutter campaigned, in part, on a platform of engaging the city in a major sustainability effort, and, upon taking office, he created the Mayor's Office of Sustainability, now a permanent part of the city's administrative structure.

The city's comprehensive plan is founded on the "five Es" of sustainability: energy, environment, equity, economy, and engagement. It has outlined three target areas for energy: to lower city government energy use by 30 percent between 2008 and 2015; to reduce citywide building energy consumption by 10 percent over this same period; and to retrofit 15 percent of the city's housing stock with insulation, air sealing, and cool roofs. The three environmental target areas include reducing greenhouse gas emissions by 20 percent, improving overall air quality to attain federal standards, and the diversion of 70 percent of solid waste from landfills. The plan's four equity targets are to manage stormwater to meet federal standards, to provide parks and recreation resources within ten minutes for 75 percent of residents, to bring local food within ten minutes of 75 percent of residents, and to increase tree coverage toward 30 percent in all neighborhoods by 2025. The three economy targets focus on reducing vehicle miles traveled by 10 percent, increasing the state of repair of the city's resilient infrastructure, and doubling the number of low- and high-skill green jobs. The single "engagement target" is to engage residents in the definition, planning, and evaluation of the results of the initiatives used to achieve the plan's targets.

Philadelphia's Local Action Plan for Climate Change is a significant part of the responsibility of Greenworks Philadelphia. Unlike many other cities, Philadelphia conceives of climate action as an explicit part of sustainability. Its greenhouse gas emission reduction goals are embedded in its environmental targets.[15] Its greenhouse gas inventory, efforts to reduce emissions, and progress toward achieving those reductions are reported in the Greenworks Philadelphia annual report.[16] Additionally, the city has worked closely with its regional transit authority, the Southeastern Pennsylvania Transit Authority (SEPTA), to coordinate emissions reduction strategies.

Although the Greenworks Philadelphia progress report itemizes dozens of specific activities, projects, and programs designed to achieve results in the fifteen target areas, including the installation of biodiesel fueling stations for city vehicles, the installation of porous pavement on city streets, and partnerships with local businesses, including an arrangement with the Philadelphia Eagles professional football team to make its stadium energy independent, three specific efforts at implementing its programs deserve additional discussion here. First, as one of Greenworks Philadelphia's equity targets, the Mayor's Office of Sustainability worked with the U.S. Forest Service to launch a local carbon offset market. This simple idea makes a personal carbon footprint calculator available to residents and provides an opportunity for residents to purchase carbon offsets; collected funds go to the Fairmount Park Conservancy to support its extensive tree-planting program.[17] Second, in order to implement its energy conservation and climate action programs, the city developed numerous initiatives to help building owners retrofit their facilities. Although many cities have created similar programs, Philadelphia has explicitly made this an equity target with the intent of making sure that the benefits of energy savings are broadly distributed across neighborhoods within the city. And third, the city took the unusual step of creating an Office of Watersheds within the Water Department to manage its water resources and wastewater with an eye toward explicitly protecting the seven watershed areas that service the city. Although all cities are serviced by watersheds and all cities have administrative agencies responsible for managing water and wastewater, Philadelphia is perhaps the first to organize and manage these administrative functions while paying such unequivocal attention to watersheds. This, of course, requires a high degree of collaboration and cooperation with other municipal water agencies.[18]

Five Cities that Seem to Take Sustainability Seriously

The next set of five selected cities profiled here provides a glimpse into the actual workings of cities' sustainability initiatives. Although their programs differ, the cities share the fact that sustainability plays a prominent role in their activities. The operational definition of sustainability varies across the cities, but all five cities seem to understand sustainability as a multidimensional concept, involving many different functional departments and activities, engaging at some level other levels of government, and requiring a relatively high level of internal coordination. All five cities have populations of nearly half a million people or more. Two of the cities, Austin and San Francisco, are fairly large, with populations of around three-quarters of a million. San Francisco, Seattle, and Portland are cities whose populations are part of much larger metropolitan areas, while Austin makes up substantial portions of its metropolitan area. All of these cities experienced population growth over the twenty-year period starting in 1990, with San Francisco (already one of the more densely populated major cities in the United States) experiencing the slowest growth.

These five cities have perhaps the most extensive commitments to sustainability policies and programs of any of the largest cities in the United States, with San Francisco, Seattle, and Portland having the top sustainability scores and Denver close behind. If American cities have made significant strides in taking sustainability seriously, it is cities in this population range that deserve the lion's share of the credit. A look at some of the central policies and programs in these cities gives an idea of the depth and breadth of their commitment.

San Francisco. The sustainability initiative in San Francisco is notable for the remarkable breadth of the city's conception of sustainability and perhaps for its lack of early success in moving sustainability issues onto the public agenda. San Francisco is also one of the few cities that incorporates a serious equity dimension in the broad view of sustainability, going well beyond the equity concerns that may be reflected in an indicators project. Overall, San Francisco is at the very top of the list of cities in terms of the numbers of programs and policies, with a sustainability index score of 35.

Sustainability in San Francisco received a major initial push in 1996 with the release of the city's Sustainability Plan.[19] This plan created the blueprint for a wide array of programs, policies, and resolutions across numerous substantive areas, including air quality, biodiversity, energy, climate change and ozone depletion, food and agriculture, hazardous materials, human health, parks, open spaces and streetscapes, solid waste, transportation, water and wastewater, the economy and economic development, and environmental justice.

The sustainability initiative, particularly the indicators project, was the product of the operation of a nonprofit organization called Sustainable City, which sought not only to develop the indicators but also to serve as an advocacy voice to help place sustainability on the city's public agenda. Largely as a result of the work of this organization, the city government's involvement has been through the city's Commission on the Environment, consisting of seven members all appointed by the mayor, which is charged with setting policy and advising all other city agencies and the Board of Supervisors. The commission works primarily with the city's Department of the Environment (often referred to as SFEnvironment), which is the central agency with any responsibility for developing and implementing the sustainability plan itself. The Department of the Environment is one of a handful of departments in the city that reports directly to the city's professional chief administrator.

Finding programmatic manifestations of the sustainability program in the city's administrative agencies is somewhat more challenging in San Francisco than in most other cities profiled here. The Commission on the Environment and the Department of the Environment are fairly active in identifying specific and narrowly targeted issues to confront and to seek approval for from the Board of Supervisors, and the department has focused much of its attention on ordinances that require, and pilot projects that achieve, greater resource efficiency in city buildings. The standard operating mode for the commission is to present specific issue resolutions to the Board of Supervisors for ratification. Over the last several years, the board has approved resolutions on such issues as discouraging the purchase of non-recycled beverage bottles, prohibiting the intentional release of balloons into the air, encouraging the use of alternatively fueled public transit vehicles, and reducing pesticides.[20]

One of the more unusual programs of the Department of the Environment is the city's biodiesel initiative. Encouraged by the Commission on the Environment and the Biodiesel Access Task Force, established in 2006, the city embarked on a major effort to promote the refining and use of biodiesel fuels, which were made up of about 20 percent refined cooking oils collected from around the city. Policies called for city vehicles to maximize their use of such fuels because they had lower greenhouse gas emissions than pure diesel fuel. The policy was designed to make biodiesel as available generally as possible, and it called for the creation of a full infrastructure and permit process to refine, distribute, store, and sell such fuels.[21] Accompanying then mayor Gavin Newsom's announcement that all 1,500 diesel vehicles had been prepared to run on diesel fuel was the disclosure of plans to build a refining facility to produce up to ten million gallons of fuel a year, a plan that came into conflict with the city's environmental justice policy.[22]

Sustainability in San Francisco seems to incorporate environmental justice or equity at a higher level than is common in the vast majority of other cities. Although equity is often described as one of the key "*Es*" in sustainability, most cities are very slow or very reticent to operationalize this concept at the policy level. San Francisco's sustainability effort focuses on environmental justice with respect to five environmental outcomes: air quality, energy, land use, food security, and health. Essentially, when the city formulates and adopts policies in these areas, and especially when it implements these policies, there is elevated cognition that officials need to be particularly sensitive to the distributional aspects of plans and programs. In one area, land use, there is reason to believe that a decision to decommission a fossil fuel–burning electricity-generating facility at Bayview–Hunters Point was motivated, at least in part, by concerns over the disproportionate effects local minority residents experienced from the air emissions.[23] Even so, these policies on equity ended up being confronted by the city's plan to build a biodiesel refinery when Hunters Point was designated as the site for this facility. This plan was blocked by the neighborhood, and eventually the area became host to a community microgrid project with emphasis on renewable energy sources.

Seattle. The city that stands at the top of virtually every list of sustainable cities, particularly those cities that have developed major indicators projects, is Seattle. The sustainability efforts in Seattle are found in both the nonprofit and governmental sectors, but the city's initiative is primarily associated with the activities of a single organization: Sustainable Seattle. This organization was founded in 1990 and began its operations in 1991. It was conceived of as a nonprofit organization (it currently operates under a 501(c)(3) tax status designation), and its origins are significantly more "grassroots" than are the sustainability initiatives in most other cities. The organization, which is governed by a board of directors and has a small staff, describes itself as a "volunteer-based civic network and forum . . . with a focus on the metropolitan city/county area" of Seattle.

The articulation of this organization's mission has changed over time, from an effort to "protect and improve [the Seattle] area's long-term health and vitality by applying sustainability to the links between economic prosperity, environmental vitality, and social equity," in 2000, to an effort "to balance concerns for social equity, ecological health, and economic vitality to create livable communities today while ensuring a healthy and fulfilling legacy for our children's children," in 2014.[24] Out of the mission has grown some six specific goals that include influencing individual and collective local actions that are thought to move the city toward greater sustainability; preparing and publishing sustainable community indicators; providing extensive information about sustainability to residents and local leaders; putting issues of sustainability on the "agenda" in people's homes, neighborhoods, places of employment, and schools, and in civic life generally; providing an open forum for "cross-community dialog" on issues of sustainability; and serving as a general resource center.

Perhaps the key defining characteristic of Sustainable Seattle, the characteristic that gave this initiative national notoriety and attention, is its Sustainable Indicators Project.[25] This project's notoriety grew not only out of the resulting indicators themselves but also out of the processes that were used to produce them. Consistent with Sustainable Seattle's goal of providing a cross-community forum for discussion of sustainability issues, the Indicators Project sought to derive its indicators through a fairly participatory process.

As impressive as the Sustainable Seattle organization and its Indicators Project have been, they tell only part of the sustainable city story in Seattle. The organization certainly articulates a goal of influencing local collective actions, but the organization does not itself have any sort of legal authority for adopting or implementing policies that promote sustainable growth. The organization can use (and has used) its sustainability indicators as a political weapon, for example, by reporting the nonattainment of specific environmental goals, but it cannot directly establish public programs that will ensure that the goals are met or that progress is made toward meeting the goals. In other words, Sustainable Seattle can measure progress toward achieving greater sustainability or the lack thereof, but it cannot directly change the city's policies and programs that affect this progress. Yet what makes the Seattle experience most impressive is the way that the city's leaders, particularly the city's administrative agencies, have begun to internalize the goals of sustainability.

In 1994, the city adopted its "Comprehensive Plan," called "Toward a Sustainable Seattle," which provides a statement of a "20-year policy plan that articulates a vision of how Seattle will grow in ways that sustain its citizens' values." This comprehensive plan represents a sustainability effort that is about as well developed and coordinated as that found in any U.S. city. The plan outlines policies that, in a fairly integrated way, affect land use, transportation, housing, capital facilities, utilities, economic development, neighborhood development and planning, human development, and cultural resources.

The Sustainable Seattle "model" or "approach" is one that prescribes the creation of a grassroots nonprofit organization that begins its initiative independent of city government or city agencies. The basic idea seems to be that once the organization takes hold, once it embarks on an indicators project and shows that it has the support of significant segments of the local population, then it can appeal to city policymakers—the mayor and city councilors—and city agency administrators to make the case that sustainability should be on the city's agenda. To local advocates of sustainability, this model or approach seems to make perfect sense. Yet to at least one observer of the Seattle experience, the inability of the nonprofit organization to directly affect sustainability itself constitutes a major shortcoming. Because the nonprofit organization possesses no legal authority for affecting public policy, and typically does not actually operate any pollution reduction programs directly, the impact of the organization on sustainability is indirect at best. This constitutes a major problem according to Jeb Brugmann, who discounts the role that this organization may have played in helping to affect the local political agenda.[26] Yet nothing in the mandatory strategic planning process in Seattle ensured that sustainability would become the cornerstone of the effort. Indeed, without the efforts of the Sustainable Seattle organization, it is entirely possible that sustainability would have played no more than a minor part in the city's planning.

Portland. Although Portland, Oregon, is not often identified as a prototypical sustainable city, there is little question that, upon examination, it possesses one of the most impressive sustainability initiatives of any major city. Portland was one of the earliest cities to become involved in explicit efforts to become more sustainable, enacting in 1993 a policy on global warming that called for the reduction of the city's carbon dioxide emissions by 20 percent from 1990 to 2010. In 1994, the city adopted a set of ten sustainable city principles that reflected the long-term commitment of the city government to pursuing a variety of specific policies. Portland's sustainability initiative is perhaps most like that found in Seattle where sustainability goals are an integral part of the city's Comprehensive Plan. The role of sustainability in the city oozes out of every ounce of the city's government operations and affects the way the government is organized and functions. The city established a single agency with central programmatic and coordinating functions, the Office of Sustainable Development, an expanded version of the office previously called the Office of Energy, and now called the Bureau of Planning and Sustainability. In conjunction with the Sustainable Portland Commission, an organization of volunteers appointed by the mayor, this bureau operates or coordinates programs on business conservation, residential conservation, global warming, solid waste and recycling, and sustainable development. Many of the clean water operations and services fall to the Bureau of Water and the Bureau of Environmental Services.

Perhaps the most important part of Portland's sustainability effort can be found in its comprehensive plan, the Portland Plan. As in Seattle's Comprehensive Plan, sustainability represents a high priority and permeates Portland's plan. Although the environment and energy constitute two of the twelve main elements in the plan, sustainability goals are threaded throughout. The plan specifies for each element, including energy and the environment, a set of goals along with the policies, programs, and actions that are necessary to achieve those goals. In 1996, for example, the plan called for the city to "promote a sustainable energy future by increasing energy efficiency in all sectors of the city by ten percent by the year 2000," goals that were apparently achieved. The goals are accompanied by specification of numerous detailed objectives, along with two-year and long-term action plans for implementing and accomplishing these goals and objectives. For example, a two-year action plan for the goal of increasing waste reduction and recycling specified that the city had to "set up recycling programs for an additional 500 multifamily buildings and 20 downtown commercial buildings." Frequently, the plan specifies which agencies are responsible for accomplishing the goals and identifies any changes in policies or ordinances that might be required to achieve them. Although the Portland Plan presents a comprehensive view of its sustainability goals, the city also works under a separate climate action plan.[27]

Denver. Denver has a fairly lengthy history of efforts to become more sustainable. Substantial support for the goal of sustainability was clearly expressed in the city's 2000 comprehensive plan, which called for specific attention to "environmental sustainability," and in its strategic transit-oriented development plan.[28] The city's sustainability efforts became formalized in 2007 when then mayor John Hickenlooper signed an executive order creating the Greenprint Denver city office and charged it with administering a full array of sustainability programs, including green building, the city's alternative fuel replacement vehicle program, waste management and recycling, water conservation, and environmental health.[29] Hickenlooper also created the Mayor's Greenprint Council, an oversight committee composed of representatives from various city agencies, experts from the University of Colorado in Denver, and others. Near the very top of the rankings reported in Table 12-1, Denver had embarked on efforts to adopt and implement thirty-three of the thirty-eight policies and programs by 2012, putting it squarely in fourth place among the largest U.S. cities.

Greenprint Denver, now implemented by the city's Office of Sustainability, works under an "action agenda," making efforts to increase city forest and tree coverage (including implementing the former mayor's challenge to plant a million trees), reduce wastes, increase reliance on renewable energy, increase green affordable housing, implement the city's green building program, expand the city's green motor fleet, promote and expand mass transit, improve the quality of water supplies and conserve them, promote green industry economic development, operate a bicycle ridership program, develop urban agriculture and a sustainable food system, implement an energy efficiency and water conservation program for low-income residents, and implement the city's climate action plan. It also operates a small business energy efficiency program.

Greenprint Denver and the Mayor's Greenprint Council have had primary responsibility for the city's climate action plan. Denver was an early signatory of the U.S. Conference of Mayors' Climate Protection Agreement. As a result, the city prepared and issued its action plan in 2007, a plan that included its greenhouse gas inventory based on 1990 and 2005 data. It also issued a one-year progress report.[30] The action plan articulated a goal of reducing per capita greenhouse gas emissions by 10 percent from 1990 levels by 2012, and it made ten specific programmatic recommendations for meeting this and subsequent targeted reductions. Until publication of the 2015 climate action plan, no climate action progress reports had been issued since 2007; also, by 2014, the climate action plan had spawned a "climate *adaptation*" plan, showing changing priorities.[31]

Although the vast majority of programs and policies related to sustainability are the responsibility of Greenprint Denver, many other agencies have programmatic responsibilities as well. Much of the city's sustainability effort is summarized in its comprehensive plans, and the Community Planning and Development Department and the Denver Planning Board have had major coordinating responsibilities for these. For example, in 2006, Denver announced a major initiative on transit-oriented development in order to facilitate the creation of urban villages, and this initiative involved other city agencies, county government, and the regional transit authority.[32] The city created a 2008 strategic plan for multimodal transportation to address the serious and growing problem of roadway congestion and reliance on personal motor vehicles for transportation.

One of Denver's most important sustainability-related accomplishments is associated with the Stapleton Development Plan. When Denver's Stapleton Airport was replaced in 1995, the city was left with a huge parcel of land available for redevelopment. Working with a number of regional partners, nonprofit groups, and governmental agencies, the city decided to embark on a $1 billion-plus effort to add well over ten thousand housing units, and to do it in a sustainable way—for example, with green building and transit-oriented planning—that was consistent with its "Green Book" sustainable development principles articulated by the Stapleton Foundation. By 2004, this redevelopment project became a full-fledged sustainability initiative.[33] Because the development is located well west of the downtown area of the city, light rail transit is intended to link residents with the city and with the new Denver International Airport, easing the need for reliance on personal motor vehicles.

Austin. In conjunction with the surrounding Travis, Williamson, and Hays Counties that constitute the greater Austin metropolitan area, Austin created an important sustainability initiative. It is important not just for its programmatic and policy elements but also because of its accomplishments in a state that does not make the pursuit of sustainability easy.[34] Austin's sustainability programs, including its Climate Protection Program, are primarily administered by its Sustainability Office.[35] The foundation of Austin's sustainability policies is found in its comprehensive plan, first called *Austin Tomorrow*, updated in 2012 as *ImagineAustin*, and last amended in 2016.[36] The Austin city council established sustainability as the central policy direction for the city's *ImagineAustin* comprehensive plan, which states that "[s]ustainability is the basis of the *ImagineAustin* vision statement and its hundreds of policies and actions developed through the input of thousands of community members." The plan provides guidance about the policies, programs, and priorities expressed by city leaders and includes sections outlining the city's desire to ensure the protection of the natural environment and open spaces, to engage in transit-oriented development and combat sprawl, and to ensure that its natural resources management is consistent with these goals. There are numerous elements to Austin's overall sustainability effort, and some of these are highlighted here.

Austin has had two sustainability indicators initiatives, one based in the larger multicounty metropolitan area and one for the city itself. The first is associated with what was originally the "Sustainability Indicators Project of Hays, Travis, and Williamson Counties," which expanded subsequently to include Bastrop, Burnet, and Caldwell Counties, the counties that constitute the metropolitan area for Austin (Austin is in Travis County).[37] Subsequently, this indicators project became known as the Central Texas Sustainability

Indicators Project. This indicators project, first developed in 1997, has more recently focused on a comprehensive array of some forty indicators and over 120 measures in nine major categories—demographics, public safety, education and children, social equity, engagement, the economy, the environment, health, and land use and mobility.[38] These indicators then became subsumed under the Community Advancement Network's Community Dashboard Report, where reference to the concept of sustainability largely disappeared.

Additionally, as the City of Austin itself moved more explicitly into sustainability efforts, it operated its own indicators project. Called "Sustainable Community," this project started in 1999 and became part of a citywide initiative to manage city government by results and to provide comprehensive reporting on government performance. The city's sustainability performance indicators covered public safety (fire and medical services, police, and the courts); youth, family, and neighborhood vitality (including health services, housing, libraries, and parks and recreation); sustainability (traffic and road maintenance, air quality, recycling and waste diversion, drinking water quality, lake and stream quality and water conservation, energy conservation, and inspections and site plan or subdivision review); and affordability.[39] These indicators were used as measures of the performance of local government, and, until 2004, results were reported annually in the City of Austin "Community Scorecard." After 2004, the performance indicators became folded into the performance management of each department and reported for the city as a whole by the Office of Sustainability.[40]

Another major component of Austin's sustainability effort is associated with its publicly owned electric utility, known as Austin Energy, and the recommendations of the Sustainable Energy Task Force. The sustainability efforts on energy use stem from the city council's resolution that 5 percent of the city's electricity should come from renewable sources by the year 2005. The utility operates a program that allows customers to elect the "GreenChoice" option by which they receive electricity generated from renewable sources at a fixed rate guaranteed for ten years, while traditional customers' rates are not guaranteed and fluctuate with the market price of fossil fuels. These renewable sources include wind, solar, and biogas, especially methane, from closed landfills. The utility owns and operates a wind turbine farm in West Texas that has generated 439 megawatts of electricity, and it purchases electricity from numerous other wind, solar, and biogas sources to provide additional renewable sources to power up to twenty thousand homes and businesses. Austin Energy also operates extensive energy conservation programs and created rebate programs for the installation of solar facilities on homes and commercial buildings.[41] In 2014, the Austin City Council passed a resolution approving a goal of zero carbon emissions from power plants by 2030, a far more ambitious goal than generating 35 percent of its electricity from renewable sources by 2020. Subsequently, the Austin Energy utility company made clear its opposition to this goal, claiming that electricity rates would skyrocket as a result.

Additionally, the city has developed and made a substantial investment in a "green building program" to provide technical information and guidance to developers concerning how to construct more environmentally friendly and energy-efficient buildings. The green building program, first established in 1991, has residential, municipal, and commercial components and includes an effort to encourage developers to engage in smart development. The Austin conception of green building, as noted in the program description, is that it "is based on a market-pull mechanism whereby the Green Building Program promotes green building practices, rates buildings that feature these practices, thus creating more demand from the public because these buildings are perceived as more attractive products for people to buy."[42]

Austin also engages in "transit-oriented development," namely, in land use planning to minimize reliance on private transportation; it has developed a "sustainable purchases protocol" for the municipal government that sets standards for city purchases of goods and services that are environmentally friendly; and it has developed a public-private partnership with the regional chamber of commerce. This last initiative, called Greater Austin@Work, is designed to foster economic development and job growth in sectors that produce fewer environmental impacts.[43]

Taking Sustainable Cities' Policies and Programs Seriously: A Summary and Thoughts for the Future

City sustainability policies span a wide array of specific programs designed to try to improve and protect the quality of the biophysical environment. These policies do this by addressing the quality of the air and by seeking to reduce greenhouse gas emissions, by trying to improve and protect access to high-quality drinking water, by managing wastewater and stormwater runoff, by managing how environmentally vulnerable or sensitive land is used, and by pursuing many other goals. When we look at efforts in these nine U.S. cities, it is clear that there is substantial variation in the extent to which cities seem to take the goal of sustainability seriously. Some cities, notably Portland, Seattle, San Francisco, and Denver, stand out as having the greatest commitment to sustainability, as is seen in their policies and programs. But all of the cities profiled here have accomplished impressive policy changes in pursuit of their sustainability goals. The exact content of their sustainability policies and programs varies, perhaps having been tailored to the specific conditions these cities face. Yet they all seem to have found ways of defining these policies so as to promote sustainability and to protect and improve the quality of the environment in ways never entertained years ago.

As these and other cities face the growing need to create or improve sustainability programs, they will discover that the challenge only gets more difficult. With two to three decades of experience, cities now face the challenge of developing a deeper understanding of what their policies and programs have accomplished. Have cities' climate protection programs really decreased their carbon and other greenhouse gas emissions? Have their energy conservation programs reduced energy consumption or altered the forms of energy their citizens consume? Has the quality of drinking water improved? These are the kinds of questions that cities and researchers need to focus on in the future.

Despite the idea that they will be able to share their experiences and find "best practices" to use as models, cities will face new environmental challenges that will undoubtedly make their work more daunting. Problems surrounding climate change—rising sea levels and increased storm surges from more intense weather events in coastal communities, drought and water shortages, and rising carbon dioxide emissions—promise to be long-term challenges. At the same time, many cities find that their efforts to pursue sustainability meet with political resistance from those who neither understand the magnitude of the environmental problems nor appreciate the governmental actions required to address them. A number of state governments, for example, have established policies barring their cities from operating sustainability or related programs. Although the U.S. federal government, particularly the U.S. Department of Energy and the U.S. Environmental Protection Agency, has provided modest support in the form of grants to help cities create sustainability programs, the future of these programs is anything but assured. Yet cities will likely continue to provide an important location for the pursuit of sustainability.

Suggested Websites

Partnership for Sustainable Communities (www.sustainablecommunities .gov) This collaborative effort on the part of the U.S. Environmental Protection Agency, the U.S. Department of Housing and Urban Development, and the U.S. Department of Transportation provides information and support to cities and towns.

ICLEI Local Governments for Sustainability USA (www.icleiusa .org) This is the American chapter of the international organization that was originally formed to help cities implement local Agenda 21 programs. It provides information and technical assistance to cities and towns that elect to become members.

STAR Communities (www.starcommunities.org/about) This nonprofit organization based in Washington, DC, provides its member cities and towns with "Sustainability Tools for Assessing and Rating Communities."

Our Green Cities (ourgreencities.com) This website and blog offers news and updates on progress in cities around the United States and provides summaries of and access to research on local sustainability policies and programs.

Smart Growth America (www.smartgrowthamerica.org) The organization advocates for a wide range of local "smart growth" policies and programs, and it provides support and advice to communities to promote sustainability leadership and coalition building.

100 Resilient Cities (www.100resilientcities.org) This nonprofit organization, started with support from the Rockefeller Foundation, provides guidance and assistance to cities around the world as they search for ways to cope with and prepare for the physical, economic, and social challenges associated with environmental changes.

U.S. Conference of Mayors Climate Protection Center (www.usmayors .org/mayors-climate-protection-center) The center provides mayors who enroll in its program with guidance, technical assistance, and "best practices" information focused on efforts to reduce carbon emissions.

International City/County Management Association—Sustainable Communities (icma.org/en/results/sustainable_communities/home) This section of the ICMA website provides members with extensive information about "best practices" and facilitates communications across cities.

Clinton Foundation—Climate Change (www.clintonfoundation.org/ our-work/by-topic/climate-change) This international effort provides technical assistance and resources to major cities around the world in order to help them reduce their air pollution and carbon emissions.

Notes

1. See Daniel A. Mazmanian and Michael E. Kraft, "The Three Epochs of the Environmental Movement," in *Toward Sustainable Communities: Transition and Transformations in Environmental Policy*, ed. Daniel A. Mazmanian and Michael E. Kraft (Cambridge, MA: MIT Press, 2009), 3–32.
2. Kent E. Portney, *Sustainability* (Cambridge, MA: MIT Press, 2015), 1–56.
3. World Commission on Environment and Development, *Our Common Future* (New York: Oxford University Press, 1987), 39.
4. Kent E. Portney, *Taking Sustainable Cities Seriously: Economic Development, the Environment, and Quality of Life in American Cities*, 2nd ed. (Cambridge, MA: MIT Press, 2013), 23–24.
5. City of New York, *OneNYC* (New York: City of New York, 2015), http://www.nyc .gov/html/onenyc/downloads/pdf/publications/OneNYC.pdf.
6. City of New York, *PlaNYC, 2011 Update* (New York: City of New York, 2011), http://www .nyc.gov/html/planyc/downloads/pdf/publications/planyc_2011_planyc_full_report.pdf.
7. Jason Corburn, *Toward the Healthy City: People, Places, and the Politics of Urban Planning* (Cambridge, MA: MIT Press, 2009).
8. City of New York, *OneNYC*, 214–51.
9. Brian Paul, "How 'Transit-Oriented Development' Will Put More New Yorkers in Cars," *Gotham Gazette*, April 21, 2010, http://www.gothamgazette.com/article/ Transportation/20100421/16/3247.
10. City of Chicago, *Adding Green to Urban Design: A City for Us and Future Generations* (Chicago: City Plan Commission, November 2008), www.cityofchicago.org/content/ dam/city/depts/zlup/Sustainable_Development/Publications/Green_Urban_Design/ GUD_booklet.pdf.
11. City of Chicago, *Eat Local, Live Healthy* (Chicago: Department of Planning and Development, November 2006), www.cityofchicago.org/content/dam/city/depts/ zlup/Sustainable_Development/Publications/Eat_Local_Live_Healthy_Brochure/ Eat_Local_Live_Healthy.pdf.

12. Chicago Department of Aviation, *Sustainable Airport Manual* (Chicago: City of Chicago, 2012), http://www.kpesic.com/sites/default/files/TM_Sustainable Airport Manual.pdf.

13. City of Chicago, *Climate Action Plan* (Chicago: City of Chicago, 2008), www .chicagoclimateaction.org/filebin/pdf/finalreport/CCAPREPORTFINALv2.pdf.

14. City of Chicago, *2015 Sustainable Chicago: Action Agenda 2012–2105 Highlights and a Look Ahead* (Chicago: City of Chicago, December 2015), https://www.cityofchicago .org/content/dam/city/progs/env/Sustainable_Chicago_2012-2015_Highlights.pdf.

15. City of Philadelphia, *Greenworks Philadelphia: A Vision for a Sustainable Philadelphia* (Philadelphia: City of Philadelphia Office of Sustainability, 2016), https://beta.phila .gov/media/20161101174249/2016-Greenworks-Vision_Office-of-Sustainability.pdf.

16. Richard Freeh and Sarah Wu, *Greenworks Philadelphia 2015 Progress Report* (Philadelphia: City of Philadelphia Office of Sustainability, 2015), https://beta.phila.gov/ media/20160419140539/2015-greenworks-progress-report.pdf.

17. See "Erase Your Trace," *Ms. Philly Organic*, August 24, 2009, http://msphillyorganic .wordpress.com/2009/08/24/erase-your-trace/.

18. See Philadelphia Water Department, Office of Watersheds, "What's on Tap," http:// phillywatersheds.org.

19. See Sustainable City, "Biodiversity," *Sustainability Plan for San Francisco*, available at www.sustainable-city.org/Plan/Biodiver/intro.htm; and Sustainable City, "Energy, Climate Change, and Ozone Depletion," *Sustainability Plan for San Francisco*, available at www.sustainable-city.org/Plan/Energy/intro.htm.

20. San Francisco Environment Commission, Meeting Minutes and Agendas, https:// sites.google.com/a/sfenvironment.org/commission/environment-commission.

21. San Francisco Environment Commission, Biodiesel Access Task Force, https://sites .google.com/a/sfenvironment.org/commission/biodiesel-access-task-force.

22. Mike Chino, "San Francisco Announces 10 Million Gallon Biodiesel Plant," *Inhabitat*, September 9, 2008, http://inhabitat.com/san-francisco-announces-10-million-gallon-biodiesel-plant/; Katie Worth, "San Francisco Falling Short on Use of Biodiesel for Public Vehicles," *San Francisco Examiner*, January 3, 2011, http://www.sfexaminer .com/san-francisco-falling-short-on-use-of-biodiesel-for-public-vehicles/.

23. ICF Jones & Stokes, *Bayview Hunters Point Community Diesel Pollution Reduction Project: Final Report* (San Francisco: Department of the Environment, February 2009), www.sfenvironment.org/sites/default/files/fliers/files/sfe_ej_bvhp_diesel_pollution_ reduction_project_report.pdf.

24. Sustainable Seattle, "About Us," www.sustainableseattle.org/about-us/.

25. Alan AtKisson, "Developing Indicators of Sustainable Community: Lessons from Sustainable Seattle," *Environmental Impact Assessment Review* 16 (1996): 337–50.

26. Jeb Brugmann, "Is There a Method in Our Measurement? The Use of Indicators in Local Sustainable Development Planning," *Local Environment* 2, no. 1 (February 1997): 59–72; Jeb Brugmann, "Sustainability Indicators Revisited: Getting from Political Objectives to Performance Outcomes—A Response to Graham Pinfield," *Local Environment* 2, no. 3 (1997): 299–302.

27. City of Portland Bureau of Planning and Sustainability, *City of Portland and Multnomah County Climate Action Plan 2009* (Portland: City of Portland, 2009), www .portlandoregon.gov/bps/article/268612.

28. See the *Denver Comprehensive Plan 2000: A Vision for Denver and Its People* (Denver: Community Planning and Development, 2000), 26, https://www.denvergov.org/ content/dam/denvergov/Portals/646/documents/planning/comprehensiveplan2000/ CompPlan2000.pdf; and *Moving People: Denver's Strategic Transportation Plan, 2008*

(Denver: Department of Public Works, 2008), https://www.denvergov.org/content/dam/denvergov/Portals/688/documents/DenverSTP_8-5x11.pdf.

29. See Mayor Michael B. Hancock, "Executive Order 123," March 11, 2013, https://www.denvergov.org/content/dam/denvergov/Portals/executiveorders/123-Sustainability-Policy.pdf.

30. Greenprint Denver Advisory Council, *City of Denver Climate Action Plan: Final Recommendations to Mayor Hickenlooper* (Denver: City of Denver, October 2007), https://www.denvergov.org/content/dam/denvergov/Portals/771/documents/EQ/Climate1/DenverClimateActionPlan_2005_Original.pdf.

31. Denver Environmental Health, *City and County of Denver Climate Adaptation Plan* (Denver: City of Denver, June 2014), https://www.denvergov.org/content/dam/denvergov/Portals/771/documents/Climate/Climate_Adaptation_Final with letter.pdf.

32. Transit Oriented Denver, *Transit Oriented Development Strategic Plan, 2014* (Denver: City of Denver, 2014), https://www.denvergov.org/content/dam/denvergov/Portals/193/documents/TOD_Plan/TOD_Strategic_Plan_FINAL.pdf.

33. Forest City Stapleton, Inc., *2004 Stapleton Sustainability Master Plan* (Denver: Forest City Stapleton, 2014), https://www.stapletondenver.com/wp-content/uploads/2014/12/Stapleton_Sustainability_Plan.pdf.

34. Steven A. Moore, *Alternative Routes to the Sustainable City: Austin, Curitiba, and Frankfurt* (New York: Lexington Books, 2007).

35. City of Austin, "City of Austin 2012 Achievements in Sustainable Buildings and Sites," August 27, 2013, www.austintexas.gov/sites/default/files/files/Public_Works/Capital_Improvement/2013-08-27_Sustainability_ReportFINAL.pdf; Lucia Athens, *Building an Emerald City: A Guide to Creating Green Building Policies* (Washington, DC: Island Press, 2010).

36. City of Austin, *ImagineAustin Comprehensive Plan* (Austin: City Council, 2016), ftp://ftp.ci.austin.tx.us/npzd/IACP_amended2016_web_sm.pdf. Original plan adopted June 15, 2012.

37. Central Texas Sustainability Indicators Project, "2012 Data Report," http://indicatorsproject.com/about/.

38. Community Action Network, *Community Dashboard 2010* (Austin: CAN, 2010), http://www.cancommunitydashboard.org/files/CANCommunityDashboard2010.pdf.

39. City of Austin, *Report on Performance Information for Fiscal Year Ended September 30, 2004* (Austin: City Council, City of Austin, 2004), www.ci.austin.tx.us/budget/03-04/downloads/performance2004.pdf.

40. City of Austin, *Performance Measures*, www.ci.austin.tx.us/budget/eperf/index.cfm. Also see City of Austin Office of Sustainability, "Organizational Sustainability: 2015 Key Performance Indicators," http://austintexas.gov/sites/default/files/files/Attachment_-_Organizational_Sustainability_KPIs_Report_Card.pdf.

41. Austin Energy, "More Than Electricity," www.austinenergy.com; See also the website of the City of Austin's Office of Sustainability, www.austintexas.gov/department/sustainability.

42. City of Austin, *Performance Measures.*

43. Austin Energy, "More Than Electricity."

Part IV

Global Issues and Controversies

Chapter 13

Global Climate Change Governance
Where to Go After Paris?
Henrik Selin and Stacy D. VanDeveer

In what seems like an annual ritual, scientists have once again declared the previous year to be one of the warmest on record. In the last 136 years, the 10 hottest years all occurred since 1998, with 2016 the warmest on record. In politics and among family members, friends, and coworkers, climate change issues and debates are visible worldwide. In the Arctic, indigenous peoples struggle to sustain their economic and cultural lives, polar bears fight to stay alive, and melting sea ice opens up new shipping lanes for oil tankers, cargo vessels, and warships. In coastal cities from Boston to Amsterdam, Dhaka, and Guangzhou, and on low-lying islands from South Asia to the South Pacific and the Gulf Mexico, people worry about the consequences of sea level rise and intensifying storm surges. Farmers from California to Cameroon grow more anxious about severe droughts and extreme weather events. In response, people participate in climate change initiatives in churches, schools, boardrooms, and public offices from city governments to the United Nations (UN), where former UN secretary-general Ban Ki-moon declared climate change "the defining issue of our time."[1] Despite strong political statements and the clear dangers of changing the climate system, international institutions and the states that drive decision making have moved slowly over the last twenty-plus years, failing to reverse global greenhouse gas (GHG) emissions.

Climate change politics and policymaking focus on both mitigation and adaptation issues. Mitigation efforts center on different ways to reduce GHG emissions. Many current mitigation policies focus on switching to less carbon-intensive energy sources (including wind, solar, and hydro power); improving energy efficiency for vehicles, buildings, and appliances; and supporting the development and deployment of technologies that help reduce GHG emissions. Adaptation efforts seek to improve the ability of human societies (broadly) and local communities (more specifically) to adjust to a changing climate (for example, to alter agricultural practices in response to seasonal and precipitation changes or to prepare urban areas in coastal regions for rising sea levels and severe weather occurrences). Complicating climate change policymaking is the fact that both mitigation and adaptation issues are fraught with difficult political, moral, and ethical challenges, as some countries contribute much more to the causes of climate change than do others, and many people and societies struggle to adapt to dangerous climatic changes they largely did not cause.

This chapter explores climate change governance across global, regional, national, and local levels. As countries struggle to formulate meaningful mitigation and adaptation policies, more aggressive action by intergovernmental forums, small communities, and individuals is necessary to meet the challenges posed by climate change causes and impacts. The next section discusses the history of climate change science and the Intergovernmental Panel on Climate Change (IPCC). This is followed by an outline of the global political framework on climate change that has developed in conjunction with the IPCC assessments, the 1992 UN Framework Convention on Climate Change (UNFCCC), the 1997 Kyoto Protocol, the 2009 Copenhagen Accord, and the 2015 Paris Agreement. Next, three important aspects of climate change politics are addressed: (1) European Union (EU) leadership and policy responses, (2) North American climate change policymaking, and (3) the challenges facing the developing world and the BRICS (Brazil, Russia, India, China, and South Africa). The chapter ends with a few remarks about the future of global climate change governance.

Science, GHG Emissions, and the IPCC

Energy from the sun reaches Earth in the form of visible light. Most of this sunlight reaches the Earth's surface while some is reflected back into space by clouds before it can get through. The sun's energy is absorbed by land and water that heats up. As the Earth's surface warms up, it gives up energy in the form of infrared radiation. Naturally occurring GHGs in the lower atmosphere trap some of this outgoing infrared radiation before it can go back into space, which makes the Earth warmer in what has been termed the greenhouse effect. GHGs have been present in the atmosphere for much of Earth's 4.5 billion-year history; without them, the planet would have average surface temperatures of approximately -20°C (0°Fahrenheit). The amount of energy that remains trapped in the atmosphere by GHGs has important long-term effects on the climate, as human activities add both naturally occurring and human-made GHG to the atmosphere.[2]

Researchers in different academic fields for over 150 years have contributed to our current—and still developing—understanding of the global climate system. American scientist Eunice Foote and British researcher John Tyndall in the 1850s studied how carbon dioxide (CO_2) and other gases in the atmosphere influence the Earth's temperature, arguing that surface temperature levels are higher with CO_2 than without CO_2 (i.e., early work establishing the dynamics of the greenhouse effect).[3] In 1896, Swedish scientist Svante Arrhenius explored what could happen to the climate system if atmospheric CO_2 concentrations increased, but he did not predict actual, significant changes. In 1938, however, British engineer Guy Stewart Callendar proposed that human CO_2 emissions were changing the climate. Furthermore, in 1956, Gilbert Plass, an American scientist, calculated that adding CO_2 to the atmosphere would have significant heat-trapping effects, contributing to a warming climate.

Science advanced when Charles David Keeling at the Mauna Loa Observatory in Hawaii began measuring actual CO_2 concentrations in open air in 1960. Before industrialization, atmospheric CO_2 concentrations were approximately 280 parts per million by volume (ppmv). Ice core data show that historical concentrations were relatively stable for several hundreds of thousands of years prior to the Industrial Revolution. Atmospheric CO_2 concentrations exceeded 400 ppmv in 2014 (far above historical levels), and they are growing at a rate of about 2 to 4 ppmv per year. While other GHGs besides CO_2 add to the warming trend, other emissions (mostly sulfate aerosols and other particulates) have a cooling effect in that they repel incoming sunlight. The future effect of particulates and changes in cloud formation are two major areas of contemporary climate change science.[4]

Current global climate changes are different from earlier alterations between warmer and cooler eras in that recent critical changes are driven by human behavior. Human activities influence both the amount of incoming energy absorbed by the Earth's surface (through land use changes including deforestation) and the amount of energy trapped by GHGs (largely by releasing CO_2 into the atmosphere through the burning of fossil fuels in manufacturing and transport, and GHGs stemming from agricultural production). Since the beginning of the Industrial Revolution in the early nineteenth century, human activities have dramatically altered the composition of GHGs in the lower atmosphere by adding to the volume of naturally occurring gases (for example, CO_2 and methane) as well as by releasing human-made GHGs (for example, hydrofluorocarbons, or HFCs). Between 1990 and 2013, global GHG emissions increased by 42.7 percent, but with enormous differences in historical and current national and per capita GHG emissions (see Table 13-1).

The 2013 data in Table 13-1 are of GHG emissions as measured in CO_2 equivalents, where the global warming potential of other GHGs is converted into that of CO_2.[5] Many GHGs, including methane and HFCs, trap much more energy in the atmosphere than does the same amount of CO_2. Thus, relatively small quantities of some highly potent GHGs contribute significantly to warming. The data also include land use changes. Approximately 10 percent of global anthropogenic CO_2 emissions stem from land use changes (mainly deforestation).[6] Including such emissions can have a major impact on the reporting of national GHG emissions—in extreme cases over a 100 percent difference. A country such as Indonesia, where deforestation is significant, gets a higher number than it would if land use changes were excluded, but a country with more sustainable forest practices and areas of reforestation, such as Costa Rica, gets lower numbers when land use changes are included, as these biological resources act as CO_2 "sinks."

In 2013, China, the United States, and the EU-28 were responsible for almost 45 percent of global GHG emissions. Middle Eastern countries, led by Kuwait at 54.47 metric tons, top the per capita emissions list. The EU-28 (7.53) have per capita emissions similar to China's (8.42), and these are less than half those of the United States (19.64) and one quarter of Canada's (25.31). These large differences result from multiple factors, including the

Table 13-1   Top Nine Global Emitters of GHG Emissions (CO_2 Equivalent), Including Land Use Change and Forestry in 2013

Country/Region	Percentage Change in Emissions 1990–2013	Percentage Share of Global Emissions	Metric Tons CO_2 Equivalent per Capita (Global Ranking of States and EU-28)
1. China	+303.1	23.7	8.42 (58)
2. United States	+12.0	12.9	19.64 (20)
3. EU-28	−14.7	7.9	7.53 (66)
4. India	+165.3	6.3	2.37 (138)
5. Indonesia	+61.6	4.5	8.60 (56)
6. Russian Federation	−29.7	4.3	14.47 (27)
7. Japan	+24.1	2.8	10.69 (49)
8. Brazil	−9.0	2.7	6.45 (75)
9. Canada	+38.8	1.8	25.31 (11)

Source: World Resources Institute, *The Climate Analysis Indicator Tool* (CAIT 2.0) online database (http://cait2.wri.org). The percentage increase for the Russian Federation is from 1992 to 2013 due to a lack of data for earlier years.

Note: Different emissions reports will vary, depending on their inclusion or exclusion of land use changes, whether CO_2 emissions or all GHGs (or carbon equivalents) are used, or as a result of slightly different estimation techniques.

scope and stringency of environmental policy, the profile of the national economy, country size and population density, public transportation infrastructure, trade patterns, consumption habits, varying access to renewable energy, and differences in energy policy. Many developing countries emit less than three metric tons per person, while high income Sweden emits less than five tons per person.

Today, most scientists agree that changes to Earth's climate system pose significant ecological, humanitarian, and economic risks. A 2016 study confirms that approximately 97 percent of published climate research agrees that humans are causing contemporary climate change.[7] Through the IPCC—established in 1988 by the World Meteorological Organization and the UN Environment Programme—thousands of climate change scientists and experts from around the world work together, tasked with assessing, summarizing, and publishing the latest peer-reviewed data and analysis. The IPCC was created to inform policymaking, but not to formulate policy. Most IPCC work is divided into three working groups (WGs). WG I studies the physical science basis of the climate system and climate change. WG II focuses on the vulnerability of socioeconomic and natural systems to climate change, the negative and positive consequences of climate change, and adaptation options. WG III examines mitigating options through limiting or preventing GHG emissions and enhancing activities that remove them from the atmosphere.

The IPCC has produced five sets of assessments with WG I reports released in 1990, 1995, 2001, 2007, and 2013–2014.[8] The first of these reports stated that, although much data indicated that human activity affected the variability of the climate system, the authors could not reach consensus. Signaling a higher degree of consensus, the 1995 report stated that the "balance of evidence" suggested "a discernible human influence on the climate." The subsequent three reports were critical in building a much higher degree of confidence within the scientific community. The 2013 report states that the human influence is clear, as the warming of the climate system (atmosphere and ocean) is "unequivocal" with atmospheric concentrations of CO_2, methane, and nitrous oxide having increased to levels unprecedented in at least the last eight hundred thousand years. Additional GHG emissions will cause further warming and changes in all components of the climate system.

The 2014 WG II report outlines a litany of impacts of climate change, including altered precipitation patterns and amounts, ice loss, sea level rise, ocean acidification, and the frequency and increased intensity of extreme weather events. Such changes already impact ecological systems and human health and societies, raising the risk of conflict. WG III reports include emissions scenarios that project possible GHG emissions levels decades into the future, based on a different set of assumptions about future levels of economic growth and the choices made by governments and citizens that affect the generation of GHG emissions. Scenarios are designed to help decision makers and planners think about how climate change may impact societies and how quickly various mitigation strategies could change future emissions. They also inform thinking about projects such as building new sewage treatment systems in a coastal area, new power plants, or the design of new water policies in drought-stricken regions. Together with reports by WG I and WG II, they make it clear that all countries face adaptation challenges, even if these vary tremendously across societies and regions.

IPCC reports are widely reviewed and cited by people in international organizations, local governments, large and small firms, environmental advocacy groups, and by scientific researchers. However, the IPCC has also come under criticism because some claims in the reports later turned out to be based on inconclusive or incorrect information. Although this leads some critics of climate change science and policy to question the integrity of the IPCC's process, the vast majority of climate change scientists support the IPCC reports and their main conclusions.

International Law and Climate Change Negotiations

International law on climate change is shaped by a complex mix of evolving scientific consensus and the material interests and values of state, nongovernmental, and private sector actors. Over two decades of global negotiations have left many frustrated and disappointed with the results and dispirited about the prospects of addressing the problem.[9] Along with a growing number of policy responses at every level of the public, private, and civil society spheres, the world's countries have adopted four major multilateral agreements: the 1992 UNFCCC, the 1997 Kyoto Protocol, the 2009 Copenhagen Accord, and the 2015 Paris Agreement. The UNFCCC was negotiated between publication of the first IPCC report and the 1992 UN Conference on Environment and Development in Rio de Janeiro, where it was adopted. It entered into force in 1994, and by 2017, 196 countries and the EU were parties to the treaty. As a framework convention, the UNFCCC sets out a broad strategy for countries to work jointly to address climate change.

Like other framework conventions, the UNFCCC defines the issue at hand, sets up an administrative secretariat to oversee treaty activities, and lays out a legal and political framework under which states cooperate over time. The UNFCCC contains shared commitments by states to continue to research climate change, to periodically report their findings and relevant domestic implementation activities, and to meet regularly to discuss common mitigation and adaptation issues at conferences of the parties (COPs). Usually, framework conventions do not include detailed regulatory commitments, leaving those issues to be addressed in subsequent agreements. Similar approaches using the framework convention–protocol model have been applied to issues such as protection of the stratospheric ozone layer, acid rain and related transboundary air pollution problems, and biodiversity loss.

The UNFCCC sets the long-term objective of "stabilization of greenhouse gas concentrations in the atmosphere at a level that would prevent dangerous anthropogenic interference with the climate system" (Article 2). The UNFCCC establishes that the world's countries have common but differentiated responsibilities in addressing climate change. This principle refers to the notion that all countries share an obligation to act, but industrialized countries and countries with economies in transition (that is, former communist countries) have a particular responsibility to take the lead because of their relative wealth and disproportionate contribution to the problem through historical emissions. These forty countries, plus the EU, are listed in Annex I of the UNFCCC. They agreed to reduce their anthropogenic emissions to 1990 levels, but no clear deadline was set for this target. The UNFCCC did not assign developing countries any GHG reduction commitments.

Responding to mounting scientific evidence about human-induced climate change in the mid-1990s, much of it presented in the second IPCC report, and to growing concern about the negative economic and social effects of climate change among environmental advocates and policymakers, the UNFCCC parties negotiated the Kyoto Protocol between 1995 and 1997. The protocol came together when the EU and U.S. negotiators struck a deal, helped along by last-minute compromises brokered, in part, by then vice president Al Gore. The Kyoto Protocol covered six GHGs: CO_2, methane, nitrous oxide, perfluorocarbons, HFCs, and sulfur hexafluoride. UNFCCC Annex I countries committed to reduce their GHG emissions collectively by 5.2 percent below 1990 levels by 2008–2012. Toward this goal, thirty-nine states had individual targets.[10] Some agreed to cut their emissions, while others merely consented to slow their emissions growth. For example, the EU-15 took on a collective target of an 8 percent reduction while the United States and Canada committed to cuts of 7 percent and 6 percent, respectively. In contrast, Iceland committed to limit its emissions at 10 percent above 1990 levels.

Annex I countries could meet their targets through different measures, including the development of national policies that lower domestic GHG emissions. They could also calculate the benefits from domestic carbon sinks that soak up more carbon than they emit by, for example, preserving forests or adopting sustainable practices such as reforestation. In addition, they could participate in transnational emissions trading schemes with other Annex I parties, develop joint implementation (JI) programs with other Annex I parties and get credit for lowering GHG emissions in those countries, or design a partnership venture with a non-Annex I country through what is known as the Clean Development Mechanism (CDM) and get credit for lowering GHG emissions in the partner country. These three options were intended to provide flexibility and reduce mitigation costs by allowing parties to cut emissions wherever it was most efficient, including in other countries.

Developing countries, lacking individual GHG reduction requirements based on the principle of common but differentiated responsibility, strongly supported the Kyoto Protocol, which entered into force in 2005. Among industrialized countries, a stark transatlantic difference emerged.[11] The EU took an early leadership role in defense of the Kyoto Protocol, succeeding in reducing GHG emissions beyond its target (see also EU section below). In contrast, the United States refused to ratify the Kyoto Protocol (and tried to convince other countries to do the same). Canada ratified the Kyoto Protocol in 2002 but announced in 2011 its official withdrawal from the agreement, after failing to curb its emissions. Both U.S. and Canadian GHG emissions have increased significantly since 1990 (see below). Australia, Japan, New Zealand, and Russia all became parties, but displayed varying levels of support.

In Bali in 2007, the UNFCCC parties launched a process to negotiate a follow-up agreement to the Kyoto Protocol, to be adopted at the 2009 COP in Copenhagen.[12] However, national leaders were unable to agree to a legally binding agreement. Instead, they settled on a Copenhagen Accord, under which countries adopted their own voluntary and widely divergent GHG targets for 2020. The Copenhagen Accord also set the goal that average global temperature increases should remain below 2°C (a target related to the UNFCCC goal to prevent dangerous anthropogenic interference with the climate system). In addition, the Copenhagen Accord noted that industrialized countries would try to mobilize $30 billion from 2010 to 2020, with the goal of reaching $100 billion a year by 2020, to support mitigation and adaptation projects in developing countries. Parties at the 2010 COP in Cancun created the Green Climate Fund as a central financial mechanism to operate alongside other bodies, including the Global Environment Facility, the World Bank, and regional development banks.

At the 2011 COP in Durban, the parties adopted the Durban Platform for Enhanced Action, launching a new round of negotiations to develop "a protocol, another legal instrument or an agreed outcome with legal force," to be concluded in 2015. The 2012 COP in Doha formulated a second Kyoto commitment period wherein Annex I countries agreed to reduce their overall GHG emissions by at least 18 percent (collectively) below 1990 levels by 2020. However, some Annex I countries—Canada, Japan, New Zealand, Russia, and the United States—refused to take on a second, formal round of Kyoto targets for 2020. Parties also added nitrogen trifluoride (NF_3) to the list of regulated GHGs, bringing the total to seven, and they extended the CDM and JI mechanisms. The 2013 COP in Warsaw and the 2014 COP in Lima laid the foundation for a global agreement in Paris in 2015, as both industrialized and developing countries for the first time moved forward with a system of GHG reduction plans for the post-2020 period.[13]

The Paris Agreement returns to the adoption of legally binding agreements, but it also builds on language in the Copenhagen Accord, setting the goal of holding global average temperature increases to well below 2°C above preindustrial levels and pursuing efforts to limit it to 1.5°C. To this end, the parties aim to reach a global peak in GHG emissions as soon as possible, as well as a balance between GHGs from anthropogenic sources and a corresponding removal by sinks between 2050 and 2100 (i.e., emissions would come down to "net zero"). Recognizing the principles of equity and common but differentiated responsibilities and respective capabilities in the light of different national circumstances, developed countries must continue to lead by undertaking economy-wide absolute GHG emission reduction targets, while developing countries are encouraged to do the same over time.

Continuing another approach from the Copenhagen Accord, the Paris Agreement allows countries to determine their own commitments. All parties should voluntarily formulate their own nationally determined contributions (NDCs) under a "pledge and review" system.[14] Importantly, NDCs are not part of the Paris Agreement but are submitted separately by each party to satisfy those countries rejecting national legally binding GHG commitments. The Paris Agreement, however, establishes a review mechanism through which countries are expected to update and strengthen their NDCs over time, coupled with a system of mandatory national reporting including on national emission sources and sinks. A first review of NDCs and their implementation is planned for 2018, while a first formal stocktaking of NDCs is scheduled for 2023 (to be repeated every five years). The hope is that this review system will encourage states to update and strengthen their various goals and implantation efforts regularly.

The Paris Agreement entered into force in 2016, demonstrating more widespread urgency than seen earlier. Collectively, implementation of the NDCs would reduce future emissions compared to policies in place before the Paris Agreement process. However, total emission cuts by the initial NDCs fall well short of those required to meet the agreed-upon temperature goals. Even if all countries were to fulfill their individual NDC pledges—which is uncertain—global average temperatures are expected to increase by between 2.6 and 3.1°C by 2100 (with some estimates higher than that).[15] An emissions pathway toward the goal of 2°C requires additional, substantial cuts, probably starting by the early 2020s. Moving forward, parties are expected to make finance flows consistent with a pathway toward low GHG emissions, and developed countries shall provide financial resources to assist developing countries. The goal of developed countries collectively providing $100 billion per year by 2020 is to be scaled up over time as part of Paris Agreement implementation. However, developed countries did not take on any individual finance targets, but they can individually determine how much they want to contribute.

Because many climatic changes are already under way and significant amounts of additional GHGs will be emitted over the coming decades, the Paris Agreement recognizes the importance of adaptation and climate-resilient development, mainly as a result from demands by developing countries. Developing countries also secured the inclusion of language on "loss and damage" as separate from adaptation. This idea is that countries contributing very little to the problem should be compensated for impacts related to climate change that cause extensive or irreversible damage, including, for example, loss of lives and property during extreme weather or the disappearance of coastal areas and small islands due to sea level rise. At the insistence of industrialized countries, however, a conference decision attached to the Paris Agreement states that such language does not constitute a legal basis for any liability or compensation. Wealthier countries secured this decision in order to avoid any clear financial or other responsibilities to compensate poorer ones for losses induced by climate change.

The Paris Agreement is widely hailed as a significant step forward by policymakers and environmental activists from many parts of the globe. Global cooperation on nearly every issue moves quite slowly, so calling Paris Agreement the "end of the beginning" for global climate politics or "good enough governance" qualifies as endorsement in international politics.[16] But it is far from perfect, and its success rests on what states and subnational and private sector actors do next. Global climate change governance is also increasingly "polycentric" as it happens at multiple levels of authority and in many types of forums beyond the UNFCCC.[17] Some decisions under the Montreal Protocol to protect the stratospheric ozone layer have substantial climate benefits, for example, as do those taken within the International Civil Aviation Organization, the International Maritime Organization, the World Bank, and the World Trade Organization—to name only a few. All of these bodies will need to do more to help curb GHG emissions if the 2°C goal is to be met. And all require committed leadership from their member states, which must continue to act more aggressively to reduce national emissions. For example, as some countries dramatically scale back coal usage, others burn more, while coal interests continue to fight curbs on CO_2 emissions virtually everywhere.[18]

EU Leadership and Policy Responses

Since the 1990s, the EU, representing the majority of the world's industrial countries, has emerged (comparatively) as a global leader in climate change politics and policymaking.[19] Even as the EU grew from fifteen members in the mid-1990s to twenty-eight members during a series of enlargements, EU bodies such as the European Commission (the administrative bureaucracy), the Council of the European Union (comprising member state government officials), and the European Parliament (of representatives elected by member state citizens) have worked together and collaborated with civil society and private sector actors to enact and implement a set of pan-European climate change and energy-related goals and policies. With a population of over five hundred million, meaning that roughly one in fourteen humans lives in the Union, the EU remains a major contributor to climate change and a major player in climate change politics and policymaking, including in the implementation of the Paris Agreement.[20]

The desire to meet the Kyoto target served as an important early impetus for EU policymakers to develop a growing number of joint policies and initiatives. The EU-15 collective Kyoto target (8 percent below 1990 GHG emission levels by 2012) was divided among member states under a 1998 burden-sharing agreement. To facilitate intra-EU policymaking and implementation, each member state took on a differentiated target under this burden-sharing approach.[21] Several of the more economically developed member states took on relatively far-reaching commitments to reduce national GHG emissions, while less wealthy member states could increase their GHG emissions in the period up to 2012, as part of these countries' efforts to expand industrial production and accelerate economic growth.

In 2009, the EU adopted a major climate and energy package in support of the so-called 20-20-20 by 2020 goals. These goals, all with a 2020 deadline, refer to a 20 percent reduction in GHGs below 1990 levels, 20 percent of the total energy consumption coming from renewable sources, and a 20 percent reduction in primary energy use compared with projected trends. The 20 percent GHG reduction goal by 2020 was submitted as the EU goal under the Copenhagen Accord and was also included in the Kyoto Protocol's second commitment period. In its NDC for the Paris Agreement, the EU raised its goals to 40 percent for GHG reduction and 27 percent for both renewable energy generation and improved energy savings, all to be achieved by 2030. The suite of policies toward the 2020 and 2030 goals also uses a burden-sharing approach in which each member state is allotted national targets.

Receiving much attention as the world's first international GHG trading scheme, the EU Emissions Trading System (ETS) serves as a main policy instrument. Ironically, the EU was opposed to GHG emissions trading during the Kyoto negotiations—an issue championed by the United States in part because of its domestic experience with emissions trading for sulfur dioxide and nitrogen oxide. The EU attempted to enact a carbon tax in the late 1990s, but this effort failed when member states could not agree on a common tax. In the face of this policy failure and the EU's need to meet its Kyoto target, EU officials developed the ETS.[22] The ETS launched with a first phase (2005 and 2007) slowly, a second trading period (2008 to 2012), and a third starting in 2013. The scheme has been significantly amended and expanded since 2005, and it now includes all twenty-eight EU members as well as Iceland, Lichtenstein, and Norway.

Currently, the ETS sets a regional cap for three GHGs—carbon dioxide, nitrous oxide, and perfluorocarbons—from over eleven thousand major point sources in power generation and manufacturing and aviation, collectively covering 45 percent of all EU GHGs.[23] The cap is designed to shrink annually so that emissions from covered sectors in 2020 will be 21 percent lower than in 2005. Every year, the EU allots emissions allowances to each participating country, which, in turn, allocates these to domestic firms. Allowances are increasingly auctioned off, rather than distributed for free, across different economic sectors. Firms can also use some emission credits generated under the CDM and JI mechanisms to meet their obligations. Those without enough allowances to cover their emissions by the end of each year are fined.

As the EU looks to maintain a prominent leadership role both globally and regionally, official EU data show that the EU-15 cut collective GHG emissions by 12.2 percent from 1990 to the 2008–2012 period, thus exceeding the Kyoto Protocol target.[24] The EU is on track to meet its 2020 GHG reduction goal, but regional GHGs are not on a strong enough downward trajectory to reach the 2030 target without further policy measures. The EU, based on current numbers and trends, seems likely to meet its 2020 renewable energy goal, but it may need additional policy action to meet the 2030 goal on renewables. The EU is also on schedule to fulfill its 2020 energy efficiency goal, and the corresponding 2030 goal can also be met if the reduction in primary energy consumption continues at the same pace as that achieved since 2005 toward the 2020 goal.[25]

North American and U.S. Climate Change Policy and Politics

In contrast to EU bodies and many EU member states, North American federal governments have been slow to act, and they have produced a much less regionally integrated response despite sharing a common market under the North American Free Trade Agreement (NAFTA).[26] The United States and Canada were viewed as laggards among industrialized countries for almost twenty years, starting in the mid- and late 1990s. Both countries' GHG emissions (excluding land use changes) are higher than in 1990—U.S. emissions by 7.0 percent and Canadian emissions by 31.8 percent in 2013. If land use changes are included, U.S. emissions increased by 12.0 percent while Canadian emissions increased by 38.8 percent.[27] In Mexico, GHG emissions increased by 71.8 percent without land use changes and 66.3 percent with land use changes between 1990 and 2013.

Even as the United States early on ratified the UNFCCC, U.S. skepticism of global climate change policy dates back to the Kyoto Protocol. Vice President Al Gore signed the Kyoto Protocol on behalf of the Clinton administration (1993–2001), although President Clinton never pushed for its ratification because of strong opposition in the U.S. Senate. President George W. Bush

(2001–2009) made rejection of the Kyoto Protocol official U.S. foreign policy. The Canadian federal government, led by Prime Minister Jean Chrétien (1993–2003), ratified the Kyoto Protocol in 2002 but failed to enact any meaningful implementation policies. In the face of growing GHG emissions, the subsequent Stephen Harper governments (2006–2015) took the very rare step of formally withdrawing Canada from the Kyoto Protocol in 2011, before the agreement's commitment period came to an end. Mexico joined the Kyoto Protocol in 2000.

At the 2009 Copenhagen COP, both the Obama administration (2009–2017) and the Harper administration opposed the idea of a legally binding agreement mandating national GHG reductions. The United States and Canada submitted identical voluntary targets under the Copenhagen Accord: a 17 percent reduction below 2005 levels by 2020. Mexico stated a goal to reduce GHG emissions by 30 percent by 2020, as compared to emission levels in a business-as-usual scenario, but only conditionally upon receiving adequate financial and technological support from developed countries. During the Durban Platform negotiations, the United States and Canada stressed that all major GHG emitters must be included in an agreement. The Obama administration, with support from Canada's new Trudeau government (2015–) as well as from the EU, China, and other countries, worked to build momentum for a more significant agreement in Paris.[28]

All three North American countries submitted NDCs in the lead-up to the Paris conference. The United States stated a goal to reduce GHG emissions by 26–28 percent below its 2005 level by 2025 and to make best efforts to reduce its emissions by 28 percent (stemming from a 2014 joint U.S.-China climate change deal that helped secure American and Chinese support for the Paris Agreement).[29] Canada, where the new government had campaigned on promises to take climate change policy more seriously, committed to reducing national GHG emissions by 30 percent below 2005 levels by 2030. Mexico intends to reduce GHG emissions by 25 percent relative to a business-as-usual baseline by 2030, which would translate into a net peaking of national emissions by 2026. Mexico also declared that this reduction target could be increased to 40 percent if it were provided external assistance at a scale commensurate to the challenge of global climate change.

North American climate change politics have changed significantly at national and subnational levels. President George W. Bush opposed mandatory national GHG reductions throughout his presidency.[30] U.S. federal policy under the Bush administration focused instead mainly on voluntary programs and the funding of scientific research and technology development. The Obama administration expressed early support for regulating GHG emissions and appointed many climate change scientists and policy advocates to government. In 2009 the Environmental Protection Agency (EPA), based on a 2007 U.S. Supreme Court ruling that CO_2 can be classified as a pollutant under the Clean Air Act, issued an endangerment finding stating that current and projected atmospheric GHG concentrations threatened the public health and welfare of current and future generations.

Obama's first term saw little regulatory action beyond increases in automobile fuel efficiency standards, as the U.S. Congress failed to pass climate change legislation. It was not until 2015 that the EPA issued a regulatory plan containing a series of measures. Chief among these was the proposal to cut national CO_2 emissions from large power plants by 30 percent below 2005 levels by 2030. The plan also supported expanded investments in renewable energy production and measures to improve energy efficiency. In addition, it stressed the need to prepare the United States for the impacts of climate change. The proposed EPA rules came under immediate scrutiny, as opponents took legal action to block their implementation. The Obama administration also raised fuel efficiency requirements for heavy trucks, proposed a set of regulations to curb methane emissions from the natural gas industry, launched a series of energy efficiency increases for appliances, denied permits to the Keystone XL pipeline, and worked with climate and energy policy leaders in various U.S. states to facilitate state-level policy development. Climate change, energy efficiency, and renewables also became priority issues in U.S. national security assessment and planning.

The 2017 inauguration of Donald Trump as U.S. president resulted in a sharp reversal of federal efforts to address climate change mitigation and adaptation (see Chapter 4). The Trump administration quickly launched initiatives to end or review Obama-era regulations aimed at reducing GHG emissions and other pollutants from power plants, the natural gas industry, and cars and heavy trucks. The administration installed climate science skeptics in leadership positions in a host of federal agencies, including the EPA; proposed deep cuts in programs related to climate change and in federal funding for climate change science and public health initiatives; and reversed the Obama decision regarding the Keystone XL pipeline. In June 2017, President Trump announced that he would withdraw the United States from the Paris Agreement. Formal notice of withdrawal can be given three years after the date of the agreement's entry into force (i.e., in November 2019), and withdrawal would come into effect one year after that. In the meantime, the Trump administration plans to cease all implementation of the nonbinding parts of the Paris Agreement, including the goals and actions outlined in the U.S. NDC and all further contributions to the Green Climate Fund.

Similar to climate change policy in the United States under George W. Bush, Canadian federal GHG policy under the Harper government did not mandate or incentivize GHG reductions. The 2015 election of Justin Trudeau, together with growing climate policy action at the provincial level, appears to have changed the direction of Canadian climate policy toward more serious emissions reductions. In 2016, the Trudeau administration in support of Canada's NDC under the Paris Agreement announced that all Canadian provinces must establish a carbon pricing scheme (e.g., a carbon tax or a cap-and-trade system) that meets a federal benchmark ("floor price") no later than 2018. If any province fails to do so, the federal government will impose its own carbon price on that province. The federal government's proposed carbon price should start at Canadian dollars (CAD) per metric ton and increase by CAD 10 each year up to CAD 50 by 2022. If fully implemented, this carbon-pricing scheme would result in a stark difference between Canadian and U.S. federal climate change policy.

Mexico, which early on engaged in modest voluntary initiatives, took several legal and political steps during the 2010s. Legislation enacted in 2012 passed Mexico's Copenhagen Accord commitment into law. This was followed in 2013 by a legal commitment to cut GHGs by 50 percent from 2000 levels by 2050 and the goal of generating 35 percent of energy from renewable sources by 2024.[31] A modest carbon tax will support Mexican GHG reductions. The 2012 and 2013 legislation gave Mexico the distinction of having the most comprehensive federal climate change law in North America, and it established Mexico as a Latin American leader in climate change policymaking and prodded other South and Central American states to move forward.[32] These federal measures alongside actions by Mexican states also form the foundation for Mexico's NDC under the Paris Agreement.

Beyond the federal level, subnational actors have developed an important and diverse set of responses (see Chapter 2). Between 2000 and 2014, energy-related CO_2 emissions fell in 35 U.S. states and increased in 15.[33] The states with the greatest reductions were Maine (−25.6%), Massachusetts (−22.6%), and Alaska (−20.9%). At the other end of the spectrum, CO_2 emissions increased by +15.2% in North Dakota and +25.2% in Nebraska. These differences stem from a host of factors, including climate, substantial variance in the sources of energy used, differential economic and population growth rates and density, diverging transportation infrastructure and needs, and large differences in state and local climate change and energy policies. Figures 13-1 and 13-2 show the extreme variance among total and per-capita energy-related CO_2 emissions in U.S. states in 2014. Illustrating the global importance of U.S. emissions, Texas, the U.S. state with highest total emissions, emitted more than Canada, Mexico, or the United Kingdom. Even a small state such as Massachusetts emits about as much as Portugal or New Zealand. The five states with the highest per capita emissions emitted between 112 (Wyoming) and 47 (Louisiana) tons per person. Meanwhile, states at the low end—New York, California, Vermont, Massachusetts, and Oregon—each emitted less than 10 tons per person.

Many U.S. states have taken policy actions in support of their own GHG reduction goals such as enacting renewable portfolio standards requiring electricity providers to obtain a minimum percentage of their power from renewable sources, formulating ethanol mandates and incentives, pushing to close coal-fired power plants, setting vehicle emissions standards, mandating the sale of more efficient appliances and electronic equipment, and changing land use and development policies to curb emissions. Several states, through their respective attorneys general, were a driving force behind the 2007 Supreme Court decision declaring CO_2 a pollutant. Especially California, building on its tradition of air pollution and energy leadership, has adopted a suite of climate change policies comparable to those of the EU. These policies aim to increase energy efficiency across the state; reduce GHG emissions

Figure 13-1 Total Energy-Related Carbon Dioxide Emissions by State, 2000–2014

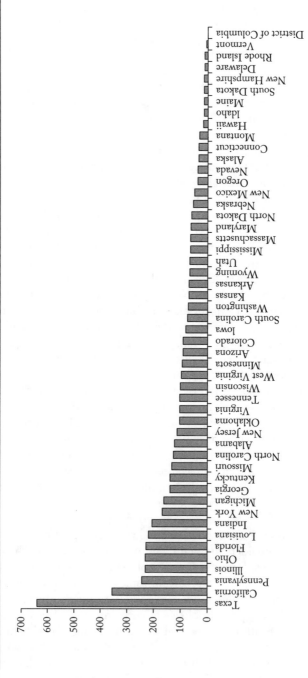

Source: U.S. Energy Information Agency, *Energy Related Carbon Dioxide Emission at the State Level, 2000–2014* (Washington DC: Department of Energy, 2017).

Figure 13-2 Per Capita Energy-Related Carbon Dioxide Emissions by State, 2000–2014

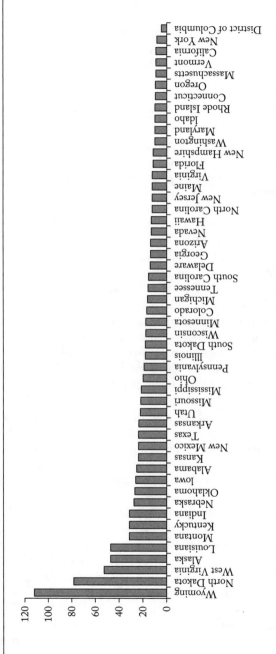

Source: U.S. Energy Information Agency, *Energy Related Carbon Dioxide Emission at the State Level, 2000–2014* (Washington DC: Department of Energy, 2017).

from power plants, homes, businesses, and transportation; and expand renewable energy generation. Among Canadian provinces, British Columbia distinguished itself (in Canada and globally) by implementing a relatively comprehensive carbon tax in 2008, which climbed to 30 CAD (or about $25) in 2012 and remained at that level through 2017.[34]

Subnational leaders also enact collaborative standards and policies. Launched in 2009, the Regional Greenhouse Gas Initiative (RGGI) creates a cap-and-trade scheme across nine states: Maryland, Maine, Vermont, New Hampshire, Massachusetts, Rhode Island, Connecticut, New York, and Delaware (New Jersey was an original member, but left in 2011). RGGI was designed to stabilize CO_2 emissions from power plants between 2009 and 2015 and to achieve a 10 percent reduction by 2019. By 2013, emissions were already far below the cap, prompting states to cut the 2014 emissions cap by 45 percent and plan for it to decline through 2020 (resulting in emissions 68 percent below the 2000–2006 average).[35] Coal use declined 58 percent from 2005 to 2015, and emissions from the electricity sector have gone down by about 45 percent.[36] Auctioning emission permits has produced over $2.6 billion for energy efficiency and other public benefits investments, saving consumers an estimated $4.6 billion and creating over 30,000 jobs.[37]

Under the Western Climate Initiative, British Columbia, California, Ontario, and Quebec work to harmonize GHG mitigation around emissions trading. In 2014, Quebec officially linked its cap-and-trade emissions scheme to California's, and Ontario plans to link its trading program to theirs in 2018. California climate change and renewable energy collaboration with Mexico expands subnational efforts into the third NAFTA member. Many Obama administration EPA proposals, if implemented, were designed to further incentivize state action and collaboration. This is not the goal of Trump administration initiatives. Canadian Prime Minister Justin Trudeau's climate change and clean energy initiatives are designed to push provinces to take more mitigation and adaptation leadership. Some provinces are also moving beyond Canada's national goal as formulated in its NDC in terms of their own GHG reduction goals. For example, Quebec's reduction goals are minus 20 percent by 2020 (from 1990 levels) and minus 37.5 percent by 2030.

In addition, large and small municipalities all over North America are taking action, both individually and through networks such as the International Council for Local Environmental Initiatives and its Cities for Climate Protection program, the U.S. Conference of Mayors' Climate Protection Agreement, the Federation of Canadian Municipalities' Partners for Climate Protection program, and the C40 group.[38] Although many municipal climate change programs are modest, cities such as New York City, Toronto, and Portland have achieved noteworthy results. North American municipalities are also increasingly developing new GHG reduction and energy efficiency programs that rely in part on innovative private financing. Additionally, a growing number of North American firms are voluntarily reducing GHG emissions and investing in low carbon technology, but it is important to note that a significant number of firms still take only limited action, while many others continue to fund lobbying efforts to prevent climate policy adoption.[39]

Even as important political and technical precedents for future climate change actions are being set all over the United States and Canada, significant public and private sector resistance to mandatory action and controls continues in North America (more so than in Europe). Polls demonstrate that U.S. voters are deeply split along partisan lines. Also, the fact that many companies are enthusiastic about Trump-era regulatory rollbacks, including auto companies that previously endorsed higher fuel efficiency standards, illustrates continuing corporate opposition to climate change policy. Some states, provinces, and municipalities also delayed or even rolled back enacted climate change policies due to combinations of local political opposition and tougher economic times during the economic downturn starting in the late 2000s. In the U.S. Congress, particularly with both chambers under Republican control after the 2016 elections, opponents of climate and clean energy policies (and of climate science) are in ascendance and determined to limit the EPA's regulatory authority (see Chapter 5)—and even its voluntary programs.

The energy futures of the North American countries are deeply linked. On the one hand, opportunities exist for much more cross-border renewable energy development and trade between both Canada and the United States and the United States and Mexico. In all three countries, the cost competitiveness of renewable energy sources such as solar and wind has improved, and renewable energy capacity and generation have increased in recent years. On the other hand, the tar sands extraction in Alberta and the related presidential executive actions to advance approval of the controversial Keystone XL pipeline system connecting Canadian oilfields with U.S. refineries and ports in the Gulf of Mexico—as well as Trump's promise to expand the extraction and use of coal and other fossil fuels—were welcomed and supported by the fossil fuel industry. Other related controversies fester: whether to expand U.S. oil, gas, and coal exports; how many new areas to open for additional fossil fuel extraction; and what, if any, subsidies to offer to renewable energy investments and production.

The Developing World and the BRICS

As the international community attempts to move forward collectively under the Paris Agreement, many developing countries face a myriad of mitigation and adaptation problems, alongside a multitude of other critical sustainable development issues. The situation of relatively vulnerable countries to climatic changes gives rise to important procedural and distributive social justice issues, from a global equity perspective.[40] Procedural justice refers to the ability of peoples and countries to partake fully in collective decision-making processes focusing on mitigation and adaptation issues, including under the Paris Agreement. Distributive justice concerns how climate change impacts or how mitigation policies affect societies and people differently, in part because countries have greatly varying domestic capacities to deal with these challenges.

For many developing countries, procedural justice issues relate to how international climate change policy is formulated and how these countries' interests are represented and taken into account. Many smaller developing countries face multiple obstacles to engaging actively in multilateral environmental negotiations and assessments.[41] These obstacles include having fewer human, economic, technical, and scientific resources with which to prepare for international negotiations or implement resulting agreements. The significant capacity differences between wealthier industrialized countries and poorer developing countries risk skewing international debates and decision making in favor of the perspectives and interests of more powerful countries, which are often interested in minimizing their own mitigation costs.

On distributive justice issues, the preambles to both the UNFCCC and the Paris Agreement recognize that many developing countries are "particularly vulnerable" to the adverse effects of climate change. For example, countries in South Asia with vast and densely populated, low-lying coastal areas, including Bangladesh and India, will experience many of the first impacts of sea level rise and increased storm intensity, as will the inhabitants of small island states. Changes in seasons and precipitation present a more acute threat to millions of poor, small-scale farmers in Africa and other tropical countries than they do to those in rich countries. Similar issues can be extended to indigenous populations all over the world, who are often among the most vulnerable in any society.[42] The IPCC's *Fifth Assessment Report* included chapters on "Human Security" and "Sustainable Development and Equity" that catalogue vast and growing risks to citizens and communities in the developing world, as well as the complexity and urgency of equity and social justice issues related to climate change causes, implications, and mitigation and adaption policymaking.[43]

The developing world has often tried to speak with one voice on climate change through the Group of 77 (G-77).[44] Evident in G-77 pronouncements is the strong interest of member states in preserving the principle of common but differentiated responsibilities as key for assigning GHG reduction requirements and in prioritizing economic development partly based upon the continued use of fossil fuels. The ability of the very diverse group of G-77 members to present a unified front has always been inconsistent, becoming more difficult in recent times. One major change over the last two decades is the rapid economic growth and increasingly assertive positions of major developing countries, often exemplified by the BRICS (Brazil, Russia, India, China, and South Africa). Despite increasing debates about whether rapidly industrializing countries such as China and India are well suited to represent the "Global South"—or even belong in such a category—Indian and Chinese officials remain attached to many of the ideas and principles associated with developing country identity in global politics.[45]

Major developing countries are under pressure to reduce GHGs. For example, low-lying islands fear Chinese emissions as much as those originating from Europe and North America, industrialized countries want a level economic playing field for their firms in international markets, and environmental organizations push for emission cuts as a central sustainable development issue. Developing country NDCs include a wide range of national goals and measures. In China, as air pollution and public health issues are becoming more salient domestically, the government is stepping up mitigation actions. These include investing heavily in greener technologies, expanding wind and solar power generation capacities, and launching pilot cap-and-trade programs.[46] Among the major goals in China's NDC are that its emissions will peak no later than 2030 and then begin to decline. India's NDC pledges to focus on renewable energy growth and adaptation. In both India and China, trends in coal use are likely to play a central role in emissions trajectories over the next decades.

Diverse NDC goals and metrics may be politically necessary, but they may also prove difficult to monitor and assess collectively. Furthermore, national GHG emissions under many NDCs are predicted to continue to grow in the short and medium terms. Finally, developing countries pay close attention to fluctuations within the Green Climate Fund and other major sources of climate finance as an important indication of the level of commitment shown by donor countries and the international community. Many, like Mexico, stipulate that fulfillment of their national GHG reduction targets is at least partially dependent on the delivery of adequate financial and technological assistance from donor countries. While there has been an increase in financial pledges, developing countries have cause to be skeptical about such pledges until funds are actually delivered. In addition, developing countries strongly argue for the principle of "additionality"—that funds going toward climate change mitigation and adaptation should be *in addition* to both development assistance and to funds going to other environmental issue areas.

Looking for Leadership

Climate change policy is developing across global, regional, national, and local governance levels, but existing initiatives are not enough to meet the Paris Agreement's temperature goals. Since the 1880s, average global temperatures have increased by 1°C, and past emissions have already built in further warming over the coming decades and centuries. The world's industrialized and developing countries do not face the same challenges, but climate change threatens all. As global GHG emissions continue to rise, the challenge of finding ways to reduce these significantly—by upwards of 80–90 percent by 2050, as is often stated—while simultaneously tackling poverty and promoting sustainable economic and social development cannot be overstated (see Chapter 14). Countries traditionally classified as developing currently account for approximately 60 percent of global annual GHG emissions, and their relative contribution continues to grow. At the same time, the vast majority of the world's poorest people live in these countries, facing growing climate-related adaptation problems that hit weaker and poorer communities much more harshly than they do stronger and richer ones. Even after global GHG emissions have been drastically reduced, researchers estimate that related climatic changes will be with us for the next thousand years.[47]

With the Trump administration declaring that the United States will withdraw from the Paris Agreement and stop implementation of measures under the NDC, the agreement loses the world's second largest GHG emitter. American withdrawal also leaves a political leadership gap. However, many other leading countries and large GHG emitters quickly criticized Trump's decision and reconfirmed their commitments to their NDCs, leaving only the United States, Nicaragua, and Syria outside of the Paris Agreement. In a sign that others are looking to fill at least part of the void left by the United States, China and the EU, only one day after Trump announced his decision, signed a declaration to forge a stronger bilateral alliance to address climate change and lead the transition to a low-carbon economy. The parties to the agreement will continue to meet annually and design rules and procedures to implement and review this agreement, with or without U.S. engagement. Yet it remains unclear exactly how the U.S. decision will shape policy decisions in other countries, as well as what kind of role U.S. representatives will play during debates and decision making at future COPs. Will U.S. representatives seek to obstruct others' progress? Or might they choose to observe or even support global cooperation more quietly, despite having declared that the United States will quit the agreement? Also unknown is what the U.S. posture on climate change will be in other global forums, such as the ozone layer protection regime, the G7/G20, and the United Nations Security Council.

Because of frustration with the UNFCCC process, even after the Paris Agreement, and disappointment in the Trump administration's decision both to leave the Paris Agreement and to reverse federal standards while supporting greater fossil fuel extraction and use, some policy advocates look to the plethora of governance experiences outside of global institutions.[48] Actors at every level of social organization are experimenting with new policies and institutions to address mitigation and adaptation needs in a myriad of ways. Research makes it clear that innovation around climate and energy collaboration is nearly infinite, but questions remain about whether this huge variety of non-state and private sector governance can meet the climate change challenge without much more significant state action in both the Global North and the Global South. This debate was reignited in the United States in the wake of the Trump administration's many federal and foreign policy actions aimed at weakening previous initiatives supportive of climate change mitigation and adaptation.

Climate finance needs are also daunting. The International Energy Agency estimates that a $53 trillion investment in energy supply and in energy efficiency is needed by 2035 to move the world toward the 2°C goal.[49] This translates into almost $2.5–3 trillion more per year up to 2035. In 2010, the World Bank calculated that the world's developing countries would need to spend between $70 to 100 billion each year between 2010 and 2050 on necessary adaptation projects under a 2°C scenario.[50] A United Nations Environment Programme (UNEP) report suggests that adaptation costs for developing countries under different emission scenarios could be even higher, between $140 and 300 billion in 2030 and rising to between $280 and 500 billion a year by 2050.[51] One thing is clear, however: the longer we delay investments in mitigation and adaptation, the larger the consequences of climate change and the higher the costs of adapting.

The scientific debate about the reality of human-induced climate change is settled, but significant disagreements remain within and among countries, and public and private sector actors, about the allocation of costs and responsibilities for cutting GHG emissions and switching to cleaner technology. International politics and national and local governments are central to addressing major climate change mitigation and adaptation challenges, but large and small firms are also critical players in their roles as investors, polluters, innovators, experts, manufacturers, lobbyists, and employers.[52] Major economic and social changes—such as the drive for low-carbon lifestyles—create both business constraints and opportunities. Collective action is required, but individual actions by consumers and citizens are needed as well. If the challenges posed by climate change are to be met, we must all take responsibility for our impact on the global climate system, using and expanding our influence over our own behavior and in our local communities, workplaces, and governments.

Suggested Websites

Center for Climate and Energy Solutions (www.c2es.org) This site offers information about international and U.S. climate change policymaking and private sector action.

EcoInternet (www.ecointernet.org) This portal, search engine, and news feed covers climate change issues.

European Commission (http://ec.europa.eu/clima) The EC site on climate action provides information about European perspectives and policy initiatives to address climate change.

Intergovernmental Panel on Climate Change (www.ipcc.ch) This panel of international experts conducts periodical assessments of scientific and socioeconomic information about climate change.

RealClimate (www.realclimate.org) This moderated forum provides commentaries on climate change science news by scientists working in different fields.

UN Climate Change Newsroom (http://newsroom.unfccc.int) This website operated by the UNFCCC Secretariat contains information about meetings and other activities organized under the UNFCCC.

Notes

1. Robert O'Neill, "Ban Ki-moon Delivers Call to Action on Global Challenges," *News*, October 22, 2008, available from the Belfer Center for Science and International Affairs, Harvard Kennedy School at http://www.belfercenter.org/publication/ban-ki-moon-delivers-call-action-global-challenges.
2. Kerry Emanuel, *What We Know about Climate Change*, 2nd ed. (Cambridge, MA: Boston Review/MIT Press, 2012).

3. Spencer R. Weart, *The Discovery of Global Warming*, 2nd ed. (Cambridge, MA: Harvard University Press, 2008); Leila McNeill, "This Lady Scientist Defined the Greenhouse Effect But Didn't Get the Credit, Because Sexism," *Smithsonian Magazine*, December 5, 2016, http://www.smithsonianmag.com/science-nature/lady-scientist-helped-revolutionize-climate-science-didnt-get-credit-180961291/.

4. For discussions about the latest developments in climate change science, see RealClimate (www.realclimate.org).

5. For a chart of different global warming potentials, see UNFCCC data at https://unfccc.int/ghg_data/items/3825.php.

6. IPCC, *Climate Change 2013: The Physical Science Basis* (Cambridge: Cambridge University Press, 2013), http://www.ipcc.ch/report/ar5/wg1/.

7. John Cook, Naomi Oreskes, Peter T. Doran, William R. L. Anderegg, Bart Verheggen, Ed W. Maibach, J. Stuart Carlton, Stephan Lewandowsky, Andrew G. Skuce, and Sarah A. Green, "Consensus on Consensus: A Synthesis of Consensus Estimates on Human-Caused Global Warming," *Environmental Research Letters* 11, no. 4 (2016): 1–7.

8. The IPCC reports and other data are available on the IPCC website (www.ipcc.ch).

9. Christian Downie, *The Politics of Climate Change Negotiations* (Northampton, MA: Edward Elgar, 2014); Harro van Asselt, *The Fragmentation of Climate Change Governance* (Northampton, MA: Edward Elgar, 2014); Thomas Hale, David Held, and Kevin Young, *Gridlock: Why Climate Change Cooperation Is Failing When We Need It Most* (London: Polity, 2013).

10. These were Australia, Austria, Belarus, Belgium, Bulgaria, Canada, Croatia, The Czech Republic, Denmark, Estonia, Finland, France, Germany, Greece, Hungary, Iceland, Ireland, Italy, Japan, Latvia, Lichtenstein, Lithuania, Luxembourg, Monaco, The Netherlands, New Zealand, Norway, Poland, Portugal, Romania, The Russian Federation, Slovakia, Slovenia, Spain, Sweden, Switzerland, Ukraine, The United Kingdom, and the United States.

11. Miranda A. Schreurs, Henrik Selin, and Stacy D. VanDeveer, eds., *Transatlantic Environment and Energy Politics: Comparative and International Perspectives* (Aldershot, UK: Ashgate, 2009).

12. Raymond Clémonçon, "The Bali Roadmap," *Journal of Environment and Development* 17, no. 1 (2008): 70–94.

13. Detailed reports about all COPs, for the UNFCCC and many other international environmental negotiations, can be found in the *Earth Negotiations Bulletin*, available at www.iisd.ca/enbvol/enb-background.htm.

14. Robert Falkner "The Paris Agreement and the New Logic of International Climate Politics," *International Affairs* 92 (5) (2016): 1107–25.

15. Joeri Rogelj, Michel de Eizen, Niklas Höhne, Taryn Fransen, Hanna Fekete, Harald Winkler, Roberto Schaeffer, Fu Sha, Keywan Riahi, and Malte Meinshausen, "Paris Agreement Climate Proposals Need a Boost to Keep Warming Well Below 2°C," *Nature* 534 (June 30, 2016): 631–39.

16. Paul Bodnar quoted in Graham Norword, "'End of the Beginning': What Was Achieved at COP-21," *NewSecurityBeat*, January 6, 2016; Joshua Busby, "After Paris: Good Enough Climate Governance," *Current History* 115, no. 777 (January 2016): 3–9.

17. Andrew Jordan, Dave Huitema, Mikael Hildén, Harro van Asselt, Tim J. Rayner, Jonas J. Schoenefeld, Jale Tosun et al., "Emergence of Policycentric Climate Governance and Its Future Prospects," *Nature Climate Change* 5 (November 2015): 977–82.

18. Tim Boersma and Stacy D. VanDeveer, "Coal after the Paris Agreement," *Foreign Affairs*, June 6, 2016.

19. Henrik Selin and Stacy D. VanDeveer, "Broader, Deeper and Greener: European Union Environmental Politics, Policies and Outcomes" *Annual Review of Environment and Resources* 40 (2015): 309–35.
20. Sebastian Oberthür, "Where to Go from Paris? The European Union in Climate Geopolitics" *Global Affairs* 2, no. 2 (2016): 119–30.
21. Henrik Selin and Stacy D. VanDeveer, *European Union Environmental Governance* (New York: Routledge, 2015).
22. Jon Birger Skjærseth and Jørgen Wettestad, *EU Emissions Trading: Initiating, Decision-Making and Implementation* (Aldershot, UK: Ashgate, 2008).
23. European Commission, *The EU Emissions Trading System (EU ETS)* (Brussels: European Commission, 2013); Selin and VanDeveer, *European Union Environmental Governance.*
24. European Environment Agency, *Trends and Projections in Europe 2013: Tracking Progress Towards Europe's Climate and Energy Targets until 2020* (Copenhagen: European Environment Agency, 2013).
25. European Environment Agency, *Trends and Projections in Europe 2016: Tracking Progress Towards Europe's Climate and Energy Targets (Copenhagen:* European Environment Agency, 2016).
26. Henrik Selin and Stacy D. VanDeveer, eds., *Changing Climates in North American Politics: Institutions, Policy Making and Multilevel Governance* (Cambridge, MA: MIT Press, 2009).
27. CAIT Climate Data Explorer, *Historical Emissions,* http://cait2.wri.org/wri.
28. Coral Davenport, "Obama Pursuing Climate Accord in Lieu of Treaty," *New York Times,* August 27, 2014.
29. White House, Office of the Press Secretary, "U.S.-China Joint Announcement on Climate Change," November 12, 2014, http://www.whitehouse.gov/the-press-office/2014/11/11/us-china-joint-announcement-climate-change.
30. Miranda A. Schreurs, Henrik Selin, and Stacy D. VanDeveer, "Conflict and Cooperation in Transatlantic Climate Politics: Different Stories at Different Levels," in *Transatlantic Environment and Energy Politics: Comparative and International Perspectives*, ed. M. A. Schreurs, H. Selin, and S. D. VanDeveer (Aldershot, UK: Ashgate, 2009), 165–85.
31. Rona Fried, "Mexico Unveils National Climate Change Strategy," *Sustainable-Business.com,* June 11, 2013, http://www.sustainablebusiness.com/mexico-unveils-national-climate-change-strategy-51628/.
32. Lisa Friedman, "Latin Americans Forge Ahead on CO$_2$ Reduction Plans," *ClimateWire,* June 9, 2014.
33. U.S Energy Information Administration, *Energy-Related Carbon Dioxide Emissions at the State Level, 2000–2014* (Washington, DC: Department of Energy, January 2017), https://www.eia.gov/environment/emissions/state/analysis/pdf/stateanalysis.pdf.
34. Stewart Elgie and Jessica McClay, "BC's Carbon Tax Is Working Well after Four Years (Attention Ottawa)," *Canadian Public Policy* 39, no. 2 (2013): 11–22.
35. See the RGGI website: www.rggi.org.
36. Michael Bradley and Christopher Van Atten, *Power Switch: The Future of the Electric Power System in the Northeast and the Disruptive Power of Innovation* (Concord, MA: MJ Badley & Associates, 2016), http://www.mjbradley.com/sites/default/files/powerswitch10-19-2016.pdf.
37. Travis Madsen and Rachel Cross, *Doubling Down on Climate Progress: The Benefits of a Stronger Regional Greenhouse Gas Initiative* (Boston, MA: Environment America, 2017).
38. Christopher Gore and Pamela Robinson, "Local Government Responses to Climate Change: Our Last, Best Hope?" in *Changing Climates in North American Politics:*

Institutions, Policy Making and Multilevel Governance, ed. Henrik Selin and Stacy D. VanDeveer (Cambridge, MA: MIT Press, 2009), 137–58.

39. Charles A. Jones and David L. Levy, "Business Strategies and Climate Change," in *Changing Climates in North American Politics: Institutions, Policy Making and Multi-level Governance*, ed. Henrik Selin and Stacy D. VanDeveer (Cambridge, MA: MIT Press, 2009), 219–40.

40. W. Neil Adger, Jouni Paavola, and Saleemul Huq, "Toward Justice in Adaptation to Climate Change," in *Fairness in Adaptation to Climate Change*, ed. W. Neil Adger, Jouni Paavola, Saleemul Huq, and M. J. Mace (Cambridge, MA: MIT Press, 2006), 1–19.

41. Pamela S. Chasek, "NGOs and State Capacity in International Environmental Nego-tiations: The Experience of the Earth Negotiations Bulletin," *Review of European Community and International Environmental Law* 10, no. 2 (2001): 168–76; Ambuj Sagar and Stacy D. VanDeveer, "Capacity Development for the Environment: Broadening the Scope," *Global Environmental Politics* 5, no. 3 (2005): 14–22.

42. Arctic Climate Impact Assessment, *Impacts of a Warming Arctic: Arctic Climate Impact Assessment* (Cambridge: Cambridge University Press, 2004).

43. W. Neil Adger, Juan M. Pulhin, Jon Barnett, Geoffrey D. Dabelko, Grete K. Hovel-srud, Marc Levy, Úrsula Oswald Spring et al., "Human Security," in *Climate Change 2014: Impacts, Adaptation, and Vulnerability—Contribution of Working Group II to the Fifth Assessment Report of the Intergovernmental Panel on Climate Change* (Cambridge: Cambridge University Press, 2014), 755–91; Marc Fleurbaey, Sivan Kartha, Simon Bol-wig, Yoke Ling Chee, Ying Chen, Esteve Corbera, Franck Lecocq et al., "Sustainable Development and Equity," in *Climate Change 2014: Mitigation of Climate Change—Contribution of Working Group III to the Fifth Assessment Report of the Intergovernmental Panel on Climate Change* (Cambridge: Cambridge University Press, 2014), 283–350.

44. Adil Najam, "The View from the South: Developing Countries in Global Environ-mental Negotiations," in *The Global Environment*, 4th ed., ed. Regina Axelrod and Stacy D. VanDeveer (Washington, DC: CQ Press, 2015).

45. Shangrila Joshi, "Understanding India's Representation of North-South Climate Pol-itics," *Global Environmental Politics* 13, no. 2 (2013): 128–47; Philip Stalley, "Prin-ciples Strategy: The Role of Equity Norms in China's Climate Change Diplomacy," *Global Environmental Politics* 13, no. 1 (2013): 1–8.

46. Joanna I. Lewis and Kelly Sims Gallagher, "Energy and Environment in China: National and Global Challenges," in *The Global Environment*, 4th ed., ed. Regina Axelrod and Stacy D. VanDeveer (Washington, DC: CQ Press, 2015); and Joanna I. Lewis, *Green Innovation in China* (New York: Columbia University Press, 2013).

47. Susan Solomon, Gian-Kasper Plattner, Reto Knutti, and Pierre Friedlingstein, "Irreversible Climate Change Due to Carbon Dioxide Emissions," *Proceedings of the National Academy of Sciences of the United States* 106, no. 6 (2009): 1704–1709, http://www.pnas.org/content/106/6/1704.full?wptouch_preview_theme=enabled.

48. Harriett Bulkely et al., *Transnational Climate Change Governance* (Cambridge: Cambridge University Press, 2014); Jennifer Green, *Rethinking Private Authority* (Princeton, NJ: Princeton University Press, 2014); Matthew Hoffmann, *Climate Gov-ernance at the Crossroads* (Oxford, UK: Oxford University Press, 2011).

49. International Energy Agency, *Special Report: World Energy Investment Outlook* (Paris: OECD/IEA, 2014), 14.

50. World Bank, *Economics of Adaptation to Climate Change: Synthesis Report* (Washington, DC: World Bank, 2010), xxvii

51. UNEP, *The Adaptation Finance Gap Report* (Nairobi, Kenya: UNEP, 2016), xii.

52. Jones and Levy, "Business Strategies and Climate Change."

Chapter 14

Environment, Population, and the Developing World

Richard J. Tobin

Environmental problems occasionally make life in the United States unpleasant, but most Americans tolerate this situation in exchange for the comforts associated with a developed economy. Most Europeans, Japanese, and Australians share similar lifestyles, so it is not surprising that they typically also take modern amenities for granted.

When lifestyles are viewed from a global perspective, however, much changes. Consider, for example, what life is like in much of the world. The U.S. gross national income (GNI) per capita was $57,540 per year, or over $1,100 per week, in 2015. In contrast, weekly incomes were less than 5 percent of this amount in thirty-two countries, even when adjusted for differences in prices and purchasing power. In several African countries, real per capita incomes are less than 2 percent of those in the United States. Much of the world's population lives on less than $2 a day. In south Asia and sub-Saharan Africa, a large share of the population's income is below this level.[1]

Low incomes are not the only problem facing many of the world's inhabitants. In some developing countries, women, often illiterate and with no formal education, marry as young as age thirteen. In Bangladesh and Niger, about a quarter of girls are married by the age of fifteen and almost two-thirds by age eighteen. In south Asia, over 40 percent of all females are married before their eighteenth birthday.[2] Many of these marriages are with much older men who have even less education than their teenage brides. During their childbearing years, women in many developing countries will typically deliver as many as five or six babies, most without skilled birth attendants. This absence is not without consequences. The likelihood that a woman will die due to complications associated with pregnancy, childbirth, or an unsafe abortion is many times higher in poor countries than in Western Europe or the United States. In Sierra Leone, as an illustration, the rate of maternal mortality is almost one hundred times higher than in the United States.

Many of the world's children are also at risk. Fewer than 6 of 1,000 American children die before the age of five; in some African countries, the infant mortality rate exceeds 80 per 1,000 children. *Every week*, as many as 130,000 children under age five die in developing countries from diseases that rarely kill Americans. Malaria, diarrhea, and acute respiratory infections cause more than half of these deaths, most of which can be easily and cheaply cured or prevented.[3]

Of the children from these poor countries who do survive their earliest years, millions will suffer brain damage because their pregnant mothers had no iodine in their diets; others will lose their sight and die because they lack vitamin A. Many will face a life of poverty, never to taste clean water, use a toothbrush or cell phone, enter a classroom, learn to read or write, visit a doctor, have access to even the cheapest medicines, or eat nutritious food regularly. To the extent that shelter is available, it is rudimentary, rarely with electricity or proper sanitary facilities. Hundreds of millions in the developing world will also become victims of floods, droughts, famine, desertification, land degradation, waterborne diseases, infestations of pests and rodents, and noxious levels of pollution because their surroundings have been abused or poorly managed.

As children in developing countries grow older, many will find that their governments cannot provide the resources to ensure them a reasonable standard of living or even a seat in a classroom. Yet all around them are countries with living standards well beyond their comprehension. The average American uses seventeen times more electricity and consumes almost 60 percent more calories per day—far in excess of minimum daily requirements—than does the typical Indian. An Indian mother might wonder why Americans consume a disproportionate share of the world's resources when she has malnourished children she cannot clothe or educate.[4] In short, life in much of the world provides an array of problems different from those encountered in developed nations. Residents of poor countries must cope with widespread poverty, scarce opportunities for employment, and a lack of development. Yet both developed and developing nations often undergo environmental degradation. Those without property, for example, may be tempted to denude tropical forests for land to farm. Concurrently, pressures for development often force people to overexploit their natural and environmental resources.

These issues lead to the key question addressed in this chapter: Can the poorest countries, with the overwhelming majority of the world's population, improve their lot through sustainable development? Sustainable development meets the essential needs of the present generation for food, clothing, shelter, jobs, and health without "compromising the ability of future generations to meet their own needs."[5] Achieving this goal will require increased development without irreparable damage to the environment.

Whose responsibility is it to achieve sustainable development? One view is that richer nations have a moral obligation to assist less fortunate ones. If the former do not meet this obligation, not only will hundreds of millions of people in developing countries suffer, but the consequences will be felt in the developed countries as well. Others argue that poorer nations must accept responsibility for their own fate because outside efforts to help them only worsen the problem and lead to an unhealthy dependence. Advocates of this position insist that it is wrong to provide food to famine-stricken nations because they have exceeded their environment's carrying capacity.[6]

The richer nations, whichever position they take, cannot avoid affecting what happens in the developing world. It is thus useful to consider how events in rich nations influence the quest for sustainable development. At least two related factors affect this quest. The first is a country's population; the second is a country's capacity to support its population.

Population Growth: Cure or Culprit?

Population growth is one of the more contentious elements in the journey toward sustainable development. Depending on one's perspective, the world is either vastly overpopulated or capable of supporting as many as thirty times its current population (about 7.5 billion in mid-2017 and increasing at an annual rate of about 80 million per year).[7] Many developing nations are growing faster than the developed nations (Table 14-1), and more than 80 percent of the world's population lives outside the developed regions. If current growth rates continue, the proportion of those in developing countries will increase even more. Between 2017 and 2050, more than 97 percent of the world's population increase, estimated to be about 2.3 billion people, will occur in the latter regions, exactly where the environment can least afford such a surge. Many of the new inhabitants will live in countries that are experiencing little, if any, economic development.

Africa is particularly prone to high rates of population growth, with some countries facing increases of 3 percent or more per year. This may not seem to be a large percentage until we realize that such rates will double the countries' populations in about twenty-four years. Fertility rates measure the number of children an average woman has during her lifetime. Eighteen of the twenty countries with fertility rates at 5 or above in 2016 were in sub-Saharan Africa. By comparison, the fertility rate in the United States was 1.8 in that year.

Although many developing countries have altered their attitudes about population growth, many have also realized the immensity of this task. The theory of demographic transition suggests that societies go through three stages. In the first stage, in premodern societies, birth and death rates are high, and populations remain stable or increase at low rates. In the second stage, death rates decline and populations grow rapidly because of vaccines, better health care, and more nutritious foods. As countries begin to reap the benefits of development, they enter the third stage. Infant mortality declines, but so does the desire or need to have large families. Population growth slows considerably.

This model explains events in many developed countries. As standards of living increased, birthrates declined. The model's weakness is that it assumes economic growth; in the absence of such growth, many nations are caught in a demographic trap. They get stuck in the second stage. This is the predicament of many countries today. In some African countries, the situation is even worse. Their populations are growing faster than their economies, and living standards are declining. These declines create a cruel paradox. Larger populations produce increased demands for food, shelter, education, and health care; stagnant economies make it impossible to provide them.

Table 14-1   Estimated Populations and Projected Growth Rates

Region or Country	Estimated Population (millions)			Rate of Annual Natural Increase (%)	Number of Years to Double Population
	Mid-2017	2030	2050		
World total	7,536	8,563	9,846	1.2	60
More developed countries	1,263	1,304	1,325	0.1	720
Less developed countries	6,273	7,259	8,520	1.4	51
United States[a]	325.4	357.7	396.8	0.4	180
Canada	36.7	41.2	47.1	0.3	180
Mexico	129.2	147.5	164.3	1.5	48
China	1,386.8	1,418.0	1,342.5	0.6	120
India	1,352.6	1,528.1	1,675.6	1.4	51
Japan	126.7	119.1	101.9	−0.2	—
Sub-Saharan Africa	1,021	1,419	2,193	2.7	27
Angola	28.6	44.3	79.6	3.6	20
Chad	14.9	22.2	36.8	3.3	22
Niger	20.6	33.5	65.6	3.8	19
Uganda	42.8	61.6	95.6	3.1	23

Source: Population Reference Bureau, *2017 World Population Data Sheet* (Washington, DC: Population Reference Bureau, 2017), www.prb.org.

a. Although rates of natural increase in the United States are modest, immigration accounts for much of the projected increase in the U.S. population.

The opportunity to lower death rates can also make it difficult to slow population growth. As of 2015, in eight African countries, the average life expectancy at birth was fifty-five years or less, compared with seventy-nine years in the United States and almost eighty-four years in Japan. If these Africans had access to the medicines, vitamins, clean water, and nutritious foods readily available elsewhere, then death rates would drop substantially. Life expectancies in these countries could be extended by twenty years or more.

There are several reasons to expect death rates to decline. Development agencies have attempted to reduce infant mortality by immunizing children against potentially fatal illnesses and by providing inexpensive cures for diarrhea, malaria, and other illnesses. These efforts have met with enormous success, and more progress is anticipated. Reduced mortality rates among children should also reduce fertility rates. Nonetheless, the change will be gradual, and millions of children will be born in the meantime. Most of the first-time mothers of the next twenty years have already been born.

The best-known population programs have been in India and China. India's family planning program started in the early 1950s as a low-key effort that achieved only modest success. The program changed from being voluntary to being compulsory in the mid-1970s. The minimum age for marriage was increased, and India's states were encouraged to select their own methods to reduce growth.

Through a variety of approaches, India has been able to cut its fertility rate significantly, but cultural and religious resistance may stifle further gains.[8] India currently adds about nineteen million inhabitants each year. If such growth continues, India could become the world's most populous country as soon as 2022.

To reduce the growth rate in China, its government once discouraged early marriages. It also adopted a one-child-per-family policy in 1979. Until the policy was relaxed in January 2016, allowing families to have two children, the government gave one-child families monthly subsidies, educational benefits for their child, preferences for housing and health care, and higher pensions at retirement. Families that had previously agreed to have only one child but then had another were deprived of these benefits and penalized financially. The most controversial elements of China's population policy involved the government's monitoring of women's menstrual cycles, forced sterilizations, and late-term abortions. The one-child policy also increased the likelihood of female infanticide in rural areas.[9]

China's initial efforts lowered annual rates of population growth considerably. Total fertility rates declined from 5.8 in 1970 to 1.6 in 2016, which is well below the replacement rate of approximately 2.1. As a result of its one-child policy, Chinese officials claimed that nearly four hundred million births have been averted.[10] More recently, voluntary decisions not to have multiple children mean that China's population is expected to decline over the next few decades.

For many years, the U.S. government viewed rapidly growing populations as a threat to economic development. The United States backed its rhetoric with money; it was the largest donor to international population programs. The U.S. position changed dramatically during the Ronald Reagan administration. Due to its opposition to abortion, the administration said the United States would no longer contribute to the United Nations Population Fund (UNFPA) because it subsidized some of China's population programs. None of the fund's resources are used to provide abortions, but the U.S. ban on contributions nonetheless continued during George H. W. Bush's administration.

Within a day of taking office, President Bill Clinton announced his intention to alter these policies, to provide financial support to the UNFPA, and to finance international population programs that rely on abortions. Just as Clinton had acted quickly, so too did George W. Bush. He reinstated Reagan's policy banning the use of federal funds by international organizations to support or advocate abortions. The cycle continued with President Barack Obama. He reversed the Bush rules and urged Congress to restore funding for the UNFPA. President Donald Trump reversed Obama's position and halted funding for the UNFPA.

Concerns about abortion are not the only reason many people have qualms about efforts to limit population increases. Their view is that large populations are a problem only when they are not used productively to enhance development. The solution to the lack of such development is not government intervention, they argue, but rather individual initiatives and the spread of capitalist, free-market economies. Advocates of this position also believe that larger populations can be advantageous because they enhance political power, contribute to economic development, encourage technological innovation, and stimulate agricultural production.[11] Other critics of population control programs also ask if it is appropriate for developed countries to impose their preferences on others.

Another much-debated issue involves increased access to abortions, and who chooses to have them. The consequences of efforts to affect population growth are not always gender neutral. In parts of Asia, male children are prized as sources of future financial security, whereas females are viewed as liabilities. In years past, the sex of newborns was known only at birth, and in most countries, newborn males slightly outnumbered newborn females. With the advent of ultrasound, however, the sex of a fetus is easily ascertained months before a child is born. This knowledge can be the basis of a decision to abort female fetuses, notably in parts of China, India, and Eastern Europe.[12]

In sum, the appropriateness of different population sizes is debatable. There is no clear answer about whether growth by itself is good or bad. The important issue is a country's and the world's carrying capacity. Can it ensure a reasonable and sustainable standard of living? Can it do so in the future when the world's population will be substantially larger?

Providing Food and Fuel for Growing Populations

Sustainable development requires that environmental resources not be overtaxed so that they are available for future generations. When populations exceed sustainable yields of their forests, aquifers, and croplands, however, these resources are gradually destroyed.[13] The eventual result is an irreversible collapse of biological and environmental support systems. Is there any evidence that these systems are now being strained or will be in the near future?

The first place to look is in the area of food production. Nations can grow their own food, import it, or, as most nations do, rely on both options. The Earth is richly endowed with agricultural potential and production. Millions of acres of arable land remain to be cultivated, and farmers now produce enough food to satisfy the daily caloric and protein needs of a world population exceeding twelve billion.[14] These data suggest the ready availability of food as well as a potential for even higher levels of production. This good news must be balanced with the realization that hundreds of millions of people barely have enough food to survive.

As with economic development, the amount of food available in a country must increase at least as fast as the rate of population growth; otherwise, per capita consumption will decline. If existing levels of caloric intake are already inadequate, then food production (and imports) must increase faster than population growth to meet minimum caloric needs. Assisted by the expanded use of irrigation, pesticides, and fertilizers, many developing countries, particularly in Asia, have dramatically increased their food production. Asia's three largest countries—China, India, and Indonesia—are no longer heavily dependent on imported food.

Other countries can point to increased agricultural production, but many of these increases do not keep pace with population growth. The consequence is that average caloric consumption declines or imports of food increase, although declining consumption and a growth in imports can happen concurrently. With frequent spikes in food and fuel prices, many countries find themselves without sufficient resources to import enough food to ensure that even minimal levels of nutrition can be maintained. As an illustration, the Food and Agriculture Organization (FAO) identified twenty-two countries in 2010, all but five in sub-Saharan Africa, that face a "protracted crisis" in food security. On average, nearly 40 percent of their populations are undernourished; their daily intake of calories is less than the minimum dietary energy required. More recently, the FAO estimated that more than 790 million people suffered from undernourishment between 2014 and 2016 and thus did not regularly consume enough food to conduct an active life.[15] These numbers included one of every four persons in sub-Saharan Africa and almost one of every two persons in some countries in the region.

Among the consequences of insufficient food are stunted growth, weakened resistance to illness and disease, and impaired learning abilities and capacity for physical labor.[16] Agricultural production can be increased, but many countries suffer a shortage of land suitable for cultivation. Other countries have reached or exceeded the sustainable limits of production. Their populations are overexploiting the environment's carrying capacity. Farmers in India, Pakistan, Bangladesh, and West Africa may already be farming virtually all the land suitable for agriculture, and the amount of arable land per capita is declining in many developing countries. Likewise, the FAO estimates that nearly a quarter of the world's population depends on land whose productivity and ecosystem functions are declining.[17] If these trends continue, millions of acres of barren land will be added to the millions that are already beyond redemption.

Shortages of land suitable for farming are not the only barrier to increased agricultural production. With more people to feed, more water must be devoted to agriculture. To feed the world's population in 2050, the amount of water devoted to agriculture will have to double between 2000 and 2050, one estimate suggests.[18] Doing so will be a challenge. All the water that will ever exist is already in existence, and much of this water is already overused, misused, or wasted in much of the world, including in the United States, one of the world's largest users of water on a per capita basis. Some countries are already desperately short of water, as frequent droughts in Africa unfortunately confirm. Farmers in many developing countries must also address the prospect that climate change will reduce their yields by as much as 10 to 20 percent by 2050.

Many developing countries rely on fish as their major source of protein. Unfortunately, the condition of many of the world's fisheries is perilous. The FAO estimates that 90 percent of the world's fish stocks are already over-fished or fully exploited and have been pushed to or beyond their biological limits. Over four hundred oxygen-starved "dead zones" have been identified in the world's oceans and coastal areas. These zones, which can barely sustain marine life, have doubled in number every ten years since the 1960s. Further evidence of a collapsing ecosystem came in mid-2011 when an international panel of marine scientists concluded that the world's oceans are at "high risk of entering a phase of extinction of marine species unprecedented in human history." The experts also concluded that degeneration in the oceans is occur-ring at a speed and rate far faster than predicted and that many of the negative impacts previously identified are more ominous than the worst predictions.[19]

It is important to appreciate, as well, that the nature of diets changes as nations urbanize. Irrespective of differences in prices and incomes, according to the International Food Policy Research Institute, "urban dwellers consume more wheat and less rice and demand more meat, milk products, and fish than their rural counterparts." This preference leads to increased require-ments for grain to feed animals, the need for more space for forage, greater demands for water, and increased pollution from animal waste. Changes in the composition of diets can be anticipated in many countries. In fact, in virtually every low-income country, urbanization is increasing faster than overall population growth (in many instances, three to four times faster).

China provides an example. Its urban population increased to nearly 800 million in 2016 from only 300 million in 1990. This means that more than 55 percent of all Chinese now live in urban areas. Government officials want to increase this proportion even further, to as much as 70 percent. In what has been called "one of the most ambitious human migration plans in history," China intends to relocate as many as 260 million people from rural to urban areas by 2020.[20] The purpose of the relocation is to stimulate economic devel-opment through increased construction and consumption.

Increased urbanization is not without its consequences. On a per capita basis, China's urban residents consumed more than four times as much beef and five times as much milk and dairy products in 2010 than did the country's rural residents.[21]

Increased demand for food also has environmental consequences. More grain must be produced to feed livestock and poultry. In a typical year, as much as 35 to 40 percent of the world's grain production is used for animal feed, but the conversion from feed to meat is not a neat one. As many as ten pounds of grain and about 1,900 gallons of water are required to produce one pound of beef. Production of beef is especially problematic for the environ-ment. In a report completed for the National Academy of Sciences in 2014, researchers concluded that beef production requires twenty-eight, eleven, and five times more land, irrigation water, and greenhouse emissions, respectively, than the average of the other livestock categories.[22] Ruminant livestock need grazing land, which is already in short supply in many areas. Throughout the world, about twice as much land is devoted to animal grazing as is used for crops. If a land's carrying capacity is breached due to excessive exploitation, then the alternative is to use feedlot production, which requires even higher levels of grain and concentrates waste products in small areas.

Relying on Domestic Production

Imports offer a possible solution to deficiencies in domestic production, but here, too, many developing countries encounter problems. To finance imports, countries need foreign exchange, usually acquired through their own exports or from loans. Few developing countries have industrial products or professional services to export, so they must rely on minerals, natural resources (such as timber or petroleum), or cash crops (such as tea, sugar, coffee, cocoa, and rubber).

Prices for many of these commodities fluctuate widely. To illustrate, prices for nickel, aluminum, natural gas, and crude oil were lower in late 2016 than in 2000.[23] To cope with oft-declining prices for crops intended for export, such as cocoa, coffee, and cotton, farmers often intensify production, which implies increased reliance on fertilizers and pesticides, or they expand the area under cultivation to increase production. Unfortunately, these seemingly rational reactions can depress prices as supply eventually outpaces demand. As the area used for export crops expands, production for domestic consumption may decline. In contrast, high prices are good for farmers but reduce affordability for cash-strapped consumers.

Opportunities exist to increase exports, but economic policies in the developed world can discourage expanded activity in developing countries. Every year, farmers in Japan, Europe, and the United States receive hundreds of billions of dollars in subsidies and other price-related supports from their governments.

The European Union provided over $110 billion in 2012 for agricultural support for its farmers, including Queen Elizabeth of the United Kingdom. In some years, 40 percent or more of its annual budget is devoted to farm subsidies. So large are these supports, the president of the World Bank once noted, that the average European cow received a subsidy of about $2.50 per day, or more than the average daily income of about three billion people.[24] Japanese cows were more privileged. They received a daily subsidy of about $7.50 per day, or more than 1,800 times as much aid as Japan provided to sub-Saharan Africa each day.

Subsidies often lead to overproduction and surpluses, which discourage imports from developing countries, remove incentives to expand production, encourage the use of environmentally fragile land, and can increase prices to consumers in countries that provide the subsidies. Rice, sugar, cotton, wheat, and peanuts are easily and less expensively grown in many developing countries, but the U.S. government subsidizes its farmers to grow these crops or imposes tariffs on their importation.

Developing countries are increasingly irritated with trade and agricultural policies that they consider to be discriminatory. In response to a complaint from Brazil, the World Trade Organization (WTO) agreed that European subsidies for sugar exports violate international trade rules. This decision followed another WTO decision in which it ruled that U.S. price supports for cotton resulted in excess production and exports as well as low international prices, thus causing "serious prejudice" to Brazil. African producers of cotton have also called for an end to government support for the production of cotton in developed countries, especially the United States, the world's largest exporter of cotton. Without access to export markets, developing countries are denied their best opportunity for development, which, historically, has provided the best cure for poverty and rapid population growth.

The Debt Conundrum

Developing countries could once depend on loans from private banks or foreign governments to help finance imports, but many low- and middle-income countries are burdened with considerable debts. A common measure of a nation's indebtedness is its *debt service*, which represents the total payments for interest and principal as a percentage of the country's exports of goods and services. These exports provide the foreign currencies that allow countries to repay their debts, which are denominated in foreign currencies, and to import food, medicines, petroleum, and machinery. When debt service increases, more export earnings are required to repay loans, and less money is available for development. Many developing nations, especially in Africa and Latin America, have encountered this problem.

The largest donors, including the United States, the World Bank, the International Monetary Fund, the African Development Fund, and the Inter-American Development Bank, have agreed to cancel the debt of the world's most indebted countries, most of which are in Africa. In exchange for this debt relief, these so-called highly indebted poor countries (HIPCs) are required to adopt reforms designed to encourage sustainable economic growth and to complete poverty reduction strategies that provide the poor with a better quality of life.

Initial reviews of the debt relief initiative have been positive. By the end of 2012, debt repayments had been reduced in thirty-six countries, nearly all in sub-Saharan Africa, by nearly $75 billion; their average debt service payments had also dropped as a result. Despite these improvements, considerable uncertainty remains. Several of the HIPCs have not been repaying the debt they owe, and the debt relief has not eliminated the risk of future "debt distress" among many of the beneficiaries.

The Destruction of Tropical Forests

The rain forests of Africa, Asia, and South America are treasure chests of incomparable biological diversity. These forests provide irreplaceable habitats for as much as 80 percent of the world's species of plants and animals.

Viable forests also stabilize soils; reduce the impact and incidence of floods; and regulate local climates, watersheds, and river systems.[25] In addition, increasing concern about global warming underscores the global importance of tropical forests. Through photosynthesis, trees and other plants remove carbon dioxide from the atmosphere and convert it into oxygen. More than one-quarter of the prescription drugs used in the United States have their origins in tropical plants.

At the beginning of the twentieth century, tropical forests covered approximately 10 percent of the Earth's surface, or about 5.8 million square miles. The deforestation of recent decades has diminished this area by about one-third. If current rates of deforestation continue unabated, only a few areas of forest will remain untouched. Humans will have destroyed a natural palliative for global warming and condemned half or more of all species to extinction.

Causes

Solutions to the problem of tropical deforestation depend on the root causes.[26] One view blames poverty and the pressures associated with growing populations and shifting cultivators. Landless peasants, so the argument goes, invade tropical forests and denude them for fuel wood, for grazing, or to grow crops with which to survive. Tropical soils are typically thin, are relatively infertile, and lack sufficient nutrients, so frequent clearing of new areas is necessary. Such areas are ill suited for sustained agricultural production.

Another explanation for deforestation places primary blame on commercial logging intended to satisfy demands for tropical hardwoods in developed countries. Whether strapped for foreign exchange, required to repay loans, or subjected to domestic pressure to develop their economies, governments in the developing world frequently regard tropical forests as sources of ready income. Exports of wood now produce billions of dollars in annual revenues for developing countries, and some countries impose few limits in their rush to the bank.

Recognizing the causes and consequences of deforestation is not enough to bring about a solution. Commercial logging can be highly profitable to those who own logging concessions, and few governments in developing countries have the capacity to manage their forests properly. These governments often let logging companies harvest trees in designated areas under prescribed conditions. All too frequently, however, these conditions are inadequate or not well enforced, often due to rampant corruption.

An Alternative View of the Problem

One cause of deforestation is the demand for tropical hardwoods in developed countries, so these countries have been under pressure to reduce that demand. Leaders of developing countries quickly emphasize how ironic it is that developed countries, whose consumption creates the demand for tropical woods, are simultaneously calling for developing countries to reduce logging and shifting cultivation. In addition, developing countries point to Europe's destruction of its forests during the industrial revolution and the widespread cutting in the United States in the nineteenth century. Why then should developing countries be held to a different standard than the developed ones? Just as Europeans and Americans decided how and when to extract their resources, developing countries insist that they too should be permitted to determine their own patterns of consumption.

Will tropical forests survive? Solutions abound. What is lacking, however, is a consensus about which of these solutions will best meet the essential needs of the poor, the reasonable objectives of timber-exporting and -importing nations, and the inflexible imperatives of ecological stability.

Fortunately, there is a growing realization that much can be done to stem the loss of tropical forests. Many countries have developed national forest programs that describe the status of their forests as well as strategies to preserve them. Unfortunately, implementation of these plans does not always parallel the good intentions associated with them. Likewise, rather than seeing forests solely as a source of wood or additional agricultural land, many countries are now examining the export potential of forest products other than wood. The expectation is that the sale of these products—such as cork, rattan, oils, resins, and medicinal plants—will provide economic incentives to maintain rather than destroy forests.

Other proposed options to maintain tropical forests include efforts to certify that timber exports are from sustainably managed forests. Importers and potential consumers presumably will avoid timber products without such certification. For such initiatives to be successful, however, exporters have to accept the certification process, and there must be widespread agreement about what is meant by sustainable management. Such agreement is still absent. In addition, no country wants to subject itself to the potentially costly process of internationally accepted certification only to learn that its forestry exports do not meet the requirements for certification or that less expensive timber is available from countries that do not participate in a certification program.

There is no shortage of separate but competing third-party certification programs. One estimate places that number at more than fifty. As one author has suggested, however, different programs may confuse consumers with less rigorously enforced but similarly named competing standards.[27] Indeed, the author suggests that logging companies encourage such confusion through their support of multiple programs. Despite the large number of certification programs, most of the forested areas that are certified—more than 80 percent—are in Europe and North America.

Other approaches to sustainable management impose taxes on timber exports (or imports). The highest taxes are imposed on logging that causes the greatest ecological damage; timber from sustainable operations faces the lowest taxes. Yet another option is to increase reliance on the community-based management of forest resources. Rather than allowing logging companies with no long-term interest in a forest to harvest trees, community-based management places responsibility for decisions about logging (and other uses) with the people who live in or adjacent to forests. These people have the strongest incentives to manage forest resources wisely, particularly if they reap the long-term benefits of their management strategies.

Still another promising initiative is the United Nations Collaborative Programme on Reducing Emissions from Deforestation and Forest Degradation (REDD) in Developing Countries, which supports nationally led REDD+ initiatives, broadening the scope of the original program. An aspect of this international program involves developed countries paying developing countries not to harvest their tropical forests. The goal is to reduce deforestation by half between 2010 and 2020, but sufficient financing for REDD and REDD+ is uncertain.

Conflicting Signals from Developed Countries

Improvements in the policies of many developing countries are surely necessary if sustainable development is to be achieved. As already noted, however, developed countries sometimes cause or contribute to environmental problems in the developing countries.

Patterns of consumption provide an example. Although the United States and other developed nations can boast about their own comparatively low rates of population growth, developing nations reply that patterns of consumption are the real culprits when it comes to sustaining the world's population. This view suggests that negative impacts on the environment are a function of not only a country's population growth but also its consumption and the technologies, such as automobiles, that enable this consumption.[28]

Applying this formula places major responsibility for environmental problems on rich nations, despite their relatively small numbers of global inhabitants. The inhabitants of these nations own and consume far more of the Earth's resources than their numbers justify. Consider that the world's richest 10 percent of adults own almost 90 percent of its total wealth whereas the bottom half of adults collectively own less than 1 percent of this wealth. For one-fifth of the world's adults, according to the *Global Wealth Report 2016*, the value of all of their assets is less than $250—compared with $344,700, the estimated mean wealth of American adults.[29] In addition, residents of developed countries consume a disproportionate share of all meat and fish and much of the world's energy, paper, chemicals, iron, and steel. One estimate suggests that people in the developed world consume, on average, about thirty-two times as many resources as do people in developing countries.[30] Put in other terms, this means that the consumption of a single American is comparable to the consumption of thirty-two Kenyans. The United States leads the world in per capita production of trash and has one of the lowest rates of recycling among developed countries.

Americans represent less than 5 percent of the Earth's inhabitants, yet they use about one-fifth of the world's energy. In 2015, the United States was both the world's largest consumer and its largest importer of petroleum.

During a typical day in the United States, about 325 million Americans consume more petroleum than the 3.25 *billion* people who live in India, Japan, and all the countries in Africa and Central and South America combined. Much of this petroleum is used to fuel Americans' love for the automobile. There are more motor vehicles than licensed drivers in the United States, and they consume more than 40 percent of the world's gasoline. An average American driver uses about five times more gasoline than the typical European. Part of the explanation is that many European cars, often designed by U.S. manufacturers, are more fuel efficient than are U.S. cars. Despite many Americans' common belief that gasoline prices are often too high, the price of gasoline in much of Western Europe is more than two to three times higher than it is in the United States.

Americans' extravagance with fossil fuels provides part of the explanation for U.S. production of about one-sixth of the emissions that contribute to global warming. The Intergovernmental Panel on Climate Change has assessed that a relatively safe level of carbon dioxide emissions is about 2.25 metric tons per person per year.[31] Each metric ton is about 2,205 pounds. With the exception of Australia, Canada, Saudi Arabia, and a few ministates, no country emits as much carbon dioxide per capita as does the United States. It produced 16.1 metric tons per capita in 2015, seven times higher than what sustainable levels of development would require. In Germany, China, and India, per capita emissions in the same year were 9.6, 7.7, and 1.9 metric tons, respectively.[32] Although China's emissions of carbon dioxide increased by over 350 percent between 1990 and 2015, a notable portion of the increase is attributable to the production of goods destined for Europe and the United States.

Americans' patterns of food consumption are also of interest. An average American consumes about 3,750 calories per day, almost the highest level in the world. Among young adults, about 25 percent of these calories are from sweetened beverages. Not surprisingly, almost three-quarters of American adults are either obese or overweight. According to the U.S. Centers for Disease Control and Prevention, no American state had a prevalence of adult obesity of more than 15 percent in 1990. By 2000, all states except Colorado exceeded this percentage. By 2015, no state had an obesity prevalence of *less* than 20 percent, and twenty-five states had rates exceeding 30 percent.[33] For these reasons, *The Economist* labeled the United States the "fattest country in the Western World." Weight-related illnesses consume as much as one-fifth of the nation's costs for medical care each year and are responsible for the deaths of more Americans each year than are motor vehicle accidents.

As much as 30 to 40 percent of all food is wasted in the United States and Western Europe. Recent research suggests that the United States spends nearly $220 billion a year growing, processing, transporting, and disposing of food that is never eaten. Wasting food has several undesirable environmental consequences. It consumes about one-fifth of all fresh water. Energy is required to produce, harvest, transport, market, and prepare food, and all of this energy is squandered when food is wasted. Food rotting in landfills contributes to emissions of greenhouse gases. As *The Economist* has noted, if the developed world reduced the food it wasted by half, the challenge of feeding the world's population in 2050 would vanish.[34]

Due to these kinds of inequalities in consumption, continued population growth in rich countries is a greater threat to the global environment than is such growth in the developing world. As the World Wildlife Fund has explained, "If everyone lived like an average resident of the USA, a total of four Earths would be required to regenerate humanity's annual demand on nature." Other experts have suggested that if Americans want to maintain their present standard of living and levels of energy consumption, their ideal population is about 50 million, far less than the mid-2017 U.S. population of about 325 million.[35]

The data just presented raise questions that merit attention. Are the world's environmental problems due to too many poor people who have few resources and who use them sparingly or to too many rich people who use more resources than their numbers justify and whose significant impact on the environment has global implications? Is it fair and equitable for the relatively small numbers of rich people to consume excessively and waste indiscriminately when hundreds of millions of people in developing countries are undernourished and undereducated, live in slums or their equivalent, are frequent victims of deadly illnesses and diseases without access to their cures, and live amidst environmental harms that they cannot escape but that would be considered scandalous and intolerable in the rich world?

Causes for Optimism?

There is cause for concern about the prospects for sustainable development among developing countries, but the situation is neither entirely bleak nor beyond hope. The rates of deforestation and population growth are slowing in many developing countries. Smallpox, a killer of millions of people every year in the 1950s, has been eradicated (except in laboratories). Polio may soon be the next scourge to be eliminated, and deaths due to AIDS, diarrhea, measles, and respiratory infections such as tuberculosis have dropped significantly.

All members of the United Nations adopted eight Millennium Development Goals (MDGs) in 2000 with the intent of achieving them by 2015. The first of these goals was to reduce the proportion of people living in extreme poverty by half between 1990 and 2015. The target was achieved in 2010. Over 1.1 billion fewer people lived in extreme poverty in 2016 than in 1990. Similarly, the mortality rate for children under five dropped by 53 percent—to forty-three deaths per one thousand live births in 2015 from ninety-one deaths per one thousand live births in 1990. Over the same period, 2.1 billion people gained access to a latrine, flush toilet, or other improved sanitation facility, and 2.6 billion gained access to a source of improved drinking water.[36]

To build on the successes of the MDGs, the world's nations established seventeen Sustainable Development Goals (SDGs) with 169 targets in late 2015. The goals, to be achieved no later than 2030, focus on economic growth, social inclusion, and environmental protection. Goal 15, as an example, seeks to protect, restore, and promote the sustainable use of terrestrial ecosystems; manage forests sustainably; combat desertification; and halt and reverse land degradation and halt biodiversity loss. Other goals address the need for sustainable consumption and for "urgent action" to combat climate change.

The MDGs and the SDGs demonstrate an increasing awareness of the need to address the problems of the developing world, but much remains to be done. Through the President's Emergency Plan for AIDS Relief (PEPFAR), as an example, the United States is the world's leader in responding to HIV/AIDS in the developing world. PEPFAR, which President George W. Bush initiated in 2003, has helped avert more than eleven million AIDS-related deaths and nearly sixteen million HIV infections worldwide. Private philanthropic support for development has also grown significantly. The Bill and Melinda Gates Foundation has provided over $35 billion to improve health, education, and the status of women in developing countries. The William J. Clinton Foundation has been similarly active and has successfully negotiated major reductions in the cost of essential drugs in many countries, assisted African farmers to improve their productivity, and worked to reduce deforestation and climate change.

Perhaps the best known target among economically developed countries is that of each country providing at least 0.7 percent (*not* 7 percent, but seven-tenths of 1 percent) of its GNI to official development assistance (ODA) to meet the needs of developing countries. The United Nations General Assembly established this target in 1970, with the expectation that donor countries would meet it by 1975. Sweden and the Netherlands were the first to do so. Despite this admirable target, only Denmark, Luxembourg, the Netherlands, Norway, Sweden, the United Arab Emirates, and the United Kingdom met or exceeded this target in 2015. Although the United States typically provides more foreign aid than any other country, its ODA is often less than 0.2 percent of the U.S. GNI, which is among the lowest percentages of the world's major donors. This situation has led some observers to label the United States as a "global Scrooge" based on its seeming unwillingness to share its wealth.

Those who think the United States should continue to scale back its ODA contributions have an ally in President Trump. His initial budget stated that it was time to prioritize the well-being of Americans and "to ask the rest of the world to step up and pay its fair share." Trump then recommended a reduction of over 30 percent in U.S. foreign assistance and that remaining assistance be focused in countries of the greatest strategic significance to the United States—rather than in countries with a high level of need. He also proposed the elimination of all U.S. funding of efforts to mitigate the effects of climate change in developing countries, including those implemented by the United Nations.[37]

Trump further proposed the termination of the McGovern–Dole International Food for Education and Child Nutrition Program. It supports education, child development, and food security in low-income, food-deficit countries around the globe. This proposal was ironic. Poor nutrition is probably the single most important threat to the world's health, and the program has helped millions of children and pregnant women avoid malnutrition. According to the Famine Early Warning System, which the United States operates, about 70 million people needed food assistance in 2017, a level deemed to be "unprecedented in recent decades." Among the 45 countries in peril, four (Nigeria, Somalia, South Sudan, and Yemen) faced a "credible risk of famine."[38] This was a prescient forecast. Millions of Yemenis encountered famine in the summer of 2017, and an outbreak of cholera among more than one-half million people in the country exacerbated the catastrophe.[39]

Is it important to assist developing countries with food and finance? Americans are often ambivalent in their answers to this question. Surveys of Americans' opinions about foreign aid present an interesting but mixed picture. More than 80 percent of those surveyed in 2008 agreed that developed countries have "a moral responsibility to work to reduce hunger and severe poverty in poor countries." Despite such support, most Americans also believe that the United States is already doing more than its share to help less fortunate countries. In surveys conducted in 2015 and 2016, respondents estimated that the average amount of the annual federal budget devoted to foreign aid is 31 percent. When told that the actual amount is less than 1 percent, nearly one-third of respondents said this was still too much. This finding contrasts with the views of people in the European Union, where a public opinion survey in 2016 found that about two-thirds of respondents favored continuing financial assistance at current levels or increasing aid, even though many European countries have some of the world's highest levels of ODA.[40]

The United States is among the world's largest donors of emergency food aid. Rather than allowing the U.S. Agency for International Development to purchase less expensive food closer to where it is needed, Congress requires that much of the food be purchased in the United States. In addition, the law requires that at least half of the food be shipped on American-flagged vessels, which are among the most expensive to use. As a result of these requirements, U.S. food aid is more expensive than it would otherwise be, and the food often arrives well after it is most needed.[41] Critics of the program also claim that the U.S. food aid destabilizes local markets and competes with farmers close to affected areas who cannot afford to donate their food.

In contrast to Americans' seeming reluctance to share their wealth, other nations have demonstrated an increased willingness to address globally shared environmental problems. The international community operates a Global Environment Facility, a multibillion-dollar effort to address global warming, the loss of biological diversity, the pollution of international waters, and the depletion of the ozone layer. The Green Climate Fund represents a similar international initiative. Created in 2010 by 194 countries, the fund provides resources for low-emission and climate-resilient projects in developing countries, especially those that are highly vulnerable to the effects of climate change, including countries in Africa and small island developing states.

Many developing nations recognize their obligations to protect their environments as well as the global commons. India's and China's commitment to reducing their emissions of greenhouse gases provide examples. India produces relatively few of these emissions on a per capita basis, but it has committed to reduce its emissions intensity by as much as 33 to 35 percent by 2030 from the levels reached in 2005. In addition, although it is facing growing demands for electricity, which could be met by burning more coal, India has committed to increasing its reliance on nonfossil fuels by 40 percent in the same year. China has pledged to reduce its carbon intensity 60 to 65 percent by 2030 compared with the levels in 2005 and has similarly pledged to increase its reliance on renewable sources of energy. China now produces more solar energy than any other country and expects to rely on renewable energy sources for 20 percent of its need by 2030. Both India and China are reducing their reliance on fossil fuels more quickly than they had previously projected, leading the *New York Times* to conclude that their progress has been "astonishing." With the withdrawal of the United States from the Paris climate agreement, China is now widely considered to be the world's champion in fighting climate change.[42]

However desirable improved environmental quality may be as an objective, poor nations cannot afford to address their environmental problems in the absence of cooperation from richer nations. Consumers in rich nations can demonstrate such cooperation by paying higher prices for products that reflect sustainable environmental management. One example of this situation would be Americans' willingness to pay higher prices for forestry products harvested sustainably. In fact, however, Home Depot found that only a third of its customers would be willing to pay a premium of 2 percent for such products.[43]

Another issue of importance is resentment in some countries toward the environmental sermons from developed countries. Climate change provides one of several examples. As leaders of several developing countries have asked, why should they slow or alter their path to development to accommodate high standards of living elsewhere? When India released a policy statement on climate change, its prime minister declared that fairness dictated that everyone deserves equal per capita emissions, regardless of where they live.[44] India is not willing, he noted, to accept a model of economic development in which some countries maintain high carbon emissions while the options available for developing countries are constrained.

President Bush once identified a growing middle class in India, which is "demanding better food and nutrition," as a cause of higher prices. The reaction from India was understandably negative. "Why do Americans think they deserve to eat more than Indians?" asked one journalist. An Indian public official characterized the U.S. position as "[g]uys with gross obesity telling guys just emerging from emaciation to go on a major diet." This characterization may be indicative of a larger concern. The perception that Americans are global environmental culprits is widespread. When people in twenty-four countries were asked in 2008 which country is "hurting the world's environment the most," majorities or pluralities in thirteen countries cited the United States.[45]

Further evidence of America's seeming lack of commitment to international environmental issues can be found in the Center for Global Development's Commitment to Development Index. The index ranks twenty-seven of the world's richest countries on their dedication to policies that benefit people living in poorer nations. In 2016, the United States ranked twenty-fourth out of these twenty-seven countries in the environmental dimension of the index.[46]

Contentious debates and inflammatory rhetoric about blame and responsibility are not productive. The economic, population, and environmental issues of the developing world dwarf those of the developed nations and are not amenable to quick resolution. Nonetheless, immediate action is imperative. Hundreds of millions of people are destroying their biological and environmental support systems at unprecedented rates to meet their daily needs for food, fuel, and fiber. The world will add several billion people in the next few decades, and all of them will have justifiable claims to be fed, clothed, educated, employed, and healthy. To accommodate these expectations, the world may need as much as 50 percent more energy in 2030 than it used in 2010.

Whether the environment can accommodate these unprecedented but predictable increases in population and consumption depends not only on the poor who live in stagnant economies but also on a much smaller number of rich, overconsuming nations in the developed world. Unless developed nations work together to accommodate and support sustainable development everywhere, the future of billions of poor people, many of whom become refugees seeking better lives, will determine the future of Americans as well.

As the authors of the Millennium Ecosystem Assessment concluded, the ability of the planet's ecosystems to sustain future generations is no longer assured.[47] Over the past fifty years, the world has experienced unprecedented environmental change in response to ever-increasing demands for food, fuel, fiber, freshwater, and timber. Much of the environmental degradation that has occurred can be reversed, but as these authors warned, "The changes in policy and practice required are substantial and not currently underway."[48]

If these experts are correct, unless the United States acts soon and in collaboration with other nations, Americans will increasingly suffer the adverse consequences of environmental damage caused by the billions of poor people we have chosen to neglect and perhaps even abandon—just as these people will suffer from the environmental damage we inflict on them. In short, there are continuing questions about whether the current economic model that depends on growth and extravagant consumption among a few privileged countries is ecologically sustainable and morally acceptable for everyone.[49]

Suggested Websites

Organisation for Economic Co-operation and Development (OECD) (www.oecd.org/development) This website provides extensive information on aid statistics and effectiveness, environment and development, and gender and development.

Population Reference Bureau (www.prb.org) The bureau is a convenient source for data on global population trends. Its annual *World Population Data Sheet* includes statistics for most of the world's nations on birth rates and death rates, per capita income, percentage undernourished, percentage in urban areas, and projected population size for 2030 and 2050.

UN Development Programme (www.undp.org) The program's website provides links to activities and reports on economic development and the environment, including the Sustainable Development Goals (SDGs).

UN Division for Sustainable Development (http://sustainable development.un.org) The "Sustainable Development Knowledge Platform" within the United Nations provides useful links to the goals and targets on sustainable development for the post-2015 development agenda.

UN Food and Agriculture Organization (www.fao.org) The FAO focuses on agriculture, forestry, fisheries, and rural development, working to alleviate poverty and hunger worldwide.

UN Population Fund (www.unfpa.org) The UNFPA funds population assistance programs, particularly family planning and reproductive health, and reports on population growth and its effects.

World Bank (www.worldbank.org) One of the largest sources of economic assistance to developing nations, the World Bank also issues reports on poverty and global economic conditions, including progress toward the SDGs. Its *World Development Indicators* include a wealth of development data.

Notes

1. World Bank, "Purchasing Power Parity National Income per Capita 2016," *World Development Indicators*, 2016, wdi.worldbank.org/table/1.1. Due to differences in the costs of goods and services among countries, GNI per capita does not provide comparable measures of economic well-being. To address this problem, economists have developed the concept of purchasing power parity (PPP). PPP equalizes the prices of identical goods and services across countries, with the United States as the base economy. For an amusing explanation of PPP, see the "The Big Mac Index" of *The Economist*, at www.economist.com/content/big-mac-index, which compares the price of a McDonald's Big Mac hamburger in nearly fifty countries.

2. UNICEF, *Ending Child Marriage: Progress and Prospects* (New York: UNICEF, 2014), http://data.unicef.org/resources/ending-child-marriage-progress-and-prospects; Population Reference Bureau, "Early Marriage Trends," *World Population Data 2015: Focus on Women's Empowerment*, November 2015, http://www.prb.org/Publications/Articles/2015/early-marriage-trends.aspx.

3. United Nations, *Millennium Development Goals Report 2013* (New York: United Nations, 2013). Archived reports are available from http://www.un.org/millenniumgoals/news.

4. Readers interested in learning about the daily challenges of poverty in the slums of India are encouraged to read Katherine Boo's prize-winning book, *Behind the Beautiful Forevers: Life, Death, and Hope in a Mumbai Undercity* (New York: Random House, 2012).

5. World Commission on Environment and Development, *Our Common Future* (London: Oxford University Press, 1987), 8, 43.

6. John N. Wilford, "A Tough-Minded Ecologist Comes to Defense of Malthus," *New York Times*, June 30, 1987, C3.

7. Population Reference Bureau, *2017 World Population Data Sheet* (Washington, DC: Population Reference Bureau, 2017), http://www.prb.org/Publications/Datasheets/2017/2017-world-population-data-sheet.aspx. For a discussion of the world's carrying capacity, see Jeroen C. J. M. Van Den Bergh and Piet Rietveld, "Reconsidering the Limits to World Population: Meta-analysis and Meta-prediction," *BioScience* 54 (March 2004): 195–204; and Erle C. Ellis, "Overpopulation Is Not the Problem," *New York Times*, September 13, 2013, A19.

8. O. P. Sharma and Carl Haub, "Change Comes Slowly for Religious Diversity in India," Population Reference Bureau, March 2009, www.prb.org/Articles/2009/indiareligions.aspx.

9. Joseph Kahn, "Harsh Birth Control Steps Fuel Violence in China," *New York Times*, May 22, 2007, A12; Jim Yardley, "China Sticking with One-Child Policy," *New York Times*, March 11, 2008, A10.

10. Leo Lewis, "China Looks to a Boom as It Relaxes One-Child Policy," *The Times* (London), November 16, 2013.

11. For example, see Julian Simon, *The Ultimate Resource* (Princeton, NJ: Princeton University Press, 1981).

12. Carl Haub and O. P. Sharma, "India's Population Reality," *Population Bulletin* 61, no. 3 (September 2006), http://www.prb.org/pdf06/61.3indiaspopulationreality_eng.pdf; Therese Hesketh and Zhu Wei Xing, "Abnormal Sex Ratios in Human Populations: Causes and Consequences," *Proceedings of the National Academy of Sciences* 103 (2006): 13271–75, www.pnas.org/content/103/36.toc.

13. Lester R. Brown, "Analyzing the Demographic Trap," in *State of the World 1987*, ed. Lester R. Brown (New York: Norton, 1987), 20–37, see page 21.

14. Per Pinstrup-Andersen, former director of the International Food Policy Research Institute, believes the world can easily feed twelve billion people. See "Will the World Starve?" *The Economist*, June 10, 1995, 39.

15. FAO, *The State of Food Insecurity in the World* (Rome, Italy: FAO, 2015), http://www.fao.org/3/a-i4646e.pdf.

16. FAO, *The State of Food and Agriculture 2007* (Rome, Italy: FAO, 2007); FAO, *Crop Prospects and Food Situation: Countries in Crisis Requiring External Assistance* (Rome, Italy: FAO, February 2008), http://www.fao.org/docrep/010/ah881e/ah881e02.htm; FAO, *The State of Food Insecurity in the World* (Rome, Italy: FAO, 2010), http://www.fao.org/docrep/013/i1683e/i1683e.pdf.

17. FAO, *Land Degradation Assessment in Drylands* (Rome, Italy: FAO, 2008).

18. Colin Chartres and Samyuktha Varma, *Out of Water: From Abundance to Scarcity and How to Solve the World's Water Problems* (Upper Saddle River, NJ: FT Press, 2011), xvii.

19. Tony J. Pitcher and William W. L. Cheung, "Fisheries: Hope or Despair?" *Marine Pollution Bulletin* 74 (September 30, 2013): 508; Robert J. Diaz and Rutger Rosenberg, "Spreading Dead Zones and Consequences for Marine Ecosystems," *Science* 321 (2008): 926–29; International Programme on the State of the Ocean, "Multiple Ocean Stresses Threaten 'Globally Significant' Marine Extinction,"

June 20, 2011, https://www.iucn.org/content/multiple-ocean-stresses-threaten-"globally-significant"-marine-extinction.

20. Bruce Kennedy, "Can China's Ambitious Urbanization Plan Succeed?" *Money Watch*, March 26, 2014, http://www.cbsnews.com/news/can-chinas-new-urbanization-plan-succeed/.

21. Zhangyue Zhou, Weiming Tian, Jimin Wang, Hongbo Liu, and Lijuan Cao, *Food Consumption Trends in China: April 2012* (Canberra: Australian Department of Agriculture, Fisheries and Forestry, 2012), http://www.agriculture.gov.au/Pages/agriculture-food/food/publications/food-consumption-trends-in-china.aspx; see also Damien Ma and William Adams, "Appetite for Destruction: Why Feeding China's 1.3 Billion People Could Leave the Rest of the World Hungry," *Foreign Policy*, October 1, 2013.

22. Gidon Eshel, Alon Shepon, Tamar Makov, and Ron Milo, "Land, Irrigation Water, Greenhouse Gas, and Reactive Nitrogen Burdens of Meat, Eggs, and Dairy Production in the United States," *Proceedings of the National Academy of Sciences of the United States* 111, no. 33, (July 2014): 11996–12001, https://doi.org/10.1073/pnas.1402183111.

23. International Monetary Fund, "Indices of Market Prices for Non-Fuel and Fuel Commodities, 2014–2017," http://www.imf.org/external/np/res/commod/Table2.pdf.

24. Statement of James D. Wolfensohn, cited in David T. Cook, "Excerpts from a Monitor Breakfast on Poverty and Globalization," *Christian Science Monitor*, June 13, 2003.

25. National Academy of Sciences (NAS), *Population Growth and Economic Development: Policy Questions* (Washington, DC: NAS, 1986), 31.

26. For discussions of the causes of deforestation, see Helmut J. Geist and Eric Lambin, "Proximate Causes and Underlying Driving Forces of Tropical Deforestation," *BioScience* 52 (February 2002): 143–50; and Noriko Hosonuma, Martin Herold, Veronique De Sy, Ruth S. De Fries, Maria Brockhaus, Louis Verchot, Arild Angelsen, and Erika Romijn, "An Assessment of Deforestation and Forest Degradation Drivers in Developing Countries," *Environmental Research Letters* 7 (2012), http://iopscience.iop.org/article/10.1088/1748-9326/7/4/044009/meta.

27. Jared Diamond, *Collapse: How Societies Choose to Fail or Succeed* (London: Penguin, 2005).

28. Paul R. Ehrlich and John P. Holdren, "Impact of Population Growth," *Science* 171 (1971): 1212–17.

29. Credit Suisse Research Institute, *Global Wealth Report 2016* (Zurich: Credit Suisse, 2016), http://publications.credit-suisse.com/tasks/render/file/index.cfm?fileid=AD783798-ED07-E8C2-4405996B5B02A32E.

30. Jared Diamond, "What's Your Consumption Factor?" *New York Times*, January 2, 2008, A19.

31. Commission on Growth and Development, *The Growth Report: Strategies for Sustained Growth and Inclusive Development* (Washington, DC: World Bank, 2008), 85–86, https://openknowledge.worldbank.org/handle/10986/6507.

32. PBL Netherlands Environmental Assessment Agency, *Trends in Global CO_2 Emissions: 2016 Report* (The Hague: PBL Publishers, 2016), http://edgar.jrc.ec.europa.eu/news_docs/jrc-2016-trends-in-global-co2-emissions-2016-report-103425.pdf.

33. Centers for Disease Control and Prevention, "Adult Obesity Facts," *Overweight and Obesity*, http://www.cdc.gov/obesity/data/adult.html.

34. ReThink Food Waste, *A Roadmap to Reduce U.S. Food Waste by 20 Percent* (New York: ReFED, 2016), refed.com/downloads/ReFED_Report_2016.pdf; "The 9-billion People Question," *The Economist*, May 26, 2011.

35. World Wildlife Fund, *Living Planet Report 2012: Biodiversity, Biocapacity and Better Choices* (Gland, Switzerland: World Wildlife Fund, 2012), 43; David and Marcia Pimentel, "Land, Water and Energy Versus the Ideal U.S. Population," *NPG Forum* (January 2005), http://npg.org/forum_series/land_water_energy_pimentel_forumpaper.pdf.

36. World Health Organization, *Fact Sheets*, http://www.who.int/mediacentre/fact sheets/en/.

37. For the quotation, see Executive Office of the President of the United States, *America First: A Budget Blueprint to Make America Great Again* (Washington, DC: Office of Management and Budget, 2018), 2; For information on the proposed reduction, see Executive Office of the President of the United States, *A New Foundation for American Greatness: Budget of the U.S. Government, Fiscal Year 2018* (Washington, DC: Office of Management and Budget, 2017).

38. FEWS Net, "Emergency Food Assistance Needs Unprecedented as Famine Threatens Four Countries," *Global Alert*, January 25, 2017, http://www.fews.net/global/alert/January 25, 2017.

39. "Deadly Combination of Cholera, Hunger and Conflict Pushes Yemen to 'Edge of a Cliff,'" *UN News Centre*, August 1, 2017, http://www.un.org/apps/news/story.asp?NewsID=57294#.WbbmeIqQyZM.

40. Bianca DiJulio, Mira Norton, and Mollyann Brodie, *Americans' Views on the U.S. Role in Global Health* (Menlo Park, CA: The Henry J. Kaiser Family Foundation, January 2016), http://kff.org/global-health-policy/poll-finding/americans-views-on-the-u-s-role-in-global-health/; and Liz Hamel, Ashley Kirzinger, and Mollyann Brodie, *2016 Survey of Americans on the U.S. Role in Global Health* (Menlo Park, CA: The Henry J. Kaiser Family Foundation, April 2016), http://files.kff.org/attachment/issue-brief-2016-survey-of-americans-on-the-u-s-role-in-global-health/; European Union, *EU Citizens' Views on Development, Cooperation and Aid*, Special Eurobarometer Report No. 455 (Belgium: DEVCO, April 2017), https://ec.europa.eu/europeaid/sites/devco/files/sp455-development-aid-final_en.pdf, 44.

41. Ron Nixon, "Typhoon Revives Debate on U.S. Food Aid Methods," *New York Times*, November 22, 2013, A3. See also Randy Schnepf, *U.S. International Food Aid: Background and Issues* (Washington, DC: Congressional Research Service, 2016), https://fas.org/sgp/crs/misc/R41072.pdf.

42. "On Climate, Look to China and India," editorial, *New York Times*, May 22, 2017, A24; Keith Bradsher, "China Turns Economic Engine Toward Clean-Energy Leadership," *New York Times*, June 6, 2017, A1.

43. "The Long Road to Sustainability," *The Economist*, Special Report: Forests, September 25, 2010.

44. Voice of America, "India Rejects Binding Commitment to Cut Greenhouse Gas Emissions," February 7, 2008, https://www.voanews.com/a/a-13-2008-02-07-voa20-66627522/556691.html.

45. Heather Timmons, "Indians Find U.S. at Fault in Food Cost," *New York Times*, May 14, 2008, C1; "Melting Asia," *The Economist*, June 7, 2008, 30; Pew Global Attitudes Project, "Some Positive Signs for U.S. Image," June 12, 2008, 65, http://www.pewglobal.org/files/pdf/260.pdf.

46. For the Commitment to Development Index, see https://www.cgdev.org/commitment-development-index.

47. Millennium Ecosystem Assessment, *Ecosystems and Human Well-Being: Synthesis* (Washington, DC: Island Press, 2005), https://www.millenniumassessment.org/documents/document.356.aspx.pdf.

48. Millennium Ecosystem Assessment, "What Are the Findings of the MA?" available from the Environment and Ecology website, http://environment-ecology.com/millennium-ecosystem-assessment/109-millenium-ecosystem-assesment.html.

49. UN Development Programme, *Human Development Report 2007/2008: Fighting Climate Change—Human Solidarity in a Divided World* (New York: UNDP, 2007), http://hdr.undp.org/sites/default/files/reports/268/hdr_20072008_en_complete.pdf.

Part V

Conclusion

Chapter 15

Conclusion
Past and Future Environmental Challenges
Norman J. Vig and Michael E. Kraft

Nobody really knows.

President Donald Trump on climate change,
Fox News, December 11, 2016

There is no Planet B

Theme of the March for Science,
April 22, 2017

More than three decades ago, we expressed concern that the Reagan administration was undermining the basic intent and integrity of the environmental legislation enacted during the "environmental decade."[1] Though lacking a clear mandate from the public or Congress, Ronald Reagan imposed an "administrative presidency" that relied heavily on the use of executive powers to roll back environmental policies (Chapter 4). He utilized the powers of appointment, budgeting, and centralized control over the regulatory bureaucracy to curtail the EPA and other agencies' capacity to implement environmental laws.

We argued then that two criteria were especially important in evaluating such presidential interventions:

> The first is *legitimacy*—does the president's action serve to further the goals embodied in relevant statutes? Does the president have an electoral mandate or public support for the political resolution of the issues that he imposes? The case for political accountability only holds if these conditions are met. The second criterion is *technical rationality*—is the president's decision compatible with a reasonable interpretation of factual evidence in the record? Or, more broadly, does the pattern of presidential intervention permit skilled professionalism as well as political responsiveness in administration?[2]

By 1983, congressional investigations had forced the resignations of Reagan's top environmental officials, including EPA administrator Anne Gorsuch and interior secretary James Watt. Congress and the courts had also blocked many of their proposed policies, although deep budget and personnel cuts had seriously undermined the professional capabilities of the EPA and other agencies. We concluded that, by the end of the first term, Reagan's attack had largely failed for lack of both legitimacy and technical rationality.[3]

Several environmental laws were in fact *strengthened* by Congress over Reagan's objections during his second term and under the subsequent Republican administration of George H. W. Bush (see Chapters 1, 4, 5, and Appendix 1). The Clinton administration further restored the budget and staff of environmental agencies (Appendix 2). Vice President Al Gore and other environmentalists in the administration attempted to build a new case for economic growth *and* environmental protection through *sustainable development*. Partly in response to issues raised in the 1980s about the efficiency of regulation, Clinton also launched a series of reforms to encourage more voluntary and collaborative approaches to decision making in both EPA regulation and public lands management. However, he failed to gain political support—and thus legitimacy—for his attempt to create an international regime to control greenhouse gas (GHG) emissions through the Kyoto Protocol of 1997 (Chapter 13).

President George W. Bush rejected the Kyoto Protocol and many of his predecessor's other reforms. Like Reagan, and to some extent Clinton, he utilized executive powers to alter policies disliked by business and industry. He and Vice President Dick Cheney promoted rapid development of energy resources, especially fossil fuels, through both executive actions and legislation. Although Bush failed to convince Congress to cut spending for natural resources and the environment, he attempted to politicize decision making throughout the bureaucracy to achieve his goals. His administration repeatedly ignored or distorted the advice of scientists and other experts on issues such as air pollution and global warming, resulting in numerous lawsuits and frequent reversals in the courts. As in the case of Reagan, his attempts to "streamline" environmental policies were limited by weak political support and lack of scientific integrity.

As explained in Chapter 4 and elsewhere in this volume, Barack Obama then utilized unilateral executive powers to expand greatly the role of government in combatting climate change and other forms of pollution. By the end of his first term, it was obvious that Congress was deadlocked on virtually all environmental issues and that the "administrative presidency" was, once again, the principal instrument for major policy change. Obama appointed highly qualified administrators, including many distinguished scientists, and based his climate policies on the Clean Air Act, as interpreted by the Supreme Court in several decisions (see Chapters 6 and 7). He also institutionalized new policies to protect the integrity of scientific evidence and to ensure its appropriate role in agency decision making. Obama's policies thus reflected the global scientific consensus on climate change and gained wide acceptance among professionals in and out of government. He played a leading role in negotiating the historic Paris Agreement on climate in 2015. His initiatives also had broad public support despite the partisan divide in Congress. In the end, however, his failure to gain congressional legitimacy for his policies raised serious doubts about their permanence and opened the door for his successor to undo them.

It is thus not surprising that President Donald Trump utilized the Reagan playbook to roll back Obama's policies. Indeed, the parallels with the

Reagan administration are striking. Through executive actions during his first hundred days in office, Trump ordered the review or elimination of nearly two dozen major environmental rules and imposed new cost-based criteria for any new regulations, proposed a budget that would cut the EPA and other agencies at least as deeply as Reagan's did, threatened the elimination of multiple agencies and programs, and specifically ordered the termination of all federal actions to control climate change (Chapter 4). Like Reagan, he placed highly partisan political appointees representing business and industry in the White House and in all agencies and departments, notably those responsible for the environment. Scott Pruitt, like Gorsuch and Watt in the Reagan administration, quickly became the leading proponent of deregulation. Like them, Pruitt was dedicated to defunding and dismantling the agency he headed.

The question once again is whether the Trump presidency can meet the fundamental criteria set out at the beginning of this chapter: *legitimacy* and *technical rationality*. In many respects, Trump's deregulation agenda is even more radical than that of Ronald Reagan.[4] His initial environmental proposals clearly lack support in public opinion and the media, and may not be upheld in Congress or by the courts.[5] The economic and scientific rationale for his policies is highly questionable as well. Because Trump has acted with little or no scientific advice in the White House, it is unlikely that policy changes will be effective or widely accepted in the intellectual and business communities that have already adapted to the global imperatives of climate change and sustainable technologies.

In the following sections, we discuss some of the major environmental challenges raised by the Trump administration and by other developments covered in this volume. We also discuss the potential for alternative approaches to environmental regulation that might both improve the effectiveness of federal policies and help to build greater consensus over the role of government. Finally, we assess the state of current environmental governance and highlight new needs for the future.

Major Issues

Most of the environmental problems discussed in earlier editions of this book are still with us—including those relating to management of public lands; control of toxic chemicals and hazardous wastes; and protection of biological diversity, endangered species, and threatened ecosystems. We focus here on three areas that have received the most attention in recent years: climate change, energy production, and air and water pollution.

Climate Change: Dire Warnings and Uncertain Future

The leading international body responsible for tracking climate change—the Intergovernmental Panel on Climate Change (IPCC)—has published five comprehensive reports since 1990, each more urgent than the last. The fifth assessment report, released in four installments in late 2013 and 2014, contained the direst warnings yet about current climate trends and future risks throughout the world.[6] The scientific report concluded that it is "extremely likely" (a greater than 95 percent chance) that human activities are "the dominant cause" of the observed global warming since the 1950s. It further documented global changes already occurring, from rapidly melting sea and land ice and rising sea levels to intense heat waves and heavy rains, strains on food production and water supplies, the deterioration of coral reefs, and threats to fish and other wildlife.[7] The final draft report recognized progress in limiting carbon emissions in some countries, but stated that these gains are being overwhelmed by growing emissions in rapidly developing countries such as China and India.[8] The report thus called for much greater commitments to both policies to mitigate emissions growth and major investments to allow social and economic adaptation to climate changes that are inevitable in the coming decades. Unless new technologies are put in place by 2030, the report argued, it will probably be too late to avoid catastrophic damage to human life on the planet.[9] "Continued emission of greenhouse gases will cause further warming and long-lasting changes in all components of the climate system, increasing the likelihood of severe, pervasive and irreversible impacts for people and ecosystems," the report stated.[10]

Recent data appear to support these projections. The years 2014, 2015, and 2016 each set new global heat records. "Temperatures are heading toward levels that many experts believe will pose a profound threat to both the natural world and to civilization."[11] The National Aeronautics and Space Administration (NASA) calculated that the planet had warmed by more than a half-degree Fahrenheit from 2013 to 2016, the largest three-year increase ever recorded. In February 2017, temperatures were running more than 50°F above normal in parts of the Arctic, threatening the survival of many native Alaskan villages.[12] Land and sea ice were melting rapidly in Greenland and around both poles.[13] Temperatures in many parts of the U.S. mainland also set dramatic new temperature records during the winter and spring of 2016–2017; for example, in February 2017, Chicago recorded multiple 70° days for the first time.[14] Scientists have also begun to link global warming to sea level rise, saltwater intrusion, and coastal storm surges;[15] heavier rainfall, flooding, and droughts;[16] increased potential for wildfires;[17] damage to infrastructures such as dams and power plants;[18] loss of ocean corals and endangered species;[19] and the spread of human diseases.[20] The correlation between climate change and certain extreme weather events, such as hurricanes, remains more controversial.[21]

The potential economic costs of climate-related property damage, loss of crops and food production, disruption of supply chains, migration of refugees, and outright conflict over natural resources could be enormous.[22] The costs of repairing damages from the hurricanes that decimated Texas, Florida and Puerto Rico in 2017 are likely to run into the hundreds of billions of dollars.[23] The Pentagon has also warned of climate threats to national security: "The pressures caused by climate change . . . are threat multipliers that will aggravate stressors abroad such as poverty, environmental degradation, political instability, and social tensions—conditions that can enable terrorist activity and other forms of violence."[24]

Scientists acknowledge that there is still considerable uncertainty about the timing and intensity of these effects. However, many of them are occurring faster than originally anticipated; for example, Arctic sea ice is melting at a far more rapid rate than previously expected and could be entirely gone by 2040.[25] This would open new shipping routes between the Atlantic and the Pacific as well as new opportunities for oil and gas exploration in the region, and could lead to increased international competition and conflict. The West Antarctic ice sheets are also collapsing into the sea, increasing the likelihood of rapid sea-level rises if adjacent ice on land is destabilized and melts.[26] And permafrost is melting faster than expected, releasing large amounts of GHG and possibly new disease vectors into the atmosphere.[27]

President Obama made a historic commitment in his negotiations with China and in the 2015 Paris Agreement to reduce U.S. carbon emissions by 26–28 percent below 2005 levels by 2025 (Chapters 4 and 13). This national pledge was based heavily on implementation of the Clean Power Plan to phase out coal-fired power plants and on raising average fuel economy standards for cars and light trucks to 54.5 miles per gallon by 2025. It is questionable whether these and other Obama policies would have enabled the United States to reach the Paris goal.[28] However, considerable progress has been made in reducing national and international GHG emissions: the Energy Information Agency estimates that U.S. energy-related emissions declined 14 percent between 2005 and 2016.[29] There is also some evidence that global emissions have leveled off, although the rate at which carbon is accumulating in the atmosphere still appears to be rising.[30] Moreover, the United Nations Environment Programme and the International Energy Agency warn that the national pledges made so far under the Paris Agreement would allow temperatures to rise well beyond the "less than 2 degrees Celsius" threshold adopted in Paris.[31] The environmental and energy policies we pursue in the future thus remain critically important.

Environmental and climate issues were hardly discussed during the 2016 presidential debates, but in campaign speeches, Trump promised to rescind the Clean Power Plan and to "cancel" the Paris accord despite protests from scientists, environmentalists, and others.[32] Once in office, the Trump administration was deeply divided over whether to repudiate the Paris accord or to stay in and reduce our national pledge.[33] After months of debate, Trump announced that the United States would withdraw from the agreement.[34] This decision, opposed by several members of the cabinet, by many business and corporate leaders, and by a majority of the American public, is likely to weaken, but not halt, global efforts to control climate change.[35] It could result in diplomatic repercussions from other countries, including our European allies, and cede leadership in development of sustainable energy technologies to other countries, notably China.[36] However, formal withdrawal would take up to four years under the terms of the agreement, and a president elected in 2020 could still possibly opt to rejoin.[37]

Despite growing scientific evidence, President Trump declared that "nobody really knows" if climate change is real and filled his administration with climate change skeptics and deniers, including several lobbyists for oil and gas companies.[38] Moreover, as noted in Chapter 4, he proposed huge budget cuts to virtually all scientific research programs related to climate change, including those of the EPA, the Department of Energy, NASA, and the National Oceanic and Atmospheric Administration (NOAA). The EPA began removing Obama-era data and scientific information from its website in April 2017, including critical data on the Clean Power Plan.[39] Scientists in and out of government feared a "climate data gap" as a result—that is, the dismantling of climate monitoring operations and loss of existing climate data. Many of those leaving government have thus collaborated in archiving data, pleading with the administration to respect the integrity of science and mobilizing public opinion to defend scientific research.[40] Tens of thousands participated in the March for Science in more than six hundred cities on April 22, 2017 (Chapter 3).

Shortly thereafter, the EPA and Interior Department began removing scientists from advisory panels and replacing them with friendlier members from business and industry.[41] They also abolished several scientific positions and committees, including the Advisory Committee for the National Climate Assessment; marginalized career scientists by transferring them to other positions; and appointed nonscientists to key scientific positions.[42] The administration has also misrepresented the findings of climate scientists, as in the Paris withdrawal announcement, and the EPA is launching its own program to challenge climate science.[43] Finally, the EPA now requires that all grant applications and awards be vetted by a political appointee to ensure that they conform to the administration's priorities.[44] Trump's apparent hostility toward research and his failure to appoint a science adviser or other scientific staff in the White House during his first months in office does not bode well for evidence-based decision making.[45]

One early test of how the administration handles scientific matters will be its response to the new National Climate Assessment, a report by thirteen federal agencies that is mandated by Congress. A draft of the report, obtained by the *New York Times* in August 2017, was filled with warnings about current climate threats and states that it is "'extremely likely' that more than half of the global mean temperature increase since 1951 can be linked to human influence."[46] Many scientists feared that the final report, released in November 2017, would be suppressed or distorted, or simply ignored.[47]

It is by no means certain that the EPA will be able to carry out many of its regulatory and policy changes (Chapter 7). Rules adopted under the Administrative Procedure Act—such as the Clean Power Plan—must be supported by extensive hearings, public comments, and a complete evidentiary record, and they are therefore difficult to change or repeal.[48] Much will depend on how the Office of Information and Regulatory Affairs (OIRA) conducts its benefit-cost analyses—especially regarding such critical matters as the social costs of carbon. Efforts to justify deregulation without a solid scientific and economic basis are not likely to succeed.[49]

Any attempt to modify rules and regulations will be subject to multiple lawsuits, which could take years to resolve (as has been the case already for Obama's power plant rule).[50] There will also be enormous resistance from many sectors of business that have built their investment plans around lower carbon footprints and new energy sources (Chapter 11). According to a recent report, "[N]early half of the Fortune 500 biggest companies in the United States have now set targets to shrink their carbon footprints."[51] The same is true of large electric utilities, which plan to close most of their coal-fired plants in favor of cleaner natural gas, wind, and solar production.[52] Many large corporations, including Apple, Google, Walmart, Anheuser-Busch, and Bank of America, have pledged to move toward total reliance on renewable energy, and far more new jobs are being created in sustainable energy technologies than in traditional fossil fuel sectors.[53] The government cannot control these market forces, especially since they are operating on a global scale.[54]

Many cities and states will also fight the administration's policy reversals (see Chapters 2 and 12). Cities account for about two-thirds of national greenhouse gas emissions. More than one thousand mayors have signed the U.S. Conference of Mayors' Climate Protection Agreement, which, among other things, calls for an 80 percent reduction in carbon emissions from their cities by 2050.[55] Over 130 American cities have also joined the Global Covenant of Mayors for Climate & Energy to support the Paris Agreement.[56] In fact, when Trump withdrew from the agreement, over twelve hundred governors, mayors, and businesses announced that they would continue their climate protection efforts, and some attempted to join the Paris accord itself.[57]

Nearly thirty states already have climate change policies such as renewable energy portfolio standards and are likely to continue them. Several states have already reduced their carbon emissions from power plants by at least 40 percent compared to 2005 levels, and some states have reduced emissions even more (see Chapter 13).[58] Several of these are among nine northeastern states that are members of the Regional Greenhouse Gas Initiative (RGGI), which began implementing a cap-and-trade system in 2009. After reducing CO_2 emissions by 40 percent from 2005 levels, the RGGI states recently agreed to reduce their power plant emissions by an additional 30 percent by 2030.[59] California is also a model for the nation and in 2016 extended its landmark climate change legislation to require a 40 percent reduction in total GHG emissions by 2030, compared to 1990.[60] Governor Jerry Brown and the California Air Resources Board have also vowed that they will fight to retain their waiver to set strict carbon emission standards for cars and light trucks if the EPA attempts to weaken federal fuel economy rules.[61] In addition, California is cooperating with Canada, Mexico, and China to maximize carbon reduction; indeed, it is "emerging as the nation's de facto negotiator with the world on the environment."[62]

A more comprehensive national approach would entail either putting a price on carbon through the taxation of fossil fuels or the establishment of a national cap-and-trade system that would gradually reduce the number of emission allowances within and across sectors (Chapter 10). A distinguished group of Republicans, led by former secretaries of state James Baker and George Schultz and former treasury secretary Henry Paulson Jr., has proposed a national carbon tax that would be returned to consumers as an annual "carbon dividend."[63] Many environmentalists and some corporations, such as ExxonMobil, also support this concept. These market-based approaches will be discussed later in the chapter.

Some energy companies are also experimenting with advanced technologies such as carbon capture and sequestration (CCS), in which carbon dioxide is removed from coal-plant emissions and pumped deeply into oil wells to aid oil recovery or for permanent storage. These and other promising energy technologies are likely to be pursued in the private sector in view of anticipated world demand.[64] Companies are also under increasing pressure from shareholders and the public to disclose more information on their exposure to climate risks and the costs they may incur in the future if their assets are "stranded" or if they are required to address climate change.[65] For example, in May 2017 ExxonMobil shareholders revolted against company management and demanded greater transparency in reporting future financial risks due to climate change. The resolution was spearheaded by the California Public Employees Retirement System (CalPERS), the nation's largest pension fund.[66] Colleges, universities, and other nonprofit organizations can also bring pressure to bear on corporations to divest stock holdings in fossil fuel companies. Hundreds of colleges and universities have also adopted a goal of net-zero emissions for their campuses, and several have already achieved it.[67]

Grassroots citizens' groups can also play an important part in bringing people together around common goals. For example, the Citizens' Climate Lobby has played a key role in addressing local climate issues in a nonpartisan manner, arranging meetings with state and national representatives, and promoting nonpartisan solutions such as a revenue-neutral carbon-fee-and-dividend system similar to that mentioned above. The group was also instrumental in creating the Climate Solutions Caucus in Congress, (Chapter 5), which in September 2017 had fifty-two members, twenty-six from each party. Members of the caucus have introduced a "Republican Climate Resolution" in the House of Representatives, with twenty cosponsors.[68] It thus seems possible that partisan gridlock over climate change may ease due to growing pressures from below.

Energy Supply: Critical Choices

However serious the potential threats of climate change, we also need an adequate and reliable supply of energy throughout the transition to lower-carbon fuels. As explained in Chapter 8, all types of energy production—including renewable sources such as wind and solar—involve environmental as well as economic trade-offs. For example, large solar installations require a great deal of land, and solar collection towers that concentrate the sun's rays to heat electricity-generating boilers also require a lot of water. Other carbon-free modes of production, such as nuclear power, present the long-term problems of waste storage and ultimate disposal. Ethanol, the production of which now accounts for 40 percent of all corn grown in the United States, may require as much energy to create as it provides for end use (see Chapter 9). Even natural gas, which releases only about half as much carbon dioxide when burned as coal, requires other forms of energy to produce and results in methane leaks and other problems that could offset the benefits of lower carbon emissions.[69] All energy production has significant impacts on water quality and quantity (Chapter 8). It is therefore important to get a balanced mix of energy sources while moving toward decarbonization.

President Obama followed an "all-of-the-above" energy strategy that encouraged the development of oil and gas production as well as of energy from renewable sources.[70] Domestic oil and gas production increased rapidly during his tenure, making the United States the world's largest producer of both.[71] Oil imports dropped from 60 percent of national consumption in 2008 to 24 percent by 2016, bringing the country much closer to "energy independence." Partly as a result of increased U.S. and Canadian production, world oil and gas prices fell dramatically, leading to rapid substitution of cleaner and cheaper natural gas for coal in electricity production.[72] This historic shift was made possible by expansion of hydraulic fracturing (fracking) of tight shale formations, notably in North Dakota and Texas but in many other states as well. Meanwhile, energy production from renewable sources such as wind and solar increased even more dramatically: wind power tripled and solar power multiplied more than 22 times during the same period. By 2016 renewable energy reached about 10 percent of the national total and was competitive with fossil fuels in many energy markets. Wind, solar, and biofuel production also employed about ten times as many workers as coal mining. This transition was clearly aided by federal government policies favoring renewable energy, but it was probably driven more by the states and by private market forces.[73] Many other countries are also moving rapidly toward clean energy.[74]

While presiding over this energy boom, President Obama also placed increasing restrictions on certain kinds of energy production. In addition to the climate change measures noted in the previous section, he tightened rules for offshore oil drilling (in the wake of the Deepwater Horizon oil spill in the Gulf of Mexico) and placed more areas off the Atlantic and Alaskan coasts off limits to new oil leasing through 2022. The Interior Department declared a moratorium on all new coal leases on public lands; issued new regulations on oil and gas fracking, including restrictions on methane flaring and emissions on public lands; and imposed a new rule to stop coal companies from dumping mining wastes into nearby streams and rivers (see Chapters 4 and 8). After years of delay, Obama also blocked construction of the Keystone XL and Dakota Access pipelines. In one of the last acts of his administration, he invoked the 1953 Outer Continental Shelf Lands Act to ban offshore oil drilling permanently along wide swaths of Alaska's coast and the Atlantic seaboard from Maine to Virginia.[75]

The other thrust of President Obama's energy policy was a strong push for energy conservation and efficiency. In addition to raising mileage standards for cars and light trucks, the new regulations establish fuel economy standards for large trucks and other heavy vehicles for the first time.[76] Standards for building construction and appliance efficiency were also tightened significantly. Consumers became more aware of energy use through programs such as Energy Star ratings for appliances and electronics. Through executive orders and memoranda, Obama also required all federal agencies, including the Department of Defense, to assess their carbon footprints and to reduce energy consumption.

President Trump's "America First" energy strategy, which was largely shaped by executives and lobbyists from the fossil fuel industries, as well as by conservative think tanks such as the Heritage Foundation, calls for the elimination of these and other restrictions and for opening vast new areas to energy production in order to achieve "energy dominance."[77] According to energy secretary Rick Perry, the United States will continue to follow an "all-of-the-above" approach to energy sources but with more emphasis on "clean" fossil fuels including coal and a new generation of nuclear power. Despite its withdrawal from the Paris Agreement, he also claimed that the United States will continue to lead the world in emission reductions and clean energy innovation under the Trump administration.[78]

The president's early actions suggested otherwise. Among them were approval of the Keystone XL and Dakota Access oil pipelines.[79] More significantly, his executive order on "Promoting Energy Independence and Economic Growth" of March 28, 2017, called on all executive departments and agencies to "immediately review existing regulations that potentially burden the development or use of domestically produced energy resources and appropriately suspend, revise, or rescind those that unduly burden the development of domestic energy resources beyond the degree necessary to protect the public interest or otherwise comply with the law." All agency heads were required to report actions in response to this demand to the director of the Office of Management and Budget (OMB) within 180 days. The order also revoked Obama's climate change plans and guidelines; ordered reviews of the Clean Power Plan and performance standards for new power plants, as well as rules on fracking and methane emissions; and ended the moratorium on coal leases on public lands.[80] More than 40 percent of all coal produced in the United States is mined on federal land, and that percentage is likely to grow as leasing is accelerated.[81]

Trump also signed a Congressional Review Act repealing the stream protection rule, and in April, the president signed executive orders that could potentially open up large areas of the Atlantic and Arctic Oceans to oil and gas leasing and could roll back the safety rules for offshore drilling.[82] Trump also pledged to eliminate restrictions on public lands, including millions of acres recently protected as national monuments. Secretary of the Interior

Ryan Zinke reviewed all monuments designated since 1996 and was expected to propose that several be reduced in size, including the 1.35-million-acre Bears Ears National Monument in Utah that was established by President Obama at the end of this term. The administration is also moving toward opening the Arctic National Wildlife Refuge in Alaska to oil and gas exploration.[83] Finally, the president's energy plan makes no mention of renewable energy, and Trump proposed cuts of more than 50 percent to Energy Department programs that support research and development on new renewable energy sources.[84]

How far Trump's deregulation campaign will go, and how effective it will be, remains to be seen. Government agencies, such as the resource bureaus of the Interior Department, may not have the technical and legal capacity to carry out such dramatic changes, nor might they see it in their self-interest to adopt policies that are strongly opposed at the local level.[85] Any attempt to reopen protected public lands such as national monuments, parks, or wildlife refuges to development will be fiercely resisted by conservation, recreation, and tourism interests—and in some cases, such as Bears Ears, by indigenous peoples.[86] Furthermore, most oil and gas extraction is now by fracking, which is regulated on private land by state and local governments. States that have mandated energy portfolios (Chapter 2) or that fear offshore oil development near their coastlines will oppose new fossil energy licensing.[87] California and New York plan to produce half of their electricity with renewables by 2030, and California is considering a plan to require utilities to produce *all* of its power with solar and wind sources by 2045.

Domestic and foreign companies that have invested heavily in renewable energy projects—many of them in red states such as Texas, Oklahoma, Idaho, Kansas, and Iowa—may also exert political and market pressure against the preferential treatment of fossil fuels.[88] One of the largest wind farms in the nation is currently being planned in Carbon County, Wyoming, formerly a center for coal mining.[89] Trump's policies may enable coal companies to expand production in the short run, but they are unlikely to revive the coal industry permanently or bring back many coal miners' jobs. In fact, a *Reuters* survey of 32 utilities in Republican states in April 2017 showed that "none plan to increase their use of coal as a result of Trump's policies."[90] The government could, however, reduce or eliminate subsidies for solar and wind power, slowing their progress.

Future energy development will largely be determined by domestic and international markets. Oil prices are set internationally, and as long as they remain relatively low, it is questionable whether companies will undertake costly projects, such as constructing the Keystone XL pipeline or launching oil rigs in risky areas like the Arctic Ocean; however, companies may well seek to obtain leases for potential future use.[91] Another possibility is the increased exportation of oil, coal, and, especially, abundant natural gas from the United States. A long-standing ban on the export of crude oil from the United States was lifted during the Obama administration, and Mr. Trump appears eager to make America a dominant global energy power. Exports of oil, coal, and liquid natural gas (LNG) are already ramping up, and some predict large future markets. But these plans also face uncertainties due to the current glut of oil and gas in the world market and to opposition to the construction of shipping facilities in some U.S. ports.[92]

Air and Water Pollution

Our current focus on energy and climate change should not blind us to more traditional environmental problems such as air and water pollution. These forms of pollution are regulated by the EPA under statutes written largely in the 1970s and, in some cases, revised in the 1980s and 1990s (see Chapters 5 and 7). As pointed out in Chapter 1, air quality has improved greatly over the decades, with aggregate emissions of the six "criteria" pollutants controlled by the Clean Air Act falling by nearly two-thirds between 1980 and 2015—despite the fact that our economy increased by more than 150 percent in real terms. Emissions of other pollutants such as hazardous chemicals and toxic metals have also declined markedly (Chapter 11). Nevertheless, air quality varies greatly in different localities and among different population groups, with many urban areas still suffering high concentrations of ozone, particulates, heavy metals, and chemicals that can cause severe health effects and even death. Nearly 40 percent of Americans still live in counties that have at least one major type of air pollution that exceeds EPA standards—in most cases excess ozone levels caused by exhaust emissions from cars, trucks, and buses, as well as factories and power plants. Many poor urban neighborhoods are especially polluted, raising environmental justice concerns.

Among the most controversial policies of the George W. Bush administration were efforts to weaken the Clean Air Act (CAA) by exempting power plants from the New Source Review (NSR) requirements of the law. Although the federal courts eventually struck down the rule in 2007, it slowed progress toward controlling the largest sources of conventional air pollutants as well as GHGs during the Bush years (Chapter 7). Two other rules required by the CAA—the Clean Air Interstate Rule (CAIR) to limit emissions from power plants that pollute neighboring states in the eastern half of the country and the Clean Air Mercury Rule (CAMR) to regulate mercury and other hazardous air emissions—were proposed by the Bush administration, but both were also found inadequate by the courts.

Under Obama, the EPA issued a new Mercury and Air Toxics Standard (MATS) in 2011, which would further tighten emission standards for mercury, lead, asbestos, and other hazardous air pollutants from coal- and oil-fired electric utility plants.[93] The Supreme Court allowed the rule to stand in March 2016, but more than a dozen states have continued to contest the EPA's regulations in the District of Columbia Circuit Court. The EPA also issued a new Cross-State Air Pollution Rule in 2011 to replace the Bush CAIR. The new rule would require power plants in twenty-seven eastern states to limit emissions of pollutants such as sulfur dioxide, nitrogen oxides, and fine particulates that affect downwind states. This rule was also upheld by the Supreme Court, but its implementation is still mired in litigation before the D.C. Circuit. Finally, in October 2015, the EPA issued its long-delayed National Ambient Air Quality Standards (NAAQS) for ozone, which lowered the acceptable amount of ground-level ozone from 75 parts per billion (set in the Bush administration) to 70 parts per billion by 2025. Although less stringent than originally proposed in 2011, these threshold limits would further reduce urban smog.[94] If implemented, the Obama regulations limiting carbon emissions from new and existing power plants would also cut emissions of all of the conventional air pollutants as well. In proposing the Clean Power Plan in June 2014, for example, the EPA stated that it would have major "co-benefits" by reducing emissions of conventional pollutants by more than 25 percent, which would avoid up to 6,600 premature deaths and 150,000 asthma attacks in children.[95]

EPA Administrator Scott Pruitt filed many of the lawsuits challenging these rules while attorney general of Oklahoma, and although he has recused himself from cases in which he was previously involved, it appears that the EPA is on a mission to restore air pollution regulations to Bush administration levels, if not to further weaken them. The Trump administration has indicated that it may attempt to roll back Obama-era regulations under the MATS and the Cross-State Air Pollution and NAAQS rules. It has begun to rescind the Clean Power Plan and threatens to lower auto emission standards. In early 2017, the EPA asked the D.C. Circuit Court to delay arguments in cases involving the ozone rule, but it reversed its position after sixteen state attorneys general, all Democrats, filed a suit challenging delay in implementing the rule.[96] It remains to be seen whether the agency will also seek to restore Bush-era regulations on New Source Review. The projected cuts of up to 40 percent in the enforcement budget of the EPA, as well as deep staff cuts and reductions in grants to states, could also gravely undermine implementation of the Clean Air Act (Chapter 7).

Much the same can be said for water pollution. During the campaign Donald Trump repeatedly promised to rescind the Waters of the United States (WOTUS) rule, which was issued in 2015 to clarify which streams, smaller tributaries, and wetlands are covered by the Clean Water Act (Chapter 9). This rule was strongly opposed by farmers, ranchers, developers, and other business interests as government "overreach" that violated local land use laws, and it was temporarily enjoined by a federal court. The EPA is in the process of withdrawing it.[97] Trump also attacked the Interior Department's 2016 stream protection rule, which was designed to limit pollution from mountaintop coal-mining operations by prohibiting the dumping of wastes into nearby streams. In this case, Republican majorities passed a Congressional Review Act repeal of the rule, and Trump signed it.[98] The administration's budget proposals also indicate that it plans to defund or eliminate major regional watershed programs such as the Chesapeake Bay Restoration Program, the Lake Champlain Basin Program, and cleanup programs for the Gulf of Mexico, Long Island Sound, Puget Sound, San Francisco Bay, and the Florida Everglades.[99]

The proposed 44 percent cut in EPA categorical grants to state and local governments, along with plans to devolve greater authority to state environmental agencies, would have especially deleterious effects on Clean Water Act programs because they are largely implemented by the states (Chapters 2 and 7). The EPA does set federal standards for effluent discharges from industries, sewage treatment plants, and other large "point" sources, but most surface water and groundwater pollution now comes from "nonpoint" or indirect sources, such as farms, city streets, golf courses, and other local activities. Agricultural operations are by far the largest of these sources, with runoff of fertilizer, pesticides, and animal waste entering streams, lakes, and groundwater. With the exception of some large concentrated animal feedlots, these operations do not require federal permits and are largely uncontrolled by state and county governments (Chapter 9). The EPA does issue guidelines for maximum allowable contamination levels of certain pollutants in surface waters and drinking water, but, again, implementing these is left to the states. Deep cuts in federal support programs are therefore likely to result in even weaker enforcement in many areas.

Urban water pollution and drinking water quality are also growing issues. The dramatic case of lead poisoning of drinking water in Flint, Michigan, which played out in 2014–2016, was not strictly an environmental issue since it stemmed from negligence in treating municipal water supplies to prevent lead from leaching into city pipes. The EPA has greatly diminished lead levels in air and water since the 1970s, reducing children's blood lead levels by over 90 percent (Chapter 1). However, millions of households across the country—especially in poor urban areas—still have elevated lead levels, exposing children to brain damage and other disease.[100]

Coal ash from power plants is another major source of water pollution. More than 100 million tons of coal ash slurry is produced annually that is laden with arsenic, mercury, lead, and other heavy metals. This waste stream is largely stored in ponds or landfills, and these have leaked into both groundwater and surface water, in some cases contaminating drinking water supplies. The EPA issued a new rule in 2015 to monitor and control the storage and disposal of these wastes, resulting in several pending lawsuits. However, Scott Pruitt has indicated that the EPA will now reconsider the rule and delay compliance deadlines for states.[101] The administration's determination to maintain coal-fired power plants thus has serious implications for water pollution as well as air pollution and climate change.

Alternative Policy Approaches

Traditional "command-and-control" regulation has been generally successful in improving environmental quality since the 1960s (Chapters 1 and 11). Nevertheless, critics of the EPA have long argued that its "one size fits all" regulations are economically inefficient and often inappropriate for specific local circumstances. Legal mandates under these rules have also resulted in endless litigation and have tended to discourage innovation and voluntary advancements that could improve outcomes (though most laws allow states to set higher standards if they choose to). Many environmental policy scholars have thus advocated new forms of "smart regulation" that utilize more flexible, less intrusive, and more cost-effective methods for reducing pollution and addressing other environmental problems.[102] Many economists, especially, have advocated market-based regimes that maximize economic efficiency and cost-effectiveness, as explained in Chapter 10. We briefly assess some of the most important of these alternative policy approaches.

Cap-and-trade systems set overall limits on the quantity of pollution emissions allowed and lower the number of allowances or permits available for use over time to meet reduction goals. Affected entities can buy and sell emission allowances, with the price being determined by the trading market (some allowances are usually auctioned off by the government or trading authority, raising funds for pollution control as well). As the cap is tightened, the price of allowances should go up, encouraging companies to cut their emissions or incur higher costs for allowances. This form of market pricing and trading gives regulated parties freedom to make their own decisions and should result in the most cost-effective way of lowering pollution. The American Clean Energy and Security Act of 2009, which passed in the House of Representatives but died in the Senate in 2010, would have established an economy-wide system of this kind to control GHGs.

Despite the act's failure, two large GHG emissions trading systems are operating today in the United States. The RGGI market, now including nine states, began operations in 2009 and the California system in 2012. As a result, some eighty million people, or one-quarter of the American population, are now covered by such systems, which have already contributed to substantial carbon emission reductions, as discussed earlier.[103] The new EPA rules for cutting emissions from coal-fired power plants proposed in 2015 were designed to encourage other states to form carbon markets, or to join the California or RGGI systems, but that now seems less likely if the Clean Power Plan is repealed.[104] However, many other countries and the European Union have such regimes, and China is planning the world's largest carbon-trading market.[105] The effectiveness of many of these systems remains to be seen, but they now appear to be the most widely utilized means of combating climate change.[106] They have also been criticized by environmental justice advocates for allowing companies to continue polluting local communities that are already at risk—often low-income minority areas.[107]

Since the failure of the climate change legislation in 2010, many economists, business leaders, and politicians of different political persuasions have endorsed *carbon taxes* as an alternative to cap and trade. In theory, putting a price on carbon or other forms of pollution via taxes or fees could achieve cost-effective outcomes similar to those of emission trading systems (Chapter 10). Taxes are also easier to administer and more transparent, thus conveying clearer signals to consumers. On the other hand, taxes do not guarantee any given level of emissions reduction and could face even greater opposition in Congress than cap and trade.

Some of these obstacles might be overcome if these taxes were revenue neutral—that is, part of a larger tax reform in which other taxes such as corporate, income, or payroll taxes were simultaneously reduced to offset the carbon tax. Such a system has been used in British Columbia, and Canada plans to extend carbon pricing systems to all provinces regardless of what the United States does.[108] Another approach, supported by many environmentalists as well as by some corporations, would rebate the taxes collected to the public in the form of an annual dividend similar to Alaska's oil revenue fund. The "conservative climate solution" proposed in early 2017 by former Republican leaders James A. Baker III, George P. Schultz, and Henry M. Paulson Jr. proposed a tax beginning at $40 per ton of carbon dioxide produced, which would raise an estimated $200 to $300 billion a year. The money would be returned to consumers as a "carbon dividend" estimated at $2,000 annually for an average family of four.[109] Such a program could also address environmental justice concerns by distributing dividends disproportionally to low-income families that would be especially hard hit by higher fuel prices. Two Democratic senators, Sheldon Whitehouse of Rhode Island and Brian Schatz of Hawaii, have proposed a somewhat similar plan as part of a broader bipartisan tax reform.[110]

Voluntary collaboration and self-policing programs are another alternative to traditional regulation. In this approach, regulated parties such as corporations or industrial sectors voluntarily agree to meet higher performance standards than required by law, in return for greater regulatory flexibility (Chapter 11). Most of these programs were created during the Clinton administration as part of its "reinventing government" initiative.[111] Although many of these experiments, such as the Performance Track program, failed to produce measurably better results than traditional regulation and have been discontinued, they did help some sectors of business and industry to improve their environmental management and reporting, and in some cases their operations. But stronger organization and governmental supervision, or effective oversight by independent bodies, appear necessary if a genuine "greening"—defined as a transformation to sustainable production—is to occur. Sectoral organizations such as trade and business associations could become more effective intermediaries if they were given stronger authority to monitor their members and enforce environmental policies. But even without such quasi-governmental devolution, all companies could be given stronger incentives to adopt management practices such as those required for ISO 14001 certification (see Chapter 11).

One key to stronger environmental performance is public *disclosure of information*. The leading example of such information disclosure is the federal Toxics Release Inventory (TRI), which has operated since the late 1980s. Over twenty thousand industrial facilities a year report on their release of some 650 toxic chemicals to the air, water, or land. The information is made available to the public in a variety of ways, including through the EPA's own TRI website.

The key assumption of such policies is that an informed public may bring some pressure to bear on poorly performing industrial facilities and their parent companies, what some have called regulation by embarrassment. It is just as likely that companies will seek to avoid such public censure by proactively altering their production processes to reduce chemical releases even if they are not subject to any regulatory requirements to do so. Although the disclosed information is often quite technical and difficult to translate into meaningful risks to the public's health, the program has led to significant decreases in the release of toxic chemicals over time, as well as to improved environmental performance on the part of industry.[112]

The success of some information disclosure programs such as the TRI led the federal government to try much the same approach with GHG releases. The EPA maintains a Greenhouse Gas Reporting Program (GHGRP) that collects and releases emissions data from facilities in forty-one different source categories and that is easily accessible by the public. Much like the TRI, the GHGRP was created under the assumption that facilities will seek to reduce their emissions precisely because the data are available to the public; the program aims to embarrass those companies that choose to do little to curtail their GHG emissions. However, it appears that the Trump administration will terminate this program. Nonprofit organizations, of course, can play a very similar role, as demonstrated by the Carbon Disclosure Project. Since 2007, it has ranked companies on their carbon emissions.

More recently, many states have begun requiring a somewhat comparable reporting of chemicals used in natural gas fracturing, largely in response to public concern over possible contamination of water supplies and other health risks. The reporting systems used to date are not as informative as they might be. Nonetheless, experience with the TRI program suggests that making this kind of information available can be very effective in improving environmental performance, especially if the reporting system is carefully designed to provide the right kind of information in a way that ordinary people can readily understand and use.[113]

Another promising policy approach, *local and regional sustainability planning*, has been used with impressive results in many cities and regions in the United States as well as in other nations. The concept of sustainability or sustainable development came into wide use following the 1987 Brundtland Commission report and later at the Earth Summit of 1992. It also was promoted heavily during the Clinton administration by the President's Council on Sustainable Development (PCSD), which focused on how communities might develop "bold, new approaches to achieve economic, environmental, and equity goals."[114]

As Chapter 12 showed, both large and small cities in the nation have embarked on intriguing programs to pursue economic development in a way that seeks to integrate environmental and equity considerations into the equation. Although some of the cities, such as Seattle, Washington, and Portland, Oregon, are well known and often celebrated for their remarkable sustainability achievements and their highly supportive local citizenry, they are by no means the only examples of successful sustainability planning. New efforts to promote sustainability are found in large cities such as New York, Chicago, and Los Angeles; midsized cities such as San Francisco, Austin, and Boston; and smaller cities such as Boulder, Colorado, and Chattanooga, Tennessee. These often include innovative programs to improve air quality, water quality, building efficiency and energy use, local transportation planning, land use, water conservation, and more. Some cities also are moving ahead in planning for adaptation to climate change.

Two other critical needs are a committed investment in *scientific research and development* and the improvement of *public education in science.* As evident throughout the book, little progress is possible on environmental challenges without strong scientific evidence to document the problems the nation faces and to identify potential solutions. The role of science is particularly important today when public trust in science and scientists appears to be in decline and political ideology often distorts scientific findings.[115] The United States historically has been highly supportive of investment in scientific research and technology development, and both Democratic and Republican administrations have given such research a high priority. Yet the Trump administration has proposed massive cuts to both basic and applied research programs. The proposed fiscal 2018 EPA budget released in May 2017 would cut science and technology spending by $282 million, almost a 40 percent reduction. Research programs in the Energy Department, Interior Department, National Science Foundation, NASA, NOAA, and other agencies would also be severely reduced or eliminated. Former Republican EPA administrators William Ruckleshaus, Lee Thomas, and William Reilly have roundly condemned these proposed cuts, yet even if Congress does not accept them, the damage to the nation's scientific leadership could be substantial.[116]

Though many different kinds of research in the natural and social sciences and engineering are needed, we hope the federal government and other organizations that invest in science follow the advice of the National Science Foundation in supporting interdisciplinary environmental research. As the Advisory Committee for Environmental Research and Education observed in 2009, the world "is at a crossroads," and human beings are stressing both natural and social systems beyond their capacity. The problems we face are complex, and our knowledge is both limited and fragmented. Solving such problems requires an unprecedented integration of knowledge from many disciplines, as well as discovery of new ways to encourage the use of knowledge in decision making and to build public understanding of the problems.[117] For example, calculation of the "social cost of carbon," a widely used metric in benefit-cost analysis, requires integration of multiple disciplines if it is to be an effective tool for policymaking.[118]

Environmental Governance for the Future

As the example of climate change makes clear, both the nation and the world need to rethink the nature of environmental governance for the twenty-first century. The governmental institutions and decision-making processes that have served us well in the past may not be as suitable for the future.

The problems we face are no longer so simple, and their causes are not as amenable to governmental intervention as was the case in the 1970s. Moreover, as we argue just above, the tools on which governments have relied, such as command-and-control regulation, need to be drawn from a more diverse public policy repertoire. It would include, for example, carefully designed market incentives such as carbon taxes, information disclosure, public education, inclusive collaborative decision making, and comprehensive local and regional planning rooted in long-term sustainability goals.[119] These new tools are not likely to replace regulation as the bedrock of environmental policy, but they may supplement it in a way that achieves better environmental results at lower cost while also reducing the burdens on business.

One message in this emerging body of work is that we need to reexamine old assumptions about government and public policy as well as the prevailing set of political values that we have embraced, particularly as they relate to individual autonomy and the limitations we place on governmental authority.[120] None of that will be easy to do in the face of determined opposition by those forces in society that fear the consequences. At a minimum, however, we need to ask about which public policies and institutional arrangements work and which do not, and about what alternatives we have to replace those that fall short. We also need to search for innovative ways to build a stronger societal capacity to identify and act on environmental problems before they reach crisis proportions.[121] Given the transboundary character of environmental problems such as climate change (and also many forms of air and water pollution), one certainty is that we will see more multilevel governance, in which the problems are addressed locally and regionally as well as nationally and internationally, at the same time. As Chapters 2, 12, and 13 make evident, state and local governments necessarily have acted independently of the federal government when it has been unable to establish sufficient political consensus to move forward with appropriate public policy. Their actions hint at the kind of multilevel governance system that is now evolving.[122]

The Trump administration has embarked on a radically different course from that of the past three decades. As argued at the beginning of this chapter, the proposed diminution of the federal role in environmental policymaking is similar to that of the Reagan experiment of the early 1980s. Overall, the Trump agenda is also likely to fail because it lacks both political legitimacy and technical-scientific rationality. The current attack on the EPA—which would reduce its budget to the lowest point in forty years in real terms—will ultimately fail as bipartisan members of Congress, governors, mayors, business leaders, universities, and a host of energized civic organizations recognize its potentially disastrous consequences. The voices of scientists, such as the thousands who marched in protest on Earth Day 2017, will be especially important in challenging the administration's failure to accept and act upon fundamental scientific knowledge regarding climate change and other issues.[123]

William D. Ruckleshaus, the first EPA administrator who was brought back by Ronald Reagan to restore the credibility and integrity of the agency in 1983, recently issued this historical warning:

To me, the E.P.A. represents one of the clearest examples of our political system listening and responding to the American people. The public will tolerate changes that allow the agency to meet its mandated goals more efficiently and effectively. They will not tolerate changes that threaten their health or the precious environment. These are the lessons President Reagan learned in 1983. We would all do well to heed them.[124]

Whether the Trump administration and its policies survive remains to be seen, given the unprecedented controversies surrounding them at this writing. Nevertheless, the nation's environmental governance will continue to evolve in coming years as congressional and presidential elections further shape the policy agenda and as public opinion ultimately determines the boundaries of change.

Notes

1. Michael E. Kraft and Norman J. Vig, "Environmental Policy in the Reagan Presidency," *Political Science Quarterly* 99, no. 3 (Fall 1984): 415–39.
2. Kraft and Vig, "Environmental Policy in the Reagan Presidency," 422.
3. For details, see Norman J. Vig and Michael E. Kraft, eds., *Environmental Policy in the 1980s: Reagan's New Agenda* (Washington, DC: CQ Press, 1984).
4. For a comparison to Reagan's Executive Order 12291, see Juliet Eilperin, "Why Trump's Order to Cut Government Regulation is Even Bolder Than It Seems," *Washington Post*, February 13, 2017. See also Nadia Popovich and Livia Albeck-Ripka, "48 Environmental Rules on the Way Out Under Trump," *New York Times*, October 5, 2017.
5. Numerous public opinion polls show that Americans—including conservatives and Republicans—support action on climate change and do not want environmental policies to be weakened. See, for example, Nadja Popovich, John Schwartz, and Tatiana Schlossberg, "How Americans Think About Climate Change, in Six Maps," *New York Times*, March 21, 2017, which shows that an average of 69 percent of adults across all congressional districts support strict CO_2 limits on existing coal-fired power plants; Christopher Borick, Barry Rabe, and Sarah Mills, "Trump's Global Warming Views Remain Elusive, but Not Those of Americans," *Brookings*, June 12, 2017; and Ed Maibach, Anthony Leiserowitz, and Jennifer Marlon, "Should the U.S. Stay in the Paris Agreement?" *US News & World Report*, June 1, 2017, which reported that Americans believed the United States should stay in the Paris climate agreement by a 5–1 majority. An international poll of 40 countries found that "in every nation surveyed, except Pakistan, a majority of respondents supported placing limits on the emissions of gases that are warming the planet." Sewell Chan, "Poll Finds Global Consensus on the Need to Curb Emissions," *New York Times*, November 6, 2015.
6. This and previous IPCC reports are available at www.ipcc.ch.
7. Justin Gillis, "Climate Panel Cites Near Certainty on Warming," *New York Times*, August 20, 2013; Gillis, "U.N. Climate Panel Seeks Ceiling on Global Carbon Emissions," *New York Times*, September 28, 2013; Gillis, "By 2047, Coldest Years May Be Warmer Than Hottest in Past, Scientists Say," *New York Times*, October 10, 2013; Gillis, "Panel Says Global Warming Carries Risk of Deep Changes," *New York Times*, December 3, 2013; Gillis, "Panel's Warning on Climate Risk: Worst Is Yet to Come," *New York Times*, March 30, 2014.

8. Justin Gillis, "U.N. Draft Report Lists Unchecked Emissions' Risks," *New York Times*, August 27, 2014.

9. Justin Gillis, "U.N. Climate Panel Warns Speedier Action Is Needed to Avert Disaster," *New York Times*, April 13, 2014.

10. Quoted in Justin Gillis, "U.N. Panel Warns of Dire Effects from Lack of Action Over Global Warming," *New York Times*, November 2, 2014. For a more recent assessment, see Chris Mooney, "These Experts Say We Have Three Years to Get Climate Change Under Control. And They're the Optimists," *Washington Post*, June 29, 2017.

11. Justin Gillis, "For Third Year, the Earth in 2016 Hit Record Heat, *New York Times*, January 19, 2017; Chris Mooney, "U.S. Scientists Officially Declare 2016 the Hottest Year on Record. That Makes Three in a Row," *Washington Post*, January 18, 2017. See also Brad Plumer and Nadja Popovich, "95-Degree Days: How Extreme Heat Could Spread Across the World," *New York Times*, June 22, 2017, for future projections.

12. Jason Samenow, "It's About 50 Degrees Warmer Than Normal Near the North Pole, Yet Again," *Washington Post*, February 10, 2017; Henry Fountain and John Schwartz, "Spiking Temperatures in the Arctic Startle Scientists," *New York Times*, December 22, 2016; Erica Goode, "A Wrenching Choice for Alaska Towns in the Path of Climate Change," *New York Times*, November 29, 2016.

13. Chris Mooney, "From Pole to Pole, Twin Sea Ice Records Have Scientists Stunned," *Washington Post*, December 6, 2016; Mooney, "NASA Took on an Unprecedented Study of Greenland's Melting. Now, the Data are Coming In," *Washington Post*, February 10, 2017; Justin Gillis, "Study Warns of a Perilous Climate Shift Within Decades," *New York Times*, March 23, 2016; Alister Doyle, "Arctic Ice Sets New Record Low for Winter: Scientists," *Reuters*, March 27, 2017.

14. Jason Samenow, "The Nation Is Immersed in Its Warmest Period in Recorded History," *Washington Post*, April 18, 2017; Jeremy White and Henry Fountain, "Spring Came Early: Scientists Say Climate Change Is the Culprit," *New York Times*, March 10, 2017; Nadja Popovich, "Hotter Summers, Once Exceptional, Become the Norm," *New York Times*, July 29, 2017; James Hohmann, "The Daily 202: Evidence of Climate Change Abounds Amid Extreme Weather in the Pacific Northwest," *Washington Post*, August 14, 2017.

15. Justin Gillis, "Greenhouse Gas Linked to Floods Along U.S. Coasts," *New York Times*, February 23, 2016; Gillis, "Global Warming's Mark: Coastal Inundation," *New York Times*, September 4, 2016; Lizette Alvarez and Frances Robles, "Worsened by Climate Change, 'King Tides' Transform Florida Life," *New York Times*, November 18, 2016; Chelsea Harvey, "One of Last Obama-Era Climate Reports Had a Troubling Update about the Rising Seas," *Washington Post*, January 23, 2017; Dale Kasler and Ryan Sabalow, "How Rising Sea Could Imperil Water Supply for Millions," *Sacramento Bee*, June 30, 2017.

16. Tatiana Schlossberg, "Wetter Storms Expected, Climate Study Says," *New York Times*, December 7, 2016; Henry Fountain, "Climate Scientists Forecast More Floods Like Louisiana's," *New York Times*, September 8, 2016; Edward Wong, "Drought Is Ravaging a Region of China," *New York Times*, June 30, 2017.

17. Justin Gillis, "Warming Seen as Lit Match in Northern Forests," *New York Times*, May 11, 2016; Tatiana Schlossberg, "Half of Rise in Fire Risk Is Tied to Climate Change," *New York Times*, October 11, 2016; Jacey Fortin, "Wildfires Choke Montana with Ash and Smoke as Drought Rages On," *New York Times*, September 8, 2017; Robinson Meyer, "Has Climate Change Intensified 2017's Western Wildfires?" *The Atlantic*, September 7, 2017, https://www.theatlantic.com/science/archive/2017/09/why-is-2017-so-bad-for-wildfires-climate-change/539130/.

18. Adam Nagourney and Henry Fountain, "A Climate Change Warning to California Dams," *New York Times*, February 15, 2017; Clifford Krauss and Hiroko Tabuchi, "Storm's Toll on Energy Industry Poses Question: Is It Time to Leave the Gulf Coast?" *New York Times*, August 30, 2017.

19. Michelle Innis, "Climate-Related Death of Coral Around World Alarms Scientists," *New York Times*, April 10, 2016; Carl Zimmer, "Study Finds Global Warming as Threat to 1 in 6 Species," *New York Times*, April 30, 2015; Erica Goode, "Warming Is Main Threat to Polar Bears, Report Says," *New York Times*, January 10, 2017; Darryl Fears, "Without Action on Climate Change, Say Goodbye to Polar Bears," *Washington Post*, January 9, 2017.

20. Coral Davenport, "White House Report Links Global Warming to Health," *New York Times*, April 5, 2016; Justin Gillis, "In Zika Epidemic, a Warning on Climate Change," *New York Times*, February 21, 2016; Brian Deese and Ronald A. Klain, "Another Deadly Consequence of Climate Change: The Spread of Dangerous Diseases," *Washington Post*, May 31, 2017.

21. See, for example, Noah S. Diffenbaugh, "Hurricane Harvey Was No Surprise," *New York Times*, August 28, 2017; and Roger Pielke Jr., "The Hurricane Lull Couldn't Last," *Wall Street Journal*, September 1, 2017.

22. Burt Helm, "The Climate Bottom Line," *New York Times*, February 1, 2015; Henry F. Paulson Jr., "The Coming Climate Crash," *New York Times*, June 22, 2014; and Robert E. Rubin, "How Ignoring Climate Change Could Sink the U.S. Economy," *Washington Post*, July 24, 2014. See also Brady Dennis, "Climate Change in the U.S. Could Help the Rich and Hurt the Poor," *Washington Post*, June 29, 2017; and Brad Plumer, "Assessing the Economic Bite from Rising Temperatures," *New York Times*, June 30, 2017.

23. Kevin Quealy, "The Cost of Hurricane Harvey: Only One Recent Storm Comes Close," *New York Times*, September 5, 2017; Stephen Leahy, "Hidden Costs of Climate Change Running Hundreds of Billions a Year," September 27, 2017, news .nationalgeographic.com/2017/09/climate-change-costs-us-economy-billions-report.

24. See Todd Stern, "Mr. Trump's Climate Decision," *Brookings*, March 6, 2017; Vera Bergengruen, "Trump May Doubt Climate Change, but Pentagon Sees It as a 'Threat Multiplier,'" *McClatchy News*, June 1, 2017, http://www.mcclatchydc.com/news/ nation-world/national/national-security/article153908824.html; and Bergengruen, "Trump's Top Aide Is Said to See Climate as a Threat," *Sacramento Bee*, August 9, 2017.

25. The Data Team, "The Decline of Arctic Sea Ice: The Arctic Could Be Free of Sea Ice by 2040, 30 Years Earlier than Previously Suggested," *The Economist*, May 1, 2017; Jugal K. Patel and Henry Fountain, "Arctic Shipping May Become Feasible, for a Price," *New York Times*, May 5, 2017; Russell Goldman, "Russian Tanker Completes Arctic Passage Without Aid of Icebreakers," *New York Times*, August 25, 2017; "The Rush to Exploit the Arctic," editorial, *New York Times*, August 27, 2017.

26. See "Antarctic Dispatches," a three-part series from the *New York Times*, May 18, 2017, https://www.nytimes.com/interactive/2017/05/18/climate/antarctica-ice-melt -climate-change-science.html.

27. Henry Fountain, "Bigger Threat to Permafrost Is Projected," *New York Times*, April 13, 2017; Fountain, "Warmer Alaska May Mean More Carbon Emissions," *New York Times*, May 9, 2017; Fountain, "A Factory of Warming at the Top of the World," *New York Times*, August 24, 2017; Brian Resnick, "Melting Permafrost in the Arctic Is Unlocking Diseases and Warping the Landscape," *Vox*, September 6, 2017, https:// www.vox.com/2017/9/6/16062174/permafrost-melting.

28. Doug Vine, "Achieving the United States' Intended Nationally Determined Contribution," Center for Climate and Energy Solutions, November 2016, https://www.c2es.org/docUploads/achieving-us-indc.pdf. The EPA projected that, even including contributions from land use and forestry and additional measures such as tougher standards for heavy-duty trucks, net reductions in U.S. GHG emissions would fall about 3.6 percent short of the 26 percent goal in 2025. However, this projection does not fully account for additional actions by cities, states, and the business sector.

29. U.S. Energy Information Administration, *Monthly Energy Review*, April 10, 2017. The transportation sector, mostly cars and trucks, now accounts for more CO_2 emissions than power generation in the United States. See Robinson Meyer, "Carbon Emissions Fell During Obama's Last Year in Office," *The Atlantic*, April 13, 2017, https://www.theatlantic.com/technology/archive/2017/04/carbon-emissions-fell-during-obamas-last-year-in-office/522945/.

30. Edward Wong, "Carbon Emissions May Have Peaked, but Data Is Hazy," *New York Times*, April 4, 2016; Justin Gillis, "Rise in Carbon Defies Slowing of Emissions," *New York Times*, June 27, 2017; Lisa Freedman, "Climate-Altering Gases Spiked in 2016, Federal Scientists Report," *New York Times*, July 13, 2017.

31. Fiona Harvey, "World on Track for 3C of Warming Under Current Global Climate Pledges, Warns UN," *The Guardian*, November 3, 2016; John Schwartz, "Climate Deal Called Too Weak to Meet Goals," *New York Times*, November 17, 2016. For an update from the IPCC, see Chelsea Harvey, "Earth Could Break Through a Major Climate Threshold in the Next 15 Years, Scientists Warn," *Washington Post*, May 9, 2017. Climate Action Tracker, a research group, estimates that the planet would warm by 2.8°C by 2100 under current pledges; see www.climateactiontracker.org/.

32. Andrew C. Revkin, "Trump's Stance on the Paris Climate Agreement is Criticized by 375 Scientists," *Dot Earth Blog*, September 21, 2016. An open letter to Trump was signed by 375 members of the National Academy of Sciences, including 30 Nobel Prize winners.

33. Coral Davenport, "Divide at White House Over the Paris Climate Agreement," *New York Times*, March 3, 2017; Chris Mooney, Brady Dennis, and Steven Mufson, "Top Trump Advisers at Odds over Paris Climate Deal," *Washington Post*, April 19, 2017; George P. Schultz and Ted Halstead, "The Business Case for the Paris Climate Accord," *New York Times*, May 9, 2017; Michael D. Shear and Diane Cardwell, "Trump Advisers Wage Tug of War Before Decision on Climate Deal," *New York Times*, May 30, 2017.

34. Michael D. Shear, "Trump Abandoning Global Climate Accord," *New York Times*, June 2, 2017; Philip Rucker and Jenna Johnson, "Trump Announces U.S. Will Exit Paris Climate Deal, Sparking Criticism at Home and Abroad," *Washington Post*, June 2, 2017; Jill Colvin, "Trump Pulls US from Global Warming Accord, to Allies' Dismay," *Associated Press*, June 1, 2017.

35. Michael D. Shear and Alison Smale, "Foreign Leaders Lament U.S. Withdrawal, but Say It Won't Stop Climate Effort," *New York Times*, June 3, 2017; Somini Sengupta, Melissa Eddy, and Chris Buckley, "As Trump Abandons Paris Agreement, Other Countries Are Defiant," *New York Times*, June 2, 2017; Jonathan Watts and Kate Connolly, "World Leaders Reject Trump's Claim Paris Climate Deal Can Be Renegotiated," *The Guardian*, June 2, 2017; Brad Plumer, "Meeting Climate Goals Was Always Hard. Without the U.S. It's Far Harder," *New York Times*, June 3, 2017. A *Washington Post–ABC News* poll conducted just after the withdrawal announcement showed that 59 percent of the public opposed the move and 28 percent approved; Scott Clement and Brady Dennis, "Post-ABC Poll: Nearly 6 in 10 Oppose Trump Scrapping Paris Agreement," *Washington Post*, June 5, 2017.

36. David E. Sanger and Jane Perlez, "Trump Hands the Chinese a Gift: The Chance for Global Leadership," *New York Times*, June 1, 2017; Keith Bradsher, "China Turns Economic Engine Toward Clean Energy Leadership," *New York Times*, June 6, 2017; Eric Roston, "If Trump Dumps the Climate Accord, the U.S. Is the Loser," *Bloomberg Business*, June 1, 2017; Philip Bump, "Nine Reasons Trump's Withdrawal from the Paris Climate Agreement Doesn't Make Sense," *Washington Post*, June 1, 2017; "A Disgraceful Exit from the Paris Pact," editorial, *New York Times*, June 2, 2017.

37. For the withdrawal timetable, see Brad Plumer, "U.S. Won't Actually Be Leaving the Paris Climate Deal Anytime Soon," *New York Times*, June 8, 2017.

38. Juliet Eilperin, "Trump Says 'Nobody Really Knows' if Climate Change is Real," *Washington Post*, December 11, 2016; Peter Baker, "No One Will Say if Trump Denies Climate Science," *New York Times*, June 3, 2017. On business conflicts of interest, see Hiroko Tabuchi and Eric Lipton, "Pruitt's E.P.A. Is Boon to Oil and Gas," *New York Times*, May 21, 2017. Eric Lipton and Lisa Freedman, "On Busy Calendar, E.P.A. Chief Puts Interests of Industries First," *New York Times*, October 3, 2017.

39. Chris Mooney and Juliet Eilperin," EPA Website Removes Climate Science Site from Public View After Two Decades," *Washington Post*, April 29, 2017; Michael Hiltzik, "Trump's EPA Has Started to Scrub Climate Change Data from Its Website," *Los Angeles Times*, May 1, 2017. The EPA archived the data, but it is more difficult to access.

40. Juliet Eilperin and Chris Mooney, "Scientists and Environmentalists Are Bracing for a Clash with Trump," *Washington Post*, December 4, 2016; Eilperin and Mooney, "Over 2,000 Scientists Urge Trump to Respect 'Scientific Integrity and Independence,'" *Washington Post*, November 30, 2016; Brady Dennis, "Scientists Are Frantically Copying U.S. Climate Data, Fearing It Might Vanish Under Trump," *Washington Post*, December 13, 2016; Steve Gorman, "U.S. Government Scientists Go 'Rogue' in Defiance of Trump," *Reuters*, January 26, 2017. For current and archived climate data, see, for example, NextGen Climate's website, saveourepa.com/climatechange.html.

41. Juliet Eilperin and Brady Dennis, "EPA Dismisses Half of Its Scientific Advisers on Key Board, Interior Suspends More Than 200 Advisory Panels in Sweeping Review," *Washington Post*, May 8, 2017; Coral Davenport, "E.P.A. Reduces Scientists' Role on a Key Panel," *New York Times*, May 8, 2017; Davenport, "E.P.A. Official Pressured Scientist on Congressional Testimony, Emails Show," *New York Times*, June 27, 2017.

42. Juliet Eilperin, "The Trump Administration Just Disbanded a Federal Advisory Committee on Climate Change," *Washington Post*, August 20, 2017; Josh Lederman, "Tillerson to Abolish Most Special Envoys, Including Climate," *Associated Press*, August 28, 2017; Joel Clement, "I'm a Scientist. I'm Blowing the Whistle on the Trump Administration," *Washington Post*, July 19, 2017; Sofia Lotto Persio, "Why Donald Trump's NASA Chief Pick Is So Controversial," *Newsweek*, September 2, 2017; Timothy Cama, "Dems Prep for Major Fight over Trump USDA Science Pick," *The Hill*, September 3, 2017.

43. John Reilly, "Trump Used Our Research to Justify Pulling Out of the Paris Agreement. He Got It Wrong," *Washington Post*, June 8, 2017; Brad Plumer and Coral Davenport, "E.P.A. Chief Is Planning a Test of Climate Science," *New York Times*, July 1, 2017.

44. Juliet Eilperin, "EPA Now Requires Political Aide's Sign-Off for Agency Awards, Grant Applications," *Washington Post*, September 4, 2017.

45. Chris Mooney, "Trump Has Filled Just 15 Percent of the Government's Top Science Jobs," *Washington Post*, June 6, 2017; Robert N. Proctor, "Climate Change in the Age of Ignorance," *New York Times*, November 20, 2016; Stuart Leavenworth, "Science Takes a Back Seat in Early Trump Administration," *Sacramento Bee*, April 25, 2017;

Jacqueline Alemany, "Science Division of WH Office Left Empty as Last Staffers Leave," *CBS News*, June 30, 2017. Presidents since Dwight Eisenhower—including Ronald Reagan—have appointed science advisers who have normally headed the White House Office of Science and Technology Policy (OSTP) and the President's. It is not clear whether Trump will retain any of these advisory mechanisms.

46. Lisa Freedman, "Climate Report Full of Warnings Awaits President," *New York Times*, August 8, 2017.

47. Chris Mooney, Juliet Eilperin and Brady Dennis, "Trump Administration Releases Report Finding 'No Convincing Alternative Explanation' for Climate Change," *Washington Post*, November 3, 2017.

48. Henry Fountain and Erica Goode, "Trump Has Options for Undoing Obama's Climate Legacy," *New York Times*, November 25, 2016; Andrew Rudalevige, "Trump Says He'll Cancel Obama's 'Unconstitutional' Executive Actions. It's Not That Easy," *Washington Post*, December 3, 2016; William W. Buzbee, "A Climate Reset?" *New York Times*, December 9, 2016; and, for a detailed example, see Bob Sussman, "Can President Trump Roll Back the Obama Emissions and Fuel Efficiency Standards for Light-Duty Vehicles?" *Brookings*, February 3, 2017.

49. See Michael Greenstone and Cass R. Sunstein, "Donald Trump Should Know: This Is What Climate Change Costs Us," *New York Times*, December 15, 2016; Rachel Augustine Potter, "How the Trump Administration Can Use Benefit Cost Analysis to Justify Deregulation," *Brookings*, August 1, 2017; and Steve Eder, "Neomi Rao, the Scholar Who Will Help Lead Trump's Regulatory Overhaul," *New York Times*, July 9, 2017.

50. John Schwartz, "Students, Cities and States Take the Global Warming Fight to Court," *New York Times*, August 11, 2017. Lisa Freedman, "As Trump Takes Aim at Obama's Clean Power Plan, a Legal Battle Looms," *New York Times*, September 29, 2017.

51. Dianne Cardwell, "Creating Their Own Green Sources," *New York Times*, August 24, 2016; Hiroko Tabuchi, "With Government in Retreat, Companies Step Up Efforts on Emissions," *New York Times*, April 26, 2017.

52. Clifford Krauss, "Production of Coal Is at Lowest in 35 Years," *New York Times*, June 11, 2016; Coral Davenport, "Coal Has Lost Its Grip on Power," *New York Times*, April 6, 2017. Since 2010, 251 of the nation's 523 coal plants have closed or are scheduled for closure. See Michael Bloomberg, "Trump's Promise to Bring Back Coal Jobs Is Worse Than a Con," *Washington Post*, May 2 2017; Davenport, "Praise for 'Clean Coal' Shows Contradictions in President's Policies," *New York Times*, July 19, 2017.

53. Nadja Popovich, "Solar and Wind, but Not Coal: Where Energy Jobs Are Growing," *New York Times*, April 26, 2017; Brian Deese, "Paris Isn't Burning: Why the Climate Agreement Will Survive Trump," *Foreign Affairs* 96, no. 4 (July/August 2017): 83–92; Barack Obama, "The Irreversible Momentum of Clean Energy," *Science*, January 13, 2017.

54. See Justin Gillis, "Weak Federal Powers Could Limit Trump's Climate-Policy Rollback," *New York Times*, January 2, 2017; David G. Victor, "What to Expect from Trump on Energy Policy," *Brookings*, November 17, 2016.

55. Ari Phillips, "Mayors Sign Climate Protection Agreement, Endorse Innovative Climate Solutions," *ThinkProgress*, June 22, 2014, https://thinkprogress.org/mayors-sign-climate-protection-agreement-endorse-innovative-climate-solutions-bcefbbe79b4b.

56. Tatiana Schlossberg, "As Trump Signals Climate Action Pullback, Local Leaders Push Forward," *New York Times*, December 16, 2016; Michael R. Bloomberg, "Climate Progress, With or Without Trump," *New York Times*, March 31, 2017.

57. Hiroko Tabuchi and Henry Fountain, "Bucking Trump, These Cities, States and Companies Commit to Paris Accord," *New York Times*, June 1, 2017; Steven Mufson, "These Titans of Industry Just Broke with Trump's Decision to Exit the Paris

Accords," *Washington Post*, June 1, 2017; Vikas Bajaj and Stuart A. Thompson, "The Green Energy Revolution Will Happen Without Trump," *New York Times*, June 20, 2017. The U.S. Conference of Mayors passed resolutions asking the federal government to rejoin the Paris Agreement and pledging to redouble their own efforts to fight climate change; see Lizette Alvarez, "Mayors, Sidestepping Trump, Vow to Fill Void on Climate Change," *New York Times*, June 27, 2017. Brad Plumer, "Fighting Climate Change Outside the Paris Accord," *New York Times*, September 21, 2017.

58. Justin Gillis and Michael Wines, "In Some States, Emissions Cuts Defy Skeptics," *New York Times*, June 7, 2014. Some of these reductions are due to factors other than carbon regulation, as noted in Chapter 10.

59. Lucas Bifera, *Regional Greenhouse Gas Initiative (RGGI)* (Arlington, VA: Center for Climate and Energy Solutions, 2013), www.c2es.org/us-states-regions/regional-climate-initiatives/rggi; "States Dare to Think Big on Climate Change," editorial, *New York Times*, August 28, 2017.

60. Jennifer Medina and Matt Richtel, "Carbon Goal in California is 'Milestone' on Climate," *New York Times*, August 26, 2016; "California Leads, Again, on Climate," editorial, *New York Times*, July 24, 2017; Brad Plumer, "California's Ambitious Agenda to Cut Greenhouse Gas Emissions," *New York Times*, July 27, 2017.

61. Adam Nagourney and Henry Fountain, "At Forefront of Climate Fight, California Plans an Offensive," *New York Times*, December 28, 2016; Hiroko Tabuchi, "California Upholds Auto Emissions Standards, Setting Up Face-Off with Trump," *New York Times*, March 24, 2017. Tabuchi, "U.S. Climate Change Policy: Made in California," *New York Times*, September 27, 2017.

62. Coral Davenport and Adam Nagourney, "Fighting Trump on Climate, California Becomes a Global Force," *New York Times*, May 25, 2017; Javier C. Hernández and Adam Nagourney, "California's Governor Steps in to Lead Charge on the Climate," *New York Times*, June 7, 2017; Ian Austen, "Canada's Climate Strategy: Work Directly with American States," *New York Times*, June 8, 2017.

63. John Schwartz, "'A Conservative Climate Solution': Republican Group Calls for a Carbon Tax," *New York Times*, February 8, 2017.

64. Henry Fountain, "Corralling Carbon Before It Belches from Stack," *New York Times*, July 22, 2014; John Schwartz, "Can Carbon Capture Technology Prosper Under Trump?" *New York Times*, January 2, 2017; Dino Grandini, "The Energy 202: Rick Perry Touts Carbon-Cutting Technology While Simultaneously Trying to Cut Its Funding," *Washington Post*, June 29, 2017.

65. Hiroko Tabuchi, "Disclose Climate Risks, Companies Are Urged," *New York Times*, December 15, 2016; Randall Smith, "Investor Demand Leads Analysts to Focus on Stock's Social and Environmental Risks," *New York Times*, December 15, 2016; Rubin, "How Ignoring Climate Change Could Sink the U.S. Economy."

66. Steven Mufson, "Financial Firms Lead Shareholder Rebellion Against ExxonMobil Climate Change Policies," *Washington Post*, May 31, 2017.

67. JLL Staff, "Why More College Campuses Are Going Carbon-Neutral," *JLL Real Views*, June 1, 2017, http://www.jllrealviews.com/industries/why-more-college-campuses-are-going-carbon-neutral/. The entire University of California system plans to reach carbon neutrality by 2025.

68. David Bornstein, "Cracking Washington's Gridlock to Save the Planet," *New York Times*, May 19, 2017. See the Citizens' Climate Lobby page entitled "Carbon Fee and Dividend Policy and FAQs," www.citizensclimatelobby.org/carbon-fee-and-dividend; and Clare Foran, "The House Republicans Calling for Climate Action in the Trump

Era," *The Atlantic*, March 15, 2017, www.theatlantic.com/politics/archive/2017/03/house-republicans-climate-change-global-warming-trump/518430/.

69. Michael Wines, "Emissions of Methane Exceed Estimates," *New York Times*, November 26, 2013; Coral Davenport, "White House Unveils Plans to Cut Methane Emissions," *New York Times*, March 28, 2014. Cheap natural gas can also replace nuclear power, raising overall carbon emissions; see Brad Plumer, "Glut of Natural Gas Pressures Nuclear Power, and Climate Goals, Too," *New York Times*, June 14, 2017.

70. White House, *Blueprint for a Secure Energy Future* (Washington, DC: White House, March 30, 2011).

71. U.S. oil production increased 78 percent from 2011 to 2015 alone due to improvements in hydraulic fracturing and horizontal drilling in previously inaccessible shale rock formations. See Alex Nussbaum, "As Trump Vows to Boost Drilling, Fracking Foes Turn to Court," *Bloomberg*, December 13, 2016.

72. Clifford Krauss and Diane Cardwell, "Climate Pact Put to Test by Drop in Price of Oil," *New York Times*, January 26, 2016; Clifford Krauss, "Oil Glut? More May Be on the Way," *New York Times*, October 6, 2016. Crude oil prices fell from over $100 a barrel to under $30 in late 2015, but recovered to around $50 by late 2016.

73. Barack Obama, "The Irreversible Momentum of Clean Energy"; Diane Cardwell, "Even as Wind Rises, It Falls Under a Political Cloud," *New York Times*, May 30, 2017; Bloomberg, "Climate Progress, With or Without Trump"; Victor, "What to Expect from Trump on Energy Policy."

74. "A Renewable Energy Boom," editorial, *New York Times*, April 4, 2016. In 2015, for the first time, renewables accounted for a majority of new electricity-generating capacity installed around the world. For an interesting example (Chile), see Maria Elena, "A Solar Saudi Arabia," *Washington Post*, March 31, 2017; Ernesto Londono, "Clean Energy in Chile: Wind, Sun and Volcanoes," *New York Times*, August 13, 2017.

75. Darryl Fears and Juliet Eilperin, "President Obama Bans Oil Drilling in Large Areas of Atlantic and Arctic Oceans," *Washington Post*, December 20, 2016; Coral Davenport, "Obama Leans on a 1953 Law to Ban Drilling," *New York Times*, December 21, 2016.

76. Coral Davenport and Aaron M. Kessler, "Proposed Rule for Big Trucks Aims at Cutting Fuel Emissions," *New York Times*, June 18, 2015. The rule was finalized in August 2016.

77. Rick Perry, Ryan Zinke, and Scott Pruitt, "Paving the Way to U.S. Energy Dominance," *Washington Times*, June 27, 2017; Steven Mufson and Chris Mooney, "Trump's 'Energy Dominance' Week Is Dominated by Misleading Claims, " *Washington Post*, June 29, 2017.

78. Perry's statement at the SelectUSA Investment Summit, Washington, DC, June 19, 2017, is available from Tom DiChristopher, "Nuclear Power on the 'Front Burner,' Says Energy Secretary Rick Perry," *CNBC*, http://www.cnbc.com/2017/06/19/nuclear-energy-is-on-the-front-burner-says-sec-rick-perry.html.

79. Clifford Krauss, "U.S., in Reversal, Issues Permit for Keystone Oil Pipeline," *New York Times*, March 25, 2017. A federal judge ordered further environmental review of the Dakota pipeline after it began operating: see Spencer S. Hsu, "Federal Judge Orders Environmental Review of Dakota Access Pipeline," *Washington Post*, June 14, 2017.

80. Coral Davenport and Alissa J. Rubin, "Trump Signs Rule to Block Efforts on Aiding Climate," *New York Times*, March 29, 2017.

81. Eric Lipton and Barry Meier, "Trump Unravels Coal Mine Limits on Federal Land," *New York Times*, August 7, 2017.

82. Juliet Eilperin, "Trump Moves to Open Atlantic Coast to Oil Drilling for First Time in More Than 30 Years," *Washington Post*, April 7, 2017; Coral Davenport, "Trump to Sign Orders That Could Expand Access to Fossil Fuels," *New York Times*, April 26, 2017; Davenport, "Trump Orders Review of Safety Rules Created After Gulf Oil Spill," *New York Times*, April 28, 2017.

83. Matthew Daly, "Trump Aims to Cut Protections for 27 National Monuments," *Associated Press*, May 6, 2017; Juliet Eilperin, "Shrink at Least 4 National Monuments and Modify a Half-Dozen Others, Zinke Tells Trump," *Washington Post*, September 17, 2017; Eilperin, "Trump Administration Working Toward Renewed Drilling in Arctic National Wildlife Refuge," *Washington Post*, September 15, 2017. It is unclear how much authority presidents have to rescind or modify monuments designated under the 1906 Antiquities Act.

84. Chris Mooney, "Trump Aims Deep Cuts at Energy Agency that Helped Make Solar Power Affordable," *Washington Post*, March 31, 2017; Brad Plumer and Coral Davenport, "Trump's Plan on Energy Calls for Deep Cuts to Innovation Programs," *New York Times*, May 24, 2017; Plumer, "Energy Department Closes Office Working on Climate Change Abroad," *New York Times*, June 15, 2017.

85. For a classic case study, see Robert F. Durant, *The Administrative Presidency Revisited: Public Lands, the BLM, and the Reagan Revolution* (Albany: State University of New York Press, 1992).

86. Terry Tempest Williams, "The Next Standing Rock?" *New York Times*, May 7, 2017.

87. California is already preparing to fight any possible new offshore oil developments by denying access to the three-mile coastal zone under state jurisdiction and to on-land construction of facilities; see Angela Hart, "State Senators Will Challenge Trump on Offshore Oil Drilling," *Sacramento Bee*, April 29, 2017. Other states are likely to follow suit.

88. Justin Gillis and Nadja Popovich, "The View from Trump Country, Where Renewable Energy Is Thriving," *New York Times*, June 8, 2017. States that voted for Trump account for 69 percent of the wind power produced in the United States. For a broader analysis and ranking of all 50 states' progress in the use of clean energy, see Union of Concerned Scientists, *Clean Energy Momentum: Ranking State Progress* (Cambridge, MA: Union of Concerned Scientists, 2017), www.ucsusa.org/EnergyProgress.

89. Coral Davenport, "As Wind Power Lifts Wyoming's Fortunes, Coal Miners Are Left in the Dust," *New York Times*, June 19, 2016; Diane Cardwell, "Wind Project in Wyoming Envisions Coal Miners as Trainees," *New York Times*, May 21, 2017. See also James Conca, "Renewable Energy Will Do Just Fine in President Trump's America," *Forbes*, November 10, 2016; and Davenport, "Energy Trends Outpace Plans for the E.P.A.," *New York Times*, December 9, 2016.

90. Ross Kerber, "'Green' Mutual Funds Bounce Back After Trump-Induced Retreat," *Reuters Business News*, May 31, 2017, https://www.reuters.com/article/us-usa-green-funds/green-mutual-funds-bounce-back-after-trump-induced-retreat-idUSKBN-18R0GB.

91. Jim Lyons, "The Rush to Develop Oil and Gas We Don't Need," *New York Times*, August 28, 2017.

92. See Clifford Krauss, "President's Preparations to Increase Gas Exports Face Glut in the Market," *New York Times*, May 2, 2017; Krauss, "Big Oil Confronts Realities of a Global Climate Effort," *New York Times*, November 8, 2016; and Linda Rudolph and Keenan McGonigle, "Oakland Rejects Coal Terminal, Sets Example on Climate

Change," *Sacramento Bee*, July 11, 2016. The potential for LNG exports is explored in Agnia Grigas, *The New Geopolitics of Natural Gas* (Cambridge, MA: Harvard University Press, 2017).

93. John M. Broder, "E.P.A. Sets Poison Standards for Power Plants," *New York Times*, December 22, 2011.

94. Coral Davenport, "New Limit for Smog-Causing Emissions Isn't as Strict as Many Had Expected," *New York Times*, October 2, 2015. Environmentalists and many scientists had argued for a lower standard of 60 parts per billion.

95. "EPA Proposes First Guidelines to Cut Carbon Pollution from Existing Power Plants," *EPA Press Release*, June 2, 2014, https://archive.epa.gov/epapages/newsroom_archive/ newsreleases/5bb6d20668b9a18485257ceb00490c98.html. See also Juliet Eilperin and Steven Mufson, "Everything You Need to Know about the EPA's Proposed Rule on Coal Plants," *Washington Post*, June 2, 2014.

96. Lisa Freedman, "E.P.A. Reverses Course on Ozone Rule," *New York Times*, August 3, 2017. However, the House of Representatives passed a Republican-backed bill that would delay implementation of the rule for eight years: see Michael Biesecker, "House Approves Delay of Obama-Era Smog Reductions, *AP News*, July 18, 2017.

97. Coral Davenport, "E.P.A. Moves to Rescind Contested Water Pollution Regulation," *New York Times*, June 27, 2017; Steven Mufson and Juliet Eilperin, "Trump Administration to Propose Repealing Rule Giving EPA Broad Authority over Water Pollution," *Washington Post*, June 28, 2017.

98. Nicholas Fandos, "U.S. Offers New Rule to Protect Streams from Coal Pollution," *New York Times*, July 17, 2015; Hiroko Tabuchi, "Republicans Move to Block Rule on Coal Mining Near Streams," *New York Times*, February 2, 2017; Lisa Lambert, "Mining Rule First to Be Killed by U.S. Congress, Others Near Chopping Block," *Reuters*, February 2, 2017.

99. Hiroko Tabuchi, "What's at Stake in the Cuts Proposed for the E.P.A.," *New York Times*, April 11, 2017; Denise Lu and Armand Emamdjomeh, "Local Programs Get the Biggest Hit in Proposed EPA Budget," *Washington Post*, April 11, 2017. Administrator Pruitt has indicated that he will not block funding for the Great Lakes Restoration Initiative. Josephine Marcotty, "EPA's Pruitt, in Departure from Trump Budget, Backs Federal Funding for Great Lakes Cleanup," *Minneapolis Star Tribune*, July 19, 2017.

100. Michael Wines, "Beyond Flint, Lead Poisoning Persists Despite Decades-Old Fight," *New York Times*, March 4, 2016; M. B. Pell and Joshua Schneyer, "The Thousands of U.S. Locales Where Lead Poisoning Is Worse than in Flint," *Reuters*, December 19, 2016, http://www.reuters.com/investigates/special-report/usa-lead-testing/.

101. Tatiana Schlossberg, "Hidden Peril of Coal Ash in the Water," *New York Times*, April 16, 2017.

102. See, for example, Robert F. Durant, Daniel J. Fiorino, and Rosemary O'Leary, eds., *Environmental Governance Reconsidered*, 2nd ed. (Cambridge, MA: MIT Press, 2017).

103. See Justin Gillis, "In Price Tag on Carbon, Plans to Save the Planet," *New York Times*, May 30, 2014, for an excellent summary. See also "Proof That a Price on Carbon Works," editorial, *New York Times*, January 19, 2016.

104. New Jersey, originally a member, may well rejoin RGGI. States such as Virginia and Pennsylvania could also join in the future.

105. Chris Buckley, "China's Leader Pushes Ahead with Big Gamble on a Carbon Trading Market," *New York Times*, June 24, 2017.

106. For an excellent detailed analysis, see Barry G. Rabe, *Can We Price Carbon?* (Cambridge, MA: MIT Press: 2018).

107. See, for example, Lara J. Cushing, Madeline Wander, Rachel Morello-Frosch, Manuel Pastor, Allen Zhu, and James Sadd, "A Preliminary Environmental Equity Assessment of California's Cap-and-Trade Program," September 2016, https://dornsife.usc.edu/PERE/enviro-equity-CA-cap-trade. The study found that "facilities that emit the highest levels of both GHGs and PM_{10} are also likely to be located in communities with higher proportions of residents of color and residents living in poverty."

108. Ian Austin, "Eye on Trump, Canada Debates Carbon Pricing," *New York Times*, December 9, 2016.

109. Schwartz, "'A Conservative Climate Solution': Republican Group Calls for a Carbon Tax"; George P. Schultz and Lawrence H. Summers, "This Is One Climate Solution That's Best for the Environment—and for Business," *Washington Post*, June 19, 2017; John Schwartz, "Exxon Mobil Lends Its Support to a Carbon Tax Proposal," *New York Times*, June 20, 2017.

110. Lisa Freedman, "Some Democrats See Campaign for Tax Overhaul as a Path to Taxing Carbon," *New York Times*, August 18, 2017.

111. Daniel J. Fiorino, *The New Environmental Regulation* (Cambridge, MA: MIT Press, 2006), Chapter 5; and Fiorino, "Regulatory Innovation and Change," in *Environmental Governance Reconsidered*, ed. Durant, Fiorino, and O'Leary, 307–36.

112. See Michael E. Kraft, Mark Stephan, and Troy D. Abel, *Coming Clean: Information Disclosure and Environmental Performance* (Cambridge, MA: MIT Press, 2011); and Robert F. Durant, "Regulation-by-Revelation," in *Environmental Governance Reconsidered*, ed. Durant, Fiorino, and O'Leary, 337–69.

113. Michael E. Kraft, *Using Information Disclosure to Achieve Policy Goals: How Experience with the Toxics Release Inventory Can Inform Action on Natural Gas Fracturing*, "Issues in Energy and Environmental Policy No. 6 (Ann Arbor, MI: CLOSUP Energy and Environmental Policy Initiative", March 2014), http://closup.umich.edu/files/ieep-2014-kraft-info-disclosure.pdf.

114. The quotation is taken from the archives of the PCSD, at http://clinton4.nara.gov/PCSD/. For a fuller history of sustainability concepts and actions, see Daniel A. Mazmanian and Michael E. Kraft, eds., *Toward Sustainable Communities: Transition and Transformations in Environmental Policy*, 2nd ed. (Cambridge, MA: MIT Press, 2009); Kraft, "Sustainability and Environmental Policy," in *Environmental Governance Reconsidered*, ed. Durant, Fiorino, and O'Leary, 75–100; and Kent E. Portney, *Taking Sustainable Cities Seriously: Economic Development, the Environment, and Quality of Life in American Cities*, 2nd ed. (Cambridge, MA: MIT Press, 2013).

115. See, for example, Aaron M. McCright, Katherine Dentzman, Meghan Charters, and Thomas Dietz, "The Influence of Political Ideology on Trust in Science," *Environmental Research Letters* 8 (2013), http://iopscience.iop.org/1748-9326/8/4/044029; Riley E. Dunlap, ed., "Climate Change Skepticism and Denial," special issue, *American Behavioral Scientist* 57, no. 6 (June 2013): 691–837.

116. William D. Ruckleshaus, Lee M. Thomas, and William K. Reilly, "Three Republican EPA Administrators: Trump Is Putting Us on a Dangerous Path," *Washington Post*, May 27, 2017. See also Christine Todd Whitman, "How Not to Run the EPA," *New York Times*, September 8, 2017. Whitman was EPA administrator under George W. Bush.

117. See Advisory Committee for Environmental Research and Education, *Transitions and Tipping Points in Complex Environmental Systems* (Washington, DC: National Science Foundation, 2009); and Michael E. Kraft and Sheldon Kamieniecki, "Research on U.S. Environmental Policy in the New Century," in *The Oxford Handbook of U.S. Environmental Policy*, ed. Sheldon Kamieniecki and Michael E. Kraft (New York: Oxford University Press, 2013), 695–712.

118. Resources for the Future, a nonpartisan research organization, has launched a new multidisciplinary initiative to update the methodology for calculating these costs, as recommended by the National Academies of Sciences, Engineering, and Medicine. See "Updating and Improving the Social Cost of Carbon," http://www.rff.org/research/collection/updating-and-improving-social-cost-carbon.

119. Mazmanian and Kraft, *Toward Sustainable Communities: Transition and Transformations in Environmental Policy*; Klyza and Sousa, *American Environmental Policy*; and Marc Allen Eisner, *Governing the Environment: The Transformation of Environmental Regulation* (Boulder, CO: Lynne Rienner, 2006).

120. See, for example, William Ophuls, *Plato's Revenge: Politics in the Age of Ecology* (Cambridge, MA: MIT Press, 2011).

121. See the following chapters in *The Oxford Handbook of U.S. Environmental Policy*, ed. Kamieniecki and Kraft: Walter A. Rosenbaum, "Capacity for Governance: Innovation and the Challenge of the Third Era," 137–63; Daniel A. Mazmanian and Laurie Kaye Nijaki, "Sustainable Development and Governance," 184–206; and Kate O'Neill, "Global Environmental Policy Making," 230–56.

122. For example, see Michele M. Betsill and Barry G. Rabe, "Climate Change and Multilevel Governance: The Evolving State and Local Roles," in *Toward Sustainable Communities: Transition and Transformations in Environmental Policy*, ed. Daniel A. Mazmanian and Michael E. Kraft, 2nd ed. (Cambridge, MA: MIT Press, 2009), 201–26; and Daniel C. Esty, "Bottom-Up Climate Fix," *New York Times*, September 22, 2014.

123. See, for example, Chris Mooney, "Scientists Just Published an Entire Study Refuting Scott Pruitt on Climate Change," *Washington Post*, May 24, 2017.

124. William D. Ruckleshaus, "A Lesson Trump and the E.P.A. Should Heed," *New York Times*, March 7, 2017.

Appendix 1 Major Federal Laws on the Environment, 1969–2017

Legislation	Implementing Agency	Key Provisions
		Nixon Administration
National Environmental Policy Act of 1969, PL 91–190	All federal agencies	Declared a national policy to "encourage productive and enjoyable harmony between man and his environment"; required environmental impact statements; created Council on Environmental Quality.
Resources Recovery Act of 1970, PL 91–512	Health, Education, and Welfare Department (later Environmental Protection Agency)	Set up a program of demonstration and construction grants for innovative solid waste management systems; provided state and local agencies with technical and financial assistance in developing resource recovery and waste disposal systems.
Clean Air Act Amendments of 1970, PL 91–604	Environmental Protection Agency (EPA)	Required administrator to set national primary and secondary air quality standards and certain emissions limits; required states to develop implementation plans by specific dates; required reductions in automobile emissions.
Federal Water Pollution Control Act (Clean Water Act) Amendments of 1972, PL 92–500	EPA	Set national water quality goals; established pollutant discharge permit system; increased federal grants to states to construct waste treatment plants.
Federal Environmental Pesticide Control Act of 1972 (amended the Federal Insecticide, Fungicide, and Rodenticide Act [FIFRA] of 1947), PL 92–516	EPA	Required registration of all pesticides in U.S. commerce; allowed administrator to cancel or suspend registration under specified circumstances.
Marine Mammal Protection Act of 1972, PL 92–532	EPA	Regulated dumping of waste materials into the oceans and coastal waters.

(Continued on next page)

Appendix 1 Major Federal Laws on the Environment, 1969–2017 (Continued)

Legislation	Implementing Agency	Key Provisions
Coastal Zone Management Act of 1972, PL 92–583	Office of Coastal Zone Management, Commerce Department	Authorized federal grants to the states to develop coastal zone management plans under federal guidelines.
Endangered Species Act of 1973, PL 93–205	Fish and Wildlife Service, Interior Department	Broadened federal authority to protect all "threatened" as well as "endangered" species; authorized grant program to assist state programs; required coordination among all federal agencies.
Ford Administration		
Safe Drinking Water Act of 1974, PL 93–523	EPA	Authorized federal government to set standards to safeguard the quality of public drinking water supplies and to regulate state programs for protecting underground water sources.
Toxic Substances Control Act of 1976, PL 94–469	EPA	Authorized premarket testing of chemical substances; allowed the EPA to ban or regulate the manufacture, sale, or use of any chemical presenting an "unreasonable risk of injury to health or environment"; prohibited most uses of polychlorinated biphenyls (PCBs).
Federal Land Policy and Management Act of 1976, PL 94–579	Bureau of Land Management, Interior Department	Gave Bureau of Land Management authority to manage public lands for long-term benefits; officially ended policy of conveying public lands into private ownership.
Resource Conservation and Recovery Act of 1976, PL 94–580	EPA	Required the EPA to set regulations for hazardous waste treatment, storage, transportation, and disposal; provided assistance for state hazardous waste programs under federal guidelines.
National Forest Management Act of 1976, PL 94–588	U.S. Forest Service, Agriculture Department	Gave statutory permanence to national forestlands and set new standards for their management; restricted timber harvesting to protect soil and watersheds; limited clear-cutting.

Carter Administration

Law	Agency	Description
Surface Mining Control and Reclamation Act of 1977, PL 95–87	Interior Department	Established environmental controls over strip mining; limited mining on farmland, alluvial valleys, and slopes; required restoration of land to original contours.
Clean Air Act Amendments of 1977, PL 95–95	EPA	Amended and extended Clean Air Act; postponed deadlines for compliance with auto emissions and air quality standards; set new standards for "prevention of significant deterioration" in clean air areas.
Clean Water Act Amendments of 1977, PL 95–217	EPA	Extended deadlines for industry and cities to meet treatment standards; set national standards for industrial pretreatment of wastes; increased funding for sewage treatment construction grants and gave states flexibility in determining spending priorities.
Public Utility Regulatory Policies Act of 1978, PL 95–617	Energy Department, states	Provided for Energy Department and Federal Energy Regulatory Commission regulation of electric and natural gas utilities and crude oil transportation systems in order to promote energy conservation and efficiency; allowed small cogeneration and renewable energy projects to sell power to utilities.
Alaska National Interest Lands Conservation Act of 1980, PL 96–487	Interior Department, Agriculture Department	Protected 102 million acres of Alaskan land as national wilderness, wildlife refuges, and parks.
Comprehensive Environmental Response, Compensation, and Liability Act of 1980 (CERCLA), PL 96–510	EPA	Authorized federal government to respond to hazardous waste emergencies and to clean up chemical dump sites; created $1.6 billion "Superfund"; established liability for cleanup costs.

Reagan Administration

Law	Agency	Description
Nuclear Waste Policy Act of 1982, PL 97–425; Nuclear Waste Policy Amendments Act of 1987, PL 100–203	Energy Department	Established a national plan for the permanent disposal of high-level nuclear waste; authorized the Energy Department to site, obtain a license for, construct, and operate geologic repositories for spent fuel from commercial nuclear power plants. Amendments in 1987 specified Yucca Mountain, Nevada, as the sole national site to be studied.

(Continued on next page)

405

Appendix 1 Major Federal Laws on the Environment, 1969–2017 (Continued)

Legislation	Implementing Agency	Key Provisions
Resource Conservation and Recovery Act Amendments of 1984, PL 98–616	EPA	Revised and strengthened EPA procedures for regulating hazardous waste facilities; authorized grants to states for solid and hazardous waste management; prohibited land disposal of certain hazardous liquid wastes; required states to consider recycling in comprehensive solid waste plans.
Food Security Act of 1985 (also called the farm bill), PL 99–198; renewed in 1990, 1996, 2002, 2008, and 2014	Agriculture Department	Limited federal program benefits for producers of commodities on highly erodible land or converted wetlands; established a conservation reserve program; authorized Agriculture Department technical assistance for subsurface water quality preservation; revised and extended the Soil and Water Conservation Act (1977) programs through the year 2008. The 1996 renewal of the farm bill authorized $56 billion over seven years for a variety of farm and forestry programs. These include an Environmental Quality Incentives Program to provide assistance and incentive payments to farmers, especially those facing serious threats to soil, water, grazing lands, wetlands, and wildlife habitat. Spending was increased substantially in 2002.
Safe Drinking Water Act of 1986, PL 99–339	EPA	Reauthorized the Safe Drinking Water Act of 1974 and revised EPA safe drinking water programs, including grants to states for drinking water standards enforcement and groundwater protection programs; accelerated EPA schedule for setting standards for maximum contaminant levels of eighty-three toxic pollutants.
Superfund Amendments and Reauthorization Act of 1986 (SARA), PL 99–499	EPA	Provided $8.5 billion through 1991 to clean up the nation's most dangerous abandoned chemical waste dumps; set strict standards and timetables for cleaning up such sites; required that industry provide local communities with information on hazardous chemicals used or emitted.

Clean Water Act Amendments of 1987, PL 100–4	EPA	Amended the Federal Water Pollution Control Act of 1972; extended and revised EPA water pollution control programs, including grants to states for construction of wastewater treatment facilities and implementation of mandated nonpoint-source pollution management plans; expanded EPA enforcement authority; established a national estuary program.
Global Climate Protection Act of 1987, PL 100–204	State Department	Authorized the State Department to develop an approach to the problems of global climate change; created an intergovernmental task force to develop U.S. strategy for dealing with the threat posed by global warming.
Ocean Dumping Ban Act of 1988, PL 100–688	EPA	Amended the Marine Protection, Research, and Sanctuaries Act of 1972 to end all ocean disposal of sewage sludge and industrial waste by December 31, 1991; revised EPA regulation of ocean dumping by establishing dumping fees, permit requirements, and civil penalties for violations.

George H. W. Bush Administration

Oil Pollution Act of 1990, PL 101–380	Transportation Department, Commerce Department	Sharply increased liability limits for oil spill cleanup costs and damages; required double hulls on oil tankers and barges by 2015; required federal government to direct cleanups of major spills; required increased contingency planning and preparedness for spills; preserved states' rights to adopt more stringent liability laws and to create state oil spill compensation funds.
Pollution Prevention Act of 1990, PL 101–508	EPA	Established Office of Pollution Prevention in the EPA to coordinate agency efforts at source reduction; created voluntary program to improve lighting efficiency; stated waste minimization was to be primary means of hazardous waste management; mandated source reduction and recycling report to accompany annual toxics release inventory under SARA in order to encourage industries to reduce hazardous waste voluntarily.

(Continued on next page)

Appendix 1 Major Federal Laws on the Environment, 1969–2017 (Continued)

Clean Air Act Amendments of 1990, PL 101–549	EPA	Amended the Clean Air Act of 1970 by setting new requirements and deadlines of three to twenty years for major urban areas to meet federal clean air standards; imposed new, stricter emissions standards for motor vehicles and mandated cleaner fuels; required reduction in emission of sulfur dioxide and nitrogen oxides by power plants to limit acid deposition and created a market system of emissions allowances; required regulation to set emissions limits for all major sources of toxic or hazardous air pollutants and listed 189 chemicals to be regulated; prohibited the use of chlorofluorocarbons (CFCs) by the year 2000 and set phaseout of other ozone-depleting chemicals.
Intermodal Surface Transportation Efficiency Act of 1991 (ISTEA, also called the highway bill), PL 102–240	Transportation Department	Authorized $151 billion over six years for transportation, including $31 billion for mass transit; required statewide and metropolitan long-term transportation planning; authorized states and communities to use transportation funds for public transit that reduces air pollution and energy use consistent with Clean Air Act of 1990; required community planners to analyze land use and energy implications of transportation projects they review.
Energy Policy Act of 1992, PL 102–486	Energy Department	Comprehensive energy act designed to reduce U.S. dependency on imported oil. Mandated restructuring of the electric utility industry to promote competition; encouraged energy conservation and efficiency; promoted renewable energy and alternative fuels for cars; eased licensing requirements for nuclear power plants; authorized extensive energy research and development.
The Omnibus Water Act of 1992, PL 102–575	Interior Department	Authorized completion of major water projects in the West; revised the Central Valley Project in California to allow transfer of water rights to urban areas and to encourage conservation through a tiered pricing system that allocates water more flexibly and efficiently; mandated extensive wildlife and environmental protection, mitigation, and restoration programs.

Food Quality Protection Act of 1996, PL 104–170	EPA	A major revision of FIFRA that adopted a new approach to regulating pesticides used on food, fiber, and other crops by requiring EPA to consider the diversity of ways in which people are exposed to such chemicals. Created a uniform "reasonable risk" health standard for both raw and processed foods that replaced the requirements of the 1958 Delaney Clause of the Food, Drug, and Cosmetic Act that barred the sale of processed food containing even trace amounts of chemicals found to cause cancer; required the EPA to take extra steps to protect children by establishing an additional tenfold margin of safety in setting acceptable risk standards.
Safe Drinking Water Act Amendments of 1996, PL 104–182	EPA	Granted local water systems greater flexibility to focus on the most serious public health risks; authorized $7.6 billion through 2003 for state-administered loan and grant funds to help localities with the cost of compliance; created a "right-to-know" provision requiring large water systems to provide their customers with annual reports on the safety of local water supplies, including information on contaminants found in drinking water and their health effects. Small water systems are eligible for waivers from costly regulations.
Transportation Equity Act for the 21st Century (also called ISTEA II or TEA 21), PL 105–178	Transportation Department	Authorized a six-year, $218 billion program that increased spending by 40 percent to improve the nation's highways and mass transit systems; provided $41 billion for mass transit programs, with over $29 billion coming from the Highway Trust Fund; provided $592 million for research and development on new highway technologies, including transportation-related environmental issues; provided $148 million for a scenic byways program and $270 million for building and maintaining trails; continued support for improvement of bicycle paths.

(Continued on next page)

Appendix 1 Major Federal Laws on the Environment, 1969–2017 (Continued)

Legislation	Implementing Agency	Key Provisions
		George W. Bush Administration
The Small Business Liability Relief and Brownfields Revitalization Act of 2002, PL 107–118	EPA	Amended CERCLA (Superfund) to provide liability protection for prospective purchasers of brownfields and small business owners who contributed to waste sites; authorized increased funding for state and local programs that assess and clean up such abandoned or underused industrial or commercial sites.
The Healthy Forests Restoration Act of 2003, PL 108–148	Agriculture Department, Interior Department	Intended to reduce the risks of forest fires on federal lands by authorizing the cutting of timber in selected areas managed by the Forest Service and the Bureau of Land Management; sought to protect communities, watersheds, and certain other lands from the effects of catastrophic wildfires; directed the Secretary of Agriculture and the Secretary of the Interior to plan and conduct hazardous fuel reduction programs on federal lands within their jurisdictions.
The Energy Policy Act of 2005, PL 109–58	Energy Department	Intended to increase the supply of energy resources and improve the efficiency of energy use through provision of tax incentives and loan guarantees for various kinds of energy production, particularly oil, natural gas, and nuclear power. Also called for expanded energy research and development, expedited building for new energy facilities, improved energy efficiency standards for federal office buildings, and modernization of the nation's electricity grid.
Energy Independence and Security Act of 2007, PL 110–140	Energy Department, Transportation Department	Set a national automobile fuel-economy standard of thirty-five miles per gallon by 2020, the first significant change in the Corporate Average Fuel Economy (CAFE) standards since 1975. Also sought to increase the supply of alternative fuel sources by setting a renewable fuel standard that requires fuel producers to use at least thirty-six billion gallons of biofuels by 2022; twenty-one billion gallons of that amount are to come from sources other than corn-based ethanol. Included provisions to improve energy efficiency in lighting and appliances and for federal agency efficiency and renewable energy use.

Obama Administration

The American Recovery and Reinvestment Act of 2009, PL 111-5	Energy Department, Transportation Department, Treasury Department	Although not a stand-alone environmental or energy policy, the economic stimulus bill contained about $80 billion in spending, tax incentives, and loan guarantees to promote energy efficiency, renewable energy sources, fuel-efficient cars, mass transit, and clean coal, including $3.4 billion for research on capturing and storing carbon dioxide from coal-fired power plants, $2 billion for research on advanced car batteries, $17 billion in grants and loans to modernize the nation's electric grid and increase its capacity to transmit power from renewable sources, and nearly $18 billion for mass transit, Amtrak, and high-speed rail.
Omnibus Public Lands Management Act of 2009, PL 111-11	Interior Department, Agriculture Department	Consolidated 164 separate public lands measures that protect two million acres of wilderness in nine states; establish new national trails, national parks, and a new national monument; provide legal status for the twenty-six-million-acre National Landscape Conservation System that contains areas of archaeological and cultural significance; and protect 1,100 miles of eighty-six new wild and scenic rivers in eight states. Together the measures constitute the most significant expansion of federal land conservation programs in fifteen years.
The Frank R. Lautenberg Chemical Safety for the 21st Century Act of 2016, PL 114-182	EPA	Modified the Toxic Substances Control Act of 1976 to require the EPA to evaluate existing chemicals and set deadlines for doing so; established a new risk-based safety standard; increased public transparency for chemical information.

Note: As of 2017, no other major laws had been approved by Congress and signed by President Trump. As always, for an update on legislative developments, consult *CQ Magazine* or other professional news sources, or Congressional Quarterly's annual *Almanac,* which summarizes key legislation enacted by Congress and describes the major issues and leading policy actors.

Appendix 2   Budgets of Selected Environmental and Natural Resource Agencies, 1980–2017 (in billions of nominal and constant dollars)

Agency	1980	1990	2000	2010	2017 (Est.)
Environmental Protection Agency (EPA) Operating Budget[a]	1.269	1.901	2.465	3.889	3.998
(Constant 2017 dollars)	3.094	3.132	3.349	4.284	3.998
Interior Department Total Budget	4.592	6.669	8.363	12.843	15.861
(Constant 2017 dollars)	11.400	10.987	11.363	14.146	15.861
Selected Natural Resource Agencies					
Bureau of Land Management	0.919	1.226	1.616	1.074	1.259
(Constant 2017 dollars)	2.241	2.020	2.196	1.183	1.259
Fish and Wildlife Service	0.435	1.133	1.498	1.588	1.562
(Constant 2017 dollars)	1.062	1.866	2.035	1.749	1.562
National Park Service	0.531	1.275	2.071	2.289	3.101
(Constant 2017 dollars)	1.296	2.100	2.814	2.521	3.101
Forest Service	2.250	3.473	3.728	5.297	4.893
(Constant 2017 dollars)	5.487	5.722	5.065	5.834	4.893

Source: Office of Management and Budget, *Budget of the United States Government,* fiscal years 1982, 1992, 2002, 2012, 2017 (Washington, DC: Government Publishing Office, 1981, 1991, 2001, 2011, and 2016), and agency websites.

Note: The upper figure for each agency represents budget authority in nominal dollars, that is, the real amount for the year in which the budget was authorized. The lower figure represents budget authority in constant 2017 dollars to permit comparisons over time. These adjustments use the implicit price deflator for the Gross Domestic Product as calculated by the Bureau of Economic Analysis, Department of Commerce.

a. The EPA operating budget, which supplies funds for most of the agency's research, regulation, and enforcement programs, is the most meaningful figure. The other two major elements of the total EPA budget historically have been Superfund allocations and sewage treatment construction or water infrastructure grants (now called state and tribal assistance grants). We subtract both of these items from the total EPA budget to calculate the agency's operating budget. The EPA and the White House define the agency's operating budget differently. They do not exclude all of these amounts and arrive at a slightly different figure. President Trump's proposed change in the fiscal 2017 budget called for a 31 percent cut in the EPA's total budget, but Congress approved only a 1 percent reduction.

For consistency, all figures in the table are taken from the president's proposed budget for the respective years, and all represent final budget authority.

Appendix 3   Employees in Selected Federal Agencies and Departments, 1980, 1990, 2000, and 2010

Agency/Department	Personnel[a]			
	1980	1990	2000	2010
Environmental Protection Agency	12,891	16,513	17,416	17,417
Bureau of Land Management	9,655	8,753	9,328	12,741
Fish and Wildlife Service	7,672	7,124	7,011	9,252
National Park Service	13,934	17,781	18,418	22,211
Office of Surface Mining Reclamation and Enforcement	1,014	1,145	622	521
Forest Service	40,606	40,991	33,426	35,639
Army Corps of Engineers (civil functions)	32,757	28,272	22,624	23,608
U.S. Geological Survey	14,416	10,451	9,417	8,600
Natural Resources Conservation Service (formerly Soil Conservation Service)	15,856	15,482	9,628	11,446

Source: U.S. Senate Committee on Governmental Affairs, "Organization of Federal Executive Departments and Agencies," January 1, 1980, and January 1, 1990; and Office of Management and Budget, *Budget of the United States Government,* fiscal years 1982, 1992, 2002, and 2012 (Washington, DC: Government Publishing Office, 1981, 1991, 2001, and 2011), and agency websites.

a. Personnel totals represent full-time equivalent employment, reflecting both permanent and temporary employees. Data for 2000 are based on the fiscal 2002 proposed budget submitted to Congress by the Bush administration in early 2001, and data for 2010 are taken from agency sources as well as the administration's proposed fiscal 2012 budget submitted to Congress in early 2011. Because of organizational changes within departments and agencies, the data presented here are not necessarily an accurate record of agency personnel growth or decline over time. The information is presented chiefly to provide an indicator of approximate agency size during different periods. Agency staffing after 2017 is likely to be less than, and sometimes far below, the 2010 levels provided in this historical table should the Trump administration budget recommendations be approved by Congress.

Appendix 4   Federal Spending on Natural Resources and the
Environment, Selected Fiscal Years, 1980–2017
(in billions of nominal and constant dollars)

Budget Item	1980	1990	2000	2010	2017 (Est.)
Water resources	4.085	4.332	4.800	6.813	5.635
(Constant 2017 dollars)	9.963	7.137	6.522	7.504	5.635
Conservation and land management	1.572	4.362	6.604	11.933	14.976
(Constant 2017 dollars)	3.834	7.186	8.973	13.144	14.976
Recreational resources	1.373	1.804	2.719	3.809	4.886
(Constant 2017 dollars)	3.349	2.972	3.694	4.195	4.886
Pollution control and abatement	4.672	5.545	7.483	10.473	8.655
(Constant 2017 dollars)	11.395	9.135	10.167	11.535	8.655
Other natural resources	1.395	2.077	3.397	6.629	8.015
(Constant 2017 dollars)	3.402	3.422	4.615	7.301	8.105
Total	13.097	18.121	25.003	39.657	42.167
(Constant 2017 dollars)	31.944	29.853	33.971	43.680	42.167

Source: Office of Management and Budget, *Historical Tables, Budget of the United States Government Fiscal Year 2017* (Washington, DC: Government Publishing Office, 2016).

Note: The upper figure for each budget category represents budget authority in nominal dollars, that is, the real budget for the given year. Figures for 1980 are provided to indicate pre–Reagan administration spending bases. The lower figure for each category represents budget authority in constant 2017 dollars. These adjustments are made using the implicit price deflator for the Gross Domestic Product as calculated by the Bureau of Economic Analysis, Department of Commerce. The natural resources and environment function in the federal budget reported in this table does not include environmental cleanup programs within the Departments of Defense and Energy, which are substantial. President Trump's budget for fiscal 2018 is likely to show sharp reductions from the numbers provided here, and the ultimate spending level will be set by Congress.

Index

Pages followed by b, f, n, or t indicate box, figure, note, or table respectively.